D0742198

Institutions and
Economic Performance

Institutions and Economic Performance

Edited by

Elhanan Helpman

Harvard University Press

Cambridge, Massachusetts

London, England

2008

Copyright © 2008 by the President and Fellows of Harvard College
All rights reserved
Printed in the United States of America

Library of Congress Cataloging-in-Publication Data

Institutions and economic performance / edited by Elhanan Helpman.—
1st ed.
p.   cm.
Includes bibliographical references and index.
ISBN-13: 978-0-674-03077-0 (cloth : alk. paper)   1. Economic
development.   2. Regional economic disparities.   3. Public
administration.   4. Social institutions.   5. Political culture.
6. Social structure.   I. Helpman, Elhanan.
HD82.I347 2008
338.9—dc22
2008003052

Contents

Part II. Theory

Part III. Contemporary Evidence

Preface

The impact of economic and political institutions on economic outcomes has interested economists and political scientists for many years. Nevertheless, the subject did not make it into the economic mainstream for a long time. Recently, however, a surge of research has provided new theoretical and empirical insights, turning this topic into a vibrant area of enquiry. This book collects original studies on institutions and economic performance, written by economists, political scientists, and economic historians, who are members of the program on Institutions, Organizations and Growth (IOG) of the Canadian Institute for Advanced Research (CIFAR). All the chapters of the book were written by members of this program, some in collaboration with other scholars. Members of the IOG program met regularly over a period of three years to discuss their work. The amount of research they produced is much too large to be collected in a single volume; it has been published in scientific journals, edited volumes and books. What we offer instead is a glimpse into this research, which is representative of the group's larger effort and, arguably, of the research agenda of this entire field.

I thank Jane Trahan for supervising the production of this book from beginning to end.

Institutions and
Economic Performance

Introduction

ELHANAN HELPMAN

Nations grow at different rates, and income per capita differs greatly across countries. Economists have studied the extent to which these differences can be explained by differences in resources, including physical and human capital. They find that, after accounting for the cumulative effect of capital inputs, large differences in income per capita remain across countries. So the natural questions are, why do total factor productivity (TFP) levels differ so much, and why do they grow at different rates in different countries?

One line of research provided important insights into the role of technological progress in explaining differences in TFP. It showed, for example, that investment in research and development (R&D) explains a substantial part of this variation, particularly in the industrial countries. However, substantial differences remain after accounting for both the accumulation of physical and human capital and R&D investment. The question is, why?

A new effort directed toward answering this question focuses on the impact of institutions on economic outcomes. Its main premise is that institutions have a direct effect on productivity, as well as an indirect effect, because they influence the form and rate of technological progress and they shape the incentives of economic and political agents. Institutions are more fundamental determinants of economic prosperity than capital accumulation or R&D investment, because they frame the environment in which these activities take place, and because they are difficult to change; one can think of institutions as a state variable that changes very slowly over time. However, not all institutions are equally difficult to change. One view holds that political institutions are more difficult to change than economic institutions, and that for this reason political institutions have a substantial impact on the evolution of economic institutions. Be this as it may, the study of institutions carries the potential for a better understanding of the determinants of human well-being. Naturally, these issues make up a rich

1

research agenda, which is only partly covered by the thirteen chapters of
this book. I believe, however, that these chapters are representative of the
larger effort in this field.

The first part of the book deals with the history of institutions, the
way they evolved over time, and the way they influenced economies. In
Chapter 1, Avner Greif hypothesizes that political, economic, and legal
institutions are inadequate for understanding economic success. He argues that administrative structures have an important influence on both
institutional and economic developments. His motivating observation is
that policymakers—be they monarchs or presidents—rely on an administration to execute their choices, implying that administrators are in a
particularly advantageous position to challenge them. It is therefore reasonable to conjecture that constitutional institutions—the rule of law, the
formulation of constitutions, and political representation—first emerge
as equilibrium outcomes in the relations between the policymakers and
powerful administrators. As in much of his work on the institutional
foundations of economic history, Greif studies equilibrium administrative
structures as self-sustaining entities, examining their stability, change, and
significance. He explores why some structures and not others lead to administrative power and constitutional institutions that are self-enforcing.
Among other insights, his analysis highlights the roles played by legal
and political institutions in fostering intra-elite cooperation, limiting the
effectiveness of the rule of law, and the distributional impact of political institutions. Greif then extends the analysis to examine the implications of different initial administrative structures on subsequent economic
and institutional change. His key conjecture is that some structures have
a comparative disadvantage in controlling non-elites and thus provide
stronger incentives for them to develop new sources of wealth. In particular, the same decentralized structures that support constitutionalism
also motivate wealth creation, and the two processes complement and
reinforce each other. The analysis thereby highlights conditions that are
conducive to a "virtuous" cycle of economic growth and constitutional development. His essay is rich in historical examples. They include Frederick
Barbarossa's relations with the German dukes in the twelfth century; King
John's conflicts with the English barons in the thirteenth century, which
led to the adoption of the Magna Carta; the Polish–Lithuanian Commonwealth, a constitutional monarchy from the sixteenth to the eighteenth
centuries; and the relations the Ottoman sultans had with their janissaries

from the fifteenth to the nineteenth centuries. He concludes by using this analysis to conjecture about the administrative foundations of the rise of the West.

In Chapter 2, Joel Mokyr takes up the institutional foundations of the Industrial Revolution in Britain. He does not challenge the now mainstream view that political developments—such as the Glorious Revolution of 1688 and other seventeenth-century developments around it, which protected property rights and placed constraints on the executive (i.e., the Crown)—played an important role in British economic success. Yet he raises a challenging question: what role have institutions played in the country's process of technological innovation and the adoption of new technologies? After all, technological change was at the heart of the Industrial Revolution, and it is not clear how the formal political institutions that emanated from the Glorious Revolution contributed to technological change. Pan-European developments, such as the Enlightenment and the growth of open science, helped Britain during the Industrial Revolution. But they cannot explain British leadership and its place at the head of the pack. Mokyr argues that formal institutions, important as they were, tell only a partial story, because informal institutions played a central role not only in fostering technological progress but also in sustaining economic growth until the mid-nineteenth century. In addition to property rights, law and order, constraints on the executive, intellectual property rights (such as patents), and financial institutions—all embodied in formal codes—there was open science, gentlemanly codes of behavior, and a high degree of trust in society, which supported the ever more complex arm's-length transactions among economic agents. Although it is hard to establish the precise mechanism that sustained this cooperative behavior, which was a predominantly middle-class phenomenon, the arguments for its existence and its contribution to British economic development are strong. Moreover, the sheer size of the British middle class on the eve of the Industrial Revolution was a contributing factor to the success of these social norms in shaping the process of change, including the acquisition of skills that set Britain ahead of other countries. All these helped transform the British economy from one of privilege and exclusion to one of open access and economic freedom.

Chapter 3, by Drelichman and Voth, discusses the impact of silver on Castilian institutions and the consequent decline of Spain. Their starting point is the resource curse, also known as the "Dutch Disease." First, the discovery of natural resources has an impact on a country's terms of trade.

Second, it leads to rent seeking and redistribution. The degree to which the struggle for rents has negative economic consequences depends on the quality of a country's institutions. The authors' main thesis is that the flow of silver influenced Castilian institutions in a way that hindered Spanish long-term economic development. Castile was a major power in western Europe after its emergence at the end of the fifteenth century as the sole victor of the Reconquista wars; and the effective merging of Castile and Aragon, under Ferdinand and Isabella in 1474, gave Castile control of the Iberian Peninsula. In subsequent years, the Crown strove to build a centralized administrative apparatus. The king presided over the Royal Council, which made the major decisions, and the royal judiciary had supremacy over local courts. In this structure, the Crown had supremacy over the nobility and the clergy. Ferdinand also obtained the right to name bishops and to control church activities in newly conquered lands. Under these circumstances the Cortes, a parliamentary body that originated in medieval times, remained the main institutional counterweight to the monarchy. Importantly, the Cortes had to approve new taxes and the renewal of extraordinary ones, but it had no jurisdiction over the use of mineral resources. Thus the silver inflow from across the Atlantic provided the Crown with revenue that was not controlled by domestic institutions, and silver became a large component of its income. This newly gained financial independence allowed Philip II, who was crowned in 1556, to restructure public finances in a way that reduced his reliance on the Cortes' consent. With the new system in place, the king could pursue expensive projects, such as the construction of monasteries, expansionist wars, and the building of the Invincible Armada. He could also leverage his financial needs with unprecedented amounts of debt. Since expenses exceeded income from silver by a wide margin, additional financing was needed from domestic sources. The king therefore used his financial commitments, and especially the need to finance troops in foreign lands, to request new taxes from the Cortes. In the evolving struggle between the Crown and the Cortes, the king managed to weaken the domestic institutions in a way that permanently damaged economic development.

Engerman and Sokoloff have argued in a series of influential papers that factor endowments had a major impact on economic development, and that they explain the divergent paths of North and South America. Their argument has several parts. First, factor endowments determined the use of slave labor, especially on plantations. Second, the use of slave labor resulted

in extreme economic and political inequality, which prevented the formation of institutions that support economic development. In other words,
regions with many slaves formed worse institutions than regions with fewer
slaves. Third, economic growth was positively correlated with the quality of
institutions; it was slower in regions with bad institutions. In Chapter 4,
Nathan Nunn examines the Engerman–Sokoloff hypothesis econometrically. Although he does not study each one of its components, he paints
a picture of mixed results. By estimating the impact of the fraction of slaves
in a country's population circa 1750 on its per capita gross domestic product (GDP) in the year 2000, he finds that within the group of New World
countries, those that had larger fractions of slaves in the mid-eighteenth
century were poorer at the end of the twentieth century. This correlation is
robust to various controls, such as initial well-being, colonial relations, and
other variables. A similar relationship holds for a smaller sample of countries from the British West Indies, for which Nunn uses slavery data from
1830. For these countries, estimates exist for plantation and urban slaves,
and both categories are found to have a negative impact on income per
capita in 2000. Finally, he finds a negative impact of slavery on economic
development across U.S. states. Evidently, these findings support the relationship between slavery and economic growth that is at the heart of the
Engerman–Sokoloff hypothesis. Yet Nunn fails to find an influence through
the *inequality channel* proposed by Engerman and Sokoloff. On the one
hand, he finds a positive correlation between land inequality in U.S. states
or counties in 1860 and the fraction of slaves in their population. But he
finds no impact of land inequality in 1860 on income per capita in 2000.
He therefore concludes that although slavery affected economic development, at least across the U.S. regions, its impact did not operate through
land inequality.

Acemoglu, Bautista, Querubin, and Robinson also study the impact of
inequality on economic outcomes, using the Engerman–Sokoloff arguments as a starting point. Yet they take a very different path. In Chapter 5,
Acemoglu et al. draw a distinction between economic and political inequality. The Engerman–Sokoloff argument starts from the effects of economic
inequality, and factor endowments that support this inequality, on economic allocations and politics. Moreover, it presumes that economic and
political inequality will be mutually self-reinforcing. While there are various reasons to expect economic and political inequality to go hand in hand,
in many societies there are marked differences between these two aspects of

inequality. These authors point out that, while in the data for U.S. states in the early part of the twentieth century, land inequality is negatively correlated with school enrollment, it is positively correlated across areas in the state of Cundinamarca in Colombia. In the United States, land inequality in 1860 had a negative effect on school enrollment in both 1870 and 1950. In Cundinamarca, the average land inequality in 1879 and 1890 had a positive effect on school enrollment in 1993. (In both cases, data availability dictates the choice of periods.) What the authors of this chapter ask, however, is whether political inequality could have played a role in driving inequality in schooling. The answer is that it did. In Cundinamarca, political inequality, as measured by the political concentration of town mayors at the end of the nineteenth century, was negatively correlated with school enrollment rates in 1993. Towns that were dominated by the same mayors or their relatives had particularly bad outcomes. Importantly, however, the rich landowners were not necessarily the dominant local politicians, because entry into politics was relatively free and open to people from many backgrounds. In fact, unlike the stylized pattern in Latin America, in Cundinamarca, land inequality was negatively correlated with political concentration (this is not to say that political power was not handsomely rewarded with private gains, because it was). The landed elite served as a counterweight to the political elite, and this provided restraint on the local executives who invested in turn in publicly beneficial projects. Acemoglu et al. propose an explanation of why land inequality may affect outcomes differently, arguing that the relationship depends on whether the polities are weakly or strongly institutionalized. In weakly institutionalized polities, in which formal political institutions do not adequately constrain the executive, economic inequality may generate an effective counterweight to the executive. In strongly institutionalized polities, economic inequality may enable the few rich to capture politics, to the detriment of the general public. The picture that emerges from this chapter about the political economy of inequality and institutions in Latin America is quite different from the conventional wisdom that has emerged from the work of Engerman and Sokoloff.

The second part of the book contains theoretical chapters, although all chapters in the last part—which deal with evidence—use theory as well. The interactions between bicameralism and staggered-term legislatures are studied in Chapter 6 by Muthoo and Shepsle. They use a standard cake-division game to examine the outcomes in different institutional structures when each chamber is in charge of half the cake. Their institutional structures include systems in which elections take place in both chambers simultaneously with no staggering, both chambers have similar staggered elections, and elections are simultaneous in one chamber and staggered in the other. In all cases the task of a legislature is to distribute the surplus (cake) across two districts. A legislator does not benefit directly from this allocation; he just enjoys rents from being in office. As a result of retrospective voting, the probability that a legislator will be reelected increases with past allocations of the cake to his district. Moreover, voters have finite memory as to past allocations. At the constitutional stage, the founding fathers choose the chamber structure, the term structure of legislators, and the allocation of proposal power. For each such structure the pure-strategy equilibrium is a Markov equilibrium. In this equilibrium the proposer takes the entire cake. This provides the benchmark result. Muthoo and Shepsle then proceed to argue that if restricted to a unicameral legislature at the constitutional stage, there are circumstances in which the founding fathers would prefer a staggered-term legislature to a simultaneous-term one. Moreover, in the baseline model, the founding fathers choose a bicameral legislature over a unicameral one. Finally, if the agenda-setting power of legislators from each district in a staggered-term chamber is the same on average as in a simultaneous-term chamber, then the founding fathers are indifferent between all possible mixes of simultaneous- and staggered-term structures of the two chambers. The baseline model is then extended in order to address various concerns. These extensions imply that two chambers lead to more bias toward the status quo than a single chamber, and that tax rates are higher in a bicameral system than in a unicameral one.

Civil wars are prevalent and they cause major economic damage. In Chapter 7, James Fearon provides a theoretical analysis of such wars. He starts the discussion with two stylized facts. First, most civil wars take the form of guerrilla conflicts. Second, poor countries are more likely to have civil wars. In fact, per capita income is the single best predictor of the probability of a civil war. To explain these regularities, Fearon constructs a game-theoretic model in which a government and a rebel group choose how many armed people to enlist. This then determines how many rebels are captured or die, while the surviving rebels tax peasants or businesses for their own benefit. Contrary to standard models of conflict, in which resources are wasted but no actors risk death, in this model, violence is an equilibrium outcome. Moreover, the model provides insight into the contest-success function, which is typically treated as a black box. In particular, the author argues that network connections among rebels can make expansion of the rebel force increasingly risky for an individual rebel. As a result, small forces have an advantage. The negative correlation between income per capita and civil wars cannot be explained in simple terms, however. In poor countries the opportunity cost of becoming a rebel is small, and there is little to be gained from fighting; in rich countries the opportunity cost is large, but there is also more to be gained. Declining marginal utility of income or risk aversion might suggest that wealthier individuals would be more reluctant to risk capture or death, yet this is insufficient to generate the empirical correlation. What is required in addition is for wealthier people to be relatively more risk averse than poorer people. In the model, the extent of rebellion is driven in large measure by the inefficiency of government counterinsurgency and the share of income that can be extracted by the guerrillas' taxation "technology" of house-to-house visits. Fearon argues that empirically both are likely to be greater in poor countries.

In Chapter 8, Grossman and Helpman study the impact of party discipline on the supply of political patronage (pork) to electoral districts. By "party discipline" they mean the degree of enforcement of electoral promises in legislative decisions. To address this issue they develop a three-stage model in which parties make electoral promises in the first stage, elections take place in the second, and legislative policymaking takes place in the third. A key feature of the model is that a party can impose costs on its legislators if they implement policies that deviate from the party's electoral promises. When these costs are zero, there is no party discipline whatsoever, and when they are infinite, a party representative implements the party's electoral promises for certain. In between, the degree of discipline varies widely. A conflict between the party and its legislators arises from the fact that the party is interested in maximizing the probability of controlling the legislature, while ex post, after being elected, a legislator is interested in supplying pork in the form of a local public good to his or her district (the electoral system is assumed to be majoritarian). In this type of polity, neither the electoral rhetoric nor the reality of pork-barrel spending bears a monotonic relationship to the degree of party discipline. In particular, promised spending per district is very high when party discipline is very low, it falls with rising discipline initially, but rises with party discipline eventually. Actual spending levels also follow a nonmonotonic pattern. And importantly, the expected welfare of voters is nonmonotonic: it is high and rising with party discipline when party discipline is high, but it can rise and eventually fall with party discipline (then rise again) when party discipline is low. One implication of this analysis is that high party discipline is desirable on welfare grounds, yet small improvements in discipline are not necessarily beneficial when discipline is low to begin with. Another implication is that the cross-sectional effects of political institutions cannot be adequately described by simple correlations between actual spending levels and measures of party discipline.

Chapter 9 closes the theory part of the book with a study by Diermeier and Fong of the "ratchet effect" of a dynamic fiscal policy. Static models of political economy have become rich in institutional detail, while dynamic models have so far suffered from highly simplified institutional structures. This state of affairs resulted from the technical difficulty of incorporating desirable institutional characteristics into dynamic political economy models. Recent advances have made this possible, however. The authors of this chapter employ a new dynamic model of legislative decision making to study the ratchet effect of government spending, which refers to the finding that government spending—as a fraction of GDP—rises during recessions but does not decline during expansions. Importantly, this is not true in all political systems. Only in one class of systems, that is, parliamentary democracies with proportional representation, is this effect present. This group includes European countries, such as Germany, Italy, the Netherlands, and Spain, but not the United Kingdom or the United States. Diermeier and Fong develop a dynamic model of parliamentary democracy with proportional representation that generates the ratchet effect. Their model has several important features. First, once a policy is enacted, it remains in force until a new law is passed. Second, the policy can be repeatedly amended during the electoral cycle by legislators with agenda-setting power. Third, due to the fact that in proportional representation systems no single party typically controls the legislature, policy formation involves bargaining among multiple parties. Fourth, as is the case in parliamentary systems, the executive has the agenda-setting power during the legislative period. The ratchet effect emerges as a result of the dynamic evolution of the status quo, and especially of entitlement programs, and asymmetries in the constraints; while it is always possible to raise spending on desired items, it is not possible to reduce spending below zero on undesirable items.

The last part of the book focuses on contemporary evidence. In Chapter 10, Anderson and Francois study the degree of formalism adopted by various groups in a Kenyan slum. This population provides a microcosm in which to explore the evolution of institutions and the determinants of their characteristics. The data come from a survey of about 520 households in the slum of Kibera (an area outside Nairobi) and include detailed information about group membership. More than 80% of the slum households sampled had members who were affiliated with informal groups. As a result, information could be obtained about the functioning of about 600 groups. This information includes such details as ethnic composition, punishment procedures, and the extent to which group relationships were formalized. Most of the groups dealt with savings, about 30% with insurance, and the rest with investment. In order to study the role of formalism in the activities of these groups, the authors distinguish between groups that are "registered" and those that are not. Registration provides a degree of external oversight. Other measures of formalism include the existence of written rules, minutes, and penalties. Some of the groups in the sample have implemented these formal procedures; others have not. The main working assumption of the study is that groups adopted formal procedures only when these procedures helped in achieving their goals. Some of the groups were formed along ethnic and kinship lines; others were not. This property provides another important source of variation. An interesting finding is that groups that formed along ethnic lines were most likely to choose formal procedures. Anderson and Francois conjecture that this resulted from the fact that it is difficult to credibly commit to discretionally punish members of one's own ethnic group or family when they break the group's rules of behavior, because one has various beneficial other relationships with such people. Under the circumstances, formal procedures make punishment more credible and therefore raise compliance with the rules. To examine this conjecture, they construct a theoretical model that incorporates these trade-offs. An important implication of the model is that kinship groups sustain cooperation without formalism when the intrinsic value of a relationship is low. When the intrinsic value of a relationship is high, however, cooperation is sustainable with or without ethnic homogeneity. But while heterogeneous groups can sustain cooperation without formal rules, homogeneous groups need them to ensure punishment. The model predicts conditions under which groups choose formal rules, and how these rules relate to membership fees and to the capacity to punish. Econometric evidence is then provided in support of these predictions.

In Chapter 11, Besley and Kudamatsu address the functioning of autocracies, which is a neglected topic in political economy. Their point of departure is the observation that autocratic regimes do not always perform badly, at least as judged by economic indicators, such as the growth rate of income per capita or other components of the human development index, that is, health and education. Given that democracy per se does not guarantee good economic performance, it is of interest to understand which features of autocratic regimes are conducive to good economic performance and which are not. Also interesting is the observation that a comparison of the density of growth rates of income per capita across democratic and nondemocratic regimes shows that nondemocratic regimes have fatter tails, both in the top and in the bottom of the distribution. This implies that nondemocratic regimes are more likely than democratic regimes to perform extremely badly or extremely well. Besley and Kudamatsu argue that economic performance depends on the accountability of political leaders, such as heads of states, and that this property can be achieved in different ways in different political regimes. While democratic regimes achieve accountability via contestability through the electoral process, autocratic regimes can also achieve accountability if a "selectorate" appoints the leader and it is powerful enough to be independent of the person in office. They develop a two-period theoretical model with two groups that face a distributional conflict, in which the selectorate has the power to keep the leader, but in which a decision to replace him triggers a contest for power in which the opposition wins the contest with positive probability. Comparing this model of autocracy to democracy, in which there are regular elections, they show that autocracy performs better than democracy if the selectorate is powerful and the distributional conflict is significant yet not too salient. In all other cases, democracy yields better results. Moreover, autocracy performs worst when the leader can hold on to power regardless of his performance. Evidently, this approach focuses attention on institutional features of political regimes that impact economic outcomes. Following this theoretical analysis, Besley and Kudamatsu examine empirically a host of autocratic regimes. Among these regimes, 35 had an annual growth rate of income per capita in the 80th percentile of the distribution. Following a series of robustness checks, 21 of these regimes survive this classification. To identify the determinants of successful autocracies, they examine a variety of correlates, such as the rate of leadership turnover, ethnic fractionalization, the availability of oil, legal origins, and the like. And in the final part of the chapter, they use the theory to interpret a variety of case studies in Brazil, China, Romania, Spain, Portugal, Thailand, Guinea, and South Korea.

Studies of the impact of democracy on growth yield inconclusive results. Aghion, Alesina, and Trebbi suggest, in Chapter 12, that the lack of robustness of this relationship may be due to the fact that democratic institutions differentially impact sectoral growth rates, depending on a sector's level of technological development and, in particular, depending on whether the sector is close or far away from the technology frontier. They develop a theoretical model to illustrate this dependence, emphasizing the impact of political institutions on the entry of new firms. Incumbents seek to prevent entry, and the political "bribes" they need to make in order to achieve this end are rising in the level of democracy. Under the circumstances, more democracy raises innovation by advanced firms but not by backward firms. As a result, improvements in democratic institutions have a larger impact on the growth of sectors that are closer to the technology frontier. This last prediction is empirically examined. Without controlling for the interaction between democracy and sectoral characteristics, the authors find no significant impact of democracy on growth. But once democracy is interacted with sectoral distance to the technology frontier, they find that democracy has a larger impact on the growth of sectors that are closer to the technology frontier and that the level of democracy has then also an independent positive effect on growth. After establishing these relationships, Aghion et al. seek to assess the extent to which the impact of democracy on sectoral growth is mediated by entry. Here the results are mixed. While exogenous measures of barriers to entry do not support this hypothesis, an endogenous measure of entry does. In this event it is not possible to establish causality, but the analysis suggests a potential role for entry in driving the impact of democracy on sectoral growth rates.

In Chapter 13, the last chapter of the book, Persson and Tabellini propose a new empirical method for estimating the impact of regime change on the growth rate of income per capita, in the wake of heterogeneous effects of regime change. Their new method consists first of estimating an equation for the probability of regime change, from democracy to autocracy or from autocracy to democracy, conditional on a variety of observable variables. The predicted probability of transition, the propensity score, is then used to match countries into groups in order to estimate within every group the impact of a regime change on the growth rate. These nonparametric matching estimates suggest that previous studies underestimated the growth effects of democracy. While standard difference-in-difference estimates yield an average growth acceleration of 0.6 percentage points after transition to democracy, the matching estimates yield an average growth acceleration of between 0.83 and 1.08 percentage points. Over the sample period this implies the difference between an 8% increase in income per capita based on the former estimate and a 13% increase based on the latter. Moreover, the difference in the growth rate between the countries that switched from autocracy to democracy was driven primarily by a decline in the growth rate of the autocracies rather than an increase in the growth rate of the newly democratized regimes. For countries that transited from democracy to autocracy, the effects were even larger. While difference-in-difference estimates yield a 0.84 percentage-point decline in the growth rate, the matching estimates suggest a decline in the growth rate between 1.6 and 2.4 percentage points. In this case the difference arises primarily from the decline in the growth rate of the countries that experienced the regime change. It follows that the two types of regime change are asymmetric, in that a switch from democracy to autocracy has a bigger negative impact on growth than the positive impact of a switch from autocracy to democracy.

Conclusion   These chapters convey an important message: institutional analysis has advanced in major ways and it has deepened our understanding of the essential determinants of human well-being. Progress in this area requires the skillful integration of several building blocks—from history, economics, political science, and other parts of the social sciences. For this reason, it does not fit well into customary research programs, which are designed along disciplinary lines. And for the same reason, progress was slow for many years. The rapid transformation of this area of inquiry in the last decade has been achieved by dismantling the disciplinary barriers, in large measure as a result of the willingness of scholars—such as those represented in this book—to learn from each other and to cooperate in advancing our common knowledge in this challenging area. As is evident from reading these chapters, despite the great progress that has been made, the resulting cumulative knowledge cannot yet effectively be used to design social, political, and economic institutions that will best serve societies with varying features. However, the way is being paved toward this goal.

— I —

History

— 1 —

The Impact of Administrative Power on Political and Economic Developments

Toward a Political Economy of Implementation

AVNER GREIF

This chapter presents a conjecture regarding the origin of constitutionalism, why it was historically insufficient to protect property rights, and why it was nevertheless positively correlated with prosperity. Theories of constitutionalism focus on constitutional rules and commonly view them as a coordination device that fosters the security of property rights. The origin of constitutionalism is the gain to property owners from coordinating on an equilibrium in which powerful rulers and the elite respect property rights.[1] Constitutionalism is a means of constraining the powerful.

History, however, suggests that constitutionalism (constitutional rules and also the rule of law and political representation) emerged to facilitate cooperation among the powerful. Constitutionalism was not a means to coordinate on an equilibrium but was an observable implication of particular equilibria. Specifically, it reflects equilibria in which a ruler, fearing sanctions by his administrators, had to take their preferences into account when making policy choices. Constitutionalism served, roughly speaking, as a means to facilitate cooperation and choice making among the powerful while reducing costly, on-the-equilibrium-path conflicts among them.

The premise of this chapter is that a ruler (e.g., a dictator, the elite, or an elected leader) who makes policy choices must rely on an administration to implement them. While the coordination theory of constitutionalism assumes that rulers can implement their choices, the premise here is that a ruler's policy choices are, in the absence of an administration to implement them, nothing but a wish. An administration is composed of individuals and organizations that are directly involved in the implementation of military, financial, legal, or other policy choices (e.g., a professional or citizens' army, militias, tax farmers, the Internal Revenue Service (IRS), feudal lords, self-governed provinces and cities, tribes, and lineages). An effective administration has the organizational capacity to execute policy choices by acting on the ruler's behalf (e.g., assembling an army, collecting taxes, or dispensing justice), making policy choices publically known, monitoring behavior, and punishing deviators.

Among its other tasks, an administration is a means to retaliate against those refusing to comply with policy choices. Administrators can therefore be in the particularly advantageous position of defying a ruler while, at the same time, reducing her capacity to retaliate against them. Indeed, military, financial, or legal administrators have often defied rulers and thereby influenced outcomes. *Administrative power* is the extent to which choices and outcomes are influenced by the administrators' capacity to defy rulers. Equilibria with different levels of administrative power exist because power increases in the cost of replacing the incumbent administrators while this cost increases in power[2] (Section 1.1).

When administrative power and gains from cooperation are sufficiently high, constitutionalism is Pareto optimal for the ruler and the administrators. The government is limited in the sense that the ruler cannot arbitrarily assign rights. The ruler's and administrators' rights are equilibrium outcomes underpinned by administrative power. Due process and equality before the law reduce costly conflicts caused by information problems, political assemblies foster cooperation (and particularly coordination on implementable choices), and gains from cooperation prevent the state from disintegrating. In such cases, the elite—those whose preferences influence policy choices—include the ruler and the administrators. (Section 1.2 presents the argument, and Section 1.3 provides historical evidence.)

This chapter's preliminary analysis of administrative power as the origin of constitutionalism suggests its promise in providing a consistent explanation for the rise, decline, and implications of constitutionalism. The administrative-power view reveals, for example, why constitutionalism rose in most of Europe (but not, for example, in Russia or China) by the fifteenth century, why rulers often protected the rights of the non-elite, and why the composition and interests of the elite changed over time and states.

In particular, the administrative-power view reveals why constitutionalism is insufficient for economic prosperity and why, nevertheless, premodern (European) constitutionalism was positively correlated with prosperity.[3] When administrative power underpins constitutionalism, those without power do not necessarily have protected rights, and welfare-related policy is biased by power considerations. Indeed, constitutional institutions benefitting the elite can be socially harmful exactly because they are "good" at fostering intra-elite cooperation in abusing the rights of the non-elite (Section 1.4).

Yet the administrative-power view reveals relations between constitutionalism and prosperity beyond the protection of property rights. Administrative power influences intra- and inter-state violence (Section 1.5), the total level of violence (Section 1.6), administrators' incentives to implement (even unauthorized) growth-enhancing policy choices (Section 1.7), and whether the nature and expected outcomes of political conflicts motivate the creation of new wealth (Section 1.8).

This analysis suggests that the historically positive correlation between constitutionalism and prosperity is due to the administrative equilibria leading to both. The administrative equilibria leading to constitutionalism also foster prosperity. They reduce overall violence, motivate administrators to implement growth-promoting choices, and lead to political conflicts favorable to the creation of new wealth. Furthermore, constitutionalism complements prosperity by providing a means for collective decision making and for peacefully providing political voice and influence to new economic groups.

Considering institutional development as reflecting the strategic problems associated with implementation differentiates this chapter from the more common *choice*-theoretic approaches to institutional development. The choice-theoretic approach assumes that rulers' choices correspond to outcomes and abstracts away from the need to implement these choices.[4] Although this assumption is often useful, we can gain from combining the analysis of choice with that of implementation (Greif 2005). Indeed, choices and implementations are interrelated: implementing choices requires an administration, and powerful administrators influence choices.[5]

Similarly, focusing on constitutions as equilibrium institutions (as in Greif 2006) differentiates this chapter from the literatures on administration: first, the literature using agency theory to study a ruler's optimal administrative forms (e.g., Levi 1989; Kiser 1999; Dixit 2006); second, the "iron triangle" literature on how the interactions between politicians, bureaucrats, and interest groups influence policy choices in democracies (e.g., McConnell 1966); and third, the literature on the determinants and impact of bureaucratic effectiveness (e.g., Wilson 1991; Evans and Rauch 1999). These important lines of work have taken legal and political institutions as given, while this chapter considers them as endogenous equilibrium outcomes.

Considering the ruler–administrators strategic problem differentiates this chapter also from the literature examining administration as a function of the relations among social groups (e.g., Greif 1998) or among rulers and their subjects (e.g., Levi 1989; Kiser 1999; Arias 2007). More generally, while Weber (1987) and Tilly (1990), among others, asserted that intra-state administrative growth is due to inter-state warfare, the analysis here highlights the reverse causal relation. Administrative equilibria influence the growth of the state—whether it disintegrates or consolidates—and whether violence prevails within or between states.

The analysis in this chapter is highly preliminary. It neither provides an explicit model, nor conducts an empirical test or rigorously integrates important considerations such as technological changes or environmental factors. As such, it represents the beginning rather than the end of a research agenda. Its only aim is to highlight the merit of developing the political economy of implementation that contends with the implications of the necessity of governing via administrators. Its key insight is that distinct initial endowments of administrative power can have profound implications on the historical trajectories of institutional and economic developments.

1.1 Administration and Administrative Power

This section defines the term "administration" as it is used in this chapter. It then differentiates between *powerful administrators* (or *powerful administrations*) who can sanction a ruler using their administrative capacity and *weak administrators* (or *ruler-controlled administrations*) who cannot.[6] It concludes by considering the technological, strategic, and structural determinants of administrative power and why multiple administrative equilibria are possible.

1.1.1 Administration

A ruler makes policy choices regarding the internal and external affairs of the state. These include the distribution of political, legal, and economic rights, processes of making legal and political decisions, and foreign policy. Whether a policymaker is a person (such as a king, dictator, or president) or a group (such as a tribe, party, ethnic group, oligarchy, republic, or theocracy), governing requires an administration. An *administration* is composed of individuals and organizations that are directly involved in the implementation of military, financial, legal, or other policy choices. An effective administration executes choices by acting on the ruler's behalf (e.g., assembling an army or dispensing justice), making choices publically known, monitoring behavior, and punishing deviators.

Because rulers have a limited physical capacity to implement policy choices, the administration at their disposal determines which of their choices will be implemented. Federal tax rates are chosen by the federal authorities, for example, but the effectiveness of the IRS determines the tax revenues that will be collected. Similarly, a ruler might choose to have an army of a certain size, but an administration is necessary to implement this choice. It must obtain the necessary funds, solicit recruits, and equip, train, and maintain them.

In studying the impact of administrations on developmental processes, it is useful to adopt the broader definition above rather than equate administrations with bureaucracies. This definition captures that administrations throughout history existed in a wide variety of forms, such as citizens' militias, mercenary armies, feudal lords, warlords, privateers, tax farmers, modern bureaucracies, temples, parishes, and self-governed provinces, colonies, cities, tribes, and clans.

1.1.2 Administrative Power

Ignoring incentive issues, administrators can use their administrative capacity to sanction the ruler by withdrawing their services, implementing another choice, or using their administrative capacity against him. (Henceforth, the term "sanction" refers to any of these actions.) Historically, administrators sometimes refused to implement choices of even seemingly mighty rulers such as Frederick Barbarossa (d. 1190), who was Emperor of the Holy Roman Empire, as well as kings of Germany, Italy, and Burgundy, and duke of Swabia. In 1174, for example, Barbarossa prepared a campaign against the Italian city-republics and asked one of his feudal lords, Henry the Lion, the duke of Saxony and Bavaria, to send his troops. Henry, however, declined and utilized his troops to secure his domain's eastern borders.[7]

Administrators have *administrative power* when their capacity to sanction a ruler influences the ruler's choices. Having influence requires the threat of sanctioning to be credible and the sanction to be sufficiently large. The larger the set of choices the administrators can influence, the higher their power. Attempts to preempt power also influence choices. For example, after the American Revolution of 1776 revealed the administrative power of the self-governed colonies to Britain, it attempted to establish Crown colonies instead.

Individuals and organizations that are not part of the state's administration might also have the capacity to sanction rulers. The expectations of such sanctions might influence rulers' choices (e.g., Greif 2005). Choices made by Chinese emperors reflected their concerns about mass peasant revolts, while those of elected officials in democracies often reflect their concerns with future votes by members of organized groups.[8] Yet, there is an important distinction between the sanctioning capacities of administrators and nonadministrators. To sanction the ruler, nonadministrators have to take *action* (e.g., revolt or vote) while potentially facing a repressive administration. In contrast, powerful administrators can impose costs on a ruler through *inaction* and only face a state apparatus that has been weakened because of their inaction. Powerful administrators therefore have a comparative advantage in sanctioning rulers.

1.1.3 Self-Enforcing Administrative Power

Different levels of administrative power can be equilibrium outcomes for a given environment and technology. Multiple equilibria exist because administrative power increases with the ruler's cost of replacing incumbent administrators and this cost increases in administrative power. (By "replacing administrators," I also mean creating an alternative administration.) To see why this is the case, ignore, for simplicity, considerations such as collective-action problems, heterogeneity in administrators' preferences, and asymmetric information.

Suppose that the cost of replacing the administrators is infinite. In this case, the administrators can implement their first-best choice with impunity because the ruler cannot retaliate against them.[9] The ruler's optimal (implementable) choice is the administrators' first-best choice. (Section 1.5 discusses the role of rulers when administrators are powerful.) If the ruler can replace the administrators with alternative ones at some cost, however, their ability to sanction that ruler is limited by the threat of replacement (and the implied retaliation). If the cost to the ruler of not implementing a particular choice is higher than the cost of replacing the noncompliant administrators by those who would comply, the incumbent administrators cannot prevent implementation. The administrators' impact on choices is lowest if the cost of replacing them is zero, in other words, if they have perfect substitutes.[10]

Environmental and technological factors influence the ruler's cost of replacing the incumbent administrators and hence their power. The power of financial administrators, for example, declines if the ruler gains an independent source of income or access to alternative financiers. High specificity of the human and physical capital required for providing administrative services implies high costs of replacing them because the set of alternative administrators is small. Fighting as a knight required a long period of training, costly equipment, and a few squires to fend against rusting. During the feudal period, therefore, European rulers could not increase their heavy cavalry force by knighting nonnobles. The federal air traffic controllers who went on an illegal strike in the United States in 1981 assumed that their special skills were of sufficient value to empower them. Their mistake was that military air traffic controllers had similar skills and hence President Reagan could replace the strikers.

The controllers' illegal strike highlights why there can be multiple equilibria in administrative power. High replacement costs render the administrators powerful, while powerful administrators can prevent choices that reduce their replacement costs. The Emperor Barbarossa, for example, faced powerful administrators—the German dukes—who gained administrative capacity during the civil war that preceded his regime. The cost of replacing them seems to have been high enough to restrict his ability to reduce their power. Following his loss in the battle of Legnano (1176) that concluded his Italian campaign, Barbarossa had to recognize the autonomy of the Italian cities. He blamed the failure on Henry's absence and, upon returning to Germany, fought and deposed Henry. But the dukes who assisted Barbarossa were the ones who devoured Henry's territories. They were sufficiently powerful to prevent Barbarossa from becoming stronger.

High costs of replacing the administrators render them powerful, and power can be used to prevent reducing replacement costs. Similarly, low replacement costs imply weak ("ruler-controlled") administrators who cannot prevent choices that will keep these costs low. In Imperial China, for example, replacement costs were low as the system was such that each administrator had close substitutes. Administrators were uniformly trained, tasks were routinized, redundant positions were created, and the communication network and protocol implied high costs of attempting to coordinate actions against the emperor. The emperor's costs of replacing an administrator were therefore low, and the administrators lacked the power to increase those costs.

Hence, there are at least two administrative equilibrium structures, one with weak and the other with strong administrations.[11] In between there are likely to be others in which neither side will find it beneficial to unilaterally change the structure. Once an administrative equilibrium corresponding to any one of these many equilibria prevails, it is *self-enforcing*. In these cases, the administrative structure—whether commissioned by a ruler, created by the administrators, or inherited from the past—will perpetuate.

1.1.4 The Limit on the Ruler's Power to Coordinate

Underpinning the assertion that an equilibrium with administrative power exists is that an administrator can use his administrative capacity to sanction the ruler. An administrator cannot have a capacity to sanction, however, if the ruler can coordinate her subjects on any self-enforcing pattern of behavior and expectations about behavior. An equilibrium with administrative power does not exist in this case because the ruler can respond to an administrator's threat by coordinating on an equilibrium in which another person is the administrator. Because it is common knowledge that everyone will follow the behavior associated with the new equilibrium, the disobedient administrator will no longer have any administrative capacity. His agents, for example, will follow the instructions of the new administrator. In other words, there is no equilibrium with powerful administrators if the ruler has a monopoly over coordinative authority or *legitimate* coordination.[12]

Yet, legitimacy itself has to be an equilibrium, and equilibria with various distributions of authority and coordinative legitimacy are theoretically possible. Such equilibria have prevailed in the past and the present and have manifested themselves in different notions of loyalty and rights. European feudal knights were expected to be and indeed often were loyal to their direct overlords and not to their kings. The commonly held belief was that they would obey their lords' choice to sanction their kings. As a matter of fact, the knights of Saxony indeed did not join Frederick Barbarossa on his Italian campaign and eventually fought alongside Henry against their emperor.

The knights' decision to join Henry in fighting the emperor is consistent with the possibility that multiple notions of loyalty can be self-enforcing. If the ruler expects some agents to be loyal to an administrator, his best response is to replace them in case of a conflict with the administrator, but if the agents expect to be replaced, their best response is more likely to support the administrator. When Henry refused to join Barbarossa's Italian campaign, the emperor could have nominated another person to replace Henry in his capacity as duke. That Barbarossa did not do so suggests that Henry's knights would not have followed the new duke and join Barbarossa in the battlefield. Their loyalty was to Henry.

The thirteenth-century barons who demanded the Magna Carta from the English king (1215) had similarly loyal knights. In the subsequent war with the king, their knights fought against him. It is difficult to imagine contemporary English soldiers fighting against the queen of England. Unlike their feudal predecessors, their loyalty is to England, not their superiors. (Arguably, the welfare state that has replaced patronage is one factor contributing to this distinction.) In short, different loyalties can be equilibrium outcomes. If an administrator's agents are loyal to him and not the ruler, the cost of replacing the administrator can be positive because he cannot be replaced through coordinating his agents.

Similarly, various beliefs and norms regarding rights and hence the scope of legitimate actions can be an equilibrium. If the scope of legitimate choices by the ruler is common knowledge, the ruler's ability to replace an administrator by coordinating the actions of the other administrators against him is diminished. The administrators are less likely to support the ruler in replacing an administrator who defied his illegitimate choice. In other words, common knowledge of choices that the ruler has a right to make coordinates the administrators to collectively sanction a ruler who made a choice he had no right to make. Such collective sanctions increase the ruler's cost of replacing an administrator who refused to implement such a choice. Collective sanctions also increase the costs of creating an alternative administration because they reduce the ruler's administrative capacity to undertake such a venture. Creating an effective new administration has historically been a costly and time-consuming matter.

Historically, rulers' investments in promoting their legitimacy suggest its importance in restricting their choices. Rulers promoted ideologies that legitimized their freedom of action. European kings invoked the divine right of kings, Chinese and Japanese emperors claimed to have mandates from heaven, and democratic leaders proclaim the legitimacy of majority rule.

Theoretically, rulers can do more than promote their legitimacy. Various administrative practices can reduce administrative power. For example, if administrative tasks are divided among relatively many administrators, each has, *ceteris paribus*, a lower capacity to sanction a ruler. The cost of replacing each administrator is lower than it would have been otherwise. First, having fewer resources for rewarding supporters reduces the set of parameters for which loyalty to that administrator is an equilibrium, and second, the higher number of administrators reduces their ability to coordinate sanctions. Choosing administrators with different interests and cultures also reduces the cost of replacing them by reducing their ability to coordinate and credibly commit to sanctioning the ruler. The cost of replacing an administrator also declines depending on the frequency of administrators' geographical rotation. Rotation undermines one's ability to cultivate loyalty among the locals. Finally, higher uniformity of administrative training, tasks, and routines also lowers this cost.

Indeed, such administrative practices that prevented administrators from acquiring a large administrative capacity, cultivating loyalty, and forming a common perception of rights were historically common. The prevalence of these measures suggests the insufficiency of coordination by rulers in eliminating administrative power. In such diverse polities as France under the Bourbon kings and China under the Qing emperors, on the one hand, and republican Genoa and Venice on the other, frequent rotation of administrators was mandatory. Muslim rulers often used slaves without local roots as administrators. The Mongol emperors of China employed foreigners, such as Marco Polo, as administrators. Administrative redundancy was created in Imperial China, as noted above, and in Communist Russia where the party's administration paralleled the state's. Although wasteful, it provided information and excess administrative capacity that limited administrative power.

The discussion so far has assumed implicitly that rulers prefer a weaker administration. Yet, rulers might benefit from increasing administrative power when it fosters commitment. The history of France provides an example. When the Bourbons came to power (1589), the Crown auctioned short-term leases to bidders who were weak because they were perfect substitutes ex ante and ex post. The Crown's expenses, however, grew faster than its revenues, and the budgetary pressure led the Crown to ex post renegotiate leases and renege on its contractual obligations. Once the farmers realized this, they made smaller bids and the budgetary crisis worsened. In response, Colbert, France's finance minister, created a strong administrator, the "Company of General Farms," in the second half of the seventeenth century. The company became the sole collector of indirect taxes and hence could more credibly threaten to halt collections if the Crown reneged on its obligations. The Crown's enhanced commitment increased revenues and resolved the budgetary crisis (Balla and Johnson 2006).

For any administration to impact outcomes, it has to be effective in implementing choices. There is nevertheless no one-to-one relationship between administrative power and other attributes of administrations such as effectiveness (capacity for and cost of implementing choices), centrality (whether decisions are made centrally and/or there are economies of scale and scope in administration), or corruption (the use of administrative posts for private gain). Some examples can illustrate the lack of one-to-one relations among these attributes and administrative power. The French Company of General Farms that collected indirect taxes was powerful and effective, while its contemporary English customs collectors were weak and effective. The Federal Reserve is a centralized and powerful administration as it is controlled by a board that cannot be arbitrarily replaced by the White House and Congress. The ideal type of Weberian bureaucracy, in contrast, is centralized but weak.

Focusing on administrative equilibria is analytically useful and empirically relevant. Yet, it is intuitive that administrative equilibria—particularly those with powerful administrators—are generally unstable. A distribution of administrative power is likely to be an equilibrium in relatively small parameter sets and hence correspondingly small exogenous shocks are likely to cause this distribution to no longer be an equilibrium outcome. Furthermore, administrative equilibria tend to undermine themselves in the sense that they lead to changes that render them self-enforcing in small parameter sets. In addition, information and coordination problems provide opportunities to rulers and administrators to shift the equilibrium in their favor. The discussion below illustrates the fragility of administrative equilibria and the associated dynamics. (See the general discussion in Greif [1998; 2006, ch. 6].)

1.2 The Origin of Constitutionalism: Theory

This section presents why and under what conditions administrative power leads to constitutionalism, namely, the rule of law, constitutional rights, and political representation. It argues that constitutionalism is an observable implication of administrative equilibria with powerful administrators.

The rule of law has several components, the first being a limited government in which the ruler is constrained from arbitrarily assigning rights. A rule of law in this sense prevails in an administrative equilibria with powerful administrators because there are rights that the ruler is better off conceding rather than demanding and triggering sanctions. (The ruler's power, if any, is due to his control over the "weak" component of his administration.) The more power the administrators have, the more rights they can secure for themselves.[13] Limited "government"—under which rulers respect predetermined customary, legal, explicit, or implicit rights—is an equilibrium outcome reflecting a balance of administrative power.

To highlight the causal relationship between administrative equilibria and other components of the rule of law (i.e., equality and due process before the law), suppose that sanctions are costly to both the ruler and administrators. Further suppose that the ruler can structure the legal processes governing disputes between himself and an administrator, and among administrators. Also suppose that there is imperfect public information. Specifically, if the ruler makes legal decisions, there is a positive probability that the administrators will interpret them as aimed at transgressing their rights or reducing their power.

Feudal Europe illustrates the relevance of this characterization of the situation. In a feudal society, decisions had to be made regarding estates held by a widow, a minor lord, or a lord who had no legal heirs. If the crown had discretion in choosing who might be entitled to marry a lord's widow, serve as a regent, or become a new lord, it could make choices that would influence the balance of administrative power. For example, a ruler could choose a lord whose preferences were more aligned with his own than with those of the administrators.

The characteristics of equilibria in such repeated, imperfect monitoring games are well known. Sanctions that are costly to the ruler and administrators will transpire on the equilibrium path whenever the administrators interpret a ruler's legal decision as aimed against them. In such cases, rulers and administrators gain from adopting decision-making processes that improve the quality of information and reduce the likelihood of conflicts. Information improves by instituting equality and due process before the law because legal decisions and processes are uniform and are conditional on the objective attributes of the situation and not on the identity of the litigants. By relinquishing discretion and respecting legal procedures with outcomes she does not control, the ruler is able to signal that her choice is not aimed at influencing power. If her expected gains from reducing conflict are larger than the expected cost of losing discretion, introducing and respecting due process and equality before the law is her best response.

Similarly, constitutional rules—charters, golden bulls, constitutions, political traditions, or basic laws—reduce conflicts on the equilibrium path. In particular, constitutional rules that specify the legal, economic, and political rights of both sides, and processes for making decisions reduce the possibility of costly misinterpretations of choices (Greif 2006).

Rulers facing powerful administrators often behaved in a manner consistent with this argument. Consider, for example, the feudal period. Even before the Magna Carta (1215) affirmed the English barons' right to be tried by their peers, English kings followed this procedure. The Magna Carta also specified processes for trial by one's peers and for handling fiefdoms that were under the supervision of regents or widows rather than an adult male lord. Similarly, Barbarossa followed the rule of law before attacking Henry. He sought legal consent for the attack from a council of dukes and attacked only after they had found Henry guilty of insubordination and declared him an outlaw. This process, most likely, was about clarifying Barbarossa's intentions rather than justice. The territory captured from Henry was given to other dukes, thereby retaining the balance of power between them and Barbarossa.

The discussion of the rule of law has so far implicitly assumed that the relative power of the ruler and the administrators is common knowledge. In reality, however, asymmetric information about each side's powers is likely to prevail. Furthermore, constitutional rules have implications beyond reducing conflicts. They also determine the allocation of gains from fewer conflicts. For these reasons, conflicts that reveal relative power and select among rules are therefore likely to transpire.

The history of the Magna Carta reflects three aspects of the above argument—that constitutional rules mitigate informational problems, that they must be self-enforcing to be followed, and that conflicts are a means to reveal relative power through which self-enforcing rules are selected. The first version of the Magna Carta was imposed on King John in 1215 by the barons, who demanded and obtained many rights when the king was militarily unprepared for confrontation. In particular, they imposed "clause 61" upon him, which specified that kings must swear an oath of loyalty to an independent baronial committee that could overrule their decisions, through force if necessary.

Later events indicate that clause 61 was not self-enforcing although the barons may have hoped to make it so by forcing King John to swear in God's name to keep it. Subsequently, John asked for and received from the Pope an annulment of his oath, gathered his forces, and invalidated the Magna Carta. The later version of the Magna Carta, confirmed by King Henry III in 1225, remained in force into the nineteenth century, and excluded clause 61. Indeed, it contained only thirty-seven clauses. Those that were not self-enforcing did not last.[14]

Administrative power leads to political representation because constitutional and other rules specifying rights are inherently incomplete "contracts." Hence, the rights and choices they specify are not likely to remain optimal to both sides as time passes. Yet, because these rules are an equilibrium outcome, neither side can *unilaterally* alter them without risking conflict. For example, a ruler risks costly retaliation if he increases taxes based on private information regarding a forthcoming external attack.

When past rights and choices are no longer optimal to both sides, their readjustment is mutually beneficial. Both the ruler and administrators can gain from coordinating on changing rights or taking other actions. Such Pareto-improving changes may be procedural (e.g., specifying a process to determine tax rates); quantitative (e.g., change in the tax rates); and/or structural, aimed at keeping the balance of power (e.g., creating militia to balance an increase in a ruler's military strength). The Magna Carta, for example, specified the process by which the king could request the imposition of a higher tax and established a baronial council to supervise the king's actions.

Political assemblies are means for changing rights and making choices to achieve Pareto-optimal outcomes for the ruler and administrators. They facilitate revealing private information, changing rights, adjusting choices, and cooperating. The assemblies will be composed of individuals with administrative capacity (e.g., nobles), the leaders of hierarchical structures (e.g., tribal leaders), or the elected representatives of horizontal structures (e.g., officials of self-governed cities).[15]

Assemblies, however, are costly to rulers because they increase administrative power by fostering coordination among the administrators. Aristotle, for one, noted that tyrants "don't allow [even] associations for social and cultural activities or anything of that kind; these are the breeding grounds of independence and self-confidence, two things which tyrants must guard against" (*Politics* 5.11). Thus, if the ruler does not gain much from changing rights and making new choices, he is better off without representative assemblies.

This implies that states with weak administrators will not have representative assemblies (although rulers may still rely on various advisory councils). The *elite* (those with formal influence over policy choices) will be constituted of the ruler and his close aides. States with powerful administrators will have assemblies representing the administrators, but only if they face an unstable environment that requires adjustments of rights and choices. In this case, the elite is composed of the ruler and the administrators. States with very powerful administrators are unlikely to have assemblies as these states disintegrate unless, due to external threats or other factors, the administrators can gain from cooperation via the state. (I return to this issue below.)

1.3   The Origin of Constitutionalism: History

While relevant evidence has yet to be systematically collected, a cursory historical examination confirms the relevance of the above argument and its predictions. In the late medieval period, constitutional monarchies and republics were the norm, not the exception, in Europe. Their most visible component is political assemblies (known as parliaments in the British Isles, *estates* in France, diets (*landtage*) in the Germanic lands, *sejm* in Poland, and *cortes* in the Iberian Peninsula). By the end of the fifteenth century, at least twenty-five national and provisional assemblies operated in the main principalities of Europe, including Scotland, England, Spain, Portugal, France, Sicily, the Netherlands, Germany, Austria, Poland, Hungary, Sweden, Denmark, and Norway (Herb 2003).

Consistent with the conjecture regarding the administrative origin of constitutionalism, these political assemblies were composed of individuals and corporate bodies with independent administrative capacity (e.g., feudal lords and self-governed cities) or they had a standing committee with administrative power.[16] Interestingly, although Japan also had powerful administrators under the Tokugawa Shogunate (1603 to 1868) it did not have an assembly. This is consistent with the argument that assemblies are established in response to the need to adjust rights. Japan was neither under external military threat nor did it trade internationally, implying it had less need for adjusting rights.

The timing of European constitutionalism also lends support to the conjecture that it is an equilibrium outcome in the relations between rulers and powerful administrators.[17] The late-medieval European states were established by rulers who had little administrative capacity. Their abilities to tax were so meager that many of them could not even support a stationary court and had to travel throughout their kingdoms to consume local products as late as the eleventh century. "The travels of the Holy Roman Emperor Conard [for that reason] in 1033 were fairly typical. He traveled some 1600 miles" (Webber and Wildavsky 1986, 168). After the eleventh century, outside raids on Europe subsided and rulers gradually acquired greater administrative capacity, mobilized larger armies, collected higher taxes, and administered justice.

Rulers faced the challenge of gaining administrative capacity in the context of intense, existential, intra-European political competition that led to the destruction of such kingdoms as Upper Burgundy and Provence. They did not have the resources to create a weak administration and therefore relied on those with administrative capacity. Among these were lords (secular and ecclesiastical), the church, and economic corporations—mainly self-governed cities (communes)—many of which had acquired administrative capacity during the period when states were incompetent. The administrative capacity to confront external threats was gained at the cost of having powerful administrators. Rulers who failed to comprehend the advantages of constitutionalism in this trade-off often paid dearly. The German emperors lost Italy and the Swiss cantons. The English, Spanish, French, Polish, and most other European rulers learned from this lesson or had the foresight to adopt constitutionalism.

Histories of individual countries similarly confirm that rulers created or summoned political assemblies when they could have gained from changing rights but feared the response of their powerful administrators to a unilateral action. The French Estates General, for example, was created in 1302 when the king, Philip the Fair, sought its consent before entering into a conflict with Pope Boniface VIII. The Estates General was composed of powerful administrators, namely the chief lords, both lay and ecclesiastical, and the representatives of self-governed towns. Afterward, it was summoned regularly when the Crown needed financial support. This was true during the Hundred Years War (1337–1453) and the Wars of Religion of the late sixteenth and early seventeenth centuries. The Estates General was not summoned, however, from 1484 to 1560 when peace generally prevailed.

Having sufficient funds without changes in rights, the Crown probably preferred not to face an assembly.

Consistent with the argument that administrators' rights are an equilibrium outcome reflecting a balance of power, they were adjusted in France when this balance had changed. This happened when the first Bourbon, Henry IV, was crowned in 1589. Because he was a powerful administrator (governing Navarre), his ascension to the throne shifted the balance of power in favor of the Crown. Indeed, Henry embarked on a campaign to take rights from administrators, particularly through the use of supervisors (*intendants*) to check on the provisional governments. Subsequent kings continued weakening these nobility-controlled governments, particularly from 1621–1661. The role of the intendants, for example, was expanded from supervision to tax collection.

The previously powerful administrators often attempted to prevent the further undermining of their power in various ways. The feudal nobility and the officers of the Parlement of Paris often revolted, but the series of failed revolts, known as the Fronde (1648–1653) revealed the new balance of power. In the absence of powerful administrators, there was no need for the Estates General, and it was not summoned after 1615. It was next summoned in 1789 when the Crown faced a financial crisis reflecting its limited success in creating an effective, yet weak, administration.

The histories of Russia and Poland similarly illustrate that constitutionalism rises and falls with administrative power and that whether a weak or a strong administration prevails will depend on the initial administrative endowment rather than technology or environment. Despite their similar endowments, Russia's constitutionalism declined over time while Poland's increased. Russia's initial administrative endowment was a weak administration, while Poland had powerful administrators.

After the Mongols conquered Russia, Moscow functioned as the tax collector for the Mongols, who bestowed the title of Grand Prince of Moscow on its ruler. The Muscovite princes, protected by the Mongols, gathered taxes while gradually developing a military and financial administration of their own. The Mongols seem to have underestimated the role of legitimacy and administrative rotation on administrative power. The Muscovite princes were administrators, with both military and taxation capacities, who served an illegitimate ruler while having the required tenure to cultivate the loyalty of their agents. These conditions favored political disintegration (secession of Russia from the Mongol Empire) and weak administrators in the new political unit.

Indeed, by the second half of the fourteenth century, the Muscovite princes revolted and gradually gained independence. Initially, the hereditary high nobility (*boyars*) retained some administrative power and gained political representation in the Boyar Duma. Consistent with the argument here, as the economic importance of the church and the cities increased, an "assembly of the land" (*zemsky sobor*) was also created (1459) with representation from the nobility, those high in the bureaucracy, the church, and the towns. Once the war with the Mongols ended, however, the princes of Moscow began to undermine these administrators' power.

Later princes, particularly Ivan III and Ivan IV, gradually restricted the boyars' power, conquered the city-republic of Novograd and eliminated its self-governance, created a standing army (the *streltsy*), and for a period ruled over about a third of Russia as their private domain. After 1654 the Assembly of the Land met only once before its last meeting in 1684. The Boyar Duma was abolished in 1711. The development of effective administration with weak administrators ended whatever small degree of constitutionalism Russia possessed.

One of the main powers facing the Russian Empire was the Commonwealth of Poland–Lithuania (Poland). It was established in 1569 through the union of Poland and Lithuania and extended over contemporary Poland, Lithuania, Belarus, Latvia, and the western part of Russia, as well as much of the Ukraine and Estonia (e.g., Stone 2001). Despite the similar technologies and natural endowments of Russia and Poland, the former was an autocracy and the latter was a constitutional monarchy from its inception until 1795 (when it was partitioned by other powers).

Poland's distinct institutional trajectory seems to reflect a different process of state formation. Polish kings did not initially function as tax collectors supported by an occupying military force. Instead, they consolidated—but did not conquer—an area governed by local aristocracies. These aristocrats did not provide the kings with the resources required for creating a ruler-controlled administration. After 1572, for example, the king was forbidden to dismiss any official and his army was restricted to 3,000 men while various magnates' armies were larger. (Section 1.4 provides additional details.)

The rule of law, constitutions, and political assemblies have historically been the observable implications of an equilibrium with powerful administrators. They were means for reducing conflicts and gaining from adjusting rights and making choices in the presence of administrative power. Clearly, constitutional institutions can emerge for similar reasons when rulers face other powerful actors and social groups. Yet, the comparative advantage of powerful administrators in sanctioning rulers, as well as historical evidence, suggests that administrative power has been particularly important in leading to constitutionalism in Europe.

1.4   Why Is Constitutionalism Insufficient for Prosperity?

This section argues that when constitutionalism is an equilibrium underpinned by administrative power, it is insufficient for prosperity because the rights of the nonpowerful are not necessarily secured while policies are biased by power considerations and the interests of the powerful.[18]

History is often invoked to claim that constitutionalism is sufficient for prosperity. Pre-modern constitutional states secured the property rights necessary for markets, thereby leading to modern economic growth. England became the canonical example, and according to this interpretation of English history, it prospered after the Glorious Revolution (1688) because the constitutionalism that followed secured rights and promoted markets (North and Weingast 1989).

Yet, after the revolution, England also witnessed some of the greatest property rights abuses in its history, such as the nineteenth-century parliamentary enclosure of the open fields (which constituted regressive confiscation of assets), higher taxation of politically unrepresented Englishmen, and land grabs in Ireland and in the colonies (e.g., O'Brien 2001; Harris 2004). Despite these abuses, England prospered, but other constitutional monarchies (as most European states were by the fifteenth century) did not.

Poland provides an example of a constitutional monarchy, which, although older than England's, is neither known for its prosperity nor for leading the transition to modern economies. Its kings were elected, and a political assembly (*sejm*) had probably existed since the twelfth century, representing the nobles, clergy, and elected local representatives. Under the Polish–Lithuanian Commonwealth (1569–1795), elections to the assembly were held every other year; the assembly was summoned every year, operated under a set of constitutional rules, elected the king, and made final decisions in legislation, taxation, budgets, and foreign affairs.

Poland's experience also suggests why constitutionalism was historically insufficient for prosperity. The rights of those without administrative power may not have been better protected than their equivalents in nonconstitutional states. The administratively powerful Polish landlords abused the rights of cities and peasants. The elected assembly prevented urban expansion by prohibiting cities from buying land and gradually increased taxation on peasants and legally subjugated them to serfdom. The situation in absolutist Russia was not much different. The Russian peasantry was similarly subjected to serfdom by the tzars. The main distinction between the two countries reflects the impact of different distributions of administrative power. In Poland, the landlords gained from serfdom, while in Russia, the central government was the major beneficiary.

As a matter of fact, constitutionalism can be socially harmful exactly because it is "good" at fostering intra-elite cooperation. In particular, constitutionalism fosters cooperation among the ruler and the administrators in abusing the rights of the non-elite. Indeed, not long after the English Parliament met for the first time, it approved tripling the poll tax that peasants paid, thereby reducing the elite's tax burden. Similarly, after the Glorious Revolution (1688), as noted above, England witnessed some of the greatest property rights abuses in its history. Better institutions for the elite do not necessarily imply good institutions for others.

More generally, rulers' incentives to protect the property rights of the non-elite are theoretically ambiguous under constitutionalism and nonconstitutionalism. At issue is how abuse impacts the balance of administrative power. On the one hand, rulers benefit from preventing abuse that increases the administrators' power. Indeed, in late medieval Europe, rulers were supposed to, and often did, protect the rights of the non-elite. The summary of Frederick Barbarossa's duty is representative. His duty "was merely to protect all the subjective rights everybody had. . . . [H]e was supposed to play [the . . .] role as law protector" (Munz 1969, 100). Similarly, Byzantine emperors successively enacted laws designed to protect small landholders from larger ones, fearing that land consolidation would undermine the military force the small landholders provided them. The eighteenth-century Austrian emperors, Maria Theresa and Joseph II, reformed the agricultural sector to the benefit of the peasants.

On the other hand, when rulers are unable to prevent abuses that increase administrators' power, they can benefit from socially inefficient policies that will check it. The Ottoman sultans enacted policies that favored their tax base in Istanbul but hindered growth in the provinces administered by governors who might have challenged them (Kivanc 2006).

Whether constitutionalism prevails or not, those making policy choices consider their impact on relative administrative power. Socially beneficial choices that undermine their powers are less likely to be chosen. Administrative power creates a wedge between the socially optimal choices and those that are optimal for rulers and administrators.[19]

Comparisons between England and the Polish–Lithuanian Commonwealth exemplify that the welfare implications of limited monarchies depend on their administrators' interests and concerns about maintaining power. In the Commonwealth, those with administrative power did not pass policies encouraging urbanization, markets, and industry, which potentially would have led to rival administrators. The administratively powerful Polish landed aristocracy pursued policies, such as serfdom, which increased their profits from export-oriented commercial agriculture without undermining their power.

In seventeenth-century England the parliamentarians were engaged in domestic agriculture, commerce, finance, and industry. Their interests lay in policies that fostered market expansion and internal demand and, following the increase in their power during the civil wars of the seventeenth century, they implemented policies that supported commercial expansion overseas. England built the largest navy in Europe, enacted the Navigation Act, gained control over the seas, and created an empire. While these policies did not initially benefit all Englishmen, they eventually contributed to general prosperity. In England, unlike the Commonwealth, the interests of those with administrative power were in line with the interest of the economy at large.[20]

Constitutionalism based on administrative power is insufficient for prosperity but it has some prosperity-enhancing attributes. Under constitutionalism, the administrators' property rights are explicit and secured and there is an institutionalized way to adjust property rights and policies. When the administrators are economic agents whose interests are aligned with economic prosperity, their political voice provides information regarding beneficial policies, their political influence contributes to rendering these policies the official ones, and their administrative capacity fosters their implementation. When the administrators are military or economic agents whose interests conflict with economic prosperity, however, their voice, influence, and capacity will be welfare reducing under constitutionalism.

The interests of the administrators, in turn, are endogenous to the administrative equilibrium. In particular, when the administrative equilibrium reduces violence and administrative power is diffused, the administrators' interests will shift toward beneficial economic policy. This issue is discussed in Section 1.6, but before turning to it, see Section 1.5, which discusses the relations between administrative power and violence.

1.5   To Revolt or to Invade? Intra-state and Inter-state Violence

It has long been recognized that an effective administration contributes to welfare and economic progress by reducing interpersonal ("private") violence. This section notes that whether an administration (effective in reducing private violence) is powerful or weak matters for other forms of violence as well. A state with a powerful administration is more likely to experience intra-state violence (for a given level of external military threat), while a state with weak administration is more likely to experience inter-state violence initiated by its ruler.

Sufficiently powerful administrators are more likely to stage a coup, revolt, or (de facto or de jure) secede, and when several powerful administrators act in this way, the state is likely to disintegrate. It is reasonable to conjecture that the expected level of intra-state violence (revolutions, coups, secessions, fighting among the administrators, etc.) increases in administrative power, in its concentration (at the hands of fewer administrators), and in the extent to which the powerful administrators are regionally based and provide military services.

Many premodern states were established through a process, which, if the above conjecture is correct, should have led to high levels of intra-state violence. States were often created by rulers who did not have the resources required to create ruler-controlled administrations but were nevertheless sufficiently talented and charismatic to mobilize tribes, nobles, or others who had administrative capacity. This is the process through which the Empire of Alexander the Great, the Empire of Attila the Hun, the Mongol Empire, and the Muslim Empire, among others, emerged. As long as such a state was expanding, the relatively few military administrators found it beneficial to cooperate. Over time, usually after the death of the first leader, gains from cooperation would decline as the empire reached its limit and the interests of administrators would diverge. The administrators would secede, quarrel over the spoils, or fight over leadership.

Upon his death, the empire of Alexander the Great disintegrated as his former generals fought over control. The Mongol Empire, the largest contiguous land empire in history, began expanding in 1206, relying on the military services of multiple Mongol, Turkish, and other tribes. It attained its largest area and disintegrated during the 1260s. The history of Russia, presented above, exemplifies how powerful administrators at the edge of an empire contributed to its disintegration. In the late fourteenth century, the Songhai played a similar role in the disintegration of the Mali empire in Africa.

I am not familiar with any theory articulating the conditions under which powerful administrators either cause the state to disintegrate or cooperate through the state. Yet, it is clear that whether powerful administrators cause the state to disintegrate or whether they maintain some political unity depends on their benefits from cooperation via the state and the ruler's ability to mobilize administrators to prevent violence (e.g., secession) by one of them. Disintegration is therefore less likely the higher is the gain from cooperation and the higher is the ruler's legitimacy.

Germany's history illustrates the importance of gains from cooperation through the state in maintaining it as one political unit. The Germanic dukes, mentioned above, progressively acquired power and independence. By the conclusion of the Thirty Years War (1648), the German Empire had disintegrated into de facto independent principalities. Yet, the Holy Roman Empire survived to the nineteenth century because it provided a means for cooperating in defense. The history of the Caliphate of Cordoba (in Spain) illustrates the importance of a ruler's legitimacy in preventing disintegration. Although Islam does not specify a legitimate process for choosing rulers, the caliphate was peacefully governed by members of the Umayyad dynasty who, as blood relatives of the prophet Mohammad, had considerable legitimacy. The Caliphate was rather successful in withstanding attacks by Christian forces. When the last member of the family, Hisham III, died in 1031, the Caliphate disintegrated into multiple rival principalities.[21]

The experience of the Caliphate reflects two reasons why rulers were useful to powerful administrators. First, succession laws specifying who is entitled to rule prevented intra-state wars over the throne. This role of succession laws is transparent in the Golden Bull (1356) issued by the German emperor. "We have promulgated, decreed and recommended for ratification the subjoined laws [governing the election of the king who will also be the emperor] for the purpose of cherishing unity among the electors, and of bringing about a unanimous election, and of closing all approach to the aforesaid detestable discord and to the various dangers which arise from it."[22] The Golden Bull explicitly named the seven prince-electors who were to choose the king. The second reason to have a king is to provide military leadership in confronting external threats. Even the Dutch Republic had a *stadtholder* who was a de facto hereditary head of state. His main task was to lead the republic in war.

Relative to powerful administrations, ruler-controlled administrations imply less intra-state violence. Ruler-controlled administrations have weak administrators, each of whom is less able to engage in intra-state violence. Administrative equilibria with weak administrators are likely to remain self-enforcing in a larger set of parameters than those with powerful administrators. Under weak administrations, larger changes in relative power are required to make the administrators powerful enough to defy the ruler.[23]

An effective ruler-controlled administration, however, provides the ruler with the resources to initiate wars with other states. The level of inter-state violence under a weak administration, may, nevertheless, be relatively low if there is a dominant, yet not aggressive state as was China in east Asia in various periods. Indeed, hegemonic peace periods saw relative prosperity. Peace, however, did not commonly prevail, and inter-state warfare, made possible by ruler-controlled administrations, further motivated each ruler to extend his administrative capacities (Tilly 1990).[24]

The economic and human costs of inter-state wars are particularly high (for a given technology and administrative equilibrium) when the interests of rulers, administrators, and the masses are aligned by ideology or economic factors. The high costs of the modern wars are partially due to nationalism and democracy which align the interests of elite and non-elite. Ireland's history illustrates the point. During World War I, general conscription was instituted in the United Kingdom of which Ireland was a part. Catholic Irish, however, supported independence and did not consider it in their interest to fight for the United Kingdom. The British recognized that without intrinsic motivation, forcing the Irish to join the army would be counterproductive and they were not drafted.

1.6   The Benefit of Midlevel Administrative Power: Reducing Overall Violence

The conditions which determine whether intra-state or inter-state violence is more prosperity-reducing are yet to be examined. Yet, the above suggests that the level of overall violence—and hence its cost—is U-shaped (given the level of external military threat). Intra-state violence increases in the administrators' power, while inter-state violence increases in the ruler's power (that is, with the administration's weakness).[25] Administrative equilibria therefore present a trade-off between intra-state and inter-state violence (that is, between social order and war).

This suggests the argument, developed in this section, that violence is lowest when the administrators' power is neither too high nor too low (henceforth, "midlevel"). In seeking to maintain their relative power, each side is motivated to check the violence beneficial to the other. The ruler (controlled administration) is sufficiently strong to reduce intra-state violence, and the administrators are sufficiently powerful to reduce inter-state violence. [26]

A necessary condition for the existence of a low-violence equilibrium is for the administrators, as a group, to have the power to restrain the ruler but be too weak to benefit from initiating intra-state violence.[27] (Greif [1998, 2006, ch. 8] and Bates, Greif, and Singh [2002] provide formal analyses.) Among the factors that make such an equilibrium more likely to exist is that the ruler controls the military administration (i.e., the military administration is weak) and powerful administrators control the state's finances. The administrators have a limited capacity to resort to violence but can nevertheless sanction the ruler by ceasing to finance the army. Recall that an administration's power declines in the number and rotation of administrators (Section 1.1). A low-violence equilibrium is therefore more likely to exist if there are relatively many military administrators who are frequently rotated and the financial administrators are stationary and either well coordinated or few in number.

The power of financial administrators can be substantial, as France's history illustrates. Colbert's response to the budgetary crisis in France in the seventeenth century was to create a strong financial administrator, the Company of General Farmers. The Crown gained because a powerful administration fostered its ability to commit to repay loans. By the eve of the French Revolution (1789), the company provided the Crown with more than one-third of its total royal tax revenues and about 40% of its operating budget. Indeed, it had gained sufficient power to block the proposed financial reforms that would have rendered it obsolete but might have prevented the Revolution (e.g., Root 1989; White 2004; Balla and Johnson 2006). Unable to reform its finances, the Crown ended up summoning the Estates General, and the Revolution followed.

The history of the Ottoman Empire illustrates the cost of failing to separate financial and military administrations and the importance of rotation in creating a weak administration. Similar to France, the Military Revolution of the seventeenth century (which increased the cost of war) led to a budgetary crisis. The Ottomans, however, responded by changing the duration of the tax farms from three years to lifetime tenure resulting in an immediate and substantial increase in revenues. Tax farmers with long tenure cultivated the loyalty of local militias, ceased paying their annual dues, and assumed, sometimes even hereditarily, political power. Only by the early nineteenth century were the Ottomans able to militarily subdue all the farmers (Balla and Johnson 2006; Hickok 1997).

In an administrative equilibrium under which the ruler and administrators constrain each other's actions, their conflicting interests regarding intra- and inter-state violence are endogenous (as mentioned in Section 1.4). Rulers bear the costs of intra-state violence but benefit from successful inter-state wars through which they gain resources to undermine administrative power. Recall, for example, the discussion of the Ottoman's success in weakening their administrators following the conquest of Constantinople. Legitimacy enhances rulers' interests in inter-state war by reducing the likelihood that defeat will lead to dethroning.

An empirical evaluation of this argument has yet to be conducted. But powerful administrators often seem to have been averse to inter-state wars initiated by their rulers. In late medieval Europe, administrators often refused to finance the "private" wars of their rulers although they were willing to finance those that were for the "benefit of the community of the realm," to use a phrase common in the sources. The English kings sought loans in Italy to finance the One Hundred Years War they initiated to regain their personal possessions in France, the French Bourbon kings had to cut deals with their feudal lords to finance their expansionist wars (Rosenthal 1998), and the Spanish Cortes refused to provide Philip II with the tax revenues required to build the Grand Armada that he sent in 1588 to conquer England.

Administrative balance of power that reduces intra-state violence influences interests in yet another way. Although the administrators can no longer gain from intra-state violence, they can gain from the economic opportunities that social order affords. The administrators' interests are transformed by the administrative equilibrium from specialization in violence to economic activities. Japan's history illustrates this process. When the Tokugawa shogunate (1603–1688) was established following a lengthy

civil war, it was a *bakufu*, meaning a "military government." Its administrators were men of arms—daimyo (lords) and samurai (warriors)—and
they were legally forbidden to engage in economic activities. The power
between the shogun and his administrators was apparently well balanced
as the period was remarkably peaceful. As time passed, however, and despite the prohibition, daimyo and samurai began engaging in economic
activities.

To summarize, intra- and inter-state violence are economically costly.
When administrative power is high, intra-state violence is more likely to
transpire, and if it is too weak, the ruler is more likely to initiate inter-
state wars. Midlevel administrative power implies that an equilibrium that
reduces both intra- and inter-state violence is more likely to exist. In the
long run, such an equilibrium can transform military administrators into
economic agents. Moreover, because midlevel administrative power entails constitutionalism, the administrators-turned-economic-agents have
an institutionalized way to influence policy choices. Economic prosperity
is more likely, because economic agents have political voice and influence.

The dynamics of such economically beneficial processes, however, can
cease if the balance of administrative power supporting low levels of violence fails to hold. This was often the case arguably because such equilibria
depend on a delicate balance of power and hence are often unstable. Temporary shocks in relative power can tilt the balance in favor of either the
ruler or the administrators.

Ottoman history illustrates how temporary shocks in relative power can
lead to new equilibria. Initially the Ottoman Empire followed the common process of relying on powerful administrators—mainly Turkish tribes
and clans, in this case—to provide military services. Civil wars were common, particularly upon the death of a sultan. This came to an end in 1453
when the Ottomans conquered Constantinople and gained the resources
and prestige to create a military force to balance (at least for a while) that
of their Turkish administrators.[28]

During the upheavals of the nineteenth century, several administrators
were able to increase their power to become independent rulers. The most
successful of them was Muhammed Ali, known as the founder of modern
Egypt. He was originally *wāli* (viceroy) of Egypt under the Ottoman rule.
He later revolted and gained international recognition of his hereditary
rights over Egypt in return for not conquering Istanbul.

1.7   Administrations, Incentives, and Economic Growth

Intensive economic growth is predicated on the introduction of new economic sectors and technologies while rulers, as discussed below, tend to make *growth-inhibiting* choices. This section presents why distinct administrative equilibria provide different incentives to administrators regarding the implementation of growth-inhibiting choices. The means used to weaken administrators provide them with strong incentives to implement these choices. In contrast, administrators with midlevel administrative power might have strong incentives to ignore growth-inhibiting choices and implement those that are *growth enhancing*.

Historically, the policy choices rulers made (as well as the choices made by very powerful administrators) were not guided by belief in the feasibility of intensive growth or a self-regulating market economy. These are relatively recent beliefs that have contributed to modern economic growth and reflect attempts to rationalize it.[29] Although premodern rulers often recognized the economic benefits of trade and the security of property rights, their policy choices were usually based on the belief that growth was extensive and the state should regulate economic activities. Policy choices therefore usually inhibited (intensive) growth.

Considerations regarding power and social order probably also led to growth-inhibiting policy choices. Rulers, and more generally the elite, have the most to lose from the rise of new economic groups that might aspire to influence policy choices. New sectors, and, more generally, economic change that might lead to new groups, are a threat. Finally, the incumbent sectors have the resources to influence policy choice and an interest in preventing the rise of competing sectors and technology.[30]

For these reasons, growth-inhibiting choices were the rule rather than the exception in premodern states. In such diverse states as Spain under the Habsburgs and Japan under the Tokugawa Shogunate, potentially productive members of society (e.g., nobles) were not allowed to be economically active. In Tokugawa Japan and in China under the Qing Dynasty, subjects were prohibited from trading abroad or immigrating overseas and alien traders' activities were restricted. Economic and social regulations in the Roman and Ottoman empires were aimed at replicating the preexisting social and economic orders. Serfdom and other forms of labor restrictions prevailed in Europe well into the modern period, while in the Muslim world (e.g., Kuran 2001, 2005) religious laws restricted contractual forms, the development of a capital market, and the formation of corporations.

The puzzling eighteenth-century European phenomenon of "Enlightened Absolutism," illustrates how rulers' fear of social change shapes choices even when the possibility of intensive growth is recognized. During the Enlightenment, the possibility of intensive growth, self-regulating markets, and economic progress was recognized. Surprisingly, however, the more absolute European rulers rather than the liberal ones were the first to alter policy choices based on these new ideas. Among them were Charles III of Spain, Joseph II of Austria, and Frederick the Great of Prussia. Why was this the case? While all European rulers were exposed to the Enlightenment, acting on these new ideas was risky. The first attempts to implement them were therefore taken by rulers who were secure in the sense of having weak administrators who were less likely to challenge them in case of failure.

Theoretically, inter-state competition might lead to the elimination of states with growth-inhibiting policies, but this was not often the case in the premodern world.[31] When rulers faced external military threats, they sought revenues to confront them. When, for example, inter-state competition became more intense in sixteenth-century Europe, it led to more, not fewer growth-inhibiting choices. Specifically, it led to mercantilism characterized by extensive and inefficient economic regulations. Prior to that, during the Warring States Period (fifth to third centuries BCE), China was divided among several competing states. To unify China (221 BCE), the rulers of the state of Qin stimulated extensive growth by encouraging fertility, immigration of peasants from other states, and expansion of cultivated land.

The impact of growth-inhibiting choices, however, depends on implementation, which, in turn, depends on the administrators' capacity and motivation. Arguably, a weak (ruler-controlled) administration will be better able to prevent the rise of new economic sectors and groups because it has been intentionally created by rulers who internalized the (perceived) costs of failing to implement choices. Monitoring and enforcement of choices by a weak administration are facilitated by the institutionalization of coordination and information-sharing routines and the ability to concentrate the state's resources (including coercive power) toward the suppression of deviants.

Furthermore, the means used to insure that administrators are weak also provide them with weak incentives for implementing growth-promoting choices on their own initiative. Tax farmers with short tenures and the frequent rotation of administrators within a centralized and hierarchical administration were the main means by which premodern states rendered administrators powerless (Section 1.1). Theoretically, such administrators have weak incentives for promoting long-term growth. They are better off collecting the greatest amount of tax or implementing growth-inhibiting choices that will foster their administrative careers. Furthermore, short-term administrators have strong incentives for preventing unauthorized behavior and private experimentations that might reveal growth-enhancing choices. Hence, the means for maintaining weak administrators also imply strong incentives for implementing growth-inhibiting choices and weak incentives for implementing growth-enhancing choices, barring those made by the ruler.

In contrast, there are conditions under which administrations with midlevel power would not prevent or even implement (unauthorized) growth-promoting choices. Consider first the case of administrative equilibrium in which the *military* administrators have midlevel administrative power. A necessary condition for such administrative equilibrium to persist is that the relative military might of the ruler and the administrators does not change over time. When this is achieved by limiting the administrators' ability to control and extract wealth from the non-elite, the latter are left relatively free to take growth-promoting actions.

Limiting the administrators' ability to control the non-elite was indeed a characteristic of Japan under the Tokugawa Shogunate (1603–1688). The shogunate is the seminal example of an orderly state with midlevel military administrators known as the daimyo (lords). The daimyo got tax revenues from their rural domains, but were prohibited from engaging in any economic activity or even staying in the tax-paying villages of their domains. The villagers were responsible for delivering the taxes to the daimyo at levels that the shogunate determined and tried to enforce. The shogun did not get tax revenues from the domains of the daimyo. With little direct administrative supervision, economic agents were freer than would otherwise have been the case to implement growth-enhancing choices.

Consider now the case of an *economic* administration with midlevel power. Theoretically, an economic administrator has an incentive to implement growth-enhancing choices, even if unauthorized, under the following condition: growth increases his expected economic income and/or administrative power by more than the expected penalty for implementing unauthorized choices. This is more likely to be the case when the administrators are stationary (and hence could benefit from investing in future growth), have administrative responsibilities beyond taxation (and hence can impact the implementation of growth-related choices), and when growth would increase the loyalty of those under their jurisdiction (and hence their administrative power).

This seems to have been the case in England after the fifteenth-century Wars of the Roses when the justices of peace became administratively important. These justices were stationary administrators, with administrative responsibility beyond taxation, and whose power depended on the cooperation of their peers. Indeed, the justices were reluctant to enforce growth-inhibiting policy choices. They administered England's counties until the nineteenth century and were responsible for keeping the king's peace. Hence they were required to enforce the law, fix wages, regulate food supplies, and maintain roads, among other duties. Despite this heavy load, the justices were unpaid. Not surprisingly, they exercised discretion in what they implemented and were more responsive to local needs than to choices made in London.

One local need had been to comply with the Old Poor Law under which local parishes were supposed to finance poor relief (through property taxes). The justices' motivation to care for the poor went beyond the need to implement the law, as paupers threatened local order. Yet, paying poor relief implied both paying more and having to collect higher taxes. The local administrators therefore sought ways to reduce poverty, and encouraging the industrialization of their parishes was one such way. Yet, early in the Industrial Revolution, the legality of employment practices in factories was often dubious at best. The local authorities, however, ignored this illegality.

More generally, contemporary observers noted the different incentives that English administrators faced in comparison to their weaker equivalents in other European states. In the fifteenth century, the Spanish ambassador reported to the king and queen of Spain, Ferdinand and Isabella, that Henry VII (1457–1509) "would like to govern England in the French fashion but he cannot" (Nef 1940, 6). By the late eighteenth century, the limited ability to enforce industrial regulations in England is well reflected in the words of a contemporary English writer who noted that "the difference between us [in England] and France consists chiefly in this: . . . we are [as] remarkable [as they] for good laws, but are shamefully neglectful in their execution" (Postlethwayt 1766, iii; cited by Nef 1940, 35).

The failure of individual administrators to implement "good laws" is not necessarily optimal for the administrators as a group. Although rational to each administrator, the rise of new economic sectors might lead to groups whose interests differ from those of the elite and whose administrative capacity reduces the incumbent elite's power. Indeed, in the long run, the rise of the industrial elite in England weakened the administrative power and political influence of the landed-elite.

Although the entry of new economic sectors might be costly to the incumbent elite, if each administrator is sufficiently small, he will not internalize this cost. In late medieval England, for example, many lords found it beneficial to establish cities on their land to increase local food demand and the value of their estates. To motivate immigration, the cities were given the right of self-governance. While beneficial to individual lords, on the national level this led to the rise of cities as powerful administrators.

Ironically, the ability of administrators to overcome collective-action problems could hinder growth by preventing growth-enhancing choices beneficial to each administrator but not to the group. In any case, administrators who are also economic agents are more likely to implement choices leading to economic sectors that complement, rather than compete, with theirs. These choices are not necessarily beneficial to others as the administrators seek private gains from their public positions. In England during its industrialization, for example, labor activists were sent to Australia by the local authorities for demanding that these authorities enforce the law.

In sum, when the administration is composed of administrators with midlevel power, there are conditions under which they have the capacity and incentive to implement or to allow others to implement (unauthorized) growth-enhancing choices. Among them are diffused administrative power, stationary administrators with responsibilities beyond taxation, administrative power that increases in the wealth of those being administered, and sufficiently many administrators to allow for experimentation and noninternalization of the systemwide implications due to the rise of new groups.

1.8   Political Conflicts, Constitutionalism, and Economic Growth

Administrative equilibria influence the nature of political conflicts aimed at altering the composition of the elite, and different political conflicts have distinct economic implications. This section describes why either powerful or weak administrations tend to lead to intra-elite conflicts over the distribution of existing wealth. Such conflicts tend to be violent and motivate wasteful preemptive measures.

In contrast, midlevel administrative power biases conflicts toward those between the elite and an economic group aspiring to join the elite (*inter-elite* conflicts).[32] The constitutionalism that midlevel administrative power implies, provides an institutionalized way to peacefully absorb the aspiring elite. The expectation that this will be the case, in turn, motivates the non-elite to pursue new sources of wealth. Because the aspiring elite brings new sources of wealth, Pareto-optimal resolutions of the conflict are more likely to exist. Constitutionalism and prosperity are mutually reinforcing.

Weak (ruler-controlled) administrations have a comparative advantage in preventing the emergence of new economic sectors (Section 1.7) and the associated groups that might challenge the incumbent elite. Inter-elite challenges are therefore less likely, and when they transpire, it is likely to be due to a growing desperation among the non-elite. Intra-elite conflicts, however, are more likely because even a ruler with weak administrators has to rely on some inner circle of elites composed of advisors, top civil administrators, generals, and so on. When random events or undermining processes alter the balance of power within this group of inner elite, *intra-elite* conflicts transpire. (The same holds in the case of powerful administrators.) Such intra-elite conflicts concern mutually exclusive shares of the same economic pie, and Pareto-improving resolutions are more likely to exist. The only institutionalized way to gain rights is through violence and by capturing the administration.

Economically wasteful intra-elite conflicts are also more likely under a weak administration because it can be captured to serve the interests of a subset of elites. In particular, a weak administration can be captured by those who interact with it on behalf of the ruler.[33] First of all, weak administrators have no power. Each is provided with incentives to implement choices made by those at upper levels in the hierarchy. Second, rulers have to allocate their finite time to many tasks. Hence, they often rely on intermediaries—such as viziers, chancellors, and prime ministers—to form and communicate choices for the administration to implement. Reliance on an intermediary is also necessary when the ruler is unable to govern due to sickness, infancy, or old age. An intermediary, however, can use his authority to implement choices that will enable him to become a de facto or de jure ruler.

For these reasons, history is rich with examples of intra-elite conflicts in states with weak administrations. Consider, for example, the Merovingian Dynasty, which was the first to rule the Frankish kingdom from the fifth to the eighth centuries. Although the administration was initially powerful and provided by the aristocrats, the Merovingians' chief officials, the mayors of the palace, were gradually able to establish and control an alternative military administration. By controlling it, the mayors became the de facto rulers and over time, the de jure rulers.

The importance of capturing the administration in the process of becoming a new ruler is reflected in a Papal Bull issued at the request of Pepin the Short, the mayor of the palace. The Bull confirmed that the person with de facto ability to implement choices should be the king, rather than the individual with the title of king. In 751, Pepin was elected king of the Franks and sent the last Merovingian king to a monastery, and the Carolingian Dynasty came to power. The Bourbons, another French dynasty, seem to have learned this lesson of history. Many of their prime ministers were members of the clergy and hence without legitimate heirs and dynastic ambitions. For the same reason, eunuchs were extensively employed in premodern administrations in such states as Byzantium, China, the Ottoman empire, and many others.

Another common means of preempting intra-elite conflicts was by providing the inner-elite with rent to motivate them to support the regime. This, however, further weakens incentives to the non-elite to create new wealth. Rent requires exclusivity of membership, which was often hereditary (e.g., Russia) or even meritocratic (e.g., China). Limiting the distribution of rent to a selective elite or promoting wasteful competition for political posts (Yang 2002) further weakens incentives to produce new wealth. Over time, low economic growth and a higher population also reduce the rent available to the elite, thereby increasing the likelihood of intra-elite conflicts.

Expectations of intra-elite conflict further motivate its members to waste resources in securing their positions in the courts, eliminating competition, and safeguarding their assets in case they lose power. A vicious cycle of economic stagnation and byzantine politics was often the result. The high costs of ex ante responses to expected intra-elite conflicts is suggested by the history of the Muslim *waqfs* (religious charities). These were established throughout the Muslim world usually by members of the elite for the explicit purpose of providing local public goods. Kuran (2001) noted that members of the elite increasingly created waqfs to protect their assets from confiscation by the state. But why was the elite fearful of the state? Where intra-elite conflicts are common, members of the elite are insecure and this insecurity implies high costs. The waqfs were legally required to invest in real estate, and this led to misallocation of resources while the rigidity of their governance prevented the effective supply of local public goods. Kuran, who documented these facts, noted that the system cost the Ottoman economy dearly.

Under administrators with midlevel power, however, growth through the rise of new economic sectors is more likely (Section 1.7), leading to the rise of new economic groups within the elite or among the non-elite. Midlevel power is therefore more likely to engender inter-elite political conflicts, potentially involving a newly emerging elite. In the Italian city-states of the late medieval period, the rise of new sectors and industries led to conflicts between the old and new elite.[34] During the English Civil War of the seventeenth century, members of Parliament involved in a new sector—the Atlantic trade—were more likely to be against the king (Jha 2006).

Inter-elite political conflicts caused by the emergence of new sectors and technologies have different economic origins and implications from intra-elite conflicts. Inter-elite conflicts are concerned with the redistribution of political rights to those who have created new wealth. They are positive-sum games. This is in contrast to intra-elite conflicts that concern the redistribution of rights and wealth from one subset of the elite to another. They are zero-sum games. Intra-elite conflicts are wasteful while inter-elite conflicts can be components of a system that fosters growth. Those who challenge the elite have something to offer in exchange for political rights, while their sources of wealth are likely to complement that of the elite (Section 1.7).

Midlevel power, leading to inter-elite conflicts, also leads to constitutionalism (Section 1.2), which provides an institutionalized means for peaceful resolution of these conflicts. Constitutionalism implies that the incumbent elite have an institutionalized way of conferring rights on the emerging elite without sacrificing their own positions. Inclusion of new groups in constitutionalism is a quantitative, rather than a qualitative, change.

If inclusion of a new economic elite is the expected outcome, the prospect of both economic and political rewards motivates the non-elite to create new sources of wealth. The expansion of constitutionalism and economic growth are therefore mutually complementary in a given period and will reinforce each other over time. This virtuous growth cycle is also more likely where the technology and environment are suitable for developing new sources of wealth (e.g., commerce) to complement elite wealth (e.g., land).

Conclusion   Common sense and historical evidence indicate that administrative power influences trajectories of political and economic development. Administrative equilibria impact constitutionalism, the composition of the elite, its policy interests, policy choices, the property rights of the non-elite, the nature and level of violence, whether growth-promoting choices (even if unauthorized) are implemented, and whether the expected outcomes of political conflicts are growth inhibiting or growth enhancing.

The preliminary analysis of this chapter suggests that constitutionalism originated in the need to govern the relations between rulers and their administrators. A ruler's policy choice is nothing but a wish in the absence of an administration to implement it. Administrators therefore have a comparative advantage in defying rulers, but there are multiple equilibria in the ruler–administrators relations. Administrative power—the administrators' ability to influence choices by the threat of sanctioning a ruler—increases in the cost of replacing the administrators, and powerful administrators can prevent choices that would reduce the cost of replacing them.

Constitutionalism is a response to administrative power. When administrative power is midlevel and hence ruler–administrator conflicts are costly to both sides, limited government is an equilibrium outcome and constitutionalism is Pareto optimal for the administrators and the ruler. Constitutional rules, equality and due process before the law, and political assemblies all reduce conflicts caused by asymmetric information; they foster cooperation and the aggregation of policy-related information. When the administration is weak (ruler controlled), it cannot sanction the ruler who thus does not benefit from constitutionalism. When the administrators are very powerful, and thus the ruler cannot sanction them, constitutionalism can still be Pareto optimal for the administrators by fostering cooperation among them against the non-elite or external threats.

The conjecture that administrative power underpins constitutionalism explains why it was not the deus ex machina of prosperity. It neither necessarily secures the property rights of those without administrative power nor guarantees prosperity-promoting policies. Policy choices are biased by interests in protecting and enhancing power. Indeed, constitutionalism might have an adverse effect on the security of property rights as it fosters the elite's ability to cooperate in abusing the rights of the non-elite. Moreover, because administrative power aligns the interests of the ruler and the non-elite, higher administrative power that leads to more constitutional rights can increase predation on the non-elite. When administrators with some power can increase it by preying on the non-elite, rulers are motivated to protect them. Increasing constitutionalism, which results from higher administrative power, implies that rulers will be less able to protect rights.

Nevertheless, constitutionalism has been positively correlated with prosperity because midlevel administrative power (sufficient for constitutionalism) is more likely to foster prosperity. First, when the administrators are economic agents whose interests are aligned with economic growth, constitutionalism provides them with the political voice and influence to pursue these interests. Second, midlevel administrative power reduces violence. High administrative power, particularly in the hands of military administrators, fosters intra-state violence while low administrative power fosters inter-state violence. Under midlevel administrative power, however, an equilibrium with low intra- and inter-state violence can exist. The administrators are too weak to revolt but sufficiently strong to prevent the ruler from initiating wars that would increase his power. Third, midlevel administrative power transforms military administrators into economic ones. When administrative power is diffused, lower intra-state violence implies a low rate of return on investment in military might.

The fourth reason that midlevel administrative power is conducive to prosperity is its impact on the incentives to implement growth-inhibiting policy choices. Such choices were common in premodern states due to wrong beliefs about the structure of the economy and concerns about social order and power. Whether growth-inhibiting choices are implemented, however, depends on the administrative equilibrium. The means of weakening the administrators, such as short tenures in each position, also motivate them to implement growth-inhibiting choices and prohibit unauthorized, growth-enhancing actions. In contrast, under certain conditions, economic administrators with midlevel power have incentives to implement or not prevent growth-enhancing (unauthorized) choices and actions. This is particularly the case for administrators who tax themselves (such as landlords, guilds, or self-governed cities), those who have broad administrative responsibilities, are based in a particular locality, and depend on the loyalty and legitimacy of their local peers.

Finally, administrative equilibria influence the nature and economic implications of political conflicts. When the administrators are weak, intra-elite political conflicts dominate because new sectors and technologies are not created and a new elite therefore does not emerge to challenge the incumbents. Midlevel administrative power biases political conflicts toward those among the inter-elite, namely, conflicts between the incumbent elite and aspiring challengers. This bias reflects that midlevel administrative power fosters the development of new economic sectors and technologies, thereby leading to the rise of new groups. Furthermore, the constitutionalism that midlevel administrative power entails, provides an institutionalized means for absorbing new elite without disenfranchising the incumbents. Growth and constitutionalism are complementary.

Yet, midlevel administrative power is inherently unstable, as either a temporary increase or decrease in power or change in its distribution can undermine it. More (or less) power can be used to further gain (or lose) power. Hence, although midlevel administrative power held by economic agents and constitutionalism prevailed in late medieval Europe, its subsequent continuation and prosperity were not preordained (Greif 2005). The instability of midlevel administrative equilibrium implied that advancement toward constitutionalism and prosperity often ceased or even reversed. If all European rulers had been successful, constitutionalism in Europe would have come to an end and Europe would have joined the ranks of the other regions where these institutions either did not emerge or did not survive to the modern period.

Historical contingencies and chance events nevertheless advanced (a progressively) small number of states toward modern constitutionalism and prosperity. Once England emerged as a liberal state, other European states adopted similar models. The beliefs inherited from their common constitutional past, such as in the legitimacy of political assemblies and the possibility of self-governance, probably facilitated this transition. Commonly held beliefs facilitated the adoption of the liberal model while popular demand—reflecting a constitutional heritage—and inter-state competition motivated its adoption by the elite.

Further research is required to develop and evaluate the merits of this comparative interpretation of distinct institutional and economic trajectories. This research will probably benefit from formalization, comparative empirical analyses, and a consideration of the impact of other distinguishing inter-state features, such as geography, the relations between secular and religious authorities, cultural distinctions (e.g., individualism and collectivism or conceptions of property rights), the unique prominence of corporations in Europe, and military technology. Moreover, in considering prosperity and growth, this research will need to examine the interplay between administrative power and the other factors that limits rulers' discretionary behavior (Greif 2005). Whatever the conclusion of this research might be, the preliminary analysis in this chapter indicates that administrative power has influenced economic and institutional developments.

This suggests new questions regarding contemporary attempts to promote constitutionalism and to advance prosperity and inter-society institutional transmission. Is administrative power important in modern states? Did the administrative structure of various colonies impact their ability to maintain constitutional institutions? Does the pre-colonial experience in constitutional institutions matter? Are administrative structures strategically manipulated to perpetuate the control of a particular elite? Is the ineffectiveness of administrations in many developing countries a way of preventing powerful administrators from constraining rulers?

More generally, in Europe, the development of constitutional institutions was gradual. It transpired in the context of having legitimate rulers and political representatives with administrative power. New post-colonial states were often supposed to become constitutional overnight, without legitimate leadership or representative assemblies with powerful administrators. Therefore, it may well be that administrative reform is a missing key ingredient in institutional reforms aimed at fostering liberal democracy. Current administrative reform focuses on the important task of making administrations more effective. What may also be needed, however, are reforms aimed at distributing administrative power in support of liberal democracy. The problem, of course, is that of implementation.

ACKNOWLEDGMENTS

This chapter greatly benefitted from comments from and discussions with Ran Abramitzky, Adi Greif, and Margaret Levi. I am also grateful to Luz Marina Arias, Avinash Dixit, Yaron Greif, Elhanan Helpman, Jim Fearon, Joel Mokyr, Ethan Segal, and an anonymous referee for helpful comments. I also thank the Canadian Institute for Advanced Research (CIFAR) for support, and members of CIFAR's Institutions, Organizations and Growth Program group for their insightful comments.

NOTES

1. See, for example, Hardin (1989), North and Weingast (1989), and Myerson (2007). For recent analyses of political representation in this line of research, see Engerman and Sokoloff (1997), Ticci and Vindigni (2006), Acemoglu and Robinson (2006), and Lezzeri and Persico (2004). See discussion in Barzel (2002). For social and cultural determinants of constitutionalism see, for example, Greif (1998), Aston and Philpin (2002), and Mokyr (2006).

2. This situation resembles the hold-up problem in interfirm relations (Williamson 1985). Most of the time administrators do not defy their rulers, but this equilibrium outcome does not indicate whether the possibility of administrative defiance impacts institutional development.

3. For correlation see De Long and Shleifer (1993). For insufficiency see, for example, O'Brien (1998), Harris (2004), and Greif (2005).

4. See, for example, North (1982, 1990), Bates (1991), Bates, Greif, and Singh (2002), Olson (1993), Acemoglu, Johnson, and Robinson (2005), and Acemoglu and Robinson (2006). Among the notable exceptions are Greif (1994, 1998, 2005), and Egorov and Sonin (2006).

5. Previous important analyses of the impact of economic or coercive powers on the rule of law assumed that agents are endowed with the ability to sanction a ruler rather than considering this ability as endogenous (e.g., Olson 1993; Bates 1991; Bates, Greif, and Singh 2002; Barzel and Kiser 1997; Haber, Maurer, and Raza 2003; Skaperdas 1992).

6. "Weakness" is vis-à-vis the ruler and not necessarily over other members of the society.

7. This argument about distinct preferences over choices differs from the argument that commitment failure is the source of failures in political bargaining (e.g., Greif 1994; Fearon 1997; Nye 1997; Acemoglu 2003).

8. Administrations may have a comparative advantage in coordinating such protests (Moe 2005). Groups with independent administrative capacity, even if not used by the ruler, are relatively effective in influencing the costs of implementing policy choices. The distribution of organizational capacity at the disposal of the ruler and other actors impacts the cost of implementing various policy choices and hence their net benefit to the ruler.

9. By "first-best" I mean their optimal choice given the technological and strategic costs of implementation.

10. Even if they have perfect substitutes, however, the multiplicity of equilibria implies that they can have power. There can be an equilibrium in which the new administrators are expected not to implement the choice either.

11. These correspond to the "coordinating" and "powerful" states in Greif (2006, ch. 8).

12. "Authority" and "legitimacy," in this context, is the commonly known belief and norms causing the ruler's subjects to follow any equilibrium strategies that he announces. See Greif (2006), particularly, section 5.4 and chapter 8.

13. There is a rich literature that examines the relations between military or production technology and the rights that one can personally secure as an equilibrium outcome when facing a predatory ruler (e.g., Olson 1993). This work differs in considering the institutional (nontechnologically) determined foundations of the rule of law as an equilibrium outcome. For previous analyses in this spirit, see Greif (1994, 1998) and Bates, Greif, and Singh (2002).

14. These 37 clauses remained in force despite the decline in the Crown's power vis-à-vis the parliament, probably because the Crown never regained the rights that were relinquished in the Magna Carta.

15. See, for example, Bates (1991), Hoffman and Norberg (2001), Barzel and Kiser (1997), and Barzel (2002).

16. For evidence and discussion, see Herb (2003). Greif (2007) develops the conjecture that the rise of limited monarchies in Europe reflects administrative power. Further evidence is that in late medieval Europe, administrators, such as cities and lords, each had particular "liberties" that specified their rights. Position-specific rights are consistent with the argument developed here.

17. It was facilitated by many factors: the fact that these administrators were often corporations (and hence "constitutional"), European individualism (which fostered institutions supporting impersonal exchange), the Roman secular legal tradition, and legitimate hereditary rulers.

18. On incentives to introduce reinforcing institutional elements that make a Pareto-optimal allocation self-enforcing, see Greif (1998, 2006).

19. Both sides have incentives to introduce reinforcing institutional elements that make a Pareto-optimal allocation self-enforcing ex post. See Greif (1998, 2006).

20. It may be that this policy was not pursued prior to the English Civil War because it could have undermined the parliamentarians' administrative power as the Crown still controlled customs revenues. Commercial expansion would have altered the balance of administrative power in the Crown's favor.

21. The subsequent conquest of Muslim Spain was facilitated by the local Muslim elite's inability to agree on an alternative ruler. I am not familiar with any theory indicating the conditions under which external threats prevent disintegration when there is no legitimate ruler.

22. The Avalon Project, http://www.yale.edu/lawweb/avalon/medieval/golden.htm. For analysis and additional evidence, see Greif (2006, ch. 8). In Russia, the assembly was rarely able to effectively object or impose its will on the tzars, yet

in 1598 and 1613 it appointed the new tzars once the previous dynasty had died out.

23. Such administrations are not forever, nevertheless. They are undermined for at least two reasons. First, the agency problem in ruler–administrator relations reduces the ruler's ability to prevent administrators from gaining power. Second, weak administrations are inflexible and bureaucratic because these features reduce the cost of replacing an administrator. They are therefore slow to adjust, and the implied ineffectiveness fosters the rise of nonstate actors with administrative power.

24. The lack of a legitimate heir can also lead to inter-state wars due to inter-state marriages among royal families. A claimant to the throne could be from another state.

25. A caveat is that rulers might strategically initiate wars to reduce administrative power.

26. The ruler's ability to prevent intra-state violence declines in administrative power, its concentration, and in the extent to which power is based on a military administration. The ruler's ability to engage in inter-state violence is higher when administrative power is lower.

27. Cultural beliefs regarding legitimate actions and loyalty are among the factors that determine whether an equilibrium with social order and security will prevail. Such an equilibrium requires that administrators consider it legitimate and that the ruler will punish administrators who harm others (e.g., by raids, failure to maintain roads or participate in defending the state).

28. It seems reasonable that the administrators' ability to prevent their powers from being undermined would increase in the uniformity of their interests and their capacity to overcome collective actions and free-rider problems. It would decrease in the extent to which the ruler is considered legitimate by those he governs and his tenure is long enough to nurture their loyalty. The creation of a relatively weak administration in France by the Bourbons in the seventeenth and eighteenth centuries, for example, was facilitated by the longevity of several monarchs.

29. Mokyr (Chapter 2, this volume) highlights the contributions of these ideas to modern growth. The discussion here relates to their origin.

30. See, for example, North (1982), Olson (1984), Greif (1998, 2006), and Acemoglu (2003).

31. By the nineteenth century, once intensive growth was better understood, this was no longer the case. European states, Turkey, and Japan made growth-promoting choices partly in response to increasing international competition.

32. The closest corresponding concepts are "political revolutions" and "social revolutions" in Skocpol (1979). Recall that under powerful administrators, intra-elite conflict can transpire as a means to signal relative power.

33. This is the case even if the coordinator doesn't have administrative power and can be replaced.

34. Inter-elite conflict also characterizes Poland's history, as already discussed, but there the administrators were powerful. Hence such conflicts do not reflect the growth-enhancing process associated with midlevel administrators.

REFERENCES

Acemoglu, Daron. 2003. "Why Not a Political Coase Theorem? Social Conflict, Commitment, and Politics." *Journal of Comparative Economics* 31(4):620–52.

Acemoglu, Daron, Simon Johnson, and James Robinson. 2005. "The Rise of Europe: Atlantic Trade, Institutional Change, and Economic Growth." *American Economic Review* 95(3):546–79.

Acemoglu, Daron, and James A. Robinson. 2006. *Economic Origins of Dictatorship and Democracy*. Cambridge: Cambridge University Press.

Arias, Luz Marina. 2007. "Public Goods Provision and Enforcement of Tax Collection: Theory and Insights from Colonial Mexico." Memo, Stanford University.

Aston, T. H., and C. H. E. Philpin, eds. 2002. *The Brenner Debate*. New edition. Cambridge: Cambridge University Press.

Balla, Eliana, and Noel Johnson. 2006. "Institutional Change in the Long-Run: The Ottoman Empire and France during the Early-Modern Period." Memo, California State University—Long Beach.

Barzel, Yoram. 2002. *A Theory of the State*. Cambridge: Cambridge University Press.

Barzel, Yoram, and Edgar Kiser. 1997. "The Development and Decline of Medieval Voting Institutions: A Comparison of England and France." *Economic Inquiry* XXXV:244–60.

Bates, Robert H. 1991. "The Economics of Transition to Democracy." *Political Science and Politics* 24:24–7.

Bates, Robert H., Avner Greif, and Smita Singh. 2002. "Organizing Violence." *Journal of Conflict Resolution* 46(5):599–628.

De Long, J. Bradford, and Andrei Shleifer. 1993. "Princes and Merchants: European City Growth before the Industrial Revolution." *Journal of Law and Economics* 36(2):671–702.

Dixit, Avinash. 2006. "Predatory States and Failing States: An Agency Perspective." Working paper, Princeton University.

Egorov, Gregory, and Konstantin Sonin. 2006. "Dictators and Their Viziers: Agency Problems in Dictatorships." Working paper, William Davidson Institute, University of Michigan, Stephen M. Ross Business School.

Engerman, Stanley L., and Kenneth L. Sokoloff. 1997. "Factor Endowments, Institutions, and Differential Paths of Growth among New World Economies." *How Did Latin America Fall Behind?* ed. Stephen Haber, 260–304. Palo Alto, CA: Stanford University Press.

Evans, Peter, and James Rauch. 1999. "Bureaucracy and Growth: A Cross-National Analysis of the Effects of 'Weberian' State Structures on Economic Growth." *American Sociological Review* 64:748–65.

Fearon, James D. 1997. "Bargaining over Objects That Influence Future Bargaining Power." Working paper, Department of Political Science, University of Chicago.

Greif, Avner. 1994. "On the Political Foundations of the Late Medieval Commercial Revolution: Genoa during the Twelfth and Thirteenth Centuries." *Journal of Economic History* 54(4):271–87.

———. 1998. "Self-Enforcing Political Systems and Economic Growth: Late Medieval Genoa." In *Analytic Narratives*, eds. Robert H. Bates, Avner Greif, Margaret Levi, Jean-Laurent Rosenthal, and Barry R. Weingast, 23–63. Princeton, NJ: Princeton University Press.

———. 2005. "Commitment, Coercion, and Markets: The Nature and Dynamics of Institutions Supporting Exchange." In *Handbook for New Institutional Economics*, eds. Claude Menard and Mary M. Shirley, chap. 28. Norwell, MA: Kluwer Academic Publishers.

———. 2006. *Institutions and the Path to the Modern Economy: Lessons from Medieval Trade.* New York: Cambridge University Press.

———. 2007. "Administrative Power Causes the Rise of Constitutionalism in Europe." Memo, Stanford University.

Haber, S., N. Maurer, and A. Razo. 2003. *The Politics of Property Rights.* Cambridge: Cambridge University Press.

Hardin, Russell. 1989. "Why a Constitution." In *The Federalist Papers and the New Institutionalism*, eds. Bernard Grofman and Donal Wittman, 100–120. New York: Agathon Press.

Harris, Ron. 2004. "Government and the Economy, 1688–1850." In *Cambridge Economic History of Britain*, eds. R. Floud and P. Johnson. Cambridge: Cambridge University Press.

Herb, Michael. 2003. "Taxation and Representation." *Studies in Comparative International Development* 38(3, Fall):3–31.

Hickok, Michael Robert. 1997. *Ottoman Military Administration in Eighteenth-Century Bosnia. The Ottoman Empire and Its Heritage*. Leiden and New York: Brill.

Hoffman, Philip T., and Kathryn Norberg. 2001. *Fiscal Crises, Liberty, and Representative Government 1450–1789*. Palo Alto, CA: Stanford University Press.

Jha, Saumitra. 2006. "Shareholding, Coalition Formation and Political Development: Evidence from 17th Century England." Manuscript, Harvard University.

Kiser, Edgar. 1999. "Comparing Varieties of Agency Theory in Economics, Political Science, and Sociology: An Illustration from State Policy Implementation." *Sociological Theory* 17:146–70.

Kivanc, Kamil. 2006. "Re-distributive Conflict as a Cause for Under-Mobilization of Economic Resources and Underdevelopment." Memo, Stanford University.

Kuran, Timur. 2001. "The Provision of Public Goods under Islamic Law: Origins, Impact, and Limitations of the Waqf System." *Law and Society Review* 35(4):841–97.

———. 2005. "Why the Islamic Middle East Did Not Generate an Indigenous Corporate Law." Manuscript, University of Southern California.

Levi, Margaret. 1989. *Of Rules and Revenues*. Berkeley: University of California Press.

Lezzeri, Alessandro, and Niccola Persico. 2004. "Why Did the Elites Extend the Suffrage? Democracy and the Scope of Government, With an Application to Britain's 'Age of Reform.'" *The Quarterly Journal of Economics* 119(2):707–65.

McConnell, Grant. 1966. *Private Power and American Democracy*. Ann Arbor: University of Michigan Press.

Moe, Terry M. 2005. "Political Control and the Power of the Agent." *Journal of Law, Economics, and Organization* 22:1–29.

Mokyr, Joel. 2006. "The Market for Ideas and the Origins of Economic Growth in the Eighteenth Century." Heineken Lecture delivered in Groningen.

Munz, Peter. 1969. *Frederick Barbarossa*. Ithaca, NY: Cornell University Press.

Myerson, Roger. 2007. "The Autocrat's Credibility Problem and the Foundations of the Constitutional State." *American Political Science Review* (forthcoming).

Nef, U. John. 1940. *Industry and Government in France and England 1540–1640*. Ithaca, NY, and London: Cornell University Press.

North, Douglass C. 1982. *Structure and Change in Economic History*. Cambridge: Cambridge University Press.

———. 1990. *Institutions, Institutional Change and Economic Performance*. Cambridge: Cambridge University Press.

North, Douglass C., and Barry R. Weingast. 1989. "Constitutions and Commitment: The Evolution of Institutions Governing Public Choice in Seventeenth-Century England." *The Journal of Economic History* 49:803–32.

Nye, John V. C. 1997. "Thinking about the State: Property Rights, Trade, and Changing Contractual Arrangements in a World with Violent Coercion." In *Frontiers of the New Institutional Economics*, eds. John N. Drobak and John Nye. Volume in honor of Douglass C. North. New York: Academic Press.

O'Brien, Patrick K. 1998. "Inseparable Connections: Trade, Economy, Fiscal State and the Expansion of Empire. In *The Oxford History of the British Empire, II, The Eighteenth Century*, ed. P. J. Marshall. Oxford: Oxford University Press.

———. 2001. "Fiscal Exceptionalism: Great Britain and Its European Rivals—From Civil War to Triumph at Trafalgar and Waterloo." Working paper 65/01, Department of Economic History, London School of Economics.

Olson, Mancur. 1984. *The Rise and Fall of Nations*. New Haven, CT: Yale University Press.

———. 1993. "Dictatorship, Democracy, and Development." *American Political Science Review* 87(3):567–76.

Postlethwayt, M. (trans.) 1766. *The Universal Dictionary of Trade and Commerce*, 3rd ed., vol. 1. London: Woodfall.

Root, Hilton L. 1989. "Tying the King's Hands: Credible Commitments and Royal Fiscal Policy during the Old Regime." *Rationality and Society* 1(Oct.):240–258.

Rosenthal, J. L. 1998. "The Political Economy of Absolutism Reconsidered." In *Analytic Narratives*, eds. R. H. Bates, A. Greif, M. Levi, J. L. Rosenthal, and B. R. Weingast, 64–108. Princeton: Princeton University Press.

Skaperdas, Stergios. 1992. "Cooperation, Conflict, and Power in the Absence of Property Rights." *American Economic Review* 84(4):720–39.

Skocpol, Theda. 1979. *States and Social Revolutions: A Comparative Analysis of France, Russia and China*. Cambridge: Cambridge University Press.

Stone, Daniel. 2001. *The Polish-Lithuanian State, 1386–1795*. Seattle and London: University of Washington Press.

Ticci, David, and Andrea Vindigni. 2006. "On Wars and Political Development: The Role of International Conflicts in the Democratization of the West." Working paper, University of California.

Tilly, Charles. 1990. *Coercion, Capital, and European States, AD 990–1992*. Cambridge, MA: Blackwell.

Webber, Carolyn, and Aaron B. Wildavsky. 1986. *A History of Taxation and Expenditure in the Western World*. New York: Simon and Schuster.

Weber, Max. [1927] 1987. *General Economic History*. New York: Greenberg.

White, Eugene. 2004. "From Privatized to Government-Administered Tax Collection: Tax Farming in Eighteenth-Century France. *Economic History Review* LVII(4):636–63.

Williamson, Oliver E. 1985. *The Economic Institutions of Capitalism.* New York: Free Press.

Wilson, James Q. 1991. *Bureaucracy: What Government Agencies Do and Why They Do It.* Reprint. New York: Basic Books.

Yang Li, Mu. 2002. "Essays on Public Finance and Economic Development in a Historical Institutional Perspective." PhD diss., Stanford University.

— 2 —

The Institutional Origins
of the Industrial Revolution

JOEL MOKYR

2.1 Introduction

The new institutional economics has, so far, had little to say about the Industrial Revolution. In their survey of institutions and modern growth, Acemoglu, Johnson, and Robinson (2005) acknowledge eighteenth-century Britain as a successful economy and, much like North and Weingast (1989) before them, search for the institutional causes in seventeenth-century political developments and in the constraints placed on the British executive (the monarchy and the royal bureaucracy) by Parliament before and after the Glorious Revolution. In this framework a grand coalition of merchants and landowners emerged, keen on protecting commerce and property. For the first time in British history, the commitment problem, in which property rights were enforced by a suitably constrained entity, approached solution.

While neither Acemoglu et al. nor North and Weingast actually say so explicitly, they imply that these reforms paved the road to the British Industrial Revolution.[1] Others are not so prudent. Mancur Olson (1982, 78–83, 128) had no doubt that "a few decades after stable and nationwide government had been established in Britain, the Industrial Revolution was on its way." In his recent survey, Kenneth Dam (2005, 84) makes the statement that "the Glorious Revolution provided a strong base for later enjoyment of the fruits of the Industrial Revolution . . . that made England arguably the wealthiest country in the world." The accounts pointing to the formal political institutions established in late Stuart and Williamite Britain rely on the notion of credible commitment: the Crown deliberately relinquished many of its prerogatives to Parliament, and thus committed itself to pay its debts and to respect the property of its citizens. At the same time, Parliament made its own commitment to sound public finance credible by not removing all of the Crown's power. One way or another, if institutions were the key to economic growth and "rule," in the formulation of Rodrik et al. (2004), they should have played a major role in the central event that triggered modern economic growth: the British Industrial Revolution.

Yet, surprisingly, there has been little effort to apply the new insights of institutional analysis to the central event of modern economic history to date, and the institutional origins of the Industrial Revolution remain poorly understood. The reason for this gap in the literature relates to two sources of confusion. One is the distinction between the events in *Britain*, which made it the leading economy in the Industrial Revolution, and developments in the larger North Atlantic economy, which refer to the Industrial Revolution in a wider area and the origins of modern growth in the West. This confusion mars much of the debate. Thus the stress on the Glorious Revolution by the institutionalists cited above, or the heavy emphasis on the fortuitous presence of useful minerals (Wrigley 1987, 1988; Pomeranz 2000), can explain the Industrial Revolution in Britain or in the Walloon areas of Belgium, but not in Switzerland or Saxony. On the other hand, emphases on modern science (Bekar, Carlow, and Lipsey 2005; Jacob and Stewart 2004) or the Enlightenment (Mokyr 2005, 2006a) stress the pan-European aspects of eighteenth-century developments that created the background for a *European* Industrial Revolution. The latter approach implies that national politics or geographical conditions may well explain Britain's lead, but not the more general economic development that led to the emergence of a multinational convergence club by 1914, in which Britain was at best a primus inter pares.[2] Institutional analysis falls somewhere in between those two approaches. Each country had its own national and local institutions, but certain institutional elements were shared, imitated, and spilled over so that a "European mode" may be discerned in the continent-wide pressures toward reform after 1750. Institutional changes were inspired by Enlightenment thought that affected much of the Western world (Mokyr 2006b). The analysis in this chapter will be concerned with the "smaller" question of Britain's leadership and will thus focus primarily on the institutional environment in Great Britain. In other Western societies, however, institutional changes before 1850 helped create the convergence club as it existed in 1914.

The second source of confusion is that the new Northian literature focuses on formal institutional transformations, in which the Crown committed to respect the property rights of the landowning and mercantile classes, made contracts more enforceable, and reduced transaction costs and uncertainty. Such an account explains growth in an economy in which institutions lubricated the wheels of commerce, finance, agriculture, and premodern artisanal manufacturing and cottage industries. It led to an improvement in the allocation of resources and the accumulation of more capital. In this fashion such changes provide an explanation of Smithian growth, in an economy with a static technology. The Industrial Revolution, however, was far more than that. Had it not been, the process of economic growth would have eventually asymptoted off into a new stationary state. In the final analysis, the Industrial Revolution rested on key technological breakthroughs and their application to production by a class of successful industrial entrepreneurs. These successes did not, moreover, lead to a new technological equilibrium but made room for the far more astonishing phenomenon of the nonconvergence of technology to a new set of dominant designs. Instead, continued improvement in technology after 1800 became the rule. How are we then to link the essence of the British Industrial Revolution to the events of 1688 and beyond, and how did institutional factors, broadly defined, help elevate Britain to the leading position it took in the Industrial Revolution?

Below I argue that the traditional emphasis on *formal* institutions has been overemphasized, and that the enforcement of property rights by the state was less crucial than the Northian interpretation has suggested. The importance of institutions extended beyond politics and formal institutions. We need to take into account "cultural beliefs" as defined by Greif (2005), which created an environment in which inventors and entrepreneurs could operate and cooperate freely. Equally important, we need to pay attention to those institutions that stimulated and encouraged technological progress and not just the growth that depends on well-functioning markets. Formal institutions such as state-enforced patent rights may have been overestimated at the expense of informal, private-order institutions.

2.2   Intellectual Property Rights and Technological Progress in the Industrial Revolution

Any institutional analysis that purports to deal with *modern* economic growth needs to recognize that what the Industrial Revolution meant was that technology increasingly became the engine of economic growth and that without it the process would inevitably have fizzled out. Which institutional structure was really conducive to technical innovation? We need to face the possibility that institutions that enhanced efficiency in a static commercial–agrarian economy were not identical to those that transformed production through rapid technological change. Secure property rights in land may have been important in a technologically static commercial economy, whereas a more dynamic economy required the flexibility provided by eminent domain and even the option to extinguish some traditional property rights if need be, such as happened through enclosure and railway acts. Credit markets like Britain's were adapted to short-term merchant credit and bills of exchange, but not necessarily for the fixed capital goods needed to set up a factory. In other words, a technologically dynamic society needs institutions that encourage creative destruction à la Schumpeter rather than those that support static efficiency. To be sure, some of those institutions may have overlapped (e.g., those that provided access to capital under high degrees of uncertainty), but on the whole, "good institutions" are historically contingent.

At first glance it would seem that the British patent system, in force since 1624, was a classic example of successful protection of intellectual property rights, and that the incentives to innovate it created were central to its economic success (North 1981).[3] The idea that technological progress depended on inventors' incentives through a patent system has become increasingly dubious on both historical and theoretical grounds (MacLeod 1988; Boldrin and Levine 2005; MacLeod and Nuvolari 2007). Our concept of intellectual property rights has been too limited and too conditioned on modern circumstances. In the centuries before the Industrial Revolution, useful knowledge, both "natural philosophy" or science (broadly defined) and "the useful arts" or technology, developed much more along a system of open science, akin to modern open-source technology (Mokyr 2006a, 2008c). While we should not altogether dismiss the role of the British patent system as an institutional factor in the Industrial Revolution, the new research casts some doubt on its strategic importance and at the same time shows the extent to which Britain's advantage over its European neighbors was limited. After all, many European nations adopted a patent law similar to Britain's after the French Revolution, and the patent system of the United States was far more user friendly (for inventors) than Britain's (Khan and Sokoloff 1998), but none of this reduced Britain's technological lead before 1850. Moreover, Moser (2007) has shown that only a small proportion of the significant inventions made in Britain by the middle of the nineteenth century were ever patented.

Eighteenth-century writers were torn between the Baconian concept of knowledge-generation as an open, cooperative activity, and the belief in the sanctity of property and individual rights. Contemporary opponents of the patent system identified it as a rent-seeking device, often used to block new entry, conveniently ignoring the fact that those who resisted patents, such as guilds, were sometimes motivated by protecting their own incumbency from unwelcome entrants (MacLeod 1988, 83, 113). It was also noted in the late seventeenth century that patentees often were not the best-qualified persons to exploit the inventions.[4] A different critique, but equally telling, was made by J. T. Desaguliers, who pointed out (1763, vol. 2, viii) that (much like modern venture capitalists), a patent was often interpreted by investors as an official imprimatur of the quality of an invention and that "several persons who have money, ready to supply boasting Engineers with it in the hope of great Returns, and especially if the project has the Sanction of an Act of Parliament to support it, and then the Bubble becomes compleat and ends in Ruin." The problem of how society should reward those who gave their time and money to develop knowledge that was of great benefit to the rest of society remained. Such rewards, it was understood, needed to be established if society was to enjoy the fruits of sustained technological progress, but how this was to be achieved remained in dispute.

Moreover, not all inventors sought the rewards of a successful patent, and certainly not many actually attained it. In Britain, the state only recognized and enforced the inventor's right (Hilaire-Perez 2000). It did not normally evaluate the invention's contribution to society. Britain's patent system, however, was not exactly inviting: it charged a patentee around £300 for the right to patent in the entire kingdom, not counting the costs of traveling to and staying in London (Khan and Sokoloff 1998).[5] Many patents were infringed upon, and judges were often hostile to patentees, considering them monopolists (Robinson 1972, 137). A considerable number of the inventors in the Industrial Revolution placed their inventions at the public's disposal, and others for one reason or another failed to secure a patent or subsequently lost it. Politicians realized that rewarding inventors who made significant contributions to the nation's technological capabilities made good public policy, unless it was done excessively and used for patronage. Thus Thomas Lombe, denied a patent extension in 1732, was awarded a substantial cash settlement by Parliament. In the first decade of the nineteenth century, Samuel Crompton, the inventor of the mule, and Edmund Cartwright, the inventor of the power loom, were also voted substantial awards by Parliament in recognition of their unpatented inventions. Such procedures were at times arbitrary (the estate of Henry Cort was denied a similar request), but they reflect a public acknowledgment that invention was costly and risky, and that if society wanted a continuous stream of technical improvements, it had to make the activity that generated innovation financially attractive.[6] It seems that the main effect of the patent system on innovation was to goad potential inventors into believing that they, too, could make as much money as successful patentees such as the Lombe brothers of Derbyshire or James Watt. Although precious few ever did, the expectation may have been enough for many.

Britain was not the only Western nation to cultivate institutions that encouraged technological progress. France and the Netherlands had patent systems in which innovations could yield considerable benefits to their propagators. The type of encouragement given to inventors in Britain differed from the French system, where government agents were put in charge of evaluating the contribution of certain inventions to the realm. The difference between the two systems can be overstated: at times the British authorities recognized the national interest in pursuing a new technology and were willing to take the initiative. An example was the Board of Longitude, established in 1714 by Parliament, which promised a large sum to the person who successfully cracked the problem of measuring longitude at sea. Almost a century later, the British Navy under the leadership of Samuel Bentham (Jeremy's brother) established the Portsmouth shipyards where the great engineer Marc I. Brunel and the instrument maker Henry Maudslay developed an advanced mass-production interchangeable-parts system for making wooden blocks for the Royal Navy. Military objectives aside, the British government normally left picking technological winners to the free market and the private sector, and the patent system reflected that attitude.

The exact impact of the patent system and other positive incentives on the technological creativity that eventually helped produce a more prosperous nation is hard to establish. Some economists have recently gone so far as to dismiss it altogether. Boldrin and Levine have argued that intellectual property rights were unimportant in bringing about economic growth, and have specifically pointed to the Industrial Revolution as a period that provides "a mine of examples of patents hindering economic progress while seldom enriching their owners and of great riches and economic successes achieved without patents" (Boldrin and Levine 2005, ch. 4, 7). Such an extreme position neglects that the patent system was important ex ante in giving would-be inventors hope for success, in a fashion not dissimilar to why people purchase lottery tickets (Dutton 1984). If no one ever won the lottery, people would stop buying tickets, but the number of winners need not be very large to keep hope alive.[7] But the continuing debate on the issue exemplifies the complexity of the institution. It also underlines the difficulty in separating exactly those elements we think of as "institutional" and those that belong properly to the category of "technological creativity."

Britain created alternative organizations that encouraged innovation and the dissemination of useful knowledge beyond the patent system. A notable example is the Society of Arts, founded in 1754, which explicitly aimed at disseminating existing technical knowledge as well as at augmenting it through an active program of awards and prizes, encouraging networking through correspondence, the publication of periodicals, and the organization of meetings.[8] Only inventions that had not been patented were eligible for one of the Society's prizes. Although such effects are hard to measure, there can be little doubt that the Society helped to stimulate invention by increasing the social standing of inventors in Britain and improving communication between creative and knowledgeable people. In 1799, two paradigmatic figures of the industrial Enlightenment, Sir Joseph Banks and Benjamin Thompson (Count Rumford), founded the Royal Institution, devoted to research and charged with providing public lectures of scientific and technological issues. Furthermore, there were the Mechanics Institutes, the first one established by Birkbeck in 1804 in London, and which spread to Scotland and then to the rest of the country. Mechanics Institutes provided technical and scientific instruction to the general public. Private institutions seem to have been quite adequate for most of Britain's needs. All in all, the British patent system was on balance a positive institution, but in no way can we credit it with giving Britain the edge that turned it into the first industrial nation.

In addition to institutions that encourage innovation, a society that hopes to benefit from technological progress needs venture capital. The traditional story is that venture capital in Britain was hard to come by because lenders tended to be conservative. Most fixed capital that embodied the new technology such as machines and engines was scraped together from private sources and from retained earnings. Yet even at the early stages of the Industrial Revolution, some of the institutions that emerged in Britain were favorable to venture capital. One such institution was the country bank, which experienced a veritable explosion in the second half of the eighteenth century. In 1750 there were no more than a dozen such banks, while in 1800 there were 370. A recent paper (Brunt 2006) has gone so far as to compare these banks to modern venture capitalists, though the analogy appears stretched. There is some evidence, however, that country bankers believed that they had inside information in high-risk industries and thus invested in them, copper mining in Cornwall being the best-known example. They failed in large numbers during crises, which indeed may be consistent with their participation in vulnerable industries. Yet again, it is important not to see the years of the Industrial Revolution through a twenty-first-century perspective. The total amount of fixed capital needed for the Industrial Revolution was not very large in the early stages, and of that, not all was high-risk capital.

2.3   Law, Order, and Institutions

Economic growth depends on law and order, but the two are not identical. Legal centralism, as Oliver Williamson has referred to it, places the law, and the state that enforces it, at the center of the stage. The issue then becomes one of credible commitment between a Hobbesian entity with a monopoly of violence, and its subjects. The subjects want the state to enforce the rules of the game but not to accumulate so much power that the state can threaten those very rights it is asked to protect. "Order" in the sense of the protection of property and contract enforcement can be attained through norms reflecting the willingness of individuals to voluntarily overcome their tendency to behave opportunistically. In that fashion they create what can be called an *economic civil society* in which reputational or other mechanisms support a world in which most people believe that it is proper to behave in a cooperative way. The key to successful economic exchanges here is not necessarily an impartial and efficient third-party enforcing agency, but the existence of a level of trust or other self-enforcing institutions within relevant networks of commerce, credit, wage-labor, and other contractual relations that support free-market activities. In other words, the state is neither necessary nor sufficient. The simple model in which it is *only* the state and threat of its justice and police systems that makes people behave cooperatively seems a poor description of any known situation.

How much of a "law-and-order society" was Britain before the Industrial Revolution? Crime was of course a serious problem in this society, though it is not easy to quantify it. The Swiss tourist de Saussure (1902, 127) found in 1726 that Britain had a "surprising quantity of robbers," but other foreign travellers also commented widely on the low levels of murder and violent crime in Britain, and one scholar feels that the murder rate in mid-eighteenth-century London would astonish a modern observer accustomed to modern American or even European cities as "remarkably low" (Langbein 1983b).[9] Yet the admittedly somewhat tenuous evidence suggests that violent crime was declining over the eighteenth century and that crimes against property moved more or less pari passu with population growth (Beattie 1974, 1986). There was also collective crime. Local rioting, either for economic or political grievances, was common. Machine breaking, bread riots, turnpike riots, or rioting against some unpopular group like Catholics, Irish immigrants, or dissenters were common. Turnpike riots, the Gordon riots of 1780, and the Bristol Bridge riot of 1793 all sowed fear in the hearts of property-owning classes. Food rioters, forgers, thieves, and those who resisted enclosures and new machinery forcibly were all threatened by execution and transport. However, daily crime that seriously endangered the accumulation of capital and the proper conduct of commerce was on the whole rare. To be sure, eighteenth-century Britain passed a myriad of draconic laws protecting property by imposing ferocious penalties on those who infringed on it.[10] The harshness of the penalties seems to suggest that violent crime and crimes against property were regarded as serious issues. Yet it also meant that the authorities were reluctant to spend resources on law enforcement, hoping that the harsh punishments could deter would-be criminals.[11] Hanoverian Britain had no professional police force comparable to the constabulary that emerged after 1830, and the court system was unwieldy, expensive, and uncertain.[12] Britain depended on the deterrent effect of draconian penalties because it had no official mechanism of law enforcement, prosecution was mostly private, and crime prevention was largely self-enforcing, with more than 80% of all prosecutions carried out by the victims. Few victims were willing to proceed with the costly and burdensome tasks of prosecuting a crime (Emsley 2005, 183–86). Patrick Colquhoun noted in 1797 that "not one in one hundred offences that is discovered or prosecuted" (1797, vii). The growing volume of both domestic and international commerce and credit was supported less by formal law and order and third-party arbitration than by private-order institutions.

If formal law enforcement was a last resort in the enforcement of contracts and the protection of property rights, how did markets function? What kept transactions costs and opportunistic behavior from mushrooming to the point where they jeopardized the levels of exchange and division of labor required for a sophisticated economy? A different way of posing the same question was expressed by the young French economist Adolphe Blanqui (1824, 326), visiting London, who wondered how a town twice the size of Paris (nearly a million people) could maintain order with only a handful of watchmen and constables. He seemed less than satisfied by the answer that the English go to bed and lock up their shops early, and was more inclined to believe that they were harder-working and more enlightened.

At closer examination, day-to-day security depended more on social conventions and self-enforcing modes of behavior than on the administration of justice by an impartial judiciary. Commercial disputes rarely came to court and were often settled through arbitration.[13] Even patent litigation was rare: out of almost 12,000 patents issued between 1770 and 1850, only 257 ever came before the courts (Dutton 1984, 71). Indeed, the number of civil cases that came to court in the eighteenth century declined precipitously relative to their mid-seventeenth-century levels: the number of cases heard at the King's Bench and Common Pleas in 1750 was only a sixth of what it was in 1670 (Brooks 1989, 364). As Figures 2.1–2.3 demonstrate, there can be little doubt that the British as a whole were becoming less litigious in the eighteenth century before things picked up again in the nineteenth century. Interpreting this fact seems less than straightforward. Does it support the view that legal institutions were becoming less important as a contract-enforcement mechanism? One could argue that if courts were extremely efficient, they might be used less.[14] Or was there a deeper social transformation? Historians such as Lawrence Stone (1985) have indeed argued that the social tensions and violence of the English world before 1650 gradually transformed it into a kinder and gentler environment in which contentiousness declined. Some contemporary commentators felt that in the late eighteenth century, behavior was slowly changing.[15]

Whether eighteenth-century Britain was really becoming a kinder and gentler place is a difficult issue, but at least within the circles of commerce,

Figure 2.1 Number of cases sent to trial: Common Pleas.

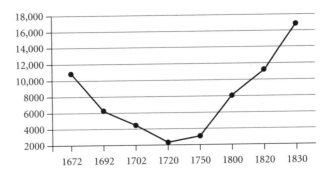

Figure 2.2 Cases in advanced stages: King's Bench.

finance, and manufacturing, trust relations and private settlement of disputes seem to have prevailed over third-party enforcement. Most business was conducted through informal codes of conduct and relied on local reputation and religious moralizing to imbue honesty and responsibility. Voluntary compliance and respect for property and rank as social norms (private-order institutions, in Greif's terminology) may have been as important as formal property rights in turning the wheels of the British economy. These norms involved a variety of signalling devices associated with "gentlemanly" codes and were commented on by contemporaries as

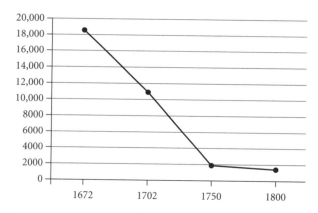

Figure 2.3 Cases in advanced stages: Court of Common Pleas.

"politeness" in a variety of contexts (Langford 2000). Economics suggests that such behavior is often associated with attempts to signal one's trustworthiness to potential partners in the market. These norms applied only to the middling classes. The laboring classes and the unwashed poor remained outside this society, so the norms did not apply to them. Hence, these classes had to be controlled by force, and the draconian laws protecting property from them reflected this need.

Observant contemporaries noted that informal institutions, that is, customs, traditions, and conventions delineating acceptable behavior were at least as important as a formal rule of law. Charles Davenant ([1699] 1771, 55) put it well—"Nowadays Laws are not much observed, which do not in a manner execute themselves"—and felt that because the magistrates did not have a strong motive to perform their duty, private persons might be relied upon "to put the laws in execution." Defoe ([1704–1713] 1938, vol. 1, 87) added caustically that "the English must be unaccountably blameable, whose Laws are the people's own Act and Deed, made at their Request . . . yet no Nation in the World makes such a jest of their Laws as the English." What Davenant and Defoe were observing was that an increasing number of people were bargaining "in the shadow of the law," that is, the parties in disputes knew what the stakes were and the (substantial) loss they would incur in case they went to trial. Yet the law itself set a guideline to dividing up the resources in dispute, and thus made the bargaining process more likely to result in cooperation, since knowledge of the law, as well as the costs of going to trial, were common to both sides, and the legal process may have become more conducive to private ordering by discouraging people from going to trial and encouraging compromise.[16] The Hobbesian view, which insists that order can be achieved only through firm third-party enforcement, may well be true for many societies (depending on many parameters, delineated by Cooter, Marks, and Mnookin [1982]), but it appears that in the century following Hobbes's death (1679) it was becoming an increasingly less apt description of social reality in Britain. What this means is that we cannot really place the efficiency of the state at the center of the stage of institutional explanations of the British economic miracle.

Indeed, the argument that Britain's advantage in leading the Industrial Revolution was due to its efficient enforcement of property rights after 1688 needs to be revisited. What mattered was that within the merchant and artisan classes there existed a level of trust that made it possible to transact with non-kin, and increasingly with people who were, if not strangers, certainly not close acquaintances. In an age when the costs of legal action went up, its availability and efficiency declined, fewer and fewer took recourse to the law and replaced it by common behavioral codes among people belonging to the same class.[17] We might have expected the reverse: the growing integration of goods and factor markets and the widening of the domestic market, and especially the increase in transactions at arm's length throughout the period of the Industrial Revolution eventually necessitated a formal system of law enforcement. But in the eighteenth century, this was far from clear.

Directions of causality are difficult to establish here. Most Enlightenment thinkers believed that the correlation between people cooperating and behaving honestly was caused by a mechanism running from prior commercialization to behavior. It was thought that commerce led to more trustworthy behavior, much like Montesquieu's influential notion of *doux commerce*, which established an association between the "gentle ways of man" and the establishment of trade (Hirschman 1977, 60).[18] But it seems more plausible that the causal arrow went primarily in the other direction, that is, that certain forms of behavior led to cooperative behavior that made market transactions possible, even at arm's length, and thus encouraged economic development.

By 1700, "gentleman" had come to mean quite different things, one a socioeconomic status, the other a code of behavior.[19] A gentleman, Asa Briggs (1959, 411) notes, was someone who accepted the notion of progress but was always suspicious of the religion of gold. An individual signalled that he was trustworthy and would not behave opportunistically because, like a true gentleman, he was not primarily motivated by greed. Gentlemanly capitalism was a way in which opportunistic behavior was made sufficiently taboo that only in a few cases was it necessary to use the formal institutions to punish deviants, since the behavior was to a large extent internalized.[20] The notion that eighteenth-century landowners were scrupulously honest or indifferent to money is a myth, but the pretension was a good signal for behavior that was less than maximally opportunistic and could thus sustain more readily cooperative trust-equilibria. The idea of a gentlemanly culture is traditionally associated with an aristocratic aversion to business and is thus often held to be antithetical to economic development.[21] But in a different sense, being a gentleman meant that one could be trusted, and gentlemanly capitalism provided a shared code, based on honor and obligation, which acted as a blueprint to prevent opportunistic behavior (Cain and Hopkins 1993). The behavior of actual country gentlemen and the moral codes believed to be associated with them and emulated if one was to be regarded as such should not be confused. Landowning parasitic drones were no more "gentlemen" than sword-wielding medieval thugs were "chivalrous." By adopting these codes, an individual signalled that he was trustworthy and would not behave opportunistically. In eighteenth-century Britain, a businessman's most important asset was perhaps his reputation as a "gentleman" even if he was not a gentleman by birth or occupation.

Economists and other social scientists have come to the conclusion that social norms of cooperation and decency can prevail even in societies with ineffective formal law enforcement (Ellickson 1991). This happens in tightly knit groups in which reputational mechanisms work effectively and social remedial norms can be applied. One such model (e.g., Spagnolo 1999) is supported by the linkage of two types of games, one a social game that lasts for a very long time and the other a one-shot economic game. If two agents face one another in both spheres, the punishment in one game may be used to induce cooperation in the other.[22] This is in some sense a formalization of the importance of trustworthiness through social networking and its effect on market efficiency. These models point to the likelihood that trust can be transferred from a social relationship into an economic relation and thus sustain cooperative outcomes in which exchange can take place and disputes are resolved even without the strict enforcement of contracts by a powerful system of impartial courts or arbiters. It is this kind of environment, whether or not one wants to refer to it as "social capital," that created the possibility of cooperation even when standard behavior in finite games would suggest that defection and dishonest behavior might have been a dominant strategy. In Britain during the Industrial Revolution, the social norms of what was perceived to be a gentlemanly culture, with an emphasis on honesty and meeting one's obligations, supported cooperative equilibria that allowed commercial and credit transactions to be consummated and partnerships to survive without the parties being overly concerned about possible defections and other forms of opportunistic behavior. Gentlemen (or those who aspired to become gentlemen) moved in similar circles and faced one another in a variety of linked contexts.

The prevalence of a social convention that defined "gentlemanly" or "polite" behavior and penalized serious deviations from it through irreparable damage to one's reputation, supplemented formal (legal) relations with a moral code that enabled an effective mode of transacting without relying on the state except in extremis. Blackstone referred to Britain as a "Polite and Commercial People." Politeness was widely equated with law-abiding behavior, and it was intuitively sensed that commercial success depended a great deal on politeness. A market economy depended on people constraining their inclination to behave opportunistically. In other words, economic agents did not play necessarily "defect" (even if that might have been in their immediate interest) and expected others to do the same. Modern economics teaches that if this is to be effective, agents need to send out costly signals that indicate to others that they are reliable and trustworthy because they belong to a class of reliable and trustworthy agents (see e.g., Posner 2000). Such signals were what "politeness" was all about: gentlemanly customs in dress, manners, housing, transportation, and speech observed by the British upper classes, and their gradual adoption by the commercial and skilled artisanal classes in the eighteenth century marks the change in British society. They helped created a gentlemanly capitalism and thus an environment in which businessmen and entrepreneurs could deal with one another and with their subordinates in a cooperative fashion that made commerce work even without the heavy hand of third-party law enforcement. In other words, what made commerce and credit possible was that middle-class people increasingly absorbed and imitated a set of behavioral norms that made them eschew opportunistic behavior that might have been personally advantageous in the very short run but socially destructive.

This kind of behavior was observed and blessed by Enlightenment thinkers.[23] The Enlightenment view associated with Montesquieu, cited above, that commerce made people more virtuous and honest, must be seen to operate in reverse: it is a sense of honesty and the importance of maintaining a gentlemanly reputation that allowed a market economy to function effectively. To be sure, the ideal of "gentleman" was not static and changed over the course of the eighteenth century, and the relation between ideal and norm on the one hand and reality on the other is always problematic. The question is not whether the preponderance of British middle-class economic agents invariably behaved like this, as much as whether it affected their behavior (and the way others expected them to behave) enough to make a growing market economy feasible without the need for incessant litigation.[24]

One issue is whether the cooperative norms of behavior were the result of the fear of social sanctions and loss of reputation, or whether they had been "internalized" into a belief in virtue and good behavior (McCloskey 2006, passim). Intellectual historians seem to favor the internalization hypothesis. Pocock (1985, 49) feels that "manners" (that is, cooperative codes of behavior) combined ethical behavior with legal concepts, "with the former predominating." Yet the importance of a good reputation in the business world of eighteenth-century Britain was clearly paramount, and Daniel Defoe was only one of many to realize this when he compared the reputation of a tradesman to that of a maiden, easily damaged by evil tongues and almost impossible to repair and described how such reputations were made and lost around the coffee house through slander (Defoe 1738, vol. 1, 197). Elsewhere he notes (ibid., 361) that a shopkeeper may borrow at better terms than a prince "if he has the reputation of an honest man." An illustration is the career of William Stout (1665–1752), whose autobiography appeared in 1851, and whose economic success was largely fueled by his meticulous reputation for honesty and generosity.[25] He covered the debts incurred by a dissolute apprentice as well as a nephew. As a Quaker, Stout may have been an unusual case, but his success in business was clearly consistent with the notion that cooperation was a remunerative strategy.

In order to function, a reputation-based system needed good information and communications, and these were provided through the many networks of friendly societies and masonic lodges that emerged all over Britain in the eighteenth century (Jacob 1997, 92–94). Such networks exist in every society, but the ones established in the eighteenth century were open and accessible to middle-class men and thus were an ideal vehicle for the transmission of the information that supported reputational mechanisms. Many of these clubs were purely social, eating and drinking clubs, or devoted to common interests and hobbies, but they clearly functioned as clearinghouses for information as well.[26] From the point of view of commercial and financial development, what mattered was the emergence of networks of merchants, industrialists, engineers, inventors, and financiers whose interactions and information exchanges (much of it in the form of gossip and rumor-mongering) were critical to the emergence of these social norms.[27] The unskilled workers and paupers were not part of these circles and thus not expected to behave the same way, but harsh as this may sound, they did not matter in this context.

2.3.1 Cooperation and the Industrial Revolution

As noted, institutions that foster cooperative behavior are conducive to efficiency and well-functioning markets, which are clearly growth enhancing. However, it is not clear how they would be instrumental in bringing about an Industrial Revolution, which was driven by innovation. One way to connect social norms and technological progress is to realize that social norms determined the way entrepreneurs interacted with their economic environment, with customers, suppliers, workers, and competitors, and to stress that within a competitive economy, many of the most successful actors were actually more cooperative than we would expect. These were norms that were increasingly important in determining the behavior of the inventors, skilled craftsmen, financiers, merchants, and the owners of the new mills and mines that defined the Industrial Revolution.

An emphasis on middle-class social norms provides us with answers to some long-debated issues regarding entrepreneurship in the British Industrial Revolution (Mokyr 2008b). The typical successful British entrepreneur in the Industrial Revolution was not so much a self-absorbed obsessive monomaniac as much as a networked and connected member of a community, his behavior constrained by its moral codes. A telltale sign of that is the diversified projects in which many entrepreneurs engaged, investing in local improvements and subscribing to projects such as roads, bridges, canals, dockworks, and later railroads.[28] They could engage in sectors they knew little about because they felt they could trust their partners (Pearson and Richardson 2001). It may thus be the case that an entrepreneurial explanation of Britain's early success is not far off the mark, but rather than look only at the incentives and characteristics of individuals, we may be advised to see how they dealt with one another.[29]

Britain was not unique in developing such social norms, but on the eve of the Industrial Revolution it had far more of a middle class than any other nation (excepting the United Provinces), and it was this bourgeoisie that was at the center of affairs. This class consisted of merchants, artisans, farmers, and mechanics, people with a mentality of acquisitiveness, a desire toward social upward mobility, and a willingness to invest in the education and well-being of their children (Doepke and Zilibotti 2007). As a result, perhaps, more of the middle-class children survived to maturity by the late seventeenth century, and this led to a slow swelling of their ranks (Clark and Hamilton 2006). These values were also followed and emulated by others, aspiring to join the good life of the better-off bourgeoisie. In Britain, more than on the Continent, the energies of this class were directed toward activities that we would regard as productive and entrepreneurial. I would add here that a middle class adopting the social norms of "gentlemen" created the environment of trust and cooperation that was necessary for the Industrial Revolution to take place. The emergence of a middle class created a demand for nonsubsistence goods, especially home furnishings and hardware, which demanded artisans with the kind of skills that were needed if the great inventors were to be able to turn their blueprints into reality.

One interesting possibility is cooperation in technological progress itself. Economic historians have found some examples of what Allen (1983) has termed "collective invention," that is, the main actors in technological innovation freely sharing information and claiming no ownership to it. There are three reasonably well-documented cases of successful collective invention: the case documented by Allen (1983) of the Cleveland (UK) iron industry between 1850 and 1875; the case documented by MacLeod (1988, 112–13, 188) of the English clock and instrument makers; and the case documented by Nuvolari (2004) of the Cornish steam-engine makers after 1800. Examples of such cases are not many, and they required rather special circumstances that were not common, and collective invention in its more extreme form, to judge from its short lifespan, was vulnerable and ephemeral.

On a more general level, however, gentlemanly capitalism generated a great deal of cooperation in the generation of technological progress. The main point to keep in mind is that most of the people who generated useful knowledge during the British Industrial Revolution did not do so *primarily* to make money. This does not mean that they were indifferent to money (though a few were independently wealthy) but rather that the game they were in was not a profit-maximizing project but a signalling game in which individuals tried to demonstrate to their peers their intellectual and technical capabilities. Useful knowledge that was not immediately patentable (and some that was) was placed in the public realm. New scientific knowledge, since the great breakthroughs of the seventeenth century, was expected to be published and made available. In earlier centuries, many natural philosophers had been keeping knowledge under a cloak of secretiveness, believing that it somehow conveyed power or gave the owner an edge in some deep and mysterious way. Such habits impeded its diffusion and access by others. The culture of secretiveness had begun to abate long before 1700, by which time the notion of "credit by priority" had been well established, as the famous quarrel between Newton and Leibniz on the origins of calculus attests.[30] Scientific discoveries of any kind were to be published, communicated, and placed in the public realm.[31] When the unusual case occurred that an eccentric scientist (e.g., John Flamsteed, the first astronomer royal, or the pathologically shy Henry Cavendish, a leading chemist of the second half of the eighteenth century) refused to do so, others would take exception.

Open science, much like open-source technology, was not practiced primarily by idealistic altruists whose objective was the warm glow from seeing humanity enriched by their knowledge (though there were some of those). It was run by ambitious and hard-working people who had clear objectives in mind. Yet the standard pecuniary incentive system central to the economic interpretation of technological change must be supplemented by a more complex one that includes peer recognition and the sheer utility of being able to do what one desires. Credit was given in terms of reputation, which correlated with university positions, court-related appointments, public honors, and sometimes a pension from a ruler or a rich citizen. Even those scientists who discovered matters of significant importance to industry, such as Claude Berthollet, Count Rumford, Joseph Priestley, or Humphry Davy, usually wanted credit, not profit.[32] Berthollet willingly shared his knowledge of the bleaching properties of chlorine with some savvy Scots, who soon were able to turn his discovery into a profitable venture. "When one loves science," wrote Berthollet to one of those Scots,

James Watt, "one had little need for fortune which would only risk one's happiness" (cited by Musson and Robinson [1969, 266]). The great engineer John Smeaton took out only one patent in his entire illustrious career; his colleague John Rennie none at all. Some entrepreneurs, too, refused to take out patents out of principle. Abraham Darby II declined to take out a patent on his coke-smelting process allegedly saying that "he would not deprive the public from such an acquisition" (cited by MacLeod [1988, 185]), and Richard Trevithick, a century later, likewise failed to take out a patent on his high-pressure engine. William Godwin noted in 1798 that "Knowledge is communicated to too many individuals to afford its adversaries a chance of suppressing it. The monopoly of science is substantially at an end. By the easy multiplication of copies and the cheapness of books, everyone has access to them" (Godwin 1798, 282–83). In that more general sense, social norms did have an effect on technology, though it is hard to quantify.

An overlooked but critical consequence of these social norms is in the formation of human capital. As I have argued elsewhere, what set Britain apart from other European countries was not its capacity to accumulate more and better science or even a higher propensity to invent, but the much higher level of *competence* of its skilled workers. Britain could draw on a large cadre of highly skilled craftsmen and technicians. These people might not have been the flashy inventors who came up with the revolutionary insights, but they were those who could read a blueprint, understood practical technicalities such as tolerance, lubrication, tension, and torque, and had experience with the qualities of iron, wood, leather, and other materials (Mokyr 2008b).[33] Harris (1992, 33) describes this knowledge as "unanalysable pieces of expertise, the 'knacks' of the trade," that is to say, knowledge that is primarily tacit and could not be learned except through experience and imitation. Harris's view may be conditioned by his expertise in the coal and iron industry, but much of the same was true in hardware, textiles, instrument making, and engineering. He notes that such skills were taken for granted at home and thus were noted mostly by foreign visitors, including industrial spies (ibid., 26; see also Harris [1998]). Harris singles out the competence of the British iron puddler, a craft requiring not only skills but experience and "almost artistic judgement," and adds that foreigners would have had a hard time importing this competence, because it was the British skilled worker who was the repository of the knowledge. He absorbed the skills needed to work with coal and iron "with the sooty atmosphere in which he lived" and would find it hard to know even what needed to be explained (Harris 1992, 28, 30). It was understood that these skills could not be readily transferred from country to country.[34]

The evidence that Britain's comparative advantage was in the skills and competence of her workmen as much as in the characteristics of her entrepreneurs is above all that it imported technological ideas and exported machines and skilled workmen, even if there were legal restrictions on those exports.[35] When it imported an invention, such as the Jacquard loom or chlorine bleaching, it improved them by a sequence of microinventions. The British paper industry, for instance, imported the Frenchman Louis-Nicolas Robert's paper-making machinery, but British mechanics such as Bryan Donkin and Henry Fourdrinier made important improvements in it. An even more telling example is that of the reverberatory furnace, first described by Vanoccio Biringuccio in 1540 in glassblowing, and adopted in Britain in the early seventeenth century. By 1700, this device had been adapted successfully to nonferrous metals by unknown British skilled workmen before its famous adaptation to iron puddling.

What were the institutional causes of Britain's high level of competence? It had precious little to do with institutions of formal education even if some of the dissenting academies were increasingly committed to teaching practical skills. Instead, it was almost entirely the result of apprenticeships. It was the product of a process of human capital formation that relied precisely on the kind of trust that contracts would be honored even if the fine details of daily contact between master and apprentice were impossible to specify, much less monitor. Britain's increasingly weak guilds had little to do with this enforcement, and indeed there is ample evidence that in many cases the process went awry. Apprentices and masters at times brought court cases against one another, and only a portion of apprentices ever completed their service (Rushton 1991; Wallis 2008). Yet here it is the atypical that may have left us the records, not the typical, and while the courts provided some kind of protection of last resort, the normal case was clearly for the contract to be carried out and most apprentices completed their terms. Those who did, on average, benefitted economically. Despite the fact that apprenticeship relationships lent themselves to opportunistic behavior (such as hold-up strategies by both master and apprentice, depending on the timing pattern of the training), the system served Britain well and supplied it with a layer of skilled artisans like no other because apprenticeship contracts were largely self-enforcing and efficient (Humphries 2003).[36] Apprenticeship took place within a "traditional network of friends, neighbours, co-religionists, and next of kin" (Humphries 2008, 11).[37] The apprentices themselves had quite a few incentives to complete their contract: only an apprentice with a completed term received the right of settlement in a county, and in those areas and trades controlled by guilds, they were barred from practicing a trade if they did not complete their term.[38] This stricture was repealed in 1814, but the institution of apprenticeship survived. It was obviously to a large extent self-enforcing rather than dependent on the letter of the law or the power of the guild. In the later nineteenth century, apprenticeship as an institution was weakened, yet it was sufficiently flexible to withstand the changes and survive until deep into the twentieth century. Apprenticeship was ideal to transmit the kind of tacit artisanal knowledge that was the essential component of competence. It was not perfect, but by all appearances it worked as a self-enforcing institution rather than as one that relied entirely on third-party enforcement (though for the social norms to work, a recourse to legal action as a *pis aller* was necessary).

To summarize, it is the complementary relation between the human capital and the social capital that explains Britain's leadership in the Industrial Revolution. The economy that could produce the technical acumen to follow up on new ideas and turn them into an economic reality was also able to create a group of entrepreneurs to exploit it, people with the ability to take advantage of the opportunities that the inventors and the mechanics created. This relationship appears in the many pairings of technical ability and businessmen. Boulton found his Watt, Clegg his Murdoch, Marshall his Murray, and Cooke his Wheatstone. These pairings were made possible by a network of information flows and personal relationships that made trust and cooperation *within a certain class of people* the default. Here, too, the importance of private order institutions seems predominant, and while they, too, existed in the shadow of the law, their success was determined by self-enforcing properties.

2.4   Formal Political Institutions

Despite the centrality of informal institutions in the argument above, the state was obviously a factor as well. How and why did British *formal* institutions help bring about an Industrial Revolution?

The issue in the premodern European economies was threefold: first, rents had to be protected from greedy and violent neighbors, both inside and outside the economy. For that reason, a third- party enforcer simultaneously charged with using its monopoly on violence to protect the economy from foreigners was essential. Second, this state itself should be prevented from expropriating so much of the rent that there would be too little left to make it worthwhile to exert much effort, so it needed to be constrained somehow. Third, once in existence, the state eventually became the rule-writing body, and its control could be used by powerful lobbies to direct a larger part of the rents to themselves through nonmarket allocations. Solving these three problems simultaneously is hard, and few nations succeeded. Britain in the period 1700–1850 gradually came closer, though the process was still far from complete by 1850.

A large literature, inspired by North and Weingast (1989), has drawn connections between formal institutions, such as constraints on the executive and "rule of law," and economic development. Yet the precise connection between the events of the Glorious Revolution and the Industrial Revolution that followed more than half a century later remains murky. The supporting evidence used by North and Weingast, pointing to a decline in the interest rates paid by the state, has been called into question (Quinn 2001; Sussman and Yafeh 2006; Stasavage 2007). But even if it was confirmed, it has never been made clear how improved borrowing conditions for the government in the first half of the eighteenth century led to technological breakthroughs more than half a century later. A further paradox appears when we compare the British with the Dutch experience. The 1688–89 revolution led to the importation of Dutch institutions and Dutch ideas (carried, in part, by the entourage of William III), and hence the experience of the two countries as the two most successful economies in the eighteenth century might be explained by these shared experiences. The problem, of course, is that the Dutch not only did not have an Industrial Revolution when Britain did, theirs was unusually late (Mokyr 1976, 2000; Van Zanden 1993; Van Zanden and Van Riel 2004). Did the institutional experience of the two nations diverge at some later point? Or is the model simply incomplete?

The sole focus on the state as the source of social order, as I have argued above, may be overemphasized. But the fundamental problem remains: an economy needs to protect rents if it is to generate them from cooperative and creative behavior. Formal institutions mattered in large part because the written formal rules and the court system established the second layer of economic cooperation when the first failed, or when conflicts needed to be resolved. More important, they wrote and rewrote the rules by which others played the economic game. The Glorious Revolution and the subsequent reforms established Parliament as a legitimate *meta-institution*: a body that could write laws that helped define the economic environment. It reduced the contestability of laws, regulations, and taxes, and had the power to repeal or amend rules that no longer worked or were recognized to be detrimental. What helped economies grow and sustain their growth was not just having the kind of institutions that were conducive to economic development, but also having the kind of *agility* that allowed institutions to change when the environment changed. As a matter of principle, there are few features of institutions that are *invariably* suitable for growth; once we are beyond the platitudes such as "law and order are better than chaos and crime," the institutional requirements for economic growth themselves change over time precisely because Smithian growth requires different institutions than Schumpeterian growth. Hence, it is important to judge not only whether an economy inherited from the past appropriate institutions that allowed it to grow, but also whether it had the flexibility to change and adapt them at relatively low cost when the need arose.

The way Britain's political system worked in the eighteenth century gave the country an agility not found elsewhere. After 1750, Parliament increasingly became concerned with its need to solve coordination and other potential market failures, and assumed new responsibilities, as indicated by its role in agricultural reforms, transportation, research (in limited areas), the regulation of weights and measures, the protection of innovators from violent resistance to new technology, and eventually with spillover effects from industrialization such as urban public health and child labor. It is this agility that gave Britain what North has called *adaptive efficiency* that other societies lacked to the same extent. Although some enlightened monarchs on the Continent were able to introduce reforms into the formal institutions of their state in the second half of the eighteenth century, most of those introduced before 1789 did not survive as more conservative ministers or successors revoked them. In the end, the Continent needed revolution and war to attain a structure that Britain had achieved over the eighteenth century without bloodshed and upheaval. It has been tempting to link the political changes of 1688–89 to subsequent changes. The Glorious Revolution once and for all solved the commitment problem: it created a set of constraints on the executive that in the view of one recent author (Dam 2005, 85) took care of the predatory ruler problem. The Bill of Rights of 1689 was followed by a string of laws that established Parliament once and for all as the institution that wrote the rules and had the power to change other institutions.[39] Parliament acquired legitimacy in the sense that when it changed the rules, even the losers in these actions would not deny its right to do so and had a responsibility to comply.[40] At the same time, Parliament was the body that had the capacity of being receptive to both the changing needs of the economy and the changing ideology and beliefs of its elite, and which could change the rules of the economic game accordingly. It imbued the British polity with the most important feature needed for economic change: institutional agility and adaptability, or in North's term, adaptive efficiency.

There is no obvious reason to infer that establishing Parliament as "the place where absolute despotic power, which must in all governments reside somewhere, is entrusted," as Blackstone noted in 1765 (1765–69, book 1, ch. 2, sec. 3), was to be a key to economic progress. After all, the newly found power of Parliament could have been (and was to a considerable extent) abused by special-interest legislation that served distributive coalitions. But parliamentary power meant that changes occurred increasingly from the top down, even if the initiative came from below. Changes in the beliefs at the top eventually affected the entire country. During the entire period under discussion, British Parliament changed British laws in accordance with what its members viewed as their own interests and Britain's perceived needs. Their idea of the national interest, however, was not invariant to the elite's ideology, which became increasingly liberal after 1760 under the influence of Enlightenment authors.[41] Parliament made the enclosure of land in recalcitrant areas possible simply by passing a set of Bills of Enclosure. It solved the coordination problems inherent in having local interests collaborate in building canals and roads by passing Turnpike Acts. It supported entrepreneurs and innovators against technologically conservative interests and those protecting their rents. It awarded pensions and prizes to inventors who had solved a problem of national importance, such as determining longitude at sea and mechanical cotton-spinning.

Moreover, in the decades after the Glorious Revolution, the overall level of energy and efficiency with which Parliament did its work increased steeply. The total number of acts passed during the rules of Charles II and James II was 564, or 20 per annum. In the 25 years between the Bill of Rights and the Hanoverian ascension (1689–1714), this number increased to 1,752 or 70 per annum; by the period 1760–1800, it rose to 8,351 or 209 per annum (Hoppit 1996, 117). It should be stressed that this legislation was mostly serving narrow and special (mostly local) interests, or serving some national rent-seeking lobby. "Specific" legislation directed at a particular place or institution remained between two thirds and three quarters of all acts throughout the period 1688–1800 (Hoppit 1996, 117). The legal historian Maitland felt that "one is inclined to call the [eighteenth] century the century of privilegia. [Parliament] seems afraid to rise to the dignity of a general proposition. . . . [I]t deals with this common and that marriage" (Maitland 1911, 393). Yet over the course of the eighteenth century, rent-seeking attempts by local and national interests started slowly to run into resistance. Many special interest groups that had legislated privileges, monopolies, exclusions, limitations on labor mobility and occupational choice, and had constructed barriers to technological innovation, found themselves on the defensive as the eighteenth century wore on and the more free-market ideas of the Enlightenment began to sink in. It was a very different Parliament in 1774 that tossed out the Calicot Act—a shameless piece of special interest legislation benefitting the wool and silk industry—from the one that had passed it in 1721 (Mokyr and Nye 2007). After 1780, Parliament increasingly used its powers to make selected dents in the rent-seeking machinery of the ancient regime under the platform of making the economy more efficient and streamlined. Parliament, rather than a venal institution that awarded the rights to the highest bidder, was becoming, in the late eighteenth century, the arbitrator of disputes between special interest groups.

Two political phenomena were at the center of this process. One was the centralization of rent seeking and lobbying. By allowing growing domestic market integration (through turnpike and canal bills, for instance), Parliament oversaw the gradual disappearance of local monopolies. By the late eighteenth century, Prime Minister William Pitt refused to meddle in local matters, which were "large areas of policy in which ministers and party politicians need not involve themselves" (Langford 1991, 205). Rent seeking and redistribution remained an essential part of the Hanoverian state until the closing years of the eighteenth century, but it became more nationwide and coordinated. Mercantilist practices had been mostly part of a complex rent-seeking alliance between crown and mercantile interests (Ekelund and Tollison 1997). Once centralized, however, the process was more amenable to changes from the top down (Mokyr and Nye 2007). The striking fact is that the Industrial Revolution was accompanied, on the whole, by a growing liberalization of economic activity.

A further way in which the state mattered in subsequent economic development is the matter of British public finance and empire. As is well recognized, the British fiscal system, based on the combination of excise taxes and government borrowing, was far sounder than elsewhere (Brewer 1989; O'Brien 1988, 2002; Stasavage 2003). North and Weingast's (1989) influential paper argued that the reforms of 1689 created a healthy institutional foundation for British public finance. The connection of this reform to subsequent economic development is, however, not clear. Its importance after 1700 is largely for what it did not do: despite the high taxes, the British state did not expropriate the surplus created by economic growth to threaten the incentives of those who created it. They could do so because taxes, while at times exorbitant, were relatively neutral and did not affect the efficiency of the economy too much. It is unclear how fiscal soundness through high excise taxes contributed materially to the Industrial Revolution, but clearly compared to what could have been, it did not get too much in the way.

Why and how did redistribution fall on hard times in Europe during and after the Industrial Revolution? There is no good theory that explains why "grabbing hands" slowly become weaker, but they clearly did in this period. Part of the reason must have been that these institutions had been very much part of the zero-sum mentality of the pre-Enlightenment world, and the notion that exclusionary rents were on the whole Pareto-dominated did not come naturally to most actors, either on the giving or the receiving end of rent-generating privileges. The areas against which British (and Continental) policymakers particularly aimed their arrows were monopolies, subsidies, labor-market restrictions, tariffs, poor relief, and price controls. By 1850, much of this regulatory machinery had been dismantled. Foreign trade, too, was regarded differently with eighteenth-century Enlightenment thought foreshadowing the insights of political economy.[42] The growing influence of the beneficial effects of trade promulgated by Smith and Ricardo made their mark on policymakers (Grampp 1987; Mokyr 2006).[43]

Enlightenment-induced changes in ideology and beliefs on the part of policymakers in charge of writing the rules played a central role in the American and French revolutions, as well as the various reforms attempted in various European nations before 1789 (Scott 1990). Reforms in Britain did not always come easily even if they did not require a Bastille. The liberal reforms of the 1780s (including the Eden treaty with France in 1786) made room for the more conservative and reactionary 1790s and early 1800s, when war with revolutionary France caused a retrenchment. But it was *reculer pour mieux sauter.* After Waterloo, the reform movement picked up steam, led by both Whigs and so-called liberal Tories, and within a few decades had dismantled much of the remaining rent-seeking apparatus. Thus, the Statute of Artificers was abolished in 1814, the enumeration clauses (that forced British colonial goods to be shipped to third markets through Britain) in the Navigation Acts were repealed in 1822, the monopoly of the East India company was ended by two parliamentary acts in 1813 and 1833, the law prohibiting the emigration of artisans was repealed in 1824, the export prohibition on machinery was weakened in 1824 and repealed in 1843, and the Bubble Act was thrown out in 1825.[44] Other exclusionary arrangements that fell out of favor were serfdom and colonial slavery, prohibitions restricting the use of certain kinds of machinery, usury laws (repealed as late as 1854 but rarely enforced long before), and similar rent-seeking relics. As Nye (2007) has argued, protection was the last vestige of privilege in the ancient regime economy to go. By the middle of the nineteenth century, it is hard to find many instances of the kind of age-of-mercantilism rent-seeking that still predominated in 1721 when Robert Walpole became the first Prime Minister. Perhaps the most telling proof of the change in political culture is the sharp decline in patronage and sinecures, that in 1750 still had been very much part of the power structure. By 1830, the Duke of Wellington said that as prime minister he commanded virtually no patronage (cited by Rubinstein 1983, 57). By the mid-1830s, the total cost of all unreformed sinecures was estimated at under £17,000, down from £200,000 two decades earlier (Harling 1995, 136). Rent seeking in all its manifestations had become socially and politically unacceptable in early nineteenth-century Britain. There is no good explanation for this decline except to attribute it to the impact of Enlightenment thought, filtering through many layers and channels to the minds of the members of the British political elite in both parties. In England the influence of the Enlightenment had been more mixed with religious sentiment than in Scotland or on the Continent. Evangelical beliefs of what was moral combined with Enlightenment notions of what was socially desirable to produce a regime that cultivated a governing style of disinterested public service. When the process was complete, by the second third of the nineteenth century, the British economy was as free of distributional institutions as any economy can ever hope to be.

The Hanoverian state did one more thing with great energy: it conducted foreign policy. In the eighteenth century this was a "blue-water" policy in the service of empire driven by hostility toward its colonial competitors.

The debate on the exact impact of the British Empire on the economy is still unresolved. But on the path to a more modern economy driven by technological progress, empire was a distraction, not a factor, the expenditures on the navy and the army a cost, not a benefit. The enormous public debt in Britain was incurred to pay for expensive wars and colonial ventures rather than to fund infrastructure. While some scholars (e.g., O'Brien 2002, 2007; Ormrod 2003) strongly feel that these hard-fisted policies materially contributed to the Industrial Revolution, others have found such an inference hard to accept (Harley 2004). The mechanisms proposed that link Britain's imperial policies to the Industrial Revolution have not been persuasive despite continuous attempts to show such connections. If Adam Smith and modern economic historians turn out to be correct in their assessment, it may well turn out to be that the fiscal structures set up by the Glorious Revolution were largely engaged in paying for a gigantic white elephant.

Mercantilist ideologies viewed economic international relations as something close to a zero-sum game, in which aggressive foreign policies were believed to pay off economically. Britain's good fortune was that its political institutions prevented these costly misadventures from ruining the economy altogether (as it did to a greater extent in its continental competitors). A direct connection between the sound public finance that formed the basis of Britain's political success and the technological progress of the Industrial Revolution seems, however, far from obvious. It must be cast in terms of things that did not happen but could have (such as a total collapse of public finance of the kind that brought about the French Revolution). Taxation was heavily skewed toward excises on middle-class goods, which may well have created a more favorable set of incentives for potential entrepreneurs who knew that they would be able to keep their profits and not have to share them with the tax collector.

British Parliament, then, was an agency that helped channel Enlightenment ideas into the realm of political action. It hardly needs to be pointed out that this change was slow, the result of a protracted struggle, hard-fought bargaining, and that victory was far from inexorable. Until at least the mid-eighteenth century, Parliament was in many ways a corrupt body, manipulated by special interests driven by rent-seeking and mercantilist ideology and some of that corruption remained in place at least until the 1832 reforms (Rubinstein 1983). But because it had the power to rewrite the rules that applied to others, Parliament could adapt to changing needs and beliefs about what was good for the nation, as well as for themselves. It remains an unanswered question why a body dominated by landlords would allow legislation that eventually undermined their de facto power base. Acemoglu, Johnson, and Robinson rightly claim that the reforms were motivated by the fear that the masses could have used their de facto power and rebelled. Whether that threat was credible is not altogether clear. Parliament seems to have had no qualms in using violence to quell organized protests and riots. It is also the case that many of the men in power believed for a long time that reforms were good for the nation and that they would be able to profit from the changing economy (Hilton 1979).

To sum up, what is most striking is what did *not* happen. The state may have had the theoretical capability to be more predatory and repressive, but was generally constrained from doing so. Taxes, while heavy in the eighteenth century and even more so during the French Wars, were levied primarily on consumption of the middle classes, whereas landowners (who had the political power to block progress) saw their relative tax burden lighten, and entrepreneurs had no real worry that the government would in some way expropriate their profits. The Industrial Revolution began to generate large surpluses and profits for entrepreneurs and those who owned the resources they needed, though the exact timing and magnitude of those surpluses are not quite clear. These surpluses could readily have been expropriated by the powerful political factions that controlled British government, and used for their own benefit or perhaps to bankroll colonial adventures. Nothing of the sort happened. Once the distractions of the Napoleonic Wars were over, the income tax was abolished with great glee, and real government spending per capita was sharply contracted.[45] After Waterloo, a more liberal creed began to replace the mercantilist instincts that had still ruled during much of the Hanoverian years. Neither the British government nor powerful special interests had more than a nibble from the gains that improving technology generated.

2.5 Institutions, Politics, and Economic Progress

Why did sustained growth not occur more often and in more places before the nineteenth century? One standard argument is that technology was constrained by the poor understanding of the fundamental principles of the natural regularities that made certain technologies work (Mokyr 2002). The alternative argument is one of negative feedback. In one version, Malthusian dynamics undid any gains in technology, institutions, and even favorable environmental shocks (Clark 2007). To that, however, we should add the underappreciated problem of negative institutional feedback and institutional inertia, which held back preindustrial societies. Jones (1988) has gone so far as to argue that growth might well have been the normal state in preindustrial societies had not institutional blockages again and again terminated it.

Before 1800, economic growth was more of a regional than a national phenomenon; throughout the preindustrial past there were some areas and cities that did well for a variety of reasons. Such local wealth gave rise to two kinds of negative institutional feedback: *internal* feedback, in which local priests, rulers, and powerful strongmen tried to extricate the rents for their own use, and *external* feedback, generated by strong but poor neighbors or more remote predators. One way or another, regions that did well through trade or manufacturing attracted someone's greed and envy. Time and again, prosperous regions in Germany, central Europe, the Low Countries, and northern Italy had their wealth physically destroyed through war; their trade impeded by tariffs, navigation acts, and privateers; or were forced to spend crippling amounts on defense. Either way, predatory warfare, continental and colonial, remained the rule during much of the eighteenth century and a direct outgrowth of the zero-sum ideology that underlay mercantilist–cameralist policies. In this world, growth, in an almost dialectical way, generated the mechanisms that undid it. After the defeat of Napoleon, such predatory wars within Europe became rare, although Europeans obviously did not include non-Western nations in their more enlightened approach to foreign policy. Whether the century of the Pax Britannica was entirely attributable to a new and less aggressive political outlook in Europe or the result of a new balance of power is unclear, but the few wars fought on European soil after 1815 (or elsewhere in the world between European colonial powers) were less predatory, destructive, and costly to the industrializing powers. As a result, the fruits of economic growth were not wasted on military spending and wars until the disasters of 1914 and beyond.

The other blockage to economic progress before the Industrial Revolution was resistance by vested interests, who had large fixed capital invested in the technological and political status quo. Acemoglu, Johnson, and Robinson (2005) raise a central question: if the income distributions in all societies were closely associated with the distribution of political power, why would anyone in a position to block change ever agree to give up this power? In Britain, the landed classes had traditionally controlled much of Parliament, after 1688 in an informal coalition with the resurgent mercantile interests. Both of these groups had a lot to gain from maintaining the status quo in which mercantilist measures channeled rents to merchants and shipping interests, and landlords received bounties on farm exports. How did this cosy arrangement slip between their fingers in the nineteenth century? In terms of political economy, the astonishing fact remains that the coalition that controlled parliament until deep into the nineteenth century, the large landlords and the merchant–financial elite, did not block the process that was to end their grip on power. Indeed, in a series of measures starting in the early 1820s and culminating in the great reform acts of 1829 and 1832, they opened the political process and provided increased political power to groups that had previously been excluded from de jure power.

Part of the answer must simply be that nobody saw it coming: the technological innovations of the Industrial Revolution transformed the British economy to a degree that was completely unforeseeable in the mid-eighteenth century. Part of the answer was that the old coalition was given a soft landing, and that eventual losers were compensated and bribed to cooperate: the Corn Laws were renewed in 1815 to maintain the income of those classes in a position to block economic reforms, and some of the old arrangements were phased out gingerly and gradually. A third part of the answer was that the old landowning class benefitted from the development, in part because of the continued rise in rents until 1815, but also because many of them were able to profit from the rise in value of urban properties, mining areas, and other real estate.[46] Economic losers who were not political losers, as Acemoglu, Johnson, and Robinson (2005, 435) maintain, would have been able to redistribute the incremental income to themselves if they retained political power. Indeed, the powerful British political elite did so, at least for a transition period long enough to absorb the shock and weaken their resistance. Finally, of course, there was the fear of rebellion. Commercial and industrial interests acquired de facto power during the Industrial Revolution, and obviously at some point those who wrote the rules had to heed their desires. As already noted, Acemoglu and Robinson (2006, 350) argue that the concessions made after 1832 (they had actually started in the mid-1820s, with the repeal of the Combination Acts), were in large part motivated by a desire to preempt a rebellion or the need to repress it violently. Such preemptive action seems plausible (the British had closely followed the unfolding events in Paris in 1830), and it is clear that the Reform Crisis of 1831–32, including the rather serious Bristol riots in October 1831, was instrumental in bringing about reform (Stevenson 1979, 221).

But the exact magnitude of the threat to overthrow the existing order remains unknown. The modest scale of British political riots, and the poor coordination between different groups, suggests that the likelihood of success was never overriding. The reforms enfranchised the middle classes but did little for the unskilled working poor, the displaced domestic workers, and paupers. Archer (2000, 93) concludes that the middle classes were as fearful of a violent revolution as any hard-line conservative. The Chartist movement, which was largely middle class and which in its early stages prompted a few outbreaks of local violence, actually followed rather than preceded the 1832 electoral reforms and led to no further franchise enlargements.[47] The year 1848 passed by relatively peacefully in Britain. On the other hand, any serious threat to the existing order would have been suppressed harshly. During the biggest threats, in the late 1790s and early 1800s, the government clamped down hard on dissidents through both legal and violent methods.

A separate role for changing ideology among the ruling elites therefore cannot be dismissed. The impact of liberal political economy, the Enlightenment's proudest offspring, on many of the policymakers of the epoch is too easy to document to ignore. The dominant figure in the "liberal Tory" government of Lord Liverpool of the 1820s was William Huskisson, an avowed Smithian, who passed a series of tariff reductions and was instrumental in reenergizing the reform movement in the 1820s.[48] The Enlightenment led to the more extreme radical reform movement of the 1820s in which ideologues like Joseph Hume and Francis Place fought for reform legislation informed and inspired by political economy as they interpreted it. The astonishing historical fact is not that such radicals were tolerated (though Place was dubbed "a bad man" for his outrageous advocacy of contraceptives; he himself sired sixteen children), but how successful they eventually proved to be in implementing their liberal programs.

The ideological background of the post-1820 reforms should not be oversimplified. We can distinguish at least three Enlightenment-inspired reform movements that were quite different in emphases and goals. Political economy and ideology differed not only on how and when mercantilism should be dismantled, but also on the fate of colonies and internal regulation. In addition to the pure Smithians, whose main guiding principle was the strong complementarity of peace, prosperity, and free trade, there were the so-called Christian political economists, who combined the logic of Enlightenment with the resurgent evangelical religion. This school helped convert the landed elites to believe in freer trade, even if their worldview was more nationalistic and cyclical than the eighteenth-century Scottish Enlightenment movement had hoped for (Howe 2002). Boyd Hilton (1977) has maintained that besides Enlightenment, there was "atonement," a religious reaction to Jacobinism that inspired some writers to support free trade for its intrinsic moral view. On their left were Ricardians and Benthamites, whose belief in free trade was more extreme and who implied that the landed aristocracy, on whose behalf the Corn Laws had passed, was essentially parasitic. Yet in the end these ideas were all elaborations and variations on the ideas of eighteenth-century Enlightenment intellectuals, and the institutional support for the emergence of the liberal market economy in the first half of the nineteenth century cannot be imagined without them.[49]

The other potentially important institutional impediment to the Industrial Revolution was resistance by the interests most directly affected by the technological changes affecting various industries after 1750. Resistance to new technology by organized or unorganized workers was a major issue in the eighteenth century and remained so during the Industrial Revolution. The groups that were on the losing end were above all domestic-industry workers who were being out-competed by factories, artisans of various levels of skills whose human capital was threatened by obsolescence, and small-scale farmers, the victims of the enclosure movement. These groups had access to a variety of effective means that were at times quite successful: from peaceful petitions to Parliament to legal strikes, to illegal rioting and machine-breaking, skilled and semiskilled workers found ways to signal their disapproval. Many of these struggles had short-term or local effects, and may well have slowed down the path of technological change in some regions.[50] The struggle over "employment" can be seen in part as one over the sunk cost in specific human capital, and in part over threatened local market power. In fact, if there was ever a serious chance of popular uprising (Acemoglu and Robinson's [2006] de facto power), this may have been it. But the state did not make many concessions; it cracked down mercilessly on rioters, siding unilaterally with innovating employers.

In the 1790s and early 1800s the world was inevitably viewed by British policymakers in harsher terms than the peaceful harmony between cooperative nations that Enlightenment writers dreamed about. The implication of this new outlook was that in a hostile world Britain could not afford to pass on technological opportunities and supported employers against workers. In 1806, a committee was appointed to decide the complaints of the West Country clothiers about the new gig mills that they felt threatened their livelihood. E. P. Thompson (1963, 528) feels that "it would be a sad understatement to say that the men's witnesses before the 1806 committee met with a frosty reception." It is telling that the final report of the committee was written by William Wilberforce, M.P., better known for his successful moral campaign against the slave trade. As the biography written by his sons recalls, Wilberforce had to mediate between the valuable men "of small capital who, with the aid of their own families, prepared the goods at home" and "enterprising capitalists." He laid down the "clear principles on which trade must be conducted" (Wilberforce and Wilberforce 1838, vol. 3, 263–67). These principles supported the employers' rights without any hesitation. There can be no doubt that the concern about foreign competition was the main motive of the men in power to refuse the demands of the anti-innovation lobbies.[51] While the report piously reiterated its conventional recognition of the "merits and value of the domestic system," it also felt that the "apprehensions about it being rooted out by the Factory System were *at present at least* wholly without foundation" (Great Britain 1806, 10, emphasis added). Above all, however, Wilberforce and his colleagues regarded as gospel that "the right of every man to employ [his] Capital according to his own discretion . . . is one of those privileges every Briton considers his birthright" (p. 12). The resistance movement went underground, but with enough determination and force on the part of the state, it had little chance to prevail. The people in power had made up their minds—the eighteenth century was over.

There are other answers to the question why the lower classes, both the working and the indigent poor, did not rebel more. British institutions provided something no other state did—a mandatory outdoor poor-relief system that remained in force until 1834. Its net effect on industrialization remains a matter of dispute (Solar 1995). The Poor Law provided a big carrot next to a large stick of violent suppression and achieved its main goal, namely domestic order. The British government, more than in any other state west of the Elbe river, was able to keep its laboring poor in their place. The Poor Law, by providing the poorest workers with a safety net and thus reducing the need to cling to land at all costs, contributed to the creation of a proletariat needed for the factories and the railroads. It also helped in smoothing the labor supply both cyclically and seasonally. In addition, the

Poor Law supported the practice of so-called pauper apprenticeships. The provision of young factory workers from workhouses run by local Poor Law guardians provided an important source of unskilled labor for the factories, especially in rural and small-town mills before 1800.[52] All the same, the magnitude of these effects is hard to ascertain and in all probability was second order.

Conclusion   What were the institutional origins of the Industrial Revolution? As argued, this question only makes sense if we distinguish the "big question" (why Europe?) from the "small question" (why Britain?). We should emphasize that the difference between Britain and its European competitors was one of degree and of timing. The question is, what kind of institutional environment, formal and informal, was most fertile to the successful sprouting of the seeds of the Industrial Revolution? The commercial environment and incentives that institutions created for the innovators and entrepreneurs who made the Industrial Revolution may have been central to Britain's leadership, even if they are harder to observe and measure than differences in the availability of coal. In part, its success was due to adaptive flexibility: the formal institutions of the British polity, rather than being "right" or "wrong," proved to be sufficiently agile to change with the changing needs of the economy. Eventually, many of these advantages were weakened, and the lead that Britain had in the Industrial Revolution was lost. To the extent that the Enlightenment and its political and economic effects were important, other European nations could take equal advantage of them.

The solution to "the commitment problem" after 1688 and the role of Parliament in constraining the executive have been at the center of the literature until now. We need, however, to be concerned with a wider set of issues than just the matter of "who shall guard the guardian." In part, the answer to the question of economic success in this age is about the informal social norms that defined the cultural beliefs of the elites, and allowed market exchange and innovation to operate in a regime of low transactions costs and reasonably self-enforcing norms of what Greif has called private-order contract-enforcement institutions. Hence, we need to consider the cultural beliefs of the political and technological elites. Cooperative behavior and trust based on gentlemanly codes allowed not just market exchange to operate but also created opportunities for new technology by allowing partnerships between inventors and entrepreneurship, and by providing Britain with a large contingent of highly skilled and dexterous craftsmen through well-functioning apprenticeships.

Institutional analysis is an important component of the emergence of modern economic growth because the British Industrial Revolution occurred in a society that overcame successfully and at comparatively low cost the institutional obstacles to sustained economic growth in earlier times. Technological inertia, negative feedback, and opportunistic behavior at both the micro and the macro levels were gradually overcome in Britain in the century after the Glorious Revolution. In addition, formal institutions, above all the changing role and orientation of Parliament, complemented the changes in informal institutions, to create an unexpected confluence of factors and circumstances that created the British Industrial Revolution. Enlightenment ideas, through a variety of mechanisms, influenced decision makers and legislators, and hence real outcomes.

Assessing the "importance" of institutions relative to other factors such as geography or demography assumes a separability that may be ahistorical. The synergy created by the interaction between the growth of useful knowledge in the eighteenth century and the formal and informal institutions that emerged side by side suggests a strong complementarity. With just technological progress but no institutional change, the process would have hit barriers that would have aborted the takeoff, as in nineteenth-century Russia. Had there been only better institutions, but no technological advances, the system would have similarly run out of steam and asymptoted off into a new stationary state (Mokyr 2006a). Sustainable and continuous economic growth needed both.

ACKNOWLEDGMENTS

Parts of this essay are based on *The Enlightened Economy* (Mokyr 2008) and other essays as cited in the text. The comments of Avner Greif, Elhanan Helpman, Deirdre McCloskey, Michael Silver, and Joachim Voth on an earlier version are acknowledged with gratitude.

NOTES

1. North (1981, 166) comes close to linking the institutional changes of the late eighteenth century with the Industrial Revolution when he maintains that it was explained by "a combination of better-specified and enforced property

rights and increasingly efficient and expanding markets." North and Weingast (1989, 831) are more prudent and wonder if arguing that without the Glorious Revolution the British economy would have followed a very different path and would not have experienced an Industrial Revolution would be "claiming too much."

2. Arguably, it could be maintained that the Industrial Revolution followed a contagion model, in which Britain was indispensable as a model to be emulated and followed, and that without its leadership, the Continent would not have been able to develop. That the British example was widely followed and imitated in various forms on the Continent cannot be denied. Britain's example shaped some of the forms of the Industrial Revolution on the Continent. But the consensus today is that France, Prussia, Belgium, Switzerland, and northern Italy followed quite different but equally successful technological and institutional trajectories. Given that much of the nineteenth-century technology was actually invented on the Continent, it seems implausible that British leadership was a necessary condition for the Industrial Revolution in the West as a whole.

3. Goethe may have been somewhat naive when he wrote that the British patent system's great merit was that it turned invention into a "real possession, and thereby avoids all annoying disputes concerning the honor due" (cited in Klemm 1964, 173). Note, however, his emphasis on honor as opposed to profit. Not so the Scottish Enlightenment writers. In his *Lectures on Jurisprudence* ([1762–66] 1978, 83, 472), Adam Smith admitted that the patent system was the one monopoly (or "priviledge" as he called it) he could live with, because it left the decision on the merit of an invention to the market rather than to officials. Smith thought, somewhat unrealistically, that if an "invention was good and such as is profitable to mankind, [the inventor] will probably make a fortune by it."

4. Andrew Yarranton, a seventeenth-century tin-plater and navigation engineer, found his business harmed by a patentee incapable of working the new technology properly (MacLeod 1988, 184).

5. The bureaucratic procedure to take out a patent was referred to by contemporaries as "cumbrous machinery." It had been little changed since it was established in 1536, and contemporaries delighted in ridiculing it, as in Charles Dickens's short story "A Poor Man's Tale of a Patent."

6. The pioneers of the paper-making machines, Henry and Sealy Fourdrinier, too, were awarded a grant of £20,000 by a Parliamentary committee (after many manufacturers testified selflessly that the continuous paper machines had been of huge benefit to their respective branches), though this amount was later reduced to £7,000 and paid as late as in 1840, when Henry was already in his seventies. Edward Jenner was voted a grant of £30,000 in 1815. The scientist

William Sturgeon, one of the pioneers of electrical technology in the 1830s, fell on hard times toward the end of his life and was awarded a one-off payment of £200 plus a small pension by Lord John Russell's government. In all these cases, and many others, there was an explicit recognition that these people had added to the well-being of the realm, in other words, they had produced positive externalities.

7. Britain's greatest post-1830 inventor, Henry Bessemer, believed that "the security offered by patent law to persons who expend large amounts of money in pursuing novel inventions, results in many new and important improvements in our manufactures" (Bessemer [1905] 1989, 82). Not all inventors concurred with this view, but if enough of them saw it this way, the British patent system deserves some credit. H. I. Dutton (1984, 203) has argued that for many inventors, patents were the only means by which they could appropriate a sufficient return for their effort and that patents thus provided security in an exceptionally risky activity. The patent law was often poorly defined and the courts unfriendly to inventors, but it remained in most cases the best incentive for inventive activity. Dutton argues that the patent laws were a "slightly imperfect" system that created an ideal system in which there was enough protection for inventors to maintain an incentive for inventions, yet was not so watertight as to make it overly expensive for users. If inventors systematically overestimated the rate of return on inventions by not fully recognizing the weaknesses of the patent system, they would have produced more innovations than in a world of perfect information. Another distinguished engineer, Richard Roberts, stressed that had it not been for the patent system, he would not have invented as much as he did, and the inventions he would have made would have lain on the shelves (Great Britain 1851, 187).

8. William Shipley, its founder, viewed its purpose as follows: "Whereas the Riches, Honour, Strength and Prosperity of a Nation depend in a great Measure on Knowledge and Improvement of useful Arts, Manufactures, Etc. . . . several [persons], being fully sensible that due Encouragements and Rewards are greatly conducive to excite a Spirit of Emulation and Industry have resolved to form [the Society of Arts] for such Productions, Inventions or Improvements as shall tend to the employing of the Poor and the Increase of Trade."

9. One attempt was made by the famous political economist and magistrate Patrick Colquhoun who tried to count the number of "individuals who live idly and support themselves by criminal or immoral pursuits." Despite his clear attempt to show the criminality of London's environment, the numbers are actually rather modest. Out of a population of 865,000 he counted 115,000 such persons. This figure seems startlingly high, until we realize that it included 50,000 "unfortunate females who support themselves by prostitution" and 10,000 "servants, male and female, out of place principally from ill be-

haviour and loss of character" not to mention 2,000 "itinerant Jews, wandering from street to street, holding out temptations to pilfer and steal" (cf. Colquhoun 1797, vii–xi).

10. By 1760, the great legal scholar Blackstone complained that "Yet, though . . . we may glory in the wisdom of the English law, we shall find it more difficult to justify the frequency of Capital Punishment to be found therein, inflicted . . . by a multitude of successive independent statutes upon crimes very different in their natures." He added that the list was so dreadful that crime victims were reluctant to press charges and juries reluctant to convict (Blackstone 1765–69, vol. 4, 18).

11. This argument has been made with great emphasis by Hay (1975), who stressed the strong class bias in eighteenth-century British criminal law. For a critique, see Langbein (1983a), who has argued effectively that the bark of these draconian criminal codes was worse than their bite.

12. Eighteenth-century law enforcement was in the hands of local magistrates and part-time local parish constables. For the rest, justice had to rely on volunteers, local informers, vigilante groups, and private associations specializing in prosecutions of felons. Some 450 such organizations were established in England between 1744 and 1856. London developed its first constables after Henry Fielding was appointed magistrate at Bow Street in 1748, and his professional assistants or thief takers became known as "Bow Street Runners." Yet it was not until after 1830 that anything remotely resembling a professional police force began to emerge in the rest of Britain, and as late as 1853, half the counties in Britain were still without police. In fact, the eighteenth-century idea of "police" was quite different from ours: the word meant something like a series of regulations and regulatory agencies for the supervision of the manners, morals, and health of society rather than a body of officers (Paley 2004).

13. Small debts could be settled through courts of voluntary arbitration known as Courts of Conscience (also known as Courts of Requests), which became increasingly popular after 1750 for settling debts without the burden of expensive court cases. These courts, significantly, were unpopular among working people who objected to the way they dealt with tallies run up in ale houses—a telltale sign that they were effective.

14. The most likely alternative to a decline in litigiousness is that courts became less accessible and more costly. On the other hand, courts enforced contracts (both written and verbal) increasingly through procedures called "actions on the case" (such as *assumpsit* for debt) in which courts enforced contracts without a formal trial (though such trials could sometimes still result). Brooks (1998, 91) adds that it is even possible that the high volume of trials in the seventeenth century may have exerted a "pedagogic effect" on debtor–creditor relationships.

15. Francis Place (1771–1854), the radical politician and reformer, for instance, noted that "the progress made in refinement of manners and morals seems to have gone on simultaneously with the improvement in arts, manufactures and commerce . . . [W]e are a much better people than we were [half a century ago], better instructed, more sincere and kind-hearted, less gross and brutal" (cited by George 1966, 18). Beattie (1986, 138–39) concurs with this view, and concludes that in 1800, British cities, and especially London, were less violent and dangerous places than in 1660.

16. The term "bargaining in the shadow of the law" originates with Mnookin and Kornhauser (1979).

17. As Brewer (1982, 214), who was one of the first to point to the importance of this phenomenon, noted, "reliability, fairness and generosity were the qualities most highly valued. . . . [T]hese attitudes oiled the wheels of commerce and enabled men to make greater profits."

18. Adam Smith, in his *Lectures of Jurisprudence*, thought he had the answer: "Whenever commerce is introduced into any country, probity and punctuality always accompany it. These virtues in a rude and barbarous country are almost unknown. Of all the nations in Europe, the Dutch, the most commercial, are the most faithfull to their word. . . . There is no natural reason why an Englishman or a Scotchman should not be as punctual in performing agreements as a Dutchman. It is far more reduceable to self interest, that general principle which regulates the actions of every man, and which leads men to act in a certain manner from views of advantage, and is as deeply implanted in an Englishman as a Dutchman. A dealer is afraid of losing his character, and is scrupulous in observing every engagement. . . . Where people seldom deal with one another, we find that they are somewhat disposed to cheat, because they can gain more by a smart trick than they can lose by the injury which it does their character" ([1757] 1978, 327).

19. Defoe (1703, 19) famously wrote that "Wealth, however got, in England makes lords of mechanics, gentlemen of rakes; Antiquity and birth are needless here; 'Tis impudence and money makes a peer." Dr. Johnson, in the same spirit, noted that "An English tradesman is a new species of gentleman" if he prospered sufficiently (Porter 1990, 50). McCloskey (2006, 294–96) traces the transformation of the word "honor" in English and French from its aristocratic sense ("reputation") to its more capitalist sense of "honesty" (reliability, truth-telling) and "politeness" ("doing the right thing") when the importance of these concepts began to increase in the eighteenth century, and discovers that the same change occurred in the Dutch language.

20. By the mid-Victorian times, this was expressed almost as a caricature by Samuel Smiles describing what really mattered for the gentleman: "The true gentleman

has a keen sense of honour, - scrupulously avoiding mean actions. His standard of probity in word and action is high. He does not shuffle or prevaricate, dodge or skulk; but is honest, upright, and straightforward. His law is rectitude - action in right lines. When he says YES, it is a law. . . . Above all, the gentleman is truthful. He feels that truth is the 'summit of being,' and the soul of rectitude in human affairs" (Smiles 1859).

21. As Daunton (1989, 125) summarizes the traditional argument, "the more an occupation or a source of income allowed for a life style which was similar to that of the landed classes, the higher the prestige it carried and the greater the power it conferred. The gentleman-capitalist did not despise the market economy but he did hold production in low regard and avoided full-time work."

22. An example of this kind of arrangement existed in Manchester in the 1820s, where the Manchester Fire and Life Assurance Company's boardroom provided "interconnected circuits of political, business, and social activities" to generate not only information underlying collective action but also regarding the reputations of the major players. Similar conditions were noted among Bristol sugar refiners in 1769 (Pearson 1991, 388).

23. John Locke, for instance, wrote in 1693 that a gentleman's upbringing should endow him with a love of virtue and reputation [and] make him from within "a good, a vertuous, and able man" and with "Habits woven into the very Principles of his Nature," not because he feared retribution but because this defined his very character (Locke [1693] 1732, 46–47). Many decades later, the French historian Hippolyte Taine, who stayed in London in 1858, summarized the concept of a gentleman as "the three syllables that summarize the history of English society" (Taine [1872] 1958, 144). The essence of the gentleman as Locke and his successors saw him "was to be his integrity" (Carter 2002, 335). Paul Langford (2000, 126) observes that one of the British aristocracy's prime characteristics was the belief in fair play and that a cheating lord was a traitor to his class.

24. The French traveler Pierre Jean Grosley noted the "politeness, civility and officiousness" of citizens and shopkeepers "whether great or little" (Grosley 1772, vol. 1, 89, 92). The eighteenth-century Italian writer and philosopher Alessandro Verri felt that London merchants were far more trustworthy than their Paris counterparts (cited by Langford 2000, 124). One French visitor to early nineteenth-century London noted that British shopkeepers were fundamentally honest, and that a child could shop as confidently as the most street-wise market shopper (Nougaret 1816, vol. 2, 12). Charles Dupin (1825, xi–xii) went as far as to attribute Britain's economic successes to the "wisdom, the economy and above all the probity" of its citizens. Reputation was critical. Prosper Mérimée, commenting on the open-access policies in the British Museum Library in 1857,

observed that "The English have the habit of showing the greatest confidence in everyone possessing character, that is, recommended by a gentleman . . . whoever obtains one is careful not to lose it, for he cannot regain it once lost" (1930, 153–54).

25. "At my begining I was too credulos and too slow in caling, and seldom made use of atturney, except to write letters to urge payments, being always tender of oppressing poor people with law charges, but rather to loose all or get what I could quietly, than give it to atturnies. And I never sued any to execution for debt, nor spend 20s in prosecuting any debter, and to loose all was more satisfaction to me than getting all to the great cost of my debtor, and to the preservation of my reputation" (Stout 1967, 120–21).

26. The extent of the spreading of these clubs is reflected by the founding of the Sublime Club of Beefsteaks devoted to carnivory in 1735. The total number of friendly societies memberships in 1800 is estimated at 600,000 (Porter 1990, 156–57). For more details, see Clark 2000.

27. Pearson (1991) documents in detail the interconnected political, social, and financial networks of Manchester's cotton elite in the post-1815 period. These tight circuits were more effective in provincial towns, where information flowed more easily than in the metropole, and may have been a contributor to the advantage that provincial towns had over the capital.

28. The great ironmonger John Wilkinson, who played such a strategic role in helping Watt cast his cylinders, invested widely outside his field of expertise such as in banks, agricultural improvements, mines, and the many canals promoted by his friend and fellow ironmaster, Richard Crawshay.

29. Recent work on the history of entrepreneurs in the United States seems to have come to the same conclusion, that networks and trust-through-connections are as important in entrepreneurial success as talent and ambition. See Laird (2006).

30. Other early examples of such priority disputes can be cited, such as the dispute between Newton and Hooke (about the inverse-square force law) or the battle between two Dutchmen, Jan Swammerdam and Reinier de Graaf, on the discovery of certain aspects of female reproduction.

31. This process has been documented in great detail by Eamon (1994, 319–50) who pointed to the influence of Francis Bacon and his followers in establishing this rule, as they realized that any progress was going to be the result of a cooperative effort. More recently Paul David (2004) has argued that open science established the quality of intellectual superstars, much in demand by courts and universities for prestige reasons.

32. A recent survey (Bowler and Morus 2005, 320–21) refers to the class of "gentlemanly specialists," men who led the development of useful knowledge but

did not make their living from it and were suspicious of anyone who did. At the same time, those who were not independently wealthy needed to find patronage either as university professors or from government, industry, or wealthy individuals.

33. Josiah Tucker, a keen contemporary observer, pointed out that "the Number of Workmen [in Britain] and their greater Experience excite the higher Emulation, and cause them to excel the Mechanics of other Countries in these Sorts of Manufactures" (Tucker 1758, 26). He must have thought of men like John Whitehurst, William Murdoch, Bryan Donkin, John Wilkinson, John Kay, Edward Troughton, not quite hall-of-fame inventors, but brilliant craftsmen. At Soho, of which a lot is known, the highly skilled "turners" were kept separate from the equally skilled fitters, and these men would require many years of apprenticeship and work as assistants (Roll 1930, 181–83).

34. The French scientist and industrialist Jean-Antoine Chaptal noted that in many branches of manufacturing, the British had become dominant, but that even after importing the machinery, the French could not compete and sold at twice the price of the British because they lacked the immense details, the customs, and the "turns of hand" (dexterity) and that while the slow progress of industry could be accelerated by learned men, there was no substitute for experience (Chaptal 1819, vol. 2, 430–31).

35. The French political economist Jean-Baptiste Say, a keen observer of the economies of his time, noted in 1803 that "the enormous wealth of Britain is less owing to her own advances in scientific acquirements, high as she ranks in that department, as to the wonderful practical skills of her adventurers in the useful application of knowledge and the superiority of her workmen" (Say [1803] 1821, vol. 1, 32–33). Another Swiss visitor, de Saussure, had noticed the same seventy-five years earlier: "English workmen are everywhere renowned, and justly. They work to perfection, and though not inventive, are capable of improving and of finishing most admirably what the French and Germans have invented" (de Saussure 1902, 218, letter dated May 29, 1727). The great engineer John Farey, who wrote an important treatise on steam power, testified a century later that "the prevailing talent of English and Scotch people is to apply new ideas to use, and to bring such applications to perfection, but they do not imagine as much as foreigners."

36. Local studies have concluded that in the eighteenth century, while masters had an incentive and opportunities to exploit and abuse the young, few apparently did so (Rushton 1991, 101). Reputation effects seem to have been important here, since apprentices without parents to protect them were in greater jeopardy of being in some way cheated by their masters.

37. Humphries (2007, 22–23) recounts a number of cases in which disputes between master and apprentice were resolved by social and reputational pressures, many of them supported by the need of the master to maintain his social relations with the parents. Her sample of hundreds of autobiographical accounts of working-class people provides a unique picture of the centrality of apprenticeship in the intergenerational transfer of human capital.

38. In 1777 the calico printers admitted that fewer than 10% of their workers had served because "the trade does not require that the men they employ should be brought up to it; common labourers are sufficient" (Mantoux [1928] 1961, 453).

39. Legislation in the 1690s and early 1700s eliminated the royal prerogative as a form of legislation and abolished the king's right to absolve certain individuals of certain laws. Other legislation established parliamentary oversight on government spending and a "civil list" that specified what royal funds would be spent on. Parliament ensured that it met regularly and an Act of Settlement assured that Parliament maintained control over the royal succession. The Act of Settlement of 1701 also established an independent judiciary, in which judges were appointed for life and could only be removed if convicted of a felony or impeached. Whether or not that really established a full "rule of law" (Dam 2005, 85) on the ground remains controversial.

40. As one historian notes, "a reverence for Parliament became an increasingly important part of élite attitudes and a vital part of élite patriotism. . . . [T]he knowledge that the institution they served was. . . . efficient [and] by the standards of the time not obstructive reassured British patricians of their polity's superiority. . . . There is evidence that even lower down the social scale Parliament inspired respect" (Colley 1992, 50, 52).

41. For examples of such influences, see Mokyr (2006b).

42. Thus Jean-François Melon, a friend of Montesquieu's, wrote in the 1730s that "the spirit of commerce and of polity are inseparable. . . . [T]he spirit of conquest and the spirit of commerce mutually exclude each other in a nation" and added that it was commerce, not violence, that supplied the "wisdom for preservation" (Melon 1738, 136–39).

43. Kindleberger (1978, 52) who admits that in some cases "free trade is the hypocrisy of the export interest" felt that "in the English case it was more a view of a world at peace, with cosmopolitan interests served as well as national."

44. As Harris (2000) has shown, the Bubble Act was primarily used as an exclusionary tool by incumbents to reduce entry and competition.

45. Total government gross income went from a peak of £69.2m in 1817 to a trough of £56.3m in 1854. The national debt peaked at £844m in 1819 and then fell to £774m in 1854. Nominal GDP went from £322m in 1821 to £718m in 1854,

thus reducing per capita taxation by 57 percent and national indebtedness by 59 percent.

46. Rubinstein's rather heroic estimate of landed and nonlanded millionaires and half-millionaires dying between 1809 and 1859 shows 179 landed millionaires versus 10 nonlanded millionaires, and 338 landed half-millionaires as compared to 54 nonlanded ones (1981, 60–65). As Rubinstein (ibid., 61) remarks, "an observer entering a room full of Britain's 200 wealthiest men in 1825 might be forgiven for thinking that the Industrial Revolution had not occurred."

47. William Lovett's Charter dated from 1838 and fizzled out after 1848, twenty tears before the next big electoral reform. The most serious outbreak of violence was the 1838 Newport riot that left fifteen people dead.

48. Huskisson "zealously and consistently subscribed to the theories of Adam Smith's teaching, [a belief] reflected in every reform in the twenties" (Brady 1967, 133). Equally well-documented is the enormous influence that *Wealth of Nations* had on other policymakers, especially after Dugald Stewart, Smith's successor at Edinburgh, turned the book into a fountainhead of wisdom (Herman 2001, 229–30; see also Rothschild 2001). Among Stewart's pupils were two future prime ministers, Palmerston and John Russell. His program was to remove all state support and protection for manufacturing and agriculture.

49. Even the aristocratic Whigs led by Earl Grey, the architect of the successful Reform Act of 1832, were motivated by a mixture of "fear of revolution, a natural desire to consolidate their power, and—above all—their own brand of patriotism" (Colley 1992, 345).

50. Thus, in Wiltshire, shearmen, through the "Wiltshire outrages" of 1802, were able to prevent the introduction of gig mills until after 1815; the machinery destroyed during the Luddite riots took some years to replace; and as late as 1830, the Captain Swing riots delayed the introduction of agricultural machinery into the South of England by many years. Randall (1991, 289) feels that the resistance, at least in some areas, gave the artisans "many extra years respite."

51. The language used by the committee is telling—"If Parliament had acted on such principles [on which the use of these particular machines is objected to] 50 years ago, the Woollen Manufacture would never have attained to half its present size. . . . [I]ts Augmentation is principally to be ascribed to the general spirit of enterprize and industry among a free and enlightened people. . . . It is likewise an important consideration . . . that we are at this day surrounded by powerful and civilized Nations, who are intent on cultivating their Manufactures and pushing their Commerce"—and specifically mentioned the worrisome evidence of such an establishment being set up in Paris. See Great Britain, 1806, 7.

52. Some of the transactions between Poor Law authorities and mill owners resembled the slave trade, for example, the purchase of seventy children from the parish of Clerkenwell by Samuel Oldknow in 1796 (Mantoux [1928] 1961, 411).

REFERENCES

Acemoglu, Daron, and James Robinson. 2006. *Economic Origins of Dictatorship and Democracy*. Cambridge: Cambridge University Press.

Acemoglu, Daron, Simon Johnson, and James Robinson. 2005. "Institutions as a Fundamental Cause of Economic Growth." In *Handbook of Economic Growth*, eds. Philippe Aghion and Steven Durlauf, 385–465. Amsterdam: Elsevier.

Allen, Robert C. 1983. "Collective Invention." *Journal of Economic Behavior and Organization* 4(1): 605–33.

Archer, John E. 2000. *Social Unrest and Popular Protest in England, 1780–1840*. Cambridge: Cambridge University Press.

Beattie, J. M. 1974. "The Pattern of Crime in England, 1660–1800." *Past and Present* 62(Feb):47–95.

———. 1986. *Crime and the Courts in England, 1660–1800*. Princeton, NJ: Princeton University Press.

Bekar, Clifford T., Kenneth I. Carlaw, and Richard G. Lipsey. 2005. *Transformations: General Purpose Technologies and Long-Term Economic Growth*. Oxford: Oxford University Press.

Bessemer, Henry. [1905] 1989. *Sir Henry Bessemer, F.R.S.: An Autobiography*. London: Institute of Metals.

Blackstone, William. 1765–69. *Commentaries on the Laws of England*. 1st ed. Oxford: Printed at the Clarendon Press. http://www.yale.edu/lawweb/avalon/blackstone/blacksto.htm.

Blanqui, Adolphe-Jérôme. 1824. *Voyage d'un jeune Français en Angleterre et en Ecosse, pendant l'automne de 1823*. Paris: Dondey-Dupré *père et fils*.

Boldrin, Michele, and David K. Levine. 2005. *Against Intellectual Monopoly*. http://www.dklevine.com/general/intellectual/against.htm.

Bowler, Peter J., and Iwan Rhys Morus. 2005. *Making Modern Science*. Chicago: University of Chicago Press.

Brady, Alexander. 1967. *William Huskisson and Liberal Reform: An Essay on the Changes in Economic Policy in the Twenties of the Nineteenth Century*. London: Oxford University Press.

Brewer, John. 1982. "Commercialization and Politics." In *The Birth of a Consumer Society: The Commercialization of Eighteenth-Century England*, eds. Neil McKendrick et al., 197–262. Bloomington, IN: Indiana University Press.

————. 1989. *The Sinews of Power: War, Money and the English State, 1688–1783.* New York: Alfred A. Knopf.

Briggs, Asa. 1959. *The Age of Improvement.* London: Longman.

Brooks, C. W. 1989. "Interpersonal Conflict and Social Tension: Civil Litigation in England, 1640–1830." In *The First Modern Society: Essays in English History in Honor of Lawrence Stone,* eds. A. L. Beier et al. Cambridge: Cambridge University Press.

————. 1998. *Lawyers, Litigation and English Society since 1450.* London: Hambledon Press.

Brunt, Liam. 2006. "Rediscovering Risk: Country Banks as Venture Capital Firms in the First Industrial Revolution." *Journal of Economic History* 66(1, March):74–102.

Cain, Peter, and Anthony G. Hopkins. 1993. *British Imperialism: Innovation and Expansion.* Harlow, Essex: Longman.

Carter, Philip. 2002. "Polite Persons: Character, Biography, and the Gentleman." *Transactions of the Royal Historical Society* 12:333–54.

Chaptal, Jean-Antoine-Claude. 1819. *De l'industrie Française.* 2 vols. Paris: Chez A.-A. Renouard.

Clark, Gregory. 2007. *Farewell to Alms: A Short Economic History of the World.* Princeton, NJ: Princeton University Press.

Clark, Gregory, and Gillian Hamilton. 2006. "Survival of the Richest: The Malthusian Mechanism in Pre-Industrial England." *Journal of Economic History* 66(3, Sep.):707–736.

Clark, Peter. 2000. *British Clubs and Societies, 1580–1800: The Origins of an Associational World.* Oxford: Clarendon Press.

Colley, Linda. 1992. *Britons: Forging the Nation, 1707–1837.* New Haven, CT: Yale University Press.

Cooter, Robert, Stephen Marks, and Robert Mnookin. 1982. "Bargaining in the Shadow of the Law: A Testable Model of Strategic Behavior." *Journal of Legal Studies* 11(2, June):225–51.

Colquhoun, Patrick. 1797. *A Treatise on the Police of the Metropolis; Containing a Detail of the Various Crimes and Misdemeanors.* 5th ed. London: Printed by H. Fry, Finsbury-Place.

Dam, Kenneth W. 2005. *The Law-Growth Nexus: The Rule of Law and Economic Development.* Washington, DC: Brookings Institution Press.

Daunton, Martin J. 1989. "Gentlemanly Capitalism and British Industry 1820–1914." *Past and Present* (122, Feb.):119–58.

Davenant, Charles. [1699] 1771. *Essay Upon the Probable Methods of Making a People Gainers in the Balance of Trade.* London: Printed for J. Knapton. Reprinted in Charles Davenant, *The Political and Commercial Works of That*

Celebrated Writer Charles D'avenant, LL.D. 2:168–382, collected and revised by Sir Charles Whitworth. London: Printed for A. Horsfield.

David, Paul A. 2004. "Patronage, Reputation, and Common Agency Contracting in the Scientific Revolution." Unpublished manuscript, August, Stanford University.

Defoe, Daniel. 1703. *A Collection of the Writings of the Author of the True-born English-man.* London (no publisher listed).

———. [1704–1713] 1938. *Defoe's Review.* Reproduced from the original editions, with an introduction and bibliographical notes by Arthur Wellesley Secord. New York: Published for the Facsimile text society by Columbia University Press.

———. 1738. *The Complete English Tradesman.* 4th ed. 2 vols. London: C. Rivington.

Desaguliers, John T. 1763. *A Course of Experimental Philosophy*, 3rd ed. 2 vols. London: Printed for A. Millar.

Doepke, Matthias, and Fabrizio Zilibotti. 2007. "Occupational Choice and the Spirit of Capitalism." Working paper, UCLA.

Dupin, Charles. 1825. *The Commercial Power of Great Britain: Exhibiting a Complete View of the Public Works of This Country.* 2 vols. London: Printed for C. Knight.

Dutton, H. I. 1984. *The Patent System and Inventive Activity during the Industrial Revolution.* Manchester: Manchester University Press.

Eamon, William. 1994. *Science and the Secrets of Nature.* Princeton, NJ: Princeton University Press.

Ekelund, Robert B. Jr., and Robert D. Tollison. 1997. *Politicized Economies: Monarchy, Monopoly, and Mercantilism.* College Station, TX: Texas A&M University Press.

Ellickson, Robert C. 1991. *Order without Law: How Neighbors Settle Disputes.* Cambridge, MA: Harvard University Press.

Emsley, Clive. 2005. *Crime and Society in England, 1750–1900.* 3rd ed. Harlow: Pearson Longman.

George, M. Dorothy. 1966. *London Life in the Eighteenth Century.* 2nd ed. Harmondsworth: Penguin Books.

Godwin, William. 1798. *Enquiry Concerning Political Justice and Its Influence on Morals and Happiness.* 3rd ed., corrected. London: Paternoster-Row, printed for G. G. and J. Robinson.

Grampp, William D. 1987. "How Britain Turned to Free Trade." *Business History Review* 61(1, Spring):86–112.

Great Britain. 1806. *British Parliamentary Papers* vol. 3, no. 268, "Select Committee on State of Woollen Manufacture of England."

———. 1851. *British Parliamentary Papers,* vol. 18, no. 486. "Select Committee of House of Lords to consider Bills for Amendment of Law touching Letters Patent for Inventions."

Greif, Avner. 2005. *Institutions and the Path to the Modern Economy: Lessons from Medieval Trade.* Cambridge: Cambridge University Press.

Grosley, Pierre Jean. 1772. *A Tour to London; or, New Observations on England, and Its Inhabitants.* By M. Grosley, translated from the French by Thomas Nugent. London: Printed for Lockyer Davis.

Harley, C. Knick. 2004. "Trade: Discovery, Mercantilism, and Technology." In *The Cambridge Economic History of Modern Britain, vol. 1,* eds. Roderick Floud and Paul Johnson, 175–203. Cambridge: Cambridge University Press.

Harling, Philip. 1995. "Rethinking 'Old Corruption,'" *Past and Present* (147, May):127–58.

Harris, John R. 1992. "Skills, Coal and British Industry in the Eighteenth Century." In *Essays in Industry and Technology in the Eighteenth Century.* Ashgate: Variorum.

———. 1998. *Industrial Espionage and Technology Transfer: Britain and France in the Eighteenth Century.* Aldershot: Ashgate.

Harris, Ron. 2000. *Industrializing English Law: Entrepreneurship and Business Organization, 1720–1844.* Cambridge: Cambridge University Press.

Hay, Douglas. 1975. "Property, Authority and the Criminal Law." In *Albion's Fatal Tree: Crime and Society in Eighteenth-Century England,* eds. Douglas Hay et al., 17–63. New York: Pantheon.

Herman, Arthur. 2001. *How the Scots Invented the Modern World.* New York: Crown.

Hilaire-Pérez, Liliane. 2000. *L'Invention Technique au Siécle des Lumiéres.* Paris: Albin Michel.

Hilton, Boyd. 1977. *Corn, Cash, Commerce: The Economic Policies of the Tory Governments 1815–1830.* Oxford: Oxford University Press.

———. 1979. "Peel: A Reappraisal." *Historical Journal* 22(3):585–614.

Hirschman, Albert O. 1977. *The Passions and the Interests.* Princeton, NJ: Princeton University Press.

Hoppit, Julian. 1996. "Patterns of Parliamentary Legislation, 1660–1800." *The Historical Journal* 39(1):109–31.

Howe, Anthony. 2002. "Restoring Free Trade: The British Experience, 1776–1873." In *The Political Economy of the British Historical Experience, 1688–1914,* eds. Donald Winch and Patrick O'Brien, 193–213. Oxford: Oxford University Press.

Humphries, Jane. 2003. "English Apprenticeships: A Neglected Factor in the First Industrial Revolution." In *The Economic Future in Historical Perspective*, eds. Paul A. David and Mark Thomas, 73–102. Oxford: Oxford University Press.

———. 2008. *Through the Mill: Child Labour and the British Industrial Revolution*. Cambridge: Cambridge University Press, forthcoming.

Jacob, Margaret C. 1991. *Living the Enlightenment: Freemasonry and Politics in Eighteenth-Century Europe*. New York: Oxford University Press.

———. 1997. *Scientific Culture and the Making of the Industrial West*. 2nd ed., New York: Oxford University Press.

Jacob, Margaret C., and Larry Stewart. 2004. *Practical Matter: Newton's Science in the Service of Industry and Empire, 1687–1851*. Cambridge, MA: Harvard University Press.

Jones, Eric L. 1988. *Growth Recurring: Economic Change in World History*. Oxford: Oxford University Press.

Khan, B. Z., and K. L. Sokoloff. 1998. "Patent Institutions, Industrial Organization, and Early Technological Change: Britain and the United States, 1790–1850." In *Technological Revolutions in Europe*, eds. Maxine Berg and Kristin Bruland, 292–313. Cheltenham, England: Edward Elgar.

Kindleberger, Charles P. 1978. *Economic Response: Comparative Studies in Trade, Finance, and Growth*. Cambridge, MA: Harvard University Press.

Klemm, Friedrich. 1964. *A History of Western Technology*. Cambridge, MA: MIT Press.

Laird, Pamela Walker. 2006. *Pull: Networking and Success since Benjamin Franklin*. Cambridge, MA: Harvard University Press.

Langbein, John H. 1983a. "Albion's Fatal Flaws." *Past and Present* (98, Feb.):96–120.

———. 1983b. "Shaping the Eighteenth-Century Criminal Trial: A View from the Ryder Sources." *University of Chicago Law Review* 50(1, Winter):1–136.

Langford, Paul. 1989. *A Polite and Commercial People: England 1727–1783*. Oxford and New York: Oxford University Press.

———. 1991. *Public Life and the Propertied Englishman, 1689–1798*. Oxford: The Clarendon Press.

———. 2000. *Englishness Identified: Manners and Character, 1650–1850*. Oxford: Oxford University Press.

Locke, John. [1693] 1732. *Some Thoughts Concerning Education*. 9th ed. London: Printed for A. Bettesworth.

MacLeod, Christine. 1988. *Inventing the Industrial Revolution: The English Patent System, 1660–1880*. Cambridge: Cambridge University Press.

MacLeod, Christine, and Alessandro Nuvolari. 2007. "Inventive Activities, Patents, and Early Industrialization: A Synthesis of Research Issues." Unpublished manuscript.

Maitland, F. W. 1911. *The Constitutional History of England.* Cambridge: Cambridge University Press. Unpublished manuscript.

Mantoux, Paul. [1928] 1961. *The Industrial Revolution in the Eighteenth Century.* Rev. ed. New York: Harper Torchbooks.

McCloskey, Deirdre N. 2006. *The Bourgeois Virtues: Ethics for an Age of Commerce.* Chicago: University of Chicago Press.

Melon, Jean François. 1738. *A Political Essay upon Commerce.* Translated, with some annotations, and remarks by David Bindon. Dublin: Printed for Philip Crampton.

Mérimée, Prosper. 1930. "Études Anglo-Americaines." In *Oevres Complétes*, vol. 8, eds. Pierre Trahard and Idouard Champion. Paris: Librairie Ancienne Honoré Champion.

Mnookin, Robert H., and Lewis Kornhauser. 1979. "Bargaining in the Shadow of the Law: The Case of Divorce." *Yale Law Journal* 88(5, April):950–97.

Mokyr, Joel. 1976. *Industrialization in the Low Countries, 1795–1850.* New Haven, London: Yale University Press.

———. 1998. "The Political Economy of Technological Change: Resistance and Innovation in Economic History." In *Technological Revolutions in Europe*, eds. Maxine Berg and Kristin Bruland, 39–64. Cheltenham: Edward Elgar Publishers.

———. 2000. "The Industrial Revolution and the Netherlands: Why Did It Not Happen?" *De Economist* (Amsterdam) 148(4, Oct.):503–20.

———. 2002. *The Gifts of Athena: Historical Origins of the Knowledge Economy.* Princeton, NJ: Princeton University Press.

———. 2005. "The Intellectual Origins of Modern Economic Growth." *Journal of Economic History* 65(2, June):285–351.

———. 2006a. "The Great Synergy: The European Enlightenment as a Factor in Modern Economic Growth." In *Understanding the Dynamics of a Knowledge Economy*, eds. Wilfred Dolfsma and Luc Soete, 7–41. Cheltenham: Edward Elgar.

———. 2006b. "Mercantilism, the Enlightenment, and the Industrial Revolution." Presented to the Conference in Honor of Eli F. Heckscher, Stockholm, May 2003. In *Eli F. Heckscher (1879–1952): A Celebratory Symposium*, eds. Ronald Findlay, Rolf Henriksson, Håkan Lindgren, and Mats Lundahl, 269–303. Cambridge, MA: MIT Press.

————. 2006c. "Mobility, Creativity, and Technological Development: David Hume, Immanuel Kant and the Economic Development of Europe." Prepared for the session on "Creativity and the Economy," German Association of Philosophy, Berlin. In *Kolloquiumsband of the XX. Deutschen Kongresses für Philosophie*, ed. G. Abel, 1131–61. Berlin 2006.

————. 2008a. *The Enlightened Economy*. New Haven, CT, and New York: Yale University Press and Penguin Press, forthcoming.

————. 2008b. "Entrepreneurship and the Industrial Revolution in Britain." In *Entrepreneurship in History*, eds. William Baumol, David S. Landes, and Joel Mokyr. Princeton, NJ: Princeton University Press.

————. 2008c. "The Market for Ideas and the Origins of Economic Growth in Eighteenth-Century Europe." [Heineken Lecture], *Tijdschrift voor Sociale en Economische Geschiedenis*, 4:3–38.

Mokyr, Joel, and John Nye. 2007. "Distributional Coalitions, the Industrial Revolution, and the Origins of Economic Growth in Britain." *Southern Economic Journal* 74(1):50–70.

Moser, Petra. 2007. "Why Don't Inventors Patent?" National Bureau of Economic Research working paper 13294.

Muldrew, Craig. 1998. *The Economy of Obligation*. New York: St. Martin's Press.

Musson, A. E., and Eric Robinson. 1969. *Science and Technology in the Industrial Revolution*. Manchester: Manchester University Press.

North, Douglass C. 1981. *Structure and Change in Economic History*. New York: Norton.

North, Douglass C., and Barry R. Weingast. 1989. "Constitutions and Commitment: The Evolution of Institutions Governing Public Choice in Seventeenth-Century England." *Journal of Economic History*, 49(4, Dec.):803–32.

Nougaret, Pierre J.-B. 1816. *Londres: La Cour et Les provinces d'Angleterre*. 2 vols. Paris: Chez Briand.

Nuvolari, Alessandro. 2004. "Collective Invention during the British Industrial Revolution: The Case of the Cornish Pumping Engine." *Cambridge Journal of Economics* 28(3):347–63.

Nye, John. 2007. *War, Wine, and Taxes: The Political Economy of Anglo-French Trade, 1689–1900*. Princeton, NJ: Princeton University Press.

O'Brien, Patrick K. 1988. "The Political Economy of British Taxation, 1660–1815." *Economic History Review* 41(1, Feb.):1–32.

————. 2002. "Fiscal Exceptionalism: Great Britain and Its European Rivals from Civil War to Triumph at Trafalgar and Waterloo." In *The Political Economy of British Historical Experience 1688–1914*, eds. D. Winch and P. O'Brien, 245–65. Oxford: Oxford University Press.

———. 2008. "Provincializing the Industrial Revolution." In *Reconceptualizing the Industrial Revolution*, ed. Jeff Horn. Cambridge, MA: MIT Press.

Olson, Mancur, 1982. *The Rise and Decline of Nations*. New Haven, CT: Yale University Press.

Ormrod, David. 2003. *The Rise of Commercial Empires.* Cambridge: Cambridge University Press.

Paley, Ruth. 2004. "Colquhoun, Patrick (1745–1820)." In *Oxford Dictionary of National Biography*, eds. H. C. G. Matthew and Brian Harrison. Oxford: Oxford University Press.

Pearson, Robin. 1991. "Collective Diversification: Manchester Cotton Merchants and the Insurance Business in the Early Nineteenth Century." *Business History Review* 65(2, Summer):379–414.

Pearson, Robin, and David Richardson. 2001. "Business Networking in the Industrial Revolution." *Economic History Review* 54(4):657–79.

Pocock, J. G. A. 1985. *Virtue, Commerce, and History*. Cambridge: Cambridge University Press.

Pomeranz, Kenneth. 2000. *The Great Divergence: China, Europe, and the Making of the Modern World Economy*. Princeton, NJ: Princeton University Press.

Porter, Roy. 1990. *English Society in the Eighteenth Century.* 2nd ed. London: Penguin Books.

Porter, Roy, and Teich Milulás, eds. 1981. *The Enlightenment in National Context*. Cambridge: Cambridge University Press.

Posner, Eric A. 2000. *Law and Social Norms*. Cambridge, MA: Harvard University Press.

Quinn, Stephen. 2001. "The Glorious Revolution's Effect on English Private Finance: A Microhistory, 1680–1705." *The Journal of Economic History* 61(3, Sep.):593–615.

Randall, Adrian. 1991. *Before the Luddites.* Cambridge: Cambridge University Press.

Robinson, Eric. 1972. "James Watt and the Law of Patents." *Technology and Culture* 13(2):115–39.

Rodrik, Dani, Arvind Subramanian, and Francesco Trebbi. 2004. "Institutions Rule: The Primacy of Institutions over Geography and Integration in Economic Development." *Journal of Economic Growth* 9(2):131–65.

Roll, Eric. 1930. *An Early Experiment in Industrial Organization.* London: Cass.

Rothschild, Emma. 2001. *Economic Sentiments: Adam Smith, Condorcet, and the Enlightenment.* Cambridge, MA: Harvard University Press.

Rubinstein, William D. 1981. *Men of Property: The Very Wealthy in Britain since the Industrial Revolution.* London: Croom Helm.

———. 1983. "The End of 'Old Corruption' in Britain 1780–1860." *Past and Present* (101, Nov.):55–86.

Rushton, Peter. 1991. "The Matter in Variance: Adolescents and Domestic Conflict in the Preindustrial Economy of Northeast England, 1600–1800." *Journal of Social History* 25(1, Autumn):89–107.

Saussure, César de. 1902. *A Foreign View of England in the Reigns of George I. & George II. The Letters of Monsieur César de Saussure to His Family*, tr. and ed. by Madame Van Muyden. London: J. Murray.

Say, Jean-Baptiste. [1803] 1821. *A Treatise on Political Economy*. 4th ed. Boston: Wells and Lilly.

Scott, H. M., ed. 1990. *Enlightened Absolutism: Reform and Reformers in Later Eighteenth-Century Europe*. Houndsmill, Basingstoke: Palgrave MacMillan.

Smiles, Samuel. 1859. *Self Help*. http://www.emotionalliteracyeducation.com/classic_books_online/selfh10.htm.

Smith, Adam. [1757] 1978. *Lectures on Jurisprudence*. Oxford: Clarendon Press.

Solar, Peter. 1995. "Poor Relief and English Economic Development before the Industrial Revolution." *Economic History Review* 48:1–22.

Spagnolo, Giancarlo. 1999. "Social Relations and Cooperations in Organizations." *Journal of Economic Behavior and Organizations* 38(1):1–25.

Stasavage, David. 2003. *Public Debt and the Birth of the Democratic State: France and Great Britain, 1688–1789*. Cambridge: Cambridge University Press.

———. 2007. "Partisan Politics and Public Debt: The Importance of the Whig Supremacy for Britain's Financial Revolution." *European Review of Economic History* 11(1):123–53.

Stevenson, John. 1979. *Popular Disturbances in England, 1700–1870*. London: Longman.

Stone, Lawrence. 1985. "The History of Violence in England: Some Observations." *Past and Present* (108, August):216–24.

Stout, William. 1967. *The Autobiography of William Stout of Lancaster, 1665–1752*. Ed. J. D. Marshall. Manchester: Manchester University Press.

Sussman, Nathan, and Yishay Yafeh. 2006. "Institutional Reforms, Financial Development and Sovereign Debt: Britain 1690–1790" *Journal of Economic History* 66(4):906–35.

Taine, Hippolyte. [1872] 1958. *Notes on England*. Translated with an introduction by Edward Hyams. Fair Lawn, NJ: Essential Books.

Thompson, E. P. 1963. *The Making of the English Working Class*. New York: Vintage Books.

Tucker, Josiah. 1758. *Instructions for Travellers*. Dublin: Printed for William Watson at the Poets Head in Carpel-Street.

Van Zanden, Jan Luiten. 1993. *The Rise and Decline of Holland's Economy*. Manchester: Manchester University Press.

Van Zanden, Jan Luiten, and Arthur Van Riel. 2004. *The Strictures of Inheritance: The Dutch Economy in the Nineteenth Century*. Princeton, NJ: Princeton University Press.

Wallis, Patrick. 2008. "Apprenticeship and Training in Premodern England." *Journal of Economic History* 68(3).

Wilberforce, Robert Isaac, and Samuel Wilberforce. 1838. *The Life of William Wilberforce, by His Sons, Robert Isaac Wilberforce and Samuel Wilberforce*. London: John Murray.

Wrigley, E. A. 1987. *People, Cities, and Wealth*. Oxford: Basil Blackwell.

———. 1988. *Continuity, Chance and Change: The Character of the Industrial Revolution in England*. New York: Cambridge University Press.

Institutions and the Resource Curse in Early Modern Spain

MAURICIO DRELICHMAN AND HANS-JOACHIM VOTH

> Our Spain has set her eyes so strongly on the business of the Indies, from where she obtains gold and silver, that she has forsaken the care of her own kingdoms; and if she could indeed command all the gold and silver that her nationals keep discovering in the New World, this would not render her as rich and powerful as she would have otherwise been.
>
> MARTÍN GONZÁLEZ DE CELLORIGO, 1600

3.1 Introduction

Reflecting upon the economic, social, and institutional decay that afflicted Castile at the turn of the seventeenth century, the pamphleteer González de Cellorigo pointed his finger at what he saw as the main culprit in his country's woes. By placing the blame for the incipient "Castilian crisis of the seventeenth century" (Thompson and Yun Casalilla 1994) on the fabulous amounts of precious metals that Spaniards extracted from their American colonies, Cellorigo became one of the first proponents of the idea known in modern economics as the "resource curse." In his view, the very gold and silver that had allowed Spain to build the most powerful empire of its time were slowly eroding its institutional foundations and economic prowess.

In the sixteenth century, Castile rose from peripheral state to the first rank of global powers. By the mid-seventeenth century it was experiencing rapid decline; since then, despite short-lived episodes of recovery, Spain remained an economic underperformer until late in the twentieth century.[1] We draw from the recent literature on the interaction between institutions and resource abundance to argue that Cellorigo's argument was largely correct: Castile suffered, essentially, from becoming too rich too fast. Before

120

the silver windfall, Castilian institutions had evolved in the direction of limiting government. Rent seeking was successfully contained through repeated bargaining between the Crown and the centers of economic activity, to the detriment of the traditional nobility and the clerical establishment. The ascendancy of the merchant classes could have well placed Castile on a path reminiscent of the English one, with a grand constitutional bargain in the end (North and Weingast 1989). Instead, Castilian institutions proved inadequate in limiting the king's powers and in preventing the negative economic outcomes and political mismanagement often associated with concentrated resource rents. There is growing evidence that the resource windfall had a negative effect on Spanish industry (Drelichman 2005b); here we argue that the silver boom also gave rise to institutions that allowed the Crown to set policy, unchecked by other stakeholders in the political game. Those institutions persisted long after the resource rents dwindled, hindering Castilian economic growth for a long time.

American silver strongly influenced much of Castilian, and indeed European, economic life in the second half of the sixteenth century. Philip II, on whose domains the sun never set, used the large inflows of American silver to run up unprecedented amounts of debt. The funds thus obtained were spent on building monumental monasteries and pursuing a string of wars all over Europe. In the New World, adventurous explorers risked (and often lost) their lives in the quest for ever richer mines. Dutch merchants and Genoese bankers, whose business depended on the liquidity created by silver, regularly bribed ship captains to learn the true amount—legal and otherwise—being imported (Morineau 1985). Long-distance traders made fortunes by shipping silver to China, where its relative price was much higher than in Europe, returning with luxury goods. The Spanish "piece of eight"—a coin modeled after the German *thaler* and eventually known as the "dollar"—became the international currency of the age.[2] Yet, given all the wealth flowing through its borders, Castile did not become as rich as one might have expected. When the decline in dynamism occurred—whether already in the late sixteenth century, or only in the later decades of the seventeenth—is now subject to debate (Alvarez Nogal and Prados de la Escosura 2007). But compared with the dynamism that characterized Spain until the 1530s, the loss of momentum was staggering. After expanding for most of the sixteenth century, the population shrank markedly at the beginning of the seventeenth (Nadal i Oller 1984); traditional export markets were lost to competitors; the Crown defaulted time and again on its debts;

and despite lavish military expenditure, most campaigns ended in fruitless victories or outright disasters. Internal fragmentation reversed many of the state-building efforts of the early sixteenth century. By 1700 the Spanish Crown and its European territories had become a prize to be contested by foreign powers in the War of the Spanish Succession.

We proceed as follows: Section 3.2 reviews the literature on the resource curse and its interaction with the institutional environment. Section 3.3 discusses the initial conditions of the Castilian economy at the beginning of the sixteenth century and the transformations it underwent prior to the silver boom. Section 3.4 describes the nature of the silver windfall, placing it in perspective relative to the economic environment of early modern Europe and comparing it to those experienced by modern-day resource-rich economies. Section 3.5 explores the different effects of the silver boom on Castilian economic development with particular emphasis on the interaction between institutions and resource revenues.

3.2   Institutions and the Resource Curse

Tracing its roots back to the dependency theory of Prebisch (1950) and Singer (1950), the "resource curse" is a loose term used to describe a variety of undesirable economic outcomes associated with natural resource abundance. The association between resource abundance and poor economic performance is extensively documented in several empirical studies (e.g., Sachs and Warner 1995; Auty 2001). The resource curse literature first emphasized the deterioration in the terms of trade and the reduction in size and scope of the manufacturing sector that normally follows a discovery or increase in the price of a natural resource (Corden and Neary 1982). This phenomenon, known as the Dutch Disease, was indeed present in Castile and Aragon between 1550 and 1580 as a result of the silver boom (Drelichman 2005b). Yet this rise in the terms of trade is an optimal response: a country that becomes richer will increase its consumption; in the face of a relatively inelastic supply of domestic factors of production, this can only be accomplished through increased imports of traded goods and a corresponding deterioration in the terms of trade. This situation is reversed if the resource abundance disappears; the Dutch Disease hence cannot account for long-term economic decline. To explain it, the literature has departed from the standard neoclassical setup in a number of ways. Rodríguez and Sachs (1999) have explored the consequences of limited access to capital markets, showing how resource-abundant countries that cannot invest abroad will experience a temporary boom in consumption and then grow at slower rates. A second approach concentrates on channels excluded from the agents' utility function when solving the decentralized optimization problem. In this vein, Wijnbergen (1984) and Krugman (1987) introduced learning-by-doing in the traded-goods sector, which erodes the comparative advantage of an economy that experiences a resource boom, and Asea and Lahiri (1999) emphasized the detrimental effects of sectoral reallocation on human capital accumulation decisions. A third strand in the literature considers the externalities that arise because of misaligned objectives between agents and governments. Among its exponents, Baland and Francois (2000) and Torvik (2002) focused on the increased incentives for rent seeking generated by resource abundance, while Tornell and Lane (1999) explored the distortions those incentives introduce in government policies. These contributions emphasize low-growth traps into which countries fall because of their reliance on natural resources; Drelichman (2005a) examines how American silver created such a problem in early modern Spain.

A more recent literature has sought to provide a comprehensive framework to explain why resources spell a curse for some countries but not for others. Mehlum, Moene, and Torvik (2006) introduce institutional quality as the central factor in determining whether a rent-seeking equilibrium, and hence a low-growth scenario, will arise or not. Robinson, Torvik, and Verdier (2006) explicitly model the incentives of politicians, as shaped by institutions, as a conduit for the resource curse.

Figure 3.1 shows the relationship between primary exports as a percentage of GNP and average GDP per capita growth rate between 1965 and 1990 using a sample of 87 countries from Sachs and Warner (1997).[3] The correlation remains negative and statistically significant after controlling for a standard vector of covariates. While the inverse correlation between resource abundance and economic growth is strong, several resource-rich countries, such as Norway, Canada, and Malaysia, have nonetheless managed to escape the resource curse. Melhum, Moene, and Torvik (2006) show that the initial institutional environment is a key determinant of the response of a country's economic performance to a resource boom.

Figure 3.2 reproduces Melhum, Moene, and Tarvik's decomposition of Sachs and Warner's data into countries with low and high institutional quality. Countries are divided according to the institutional quality score

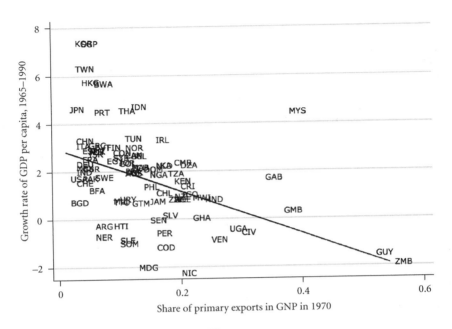

Figure 3.1 The resource curse.

from Knack and Keefer (1995). Countries with a score of .68 and above are considered to have institutions of high quality.

Figure 3.2 illustrates how the resource curse result is driven by countries with low institutional quality. The correlation, which remains strong in the top panel, all but disappears among countries with institutions that limit the ability of governments to extract economic rents or expropriate businesses and individuals. In Section 3.3 we document how a series of constitutional-level events in the early sixteenth century lowered the overall quality of Castilian institutions, paving the way for negative economic growth outcomes in the wake of the silver discoveries.

The literature has so far sidestepped the question of whether there might be a feedback mechanism from resources to institutions. Sachs and Warner (1995, 19–20) failed to find an effect of resource abundance on an index of bureaucratic efficiency, which they used as their measure of institutional quality. This result has been accepted even by subsequent works that challenged many of the remaining claims of Sachs and Warner (e.g., Mehlum, Moene, and Torvik 2006, 3). While we do not aim to close this gap in the

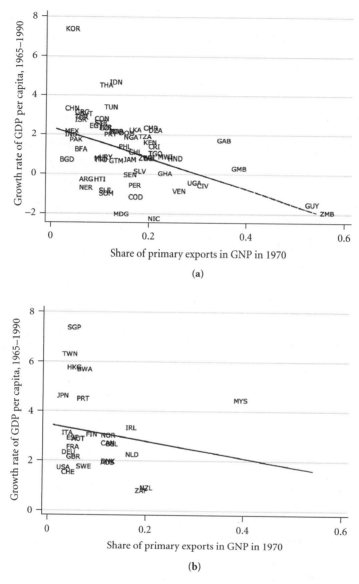

Figure 3.2 Resources and GDP growth by country institutional quality: (a) countries with low institutional quality; (b) countries with high institutional quality.

literature, we point to an important counterexample by showing that constraints on the monarch's power failed to increase as a direct result of its resource windfall.

3.3   Castile's Endowments and Institutions in the Early Sixteenth Century

At the end of the fifteenth century, Castile was positioned to become a dominant power in western Europe. It had emerged from the seven-centuries-long Reconquista wars as the lone victor, absorbing Arab territories and competing Christian crowns alike, and establishing its undisputed hegemony over the Iberian Peninsula. Although Spain did not formally become a unified polity until the eighteenth century, the two major crowns of Castile and Aragon were effectively merged under Ferdinand and Isabella in 1474, and the remaining territories of present-day Spain followed shortly thereafter. From the sixteenth century onward, the unified crowns were usually considered a single polity and referred to as "The Spains" or "The Hispanic Monarchy." While Aragon did maintain some degree of fiscal independence, it never came close to overshadowing Castilian hegemony. The sheer size of its territory, population, and resources assured Castile a comfortable position as the center of Iberian power.

3.3.1 Geography

Castile's geography was always decried as one of the major factors hindering its economic development. Large areas of Spain are rocky, mountainous, or outright barren; the country's average altitude is 600 meters above sea level, and 45% of the territory is unfit for agriculture still today. Large mountain chains crisscross the peninsula, making overland transport difficult, slow, and expensive. Of all the places at risk of experiencing resource-led growth, Castile certainly ranked at the bottom of the list.

Yet that same geography had its advantages. The rugged terrain protected Castile's borders. In the entire second millennium, very few foreign armies managed to gain a foothold on Spanish soil. Only Napoleon's attempt in 1809 culminated in a relatively successful invasion, and even then, a short-lived one. On the climatic front, the combination of mild winters in the south and cool summers in the highlands was ideal for the breeding of merino sheep; Castile thus had a formidable comparative advantage in fine wool, one of the premium traded commodities of the late Middle Ages and early modern period.[4] By supplying the Dutch upscale textile-manufacturing sector, Castilian wool fueled one of Europe's largest cross-border trades; the commercial networks it created quite possibly contributed to the continuing prosperity of the Cantabric coast and the Basque country long after Spain's golden age was past (Grafe 2001).

Perhaps Castile's most significant geographical feature in terms of its potential for economic growth in early modern times was its extensive Atlantic coastline. Access to the Atlantic has been identified as one of the major forces behind trade-friendly institutional reform in western Europe; it appears to correlate with subsequent economic performance (Acemoglu, Johnson, and Robinson 2005b). While once-thriving Aragon languished as the Mediterranean trading economy lost steam, Castile was superbly positioned to take advantage of the Atlantic's dynamism.

3.3.2 Initial Institutions

The combined strength of Castile and Aragon under the Catholic Kings (r. 1474–1516) effectively put an end to internecine warfare and, with the conquest of Granada in 1492, unified the territory of modern Spain under a single central monarchy. The joint monarchy benefited from the advantages the military revolution conferred on centralized states, as the increased scale of warfare favored larger political units endowed with widespread taxing and spending ability.[5] Relying on the strength of their cannons and the effectiveness of their infantry, Ferdinand and Isabella quickly moved to dismantle the remnants of medieval political organization, concentrating power in their hands and sketching the major traits of a modern nation state.

Having put an end to internecine wars, the Crown proceeded to transform itself into a strong executive through three clearly defined sets of reforms: it created a career bureaucracy, which reserved the key decision-making posts for competent and trusted advisors rather than for members of the noble families; it strengthened the royal judiciary, putting an end to a myriad of overlapping of jurisdictions; and it reeled in the nobility and the church, largely neutering their influence in government affairs.

Starting in the late fifteenth century, the Crown established collegiate advisory bodies (the councils), staffed them with a mix of professional bureaucrats and power brokers, and charged them with overseeing specific areas of public administration. The number of councils grew steadily during the first half of the sixteenth century; by the time Philip II ascended to the throne in 1556, they had become a veritable ministerial array with competencies in every area of government (Artola 1988).[6] All major decisions eventually rested with the Royal Council, presided over by the king himself. The council system ensured that a number of key positions would be filled with persons who had accumulated some expertise in their specific area of public administration while limiting the access to government formerly enjoyed by the hereditary nobility.

The Catholic Kings also recast the medieval chancery into the system of royal chancery courts with appellate jurisdiction over all judicial matters. This established the supremacy of the royal judiciary over a myriad of competing local, regional, ecclesiastical, and special jurisdictions (Kagan 1981). Royal chancery judges could be appointed and removed at will by the monarch; since most viewed their position as an intermediate step in the quest for a seat on a council, their actions tended to closely reflect the will of the Crown (Martín Postigo and Domínguez Rodríguez 1990). To further assure the Crown's desired outcome in any litigious proceedings, the Royal Council remained the ultimate judiciary authority in the kingdom.

The Crown completed the consolidation of its power by asserting its supremacy over the nobility and the clergy, relegating them to positions far from the spheres of power whenever possible and ensuring they responded to royal wishes when not. In one of the brilliant strokes that would make him the model for Machiavelli's *Il Principe*, Ferdinand obtained from Pope Innocent VIII the right to nominate the bishops and control all church activities in future conquered lands, including the southern kingdom of Granada and the still-undiscovered New World. The right, known as *patronato*, extended in practice to all of Spain, with the pope regularly confirming the Crown's nominees to the lucrative ecclesiastical offices. In exchange for assisting the papacy with its military and diplomatic needs in Europe, the king had become the political head of the Spanish church. The importance of this achievement cannot possibly be understated: under the Catholic Kings the Spanish church controlled perhaps three times as much revenue as the Crown (Elliott [1963] 1990, 99–110). While in subsequent decades the state expanded by leaps and bounds, the Habsburg kings continued to rely on the rights acquired by Ferdinand to regularly tap ecclesiastical revenues in the pursuit of their fiscal, political, and military goals.

The Catholic Kings also conducted a purge of the noble ranks by revising most of the privileges granted by their predecessor and replacing noble Crown officials with advisors appointed on the basis of merit—including a few Jewish ones. Although the wealthy noble households did retain varying degrees of influence well into the Habsburg period, their participation in government was always under the close oversight of the Crown. The early modern Castilian monarchy was thus remarkably free from the palace intrigues and conspiracies that had plagued its medieval predecessors, and only during the disintegration of the Habsburg regime in the late seventeenth century did noble infighting again play a significant role in government. The middle and lower nobility stopped being a relevant force altogether in the first quarter of the sixteenth century, with their higher-ranking members at best exerting some political influence at the local level (Domínguez Ortiz 1985; Drelichman 2007).

With the traditional power brokers under royal control, the one remaining check on the monarchy were the Cortes, a quasi-parliamentary body dating from the late medieval period. The original conception of the Cortes was that of the voice of the "kingdom" in front of the king. While prior to the sixteenth century they sometimes included the participation of the nobility and the clergy as separate "estates," by the Habsburg period only the representatives of the 18 principal cities of Castile retained full voting rights (Thompson 1976, 147). The Cortes were thus well positioned to become an instrument of the urban merchant elites, the elements defending property rights and limiting absolutist power in Britain and the Netherlands (Weber 1968; Acemoglu, Johnson, and Robinson 2005a).

Besides voicing the concerns of the Kingdom and swearing in monarchs and heirs to the throne, the original role of the Cortes was to grant their assent to new taxes or to the renewal of extraordinary ones. In their medieval origin, this meant approving increases in the direct taxes paid by the cities (*servicios*) and, later on, voting the sales taxes known as *alcabalas;* taken together, these levies accounted for the majority of Crown income in the late medieval period.

The centralizing drive of the late fifteenth century reduced the influence of the Cortes by bringing additional revenue under the exclusive control of the monarchy. Ecclesiastical levies, royal monopolies, and the sale of royal jurisdictions were the most common devices employed by the Crown to bolster its finances without having to seek parliamentary consent; forced loans were also used on occasion. These so-called arbitrary measures (*arbitrios*) could go only so far in filling the royal coffers, and an ambitious foreign policy required vastly greater resources. Given the strength of the Cortes, it would have been natural for the Habsburgs to strike a quid-pro-quo bargain that would have seen rising tax revenues exchanged for greater institutional constraints on the Crown. This bargain was never struck. In the following sections we explore the dynamics of this process and the role American treasure played in it.

3.4   The Resource Boom

As the age of exploration started in earnest, Castile quickly traded its golden fleece for a silver spoon. The initial contacts with Mesoamerican cultures convinced Spaniards that the American continent held large deposits of precious metals. While the Crown moved to create a colonial trading monopoly centered on the city of Seville, it also adopted a laissez-faire approach to exploration and exploitation of the New World. Private entrepreneurs could set up their own extractive operations as long as they traded exclusively through Seville and paid a flat 20% tax on their production—the "royal fifth." This created powerful incentives that fueled half a century of epic explorations and tragic warfare. While gold proved to be disappointingly scarce, by the mid-sixteenth century, industrial-scale exploitation of the largest silver reserves in the world at Potosí, in present-day Bolivia, was under way. A chemical smelting method suited to their particular ore was quickly developed, and a system of treasure fleets was devised to carry the metal across the Atlantic. The size of the convoys swelled to over one hundred ships at their peak, becoming the largest long-distance trading operation of the time. It turned out to be remarkably well protected against both pirates and natural disasters. Its success guaranteed the effectiveness of Seville's trading monopoly.

Figure 3.3, based on the classic reconstruction of treasure imports by Earl Hamilton (Hamilton 1934), shows the Crown's portion of the bullion reaching Spain in constant terms, between 1500 and 1650, by five-year periods.[7]

Hamilton obtained his figures from the records of the *Casa de la Contratación*, the body charged with overseeing all trade with the Indies. His figures were often criticized for relying on official statistics, and hence not taking smuggling into account (e.g., Morineau 1985). Since we are inter-

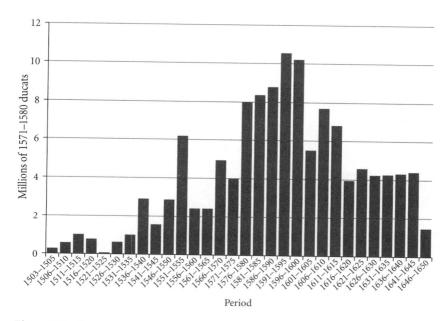

Figure 3.3 Crown treasure, 1500–1650, at five-year intervals. *Source:* Hamilton (1934), Drelichman (2005b).

ested only in the Crown's share of treasure, his methodology turns out to be ideal for our purposes.

To put the magnitude of the silver revenues in perspective, cost estimates of the entire "enterprise of England," which ended with the disaster of the Invincible Armada, are pegged at around 10 million ducats (Parker 1998, 269); yearly Crown revenues at the end of the sixteenth century were also in the neighborhood of 10 million ducats. According to Hoyle (1995), Henry VIII's sales of confiscated church lands yielded £375,000 over six years. Even using the conversion rates that prevailed prior to the Henrician debasements, this sum cannot have exceeded 4 million ducats, an amount dwarfed by the Habsburgs' quinquennial silver revenues.

Silver quickly became a very substantial component of the Crown's income. Figure 3.4 shows that the share of revenue accounted for by colonial sources (composed almost exclusively of silver taxes and mining) hovered in the neighborhood of 15% in the third quarter of the sixteenth century. It later climbed to between 20% and 25%, even as total Crown revenue more than trebled during the same period.

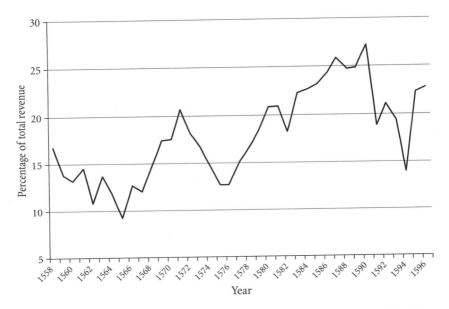

Figure 3.4 Revenue from colonies in America (Indies) as a percentage of total Crown revenue (four-year moving average). *Source:* Ulloa (1977), Drelichman and Voth (2007).

Table 3.1 offers some further perspective on the magnitude of the revenues the Spanish Crown derived from silver mining by presenting an asynchronous comparison with modern resource-rich economies. The left panel ranks hydrocarbon-rich economies by hydrocarbon-derived revenues as a percentage of total government revenues; the right panel does the same for mining-rich economies. All magnitudes for modern economies are 2000–2003 averages; those for Castile are measured at the 1587–1589 peak.

At the apogee of the silver boom, Castile derived 29% of its total fiscal revenue from the taxation of colonial silver imports. When compared to modern mining-rich economies this would place her only second to Botswana and its diamond revenue, and well above other mining giants. Although no early modern economy could possibly approach the scope of a modern petro-state, the size of the silver windfall would also have been large enough to propel Castile above the 20% threshold used by the IMF to classify an economy as hydrocarbon-rich. In that category, the share of

Table 3.1 Government revenues from hydrocarbon and mineral sources in selected resource-rich countries, as a percentage of total fiscal revenue

Hydrocarbon-rich countries	Hydrocarbon revenue as % of total fiscal revenue (2000–2003 average)	Mineral-rich countries	Mineral resources	Mineral revenue as % of total fiscal revenue (2000–2003 average)
Colombia	9.0	Sierra Leone	Diamonds	0.5
Kazakhstan	21.0		bauxite,	
Norway	24.4		rutile	
Ecuador	26.4	Jordan	Phosphates,	1.6
Cameroon	26.6		potash	
Trinidad and Tobago	27.4	Chile	Copper	3.9
Castile 1587–89	**29.0**	Kyrgyz Republic	Gold	4.1
Indonesia	31.3	Mongolia	Copper, gold	6.1
Vietnam	31.8	Namibia	Diamonds	10.0
Mexico	32.2	Mauritania	Iron ore	10.6
Russia	39.7	Papua New Guinea	Gold	16.1
Venezuela	52.7	Guinea	Bauxite/	18.3
Iraq	58.4		alumina	
Iran	59.3	**Castile 1587–89**	**Silver**	**29.0**
Bahrain	71.2	Botswana	Diamonds	56.2
Qatar	71.3			
Libya	72.5			
United Arab Emirates	76.1			
Nigeria	77.2			
Saudi Arabia	81.6			
Equatorial Guinea	84.0			
Brunei Darussalam	85.8			

Source: International Monetary Fund (2005)

natural resources in Castilian revenues would exceed those of Norway and Kazakhstan, and fall slightly short of those of Indonesia and Mexico, with Russia not much further away.

The silver windfall had an enormous impact on the economy of Castile, Europe, and indeed the whole world. The silver price differentials between Europe and the Far East fueled a vibrant long-distance trade, bringing large quantities of oriental luxury goods to Europe and prompting some scholars to identify in it the "birth of globalization" (Flynn and Giráldez 2004). The bullion that was retained in Europe roughly doubled the monetary stock in the course of a century; the ensuing "price revolution," a sustained increase in the price level of virtually all European economies, had wide-ranging effects on fiscal systems, trading arrangements, and monetary institutions (Hamilton 1934; Flynn 1978; Fisher 1989). The strongest effects of the resource windfall were naturally felt in Castile itself. Silver was perhaps the most perfectly tradable commodity of the time. The large increase in its supply, coupled with the new sources of demand from the Far East and the expectation of future mineral discoveries prompted factors of production to be diverted from export industries, such as fine wool and manufactures, and into the extraction and service industries associated with the silver trade. This classic case of Dutch Disease afflicted Castile for much of the second half of the sixteenth century (Forsyth and Nicholas 1983; Drelichman 2005b); in the following section we argue that the resource boom had costs in terms of economic and political development that went far beyond allocative and balance-of-payments effects.[8]

3.5   The Interaction between Resources and Institutions: A Political Resource Curse

Starting in the early years of the exploration of Spanish America and at least until the end of the sixteenth century, precious metals were indissolubly tied to the financing of the monarchy. As early as 1519, in an episode emblematic of what was to follow, Charles V used the first gold plundered from the Aztec empire to pay for the expenses of the fleet that carried him to claim the imperial crown. Although the Cortes had voted to authorize the voyage, the cities disavowed their representatives amidst allegations of vote buying and heavy-handedness by the king. The ensuing revolt, known as the *comunidades*, was led by the wealthy urban elites and petty nobles in an ultimately doomed attempt to stall the centralizing drive of the monarchy.

Although the revolt prevented the collection of the special levy to fund the voyage, the king nonetheless forged ahead using the Mexican loot (Parker 1999, 135). As the mines of Potosí and Zacatecas entered production in the late 1540s, American silver became the cornerstone of a financial system that allowed the Spanish Crown to project its power across the known world without the need to bargain with its subjects for additional resources.

3.5.1 Silver and Crown Financing

Under Charles V, the Crown's main financial instruments were short-term loans, called *asientos*, contracted mainly with the Fugger and Welser banking families. Charles first used a Fugger loan to bribe the grand electors that elevated him to the throne of the Holy Roman Empire over the aspirations of Francis I of France.[9] Subsequent *asientos* were contracted all over Europe, and used to pay for the armies and fleets that attempted, with mixed success, to establish the Habsburg Empire as the hegemonic power of the time.

Charles' *asientos* were uncollateralized; his credit rested exclusively on his reputation and on his repayment capacity.[10] The Golden Bull, the constitutional document of the Holy Roman Empire, severely limited his ability to use imperial revenues, and altogether prevented him from spending them outside the empire's borders.[11] Charles was not bound by any such constraints with regards to Castilian silver, which he leveraged to finance his geopolitical designs. Figure 3.5 shows how short-term borrowing and treasure imports grew in almost complete lockstep during his reign.

A similar pattern arose during the reign of Philip II, who succeeded Charles in 1556. Philip's accession to the throne was soon followed by the first suspension of payments on short-term debt, a result of the enormous expenses incurred by the emperor in the Franco-Habsburg wars. Although the default interrupted lending for almost a decade, the rapid increase in the growth rate of American remittances around the same time allowed Philip to regain access to capital markets and engineer a new system of government finance that relied as little as possible on the consent of the Cortes. In the new scheme, devised by several Genoese banking families, short-term loans were collateralized by perpetual bonds, known as *juros*. The bankers typically had the right to sell the bonds among the Castilian rentier classes, thus effectively acting as the financial intermediaries of the Crown. Service

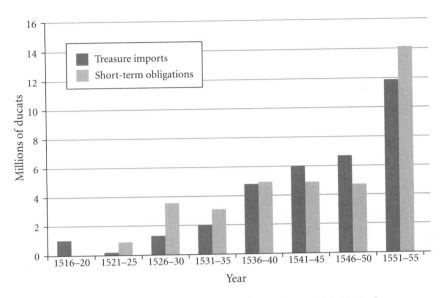

Figure 3.5 Treasure imports and short-term borrowing, 1516–1555. *Source:* Drelichman (2005a).

of *juros* was guaranteed by existing tax revenues, while the revolving payments on short term *asientos* were met out of silver revenues.[12] The system allowed the Crown to pursue ever more expensive projects: the War of the Holy League, the construction of the Escorial monastery, the Dutch War of Independence, and the Invincible Armada were all financed during periods of heavy borrowing through *asientos*.

Figure 3.6 plots the yearly interest payment on *juros*, known as the *situado*, and the annualized amount of silver revenue received by the Crown. The correlation between the two series leaves no doubt as to the role of American treasure in anchoring the financial system of the monarchy.

Silver revenue allowed Philip to contract unprecedented amounts of debt. Artola's (1982) data for 1598 show that the value of outstanding *juros* was seven times annual Crown revenue. In comparison, the debt incurred by Henry VIII's in the wake of the Dissolution of the Monasteries was only twice his annual revenues, a ratio from which England did not significantly depart until the Glorious Revolution (Hoyle 1995). In absolute terms, the magnitude of Henrician debt was somewhere in the order of one sixth of what Charles V managed to borrow, and a mere one sixteenth of

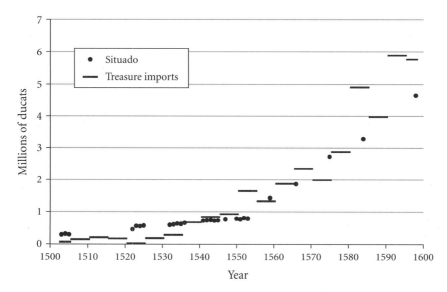

Figure 3.6 Treasure imports and long-term debt, 1500–1600. *Source:* Drelichman (2005a).

what Philip II eventually owed. Since Castile had roughly one-and-a-half times the population of England, the gap is very large even in per capita terms. If we accept Yun's estimate putting Castilian fiscal pressure at 9% of GDP by 1600 (Yun Casalilla 2002, 79–80), the long-term debt of turn-of-the-century Castile would have exceeded 60% of GDP. Measurement error and the relative usefulness of the concept of GDP in the early modern period preclude the use of these figures in comparisons with present-day economies. The fact remains that this was a magnitude no contemporary ruler could remotely approach, and that not even England and its investor-friendly institutional reforms could match until the end of the eighteenth century.

3.5.2 *The Crown and the Cortes*

Silver remittances could not cover all the expenses of the Crown; in fact, even at the peak of extraction, they never exceeded one-third of total Crown revenue. What silver did, however, was to allow the Crown to spend freely using borrowed funds and present the Cortes with the bill after the fact.

In the second half of the sixteenth century, the Crown resorted twice to the same "hard-ball" bargaining. The large costs of warfare under the Habsburg kings were financed with German or Genoese credit. Those loans were collateralized with *juros*, the service of which was guaranteed by Castilian tax streams. None of these maneuvers required the approval of the Cortes. Once the outstanding debt outstripped the servicing capacity afforded by the existing tax base and the flow of silver, the Crown declared a suspension of payments and urged the Cortes to approve an increase in indirect taxation. Long delays or outright refusals to approve the requested tax increases would have resulted in a rapid deterioration of the military situation abroad, a political cost the Cortes were seldom prepared to shoulder. Also, debt holders in the cities—many of them of elevated social status—were affected by the default, and probably saw a tax rise as a much smaller evil than a continued moratorium.

The first such episode was triggered by the suspension of payments of 1575.[13] The proximate cause of the spiraling debt was the flare up of the Dutch Revolt, as the heavy-handed tactics of the Duke of Alba resulted in both an increase in military costs and a loss of tax revenue to the rebels. Philip convened the Cortes and requested a threefold increase in the value of the *alcabalas*, a sales tax that was normally farmed out to city governments in exchange for fixed annual payments.[14] While the negotiations dragged on, several regiments of the Army of Flanders, not having been paid for over a year, decided to sack the loyal city of Antwerp in an episode known as the Spanish Fury. The sack of Antwerp cost the Spaniards the support of the Flemish population in their war against the Dutch, and caused the revolt to spread. In its wake, the Cortes yielded to most of the king's requests, granting a doubling of the *alcabalas*, with an additional extraordinary levy to be disbursed in the first two years. Although they had tried their best to forestall the king's demands, in the end the Cortes walked away with few concessions and no additional control over the Crown's expenditures.

One might ask whether silver was instrumental in this outcome. The Cortes were ultimately forced to grant a tax increase, and the Crown managed to collect it, pointing to some slack in Castile's fiscal capacity before 1577. Couldn't Philip II have borrowed against these future tax revenues, used the proceeds to lead Castile into the same expensive campaigns, and confronted the Cortes for money down the road? We argue that the nature of the early modern sovereign debt markets ruled out such a scenario.

Sixteenth-century monarchs who wanted to venture into the international credit markets had two options. The first one was to hand over control over the revenue sources that guaranteed repayment, in the style of a tax farm. This usually happened in the framework of a multiyear arrangement and secured the lowest interest rates. Castilian *juros* were usually issued under such arrangements. The alternative was uncollateralized borrowing, which commanded much higher interest rates and hence was generally used for short-term loans. Monarchs who tried this route found that bankers held them to a fairly stringent credit ceiling—Henry VIII never managed to borrow more than twice his annual revenues in this fashion, nor did Charles V before silver started pouring in.[15] American bullion backed the promises of Castilian kings with a large and reliable source of revenue. By increasing the resources that accrued directly to the Crown, it decreased the perceived risk of lending to it on an uncollateralized basis. Genoese bankers would not have lent to Philip II on the chance that he might later convince the Cortes to pay up; they took a calculated gamble in lending to him because the steady silver flows meant that the Crown would be liquid enough to repay a good part of the loans. These operations were still considered very risky. The interest rates of some *asientos* reached well above 20% in times of uncertainty, and the bankruptcies attest that repayment was far from guaranteed. But silver allowed borrowing to take place, war to be declared, and Philip to lead Castile into military adventures that left the Cortes little choice but to grant the additional taxes required to shore up the situation. Had silver never been found, it is hard to conceive how Castile could have funded its ambitious military ventures unless the Cortes had granted prior consent. The resistance the Cortes exhibited to royal requests even in the most dire of times suggests that it was very unlikely that such consent would have been granted lightly.

As the session of the Cortes was winding down, the 1577 treasure fleet brought the largest amount of bullion in a single shipment up to that time, starting the run-up to the peak of the 1590s. The additional silver and the extraordinary levy provided the king with the resources to settle the defaulted debt with his bankers, while the doubling of the *alcabalas* provided him with unencumbered tax streams he could use as collateral for new *juros* issues. Lending resumed as early as 1578, infusing renewed vigor into the military campaign in the Dutch provinces.

Nothing seemed to change in the second half of Philip's reign. The Crown continued to spend enormous sums in building the Royal Monastery of El

Escorial, fighting the Dutch rebels, and outfitting the Invincible Armada. Its defeat in 1588 cost Castile a full year's worth of revenue, and prompted Philip to again convene the Cortes and ask for an emergency tax to protect Castile from the imminent threat of a British invasion.[16] The *millones*, as the new excises were collectively called, departed from the previous tradition in that the Cortes succeeded, at least in principle, in attaching strings to their renewal (Jago 1981). The *millones* scheme consisted of multiyear agreements negotiated between the Crown and the Cortes. The new taxes were collected at the local level, and were transferred to the Crown provided that the conditions in the previous agreement had been met. In theory, the cities retained administrative control over the funds, and the compliance with the conditions was overseen by an independent commission dominated by representatives of the cities.

The revival of parliamentary authority took place mainly on paper, and did not make itself felt in the Crown's coffers. Although the *millones* commission repeatedly sought instruments to control the destiny of the funds that fell under its oversight, it never gained the ability to restrain the Crown from diverting them to its preferred uses. Starting in the 1620s, the king managed to gradually pack the commission with his own representatives. As the Crown declared its sixth bankruptcy in 1647, the commission was absorbed by the Council of Finance (Jago 1981), under the direct control of the Crown. The following year the Treaty of Westphalia would mark the end of Castile's imperial adventures and usher in a period of internal strife and disintegration of state institutions. The Cortes never recovered their lost influence, and after 1663 they were only convened on ceremonial occasions.

Conclusion   At the dawn of the early modern age, Castile had developed all the major traits of a nation state, second perhaps only to Britain. The monarchy had been able to use its newfound military might to concentrate power in its hands, largely containing or eliminating the influence of the medieval "estates" of the clergy and the church. The one medieval institution to emerge with its attributes largely unaltered was the Cortes. Composed of representatives of the merchant and urban elites, it was also the institution that harbored the best prospects for becoming a meaningful check on the power of the Crown.

The relationship between the Crown and the Cortes was always a tense one, as the two competed for the power to raise revenues and the prerogative of deciding their uses. What might have been the outcome of this political game had Castile not stumbled upon the mines of Potosí is a counterfactual that defies analysis. We have nonetheless illustrated how the silver windfall allowed the Crown to skirt the issue altogether, resorting to the Cortes only in emergency situations and forcing them to deal with a fait accompli.

We interpret the political evolution of sixteenth-century Castile as the effect of a large natural-resource windfall in the context of an institutional environment that, while advanced for its time, was not designed to handle a shock of the magnitude of American silver. Although the prerogatives of the Cortes were well established in regard to the traditional medieval taxes, the constitutional structure of Castile did not contemplate the possibility of large expansions of the revenue base. Silver revenues thus fell under the exclusive control of the Crown, which leveraged them to pursue its imperial program, unchecked by the representatives of its kingdom.

The development of Castilian institutions was in many ways the exact opposite to that in Britain and the Netherlands, whose constitutional arrangements emerged from the need to grapple with scarcity. British and Dutch economic growth and financial development were a consequence of institutions that limited the power of the monarch (North and Weingast 1989); Castilian financial sophistication and recklessness arose from a natural-resource windfall that handed unprecedented spending power to the Crown. With the exception of the six years surrounding the Dissolution of the Monasteries, Henry VIII's warring instincts were constantly reined in by the state of his finances (Hoyle 1995); Charles V and Philip II's belligerence, on the other hand, was encouraged by the sheer size of the financial resources at their disposal.

Castile acquired a global empire riding the wave of its silver boom, but subsequently failed to find permanent sources of income to sustain its ambitions. As silver revenue dwindled in the early seventeenth century, the Castilian tax base was stretched to its limits, further harming development and growth. Despite the crushing level of taxation, the demise of Spanish dominance could not be postponed for long. The burghers in the major Castilian cities failed to push through reforms that would have established some degree of control over expenditures, while continuous warfare undermined any chance of fiscal consolidation. This equilibrium persisted even in the face of growing external threats and internal strife. American silver paid for Castile's heady days of glory and power; through its effect on institutions, the windfall may also have sentenced it to long centuries of decline.

ACKNOWLEDGMENTS

We thank Avner Greif, Leandro Prados de la Escosura, Blanca Sánchez Alonso, participants at the EREH conference in Lund (2007), and members of the Institutions, Organizations, and Growth Program of the Canadian Institute for Advanced Research (CIFAR) for their insightful comments, and Isaac Holloway for research assistance. Financial support from CIFAR, the Social Sciences and Humanities Research Council of Canada (SSHRC), and the Spanish Ministry of Education is gratefully acknowledged.

NOTES

1. The decline of Spain in the seventeenth century has continued to attract scholarly attention at a steady pace. For three recent examples see Marcos Martín (2000), Kamen (2003), and Yun Casalilla (2004). Allen (2001) provides a long-run comparative analysis of the economic performance of several European economies, including Spain.

2. Spanish silver fueled the first truly global trade, flowing from mines in Mexico and Peru to Seville, continuing on to European commercial centers, and often ending up in the Far East, where Chinese demand for monetary uses kept its price high. See Flynn and Giráldez (2004) for further discussion.

3. The full dataset is available from http://www.cid.harvard.edu/ciddata/ciddata.html.

4. The wool industry at its early sixteenth-century peak counted upward of three million sheep, compared with a population of barely over four million people. The production, processing, trading, and exporting of Merino wool was the economic engine of Northern Castile, prompting scholars to refer to the industry as "Spain's golden fleece" (Phillips and Phillips 1997).

5. See Tilly (1990) and Brewer (1988) for an articulation of the relevance of taxation and military expenditure to the development of nation states. Parker (1976) discusses the military revolution of the sixteenth century at length.

6. Philip II could count on a Royal Council (known as the Council of Castile), and one each for Aragon and Navarre; later on he would add councils for Italy, Flanders, Borgogne, Portugal, and a separate chamber for Castile. Foreign policy was overseen by the councils of state and war; religious and nobility matters by the councils of the Inquisition and military orders; responsibility for

financial matters resided with the councils of finance and crusade; and colonial affairs were in the hands of the council of Indies.

7. The nominal figures are deflated by the silver price index in Hamilton (1934).

8. Drelichman (2005b) thoroughly documents how Castile sharply increased consumption following the silver discoveries, and later reduced it when the remittances failed to live up to the original expectations.

9. See Cohn (2001) for further details on Charles' use of short-term loans to secure the imperial crown.

10. The standard reference on Charles' bank loans is Carande (1987).

11. A discussion of the Golden Bull, together with an English translation of the Latin text, can be found in Henderson (1910). Chapters IX and X limit the authority of the emperor in matters of taxation and expenditure. The Bull was staunchly enforced by the German princes.

12. For a detailed description of the sovereign lending system of Philip II, see Ruíz Martín (1965).

13. For a discussion of the dynamics of the 1575 bankruptcy and the 1577 settlement see Lovett (1980; 1982).

14. The king founded his request in his legal right to collect sales taxes on every transaction in the kingdom at a 10% rate, while the payments contracted with the cities implied a rate of between 2% and 3%. Should the Cortes refuse to comply, the king's threat was to not renew the tax farms and to collect the tax at its full 10% rate. The cities' representatives, knowing that the king lacked the administrative structure to follow up on his threat, refused to budge, and the negotiations dragged on (Jago 1985).

15. We only consider "true" sovereign borrowing, in which the king has no ability to exert violence over the lenders—although he may default if he so wishes. Early modern monarchs often resorted to forced loans, which amounted to confiscation of a part of the interest and, on occasion, of the entire capital as well. Since this type of lending was not voluntary, we consider it as a form of prerogative taxation rather than a freely contracted financial obligation, and hence exclude it from our analysis of lending.

16. Estimates of the cost of Philip's military campaigns can be found in Parker (1998).

REFERENCES

Acemoglu, Daron, Simon Johnson, and James Robinson. 2005a. "Institutions as the Fundamental Cause of Long Run Growth." In *Handbook of Economic Growth*, eds. P. Aghion and S. Durlauf. Amsterdam: Elsevier.

————. 2005b. "The Rise of Europe: Atlantic Trade, Institutional Change, and Economic Growth." *American Economic Review* 95(3):546–79.

Allen, Robert C. 2001. "The Great Divergence in European Prices and Wages from the Middle Ages to the First World War." *European Review of Economic History* 38(4):411–47.

Alvarez Nogal, Carlos, and Leandro Prados de la Escosura. 2007. "Searching for the Roots of Retardation: Spain in European Perspective, 1500–1850." Working Papers in Economic History 07–06. Madrid: Universidad Carlos III de Madrid.

Artola, Miguel. 1982. *La Hacienda del Antiguo Régimen*. Madrid: Alianza.

————. 1988. "El Estado." In *Enciclopedia de Historia de España*, ed. M. Artola. Madrid: Alianza.

Asea, Patrick K., and Amartya Lahiri. 1999. "The Precious Bane." *Journal of Economic Dynamics and Control* 23:823–49.

Auty, Richard M. 2001. *Resource Abundance and Economic Development*. Oxford: Oxford University Press.

Baland, Jean-Marie, and Patrick Francois. 2000. "Rent-Seeking and Resource Booms." *Journal of Development Economics* 61:527–42.

Brewer, John S. 1988. *The Sinews of Power*. Cambridge, MA: Harvard University Press.

Carande, Ramón. 1987. *Carlos V y sus banqueros*. 3rd ed., 3 vols. Barcelona: Crítica.

Cohn, Henry J. 2001. "Did Bribes Induce the German Electors to Choose Charles V as Emperor in 1519?" *German History* 19:1–27.

Corden, W. Max, and J. Peter Neary. 1982. "Booming Sector and De-Industrialization in a Small Open Economy." *The Economic Journal* 92:825–48.

Domínguez Ortiz, Antonio. 1985. *Las clases privilegiades en el Antiguo Régimen*. Madrid: ISTMO.

Drelichman, Mauricio. 2005a. "All that Glitters: Precious Metals, Rent Seeking, and the Decline of Spain." *European Review of Economic History* 9(3):313–36.

————. 2005b. "The Curse of Moctezuma: American Silver and the Dutch Disease." *Explorations in Economic History* 42(3):349–80.

————. 2007. "Sons of Something: Taxes, Lawsuits and Local Political Control in Sixteenth-Century Castile." *The Journal of Economic History* 67:608–42.

Drelichman, Mauricio, and Hans-Joachim Voth. 2007. "The Sustainable Debts of Philip II: A Reconstruction of Spain's Fiscal Position, 1560–1598." Working paper, University of British Columbia.

Elliott, John H. [1963] 1990. *Imperial Spain, 1469–1716*. London: Penguin Books.

Fisher, Douglas. 1989. "The Price Revolution: A Monetary Interpretation." *Journal of Economic History* 49(4):883–902.

Flynn, Dennis O. 1978. "A New Perspective on the Spanish Price Revolution: The Monetary Approach to the Balance of Payments." *Explorations in Economic History* 15(4):388–406.

Flynn, Dennis O., and Arturo Giráldez. 2004. "Path Dependence, Time Lags and the Birth of Globalisation: A Critique of O'Rourke and Williamson." *European Review of Economic History* 8(1):81–108.

Forsyth, Peter J., and Stephen J. Nicholas. 1983. "The Decline of Spanish Industry and the Price Revolution: A Neoclassical Analysis." *Journal of European Economic History* 12(3):601–10.

Grafe, Regina. 2001. "Northern Spain between the Iberian and the Atlantic Worlds: Trade and Regional Specialisation, 1550–1650." Unpublished PhD diss., London School of Economics and Political Science, London.

Hamilton, Earl J. 1934. *American Treasure and the Price Revolution in Spain, 1501–1650*. Cambridge, MA: Harvard University Press.

Henderson, Ernst F. 1910. *Select Historical Documents of the Middle Ages*. London: George Bell and Sons.

Hoyle, Richard. 1995. "War and Public Finance." In *The Reign of Henry VIII: Politics, Policy, and Piety*, ed. D. McCulloch. Houndmills, Basingstoke, Hampshire: Macmillan.

International Monetary Fund. 2005. "Guide on Resource Revenue Transparency." June. http://www.imf.org/external/pubs/ft/grrt/eng/060705.htm.

Jago, Charles. 1981. "Habsburg Absolutism and the Cortes of Castile." *The American Historical Review* 86:307–26.

———. 1985. "Philip II and the Cortes of Castile: The Case of the Cortes of 1576." *Past and Present* (109):24–43.

Kagan, Richard L. 1981. *Lawsuits and Litigants in Castile, 1500–1700*. Chapel Hill, NC: University of North Carolina Press.

Kamen, Henry. 2003. *Empire: How Spain Became a World Power, 1492–1763*. New York: Harper Collins.

Knack, Stephen, and Philip Keefer. 1995. "Institutions and Economic Performance: Cross-Country Tests Using Alternative Institutional Measures." *Economics and Politics* 7(3):207–27.

Krugman, Paul. 1987. "The Narrow Moving Band, the Dutch Disease and the Competitive Consequences of Mrs. Thatcher." *Journal of Development Economics* 27:41–55.

Lovett, A. W. 1980. "The Castilian Bankruptcy of 1575." *The Historical Journal* 23:899–911.

———. 1982. "The General Settlement of 1577: An Aspect of Spanish Finance in the Early Modern Period." *The Historical Journal* 25(1):1–22.

Marcos Martín, Alberto. 2000. *España en los siglos XVI, XVII y XVIII*. Barcelona: Crítica.

Martín Postigo, María de la Soterraña, and Cilia Domínguez Rodríguez. 1990. *La sala de hijosdalgo de la Real Chancillería de Valladolid*. Salamanca: Ambito.

Mehlum, Halvor, Karl Moene, and Ragnar Torvik. 2006. "Institutions and the Resource Curse." *Economic Journal* 116:1–20.

Morineau, Michel. 1985. *Incroyables gazettes et fabuleux metaux*. London: Cambridge University Press.

Nadal i Oller, Jordi. 1984. *La población española: siglos XVI a XX*. First corrected and augmented ed. Barcelona: Ariel.

North, Douglass C., and Barry R. Weingast. 1989. "Constitutions and Commitment: The Evolution of Institutional Governing Public Choice in Seventeenth-Century England." *Journal of Economic History* 49(4):803–32.

Parker, Geoffrey. 1976. "The Military Revolution, 1560–1600—A Myth?" *The Journal of Modern History* 48:195–214.

———. 1998. *The Grand Strategy of Philip II*. New Haven, CT, and London: Yale University Press.

———. 1999. "The Political World of Charles V." In *Charles V and His Time, 1500–1559*, ed. H. Soly. Antwerp: Mercatorfonds.

Phillips, Carla Rahn, and William D. Phillips, Jr. 1997. *Spain's Golden Fleece: Wool Production and the Wool Trade from the Middle Ages to the Nineteenth Century*. Baltimore, MD, and London: The Johns Hopkins University Press.

Prebisch, Raúl. 1950. *The Economic Development of Latin America and Its Principal Problems*. New York: United Nations.

Robinson, James A., Ragnar Torvik, and Thierry Verdier. 2006. "Political Foundations of the Resource Curse." *Journal of Development Economics* 79(2):447–68.

Rodríguez, Francisco, and Jeffrey Sachs. 1999. "Why Do Resource-Abundant Economies Grow More Slowly?" *The Journal of Economic Growth* 4:277–303.

Ruíz Martín, Felipe. 1965. "Un expediente financiero entre 1560 y 1575. La hacienda de Felipe II y la Casa de Contratación de Sevilla." *Moneda y Crédito* 92:3–58.

Sachs, Jeffrey D., and Andrew M. Warner. 1995. "Natural Resource Abundance and Economic Growth." National Bureau of Economic Research working paper 5398.

———. 1997. "Sources of Slow Growth in African Economies." *Journal of African Economies* 6(3):335–76.

Singer, Hans. 1950. "The Distribution of Gains between Investing and Borrowing Countries." *American Economic Review* 40:473–85.

Thompson, I. A. A. 1976. *War and Government in Habsburg Spain, 1560–1620*. London: The Athlone Press.

———. 1994. "Castile: Polity, Fiscality, and Fiscal Crisis." In *Fiscal Crises, Liberty, and Representative Government, 1450–1789*, eds. P. T. Hoffman and K. Norberg. Palo Alto, CA: Stanford University Press.

Thompson, I. A. A., and Bartolomé Yun Casalilla. 1994. *The Castilian Crisis of the Seventeenth Century*. Cambridge: Cambridge University Press.

Tilly, Charles. 1990. *Coercion, Capital, and European States, AD 990–1992*. Oxford: Oxford University Press.

Tornell, Aaron, and Philip R. Lane. 1999. "The Voracity Effect." *American Economic Review* 89:22–46.

Torvik, Ragnar. 2002. "Natural Resources, Rent Seeking, and Welfare." *Journal of Development Economics* 67:455–70.

Ulloa, Modesto. 1977. *La hacienda real de Castilla en el reinado de Felipe II*. 2nd ed. Madrid: Fundación Universitaria Española, Seminario Cisneros.

Weber, Max. 1968. *Economy and Society: An Outline of Interpretive Sociology*. Berkeley: University of California Press.

Wijnbergen, Sweder van. 1984. The Dutch Disease: A Disease after All? *The Economic Journal* 94:41–55.

Yun Casalilla, Bartolomé. 2002. El Siglo de la Hegemonía Castellana (1450–1590). In *Historia Económica de España, Siglos X-XX*, eds. F. Comín, M. Hernández, and E. Llopis. Barcelona: Crítica.

———. 2004. *Marte contra Minerva. El precio del imperio español, c. 1450–1600*. Barcelona: Crítica.

— 4 —

Slavery, Inequality, and Economic Development in the Americas

An Examination of the Engerman-Sokoloff Hypothesis

NATHAN NUNN

4.1 Introduction

In a series of influential papers (Engerman and Sokoloff 1997, 2002, 2006; Sokoloff and Engerman 2000), economic historians Stanley Engerman and Kenneth Sokoloff argue that the different development experiences of the countries in the Americas can be explained by initial differences in factor endowments, which resulted in differences in the use of production based on slave labor. The authors argue that reliance on slavery resulted in extreme economic inequality, and this in turn hampered the evolution of institutions necessary for sustained, long-term economic growth. The authors hypothesize that inequality adversely affected the development of important institutions such as voting rights (Engerman and Sokoloff 2005b), taxation (Sokoloff and Zolt 2007), and the provision of public schooling (Mariscal and Sokoloff 2000).

In this chapter, I empirically examine two parts of Engerman and Sokoloff's hypothesis: (1) that large-scale plantation slavery resulted in economic inequality, and (2) that this resulted in subsequent underdevelopment.[1]

In Section 4.2 of the chapter, I test for the reduced-form relationship between large-scale plantation slavery and economic underdevelopment. This is done by examining whether there is evidence that countries that relied most heavily on slave use in the late eighteenth and early nineteenth centuries are poorer today. I test for this relationship looking across former New World economies, and across counties and states within the United

States. In both settings, I find a significant negative relationship between past slave use and current economic performance. I also examine whether large-scale plantation slavery appears to have been particularly damaging for economic development. I do not find any evidence that large-scale slavery was more detrimental for growth than other forms of slavery. Instead, the evidence suggests that all forms of slavery were detrimental, and that if any form of slavery was particularly detrimental, it was actually small-scale nonplantation slavery.

In Section 4.3 of the chapter, I examine whether, consistent with Engerman and Sokoloff's hypotheses, the negative relationship between slavery and income can be explained by slavery causing extreme economic inequality, which adversely affected economic growth. Looking within the United States, I find that slavery in 1860 is positively correlated with land inequality in the same year, but I do not find that initial land inequality had any subsequent effect on economic development. In addition, I do not find that the effect of slavery on inequality is able to account for the estimated effect of slavery on economic development.

Overall, the results of this chapter support Engerman and Sokoloff's basic assertion that slavery was detrimental for economic development. However, the data do not show that large-scale plantation slavery was particularly detrimental for development, and it does not appear that slavery's adverse effect on subsequent economic performance is because of its impact on initial economic inequality.

4.2 Testing the Reduced-Form Relationship: Plantation Slavery and Economic Development

4.2.1 Looking within Former New World Countries

To construct measures of the prevalence of slave use in each New World country, I use historic population data from a variety of sources, most often population censuses. These data and their sources are described in detail in the appendix. As my measure of the prevalence of slavery, I use the fraction of each country's total population that is in slavery in 1750. It is important to note that I am not using the proportion of the population that is of African descent. Included in the category of slaves are enslaved Africans and enslaved Native Americans, while free Africans are not included. One could

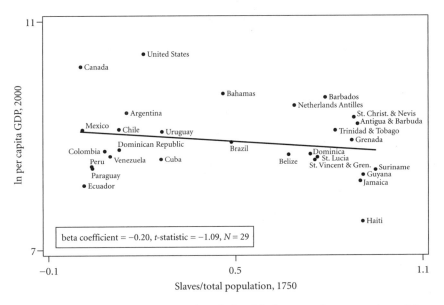

Figure 4.1 Bivariate plot showing the relationship between the proportion of the population in slavery in 1750 S_i/L_i and the natural log of per capita GDP in 2000 $\ln y_i$.

also construct estimates of the proportion of a population that was African, but this is a much less precise measure of the variable of interest.

As a measure of economic development, I use the natural log of per capita GDP in 2000. The sample includes 29 former New World countries for which income, population, and slave data are available.

The relationship between current income and the proportion of the population in slavery in 1750 is shown in Figure 4.1. In the raw data one observes weak evidence that slavery may have adversely affected economic development. There is a negative, but statistically insignificant, relationship between past slave use and current income.

I further examine this relationship by estimating the following equation, which also controls for other potentially important determinants of economic development:

$$\ln y_i = \alpha + \beta_S \, S_i/L_i + \gamma \, L_i/A_i + \mathbf{I}'\delta + \varepsilon_i. \tag{4.1}$$

The subscript i indexes countries, y_i is per capita GDP in 2000, S_i/L_i is the proportion of slaves in the total population in 1750, L_i/A_i is the population density in 1750, and **I** denotes colonizer fixed effects for former French, British, Spanish, Portuguese, and Dutch colonies. The fixed effects are included to capture an important part of Engerman and Sokoloff's overall argument. The authors argue that although Spanish colonies did not have large numbers of slaves, they were still characterized by high levels of inequality. Primarily because large native populations survived European contact, the Spanish adopted the native practice of awarding property rights over land, labor, and minerals to a small elite.[2] To capture this Spanish effect, I include a fixed effect for countries that are former Spanish colonies. I also include fixed effects for the nationalities of the other colonizers, which will capture other differences in colonial strategies that may be important for economic development.

The coefficient of interest in equation (4.1) is β_S, the estimated relationship between past slave use and current income. A concern when interpreting this coefficient is whether the estimated effect is actually causal. In this setting, the core issue is that initial country characteristics affected the use of slave labor, and that these initial conditions may either persist, affecting income today, or they may have affected the past evolution of income through channels other than slave use. It may be that countries with characteristics that were least favorable for economic growth have been most likely to use slave labor. If this is the case, then this will tend to bias the estimated relationship between slave use and income downward, and we may falsely conclude that slavery was bad for subsequent economic development even if this is untrue.

Because of the lack of availability of historic data for all countries in the sample, I am unable to control for all of the initial country characteristics that I would like to control for. However, one measure that is available is initial population density (L_i/A_i), which I include as a control in equation (4.1). The variable is meant to capture the economic prosperity of each country in 1750, which was in turn determined by a host of factors such as climate, soil quality, and the distance to international markets.[3] The variable will also be positively correlated with the future growth potential of a country at the time. This is because both voluntary and forced migration would have been determined, at least in part, by the expected future profitability of the colonies. Labor would have migrated to where the current and future returns to labor were the highest.[4]

OLS estimates of equation (4.1) are reported in Table 4.1. The first column reports estimates of equation (4.1) with colonizer fixed effects only,

Table 4.1 Slavery in 1750 and current income across former New World economies

Dependent variable: ln y_i	(1)	(2)	Omit USA, CAN (3)	Omit USA, CAN, HTI (4)
Fraction slaves, S_i/L_i	−2.31***	−2.63***	−1.43*	−1.43*
	(.47)	(.42)	(.74)	(.74)
Population density, L_i/A_i		.61***	.59**	.59***
		(.21)	(.20)	(.20)
Colonizer fixed effects	Yes	Yes	Yes	Yes
R^2	.53	.66	.53	.37
Number of observations	29	29	27	26

Note: The table reports OLS estimates of equation (4.1). The dependent variable is the natural log of per capita GDP in 2000, ln y_i. The unit of observation is a country. Coefficients are reported with standard errors in parentheses. The ***, **, and * indicate significance at the 1%, 5%, and 10% levels. "Fraction slaves, S_i/L_i" is the number of slaves in the population divided by the total population, measured in 1750. "Population density, L_i/A_i" is the total population in 1750 divided by land area. The colonizer fixed effects are for Portugal, England, France, Spain, and the Netherlands.

while the second column reports the fully specified estimating equation, also controlling for initial population density. In both specifications the estimated coefficient for S_i/L_i is negative and statistically significant. The magnitudes of the estimated coefficients, as well as being statistically significant, are also economically large. As an example, consider Jamaica, where 90% of its population was in slavery in 1750. Today Jamaica is relatively poor, with an average per capita GDP of $3,640 (measured in 2000).[5] According to the estimates of column 2, if Jamaica had relied less on slave production so that the total proportion of slaves in its economy was only 46%, which was the proportion of slaves in the Bahamas at the time, then Jamaica's income would be $11,580, rather than $3,640. This is an increase of well over 200%. An additional way to assess the estimated magnitude of β_S is to calculate standardized beta coefficients. The calculated beta coefficient for S_i/L_i in column 2 is −1.51, which is extremely large. A one standard deviation decrease in S_i/L_i results in an increase in ln y_i of over 1.5 standard deviations.

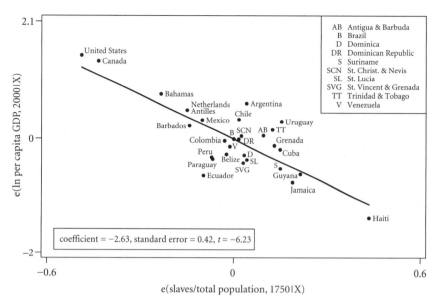

Figure 4.2 Partial correlation plot showing the relationships between the proportion of slaves in the population in 1750 S_i/L_i and the natural log of per capita GDP in 2000 ln y_i.

The partial correlation plot for S_i/L_i from column 2 is shown in Figure 4.2. Although no single observation appears to be clearly biasing the results, Canada and the United States appear to be particularly important observations. One may be concerned that the estimates may simply be reflecting differences between Canada and the United States, and all of the other New World economies. If so, the estimated relationship between slavery and economic development may be driven by other differences between the two groups, such as climate or the extent of European settlement.

Because of this concern, in the third column of Table 4.1, I reestimate equation (4.1) after omitting Canada and the United States from the sample. As shown, the magnitude of the estimated coefficient for S_i/L_i decreases, but it remains statistically significant. These results show that even ignoring Canada and the United States, one still observes a negative relationship between past slave use and subsequent economic development. This is significant because the evidence presented in Engerman and Sokoloff (1997, 2002, 2006) and Sokoloff and Engerman (2000) generally relies on comparisons between Canada and the United States, and the other less-developed countries in the Americas. The results here show that even looking within the latter group, one still observes a link between slavery and economic development. The final column also omits Haiti, which from Figure 4.2 is also a potentially influential observation. The results show that even after dropping all three countries from the sample, one still observes a significant negative relationship between slavery and subsequent income.

Given the admittedly sparse set of control variables in the estimating equation, the results presented here do not prove with certainty that slavery adversely affected subsequent economic development. However, they do provide very suggestive evidence, showing that the patterns that we observe in the data are consistent with the general argument put forth by Engerman and Sokoloff.

4.2.2 Looking within the British West Indies

In this section, I examine an even smaller sample of 12 countries that were part of the British West Indies. The sample includes Antigua and Barbuda, Bahamas, Belize, Dominica, Grenada, Guyana, Jamaica, St. Christopher and Nevis, St. Lucia, St. Vincent and the Grenadines, Trinidad and Tobago, and Barbados. Although this is a much more restricted sample, there are a number of benefits to examining this smaller group of countries. First, the data are all from one source, British census records, all of which are recorded and summarized in Higman (1984). Because all data are from slave censuses that were conducted by the British government using the same procedures and administration, the data and information collected are quite reliable, and any biases or errors that may exist will be similar across all countries (Higman 1984, 6–15). Second, the sample of countries is homogenous in many dimensions. They are all small former British colonies located in the Caribbean. As a result, many of the omitted factors that could potentially bias the estimates of interest, such as differences in culture, geography, or historical experience, are diminished by looking at this more homogenous sample.

The final benefit is that much more information is available for each country. Specifically, information on the size of plantations and on the use of slaves is available. This allows us to consider more deeply the hypotheses in Engerman and Sokoloff's work. To this point, we have examined the relationship between slave use and economic development, finding that, consistent with their analysis, past slave use is associated with current underdevelopment. With the data from Higman we can begin to examine the potential channels behind this relationship. Because the hypothesized channel in Engerman and Sokoloff works through economic inequality, the authors focus almost exclusively on the adverse effect of slavery on large-scale plantations. Their argument is that this form of slavery resulted in economic inequality, poor institutions, and economic stagnation.

Using Higman's data on slave use and the size of slave holdings, I examine whether the negative relationship between slave use is driven by large-scale plantation slavery rather than other forms of slavery. I do this by allowing the relationship between slavery and income to differ depending on the manner in which the slaves were used. I divide the total number of slaves in each society into two groups, plantation slaves and slaves not working on plantations, and calculate two measures of slavery: the proportion of the population that are slaves working on plantations, denoted S_i^P/L_i, and the proportion of the population that are slaves but do not work on plantations, S_i^{NP}/L_i. The plantation slaves include those working on sugar plantations, coffee plantations, cotton plantations, or in other forms of agriculture. Nonplantation slaves are slaves that are either working in urban areas or in industries, such as livestock, salt, timber, fishing, and shipping.[6] In the sample, the mean value of S_i^P/L_i is .61 and of S_i^{NP}/L_i is .13. This reflects the fact that in the Caribbean, the primary use of slaves was for manual labor on sugar, coffee, or cotton plantations. The two slavery measures are negatively correlated, with a correlation coefficient of $-.90$. This is a result of the fact that, holding the total number of slaves constant, increasing the number of slaves in one occupation decreases the number in the other.

Using the two measures of slavery, I estimate a less restrictive version of equation (4.1), where the two types of slavery are allowed to have different effects on economic development:

$$\ln y_i = \alpha + \beta_P \, S_i^P/L_i + \beta_{NP} \, S_i^{NP}/L_i + \gamma \, L_i/A_i + \varepsilon_i. \qquad (4.2)$$

To see that equation (4.2) is simply a less restrictive version of equation (4.1), note that if we restrict the two coefficients to be equal, $\beta_P = \beta_{NP}$, then equation (4.2) reduces to equation (4.1). The only difference is that in equation (4.2), the colonizer fixed effects drop out because all of the countries in the sample are former British colonies.

The slavery data are now from 1830 rather than 1750. Although the total number of slaves and free persons are available for both 1750 and 1830,

Table 4.2 Slavery and income within the British West Indies

Dependent variable: ln y_i	1750 (1)	1830 (2)	1830 (3)	1830 (4)
Fraction of population that are				
Slaves, S_i/L_i	−2.42***	−2.24**		
	(.74)	(.93)		
Nonplantation slaves, S_i^{NP}/L_i			−6.55**	
			(2.06)	
Plantation slaves, S_i^P/L_i			−3.84***	
			(1.04)	
Slaves on holdings with 10 slaves or less, S_i^S/L_i				−20.92***
				(3.82)
11 to 200 slaves, S_i^M/L_i				−5.32***
				(.95)
201 slaves or more, S_i^L/L_i				−8.12***
				(1.30)
Population density, L_i/A_i	.24***	.21***	.20***	.36***
	(.06)	(.07)	(.06)	(.03)
F-test of equality (p-value)			.06	.00
R^2	.69	.55	.73	.96
Number of observations	12	12	12	11

Note: The table reports OLS estimates of equations (4.1), (4.2), and (4.3). The dependent variable is the natural log of per capita GDP in 2000, ln y_i. Coefficients are reported with standard errors in parentheses. The ***, **, and * indicate significance at the 1%, 5%, and 10% levels. In column 1, all variables are measured in 1750, and in columns 2–4, all variables are measured in 1830. The null hypothesis of the reported F-test is the equality of the coefficients for the slavery variables.

the number of slaves disaggregated by slave use is only available for 1830. Because by 1830 none of the countries in the sample had abolished slavery, the proportion of slaves in 1830 is a good approximation of the use of slaves in the years prior to this date. This can be seen from the fact that the correlation between the proportion of the population in slavery in 1750 and in 1830 within the sample is .74. In addition, estimates of equation (4.1) are similar whether the 1750 data or the 1830 data are used. These estimates are reported in columns 1 and 2 of Table 4.2.

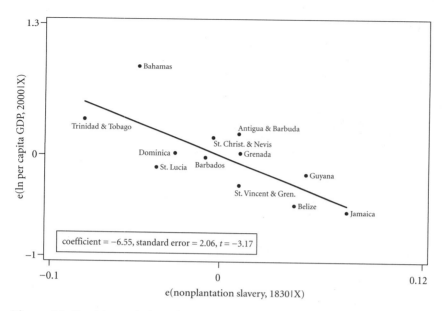

Figure 4.3 Partial correlation plot showing the relationship between nonplantation slavery S_i^{NP}/L_i and the natural log of per capita GDP in 2000 $\ln y_i$.

Estimates of equation (4.2) are reported in the third column of Table 4.2. Both slavery variables enter with negative coefficients, and both coefficients are statistically significant. These results confirm the previous negative relationship between slave use and economic development. However, the relative magnitudes of the coefficients do not support Engerman and Sokoloff's focus on the detrimental effects of large-scale plantation agriculture. According to the estimated magnitudes, it is not the use of slaves on large-scale plantations that has the greatest negative impact on development, but the use of nonplantation slaves.

The partial correlation plots for the two slavery variables are shown in Figures 4.3 and 4.4. From the plots it is apparent that neither relationship is being driven by a small number of outlying observations. Both relationships appear robust.

Next, I consider an alternative way of cutting the slavery data, and examine whether the effect of slavery differs depending on the size of slave holdings. Higman provides data on the number of slaves that are held on slave holdings with (1) 10 slaves or less, (2) 11 to 50 slaves, (3) 51 to 100 slaves, (4) 101 to 200 slaves, (5) 201 to 300 slaves, or (6) 301 slaves or

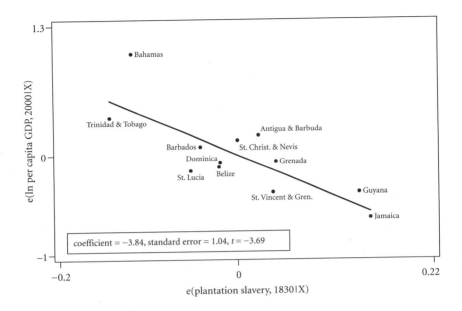

Figure 4.4 Partial correlation plot showing the relationship between plantation slavery S_i^P/L_i and the natural log of per capita GDP in 2000 $\ln y_i$.

more.[7] Because of the small number of observations available, I aggregate the holdings into three categories: (1) small-scale holdings of 10 slaves or less, (2) medium-scale holdings with 11 to 200 slaves, and (3) large-scale holdings with 201 slaves or more. I then calculate the proportion of the population that are slaves held on small-scale holdings S_i^S/L_i, medium-scale holdings S_i^M/L_i, and large-scale holdings S_i^L/L_i.[8]

These measures provide an additional way of examining Engerman and Sokoloff's hypothesis that the detrimental impact of slavery arose because it was associated with economic inequality arising because of the existence of large-scale slave plantations. Across the countries in the sample, there is a strong positive relationship between the size of slave holdings and the use of slaves on plantations. This can be seen from Table 4.3, which reports the correlation coefficients between the two measures of slave use, disaggregated by occupation, and the three measures of slave use, disaggregated by size of slave holdings. A clear pattern is apparent. The fraction of the population that is comprised of plantation slaves is negatively correlated with the

Table 4.3 Correlations between slave-holding size and slave occupation across countries within the British West Indies

	S_i^S/L_i	S_i^M/L_i	S_i^L/L_i
S_i^P/L_i	−.808	.881	.494
	(.00)	(.00)	(.12)
S_i^{NP}/L_i	.649	−.843	−.232
	(.03)	(.00)	(.49)

Note: Pairwise correlation coefficients are reported with p-values in parentheses. Each correlation is estimated across 11 countries.

fraction of the population that is comprised of slaves on small-scale holdings, and positively correlated with the fraction of the population that is comprised of slaves on medium- and large-scale holdings. These correlations confirm that the size of slave holdings variables provides an alternative indicator of the use of slaves on large-scale plantations. The relationship between slave-holding size and the use of slaves is also shown in Higman (1984, 104–6), where average slave-holding size by slave use is provided for five of the colonies. The largest holdings tended to be on sugar plantations, followed by coffee and then cotton. The smallest holdings were for slaves working in the livestock industry.

Allowing the effect of slavery to differ by the size of slave holdings yields the following estimating equation:

$$\ln y_i = \alpha + \beta_S \, S_i^S/L_i + \beta_M \, S_i^M/L_i + \beta_L \, S_i^L/L_i + \gamma \, L_i/A_i + \varepsilon_i. \quad (4.3)$$

As before, this equation is simply a more flexible version of equation (4.1).

OLS estimates of equation (4.3) are reported in column 4 of Table 4.2.[9] The results again support the notion that slave use was detrimental for economic development, but they do not support Engerman and Sokoloff's focus on the negative effects of large-scale slave holdings. Contrary to the prediction that large-scale slavery should have the largest impact on development, the estimates suggest that it is in fact small-scale slavery that has the largest impact. The magnitude of the small-scale coefficient is nearly four times the magnitude of the medium-scale coefficient, and over twice the magnitude of the large-scale coefficient. As well, these differences are statistically significant. The null hypothesis of the equality of the coefficients for S_i^S/L_i, S_i^M/L_i, and S_i^L/L_i is rejected at any standard significance level.

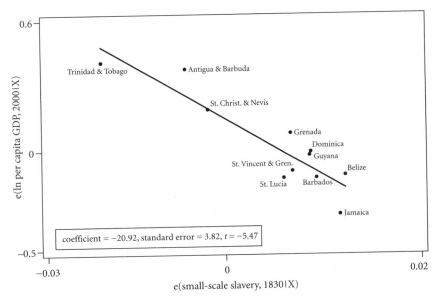

Figure 4.5 Partial correlation plot showing the relationship between small-scale slavery S_i^S/L_i and the natural log of per capita GDP in 2000 ln y_i.

The partial correlation plots, reported in Figures 4.5–4.7, show that the relationships between each of the three slavery variables and income appear robust. None of the relationships are driven by outlying observations.

Overall, these results confirm the previous findings in Section 4.2.1. Looking within the British West Indies, the data provide support for Sokoloff and Engerman's hypothesis that slavery adversely affected subsequent economic development. However, they do not support their emphasis on the adverse effects of large-scale plantation slavery. According to the estimates, all forms of slavery are detrimental for economic development, and if anything small-scale slavery, not large-scale slavery, was more detrimental. There is no evidence that large-scale plantation slavery was more detrimental than other forms of slavery.

4.2.3 Looking within the United States

I now turn to a different source of evidence and compare the relative development of counties and states within the United States. Using information on the number of slaves and free persons in each county and state in each

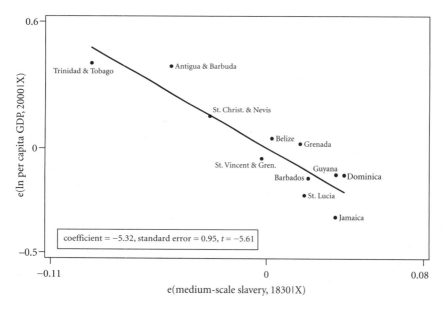

Figure 4.6 Partial correlation plot showing the relationship between medium-scale slavery S_i^M / L_i and the natural log of per capita GDP in 2000 ln y_i.

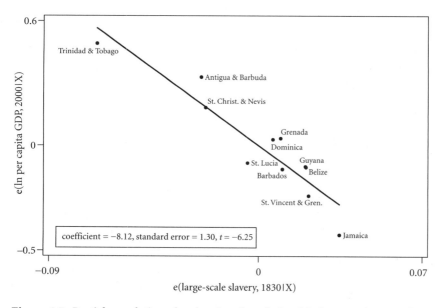

Figure 4.7 Partial correlation plot showing the relationship between large-scale slavery S_i^L / L_i and the natural log of per capita GDP in 2000 ln y_i.

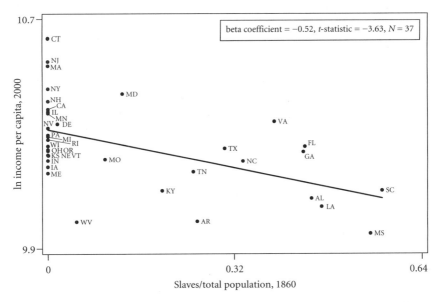

Figure 4.8 Bivariate plot showing the relationship between the proportion of the population in slavery 1860 S_i/L_i and the natural log of per capita income in 2000 $\ln y_i$.

decade between 1790 and 1860, I again examine Engerman and Sokoloff's assertion that domestic slavery was detrimental for subsequent economic development. Population data for slaves and free persons are taken from the U.S. decennial censuses, while income data are from the BEA's *Regional Economic Accounts*.

The cross-state relationship between the proportion of the population in slavery in 1860, the year for which data are available for the largest number of states, and the natural log of per capita income in 2000 is shown in Figure 4.8. The figure shows a clear negative relationship between slave use and subsequent economic performance.

I explore this relationship further in Table 4.4. Each column of the table reports the estimated relationship between slavery in each decade between 1790 and 1860 and log per capita income in 2000, controlling for initial population density measured in the same year as slavery. The top panel of the table reports the relationship between the proportion of the population in slavery and per capita income across U.S. states. The number of observations begins at 17 in 1790 (the first column) and increases each decade

Table 4.4 Slavery and income across counties and states within the United States

Dependent variable: ln y_i	1790	1800	1810	1820	1830	1840	1850	1860
				State-level regressions				
Fraction slaves, S_i/L_i	-.13	-.10	-.11	-.28*	-.29**	-.27**	-.34**	-.33***
	(.24)	(.23)	(.20)	(.15)	(.14)	(.13)	(.13)	(.11)
Population density, L_i/A_i	.52**	.57***	.52***	.46***	.40***	.33***	.19**	.16***
	(.20)	(.19)	(.17)	(.13)	(.11)	(.10)	(.07)	(.05)
R^2	.38	.43	.44	.53	.53	.48	.42	.43
Number of observations	17	18	19	25	27	30	33	37
				County-level regressions				
Fraction slaves, S_i/L_i	-.28**	-.21*	-.15	-.17*	-.19**	-.24***	-.23***	-.22***
	(.11)	(.12)	(.10)	(.10)	(.09)	(.08)	(.08)	(.07)
Population density, L_i/A_i	.09***	.06***	.04***	.03***	.02**	.01***	.007***	.004***
	(.01)	(.01)	(.007)	(.006)	(.003)	(.002)	(.001)	(.001)
R^2	.17	.13	.10	.09	.09	.09	.08	.07
Number of observations	283	400	521	739	964	1,273	1,588	2,014

Note: The dependent variable is the natural log of per capita income in 2000, ln y_i. Coefficients are reported with standard errors in parentheses. For the county-level estimates the standard errors are clustered at the state level. The ***, **, and * indicate significance at the 1%, 5%, and 10% levels. Population density L_i/A_i is measured in the same year as slavery.

to 37 in 1860 (the last column). The reason that the 1790 estimates include 17 states when only 13 states had joined the Union is that census data are also available for West Virginia, Kentucky, Maine, and Vermont. In 1790 West Virginia and Kentucky were part of Virginia, while Maine was a part of Massachusetts. Therefore, data are available for these three areas that later became independent states. In addition, data are also available for the Vermont Republic, which joined the Union a year later in 1791, becoming the state of Vermont.[10]

All of the estimated coefficients for the fraction of population in slavery S_i/L_i are negative. For the three decades prior to 1820 the coefficients are statistically insignificant, while for the five decades after 1810 the coefficients are statistically significant. The insignificance of the results for the first three decades is because three important slave states (Louisiana, Mississippi, and Alabama) did not join the Union until the decade after 1810. This can also be seen in Figure 4.8. If one omits these three states, the negative relationship is weakened substantially.

The magnitudes of the estimated coefficients are large. When controlling for initial population density, the calculated beta coefficients range from −.09, for 1790, to −.41, for 1860. According to the 1860 estimates, if in 1860 South Carolina had no slavery, rather than 57% of its population in slavery, then its average per capita income in 2000 would have been $29,400 rather than $24,300. This is an increase in income of over 20%.

The second panel of Table 4.4 reports the same estimates looking across counties rather than states. As in the state-level regressions, the coefficient estimates for S_i/L_i are negative. To be as conservative as possible, I allow for nonindependence of counties within a state and report standard errors clustered at the state level. This tends to at least double the reported standard errors. The coefficient estimates are negative and statistically significant for every year except 1810. Again, the coefficients are also economically large. The calculated beta coefficients range from −.13 to −.23.

The estimated relationship between slave use and subsequent economic performance reported in Table 4.4 is consistent with the recent findings of Mitchener and McLean (2003) and Lagerlöf (2005). Mitchener and McLean (2003) estimate the relationship between slave use and subsequent labor productivity across U.S. states, and find a significant negative relationship between the fraction of the population in slavery in 1860 and average labor productivity in the decades after this date. Lagerlöf (2005), looking across U.S. counties, also documents a negative relationship between past slave use, measured in 1850, and subsequent per capita income measured in 1994.

The 1860 Census also reports the total number of slave holders that hold the following number of slaves: 1, 2, 3, 4, 5, 6, 7, 8, 9, 10–14, 15–19, 20–29, 30–39, 40–49, 50–69, 70–99, 100–199, 200–299, 300–499, 500–999, and 1,000 and over. Because the census only reports information on the size of holding of each slave holder and not of each slave (as in the Higman data), I can only calculate the number of slaves held on each size of holding when the exact number of slaves per holder is given, which is only for holdings with less than 10 slaves. Therefore, although I can separate small-scale holdings (9 slaves or less) from medium- or large-scale holdings, I am unable to separate slaves held on medium-scale holdings (10 to 199 slaves) from those held on large holdings (200 slaves or more).[11]

Using the census data, I construct two measures of slavery: the proportion of the population that is comprised of slaves held on small-scale holdings S_i^S/L_i, and the proportion of the population that are slaves held on medium- or large-scale holdings S_i^{ML}/L_i. As before, I allow the two types of slavery to affect economic development differently:

$$\ln y_i = \alpha + \beta_S \, S_i^S/L_i + \beta_{ML} \, S_i^{ML}/L_i + \gamma \, L_i/A_i + \varepsilon_i. \qquad (4.4)$$

The subscript i indexes either counties or states, and as before, $\ln y_i$ and L_i/A_i denote log income in 2000 and initial population density.

Table 4.5 reports the estimates of equation (4.4). The first column reports estimates where a state is the unit of observation. The coefficients for S_i^S/L_i and S_i^{ML}/L_i are both negative, but neither is statistically significant. Their insignificance appears to be the result of multicollinearity. The correlation between S_i^S/L_i and S_i^{ML}/L_i is .87. Although neither coefficient is individually significant, jointly the two coefficients are significant. An F-test of their joint significance is able to reject the null hypothesis that both coefficients are jointly equal to zero at the 2% level. This can also be seen from the R^2, which increases from .28 to .43, when the two variables are included in the estimating equation.

Turning to the point estimates, I find that contrary to Engerman and Sokoloff's hypothesis, there is no evidence that large-scale slavery is more detrimental for development than small-scale slavery. Although these point estimates do not support Engerman and Sokoloff's focus on large-scale plantation slavery, it is possible that the data are not sufficiently rich to

Table 4.5 Slavery and income within the United States

Dependent variable: ln y_i	State-level regressions (1)	County-level regressions (2)
Fraction of the population that are slaves		
On holdings with 9 slaves or less, S_i^S/L_i	−.41	−.24
	(.99)	(.25)
On holdings with 10 slaves or more, S_i^{ML}/L_i	−.31	−.22***
	(.26)	(.06)
Population density, L_i/A_i	.16***	.004***
	(.05)	(.0006)
F-test of equality (p-value)	.93	.94
R^2	.43	.07
Number of observations	37	2,014

Note: The dependent variable is the natural log of per capita income in 2000, ln y_i. Coefficients are reported with standard errors in parentheses. The ***, **, and * indicate significance at the 1%, 5%, and 10% levels. For the county-level estimates, the standard errors are clustered at the state level. In column 1 the unit of observation is a U.S. state, and in column 2 the unit of observation is a U.S. county. The slavery and population density variables are measured in 1860.

identify the more harmful effects of medium- or large-scale slavery relative to small-scale slavery. For this reason, I also examine county-level data, which provide finer variation that can help to better identify the differential effects of slavery. At the county level, the collinearity between S_i^S/L_i and S_i^{ML}/L_i is .65, which is lower than the correlation at the state level.

Column 2 reports county-level estimates. Again, the results do not provide a clear indication that large-scale slavery had a worse impact on economic development relative to other forms of slavery. The estimated coefficients for both S_i^S/L_i and S_i^{ML}/L_i are negative. Looking at the magnitudes, small-scale slavery is estimated to be slightly worse for economic development than large-scale slavery, although the difference between the two coefficients is not statistically different from zero. Looking at the statistical significance of the coefficients, it is only medium- and large-scale slavery that is statistically different from zero. Therefore, the results appear mixed and differ depending on whether one considers the magnitudes of the estimated coefficients or their statistical significance. As before, the evidence does not clearly indicate that large-scale plantation slavery was more detrimental for economic development than other forms of slavery.

Overall, the results of this section show that, either looking across New World economies, or across counties and states within the United States, there is a negative relationship between past slave use and current economic development. However, the results do not provide support for the view that large-scale plantation agriculture was particularly detrimental. All forms of slavery—smaller-scale nonplantation forms of slavery and large-scale plantation slavery—appear to have had similarly detrimental effects on economic development.

4.3 Testing Specific Channels of Causality

I now turn to the specific channels of causality underlying the negative relationship between slavery and economic development. Recall that Engerman and Sokoloff's argument is that plantation slavery resulted in increased economic inequality, which resulted in subsequent economic underdevelopment. This chain of causality is illustrated in Figure 4.9.

In the previous section, I simultaneously examined both parts of their argument, testing for a reduced-form relationship between slavery and economic development. In this section, using data on the distribution of land holdings from the 1860 U.S. Census, I examine Engerman and Sokoloff's argument that slavery was detrimental because of its effect on initial economic inequality. That is, I examine separately both hypothesized relationships from Figure 4.9: (1) that plantation slavery resulted in increased economic inequality, and (2) that inequality resulted in economic underdevelopment. The first hypothesis is examined in Section 4.3.1, and the second is examined in Section 4.3.2.

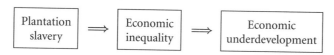

Figure 4.9 Testing the channels of causality in Engerman and Sokoloff's hypothesis.

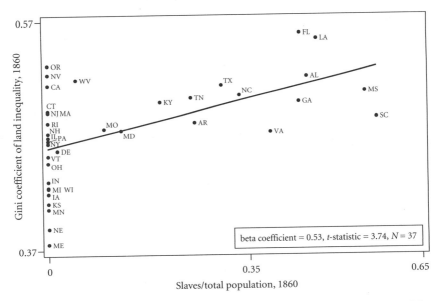

Figure 4.10 Bivariate plot showing the relationship between the proportion of the population in slavery in 1860 and the Gini coefficient of land inequality in 1860.

4.3.1 Testing Relationship 1: Plantation Slavery ⇒ Economic Inequality

The 1860 U.S. Census provides data on the number of farms, in each county and state, that are in each of the following seven size categories: (1) 9 acres or less, (2) 10 to 19 acres, (3) 20 to 49 acres, (4) 50 to 99 acres, (5) 100 to 499 acres, (6) 500 to 999 acres, and (7) 1,000 acres or more. I use this information to construct, for each county and state, the Gini coefficient of land inequality in 1860. Full details of the construction are provided in the appendix.

I examine whether the data support Engerman and Sokoloff's view that slavery resulted in increased economic inequality by first considering the unconditional relationship between the proportion of the population in slavery in 1860 and land inequality in 1860. Figure 4.10 shows this relationship across states. Consistent with their view, one observes a positive, statistically significant relationship between slavery and inequality.

The relationship is examined further in Table 4.6. Column 1 reports the bivariate relationship between slavery and inequality shown in Figure 4.10. In column 2, I control for population density in 1860, which, as before, is

Table 4.6 Slavery and land inequality within the United States

Dependent variable: Land inequality	State-level regressions		County-level regressions	
	(1)	(2)	(3)	(4)
Fraction slaves, S_i/L_i	.12***	.13***	.09***	.09***
	(.03)	(.03)	(.03)	(.03)
Population density, L_i/A_i		.02		−.0005***
		(.02)		(.0002)
R^2	.29	.32	.07	.07
Number of observations	37	37	1,933	1,933

Note: The dependent variable is the Gini coefficient of land inequality in 1860. Coefficients are reported with standard errors in parentheses. For the county-level estimates, the standard errors are clustered at the state level. The ***, **, and * indicate significance at the 1%, 5%, and 10% levels. In columns 1 and 2 the unit of observation is a U.S. state, and in columns 3 and 4 the unit of observation is a U.S. county.

meant to proxy for initial prosperity. Because it is unclear whether we expect to find a relationship between population density and land inequality, and if so, whether we expect it to be positive or negative,[12] I report estimates both without and with controls for initial population density. The even-numbered columns report estimates controlling for population density, while the odd-numbered columns do not control for population density. In column 2, the estimated coefficient for S_i/L_i is positive and highly significant, confirming the result from column 1.[13] Columns 3 and 4 provide the same estimates at the county level.[14] Both coefficients are positive and statistically significant, showing that at the county level we also observe a positive relationship between slavery and land inequality in 1860. The estimated magnitudes are also very large. The calculated beta coefficient for the state-level estimates is .59 (column 2), while the beta coefficient for the county-level estimates is .26 (column 4).

These results are consistent with the first relationship in Figure 4.9: that slavery caused increased economic inequality. In 1860, the states and counties with the largest proportion of slaves in their population also had the most unequal distribution of land holdings.

Within the United States, economic inequality is very persistent even in the long run. This can be seen from Figure 4.11, which shows the cross-state relationship between the Gini coefficient of land inequality in 1860 and the

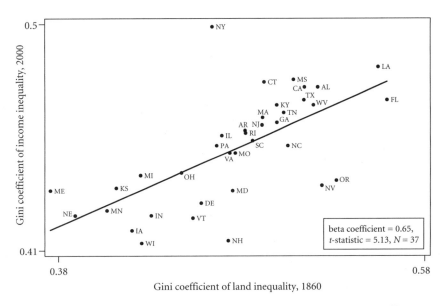

Figure 4.11   Bivariate plot showing the relationship between the Gini coefficient of land inequality in 1860 and the Gini coefficient of income inequality in 2000.

Gini coefficient of income inequality in 2000. The relationship between the two measures of inequality is remarkably strong.

Because of the persistence of economic inequality, there is a strong relationship between past slave use and current economic inequality. This is shown in Figure 4.12, where a clear positive relationship between slavery in 1860 and current income inequality is apparent. Although not reported here, this result is robust to controlling for initial population density. This suggests that within the United States, not only did slavery result in economic underdevelopment (as was shown in Section 4.2.3), but it also resulted in increased economic inequality.[15]

4.3.2 Testing Relationship 2: Economic Inequality ⇒ Economic Underdevelopment

The second part of Engerman and Sokoloff's hypothesis is that the economic inequality that arose because of slavery resulted in economic underdevelopment. They argue that inequality resulted in domestic institutions that advantaged the elites, rather than providing the foundation necessary for sustained economic growth. In columns 1 and 4 of Table 4.7, I

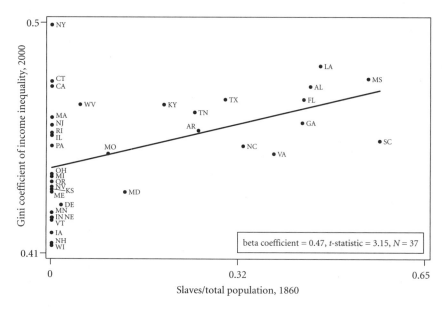

Figure 4.12 Bivariate plot showing the relationship between the proportion of the population in slavery in 1860 and the Gini coefficient of income inequality in 2000.

empirically test for a relationship between initial economic inequality and subsequent economic development. The columns report the estimated relationship between the Gini coefficient of land inequality in 1860 and income in 2000, controlling for initial population density. Column 1 reports estimates at the state level, while column 4 reports estimates at the county level. In both specifications, the estimated coefficient for land inequality is negative, but statistically insignificant. Although the sign of the coefficient is consistent with inequality adversely affecting development, its insignificance shows that statistically its estimated effect is not different from zero.

There is also a second testable prediction that follows from Sokoloff and Engerman's argument. According to their hypothesis, the estimated relationship between slavery and economic development (which was reported in Table 4.4) should be accounted for by the relationship between initial inequality and economic development. The remaining columns in Table 4.7 test this prediction of their theory. Columns 2 and 5 revisit the estimated relationship between slavery and economic development previously reported in Table 4.4. Column 2 simply reproduces the 1860 state-level estimates, and column 5 reestimates the county-level regressions, using a

Table 4.7 Slavery, land inequality, and income within the United States

Dependent variable: ln y_i	State-level regressions			County-level regressions		
	(1)	(2)	(3)	(4)	(5)	(6)
Gini coefficient of land inequality	−.46 (.51)		.45 (.55)	−.11 (.11)		.07 (.11)
Fraction slaves, S_i/L_i		−.33*** (.11)	−.39*** (.13)		−.23*** (.07)	−.24*** (.07)
Population density: L_i/A_i	.21*** (.06)	.16*** (.05)	.15*** (.05)	.004*** (.0006)	.004*** (.0006)	.004*** (.0006)
R^2	.30	.43	.45	.03	.08	.08
Number of observations	37	37	37	1,933	1,933	1,933

Note: The dependent variable is the natural log of per capita income in 2000, ln y_i. Coefficients are reported with standard errors in parentheses. For the county-level estimates the standard errors are clustered at the state level. The ***, **, and * indicate significance at the 1%, 5%, and 10% levels. In columns 1–3 the unit of observation is a U.S. state, and in columns 4–6 the unit of observation is a U.S. county.

slightly smaller sample of counties for which land inequality data are also available. Because farm-size data are missing for the counties of Nebraska and Nevada, they are not included in the sample. This results in a reduction in the sample size from 2,014 to 1,933 counties. As shown, one still finds a negative relationship between slavery and income among this smaller sample of counties.

Columns 3 and 6 test whether the estimated relationships between slavery and income in columns 2 and 5 can be accounted for by the relationship between land inequality and income. This is done by including both the Gini coefficient of land inequality and the fraction of slaves in the population as explanatory variables in the estimating equation. If slavery affects income only through its effect on initial economic inequality, then controlling for inequality should significantly reduce the estimated relationship between slavery and income. The results show that this is not the case. At both the state and the county levels, the inclusion of the land inequality measure actually increases the magnitude of the estimated coefficient for S_i/L_i, rather than decreasing it. At the state level, the estimated effect increases from −.33 to −.39, and at the county level, the effect increases from −.23 to −.24. The results, therefore, do not support Engerman and

Sokoloff's argument that slavery adversely affected economic development because it resulted in initial inequality.

The results in Table 4.7 show clearly that land inequality in 1860 is uncorrelated with income in 2000. These results are particularly interesting given that others have found evidence that early land inequality had adverse effects on outcomes measured in the early 1900s. Ramcharan (2006) finds a negative relationship between early land inequality and per capita education expenditures in 1930, and Acemoglu et al. (2008) document a negative relationship between land inequality in 1860 and school enrollment in 1950. The estimates from Table 4.7 suggest that the effects documented by Ramcharan (2006) and Acemoglu et al. (2008) died out by the end of the twentieth century. This is not surprising given that beginning in the 1940s, average incomes in the southern states began to catch up to the northern states (Wright 1987) and given the fact that the black-white education gap and the black-white wage gap have both decreased significantly since 1940 (Smith and Welch 1989).

The results of Section 4.3 are best summarized by returning to Figure 4.9. There is evidence of the first relationship in the diagram. Slavery in 1860 is associated with greater land inequality in the same year. This was shown in Table 4.6. Further, as a result of the persistence of economic inequality, there is also a strong positive relationship between slavery and current income inequality. However, I do not find evidence for the second relationship in Figure 4.9. The results of Table 4.7 show that land inequality in 1860 is not correlated with income in 2000. They also show that the positive relationship between slavery and inequality is unable to explain the negative relationship between slavery and economic development. Instead, the data suggest that slavery had two distinct impacts. First, slavery resulted in lower long-term economic growth, and second, slavery resulted in greater initial inequality, which has persisted until today. These two effects appear to be unrelated. Contrary to Engerman and Sokoloff's hypothesis, it was not because slavery increased initial economic inequality that it was detrimental for economic development.

Although these results take us a step toward better understanding the long-term impacts of slavery in the Americas, an important question remains. If the relationship between past slave use and current income is not through the channel hypothesized by Engerman and Sokoloff, then what explains the relationship? One possibility, which is highlighted by Acemoglu et al.'s (2008) Chapter 5 in this book, is that what may have been important for long-term economic development was political inequality, not economic inequality. The authors, looking within Cundinamarca, Colombia, show that economic and political inequality are not always strongly correlated, and that they can diverge in significant ways. When examining the relationship between inequality and economic development, they find that one reaches very different conclusions depending on whether one looks at economic inequality or political inequality. It is possible that the results reported here would be very different if political inequality, rather than economic inequality, was examined.

A second possibility follows from Wright (2006), who argues that slavery's long-term effects are best understood by comparing its property rights institutions to those that arise from a production system based on free labor. Because slavery provided slave owners with property rights over labor, which allowed them to relocate labor as necessary, the slave states did not have a strong incentive to provide the public goods and institutions necessary to attract migrants (Wright 2006, 70–77). This channel is similar to Engerman and Sokoloff's, but is different in a subtle yet important way. It is not economic inequality that caused the subsequent development of poor institutions. Rather, it was slavery itself. Through the purchase and sale of slaves, involuntary migration could substitute for voluntary migration, and therefore, the growth-promoting domestic institutions needed to attract free labor were not developed.

Conclusion   This chapter has examined the core predictions that arise from a series of influential papers written by Stanley Engerman and Kenneth Sokoloff (e.g., Engerman and Sokoloff 1997, 2002, 2006; Sokoloff and Engerman 2000). Examining the relationship between past slave use and current economic performance, I find evidence consistent with their general hypothesis that slavery was detrimental for economic development. Looking either across countries within the Americas or across states and counties within the United States, one finds a strong significant negative relationship between past slave use and current income. However, contrary to the focus of their argument, the data do not show that large-scale plantation slavery was more harmful for growth than other forms of slavery. Instead, the evidence suggests that all forms of slavery were detrimental, and that large-scale slavery, if anything, was less deterimental than small-scale slavery.

Turning to their hypothesized channels of causality, I examined whether the relationship between slavery and income can be explained by slavery's effect on initial economic inequality. Looking within the United States, I found that, consistent with their hypothesis, slave use in 1860 is positively correlated with land inequality in the same year. Because of the persistence of inequality over time, past slave use is also positively correlated with current income inequality. Thus, the data suggest that slavery had a long-term effect on inequality as well as income. However, after examining the relationship between slave use, initial inequality, and current income, I found that slavery's effect on initial economic inequality is unable to account for any of the estimated relationship between slavery and economic development. Contrary to their hypothesis, slavery's adverse effect on economic development does not appear to be because of its effect on initial economic inequality.

DATA APPENDIX

Data on country-level per capita GDP in 2000 are from World Bank (2006). For countries with missing income data, converted income data from the Penn World Tables or Maddison (2003) were used when possible. For both series, data are measured in PPP-adjusted dollars. State- and county-level per capita income in 2000 are from the BEA's *Regional Economic Accounts*. The county-level data are from Table CA1-3 located at www.bea.gov/regional/reis/, and the state-level data are from Table SA1-3 at www.bea.gov/regional/spi/.

Population density is measured in hundreds of persons per square kilometer in the cross-country regressions, and hundreds of persons per square mile in the county- and state-level regressions. Country-level land-area data are from Harvard's *Center for International Development's Geography Database* located at www.cid.harvard.edu/ciddata/geographydata.htm. Land-area data for U.S. states and counties are from the U.S. Bureau of the Census (2006).

The country-level slave and free populations data used in Section 4.2.1 are from a variety of sources. All data are from 1750 or the closest available year. Figures for Barbados, Saint Christopher and Nevis, Antigua and Barbuda, Jamaica, Cuba, Dominica, Saint Lucia, Saint Vincent and the Grenadines, Trinidad and Tobago, Grenada, Guyana, Belize, Bahamas, Haiti, Suriname, Netherlands Antilles, and the Dominican Republic are from Engerman and Higman (1997). All figures are for 1750. Data for Canada are from the 1784 Census of Canada, http://www.statcan.ca/

english/freepub/98-187-XIE/geo1.htm. Data for the United States are for 1774 and are from Jones (1980). Brazilian data are for 1798 and are taken from Simonsen (1978, 54–57). Chilean data are from 1777 and are from Sater (1974). The figures for Colombia are for 1778 and are from McFarlane (1993, 353). Data for Ecuador are for 1800 and are from Restrepo (1827, 14). Mexican data are for 1742 and are from Aguirre Beltran (1940, 220–23). Peruvian data are for 1795 and are from Rugendas (1940). Data from Paraguay are for 1782 and are from Acevedo (1996, 200–206). Venezuelan data are for 1800 and are taken from Figueroa (1983, 58). Data for Uruguay are for the city of Montevideo in 1800 and are taken from Williams (1987). Data for Argentina are for the city of Buenos Aires in 1810 and are from Rout (1976, 91, 95) and Johnson, Socolow, and Seibert (1980).

Slave and free populations data for counties and states within the United States are from the 1790 to 1860 decennial censuses of the United States. The data have been digitized and can be accessed at http://fisher.lib.virginia.edu/collections/stats/histcensus/. The data on the size of slave holdings and the size of farms in 1860 are also from this source.

The Gini coefficient of income inequality for each state in 2000 is from the U.S. Census Bureau. I approximate income inequality in 2000 using inequality in 1999, which is the closest year for which the inequality measures are available. The data were accessed from Table S4 available at www.census.gov/hhes/www/income/histinc/state/state4.html.

The Gini coefficient of land inequality is calculated using information about the size of each farm in the 1860 U.S. Census. The number of farms in each county is available for the following farm sizes: (1) 9 acres or less, (2) 10 to 19 acres, (3) 20 to 49 acres, (4) 50 to 99 acres, (5) 100 to 499 acres, (6) 500 to 999 acres, and (7) 1,000 acres or more. Because for each category I do not know the mean farm size, I use the median size of the category. For the category 1,000 acres or more, I use 1,000 acres. The Gini coefficients are calculated using the Stata program *ineqdec0* written by Stephen P. Jenkins. The formula for calculating the Gini coefficient is

$$1 + (1/n) - \frac{2 \sum_{i=1}^{n} (n - i + 1) a_i}{n \sum_{i=1}^{n} a_i},$$

where n is the number of farms, a_i is farm size, and i denotes the rank, where farms are ranked in ascending order of a_i.

ACKNOWLEDGMENTS

I thank Daron Acemoglu, Elhanan Helpman, Jim Robinson, Daniel Trefler, and seminar participants at the Institutions, Organizations, and Growth Program meeting of the Canadian Institute for Advanced Research (CIFAR) for valuable comments. I also thank Maira Avila, Yan Carrière-Swallow, and Wendy Bo Wu for excellent research assistance.

NOTES

1. I do not examine the first component of their argument, that natural resources, such as soils suitable for plantation agriculture, were an important determinant of slave use in the colonies. The link between geography and slavery, across counties within the United States, has been examined by Lagerlöf (2005). He finds temperature, elevation, and precipitation to all be important determinants of slave use.

2. See Engerman and Sokoloff (2005a, 4) or Sokoloff and Engerman (2000, 221–22) for details.

3. See Acemoglu, Johnson, and Robinson (2002) for evidence showing that population density is highly correlated with per capita income.

4. For more on this point see the discussions in Wright (2006, 29–30) and in Sokoloff and Engerman (2000, 220).

5. Per capita GDP is measured in purchasing power parity (PPP) adjusted dollars. By this measure the per capita GDP of the United States in 2000 was $33,970.

6. The category of nonplantation slaves can be further disaggregated between urban slaves and those working in industry. The results are qualitatively identical to what is reported here if this distinction is also made. As well, one could alter the category of plantation slaves to not include slaves that worked in "other forms of agriculture." Again, the results are similar if this alternative classification is chosen.

7. Higman (1984, 100–104) provides a detailed discussion of the difficulty of identifying a slave holding in the data. Slave holdings are identified from each registration return of the slave censuses. Slave owners who owned multiple plantations may have filled out a different form for each location. Also, if multiple owners owned slaves at one plantation, then these slaves may be identified as being in one slave holding.

8. The conclusions reported here do not depend on the assumptions made in creating the categories. Alternatively, one could choose different cutoffs for the slave-holding categories, or one could choose to create two categories rather than three, and the same conclusions would be obtained.

9. In this regression, the sample size is reduced from 12 to 11 countries because slave-holding size data are unavailable for the Bahamas.

10. Similarly, in 1800 there are 18 observations even though only 16 states had joined the Union by this time. This is because of West Virginia and Maine.

11. Note that because of these same data limitations, the definition of "small scale" is slightly different than it was in Section 4.2.2. Here the definition of "small scale" is 9 slaves or less, while the definition in Section 4.2.2 was 10 slaves or less.

12. The empirical evidence of the relationship between income and inequality across countries in the twentieth century is very mixed. Some studies find a positive relationship (e.g., Forbes 2000), others find a negative relationship (e.g., Easterly 2007), and others find both (e.g., Barro 2000).

13. As before, one can disaggregate slaves into those held on small-scale holdings and those held on medium- or large-scale holdings. Doing this one finds that the relationship between slavery and land inequality is not driven by large-scale slavery, but by small-scale slavery. Echoing the findings earlier in the chapter, these results show that although slavery may have resulted in economic inequality, it is not a result of the particularly detrimental effects of large-scale plantation slavery.

14. Because farm-size data are unavailable at the county level for Nebraska and Nevada, there are now only 1,933 observations in the county-level regressions.

15. A related finding has been documented by Lagerlöf (2005), who shows that across U.S. counties, the current income differential between blacks and whites is positively correlated with the proportion of the population in slavery in 1850.

REFERENCES

Acemoglu, Daron, María Angélica Bautista, Pablo Querubín, and James A. Robinson. 2008. "Economic and Political Inequality in Development: The Case of Cundinamarca, Colombia." Chapter 5, this volume.

Acemoglu, Daron, Simon Johnson, and James A. Robinson. 2002. "Reversal of Fortune: Geography and Institutions in the Making of the Modern World Income Distribution." *Quarterly Journal of Economics* 117:1231–94.

Acevedo, Edberto Oscar. 1996. *La Intendencia del Paraguay en el Virreinato del Río de la Plata.* Buenos Aires: Ediciones Ciudad Argentina.

Aguirre Beltran, Gonzalo. 1940. *La Poblacion Negra de Mexico, 1519–1810.* Mexico City: Fondo de Cultura Economica.

Barro, Robert J. 2000. "Inequality and Growth in a Panel of Countries." *Journal of Economic Growth* 5.

Easterly, William. 2007. "Inequality Does Cause Underdevelopment." *Journal of Development Economics* 84:755–76.

Engerman, Stanley L., and B. W. Higman. 1997. "The Demographic Structure of the Caribbean Slave Societies in the Eighteenth and Nineteenth Centuries." In *General History of the Caribbean, Volume III: The Slave Societies of the Caribbean*, ed. Franklin W. Knight, 45–104. London: UNESCO Publishing.

Engerman, Stanley L., and Kenneth L. Sokoloff. 1997. "Factor Endowments, Institutions, and Differential Paths of Growth among New World Economies: A View from Economic Historians of the United States." In *How Latin America Fell Behind*, ed. Stephen Haber, 260–304. Palo Alto, CA: Stanford University Press.

———. 2002. "Factor Endowments, Inequality, and Paths of Development among New World Economies." Working paper 9259, National Bureau of Economic Research.

———. 2005a. "Colonialism, Inequality, and Long-Run Paths of Development." Working paper 11057, National Bureau of Economic Research.

———. 2005b. "The Evolution of Suffrage Institutions in the Americas." *Journal of Economic History* 65:891–921.

———. 2006. "The Persistence of Poverty in the Americas: The Role of Institutions." In *Poverty Traps*, eds. Samuel Bowles, Steven N. Durlauf, and Karla Hoff, 43–78. Princeton, NJ: Princeton University Press.

Figueroa, Federico Brito. 1983. *La estructura económica de Venezuela colonial.* Universidad Central de Venezuela, Ediciones de la Biblioteca, Caracas.

Forbes, Kristin. 2000. "A Reassessment of the Relationship between Inequality and Growth." *American Economic Review* 90:869–87.

Higman, Barry W. 1984. *Slave Populations of the British Caribbean, 1807–1834.* Baltimore, MD: The Johns Hopkins University Press.

Johnson, Lyman L., Susan Migden Socolow, and Sibila Seibert. 1980. "Población y Espacio en el Buenos Aires del Siglo XVIII." *Desarrollo Económico* 20:329–49.

Jones, Alice Hanson. 1980. *Wealth of a Nation to Be.* New York: Columbia University Press.

Lagerlöf, Nils-Petter. 2005. "Geography, Institutions and Growth: The United States as a Microcosm." Mimeo, York University.

Maddison, Angus. 2003. *The World Economy: Historical Statistics.* Paris: Organisation for Economic Co-operation and Development.

Mariscal, Elisa, and Kenneth L. Sokoloff. 2000. "Schooling, Suffrage, and the Persistence of Inequality in the Americas, 1800–1945." In *Political Institutions and Economic Growth in Latin America: Essays in Policy, History, and Political Economy*, ed. Stephen Haber, 159–218. Palo Alto: Hoover Institution Press.

McFarlane, Anthony. 1993. *Colombia before Independence: Economy, Society, and Politics under Bourbon Rule.* New York: Cambridge University Press.

Mitchener, Kris James, and Ian W. McLean. 2003. "The Productivity of U.S. States since 1880." *Journal of Economic Growth* 8:73–114.

Ramcharan, Rodney. 2006. "Inequality and Redistribution: Evidence from U.S. Counties and States, 1890–1930." Mimeo, International Monetary Fund.

Restrepo, José Manuel. 1827. *Historia de la Revolución de la República de Colombia en la América meridional,* vol I. Paris: Bensanzon.

Rout, Leslie B. Jr. 1976. *The African Experience in Spanish America.* London: Cambridge University Press.

Rugendas, João Maurício. 1940. *Viagem Pitoresca através do Brasil.* São Paulo: Livraria Martins.

Sater, William F. 1974. "The Black Experience in Chile." In *Slavery and Race Relations in Latin America,* ed. Robert Brent Toplin, 13–50. Westport: Greenwood Press.

Simonsen, Roberto Cochrane. 1978. *Historia Economica do Brasil: 1500/1820.* Sao Paulo: Companhia Editora Nacional.

Smith, James P., and Finis R. Welch. 1989. "Black Economic Progress after Myrdal." *Journal of Economic Literature* 27:519–64.

Sokoloff, Kenneth L., and Stanley L. Engerman. 2000. "History Lessons: Institutions, Factor Endowments, and Paths of Development in the New World." *Journal of Economic Perspectives* 14:217–32.

Sokoloff, Kenneth L., and Eric M. Zolt. 2007. "Inequality and the Evolution of Institutions of Taxation: Evidence from the Economic History of the Americas." In *The Decline of Latin American Economies: Growth, Institutions, and Crises,* eds. Sebastian Edwards, Gerardo Esquivel, and Graciela Márquez, 83–136. Chicago: University of Chicago Press.

U.S. Bureau of the Census. 2006. *County and City Data Book, 2000.* Washington, DC: U.S. Department of Commerce, Bureau of the Census.

Williams, John Hoyt. 1987. "Observations on Blacks and Bondage in Uruguay, 1800–1836." *The Americas* 43:411–27.

World Bank. 2006. *World Development Indicators.* Washington, D.C.: World Bank.

Wright, Gavin. 1987. "The Economic Revolution in the American South." *Journal of Economic Perspectives* 1:161–78.

———. 2006. *Slavery and American Economic Development.* Baton Rouge, LA: Louisiana State University Press.

— 5 —

Economic and Political Inequality in Development: The Case of Cundinamarca, Colombia

DARON ACEMOGLU, MARÍA ANGÉLICA BAUTISTA,
PABLO QUERUBÍN, AND JAMES A. ROBINSON

5.1 Introduction

A large and growing academic literature argues that economic inequality has adverse effects on economic development, for example, because of the effects of imperfect capital markets, through demand externalities, or because of political economy factors.[1] A recently emerging consensus, exemplified by Engerman and Sokoloff (1997), maintains that the divergent economic paths of North and South America are a consequence of their different levels of economic inequality. This consensus asserts that the main difference between the two parts of the American continent was in economic inequality that emerged during the colonial period and persisted to the nineteenth century, and links the current economic difficulties of South American nations to their greater inequality.

A major empirical challenge for this view, however, is that economic inequality is also correlated with many other potential determinants of long-run development. Most important for the focus of this chapter, economic inequality may be associated with political inequality, in the sense that collective choices reflect the wishes and interests of a small subsection of the society. Theoretically, we may expect economic inequality to lead to political inequality (as the economically powerful become politically more influential), but the reverse link is at least as important, as those with political power will be able to amass greater economic wealth. To illustrate this point, note that there is a negative relationship between land inequality and development not only when we compare the United States to South America, but also across the U.S. states. For example, Figure 5.1 shows a plot

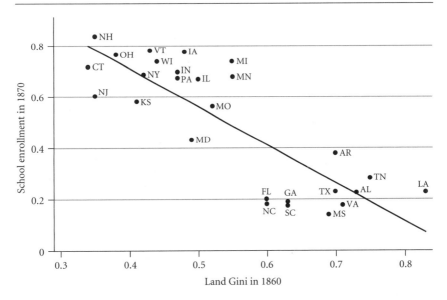

Figure 5.1 Land Gini and school enrollment in the United States (1870). The land
Ginis for the U.S. south and north were constructed from the complete Gallman–
Parker and Bateman–Foust samples, respectively, from the microdata of the 1860
U.S. census. School enrollment constructed from the 1870 census as number of
persons attending school over population between 5 and 18 years old.

of the land Gini in each U.S. state in 1860 against total school enrollment
in 1870 (see below for data details). There is a clear negative relationship,
with the more unequal southern states having lower enrollments. Figure 5.2
plots the relationship between the land Gini in 1860 against the enrollment rate in 1950 and shows that this relationship persists to the twentieth century.[2] Do these correlations establish that there is an adverse effect
of economic inequality on schooling? While this is a possibility, one also
has to bear in mind that the U.S. states with greater economic inequality
are also those with greater political inequality. For example, the southern
states were not only more unequal economically, but exhibited a very high
degree of political inequality, with a large fraction of the population disenfranchised and large planters controlling politics directly or indirectly.
Therefore, one can imagine that it might be the relationship between political inequality and economic outcomes that underlies the patterns shown
in Figures 5.1 and 5.2. Political inequality may retard development because

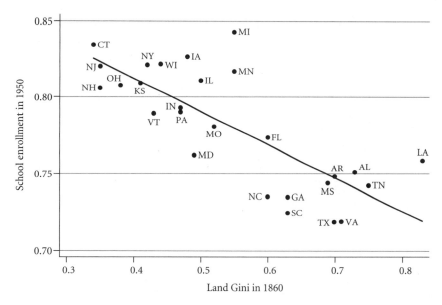

Figure 5.2 Land Gini and school enrollment in the United States (1950). The land Ginis for the U.S. south and north were constructed from the complete Gallman–Parker and Bateman–Foust samples, respectively, from the microdata of the 1860 U.S. census. School enrollment constructed from the 1950 census as number of persons between 5 and 18 years old attending school over total population between 5 and 18 years old.

elites who control politics may create rents for themselves, impede entry (Acemoglu 2008), and have little interest in the provision of public goods, including schooling (Bates 1981). Political inequality will also tend to be associated with the absence of political competition and accountability, two factors that help to guarantee that political systems generate desirable outcomes.[3]

Is it economic or political inequality that matters for long-run development? And how does inequality in general interact with the institutional structure of a society in shaping its development path? These questions are made interesting in part because even though it is typically asserted that economic and political inequality go hand in hand, particularly in Latin America and across the U.S. states, this is not necessarily so everywhere else in the world, or even, as we show, in Colombia. For example, in much of sub-Saharan Africa since independence, measured economic inequality has been quite low, but political inequality has been severe with rule by long-running autocrats or small cliques, most clearly in the Sudan, Angola, the Congo, Malawi, Côte d'Ivoire, Togo, and the Cameroon. This combination led to disastrous development outcomes. In contrast to the African cases, development in South Korea and Taiwan seems to have taken place precisely in the context of economic equality, but under dictatorial regimes, with political power concentrated in the hands of a small elite. Finally, there are examples of rapid development with high economic inequality but relative political equality, such as Mauritius in the 1970s and 1980s. It is therefore important to attempt to "unbundle" the separate effects of economic and political inequality on long-run development both to gain a better understanding of the causes of the process of economic development and to evaluate the newly emerging conventional wisdom about the sources of underdevelopment in Latin America.

Despite the importance of the aforementioned questions, they have not been tackled by the existing literature. The early cross-country work finds a negative correlation between economic inequality and growth (for example, Alesina and Rodrik 1994; Persson and Tabellini 1994; Perotti 1996), but as noted above, this work does not distinguish between political and economic inequality, which are often highly correlated. Moreover, even the negative correlation between economic inequality and subsequent growth appears to be nonrobust (Barro 2000; Forbes 2000; Banerjee and Duflo 2003).[4] There is also microevidence on the relationship between economic inequality and development, for example Benjamin, Brandt, and Giles (2006). The issue of the effects of political inequality has not been systematically addressed, however, except to the extent that it can be associated with the absence of democracy. While some theoretical papers suggest that democracy ought to be good for development (Acemoglu and Robinson 2000b; Lizzeri and Persico 2004), others argue the relationship is ambiguous (Acemoglu 2008) and the empirical literature mostly finds no effects (Barro 1997), though Bond et al. (2005) and Persson and Tabellini (2006) find a positive effect of the cumulative democratic history of a country on economic growth.

In this chapter we investigate the influence of economic and political inequality on long-run development using microdata from the state of Cundinamarca in Colombia. Our focus is the critical period of development in the late nineteenth century when Latin American economies began to grow and integrate with the world market. Cundinamarca provides a natural setting for such an investigation since it was the center of the largest pre-Columbian civilization in Colombia, the Muiscas. It also contains Bogotá, the capital of both colonial and independent Colombia. In many ways, Cundinamarca was at the heart of the Spanish colonial system. Our investigation is made possible by unique data on nineteenth-century land ownership. In 1879 and 1890, the state of Cundinamarca undertook comprehensive land censuses (*catastros*), which recorded the identity of each landowner in the state, the name of their farm, and the value of their land. We use these data to construct Gini coefficients for the distribution of landed wealth. The *land Gini* is both a natural and easy-to-interpret measure of economic inequality, and it is used commonly in the literature. Moreover, by focusing on land inequality, we can capture the major source of economic inequality in South America emphasized by Engerman and Sokoloff (1997).[5]

To measure political inequality, we collected data on the identity of all of the mayors of the municipalities of Cundinamarca for the period 1875 to 1895. Specifically, we construct an index of *political concentration*, which measures the extent to which political officeholding was monopolized by individuals. Throughout this period, the right to vote in Cundinamarca was restricted by property and literacy requirements. Nevertheless, the distribution of political power varied a lot across different municipalities of Cundinamarca, with some having frequent turnover of mayors, while in others the same family or small group of families kept power for extended periods.[6]

Finally, our data also enable us to investigate another interesting, related question, the developmental implications of the overlap between economic and political power. In particular, having both political and economic power concentrated in the hands of a small group of individuals creates both benefits (since the politicians are willing to choose policies that encourage investment as this increases the value of their own assets) as well as costs (since a greater degree of elite control of politics and the economy can lead to the existence of a landed oligarchy, which may be costly for development).[7] We investigate these questions by constructing an index of *overlap*, which measures the extent to which large landowners and politicians were the same people.[8]

The main results of the chapter are as follows. First, by way of comparison, using microdata from the 1860 U.S. census, we show that while the distribution of landed wealth in Cundinamarca was considerably more

unequal than in northern U.S. states, it was less unequal than in the U.S.
South.[9] More important and somewhat surprising, we find a negative association between land inequality (land Gini) and political concentration
across municipalities in Cundinamarca. Though this is inconsistent with
the stylized picture that, at least in Latin America, political and economic
inequality often covary, it is actually consistent with the historical literature on Colombia, which stresses that politics was a career open to people
of many backgrounds (see Safford 1972, 1974; Deas 1993; and Uribe-Uran
2000).

Our second set of results is rather surprising. When we look at current
outcomes, we find that land Gini (economic inequality) is *positively* associated with good outcomes. For example, areas that were more unequal in the
late nineteenth century have higher levels of secondary and primary school
enrollment, lower poverty, and higher urbanization. Figure 5.3 shows the
relationship between the land Gini at the end of the nineteenth century
and contemporary secondary school enrollment in Cundinamarca. In contrast to Figures 5.1 and 5.2 for the United States, there is now a positive
relationship. A natural concern is that this positive relationship may reflect the effect of some omitted factors, such as higher land quality in places
with higher inequality. We attempt to deal with potential sources of omitted variable bias by controlling for a rich set of geographic characteristics
and current land inequality. Overall, our results suggest that the relationship shown in Figure 5.3 is relatively robust. We also find similar results
when we look at outcomes at intermediate dates, such as data from the 1937
census. The estimated effects are also large economically. For instance, the
historical land Gini, on its own, accounts for about 30% of the variation in
the contemporary outcome variables.

Even though this correlation does not establish a causal effect, it is difficult to rationalize with theories that argue for a direct causal link from
economic inequality to long-run economic development, such as that in
Engerman and Sokoloff (1997). This is particularly challenging to the view
that greater land inequality will have negative effects on economic development by depressing education, for example, as articulated by Galor
and Zeira (1993), Benabou (2000), Engerman and Sokoloff (1997), Galor,
Moav, and Vollrath (2006), and Ramcharan (2006). Our evidence shows
that land inequality is uncorrelated with literacy in 1937 and has a positive
effect on primary and secondary school enrollment in 1993.

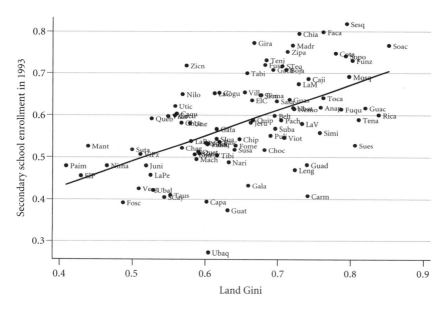

Figure 5.3 Land Gini and secondary school enrollment in Cundinamarca. Land Gini is the average Gini coefficient for 1879 and 1890 constructed from the *catastros*. Secondary school enrollment was constructed from the 1993 census as fraction of children between 12 and 18 years old attending school.

When we turn to political variables, however, we find a fairly robust negative relationship between political concentration (our measure of political inequality) and good economic outcomes. Figure 5.4, for example, shows a significant negative relationship between our index of political concentration at the end of the nineteenth century and secondary school enrollment today. In contrast, we find no robust effect of the overlap measure discussed above on either long-term or medium-term outcomes.

Though difficult to reconcile with the conventional wisdom, our findings are consistent with other strands of research, including both the historical literature on Colombia and Latin America and work by Bates (1981) on the political economy of Africa. Bates (1981) documented that economic policy in post-independence Kenya was more conducive to better economic outcomes than in Ghana because of the balance of power between politicians and economic elites in the former country. In Ghana, smallholders growing cocoa could not solve the collective action problem and were unable to

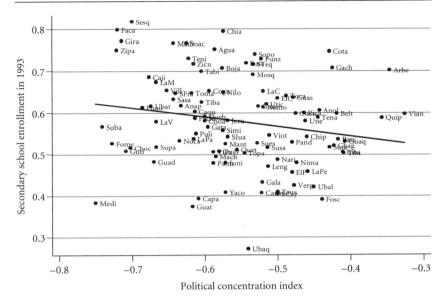

Figure 5.4 Political concentration and secondary school enrollment in
Cundinamarca. Political concentration index defined as the negative of the
number of different individuals in power between 1875 and 1895, over the number
of mayor appointments for which data is available. Secondary school enrollment
was constructed from the 1993 census as fraction of children between 12 and 18
years old attending school.

restrain politicians from engaging in costly clientelism and choosing highly
distortionary economic policies. In Kenya, mostly as a legacy of white settlement in the highlands, farm sizes were larger and an agricultural elite was
able to organize and check the power of the politicians in Nairobi. In consequence, better policies and economic outcomes resulted. Therefore, Bates's
comparison of Ghana versus Kenya provides an example in which greater
(land) inequality led to better economic outcomes.[10]

In this light, a possible interpretation for our results is that powerful
and rich landowners may be creating checks against the most rapacious
tendencies of politicians. Consequently, in the municipalities with major
landowners, distortionary policies that could be pursued by politicians
were limited, and this led to better economic outcomes. This interpretation
is also consistent with the negative association between political inequal-

ity and economic outcomes (as well as the negative relationship between economic and political inequality we find in Cundinamarca). Though plausible, this explanation is in stark contrast both to the conventional wisdom about the source of underdevelopment in Latin America and to the insights of many economic models emphasizing the negative effects of inequality by restricting access to credit or through political economy mechanisms. As a check on the plausibility of our interpretation, we use the microdata from the Cundinamarca land censuses to construct a separate *overall land Gini*. While the standard measure of the land Gini captures inequality among landowners, the overall land Gini measures inequality in the entire population, assigning zero land holdings to families without any land. According to Bates's hypothesis, it should be land inequality among landowners—that is, the standard land Gini—that should have a positive effect, while overall land Gini should have no impact on economic outcomes. According to the Engerman–Sokoloff-type hypotheses and to economic models emphasizing the adverse effects of inequality, both of these measures should have a negative effect on economic development. We find that when both measures are included together, it is inequality among landowners—the standard land Gini—that has a positive effect on subsequent economic outcomes, while the overall land Gini has a small negative and insignificant impact.

One question raised by our interpretation is the source of the difference between the results we find in Cundinamarca and the patterns across U.S. states in the nineteenth century, where land inequality appears to be strongly negatively correlated with economic outcomes. We believe that the answer to this question may lie in the differences in the level of political development between the United States and Colombia. Like twentieth-century Africa, Colombia in both the nineteenth and twentieth centuries can be characterized, in the terminology of Acemoglu, Robinson, and Verdier (2004), as "weakly institutionalized" in the sense that political institutions placed few constraints on what actions politicians could take. Bates's insight was that in such circumstances, land inequality may be associated with better outcomes because, at least when landed elites are distinct from politicians, such elites can check the power of politicians. In the central areas of Cundinamarca, where landed elites were more consolidated and land inequality higher, they were able to constrain politicians. In consequence political concentration was lower. In more peripheral areas of the department, it was easier for politicians to consolidate their hold on power since there was no strong economic elite to counterbalance their power. When unchecked, politicians were less accountable and, as we show, were able to accumulate large amounts of land and wealth. The resulting political economy also appears to have involved a severe lack of public goods provision. In contrast, the relationship between inequality and economic outcomes appears to be different in strongly institutionalized environments such as the United States. Here, political institutions place certain constraints on politicians so that having a strong, landed elite is not necessary as a check against politicians and does not necessarily create a tendency for better outcomes. Rather, and possibly consistent with the U.S. evidence, in such environments, greater inequality may have negative economic or political consequences (for example, in the extreme, via "political capture," as in Acemoglu and Robinson [2006b] or Acemoglu, Ticchi, and Vindigni [2006]). This description is broadly consistent with the situation in the U.S. South. Landed elites in the southern United States, both in the pre- and post-bellum periods, tended to have more say in politics and were able to use their power strategically to generate rents for themselves, by creating a low-wage, low-skill labor market and by underinvesting in education so as to make the plantation labor force easier to control and less mobile (Wright 1986; Margo 1990).

Therefore, the overall pattern that emerges from this interpretation is one that can be summarized schematically as follows:[11]

	High economic inequality	Low economic inequality
Weakly institutionalized policies	Better property rights *Examples:* Kenya, Central Cundinamarca	Worse property rights *Examples:* Ghana, Peripheral Cundinamarca
Strongly institutionalized policies	Captured politics *Example:* Southern United States	Competitive politics *Example:* Northern United States

Our final set of results also provides support for the interpretation presented above. We exploit the microdata on land holdings and the identity of politicians to investigate the mechanism via which political inequality might be affecting economic outcomes. In particular, we use linear and quantile regressions to document that those with political power are able to increase the value of their land holdings much more rapidly than others. In particular, an individual who remains a politician for four years *triples* the value of his landholdings relative to other landowners. This is a very large effect, suggesting that politicians are able to use their position in order to increase their wealth substantially. These results illustrate a direct mechanism through which political power played an important role in the allocation of economic resources in nineteenth-century Cundinamarca.[12] Finally, consistent with these results, we also find that those with political power seem to be significantly more likely to acquire additional land than those with land are to become politicians.

Overall, even though what we present in this chapter are historical correlations (not necessarily estimates of causal effects or structural parameters), they are both challenging to the conventional wisdom and paint a picture very different from those obtained from cross-country studies and from the within-the-U.S. variation shown in Figures 5.1 and 5.2. At least for Cundinamarca (and as we will show below, for Colombia as a whole), there is no evidence that greater land inequality is associated with bad economic outcomes. On the contrary, greater land inequality more than 120 years ago has a positive predictive power for economic outcomes today, even after controlling for current land inequality and a variety of geographic controls. In contrast, greater monopolization of political power in the hands of particular families or individuals during the nineteenth century seems to be robustly associated with worse outcomes today.

The chapter proceeds as follows: In Section 5.2 we describe the historical and institutional setting of Cundinamarca and some of the relevant literature. Section 5.3 describes the historical and contemporary data we use in this chapter and introduces the measures of land Gini, political concentration, and overlap. Section 5.4 compares land inequality in Cundinamarca to inequality in U.S. states around the same time. In Section 5.5 we examine the correlations between these variables and long-run outcomes in 1937 and 1993. Sections 5.6 and 5.7 examine the dynamics of wealth accumulation and political office holding. A conclusion follows.

5.2   The Setting

In this section, we provide some relevant background information about the history and institutions of Cundinamarca and Colombia and discuss in more detail the relationship between our work and the relevant historical and social scientific literatures. The modern department of Cundinamarca[13] was the heart of the Muisca civilization at the time of the conquest of Colombia, and the capital of Colombia, Bogotá, is located in the middle of the department. Since the greatest density of indigenous peoples was in Cundinamarca and the neighboring department of Boyacá, Spanish colonial institutions originated here, and the first grants of *encomienda*, the institution that allocated the labor and tribute of indigenous peoples to conquistadors, were given by the conquistador Gonzalo Jiménez de Quesada in this region beginning in 1538.[14] Subsequently, large haciendas emerged in Cundinamarca, and throughout the colonial period the department remained at the heart of state and society in the Spanish province of New Grenada.[15] This situation persisted after independence, with Bogotá remaining the capital, and in the period we study, Cundinamarca was clearly at the heart of national politics and the home of a great deal of the most important sections of the political elite.[16]

From at least the 1850 presidential election onward political conflict in Colombia coalesced around two parties, the Conservatives and Liberals. In 1850 the Liberals won the presidency for the first time, and José Hilario López became president. From then until 1885, the Liberals controlled the central state except for a brief period after 1856 when they lost a presidential election, held under universal male suffrage (Bushnell 1971), to the Conservatives. The Liberals shortly afterward reclaimed control through a brief civil war and wrote a new liberal constitution at Rionegro in 1863.[17] The Rionegro constitution was highly federal, and the right to determine who could vote was delegated to the states.

In 1885 there was another civil war between the parties, and power switched to the Conservatives until 1930. This period, known as the Regeneración (Regeneration) led to the rewriting of the constitution and an undoing of many of the policies promoted by the Liberals. In particular, federalism was abolished and power was centralized to the national state. There were also important changes in economic policies, for example, a significant increase in tariffs and a general movement away from free trade.[18] The Liberal election victory of 1930 led to the introduction of universal male suffrage in 1936 and the introduction of more progressive social and labor market policies, but it also led to increasing political polarization between the parties that culminated in the victory of Conservative Mariano

Ospina in 1946 followed by a partisan civil war (the so-called La Violencia), which led to a military coup in 1953. The parties negotiated a return to democracy in 1958.

There are many interpretations of long-run development in Colombia from various perspectives. The nineteenth-century Liberal politicians and intellectuals, such as Manuel Murillo Toro, Salvador Camacho Roldán, José María Samper, and Miguel Samper, wrote extensively on economic matters and promoted a version of classic nineteenth-century liberalism as the way to modernize and develop the country. Vestiges of the colonial system were one of the main things they criticized. During the Liberal period between 1850 and 1885, tariffs were cut, monopolies abolished, the remnants of colonial institutions such as slavery finally destroyed, and church lands were expropriated. However, the Liberal period also generated significant economic and political instability, and McGreevey (1970) argues that there was a notable increase in inequality during this era. Despite transitory booms, it was only with the sustained expansion of the coffee economy from the 1880s onward that economic growth began in Colombia. Growth has been sustained but slow ever since, and after 1900, Colombia has remained at about 18% of U.S. GDP per capita (Robinson and Urrutia 2007). The development of the coffee industry was linked most famously to a frontier expansion into the current states of Caldas, Risaralda, and Quindío, which is typically characterized as rather egalitarian by Latin American standards (the classic work is by Parsons [1949]).

For our focus, the institutions governing the selection of mayors and their powers are essential. During the Liberal period, mayors were appointed by the departmental governors who were themselves elected. After 1885 and the centralization of power, governors still appointed mayors but were themselves appointed by the president of the republic. Municipal councilors were elected throughout the entire period. The centralized appointment of mayors was only abandoned in 1986. Before 1885 the governor of Cundinamarca was a Liberal[19] except for a brief period in 1867 when a Conservative, Ignacio Gutiérrez, was elected only to be replaced with a Liberal by the federal government in 1868 (Delpar 1981, 96). After 1880 the governor was a more moderate Liberal from the camp of President Rafael Núñez (called Independents), and by the time of Núñez's second presidency after 1884, Independents were cooperating with Conservatives in the department (Park 1985, 250). Under the Political and Municipal

Code of 1858 (Estado de Cundinamarca 1859), mayors were appointed each year along with a substitute, and the term of the mayor was six months after which he would be replaced by the substitute for six months. Article 130 of the code says, "At the end of each term, the substitute becomes the mayor and executes the functions in the next period; only in extraordinary cases there will be a new appointment of the mayor, since in ordinary cases the only appointment that can take place is the one for the substitute each semester." In practice, however, repeated terms for the same mayor were common. For example, in Suesca, Rafael Olaya was mayor continually from 1871 to 1883 (Olaya was also the fifth largest landowner in the municipality with land worth 24,000 pesos in 1879 when the mean value of land in the municipality was 1,429 pesos). After 1885, the law was changed so that the term of a mayor became one year and mayors could be officially reappointed (Estado de Cundinamarca 1889, article 227).

In terms of the power and responsibilities of the mayor, article 127 of the 1858 code says that "The mayor is the highest figure of the public administration in the District, and as the representative of the Executive Power he is in charge of the execution of the laws in the District." Mayors were in charge of raising property taxes ("rents") to fund schools, and article 298 of the 1858 code states that there "Is an obligation for every city, village or parish to maintain a public primary school for boys and another one for girls." Taxes were also supposed to pay for the police and for public works such as the maintenance of roads and bridges. Mayors therefore had a large number of tasks with respect to the enforcement of laws and the provision of public goods, and Cruz Santos (1965, vol. I, 519) estimates that in 1869–70 about 23% of total government expenditures were decided at the municipal level.

One of the most important parts of the mayors' responsibilities, from the point of view of this chapter, was their role in adjudicating land disputes. During the nineteenth century, large areas of government-owned land, or *baldíos*, were distributed to individuals in Colombia and there were constant disputes over the title to lands. Although the right to "regulate the distribution or destiny of uncultivated lands" (Estado de Cundinamarca 1889, article 208) was delegated to the municipal councils, the secondary literature on this makes it very clear that mayors played a pivotal role in determining the outcome of these conflicts, probably because they were in charge of the police. Palacios' (1980) seminal work on the evolution of the coffee economy in Colombia has an extensive discussion of the allocation of land and property rights, noting that "local control of power was the sine qua non in this process of distribution" (p. 186). Although national laws gave squatters the chance to file for title in government lands if no other previous title existed, the reality was that many government lands were expropriated by those who controlled the instruments of local political power. LeGrand (1986, 73) notes, "By their compliance with or disregard of legal prescriptions, municipal authorities shaped the expression and resolution of the public land conflicts. Given their strategic position in the bureaucratic hierarchy, they also played a significant role in interpreting the issues involved in any given dispute to authorities at higher levels." Mayors and local police were the people who evicted squatters and supported or denied claims to land ownership. Both Palacios (1980, 185–95) and LeGrand illustrate this with many stories. For instance, LeGrand describes the typical way in which squatters would be forced to recognize the title of the politically powerful: "Once entrepreneurs had established property rights over the land, whether through grants or by illegal means, they then took action to deprive the settlers living there of their independence. Accompanied by the local mayor or a police patrol, they informed the settlers who had opened the land that they had mistakenly occupied private property" (p. 58).

Who were these mayors? Christie (1979, 50) in his study of local political bosses—*gamonales* (also known as *caciques*)—argues, "Only sometimes were they the largest landowners," and LeGrand (1986, 73) asserts, "Large landowners, for the most part, declined to occupy local political posts." One interesting source on these matters is Rufino Gutiérrez who in his capacity as prefect visited many municipalities of Cundinamarca in 1886 and 1887 and subsequently wrote a memoir (Gutiérrez 1920).[20] Gutiérrez (pp. 90–91) points out that few mayors were important landowners, but instead tended to be small landowners. He argues that the major landowners used their influence to get mayors appointed who would favor their interests (see also Deas [1971], on local politics). These conclusions are consistent with the general historiography on Colombia, which, following Safford (1972, 1974), has played down the political role of large landowners. Though Colombia did have land-owning caudillos like José Maria Obando and Tomás Mosquera, this literature claims that, by and large, politics was a career in nineteenth-century Colombia and attracted people from all backgrounds (see also Uribe-Uran 2000). Our empirical findings are partially consistent with this view. We find that there were many non-land-owning mayors (often using their powers to enrich themselves), though there was also some overlap between landowners and politicians. Indeed in a number of municipalities, there were close links between the largest landowners and local politics. In addition to the case of Suesca discussed above, in Fomeque the largest landowner, Manuel Pardo Rojas (land valued at 20,020 pesos in 1879 when the mean land value of landholdings in the municipality was 989 pesos) was mayor six times. In Une, Simon Rojas (land holding of 3,500 pesos when the mean was 883 pesos) was mayor ten times between 1873 and 1883. There are many other examples of mayors belonging to the top quintile of the land distribution.

Moreover, as Christie (1979, 1986) himself showed, elite families were heavily involved in local politics. Christie, in his reexamination of the nature of frontier expansion in nineteenth-century Colombia, compiled a list of the mayors and members of the local councils of all the municipalities of Viejo Caldas up until 1905. Using documents on the history of Manizales and other municipalities, Christie was able to determine the 27 most prestigious families who were also owners of great land concessions in the region. Matching the official posts with the last names of these families, he estimated that during the period between 1827 and 1905, more than 2,500 out of the 3,500 positions available were occupied by members of these families. When doing the same exercise but for the year 1920 this time, Christie found that 75% of the mayors came from the same families.

What do we know about the process by which mayors were appointed? Though we do not have direct evidence on this, the most likely process that drove the appointments is that governors had to respect local power structures and local *gamonales* and *caciques*. Neither the central state nor the department of Cundinamarca had military forces that were sufficient to intervene effectively in local politics, and in practice it was probably impossible to overturn local power structures, even had there been an incentive. Evidence supporting this interpretation comes from the dramatic shift in power with the Regeneración in 1885 in which the Conservatives replaced the Liberals at the national level (see Mazzuca and Robinson 2006). Even though at the national level the Conservatives drove the Liberals out of the legislature to such an extent that in the 1890s there was only one Liberal, Rafael Uribe Uribe, in the legislature, in most municipalities the same mayors were appointed before and after the Regeneración. Additional evidence consistent with this pattern comes from the *memorias* of Gutiérrez. Gutiérrez records that he was called urgently to visit Choachi and found that the public administration was in terrible shape. He notes that "the person that by that time was the Mayor, Mr. Patrocinio Pardo, did not satisfy the position, for several justified reasons, [and] we demanded his resignation and appointed his substitute Mr. Pedro Angel Garcia" (Gutiérrez 1920, 51). Though Gutiérrez may have removed Patrocinio Pardo, he was back as mayor in 1890, 1891, and 1893, and had previously been mayor in 1878 and 1881. Pedro Angel García (who was in the top quintile of the land distribution with land of 2,180 pesos when the municipal average was 874 pesos) served as mayor nine times between 1871 and 1891, and several other members of the Pardo and García families did as well. The fact that Patrocinio Pardo could be removed for incompetence but was quickly reappointed is consistent with the interpretation that the governor, who made the appointments, had to recognize the power of local elites. The situation appears to have been similar in Suesca. Rafael Olaya was removed from the office of mayor in 1873 for manipulating *adhesiones*—endorsements or declarations of support for different political candidates (Delpar 1981, 102). But our data show that he was immediately reappointed. Another interesting example comes from Deas' (1977) study of the Hacienda Santa Bárbara in Sasaima. Though he points out that Sasaima was and is a Conservative municipality (p. 286), the first person appointed mayor after the Regeneración was Felipe Castellanos with Esteban García as his alternate. Yet both of these people had been appointed in the Liberal period, Castellanos as mayor in 1879 and 1883 and García in 1880. The probable interpretation of this is that even Liberals had to appoint Conservative mayors in Sasaima.

Finally, the degree of political concentration in Cundinamarca, which we will exploit and document further below, is illustrated by a few prominent examples. For instance, in Viani, out of 44 mayors who held office, half of them corresponded to only 4 individuals, and 25 out of the 44 came from either the Bonilla or Hernandez family. In Arbelaez, the Rodriguez family was in power in every single year for which we have data. With the exception of 1888, Ramon Rodriguez was the mayor in every year between 1887 and 1895. In Quipile, only 3 individuals account for 20 of the 44 mayor appointments that were recorded. Francisco Escobar was the mayor during the 1880–84 period and Genaro Mendieta was from 1888 to 1895. In La

Calera, a municipality founded by Don Pedro de Tovar in 1765, half of the
mayor appointments came from the Tovar family, which was in power every
year during the 1875–95 period (except in 1889). In Guasca, almost 70%
of the 51 mayor appointments came from only 3 families, and the Acosta
and Rodriguez families were in power during most of the period. Similarly,
most of Cucunubá's mayors came from the Gómez family, which was in
power during 1875–81 and 1887–95. Today, much of Cucunubá is owned
by Pedro Gómez. These are only a few examples that illustrate the way in
which power in many municipalities was concentrated in the hands of a
few families and individuals.

5.3   The Data

5.3.1 Cadastral Data and the Land Gini

Our basic source of data on economic inequality in nineteenth century
Cundinamarca is the cadastral (land census) data collected by the state of
Cundinamarca in 1879 and 1890.[21] The cadastral information was collected
by state officials for tax purposes and provides information on the location,
owners, and value of every plot with value above $25 Colombian pesos
in 1879 and above $100 in 1890. The censoring values for each land cen-
sus are low, so we have information for most plots. In 1879, there were
15,478 landowners in Cundinamarca, and this number increased to 18,598
in 1890. We have no real information about the reliability of these data
though Camacho Roldán (1892) praises the 1868 data as being accurate.
Gutiérrez (1920) noted in his visit to Usme in 1886 that the value of lands
for that municipality in the *catastro* was low relative to his own expectations, but he does not systematically record views on this for all the places
he visited.

We will construct two measures of land inequality. The first is the standard measure of the *land Gini* coefficient, which measures land inequality
among landowners. For each municipality at each date, we construct the
Gini coefficient using the standard formula

$$g_{mt} = \frac{1}{n_t^2 \bar{y}_t} \sum_{i=1}^{n_t} \sum_{j=1}^{n_t} |y_{i,t} - y_{j,t}|, \tag{5.1}$$

where $i = 1, ..., n_t$ denotes land owners at time t, $y_{i,t}$ is the value of land owned by individual i at time t, and $\bar{y}_t = \frac{1}{n_t} \sum_{i=1}^{n_t} y_{i,t}$ is the average value of land at time t. Throughout most of our analysis, we average the Gini coefficients across the two dates for each municipality to arrive at our main measure of (average) *land Gini*. The average Gini over this entire period was 0.65 (see Table 5.1 below). If we look at the two land censuses separately, we find that the land Gini was 0.64 in 1879 and increased slightly to 0.66 in 1890.[22]

Despite its widespread use, the land Gini suffers from an obvious problem. An area in which all land is held by two very large landowners will have a low value of the land Gini, because land is equally distributed among landowners. But if we looked at the population as a whole, there would be a tremendous amount of land inequality. To alleviate this problem, we construct an alternative measure, *overall land Gini*, which again computes equation (5.1), but uses the total number of families and assigns zero land holdings to the families who do not appear in the *catastro*.[23] We start our analysis with the land Gini and then show how controlling for both the land Gini (among landowners) and overall land Gini affects the results.[24]

In Figure 5.5, we superimpose the distribution of the land Gini on a map of Cundinamarca. This figure is useful both to show the geographic structure of Cundinamarca and the distribution of municipalities, and also depicts the variation in land inequality. Darker areas in the figure correspond to higher values of the land Gini (as indicated in the legend to the figure). The picture reveals that land inequality tends to be higher in the series of intermontane basins to the west and north of Bogotá, but it is also high in the far-western municipalities, which are down in the valley of the Magdalena river.

5.3.2 Political Concentration

To measure political inequality, we collected data on politician (mayor) names from the *Registro del Estado* and *Gaceta de Cundinamarca*, official newspapers that published the names of principal and substitute mayors appointed in each municipality. We were able to find a total of 4,763 mayor appointments between 1875 and 1895.[25] Each appointment, however, does not correspond necessarily to a different individual, for the same individuals were sometimes reappointed in many years. Hence, the 4,763 different

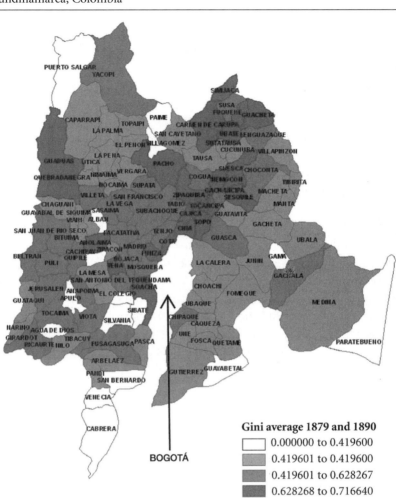

Figure 5.5 Land Gini in Cundinamarca. Land Gini is the average Gini coefficient
for 1879 and 1890 constructed from the *catastros*.

appointments we collected correspond to 2,300 different individuals during this period. A striking fact is the large number of mayors. While in principle, 2 mayors (principal and substitute) should be appointed per year in each municipality, an average of 2.9 appointments per municipality was observed. This is because there are resignations and replacements in some years.

We used these data to construct a measure of the concentration of political power. Our measure of political concentration for municipality m at time t is computed as

$$p_{mt} = -\frac{\text{Number of Different Individuals in Power}_{mt}}{\text{Number of Mayor Appointments}_{mt}}.$$

The negative sign in front is introduced so that higher values of the index correspond to higher political concentration (thus making the interpretation of the coefficients easier). Consequently, our political concentration index takes a value of -1 when there is very low political concentration, and values close to 0 for high levels of concentration. We computed this index for the whole period 1875–1895. Table 5.1 will show that the mean of this variable is -0.56.

Figure 5.6 is similar to Figure 5.5 and maps political concentration across the municipalities of Cundinamarca. Now darker areas correspond to higher levels of political concentration. This figure shows that places with higher levels of political concentration are spread out all over the state. They range from municipalities like Beltran in the Magdalena River valley in the west, to Ubala, which is on the eastern slopes of the cordillera. Also highly concentrated are the southern coffee-growing municipality of Arbelaez, founded in the mid-nineteenth century, and the northern municipality of Sutatausa, an area of dense Muisca settlement and one of the first municipalities to be founded in Cundinamarca.

5.3.3 Measuring the Overlap of Wealth and Political Power

In addition to our basic measures of economic and political inequality, we constructed a measure of the overlap between political officeholding and landed wealth. To do this we classified the individuals in our sample according to whether they were politicians, rich, or both. We define an individual as being both rich and a politician if we can find an exact match of the first

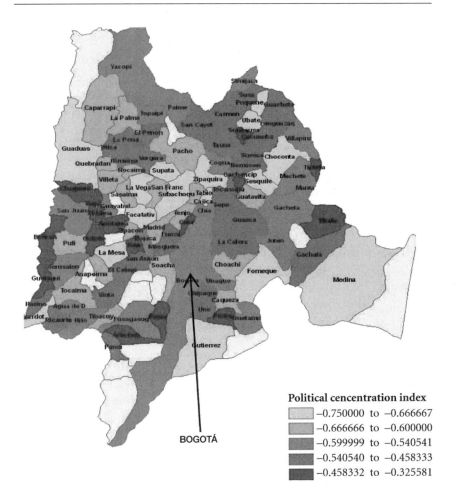

Figure 5.6 Political concentration index in Cundinamarca. Political concentration index defined as the negative of the number of different individuals in power between 1875 and 1895, over the number of mayor appointments for which data is available.

and last name among the top 25% richest landowners in the *catastro* and in the list of mayors *within* each municipality. Naturally, this procedure may lead to an overstatement of overlap if we match two different persons with the same first and last name, though this appears to be unlikely within a municipality. On the other hand, there are various reasons for understating overlap, since rich landowners may be politicians in neighboring municipalities or they may have substantial political influence without becoming mayors themselves.

To construct our measure of overlap, let us introduce some notation. Let N_{mt} be the set of adult males living in municipality m at time t, L_{mt} be the set of adult males without any substantial landholdings or political power, R_{mt} be the rich, that is those with substantial landholdings, and finally, let P_{mt} be those with political power (mayors). It is clear that

$$N_{mt} = L_{mt} \cup R_{mt} \cup P_{mt}.$$

Let $\#R_{mt}$ be the number of individuals in the set R_{mt}, and define $\#N_{mt}$, $\#P_{mt}$, $\# \left(R_{mt} \cup P_{mt} \right)$, and $\#L_{mt}$ similarly. Since we can directly compute $\#P_{mt}$ and $\#R_{mt}$, and observe $\#N_{mt}$, the number of individuals who are neither rich nor politicians can be computed as

$$\#L_{mt} = \#N_{mt} - \# \left(R_{mt} \cup P_{mt} \right).$$

For the purposes of our analysis, we define individuals whose land plots are in the top 25% most valuable plots as "rich landowners." In these calculations, we compute the thresholds for the entire region (and not for each municipality separately) so as to exploit the variation in the presence of big landowners driven by inequality across regions that we want to take into account.[26] In calculating the number of rich landowners in each municipality, we use the *catastros* for 1879 and 1890. For politicians, we use neighboring dates to these, so that for 1879, any individual who was a mayor between 1877 and 1882 is considered a politician, and for 1890, we look at the window from 1888 to 1892.

Our measure of overlap in municipality m at time t is computed as

$$o_{mt} = \frac{\# \left(R_{mt} \cap P_{mt} \right)}{\# \left(R_{mt} \cup P_{mt} \right)}.$$

Our main measure of overlap is the average of this index for the two dates 1879 and 1890. Table 5.1 will show that the mean of this variable is 0.07, so that 7% of rich landowners and politicians were both rich and in power.

5.3.4 Data on Outcomes

We have two sets of outcome variables. The contemporary data are from the 1993 population census and the Colombian statistical agency DANE (Departamento Administrativo Nacional de Estadística).

We constructed two basic education variables from the 1993 census: primary school enrollment, which was calculated as the number of children attending school that are between 7 and 11 years old divided by the total number of children that are between 7 and 11 years old in the municipality; and secondary school enrollment, defined as the number of children attending school that are between 12 and 17 years old divided by the total number of children that are between 12 and 17 years old in the municipality. The descriptive statistics in Table 5.1 will show that there is much more variation across municipalities in secondary school enrollment, motivating our focus on this measure (though we will also show results using primary school enrollment).

Figure 5.7 is similar to Figures 5.5 and 5.6 and maps the secondary enrollment data across the Cundinamarca municipalities. Darker areas now indicate higher enrollment. It is evident from this figure that enrollment is higher closer to Bogotá and particularly on the Sabana de Bogotá.

We also used the 1993 census to construct a measure of urbanization, defined as the proportion of the population in urban areas. The census reports urban population for each municipality, so we simply divided this by the total population of the municipality. Each municipality has one urban area, the *cabecera*, where the municipal government buildings are located (other subdistricts of the municipality are called *veredas*), so urban population is the population of the *cabecera*.

Finally, the 1993 census also provides an index of poverty, referred to as unsatisfied basic needs (which has the Spanish acronym NBI—Necesidades Básicas Insatisfechas) and used commonly in Colombia and in other Latin American countries. In this index, a household is counted as having unsatisfied basic needs if it meets any one of five different criteria. These are (1) inadequate dwelling, such as when the floor is composed of soil or

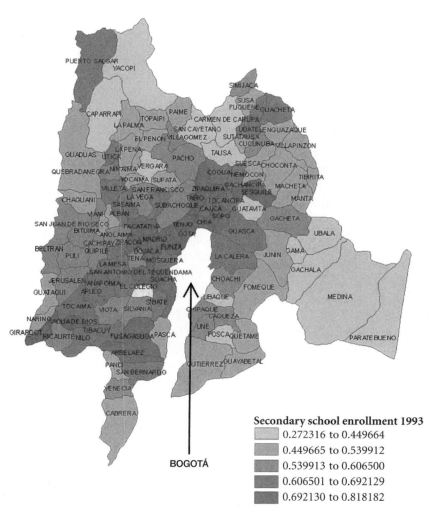

Figure 5.7 Secondary school enrollment in Cundinamarca. Secondary school enrollment constructed from the 1993 census as fraction of children between 12 and 17 years old attending school.

the house is made of precarious building materials; (2) the household's
dwelling lacks basic services, such as piped water, sewers, or toilets; (3) the
household is overcrowded, which is defined as one where the number of
people per bedroom is greater than three; (4) the household is characterized by inadequate school attendance, which is indicated by a child between
7 and 11 years old who does not attend school; and (5) the household has
high economic dependence, meaning that the head of the household has
less than a fourth-grade education and has more than three dependents.
The indicator we use is the proportion of households in a municipality with
unsatisfied basic needs.

For the medium-term outcomes, we used data from the 1937 population
census. While there are no data on educational enrollment in this census,
we measured the proportion of adults who were literate. We also calculated
urbanization in 1937 in exactly the same way as we did in 1993. Finally, the
1937 census also records for each municipality the total number of buildings and also the number of buildings that lack access to electricity, water,
and sewage. We therefore constructed the fraction of buildings without access to all public services by combining these two pieces of information,
which provides us with a measure of noneducational public-goods provision.

We use a variety of exogenous control variables in the regressions in order to ensure that our results are not driven by omitted differences in the
quality or productivity of land. Our controls include altitude of the municipality (in meters above sea level), the distance of the municipality to
Bogotá (in kilometers), area (in squared kilometers), and average rainfall
(in millimeters). All of these data were obtained from Instituto Geográfico
Agustin Codazzi in Bogotá. Distance to Bogotá may be particularly important, since Figure 5.5 suggests that there are a number of municipalities near
Bogotá that have relatively high land inequality. We check the robustness of
our results to including high-degree polynomials in distance to Bogotá that
would capture any nonlinear effect of this variable.

Finally, we also control for the year of foundation of a municipality (from
Bernard and Zambrano 1993). While the highlands of Cundinamarca were
settled in the sixteenth century, much of the lower western and eastern
slopes were only settled in the mid-nineteenth century in a process of frontier expansion. This frontier expansion was associated with the spread of
the coffee economy (see Rivas [1946] or Palacios [1980] for discussion) and

the determination of property rights in land, and the nature of the societies that formed in the nineteenth century may be quite different from those founded during the colonial period (see Jiménez [1985] for a detailed treatment of one such municipality, Viotá). We include the foundation date in some of our regressions to control for this source of omitted variable bias.

5.3.5 Descriptive Statistics and Correlations

Table 5.1 shows descriptive statistics for our entire sample and also for subsamples created according to land Gini and political concentration (both average values over the two dates and the subsamples were created by dividing the sample according to median values). A number of features are notable in this table. First, the land Gini at the end of the nineteenth century was quite high, 0.65. Moreover, it still continues to be very high today (third row). The standard deviation of this variable indicates that there is considerable variation in the extent of land inequality within Cundinamarca. The same applies to the extent of political inequality. Also, as noted above, the outcome variables also show considerable variation, except primary school enrollment, which is very high in most municipalities and thus exhibits less variation than the other outcome variables.

Table 5.1 also shows descriptive statistics by dividing the sample into low and high land inequality areas (columns 2 and 3) and into low and high political concentration areas (columns 4 and 5). The comparison of columns 2 and 3 shows that all economic outcomes are better in high land inequality areas. For example, secondary school enrollment is 65% in high land inequality areas, whereas low land inequality areas have only 52% secondary school enrollment. In contrast, when we turn to political concentration, low political concentration areas have better economic outcomes. For example, secondary school enrollment is 60% in low political concentration areas and 56% in high political concentration areas. These differences are consistent with the patterns shown in Figures 5.3 and 5.4, and the regression analysis will show that these differences are relatively robust to controlling for a variety of geographic and other controls.

Table 5.2 describes our data further by showing the correlation matrix among our main historical explanatory variables, the land Gini at the end

Table 5.1 Descriptive statistics

	All municipalities (1)	Low land inequality (2)	High land inequality (3)	Low political concentration (4)	High political concentration (5)
Land Gini	0.65	0.57	0.73	0.66	0.65
	(0.10)	(0.06)	(0.05)	(0.09)	(0.10)
Overall land Gini	0.86	0.83	0.90	0.86	0.87
	(0.07)	(0.07)	(0.05)	(0.07)	(0.07)
Contemporary land Gini	0.67	0.63	0.73	0.69	0.66
	(0.09)	(0.07)	(0.08)	(0.09)	(0.09)
Political concentration index	−0.56	−0.53	−0.57	−0.64	−0.48
	(0.10)	(0.08)	(0.10)	(0.06)	(0.06)
Overlap	0.07	0.07	0.06	0.05	0.08
	(0.04)	(0.04)	(0.04)	(0.03)	(0.04)
Secondary school enrollment	0.58	0.52	0.65	0.60	0.56
	(0.11)	(0.09)	(0.09)	(0.11)	(0.10)
Primary school enrollment	0.83	0.83	0.86	0.84	0.84
	(0.06)	(0.05)	(0.07)	(0.08)	(0.05)
Urbanization (1993)	0.31	0.22	0.41	0.35	0.26
	(0.23)	(0.13)	(0.28)	(0.26)	(0.20)
Unsatisfied basic needs	0.40	0.44	0.33	0.37	0.42
	(0.14)	(0.13)	(0.11)	(0.14)	(0.14)
Literacy rate	0.40	0.40	0.41	0.42	0.38
	(0.12)	(0.12)	(0.10)	(0.13)	(0.10)
Urbanization (1937)	0.17	0.12	0.20	0.20	0.14
	(0.18)	(0.10)	(0.18)	(0.22)	(0.13)
Share of buildings without access to public services	0.91	0.95	0.88	0.88	0.94
	(0.12)	(0.07)	(0.13)	(0.16)	(0.08)
Distance to Bogotá	88.23	93.49	77.96	85.84	90.53
	(45.00)	(38.74)	(48.35)	(44.28)	(46.01)

Note: Values are averages with standard deviations in parentheses. Land Gini is the average land value Gini coefficient for 1879 and 1890 constructed from the *catastros*. Overall land Gini is the average land value Gini coefficient for 1879 and 1890 constructed from the *catastros* taking into account landless families (see text for details). Political concentration index measured as the negative of the number of different individuals in power between 1875 and 1895 over number of mayor appointments for which data is available. Overlap is of the nineteenth century, the overall land Gini at the end of the nine-teenth century, the contemporary land Gini, the political concentration index, and the overlap variable, as well as our main outcome variables. This table shows that there is a negative correlation between political and economic inequality, which is the opposite of the pattern that appears in the nineteenth-century United States (where political inequality also ap-pears to be higher in the more unequal South). This contrast between the United States and Cundinamarca confirms the discussion in Section 5.1. In any case, the correlation between the two variables is not very large (correlation coefficient −0.25), giving us an opportunity to determine the separate correlation between political and economic inequality and economic outcomes. Overlap is even less correlated with these two vari-ables.

The outcome variables are also correlated with each other, though not very highly so. For example, the correlation between urbanization and pri-mary school enrollment is only 0.23. This implies that there is independent information in all of these outcome variables, and considerable indepen-dent variation in our basic inequality variables.

Table 5.1 *(notes)*

measured as fraction of rich landowners and politicians that are both landowners and politicians (average for 1879 and 1890). Contemporary land Gini corresponds to Gini coefficient of land value for 2002 constructed from IGAC *catastros*. Secondary school enrollment is constructed from the 1993 census as fraction of children between 12 and 17 years old attending school. Primary school enrollment also constructed from the 1993 census as fraction of children between 7 and 11 years old attending school. Unsatisfied basic needs constructed from the 1993 census as fraction of households with unfulfilled basic needs (see text for details).

Urbanization figures constructed from the corresponding year censuses as fraction of total population living in urban areas. Literacy rate constructed from the 1937 census as number of literate individuals over total population. Fraction of buildings without access to public services also constructed from the 1937 census as fraction of buildings without access to electricity, water, and sewage. Distance to Bogotá is measured in kms. Column 1 reports figures for all municipalities. Column 2 reports figure for the 49 municipalities with land Gini below its median value while column 3 reports figures for the 49 municipalities with land Gini above its median value. Column 4 reports figures for the 56 municipalities with political concentration index below its median value and column 5 reports figures for the 56 municipalities with political concentration index above its median value.

Table 5.2 Correlation matrix

	Land Gini	Overall land Gini	Contemporary land Gini	Political concentration index	Overlap	Secondary school enrollment	Urbanization (1993)	Unsatisfied basic needs
Land Gini	1.00							
Overall land Gini	0.48	1.00						
Contemporary land Gini	0.60	0.23	1.00					
Political concentration index	−0.25	−0.05	−0.26	1.00				
Overlap	−0.08	−0.05	−0.04	0.43	1.00			
Secondary school enrollment	0.54	0.16	0.56	−0.30	−0.09	1.00		
Urbanization (1993)	0.47	0.11	0.59	−0.30	−0.10	0.64	1.00	
Unsatisfied basic needs	−0.56	0.09	−0.49	0.37	−0.03	−0.67	−0.47	1.00

Note: Land Gini is the average land value Gini coefficient for 1879 and 1890 constructed from the *catastros*. Overall land Gini is the average land value Gini coefficient for 1879 and 1890 constructed from the *catastros* taking into account landless families (see text for details). Contemporary land Gini corresponds to Gini coefficient of land value for 2002 constructed from IGAC *catastros*. Political concentration index measured as the negative of the number of different individuals in power between 1875 and 1895 over number of mayor appointments for which data is available. Overlap is measured as fraction of rich landowners and politicians that are both landowners and politicians (average for 1879 and 1890). Secondary school enrollment is constructed from the 1993 census as fraction of children between 12 and 17 years old attending school. Urbanization constructed from the 1993 census as fraction of total population living in urban areas. Unsatisfied basic needs constructed from the 1993 census as fraction of households with unfulfilled basic needs (see text for details).

5.4   The Inequality of Wealth: Cundinamarca and the United States

As discussed in Section 5.1, a recently emerging consensus relates the current differences in economic outcomes between the United States and South America to nineteenth-century differences in inequality (especially land inequality). Was land more unequally distributed in Cundinamarca than in the United States in the nineteenth century? In this section, we will see that the answer to this question is more nuanced than typically presumed. Cundinamarca appears to be substantially more unequal than the northern United States, but more equal than the U.S. South.

To provide a comparison of land inequality between Cundinamarca and the United States in the nineteenth century, we compare our land inequality data (described above) with U.S. microdata from the 1860 land census provided in the Gallman–Parker and Bateman–Foust samples. These data, which are downloadable from the Inter-university Consortium for Political and Social Research (ICPSR) website (www.icpsr.umich.edu), comprise two famous random samples taken from the 1860 census. The Gallman–Parker sample contains variables recorded for 5,228 farms located in the major cotton-producing counties of the South (see, e.g., Schaefer and Schmitz 1985; Schmitz and Schaefer 1986). The farms were selected from the 1860 manuscript census schedules by a sample of all farms in 405 southern counties that each produced over 1,000 bales of cotton in 1860. This resulted in a 1.67 percent sample of all farms in the major cotton-growing counties of the eleven states of the confederacy. We use the data on the value of the farms in dollars. The Bateman–Foust sample (see Bateman and Foust 1974) contains demographic, occupational, and economic information for over 21,000 rural households in the northern United States. The data were obtained from the agricultural and population schedules of the 1860 census and cover all households in a single township from each of 102 randomly selected counties in 16 northern states. We again use the data on the dollar value of farms. Together these datasets give us a picture of land distribution in both the northern and southern United States in 1860.

Our calculations using these samples are reported in Table 5.3. In particular, we compute the land Gini for individual states and for the North, the South, and the entire United States. The picture that emerges from the comparison of the numbers in Table 5.3 to those in Table 5.1 is interesting. As expected, northern U.S. states are considerably more equal than

Table 5.3 Land inequality in U.S. states (1860)

State	Land Gini	No. observations	Average land value
Panel A. Northern states			
Connecticut	0.34	259	3,421
Illinois	0.50	1,563	2,659
Indiana	0.47	5,020	2,534
Iowa	0.48	825	2,066
Kansas	0.41	623	1,702
Maryland	0.49	534	2,097
Michigan	0.55	1,516	1,544
Minnesota	0.55	379	983
Missouri	0.52	1,180	1,745
New Hampshire	0.35	807	1,860
New Jersey	0.35	362	5,274
New York	0.42	4,043	3,888
Ohio	0.38	851	3,381
Pennsylvania	0.47	2,465	3,722
Vermont	0.43	147	3,327
Wisconsin	0.44	544	1,748
Total northern states	0.47	20,821	2,820
Panel B. Southern states			
Alabama	0.73	1,005	3,223
Arkansas	0.70	434	3,048
Florida	0.60	65	2,162
Georgia	0.63	818	3,459
Louisiana	0.83	225	18,197
Mississippi	0.69	707	4,491
North Carolina	0.60	391	2,548
South Carolina	0.63	524	4,293
Tennessee	0.75	465	5,986
Texas	0.70	551	3,340
Virginia	0.71	42	3,555
Total southern states	0.72	5,055	4,514
Total U.S. states	0.58	25,876	3,333

Note: The land Ginis for the U.S. South and North were constructed from the complete Gallman–Parker and Bateman–Foust samples, respectively, from the microdata of the 1860 U.S. census.

Cundinamarca. For example, Connecticut has the lowest land Gini of 0.34, compared to the land Gini of 0.65 in Cundinamarca. However, contrary to the widespread notion that Latin America is substantially more unequal than the United States, all southern states, except Florida, Georgia, and the Carolinas, are more unequal than Cundinamarca. For example, the land Gini in Louisiana is 0.83, considerably higher than that of Cundinamarca. The average land Gini in the South is 0.72, which is also greater than the Gini for Cundinamarca, 0.65.

5.5   Inequality and Long-Run Development in Cundinamarca

We now examine the consequences of wealth inequality, political concentration, and overlap for long-run development outcomes. To do this we exploit the cross-sectional variation within the municipalities in Cundinamarca. Throughout the section, we estimate cross-sectional ordinary least squares (OLS) regressions of the following form

$$y_m = \alpha g_m + \beta p_m + \gamma o_m + \mathbf{x}'_m \delta + u_m, \tag{5.2}$$

where y_m is some measure of development in municipality m, $\mathbf{x}_m$ is a vector of covariates, and u_m is an error term, capturing all other omitted factors, with $E\left(u_m\right) = 0$ for all m. In (5.2) the main objects of interest are the coefficients on the land Gini, denoted by g_m, the extent of political concentration, denoted by p_m, and the degree of overlap, denoted by o_m, in municipality m. We report regressions in which each of these variables features separately and then together. We start by looking at the effect of these variables on contemporary outcomes and then turn to their effect on 1937 outcomes. A key concern in all of these regressions is omitted variable bias. For this reason, the vector $\mathbf{x}_m$ will control for a rich set of covariates, especially for measures of differences in land quality across municipalities.

5.5.1 Contemporary Outcomes

Tables 5.4 and 5.5 examine the relationship between our four contemporary outcome variables and historical land inequality, political concentration, and overlap. Panel A of Table 5.4 is for secondary school enrollment, while Panel B is for primary school enrollment. Column 1 shows the bivariate relationship between land Gini and secondary school enrollment without any other controls. There is a strong *positive* association, indicating that municipalities that were more unequal at the end of the nineteenth century have higher levels of secondary school enrollment today. This relationship in column 1 is the same as that shown in Figure 5.3 in Section 5.1. The coefficient estimate is equal to 0.61, and is highly significant with a standard error of 0.09. The R^2 of this bivariate regression is 30%, indicating a large and significant correlation between historical land inequality and secondary schooling. As a different way of gauging the quantitative significance of this correlation, recall from Table 5.1 that the standard deviation of land Gini is 0.10 in the entire Cundinamarca. The coefficient estimate implies that we expect a municipality with one standard deviation greater land Gini than the mean to have approximately 0.06 percentage points higher secondary school enrollment. Relative to the mean of this variable in Cundinamarca, 0.58, this translates into a 10% increase, which is substantial.

The main threat to the interpretation of the relationship between land inequality and contemporary economic outcomes is that municipalities with greater inequality may have higher-quality lands or other sources of higher incomes. While we cannot control for all possible sources of omitted variable bias, we can check the robustness of this correlation to a range of geographic controls that should capture differences in land quality. Column 2 attempts to do this by adding altitude, distance to Bogotá, amount of rainfall, and also the historical variable, the year of foundation of the municipality. After including these controls, there is still a positive association between the land Gini and secondary schooling, though the coefficient is slightly smaller now, 0.48 (standard error = 0.10).

Column 3 of Table 5.4 looks at the relationship between the political concentration index and secondary school enrollment. Here we see a statistically significant (though somewhat weaker) *negative relationship*, corresponding to the pattern shown in Figure 5.4 in Section 5.1. The coefficient estimate, −0.36, is highly significant with a standard error of 0.11. The quantitative magnitude of this effect is also somewhat smaller than the magnitude associated with the land Gini; the coefficient estimate implies that a municipality with one standard deviation above the mean political concentration index tends to have 3.6% lower secondary school enrollment in 1993. Column 4 demonstrates that this relationship is robust to including geographic controls, and the magnitude of the effect is only slightly smaller, −0.35 (standard error = 0.10), than in column 3.

Table 5.4 OLS regressions for long-term outcomes

	(1)	(2)	(3)	(4)	(5)	(6)	(7)	(8)	(9)	(10)
Panel A			*Dependent variable: Secondary school enrollment*							
Land Gini	0.61	0.48					0.44	0.44	0.28	0.16
	(0.09)	(0.10)					(0.09)	(0.09)	(0.11)	(0.10)
Political			−0.36	−0.35			−0.27	−0.27	−0.22	−0.22
concentration			(0.11)	(0.10)			(0.10)	(0.11)	(0.11)	(0.11)
index										
Overlap					−0.27	−0.43		−0.01	−0.07	−0.13
					(0.29)	(0.24)		(0.23)	(0.19)	(0.19)
Contemporary									0.38	0.37
land Gini									(0.13)	(0.11)
Geographic controls	No	Yes	No	Yes	No	Yes	Yes	Yes	Yes	Extended
Observations	92	92	94	93	93	93	92	92	92	92
R^2	0.30	0.45	0.09	0.37	0.01	0.32	0.50	0.50	0.54	0.61
Panel B			*Dependent variable: Primary school enrollment*							
Land Gini	0.19	0.11					0.10	0.10	0.12	0.05
	(0.06)	(0.05)					(0.05)	(0.05)	(0.06)	(0.05)
Political			−0.08	−0.09			−0.07	−0.11	−0.11	−0.08
concentration			(0.07)	(0.05)			(0.05)	(0.06)	(0.06)	(0.06)
index										
Overlap					0.04	0.02		0.17	0.18	0.12
					(0.16)	(0.12)		(0.14)	(0.14)	(0.13)
Contemporary									−0.04	0.00
land Gini									(0.07)	(0.06)
Geographic controls	No	Yes	No	Yes	No	Yes	Yes	Yes	Yes	Extended
Observations	92	92	94	93	93	93	92	92	92	92
R^2	0.09	0.52	0.01	0.51	0.00	0.49	0.53	0.54	0.54	0.60

Note: Robust standard errors in parentheses. Secondary school enrollment is constructed from the 1993 census as fraction of children between 12 and 17 years old attending school. Primary school enrollment also constructed from the 1993 census as fraction of children between 7 and 11 years old attending school. Land Gini is the average land value Gini coefficient for 1879 and 1890 constructed from the *catastros*. Political concentration index measured as the negative of the number of different individuals in power between 1875 and 1895 over number of mayor appointments for which data is available. Overlap is measured as fraction of rich landowners and politicians that are both rich landowners and politicians (average for 1879 and 1890). Rich landowners are defined as those with landholdings among the top 25% most valuable plots. Contemporary land Gini corresponds to Gini coefficient of land value for 2002 constructed from IGAC *catastros*. Geographic controls include altitude (in mts above sea level), distance to Bogotá (in kms), area (in sq. kms), rainfall (in mms), and year of foundation. A quartic in distance to Bogotá and land value per square km (average for 1879 and 1890) are included in column 10.

Table 5.5 OLS regressions for long-term outcomes

	(1)	(2)	(3)	(4)	(5)	(6)	(7)	(8)	(9)	(10)
Panel A			*Dependent variable: Urbanization in 1993*							
Land Gini	1.11	0.79					0.71	0.71	0.21	0.06
	(0.23)	(0.21)					(0.21)	(0.20)	(0.23)	(0.23)
Political			−0.77	−0.57			−0.44	−0.33	−0.15	−0.26
concentration			(0.26)	(0.27)			(0.29)	(0.32)	(0.28)	(0.27)
index										
Overlap					−0.65	−1.07		−0.51	−0.73	−0.32
					(0.66)	(0.55)		(0.65)	(0.56)	(0.46)
Contemporary									1.23	0.97
land Gini									(0.28)	(0.28)
Geographic	No	Yes	No	Yes	No	Yes	Yes	Yes	Yes	Extended
controls										
Observations	92	92	94	93	93	93	92	92	92	92
R^2	0.22	0.36	0.09	0.31	0.01	0.30	0.38	0.39	0.50	0.60
Panel B			*Dependent variable: Unsatisfied basic needs*							
Land Gini	−0.72	−0.49					−0.44	−0.44	−0.35	−0.21
	(0.12)	(0.12)					(0.11)	(0.11)	(0.13)	(0.11)
Political			0.51	0.36			0.28	0.41	0.38	0.33
concentration			(0.12)	(0.11)			(0.11)	(0.12)	(0.12)	(0.12)
index										
Overlap					−0.11	−0.03		−0.62	−0.58	−0.60
					(0.35)	(0.26)		(0.25)	(0.23)	(0.24)
Contemporary									−0.23	−0.33
land Gini									(0.13)	(0.14)
Geographic	No	Yes	No	Yes	No	Yes	Yes	Yes	Yes	Extended
controls										
Observations	92	92	94	93	93	93	92	92	92	92
R^2	0.31	0.57	0.14	0.51	0.00	0.45	0.61	0.63	0.64	0.69

Note: Robust standard errors in parentheses. Urbanization constructed from the 1993 census as fraction of population living in urban areas. Unsatisfied basic needs constructed from the 1993 census as fraction of households with unfulfilled basic needs (see text for details). Land Gini is the average land value Gini coefficient for 1879 and 1890 constructed from the *catastros*. Political concentration index measured as the negative of the number of different individuals in power between 1875 and 1895 over number of mayor appointments for which data is available. Overlap is measured as fraction of rich landowners and politicians that are both rich landowners and politicians (average for 1879 and 1890). Rich landowners are defined as those with landholdings among the top 25% most valuable plots. Contemporary land Gini corresponds to Gini coefficient of land value for 2002 constructed from IGAC *catastros*. Geographic controls include altitude (in mts above sea level), distance to Bogotá (in kms), area (in sq. kms), rainfall (in mms), and year of foundation. A quartic in distance to Bogotá and land value per square km (average for 1879 and 1890) are included in column 10.

Columns 5 and 6 show that there is a negative but not always significant relationship between overlap and school enrollment. For example, without covariates, the relationship is insignificant, and it becomes marginally significant at 5% when the geographic controls are included.

Columns 7 and 8 look at the effect of land Gini and the political concentration index when they are included together. Both variables continue to be significant, and, together with the geographic controls, they explain about 50% of the variation in secondary schooling across Cundinamarca municipalities.

Finally, in columns 9 and 10, we add further controls in order to deal with potential omitted variable concerns. Column 9 adds the contemporary land Gini. Interestingly, this is also significant and positive, but the historical land Gini continues to be positive and significant (coefficient = 0.28, standard error = 0 .11), while the political concentration index continues to be negative and significant (coefficient = −0.22, standard error = 0.11).

Column 10 is the most demanding specification and adds a quartic in distance to Bogotá in order to flexibly control for differences in the quality of land plots that may be near Bogotá. In this column we also control for the best proxy for differences in land quality across municipalities, the average land value per square kilometer from the land censuses. The quartic in the distance to Bogotá is useful since Figure 5.5 showed that land inequality is higher in many of the municipalities that are near Bogotá. Average land value is the market's perception of differences in land quality at the end of the nineteenth century and should be a "sufficient statistic" for these differences. Moreover, differences in average land value will also indirectly control for differences in tax revenues across municipalities, a major source of revenue and thus of fiscal capacity of municipalities.[27] The addition of these variables reduces the effect of the land Gini to 0.16 (standard error = 0.10), which is no longer significant at 5%, but the effect of the political concentration index remains unchanged and still significant at 5%.

One concern may be that Cundinamarca is atypical and some unobserved heterogeneity is responsible for the positive relationship between land inequality and secondary school enrollment. In fact, the results in Panel A of Table 5.4 show not only a positive relationship between the historical land Gini and secondary enrollments today, but also a positive association between contemporary land inequality and schooling. As a check for whether Cundinamarca is atypical in terms of the relationship between

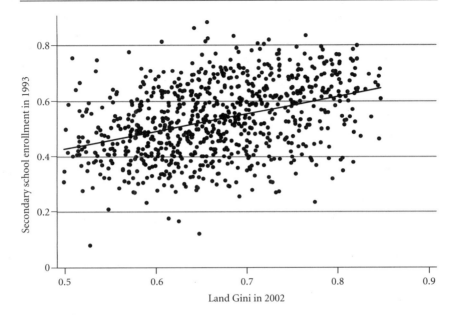

Figure 5.8 Contemporary land inequality and secondary school enrollment in
Colombia. Land Gini constructed from the 2002 IGAC *catastros*. Secondary school
enrollment constructed from the 1993 census as fraction of children between 12
and 18 years old attending school.

land inequality and schooling, we looked at the contemporaneous relationship between these two variables for all Colombian municipalities.[28]
Figure 5.8 shows the relationship between land Gini in 2002 and secondary
school enrollment in the whole of Colombia.[29] Consistent with the patterns for Cundinamarca, there is a positive relationship, and in fact the
magnitude of this relationship is very similar to that which we find in Cundinamarca. This gives us some confidence that the relationship within Cundinamarca is not an aberration, and whatever factors are responsible for the
positive association between land inequality and education within Cundinamarca seem to be present when we look at the whole of Colombia.

Panel B repeats the same regressions as in Panel A, with primary school
enrollment. The overall pattern is the same, except that all of the variables
are less significant than in Panel A, and both land Gini and the political
concentration index are no longer significant in column 10 when all of the

controls, including the contemporary land Gini and the quartic in distance to Bogotá, are included. These weaker results probably reflect the fact that, as noted above, primary enrollment is already high in most municipalities.

Panel A of Table 5.5 looks at urbanization, which is a crude but useful proxy for overall development in a municipality. The results in this table are broadly similar. There is a positive effect of the land Gini on urbanization, though this effect becomes insignificant in columns 9 and 10. The relationship between political concentration and urbanization is also negative and significant when we do not include additional controls, but becomes insignificant in columns 9 and 10.

When we turn to our index of poverty in Panel B of Table 5.5, the results are more robust. In all columns, there is a negative and significant relationship between the land Gini and poverty and a positive and significant relationship between the political concentration index and poverty. In particular, even in column 10, where we control for a quartic in distance to Bogotá and for average land values, a higher land Gini is associated with lower poverty, and higher political concentration is associated with significantly higher poverty.

Overall, we conclude that, contrary to the conventional wisdom about the nature of long-run development in Latin America, there is no evidence that higher land inequality is related to bad economic outcomes. On the contrary, in most of our specifications there is a positive and significant relationship between land inequality and good economic outcomes. Instead, there seems to be a fairly robust negative relationship between political inequality and education and a positive relationship between political inequality and poverty. The results in Tables 5.4 and 5.5 also indicate that the comparatively worse development in municipalities with lower land inequality and higher political concentration might be working partly through lower provision of public goods, such as schooling, in these areas.[30]

5.5.2 Medium-Term Outcomes from the 1937 Census

We next turn to the effect of the land Gini, political concentration, and overlap from the late nineteenth century on medium-term (1937) outcomes. This exercise is interesting for a number of reasons. First, looking at the 1937 outcomes is a useful robustness check on the results presented in Tables 5.4 and 5.5. Second, the effect on medium-term outcomes might be informative about the mechanisms through which economic and political inequality might be affecting economic development.

The results with the 1937 outcomes are presented in Tables 5.6 and 5.7. In all cases, we report regressions of the form (5.2) again, with the only difference being that the different dependent variables are now those that are available in the 1937 census.

Panel A of Table 5.6 examines the impact of the land Gini, political concentration, and overlap on adult literacy. A greater land Gini is associated with higher literacy in column 1, but this relationship disappears once we control for the standard geographic covariates in column 2. In contrast, there is a robust negative relationship between political concentration and literacy with or without the covariates (shown in columns 3 and 4).

Columns 5 and 6 show that although the estimated coefficient on overlap is negative, it is not statistically significant. Columns 7, 8, and 9 include the land Gini and the political concentration index together, and column 9 also includes the quartic in the distance to Bogotá and our proxy for differences in land quality and average land value. In all cases, there is no relationship between literacy and the land Gini, but there is a robust and statistically significant negative effect of political concentration on literacy. Consequently, we conclude that the negative effect of higher political inequality on medium-term educational outcomes is relatively robust.

Panel B of Table 5.6 examines urbanization in 1937. The results here are similar to those for urbanization in 1993. The land Gini has a significant positive coefficient. Political concentration and overlap are also significant and have the same sign as in the other tables, though they become less significant when entered together with the land Gini. When all of these variables, as well as the quartic in distance to Bogotá and average land values, are included together in columns 7, 8, and 9, the results become insignificant, though the quantitative effect of the political concentration index is similar to earlier columns.

Finally, Table 5.7 looks at a direct measure of public goods provision for 1937, the fraction of buildings without access to public services. This variable is informative about whether the effects of land inequality and political concentration might be working by affecting the extent of public goods provision in different municipalities. Column 1 shows that greater land inequality is associated with better outcomes (greater access to public services). This effect remains statistically significant when covariates are added in column 2, though the size of the coefficient falls by one half.

Table 5.6 OLS regressions for medium-term outcomes

	(1)	(2)	(3)	(4)	(5)	(6)	(7)	(8)	(9)
Panel A			*Dependent variable: Literacy rate in 1937*						
Land Gini	0.27	0.09					0.04	0.04	0.00
	(0.11)	(0.11)					(0.11)	(0.11)	(0.13)
Political			−0.31	−0.27			−0.27	−0.30	−0.29
concentration			(0.11)	(0.12)			(0.12)	(0.12)	(0.14)
index									
Overlap					−0.16	−0.19		0.17	0.21
					(0.31)	(0.28)		(0.29)	(0.34)
Geographic	No	Yes	No	Yes	No	Yes	Yes	Yes	Extended
controls									
Observations	97	91	99	92	98	92	91	91	91
R^2	0.05	0.26	0.06	0.30	0.00	0.26	0.30	0.30	0.31
Panel B			*Dependent variable: Urbanization in 1937*						
Land Gini	0.42	0.31					0.24	0.24	−0.02
	(0.13)	(0.13)					(0.12)	(0.12)	(0.15)
Political			−0.43	−0.47			−0.42	−0.37	−0.32
concentration			(0.20)	(0.24)			(0.25)	(0.27)	(0.31)
index									
Overlap					−0.67	−0.73		−0.24	0.16
					(0.37)	(0.40)		(0.39)	(0.36)
Geographic	No	Yes	No	Yes	No	Yes	Yes	Yes	Extended
controls									
Observations	98	92	100	93	99	93	92	92	92
R^2	0.08	0.14	0.06	0.18	0.03	0.13	0.20	0.20	0.35

Note: Robust standard errors in parentheses. Literacy rate constructed from the 1937 census as number of literate individuals over total population. Urbanization constructed from 1937 census as fraction of population living in urban areas. Land Gini is the average land value Gini coefficient for 1879 and 1890 constructed from the *catastros*. Political concentration index measured as the negative of the number of different individuals in power between 1875 and 1895 over number of mayor appointments for which data is available. Overlap is measured as fraction of rich landowners and politicians that are both landowners and politicians (average for 1879 and 1890). Rich landowners are defined as those with landholdings among the top 25% most valuable plots. Geographic controls include altitude (in mts above sea level), distance to Bogotá (in kms), area (in sq. kms), rainfall (in mms), and year of foundation. A quartic in distance to Bogotá and land value per square km (average for 1879 and 1890) are included in column 9.

Table 5.7 OLS regressions for medium-term outcomes

	(1)	(2)	(3)	(4)	(5)	(6)	(7)	(8)	(9)
Panel A			*Dependent variable: Fraction of buildings*						
			without access to public services						
Land Gini	−0.41	−0.23					−0.17	−0.16	−0.03
	(0.09)	(0.08)					(0.07)	(0.07)	(0.08)
Political			0.46	0.41			0.38	0.35	0.35
concentration			(0.14)	(0.17)			(0.17)	(0.20)	(0.23)
index									
Overlap					0.55	0.61		0.17	−0.07
					(0.26)	(0.22)		(0.23)	(0.21)
Geographic	No	Yes	No	Yes	No	Yes	Yes	Yes	Extended
controls									
Observations	97	91	98	92	98	92	91	91	91
R^2	0.13	0.25	0.16	0.33	0.03	0.26	0.36	0.36	0.44

Note: Robust standard errors in parentheses. Fraction of buildings without access to
public services constructed from the 1937 census as fraction of buildings without access
to electricity, water, and sewage. Land Gini is the average land value Gini coefficient for
1879 and 1890 constructed from the *catastros*. Political concentration index measured as
the negative of the number of different individuals in power between 1875 and 1895 over
number of mayor appointments for which data is available. Overlap is measured as fraction
of rich landowners and politicians that are both landowners and politicians (average for
1879 and 1890). Rich landowners are defined as those with landholdings among the top 25%
most valuable plots. Geographic controls include altitude (in mts above sea level), distance
to Bogotá (in kms), area (in sq. kms), rainfall (in mms), and year of foundation. A quartic in
distance to Bogotá and land value per square km (average for 1879 and 1890) are included in
column 9.

Columns 3 and 4 show that there is a negative relationship between
political concentration and public goods provision in 1937 with or without
covariates. In this case, the magnitude of the coefficient is also relatively
insensitive to whether or not covariates are included. Columns 5 and 6
then show that higher overlap is also significantly correlated with worse
outcomes. However, this effect is not robust to the inclusion of economic
and political inequality. The effect of the land Gini continues to be negative
and significant in columns 7 and 8, but not significant in column 9. The
coefficient on political concentration index remains similar even with the
extended set of controls, though because of the larger standard errors, it is
only significant at 10%.

Overall, the results from the 1937 census are broadly consistent with the patterns for contemporary outcomes and indicate that municipalities with greater economic inequality fare better in terms of economic outcomes and public goods provision, while those with greater political inequality do worse.

5.5.3 Corroborating the Mechanism

The results presented so far are the opposite of much of the recent literature on underdevelopment in Latin America and also inconsistent with the literature in economics emphasizing the negative effects of inequality on economic growth working through either credit market mechanisms or political economy. In Section 5.1, we suggested a potential interpretation for these patterns based on Bates's (1981) seminal work on Africa. Bates showed how greater land inequality in Kenya relative to Ghana led to better policies and outcomes, because it prevented politicians from pursuing highly distortionary policies that would have led to the collapse of agricultural markets in many African countries. We argued that in weakly institutionalized polities such as post-colonial Africa or nineteenth-century Colombia, economic inequality might have been a useful counterbalance against the unchecked power of political elites.

Is there any way to corroborate this story? In the next section, we will document that politicians in Cundinamarca indeed appear to have used their political power to amass very significant wealth. Another way of checking our story is to distinguish between the land Gini (land inequality among landowners) and the overall land Gini (inequality among all families) as described in Section 5.3.1. In Table 5.8 we repeat our main regressions, including the land Gini together with the overall land Gini. We only show the specifications with the standard geographic controls and the specification with the extended set of controls (quartic in distance to Bogotá and average land value). In all of the regressions, we drop the overlap measure, since it is almost always insignificant and not central to this discussion. Panel A of the table shows the long-term outcomes, while Panel B is for medium-term outcomes.

The overall picture that emerges is very interesting. In all cases, a higher land Gini is associated with better outcomes both in the long run and in the medium run. In contrast, overall land inequality has the opposite sign, though it is typically insignificant. Political concentration maintains

Table 5.8 OLS regressions for long- and medium-term outcomes

	(1)	(2)	(3)	(4)	(5)	(6)	(7)	(8)
Panel A: Long-term				*Dependent variable*				
outcomes	Secondary school enrollment		Primary school enrollment		Urbanization (1993)		Unsatisfied basic needs	
Land Gini	0.30	0.14	0.20	0.13	0.26	0.07	−0.50	−0.34
	(0.13)	(0.12)	(0.07)	(0.07)	(0.28)	(0.31)	(0.16)	(0.16)
Overall	−0.03	0.04	−0.19	−0.15	−0.07	−0.02	0.34	0.23
land Gini	(0.13)	(0.15)	(0.08)	(0.07)	(0.28)	(0.29)	(0.17)	(0.17)
Political	−0.23	−0.24	−0.07	−0.06	−0.31	−0.32	0.25	0.22
concentration index	(0.09)	(0.10)	(0.05)	(0.05)	(0.25)	(0.26)	(0.10)	(0.11)
Contemporary	0.37	0.37	−0.05	−0.02	1.19	0.95	−0.22	−0.33
land Gini	(0.13)	(0.11)	(0.07)	(0.06)	(0.29)	(0.27)	(0.14)	(0.14)
Geographic controls	Yes	Extended	Yes	Extended	Yes	Extended	Yes	Extended
Observations	92	92	92	92	92	92	92	92
R^2	0.54	0.60	0.55	0.61	0.49	0.60	0.64	0.67

Panel B: Medium-term			*Dependent variable*			
outcomes			Urbanization (1937)		Lack of public services	
	Literacy rate					
Land Gini	0.22	0.22	0.43	0.14	−0.28	−0.11
	(0.13)	(0.16)	(0.15)	(0.24)	(0.08)	(0.14)
Overall	−0.41	−0.41	−0.43	−0.30	0.25	0.16
land Gini	(0.17)	(0.17)	(0.21)	(0.28)	(0.14)	(0.18)
Political	−0.26	−0.27	−0.41	−0.30	0.38	0.34
concentration index	(0.12)	(0.14)	(0.24)	(0.27)	(0.17)	(0.20)
Geographic controls	Yes	Extended	Yes	Extended	Yes	Extended
Observations	91	91	92	92	91	91
R^2	0.34	0.34	0.22	0.36	0.38	0.45

Note: Robust standard errors in parentheses. Land Gini is the average land value Gini coefficient for 1879 and 1890 constructed from the *catastros*. Overall land Gini is the average land value Gini coefficient for 1879 and 1890 constructed from the *catastros* taking into account landless families (see text for details). Political concentration index measured as the negative of the number of different individuals in power between 1875 and 1895 over number of mayor appointments for which data is available. Contemporary land Gini corresponds to Gini coefficient of land value for 2002 constructed from IGAC *catastros*. Secondary school its negative effect on long-run and medium-run outcomes and is typically significant. Therefore, the results in this table suggest that what matters is not overall inequality (as would be the case in models with credit market constraints), but the extent of inequality among landowners. This is consistent with the interpretation that better economic outcomes emerge when there exists a group of significant landowners that can counterbalance the effect of politicians.

5.6 Political Power and Land Accumulation

The evidence presented so far established a range of interesting correlations between historical variables and the economic development of different municipalities in Cundinamarca. While we are unable to conclude that these correlations correspond to the causal effects of economic and political inequality on economic development, they suggest some interesting patterns that need to be investigated further. One possible area of study is to see whether various first-order mechanisms via which political power might affect economic outcomes are present. In particular, is it the case that individuals with greater political power are able to use this for their own economic benefit?

The data suggests that both for 1879 and 1890, landowners with political power have on average more valuable land plots than nonpolitician landowners. For 1879, landholdings of a nonpolitician landowner were worth $1,770 on average while the average was $3,022 for landowning

Table 5.8 *(notes)*

enrollment is constructed from the 1993 census as fraction of children between 12 and 17 years old attending school. Primary school enrollment also constructed from the 1993 census as fraction of children between 7 and 11 years old attending school. Unsatisfied basic needs constructed from the 1993 census as fraction of households with unfulfilled basic needs (see text for details).

Urbanization figures constructed from the corresponding year censuses as fraction of total population living in urban areas. Literacy rate constructed from the 1937 census as number of literate individuals over total population. Lack of public services is fraction of buildings without access to public services constructed from the 1937 census as fraction of buildings without access to electricity, water and sewage. Geographic controls include altitude (in mts above sea level), distance to Bogotá (in kms), area (in sq. kms), rainfall (in mms), and year of foundation. Extended geographic controls include the former plus a quartic in distance to Bogotá and land value per square km (average for 1879 and 1890).

politicians. The corresponding figures for 1890 are \$2,915 and \$5,726 respectively. The same pattern applies when we look at the percentage change in land value between the two *catastros*. While the value of land for non-politician landowners increased on average 99% between 1879 and 1890, plots for politicians increased, on average, 209%.[31]

More interesting than this cross-sectional comparison would be to investigate whether politicians increased their land holdings (or the value of their land) more than other landowners and by how much. We are able to do this by using our microdata. In particular, we restrict the sample to landowners that were present in both censuses and investigate whether those that have held political power saw the value of their lands increase. We measure the extent of political power by the number of years that an individual was in power between 1879 and 1890 (thus creating a continuous measure of political power). We denote this measure by n_{mi}, the number of years that individual i was in power in municipality m. We start with the simple OLS regression of the form

$$\Delta v_{mi} = \lambda n_{mi} + \mathbf{x}'_m \mu + \varepsilon_{mi}, \tag{5.3}$$

where the dependent variable Δv_{mi} is the percentage change in the value of land held by landowner i in municipality m. The coefficient of interest is λ, which measures the relationship between the number of years the politician has been in power, n_{mi}, and the change in land value. Once again $\mathbf{x}_m$ refers to a vector of control variables, all of them defined at the municipality level (since we do not observe any individual characteristics). Also ε_{mi} is an error term with the usual properties.

The results of this exercise are reported in the first three columns of Table 5.9. The first column does not include any geographic controls. The second column includes the standard geographic controls, while the third column also adds a full set of municipality fixed effects (so that identification comes only by comparing politicians and landowners within each municipality). Panel A of this table reports the results of this regression on a balanced panel consisting of 6,391 individuals that were landowners both in 1879 and in 1890. When we include geographic controls, the sample is down to 6,156 landowners. Columns 1–3 show that one more year in power is associated with approximately 50% higher land values, which is a very large effect. The estimates in all three columns are highly statistically significant. This estimate suggests that an individual who remains in power for

Table 5.9 OLS and quantile regressions for % change in land value

	(1)	(2)	(3)	(4)	(5)	(6)	(7)	(8)	(9)	(10)	(11)	(12)

Panel A: Balanced sample for all landowners. Dependent variable is % change in land value between 1879 and 1890.

	OLS regressions			Quantile regression								
				Quantiles								
				0.15	0.25	0.35	0.45	0.50	0.55	0.65	0.75	0.85
Number of years in power between 1879 and 1890	0.50	0.47	0.42	0.03	0.06	0.15	0.23	0.27	0.29	0.44	0.65	1.02
	(0.09)	(0.09)	(0.08)	(0.02)	(0.01)	(0.01)	(0.01)	(0.02)	(0.02)	(0.04)	(0.04)	(0.07)
Geographic controls	No	Yes	Extended	Yes	Yes	Yes	Yes	Yes	Yes	Yes	Yes	Yes
Observations	6,391	6,156	6,156	6,156	6,156	6,156	6,156	6,156	6,156	6,156	6,156	6,156
R^2/pseudo R^2	0.01	0.01	0.05	0.00	0.00	0.01	0.01	0.01	0.01	0.01	0.01	0.02

Panel B: Balanced sample for landowning politicians. Dependent variable is % change in land value between 1879 and 1890.

	OLS regressions			Quantile regression								
				Quantiles								
				0.15	0.25	0.35	0.45	0.50	0.55	0.65	0.75	0.85
Number of years in power between 1879 and 1890	0.28	0.29	0.29	0.04	0.05	0.08	0.10	0.13	0.19	0.23	0.48	0.53
	(0.16)	(0.16)	(0.18)	(0.06)	(0.04)	(0.06)	(0.05)	(0.08)	(0.08)	(0.11)	(0.14)	(0.22)
Geographic controls	No	Yes	Extended	Yes	Yes	Yes	Yes	Yes	Yes	Yes	Yes	Yes
Observations	560	528	528	528	528	528	528	528	528	528	528	528
R^2/pseudo R^2	0.01	0.01	0.17	0.01	0.00	0.00	0.00	0.01	0.01	0.01	0.01	0.03

Note: Standard errors in parentheses. The sample in panel A consists of individuals that appeared as landowners both in 1879 and 1890 in the same municipality. The sample in panel B consists of individuals that appeared as landowners both in 1879 and 1890 and were politicians in any given year between 1879 and 1890. Geographic controls include altitude (in mts above sea level), distance to Bogotá (in km), area (in sq. kms), rainfall (in mms), and year of foundation. Extended controls in column 3 include geographic controls and municipality dummies.

four years increases the value of his land holdings by 200% relative to other landowners. This is truly a large effect and shows how important political power appears to have been in nineteenth-century Cundinamarca.

Panel B of Table 5.9, on the other hand, focuses on within-politician variation, and restricts the sample to a balanced panel of individuals that were landowners in both states and politicians at some date in between. This leaves us with a sample of 560 individuals, out of which 32 are lost when we restrict the sample to municipalities for which we have all the geographic controls. In this case again, there is a positive association between number of years in power and the change in land value in both columns, though this relationship is now only significant at 10%. While the relationship is slightly imprecise, the magnitude of the effect continues to be large. An additional year in power is associated with an additional increase in land value of 29 percentage points.[32]

The effect of political power on land values may be different for different politicians. For example, some politicians may be more corrupt than others, or some politicians may focus their energy in self-enrichment in other spheres of economic life. To investigate this issue, we estimate standard quantile regressions (Koenker and Bassett 1978). In particular, we report regressions from the quantile regressions of the form:

$$\Delta v_{mi} = \lambda(\tau) n_{mi} + \mathbf{x}_m' \mu(\tau) + \varepsilon_{mi}(\tau), \tag{5.4}$$

where τ refers to the quantile in question. This regression estimates a separate vector of coefficients, $\lambda(\tau)$ and $\mu(\tau)$, for each quantile, indicating how political power has different effects depending on the (residual) distribution of changes in land value of the politician. Given the moderate number of observations we have (approximately 6,000 in Panel A and only 528 in Panel B), we look at non-extreme quantiles, 0.15, 0.25, ..., 0.85.

Consistent with our expectations, we find much larger effects of political power on land value changes at higher quantiles. For example, in Panel A, while the effect at the median is 0.27 (standard error = 0.02), the effect at the 75th percentile is 0.65 (standard error = 0.04), and at the 85th percentile it is even significantly larger, 1.02 (standard error = 0.07). These results are also plotted in Figure 5.9, which shows the monotonically increasing effect as we look at higher quantiles. The results in Panel B confirm the same pattern.

Our interpretation of these is that those with political power are able to amass greater economic wealth, either by acquiring more land or by in-

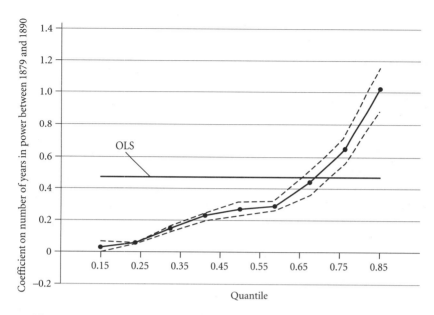

Figure 5.9 Land accumulation and political power: Quantile regressions.

creasing the value of their land, and this effect is especially pronounced when we look at heterogeneity among landowners. Naturally, these micro-data regressions do not establish causality either, and part of the effect may reflect unobserved heterogeneity (for example, those with greater ability being selected into politics and also able to increase the value of their lands). Nevertheless, we find these results encouraging for hypotheses emphasizing the importance of political power and political inequality. In addition, we believe these results are very consistent with the idea that in places where their power was not checked by landed elites, politicians were able to use their power in socially inefficient ways, possibly by expropriating land and or by targeting public services, such as roads, to increase the value of the land they held.

5.7 The Dynamics of Wealth and Political Power

As a final check on the relationship between political power and economic wealth, we also investigate whether politicians are likely to become landowners and how this compares to the likelihood of economically wealthy individuals becoming politicians. In particular, let $r_{it} \in \{0, 1\}$ be an indicator for whether individual i is a rich landowner at time t, while

$p_{it} \in \{0, 1\}$ is an indicator for whether individual i is a politician at time
t. We also use $p_{it}^o = 1$ to denote an individual who is a politician but not a
rich landowner at time t, and $r_{it}^o = 1$ to denote a rich landowner at time t
who is not a politician. Finally, $l_{it} = 1$ denotes an individual who is neither
a rich landowner nor a politician.

We are interested in the likelihood that a politician who is not a rich
landowner becomes a rich landowner, which can be expressed as
$\Pr\left[r_{it+1} | p_{it}^o\right]$. However, rather than looking at this conditional probability,
it is more natural and informative to normalize this with the probability
that an individual who is neither a politician nor a rich landowner becomes
a rich landowner, $\Pr\left[r_{it+1} | l_{it}\right]$. Consequently, the first measure of interest is

$$\frac{\Pr\left[r_{it+1} | p_{it}^o\right]}{\Pr\left[r_{it+1} | l_{it}\right]}.$$

Our main interest is to compare this ratio to the likelihood that a rich
landowner who is not a politician initially becomes a politician, which is
defined similarly as

$$\frac{\Pr\left[p_{it+1} | r_{it}^o\right]}{\Pr\left[p_{it+1} | l_{it}\right]}.$$

Finally, we can also look at

$$\frac{\Pr\left[r_{it+1} | r_{it}^o\right]}{\Pr\left[r_{it+1} | l_{it}\right]} \quad \text{and} \quad \frac{\Pr\left[p_{it+1} | p_{it}^o\right]}{\Pr\left[p_{it+1} | l_{it}\right]}$$

to measure persistence in landowning and political status again for comparison.[33]

Table 5.10 shows 2×2 matrices of these ratios for Cundinamarca and
for the nine provinces (which are made up of the municipalities we have
studied until now). We compute the standard errors for these ratios by
bootstrapping.[34] The results in Table 5.10 show that in Cundinamarca as
a whole, and in eight out of the nine provinces, the probability of transitioning from being a politician to landowner is greater than the probability
of transitioning from being a landowner to a politician (in both cases normalized by the probability of transition of a nonlandowner nonpolitician).
Moreover, this difference is statistically significant (at 5% or less) for the

Table 5.10 Conditional probability ratios

(a) Bogotá				(b) Choconta		
Ratios	r_{it}^o	p_{it}^o		Ratios	r_{it}^o	p_{it}^o
$\dfrac{\Pr[r_{it+1}\vert\bullet]}{\Pr[r_{it+1}\vert l_{it}]}$	13.58 (1.61)	4.54 (1.26)		$\dfrac{\Pr[r_{it+1}\vert\bullet]}{\Pr[r_{it+1}\vert l_{it}]}$	80.70 (15.98)	22.94 (10.52)
$\dfrac{\Pr[p_{it+1}\vert\bullet]}{\Pr[p_{it+1}\vert l_{it}]}$	1.98 (0.89)	15.66 (4.06)		$\dfrac{\Pr[p_{it+1}\vert\bullet]}{\Pr[p_{it+1}\vert l_{it}]}$	14.74 (7.193)	3.52 (18.87)

(c) Facatativa				(d) Guaduas		
Ratios	r_{it}^o	p_{it}^o		Ratios	r_{it}^o	p_{it}^o
$\dfrac{\Pr[r_{it+1}\vert\bullet]}{\Pr[r_{it+1}\vert l_{it}]}$	35.44 (4.43)	16.28 (4.66)		$\dfrac{\Pr[r_{it+1}\vert\bullet]}{\Pr[r_{it+1}\vert l_{it}]}$	71.33 (11.37)	23.77 (6.68)
$\dfrac{\Pr[p_{it+1}\vert\bullet]}{\Pr[p_{it+1}\vert l_{it}]}$	21.34 (11.78)	50.02 (32.16)		$\dfrac{\Pr[p_{it+1}\vert\bullet]}{\Pr[p_{it+1}\vert l_{it}]}$	9.38 (3.52)	40.43 (12.58)

(e) Guatativa				(f) Oriente		
Ratios	r_{it}^o	p_{it}^o		Ratios	r_{it}^o	p_{it}^o
$\dfrac{\Pr[r_{it+1}\vert\bullet]}{\Pr[r_{it+1}\vert l_{it}]}$	76.04 (13.25)	23.11 (7.86)		$\dfrac{\Pr[r_{it+1}\vert\bullet]}{\Pr[r_{it+1}\vert l_{it}]}$	45.25 (8.47)	17.05 (7.07)
$\dfrac{\Pr[p_{it+1}\vert\bullet]}{\Pr[p_{it+1}\vert l_{it}]}$	20.28 (9.64)	41.71 (22.75)		$\dfrac{\Pr[p_{it+1}\vert\bullet]}{\Pr[p_{it+1}\vert l_{it}]}$	5.93 (2.61)	36.85 (15.65)

(g) Tequendama				(h) Ubate		
Ratios	r_{it}^o	p_{it}^o		Ratios	r_{it}^o	p_{it}^o
$\dfrac{\Pr[r_{it+1}\vert\bullet]}{\Pr[r_{it+1}\vert l_{it}]}$	34.97 (4.28)	7.33 (2.46)		$\dfrac{\Pr[r_{it+1}\vert\bullet]}{\Pr[r_{it+1}\vert l_{it}]}$	39.60 (6.13)	22.63 (5.93)
$\dfrac{\Pr[p_{it+1}\vert\bullet]}{\Pr[p_{it+1}\vert l_{it}]}$	2.58 (1.16)	27.56 (7.47)		$\dfrac{\Pr[p_{it+1}\vert\bullet]}{\Pr[p_{it+1}\vert l_{it}]}$	7.80 (3.62)	30.15 (15.05)

(i) Zipaquira				(j) Cundinamarca		
Ratios	r_{it}^o	p_{it}^o		Ratios	r_{it}^o	p_{it}^o
$\dfrac{\Pr[r_{it+1}\vert\bullet]}{\Pr[r_{it+1}\vert l_{it}]}$	32.95 (3.81)	18.01 (4.53)		$\dfrac{\Pr[r_{it+1}\vert\bullet]}{\Pr[r_{it+1}\vert l_{it}]}$	39.19 (1.86)	14.55 (1.41)
$\dfrac{\Pr[p_{it+1}\vert\bullet]}{\Pr[p_{it+1}\vert l_{it}]}$	6.35 (2.36)	53.22 (18.75)		$\dfrac{\Pr[p_{it+1}\vert\bullet]}{\Pr[p_{it+1}\vert l_{it}]}$	6.48 (0.87)	34.48 (4.25)

Note: Bootstrapped standard errors in parentheses.

whole of Cundinamarca and for the four larger provinces. This finding is also consistent with our interpretation that political power is important in obtaining economic rents and resources. In contrast, there seems to be a smaller role of wealth in enabling individuals to become politicians. This pattern therefore strengthens our overall conclusion that a more systematic study of the consequences of political power and of political inequality on economic outcomes and economic development is necessary.[35]

Conclusion   What is the effect of economic inequality on long-run economic development? This question is central for many theories of comparative development and has gained further attention by recent emphasis from Engerman and Sokoloff (1997) and others that the roots of the different economic performances of the north and south of the American continent are in their different levels of economic inequality in the nineteenth century. Most existing investigations of this question look at cross-country data (or cross-state and cross-village data) and do not distinguish between economic and political inequality. However, many theories suggest that economic inequality is likely to lead to political inequality, so that political power should be concentrated in the hands of those who are rich, while other equally plausible theories suggest that political inequality, the concentration of political power in the hands of a few, is likely to lead to economic inequality as the politically powerful use politics to become richer. Consequently, we expect the Latin American societies in the nineteenth century not only to be economically more unequal, but also to feature greater levels of concentration of political power in the hands of a few. Nevertheless, neither existing theoretical discussions nor existing empirical studies distinguish the potentially different roles of economic and political inequality. Understanding whether it is economic or political inequality that matters for economic development is important both to understand the mechanics of long-run development and also because outside of the Americas, there are instances of societies with relatively equal distributions of economic resources but high degrees of political inequality (e.g., many countries in sub-Saharan Africa and East Asia).

In this chapter, we used unique data from nineteenth-century Colombia to undertake a first investigation of the relative and potentially distinct roles of economic and political inequality on long-run development. Using land censuses (*catastros*) from 1879 and 1890, we constructed measures of land inequality (land Gini) and we collected information on the identity of mayors in each of the municipalities in Cundinamarca from which we constructed an index of political concentration.

Our data indeed confirm that Cundinamarca is more unequal than the northern United States in the nineteenth century. However, perhaps somewhat surprisingly, we find that Cundinamarca is more equal than the U.S.

South. Even more surprising, we find that across Cundinamarca municipalities, there is a negative association between political and economic
inequality. Though perhaps political inequality can be conceptualized and
measured in other ways, what we find certainly suggests that the conventional wisdom is too simplistic. Moreover, and again very differently from
the recently emerging consensus about the sources of comparative development within the Americas, we find a positive association between economic
(land) inequality and long-run development. Municipalities with greater
land inequality are those that supply more public goods and are more edu-
cated and urbanized today. In contrast, we find a relatively robust negative
relationship between political inequality and economic outcomes. We also
show that politically powerful individuals appear to have been much more
likely to become landowners and to have increased the value of their lands
substantially.

   Our interpretation of these results is that in weakly institutionalized polities, such as nineteenth- and twentieth-century Colombia, economic inequality may be a useful counterbalance against the most rapacious policies that may be pursued by political elites. This interpretation is consistent both with the negative effect of political concentration (inequality)
on long- and medium-term outcomes in Cundinamarca, with the evidence
presented by Bates (1981) for Africa, and with the additional results we presented above, suggesting that it is inequality among landowners, not overall
inequality, that has the positive effect on various economic outcomes. Although this interpretation is consistent with our findings and plausible in
view of the experiences of other countries with weakly institutionalized
polities, it is very different from the conventional wisdom in the studies
of underdevelopment in Latin America and from the conclusions of the recent economic literature focusing on the effects of inequality on economic
growth. Nevertheless, our results do not provide a direct test of this interpretation, and whether this perspective is useful for understanding the relationship between inequality and economic growth and the development
path of Latin America remains an open research question.

   It should also be emphasized that all of the results presented in this
chapter, striking though they may be, are historical correlations. While we
control for a variety of geographic factors and other municipality characteristics, we cannot be sure that these associations correspond to the causal
effect of land inequality and political concentration on long-run economic
development. Nevertheless, given the robustness and the magnitudes of

these patterns, they call for more nuanced theories of comparative development. At the very least, theories that emphasize the importance of economic inequality should be able to explain these robust correlations. Therefore, irrespective of whether the correlations presented here have a causal component and of whether the interpretation we offer is the correct explanation of the patterns observed in Cundinamarca, the evidence strongly suggests that in addition to the emphasis on economic inequality, there should be more research to understand the effects of politics and political inequality on economic outcomes in comparative development.

ACKNOWLEDGMENTS

We would particularly like to thank Malcolm Deas for introducing us to the Catastros de Cundinamarca and for his extraordinary generosity with his time and knowledge of Colombian history. We also thank Peter Evans for discussions, and conference participants at Brown, the Canadian Institute for Advanced Research, the All-U.C. Economic History conference at U.C. Davis, IMF, the Kennedy School, Maryland, MIT, and the World Bank for useful suggestions, particularly Allan Drazen, Daniel Trefler, and Michael Walton. We are also grateful to Catalina Bautista, Leopoldo Fergusson, María Alejandra Palacio, Diana Rodriguez, and Olga Lucía Romero for help in putting together the data on which this research is based.

NOTES

1. On the effect of inequality because of its interactions with imperfect capital markets see, for example, Banerjee and Newman (1993) or Galor and Zeira (1993). For the impact of inequality through the composition of aggregate demand, see, for example, Murphy, Shleifer, and Vishny (1989). More important for the application of these theories to Latin America and for the focus of the present chapter are the political economy mechanisms linking inequality to economic development (see, among others, Meltzer and Richard [1981]; Alesina and Rodrik [1994]; Persson and Tabellini [1994]; Benabou [2000]). In addition, some authors emphasize the link between inequality and political instability (Alesina and Perotti 1996) and on incentives to invest in education (Bourguignon and Verdier 2000; Galor, Moav, and Vollrath 2006). See Benabou (1996) and Aghion, Caroli, and García-Peñalosa (1999) for surveys of this literature.

2. A similar relationship between land inequality and education across U.S. states during the mid-twentieth century is documented in Galor, Moav, and Voll-

rath (2006) and Ramcharan (2006). However, consistent with Nunn's (2007) results on the relationship between land inequality and income today, we find that the relationship between land inequality in the nineteenth century and current educational attainment is much weaker. This presumably reflects the rapid convergence of southern states to the U.S. average in terms of education and income per capita over the past 50 years following the major educational and political reforms in the South. The fact that the relationship between historical economic inequality and educational attainment has disappeared in less than half a century following political reforms further bolsters our evidence from Cundinamarca suggesting that political inequality is as important as, or more important than, economic inequality in shaping comparative development.

3. Acemoglu and Robinson (2000a, 2006a) also suggest that in societies with significant political inequalities, those with political power may block the introduction of new technologies or underinvest in public goods because of the fear that this will erode their political power.

4. To deal with the ubiquitous omitted variable biases in such regressions, Easterly (2007) instruments inequality with the extent of land suitable for growing sugarcane and finds a negative effect on growth. Since the presence of sugar plantations may create negative effects through a variety of channels, including political inequality, this evidence does not establish that it is economic inequality that matters or that there is a causal effect from overall economic inequality to growth.

5. Though some of these data have been discussed by historians, for example Jiménez (1985), and Palacios (1981) provided an analysis of the 1879 data for the entire department, we are the first to study these data more systematically and examine the long-run consequences of land inequality in Cundinamarca.

6. We calculated political concentration both at the level of individuals and, by aggregating last names, to the level of families. However, the results with families were very similar, and in this chapter we report results only with individuals.

7. Classic works that emphasize the cost of landed oligarchy in Latin America include Stein and Stein (1970), Gilbert (1977), Stone (1990), and Paige (1997). See Schwartz (1996) for a review of the facts and issues. Acemoglu (2008) and Acemoglu and Robinson (2006b) present models in which such concentration of power can lead to adverse effects. On the other hand, many simple political economy models suggest that congruence of interests between the politically and economically powerful may be good for economic development (see, for example, Acemoglu 2007).

8. There is an interesting literature that indirectly speaks to this issue. This literature finds that connections between politicians and firms tend to raise the asset prices of firms (Fisman 2001; Johnson and Mitton 2003; Faccio 2006), get them

preferential access to loans from government banks (Khwaja and Mian 2005), or policy favors (Bertrand et al. 2006). Bertrand et al. (2006) also find that politically connected firms alter their decisions in response to political incentives. However, this literature has not looked at the implications of these linkages for development outcomes.

9. This in itself is important. We know little about the basic historical facts on comparative wealth inequality in Latin America, and what we do know is not always consistent with the view espoused by Engerman and Sokoloff (1997) that Latin America always had greater economic inequality than the United States (see Jones 1980; Johnson 1994). Most notably, Coatsworth (1998) argues that greater inequality in Latin America is a relatively recent phenomenon associated with the economic developments of the late nineteenth century, leading to some group of politically powerful individuals monopolizing large productive stretches of land. Our result that land inequality in the U.S. South was greater than in Cundinamarca provides support for this viewpoint.

10. Our findings and this interpretation are also consistent with Coatsworth (1998, 2005) and Nugent and Robinson (2002), who have emphasized that economic inequality in Latin America is better thought of as an outcome of the unequal distribution of political influence. In turn these more general arguments echo a large literature by historians, for instance Solberg (1969) or McCreery (1994).

    Our results are also consistent with Banerjee and Somanathan's (2006) finding that higher land inequality is associated with greater public goods provision in India. They suggest that this may be because higher land inequality allows landowners to solve their collective action problems.

11. Our discussion and the schematic summary above represent the U.S. South as "strongly institutionalized." An alternative is to view the U.S. South, just as the nineteenth-century Colombia, as weakly institutionalized. In this case, the outcomes in the U.S. South are the intermediate outcomes generated by highly unequal, weakly institutionalized polities, which are inferior to those arising in strongly institutionalized polities such as the U.S. North. This alternative perspective is consistent with all the results we present in this chapter and with our general interpretation, though we believe that the power of the federal state in the United States in the nineteenth century put certain real restrictions on politics in the South and justifies our schematic representation of the South as strongly institutionalized.

12. A number of caveats are once again important to note. First, unobserved heterogeneity in the talents of different individuals might be responsible for some of these results. Second, our regressions are not informative about whether this process of political power leading to economic wealth is efficient or inefficient.

13. The name for the department stems from an Indian phrase "Kundur marqa," which means the "Condor's nest."

14. The best overviews of the colonial period are Colmenares (1973), Melo (1996) and the early chapters of Safford and Palacios (2001).

15. Some narrative information on the emergence of haciendas in central Cundinamarca is in Pardo Umaña (1946) and Villamarin (1975).

16. Key Conservative presidents such as Miguel Antonio Caro (president between 1894 and 1898) and José Manuel Marroquín (president between 1900 and 1904), both of whom appear in the 1890 catastro, lived their entire lives on the Sabana de Bogotá, the intermontane plain on which Bogotá sits.

17. The best overviews of politics in this period are Delpar (1981) and Park (1985).

18. For overviews of the politics of this period see McGreevey (1970), Bergquist (1978), Posada-Carbó (1997), or Mazzuca and Robinson (2006).

19. Even though the period before 1885 was dominated at the national level by Liberals, Conservatives controlled the states of Antioquia and Tolima.

20. Article 115 of the 1858 Municipal Code states that "The Prefect, as political representative of the Executive Power, is in charge of the Political administration of the Department and the Corregidores and Alcaldes are subject to him." Article 116 continues that the Prefect will "visit all the Districts of the Department once in a year and find out if the laws have been implemented and enforce them for a better execution."

21. Cundinamarca also undertook such catastros in 1868 and in 1915. Unfortunately, we have been unable to locate these data, possibly because the state archive of Cundinamarca was burned down in April 1948 in the rioting that followed the assassination of the Liberal politician Jorge Eliécer Gaitan, though see Camacho Roldán (1892) for a discussion of the 1868 data. The departments of Tolima and Santander also conducted several catastros in the nineteenth century, but we have also been unable to find these data.

22. There were however, striking cases of land inequality such as those of Fontibón, formerly the site of the encomienda of Jiménez de Quesada, which had a Gini coefficient of 0.857 in 1879, and Ricaurte with a Gini coefficient of 0.891 in 1890.

23. Since the nineteenth-century censuses do not provide information on the number of families or households, but only on the number of individuals, we used the estimate of 10 members per family provided by Gomez (1969) to convert the number of individuals in a municipality into the number of families. We then calculated the number of landless families by subtracting the total number of landowners from the total number of families.

24. We are only able to compute the overall land Gini for Cundinamarca at the end of the nineteenth century. We do not have microdata for Cundinamarca or the

rest of Colombia today; thus the contemporary land Gini numbers we use below
are for inequality among landowners.

25. Information was not reported for every single municipality in every year, but
there does not appear to be any systematic bias in this.

26. We have also computed an alternative measure where individuals whose land
plots are in the top 50% most valuable plots are counted as "rich landowners,"
with very similar results. To save space, we do not report these results.

27. We do not have data on current land values or average income differences across
municipalities. Even if we had such data, it would not be appropriate to include
these as controls in our regressions, since average income in a municipality
is partly an outcome of education and public goods provision, which we are
attempting to explain with historical measures of economic and political inequality.

28. We cannot look at the relationship between historical land Gini and schooling
for the whole of Colombia, since the historical data on land distribution are
only available for Cundinamarca.

29. In particular, Figure 5.8 shows the relationship excluding "outliers," that is municipalities with the highest 2.5% and lowest 2.5% values for the land Gini.
The relationship is very similar without excluding these extreme values, though
the basic pattern in the figure is harder to see. The same results can be seen
from simple regression analysis. Within Cundinamarca, a regression of secondary school enrollments on contemporary land Gini gives a coefficient of
0.67 (standard error = 0.09). For the entire Colombia, the same regression leads
to a coefficient of 0.57 (standard error = 0.04) without excluding municipalities
with extreme values of the Gini, and to a coefficient of 0.63 (standard error =
0.05) when these extreme values are dropped. The coefficients are very similar when we include the standard geographic controls. In addition, including a
full set of department (region) fixed effects leaves the relationship between the
land Gini and secondary school enrollment essentially unchanged (coefficient
= 0.53, standard error = 0.04).

30. We tried a number of different identification strategies to estimate the causal
effect of political concentration on development outcomes using instrumental
variables. All of these tried to exploit the idea that political concentration represented the legacy of the political monopoly of colonial elites. We first looked
directly at the colonial elite, that is, all of the Spaniards granted *encomiendas*
in the sixteenth century and those working for the colonial state in 1794, and
matched their last names to the names of mayors at the end of the nineteenth
century. Even though there were a number of matches, this variable turned
out not to have much predictive power for political concentration. We then
looked directly at where the grants of *encomiendas* were and at the density of

the tributary Indian population in the sixteenth century, but we found these to be uncorrelated with political concentration. We finally looked more generally at other measures of the colonial legacy, such as the presence of the colonial state, measured by the location of tax collectors or state monopolies. Again this turned out to be uncorrelated with political concentration.

31. Since we do not have a price index for this period, all of these changes are nominal.

32. In some sense, the difference in the magnitudes between the two panels corresponds to the difference in "intensive" and "extensive" margins. Panel B only exploits the intensive margin, the within-politician variation, and thus has a lower effect of an additional year in power on land values, whereas Panel A includes the sum of the intensive and extensive margins.

33. There are naturally many other ratios of conditional probabilities we can look at, for example,

$$\frac{\Pr\left[r_{it+1}|r_{it}\right]}{\Pr\left[r_{it+1}|l_{it}\right]} \text{ and } \frac{\Pr\left[r_{it+1}|p_{it}\right]}{\Pr\left[r_{it+1}|l_{it}\right]},$$

but the four that we focus on are sufficiently informative for our purposes.

34. The standard errors were computed via nonparametric bootstrapping with 500 replications.

35. One caveat is that when we look at individuals who are both landowners and politicians in 1879, they have the highest probability of (still) being a landowner or remaining a politician in 1890.

REFERENCES

Acemoglu, Daron. 2007. "Modelling Inefficient Institutions." In *Advances in Economics and Econometrics*, 3 vols. Ninth World Congress of the Econometric Society, eds. Richard Blundell, Whitney Newey, and Torsten Persson. New York: Cambridge University Press.

———. 2008. "Oligarchic vs. Democratic Societies." *Journal of the European Economic Association* 6(1):1–44.

Acemoglu, Daron, and James A. Robinson. 2000a. "Political Losers as a Barrier to Economic Development." *American Economic Review* 90:126–30.

———. 2000b. "Why Did the West Extend the Franchise? Democracy, Inequality and Growth in Historical Perspective." *Quarterly Journal of Economics* 115:1167–99.

———. 2006a. "Economic Backwardness in Political Perspective." *American Political Science Review* 100:115–31.

————. 2006b. "Persistence of Power, Elites and Institutions." NBER working paper #12108.

Acemoglu, Daron, James A. Robinson, and Thierry Verdier. 2004. "Kleptocracy and Divide and Rule: A Theory of Personal Rule." *Journal of the European Economic Association* 2:162–92.

Acemoglu, Daron, Davide Ticchi, and Andrea Vindigni. 2006. "Emergence and Persistence of Inefficient States." NBER working paper #12748.

Aghion, Philippe, Eva Caroli, and Cecilia García-Peñalosa. 1999. "Inequality and Economic Growth: The Perspective of the New Growth Theories." *Journal of Economic Literature* 37:1615–60.

Alesina, Alberto, and Roberto Perotti. 1996. "Income Distribution, Political Instability and Investment." *European Economic Review* 40:1203–25.

Alesina, Alberto, and Dani Rodrik. 1994. "Distributive Politics and Economic Growth." *Quarterly Journal of Economics* 109:465–90.

Banerjee, Abhijit, and Esther Duflo. 2003. "Inequality and Growth: What Can the Data Say?" *Journal of Economic Growth* 8:267–99.

Banerjee, Abhijit, and Andrew F. Newman. 1993. "Occupational Choice and the Process of Development." *Journal of Political Economy* 101:274–98.

Banerjee, Abhijit, and Rohini Somanathan. 2006. "Political Economy of Public Goods: Some Evidence from India." Unpublished, Department of Economics, MIT.

Barro, Robert J. 1997. *The Determinants of Economic Growth: A Cross-Country Empirical Study.* Cambridge, MA: MIT Press.

————. 2000. "Inequality and Growth in a Panel of Countries." *Journal of Economic Growth* 5:5–32.

Bateman, Fred, and James D. Foust. 1974. "A Sample of Rural Households Selected from the 1860 Manuscript Censuses." *Agricultural History* 48:75–93.

Bates, Robert H. 1981. *Markets and States in Tropical Africa.* Berkeley: University of California Press.

Benabou, Roland. 1996. "Inequality and Growth." *NBER Macroeconomics Annual,* 11–73.

————. 2000. "Unequal Societies: Income Distribution and the Social Contract." *American Economic Review* 90:96–129.

Benjamin, Dwayne, Loren Brandt, and John Giles. 2006. "Inequality and Growth in Rural China: Does Higher Inequality Impede Growth?" Unpublished, Department of Economics, University of Toronto.

Bergquist, Charles W. 1978. *Coffee and Conflict in Colombia, 1886–1910.* Durham, NC: Duke University Press.

Bernard, Olivier, and Fabio Zambrano. 1993. *Ciudad y Territorio: El Proceso de Poblamiento en Colombia*. Bogotá: Academia de Historia de Bogotá.

Bertrand, Marianne, Francis Kramarz, Antoinette Schoar, and David Thesmar. 2006. "Politically Connected CEOs and Economic Outcomes: Evidence from France." Unpublished.

Bond, Philip, William Barndt, John Gerring, and Carola Moreno. 2005. "Democracy and Growth: A Historical Perspective." *World Politics* 57:323–64.

Bourguignon, François, and Thierry Verdier. 2000. "Oligarchy, democracy, inequality and growth." *Journal of Development Economics* 62:285–313.

Bushnell, David. 1971. "Voter Participation in the Colombian Election of 1856." *Hispanic American Historical Review* 51:237–49.

———. 1993. *The Making of Modern Colombia: A Nation in Spite of Itself*. Berkeley: University of California Press.

Camacho Roldán, Salvador. 1892. "Catastro del Estado de Cundinamarca, 1868." In *Escritos Varios de Salvador Camacho Roldán*, vol. 1. Bogotá: Librería Colombiana.

Christie, Keith H. 1978. "Antioqeño Colonization in Western Colombia: A Reappraisal." *Hispanic American Historical Review* 58:260–83.

———. 1979. "Gamonalismo in Colombia: An Historical Overview." *North/South: Canadian Journal of Latin American Studies* 4:42–59.

———. 1986. *Oligarcas, campesinos y política en Colombia: aspectos de la historia socio-política de la frontera antioqueña*. Bogotá: Universidad Nacional de Colombia.

Coatsworth, John H. 1998. "Economic and Institutional Trajectories in Nineteenth-Century Latin America." In *Latin America and the World Economy since 1900*, eds. John H. Coatsworth and Alan M. Taylor. Cambridge, MA: Harvard University Press.

———. 2005. "Structures, Endowments, and Institutions in the Economic History of Latin America." *Latin American Research Review* 40:126–44.

Colmenares, Germán. 1973. *Historia Economica y Social de Colombia, 1537–1719*. Bogotá: Tercer Mundo Editores.

Cruz Santos, Abel. 1965. *Economía y hacienda pública*, 2 vols. Bogotá: Ediciones Lerner.

Deas, Malcolm. 1971. "Algunas Notas sobre la Historia del Caciquismo en Colombia." *Revista del Occidente* 127:118–40.

———. 1977. "A Colombian Coffee Estate: Santa Bárbara, Cundinamarca, 1870–1912." In *Land and Labour in Latin America: Essays on the Development of Agrarian Capitalism in the Nineteenth and Twentieth Centuries*, eds. Kenneth Duncan and Ian Rutledge. New York: Cambridge University Press.

———. 1993. *Del poder y la gramática: y otros ensayos sobre historia, política y literatura colombianas*. Santafé de Bogotá: Tercer Mundo Editores.

Delpar, Helen. 1981. *Red against Blue: The Liberal Party in Colombian Politics, 1863–1899*. Tuscaloosa, AL: University of Alabama Press.

Easterly, William. 2007. "Inequality Does Cause Underdevelopment: Insights from a New Instrument." *Journal of Development Economics* 84(2):755–76.

Engerman, Stanley L., and Kenneth L. Sokoloff. 1997."Factor Endowments, Institutions, and Differential Growth Paths among New World Economies." In *How Latin America Fell Behind*, ed. Stephen Haber. Palo Alto, CA: Stanford University Press.

———. 2005. "The Evolution of Suffrage Institutions in the New World." *Journal of Economic History* 65:891–921.

Estado de Cundinamarca. 1859. *Los doce Códigos del Estado de Cundinamarca*. Bogotá: Echeverría.

———. 1889. *Ordenanzas del departamento de Cundinamarca: expedidas por la asamblea de 1888 y códigos, de policía y político municipal seguidos de algunas leyes nacionales y decretos del poder ejecutivo*. Bogotá: Imprenta de la Luz.

Faccio, Mara. 2006. "Politically Connected Firms." *American Economic Review* 96:369–86.

Fisman, Raymond. 2001. "Estimating the Value of Political Connections." *American Economic Review* 91:1095–1102.

Forbes, Kristen J. 2000. "A Reassessment of the Relationship between Inequality and Growth." *American Economic Review* 90:869–87.

Gallman, Robert E. 1969. "Trends in the Size Distribution of Wealth in the Nineteenth Century: Some Speculations." In *Six Papers on the Size Distribution of Wealth and Income*, ed. Lee Soltoro. NBER, Studies in Income and Wealth, 33:1–30.

Galor, Oded, Omer Moav, and Dietrich Vollrath. 2006. "Inequality in Land Ownership, the Emergence of Human Capital Promoting Institutions and the Great Divergence." Brown University, working paper #2006-14.

Galor, Oded, and Joseph Zeira. 1993. "Income Distribution and Macroeconomics." *Review of Economic Studies* 40:35–52.

Gilbert, Dennis L. 1977. *The Oligarchy and the Old Regime in Peru*. Ithaca, NY: Cornell University Press.

Gomez, Fernando. 1969. "Análisis de los Censos de Población del Siglo XIX en Colombia." Tesis de Grado, Bogotá, Universidad de los Andes.

Gutiérrez, Rufino. 1920. *Monografías*. Bogotá: Imprenta nacional.

Jiménez, Michael F. 1985. "The Limits of Export Capitalism: Economic Structure, Class and Politics in a Colombian Coffee Municipality, 1900–1930." Unpublished PhD Diss., Department of History, Harvard University.

Johnson, Lyman L. 1994. "The Distribution of Wealth in Nineteenth-Century Buenos Aires Province." In *The Political Economy of Spanish America in the Age of Revolution*, eds. Kenneth J. Adrien and Lyman L. Johnson. Albuquerque, NM: University of New Mexico Press.

Johnson, Simon, and Todd Mitton. 2003. "Cronyism and Capital Controls: Evidence from Malaysia." *Journal of Financial Economics* 67:351–82.

Jones, Alice H. 1980. *Wealth of a Nation to Be: The American Colonies on the Eve of the Revolution*. New York: Columbia University Press.

Khwaja, Asim I., and Atif Mian. 2005. "Do Lenders Favor Politically Connected Firms? Rent Provision in an Emerging Financial Market." *Quarterly Journal of Economics* 120:1371–1411.

Koenker, Roger, and Gilbert Bassett. 1978. "Regression Quantiles." *Econometrica* 46:33–50.

LeGrand, Catherine. 1986. *Frontier Expansion and Peasant Protest in Colombia, 1850–1936*. Albuquerque, NM: University of New Mexico Press.

Lizzeri, Alessandro, and Nicola Persico. 2004. "Why Did the Elites Extend the Suffrage? Democracy and the Scope of Government, with an Application to Britain's 'Age of Reform.'" *Quarterly Journal of Economics* 119:707–65.

Margo, Robert A. 1990. *Race and Schooling in the South, 1880–1950: An Economic History*. Chicago: University of Chicago Press.

Mazzuca, Sebastián, and James A. Robinson. 2006. "Political Conflict and Power-Sharing in the Origins of Modern Colombia." NBER working paper #12099.

McCreery, David. 1994. *Rural Guatemala, 1760–1940*. Palo Alto, CA: Stanford University Press.

McGreevey, William P. 1970. *An Economic History of Colombia*. New York: Cambridge University Press.

Melo, Jorge Orlando. 1996. *Historia de Colombia: La Dominación Española*. Bogotá: Biblioteca Familiar.

Meltzer, Allan H., and Scott F. Richard. 1981. "A Rational Theory of the Size of Government." *Journal of Political Economy* 89:914–27.

Murphy, Kevin J., Andrei Shleifer, and Robert W. Vishny. 1989. "Income Distribution, Market Size and Industrialization." *Quarterly Journal of Economics* 104:537–64.

Nugent, Jeffery B., and James A. Robinson. 2002. "Are Endowments Fate?" CEPR discussion paper #3206.

Nunn, Nathan. 2007. "Slavery, Inequality, and Economic Development in the Americas: An Examination of the Engerman-Sokoloff Hypothesis." Mimeo, University of British Columbia.

Paige, Jeffrey M. 1997. *Coffee and Power: Revolution and the Rise of Democracy in Central America*. Cambridge, MA: Harvard University Press.

Palacios, Marco. 1980. *Coffee in Colombia, 1850–1970: An Economic, Social, and Political History*. New York: Cambridge University Press.

———. 1981. "La Propiedad Agraria en Cundinamarca, 1880–1970: Un Esbozo sobre la Sociedad de las Tierras Templadas." Unpublished, El Colegio de México.

Pardo Umaña, Camilo. 1946. *Las Haciendas de la Sabana*. Bogotá: Editorial Kelly.

Park, James W. 1985. *Rafael Núñez and the Politics of Colombian Regionalism, 1863–1886*. Baton Rouge, LA: Louisiana State University Press.

Parsons, James J. 1949. *Antioqueño Colonization in Western Colombia*. Berkeley: University of California Press.

Perotti, Roberto. 1996. "Growth, Income Distribution, and Democracy: What the Data Say." *Journal of Economic Growth* 1:149–87.

Persson, Torsten, and Guido Tabellini. 1994. "Is Inequality Harmful for Growth?" *American Economic Review* 84:600–621.

———. 2006. "Democratic Capital: The Nexus of Political and Economic Change." NBER working paper #12175.

Posada-Carbó, Eduardo. 1997. "The Limits of Power: Elections under the Conservative Hegemony in Colombia, 1886–1930." *Hispanic American Historical Review* 77:245–79.

Ramcharan, Rodney. 2006. "Inequality and Redistribution: Evidence from US Counties and States, 1890–1930." Unpublished, International Monetary Fund.

Rivas, Medardo. 1946. *Los trabajadores de tierra caliente*. Bogotá: Ministerio de Educación de Colombia.

Robinson, James A., and Miguel Urrutia, eds. 2007. *Economía Colombiana del Siglo XX: Un Análisis Cuantitativo*. Bogotá and México D.F.: Fondo de Cultura Económica.

Safford, Frank R. 1972. "Social Aspects of Politics in Nineteenth-Century Spanish America: New Grenada, 1825–1850." *Journal of Social History* 5:344–70.

———. 1974. "Bases for Political Alignment in Early Independent Spanish America." In *New Approaches to Latin American History*, ed. Richard Graham. Austin: University of Texas Press.

Safford, Frank R., and Marco Palacios. 2001. *Colombia: Fragmented Land, Divided Society*. New York: Oxford University Press.

Schaefer, Donald, and Mark Schmitz. 1985. "The Parker-Gallman Sample and Wealth Distributions for the Antebellum South: A Comment." *Explorations in Economic History* 22:220–26.

Schmitz, Mark, and Donald Schaefer. 1986. "Using Manuscript Census Samples to Interpret Antebellum Southern Agriculture." *Journal of Interdisciplinary History* 17:399–414.

Schwartz, Stuart B. 1996. "The Landed Elite." In *The Countryside in Colonial Latin America*, eds. Louisa Schell Hoberman and Susan Migden Socolow. Albuquerque, NM: University of New Mexico Press.

Solberg, Carl E. 1969. "A Discriminatory Frontier Land Policy: Chile, 1870–1914." *The Americas* 26:115–33.

Stein, Stanley J., and Barbara H. Stein. 1970. *The Colonial Heritage of Latin America*. New York: Oxford University Press.

Stone, Samuel Z. 1990. *The Heritage of the Conquistadors: Ruling Classes in Central America from the Conquest to the Sandinistas*. Lincoln, NE: University of Nebraska Press.

Uribe-Uran, Victor. 2000. *Honorable Lives: Lawyers, Families and Politics in Colombia, 1780–1850*. Pittsburgh, PA: University of Pittsburgh Press.

Villamarin, Juan A. 1975. "Haciendas en la Sabana de Bogotá, Colombia, en la Época Colonial: 1539–1810." In *Haciendas, Latifundios y Plantaciones en América Latina*, ed. Enrique Florescano. Mexico: Siglo Veintiuno Editores.

Wright, Gavin. 1986. *Old South, New South*. New York: Basic Books.

— II —

Theory

— 6 —

The Constitutional Choice
of Bicameralism

ABHINAY MUTHOO AND KENNETH A. SHEPSLE

6.1 Introduction

Studies of political economy in recent years have placed emphasis on the operating characteristics of political and economic institutions. The premise of this work is that constitutional features of the political economy provide a structure of institutional incentives inducing equilibrium behavior and practices by optimizing agents. At both the theoretical and empirical levels there are comparisons in the literature of the equilibrium tendencies of classes of political arrangements (see, for example, Persson and Tabellini [2000, 2005], respectively). Political agents behave differently (targeting benefits, producing public goods, regulating the economy, extracting rents), and the effects of their collective choices differ (size and composition of spending, level of debt, productivity and growth of the economy) in presidential and parliamentary regimes, in unicameral and bicameral legislatures, under majoritarian and proportional electoral systems, and more generally in autocratic and democratic political economies. This research has made clear that explanations of collective choice require attention to institutional building blocks in order to anticipate equilibrium performance under different configurations. These explanations, in turn, provide a rational basis for ex ante constitutional decisions.

To date, most of the work has entailed comparisons between broad institutional regimes. Empirical work demonstrates that even crude distinctions, like that between majoritarian and proportional electoral arrangements, uncover systematic differences in the form of behavior and the content of outcomes. In the present chapter we extend this style of analysis but focus on some microinstitutional differences.

We take a garden-variety instance of distributive politics—a divide-the-cake stage game—and explore dynamic extensions in different institutional contexts. In one institutional setting, there is repeated play of the stage game in a unicameral legislative body, where each period of play is separated by an election in which all legislators face renewal. In a second setting, the term length for the unicameral body is two periods, the stage game is played once in each of two periods, there is an election at the end of each period (as in the first setting), but with only a subset of legislators facing reelection in that period. The first setting entails *simultaneous* legislator reelection, while the second setting captures the incentives faced by legislators in a *staggered-term* legislature. The analysis of these settings permits us to unpack the "electoral connection" under varying institutional conditions.

We then combine these building blocks into an analysis of bicameralism. We establish the operating characteristics of a dual legislature, each chamber responsible for dividing half a cake, when both are simultaneous-term bodies, both are staggered-term bodies, and when there is one chamber of each type.[1] These positive results allow us to consider how features of political institutions should initially be arranged at a "constitutional moment." Our basic bicameralism model also permits us to move beyond simple distributive-politics tasks, like dividing a cake, to incorporate consideration of taxation and public goods.

The analysis of bicameralism is of interest in its own right inasmuch as we observe single-period term, multi-period term, simultaneous-election, and staggered-election legislatures, individually and in bicameral combination, empirically. A second virtue of this approach is that it provides a foundation for assessing whether generalizations drawn on the basis of relatively broad institutional distinctions, as is common in the current literature, are robust to finer-grained distinctions. Finally, we are in a position to explore endogenous institutional choice.

6.2   Bicameralism: Conventional Accounts

There is a wealth of historical material on the emergence and evolution of legislative bodies, principally as advisors to (and later providers of protection from) rulers. We provide a sketch of this history as it pertains to bicameralism below. Following this, we review some of the models of bicameral legislative choice. We shall see that there are a number of models of bicameralism related to our own. The main shortcomings of these models, however, are in not exploring dynamic extensions and in not taking variation in term structure across chambers into account. In effect, bicameralism is modeled as joint choice by two symmetric, essentially identical chambers. Our own approach makes dynamics and term structure central elements, and we trace the consequences of these in succeeding sections. (There are virtually no theoretical papers, though an occasional empirical one, on the distinction between simultaneous-term and staggered-term chambers.)

6.2.1 Historical Backdrop

The historical roots of bicameralism extend back at least as far as the classical societies of Greece and Rome. These were not instances of dual legislative chambers by which we know modern bicameralism, but more like advisory bodies to the ruler. There is evidence of these in Athens, Sparta, Crete, Carthage, and early Rome (Tsebelis and Money 1997). They did sometimes assume a quasi-representative character, with assemblies representing different classes of citizen. Set next to such "representative" assemblies were smaller councils of advisors to the ruler, thus giving the institutional arrangement the nominal appearance of bicameralism. Early Rome, in fact, had a council of elders to advise the ruler, that has given modern upper chambers their name—the Senate. Arrangements such as these appeared in Europe throughout and beyond the first millenium, with religious bodies often overlayed on, or thoroughly integrated with, secular ones.

As the "mother of parliaments," Britain developed some of the earliest institutional practices that came to be imitated throughout the Western world. By the ninth century, Angles and Saxons had firmly established a presence in England and governed via quasi-military organizations. Various "courts" were established (courts of law, the hundreds court, the shire court) that different classes of individuals were expected to attend upon a summons from the ruler. In these settings the judicial, the legislative, and the administrative were blended as disputes were resolved, laws enacted, and decisions implemented. Over the next several centuries, these sometimes advisory, often military-like bodies morphed into a pair of legislative chambers. One contained geographically based representatives (e.g., two knights from each shire) and the other, privileged or entitled individuals (earls, dukes, lords, etc.). By the end of the thirteenth century, an arrangement of two chambers, one of which consisted of "(s)elected" local representatives and which met with some regularity, was firmly in place. Of great significance for the political importance of a separate powerful legislature was the written commitment by King John in 1215 to seek consent from the parliament to levy taxes above and beyond those to which he was entitled by feudal prerogative. This provided elites a focal venue for coordination to protect themselves from royal exploitation. While we cannot develop the subsequent history in any detail (see Gneist [1886] for a thorough account), we should note that over the next five centuries the British parliament was transformed from an institution summoned into being at the discretion of the ruler to one that met on regular occasions and developed an existence and policy inclinations independent of the ruler's wishes.

By the end of the bloody seventeenth century, following civil war, regicide, experimentation with a republic, restoration of the monarch, and a second deposing, power had permanently shifted from the king to the parliament, the latter now a bicameral body that met regularly. The upper chamber, Lords, consisted of hereditary and life peers (whose number varied with the disposition of the king to create them). The lower chamber, Commons, represented individuals satisfying a substantial property requirement (essentially the "gentry"). It is estimated that the electorate of mid-seventeenth century England and Wales was 160,000 (Gneist 1886, 285). Thus, a legislature consisting of two chambers that met regularly and whose consent was necessary for most initiatives of the ruler, especially the provision of supply, was firmly in place. At this same time England's North American colonies were crafting institutions of their own. With some exceptions, they produced colonial legislatures that had the look and feel of the mother-country parliament back in London.[2]

The innovation of the United States Constitution, late in the eighteenth century, was the creation of a bicameral arrangement that replaced a class basis for chamber representation with a modified federal basis. The "great compromise" of the Constitutional Convention of 1787 allowed for lower-chamber representation based on population and upper-chamber representation based on equality among the states. It also adopted the principal of "partial renewal" for the upper chamber in which, because the term of a senator was six years and that of a representative two, only a fraction of senators would be subject to replacement at the end of each two-year Congress. (The entire House is subject to renewal at the conclusion of a Congress.) Thus the House is a *simultaneous-term (full-renewal) chamber* and the Senate is a *staggered-term (partial-renewal) chamber*.

British class-based bicameralism and American federal-based bicameralism were the two prevailing models that proved influential in the nineteenth century as many continental European countries moved away from absolutism to representative democracy. One pattern, following the British experience, was for some form of Estates General of medieval origin, with a number of privileged classes or categories represented in separate chambers (often serving in no more than a consultative capacity to the monarch) to transform itself into dual legislative chambers. The upper chamber served to empower and protect a landed aristocracy or other elite from the potential predations of the popular chamber. Another pattern, following the American example, applied to confederations. Many of these, as reported in Tsebelis and Money (1997, 31–32), actually began as unicameral, its members essentially ambassadors from the territorial units of the confederation. The pressure of republicanism and popular participation in the wake of the French and American revolutions transformed these arrangements into bicameral structures, preserving the representation of local units in one chamber and adding popular representation in the other. In each of these patterns, established centers of power, whether landed elites, the bourgeoisie, or local governmental units, protected themselves in a second chamber while extending popular representation in a first chamber. As noted by Lascelles (1952, 202–3), "Of course, no second chamber can stop a revolution but it can check the abuse of power by constitutional means or the use of it in an oppressive manner. . . . "

We conclude this historical tour with some brief observations about the last century and the contemporary scene. Bicameralism, as we have seen, emerged as a medieval development (with traces of more ancient roots) but has been mainly a modern phenomenon associated with the rise (or re-creation) of the state. Important dates are 1215 and 1688 in England, 1787 in the United States, 1789 in France, the nineteenth century in the rest of western Europe, and the last decade of the twentieth century in eastern Europe. By the end of the twentieth century, bicameralism was mainly associated with large, rich countries. In 183 parliamentary democracies counted by Patterson and Mughan (1999), 122 are unicameral and mostly small; 61 are bicameral and mostly large. (They also note that most municipalities around the world have unicameral councils.) In a report posted on the website of the French Senat (2000), it is noted that there has been a near doubling of the number of bicameral legislatures in the last 25 years— presumably an effect of the spread of democracy to former Communist states in eastern Europe. It also notes that of the fifteen countries with the highest GDP, only two (China and Korea) are unicameral.

6.2.2 Rationales for Bicameralism

We are, of course, not the first to explore the operating characteristics or examine the normative attractions of bicameralism. Why bicameralism? This is really two questions: Why is there more than one legislative chamber? And why no more than two legislative chambers? As we shall see, the literature addresses the first question but not the second.

An early explanation for bicameral legislative arrangements emerged from *realpolitik*. Whether an explicit compromise as developed in the U.S. Constitutional Convention, or an implicit recognition by existing elites as happened in much of Europe, the emergence of new sources of political power or the threat of political challenges to the established order induced institutional accommodation. This accommodation often took the form of balancing competing bases for representation. Dual legislative chambers, in effect, provided a more convenient and flexible institutional solution than attempting to house alternative representational considerations under a single institutional roof.[3] In suggesting that *representational diversity* is a force for bicameralism, Patterson and Mughan (1999, 10) point out that, circa 1990, 54 of 66 unitary democracies were unicameral while 18 of 19 federal democracies were bicameral. And, as we noted above, they also suggest that a unicameral structure is associated with smaller, and presumably more homogenous, polities while bicameralism is associated with larger, heterogeneous polities.

The most comprehensive set of claims in favor of bicameralism is the one offered in *Federalist #62* and *#63* (Hamilton, Jay, and Madison n.d.).[4] Their first claim is that the upper chamber is a check on popular passions and thus on the possibility of *majority tyranny*.

> In this point of view, a senate, as a second branch of the legislative assembly, distinct from, and dividing the power with, a first, must be in all cases a salutary check on the government. It doubles the security to the people, by requiring the concurrence of two distinct bodies in schemes of usurpation or perfidy, where the ambition or corruption of one would otherwise be sufficient (Hamilton, Jay, and Madison n.d., no. 62, 403).

Riker (1992), too, emphasizes the control of majority tyranny, claiming that a bicameral structure is more appropriate than other devices. He concedes, however, that other constitutional features accomplish this purpose—a unitary legislature with a supermajority decision rule, an independent executive, proportional representation (diminishing the likelihood of a single majority party), judicial veto power—but presents deficiencies in each relative to bicameralism (which we take up in the next section).

The second claim for bicameralism from Hamilton and Madison revolves around the virtues of *delay*. Numerous bodies, like most lower chambers, are subject to sudden impulses that less numerous bodies are able to check through deliberation and patience. Members of the lower chamber may, given their short terms, be impulsive and prone to quick fixes to problems that would better yield to a more deliberative and considered treatment. Thus, the combination of smaller size and longer terms provides the Senate with the inclination toward delay. Of course it should be observed that, as advocates for the Constitution, Hamilton and Madison did not balance their analysis with an assessment of the costs of delay, or what today would be called *gridlock*.

Nevertheless, as also emphasized by Riker (1992) and Levmore (1992), bicameralism renders change more difficult than unicameralism. Their argument is that it takes longer to broker a deal to change the status quo because acceptable changes are harder to find in a bicameral arrangement than in a unicameral one.[5] As a corollary of delaying change by making it more difficult, bicameralism also reduces the prospect of arbitrary change, something that is more problematical for multidimensional decisions in a simple majority-rule institution with no Condorcet winner.[6]

A third rationale for bicameralism offered up by Hamilton and Madison is related to *agent types* on the one hand and the specific tasks often performed by upper chambers on the other. They observe:

> It is not possible that an assembly of men called for the most part from pursuits of a private nature, continued in appointment for a short time, and led by no permanent motive to devote the intervals of public occupation to a study of the laws, the affairs, and the comprehensive interests of their country, should, if left wholly to themselves, escape a variety of important errors in the exercise of their legislative trust (Hamilton, Jay, and Madison n.d., no. 62, 404).

By contrast, politicians with longer terms are in a position to accumulate substantive expertise and human capital relevant to governing. Thus, it should come as no surprise that upper chambers frequently have responsibility to review and revise the work of the lower chamber. Indeed, in many upper chambers they may *only* review and revise matters related to the raising of revenue. In effect, the second chamber provides a second opinion. (And, in those political systems where power has shifted dramatically to the lower chamber, the upper chamber is often restricted to a role of review and revision for all legislation.)

Fourth, and related, the authors of *The Federalist* regarded stability in policy and in government as a virtue. "No government, any more than an individual, will long be respected without being truly respectable; nor be truly respectable, without possessing a certain portion of order and stability" (Hamilton, Jay, and Madison n.d., no. 62, 407). Longer terms for the upper chamber mean more experienced members, a more stable membership, and a greater willingness to think long term.

Fifth, Hamilton and Madison further emphasize time horizon and limited discounting of the future associated with the upper chamber. The lower chamber, given their shorter leash, is bound to be focused on the short term. So, while frequent elections maintain popular control over politicians, they have a dark side. A second chamber, on a different and lengthier electoral calendar, is a partial corrective. They note that "the proper remedy for [a short-term–oriented lower chamber] must be an additional body in the legislative department, which, having sufficient permanency to provide for *such objects as require a continued attention,* and a train of measures, may be justly and effectually answerable for the attainment of those objects" (Hamilton, Jay, and Madison n.d., no. 63, 409; emphasis added).

We have presented the liberal canon of justifications for bicameralism—representational diversity, checks on majority tyranny, the virtues of delay, the need for experienced and knowledgeable legislative politicians while not sacrificing proximity to popular sentiments, the benefits of review and revision, stability of the political class, and longer time horizons and a willingness to devote energy to "such objects as require a continued attention." The justifications are suggestive . . . up to a point. They demonstrate why a single legislative chamber may be at a disadvantage, but they justify neither why a second chamber is sufficient nor, in failing to explore alternative remedies, whether it is necessary. We turn to some of the modeling literature for views on these issues.

6.3   Modeling Literature

6.3.1   Bicameralism

There are many models of legislatures and their internal arrangements, but few take up the issue of bicameralism. Indeed, most political economy models include a legislature that looks either like the U.S. House of Representatives with its elaborate internal structure and nuanced procedures, or like a continental lower chamber with a cabinet supported (typically) by a multiparty coalition. Explicit treatments of bicameralism are rare.

Riker (1992) attempts to provide insights about bicameralism developed from more formal considerations.[7] Riker is obsessed with majority preference cycles. Their very existence means that majority decisions are arbitrary and can only be arrived at by contrivance (e.g., agenda manipulation). Since they almost always exist in multidimensional policy spaces, Riker concludes that simple majority decision making is tyrannical, precisely the worry expressed about unicameral legislatures in *The Federalist*. He then explores, mainly via abstract examples, how several institutions might alleviate this condition. If, in a multidimensional set up, the winset of any status quo is non-empty under simple majority rule, the winset for that status quo under a supermajority criterion is nested within the simple majority winset. This, Riker claims, ameliorates majority tyranny and increases the prospects for delay. Likewise, he shows that the intersecting winsets of multiple chambers have a similar effect.[8] However, and this is his "pitch" for bicameralism, unidimensional decisions, in which single-peaked preferences assure the absence of preference cycles and the existence of a majority-rule optimum, are handled more effectively by bicameral arrangements than any of his other proposed institutions.

> So we have reached the new normative justification of bicameralism. As against unicameralism, bicameralism works to minimize majority tyranny. As against other methods of delay, it allows majority decision when an unequivocal majority choice exists. Thus it captures the advantages and avoids the disadvantages of the method of majority rule (Riker 1992, 113).[9]

Levmore (1992) is also deeply troubled by preference cycles under simple majority rule and the opportunities for mischief this affords an agenda setter (or head of a majority party) in a unicameral legislative body. The advantage of bicameralism he identifies has to do with the sequencing of votes when two bodies must concur. An agenda setter in one chamber may well be able to sequence votes to obtain a result he desires. But if that result must then be considered by a second chamber, whose agenda setter has objectives of her own, then the first agenda setter's leverage is reduced— "At the very least, if the two chambers consider an issue simultaneously, one chamber's agenda setter will be at the mercy of the order of consideration in the second chamber. Bicameralism can thus be understood as an antidote to the manipulative power of the convenor, or agenda setter, when faced with cycling preferences" (Levmore 1992, 147–48).

The arguments of Riker and Levmore are casual, driven mainly by example, and seem contrived to some (see Tsebelis and Money [1997], ch. 9). They seek to justify bicameralism. Most of the modeling literature, on the other hand, seeks to trace the implications of bicameralism. We will be brief in describing some of these results.

It is well known that the existence of a non-empty majority core in a multidimensional spatial model is a zero-probability event. Hammond and Miller (1987) show conditions that produce a non-empty *bicameral* core— the set of points that cannot be defeated by concurrent majorities in both chambers.[10] Tsebelis and Money (1997) employ cooperative game theory concepts (core, yolk, uncovered set), like Hammond and Miller, to identify bicameral equilibria under conditions of bargaining between the chambers. They explore Rubinstein–Baron–Ferejohn bargaining between agents of the two chambers (as in a conference or navette procedure). Both moral hazard and impatience figure in this.[11] In a more general framework, Diermeier and Myerson (1999) provide an elegant treatment of "strategic" organizational design. Taking constitutional features as given—unicameral or multicameral legislature, independence of executive, distribution of agenda power and veto power across constitutional players—they examine how a chamber will strategically arrange its own internal organization in order to accomplish chamber-specific goals.[12] Their general approach is very appealing for it accommodates a variety of ways in which "hurdles" may be put in place, ranging from disciplined legislative parties to committee systems to committee chairs with veto power to strong floor leaders. This enables comparisons across nominally different organizational features in terms of the hurdles they imply and thus the extraction capabilities from special interests they constitute.

6.3.2 Staggered Terms

In every treatment of bicameralism with which we are familiar, there is no recognition of the near-universal regularity that membership conditions vary across the chambers. For example, nearly all lower chambers are elected. In contrast, of the 72 two-chamber legislatures identified on the French Senat website in 2000, 36 have fully elected upper chambers, 18 are partially elected, and 18 are fully appointed. Eighteen percent have term lengths of four years; 31% have five years; 24%, six years; 7%, more than six years; and the remainder are mixed. And lower chambers tend to have shorter term lengths (whether fixed or determined endogenously by the discretionary calling of elections). Bicameral chambers, in short, are not copies of each other.

Of special interest to us in the present chapter is the fact that many upper chambers not only have longer terms than lower chambers, they also do not "fully renew" themselves at each election occasion. One third of the members of the U.S. Senate, for example, face renewal of their six-year terms every two years. This means that while all members of the lower chamber are "in cycle" every election—this is the defining property of a simultaneous-term legislature—only a third of senators are. This, in turn, means that in intrachamber politics, senators may condition their choices and actions on each other's location in the electoral cycle, something simultaneous-term lower-chamber members cannot do.

Alas there are virtually no models of bicameralism incorporating differential membership conditions across chambers.[13] The model that we develop in the present chapter addresses some of these microfeatures.

6.4 Theoretical Features of the Baseline Model

In order to focus attention initially on some of the core features of our framework and establish a few of our main points in as simple a setup as possible, we first study a baseline model with two restrictive features, one concerning the economic environment and the other concerning the legislative structure. With respect to the former, we assume that in each period there is an exogenously given, fixed economic surplus, or cake, to be allocated as pork across political districts. Thus, we suppress the underlying, general fiscal-policy problem of taxation (that determines the size of the cake) and its allocation between district-specific amounts of pork and national public goods. With respect to the latter, we assume that if there are two (or more) chambers in the legislature, then they are identical except possibly with respect to their term structures. Section 6.7 on extensions considers somewhat richer environments.

6.4.1 Term Structure

We consider an infinitely lived legislature that is founded in period −1. At that time the "founding fathers" jointly determine and commit to various elements of its institutional structure, as described in Section 6.4.5. At this constitutional moment, there are no legislators present. The legislature starts operating from period 0 onward. In each period t (where $t = 0, 1, 2, 3, \ldots$) there are two legislators in a chamber (of either a unicameral or a bicameral legislature), each elected from a separate electoral district.[14]

We will begin our analysis with a simultaneous-term, unicameral legislature (in which both legislators come up for reelection in the same period), and then compare it to a staggered-term, unicameral legislature (in which the two legislators come up for reelection at different dates). In the context of our baseline model, this will prove pretty straightforward to do, but it will illustrate some of the calculations at work and allow us to zero in on the importance of the determination and allocation of agenda power (formally captured by recognition probabilities). We then study the more interesting case of a bicameral legislature. A main aim in this part of the analysis is to explore the circumstances, if any, under which a bicameral legislature is preferred (and hence selected by the founding fathers at the constitutional moment) over a unicameral legislature.

Our model of elections is described in Section 6.4.2. The policy context in each period concerns the sharing of an economic surplus. We stylize this as the allocation of a cake of unit size between the two districts. In the context of a unicameral legislature, the two legislators negotiate over the partition of this whole cake. But in a bicameral setting, each of the two chambers independently divides half of the cake.[15] Note that the legislative task is exclusively one of distribution. There are no public goods in this baseline model, and the surplus is treated as exogenous. The bargaining procedure (which in particular embodies the distribution of proposal power between the legislators within a chamber) is described in Section 6.4.3. If an agreement is struck, then the agreed shares of the cake flow to the districts. The legislators receive no direct benefit from any portion of this cake. A legislator simply receives a fixed payoff $b > 0$ in each term he serves in office. Any share of the cake that he negotiates for his district, however, may help his reelection prospects.

6.4.2 Elections

The likelihood of a legislator being reelected depends on a variety of factors. Even when such factors are taken into account, some uncertainty about the election outcome remains. Let Π therefore denote the probability that an arbitrary legislator (in an arbitrary period) is reelected. We explicitly incorporate a key idea about this probability of being reelected, the notion of *retrospective voting* (Fiorina 1981). Voters care about the legislator's past performance in office when deciding whether or not to reelect him. We formalize this idea by positing that Π depends on the amounts of cake he obtained for his constituents during his most recent term of office. When that term consists of two periods, then we write this as $\Pi(x_1, x_2)$, where x_1 and x_2 are the amounts of cake obtained by the legislator during the first and second periods, respectively, in his most recent two-period term of office. And when the term of office consists of a single period, then we write this simply as $\Pi(x)$.

It is natural to assume that receiving more cake does not make a voter worse off, and thus does not decrease a legislator's chances of getting reelected. However, it may be that for some increases, the chances are unaffected, hence, the following assumption.

Assumption 6.1 *(Weak Monotonicity)   The probability Π that a legislator is reelected is nondecreasing in its argument(s).*

In summary, our model of elections comes in reduced form and is characterized by the probability-of-reelection function Π satisfying assumption 6.1. Thus, the probability-of-reelection function is exogenously given (i.e., in particular the voting rule and voter behaviour are not explicitly modelled).[16]

6.4.3 Bargaining Power

The procedural rules that influence the determination of the negotiated partition of the cake are a key part of the institutional structure of the legislature, pinning down the allocation of power (proposal power in particular) between the two legislators. Our framework abstracts from many of the details of real institutions through which power is derived (such as membership on committees or floor leadership positions), capturing the allocation of bargaining power in a simple manner.

For each chamber, we posit a random proposer, "take-it-or-leave-it-offer" format. Let $\theta_i \in [0, 1]$ denote the probability with which the legislator from district i $(i = 1, 2)$ is recognized, and makes an offer of a partition of the cake that the chamber in question has available, where $\theta_1 + \theta_2 = 1$. If the offer is accepted, agreement is struck. But if the offer is rejected, then bargaining terminates, no agreement is reached, and no cake is obtained (in the period in question) by either district from this chamber.

The recognition probabilities can depend on several factors including the following: (a) the population size of the two districts, with the larger-sized district possessing higher recognition probability (which captures the notion that larger-sized districts have a larger number of legislators), (b) the seniority of the legislators (with, for example, recognition probability increasing with seniority), and (c) in the case of a staggered-term chamber, the positions of the legislators in the "electoral cycle" (with recognition probabilities in a period increasing with proximity to the election date).

We adopt the convention that an offer designates the share going to the proposer. It is therefore convenient to use the word "demand" rather than "offer." We adopt the following regularity assumptions.

Assumption 6.2 *(Tie Breaking)   (i) When indifferent between accepting or rejecting a demand, a legislator accepts it. (ii) When indifferent between making one of several demands, a legislator selects the one that allocates the largest share of the cake to him.*

For future reference, it may be noted that the expected payoff to a legislator who is reelected on each occasion with a constant probability $\pi \in [0, 1)$ equals $b/(1 - \pi)$. Notice that, without much loss of generality, we do not endow legislators with a discount factor.[17]

6.4.4 Informational Structure

How much information does any legislator have in any given period about the history of play? The issue is especially pertinent here since every legislator faces reelection, and with positive probability is replaced by a newly minted legislator. While the legislature is an infinitely lived body, operating over an indefinite number of periods, legislators come and go. As such, a legislator may not know all of the important or relevant bits of the history of play at any given period. In this chapter, we posit a *default information regime*, one in which legislators have imperfect information about the history of play.

Assumption 6.3 *(Imperfect Information)*   *For any t there exists a finite T > t such that legislators in period T and onward do not know of the actions taken by the legislators in periods s ≤ t.*

This formalization of imperfect information is implied by agents with finite memory; the length can vary across legislators. Assumption 6.3 implies that information about a past action is lost for sure some finite number of periods in the future.[18]

An altogether different kind of information concerns what a legislator knows about the game form, the payoffs, and various parameters. Throughout this chapter we adopt the *complete information* assumption: that is, there is common knowledge amongst all legislators about the game itself.

6.4.5 Founding Fathers' Problem

At the constitutional moment in period −1, the founding fathers select the institutional structure of the legislature. In particular, they jointly choose (a) chamber structure (unicameral or bicameral), (b) term structure (simultaneous, staggered, or mixed), and (c) the allocation of proposal power (recognition probabilities in each chamber). These features are institutionalized through appropriate constitutional mechanisms, which determine legislative procedures and rules.

The choices are made so as to optimize over the founding fathers' joint interests. We assume that the founding fathers respectively represent the interests of the two districts, and that for each district, the voters across time have the same preferences. We can therefore identify one infinitely lived principal per district. Let $u_i(c)$ denote the per-period utility obtained by the principal from district i ($i = 1, 2$) when her consumption is c in the period in question, and let $\delta_i < 1$ denote the per-period discount factor used by her to discount future utility. We assume that u_i is strictly increasing and strictly concave in c. The latter feature captures the notion that the principals (voters, citizens) are strictly risk averse.

6.4.6 Comparisons

Our main objective is to compare and contrast the properties of the equilibrium outcomes in legislatures with one or two chambers consisting of agents serving under a staggered-term or simultaneous-term structure. For a simultaneous-term legislature, a term consists of one period with an election taking place at the end of the period. In contrast, a term of office in a staggered-term body consists of two periods with elections taking place at the end of every period. The important difference is that both simultaneous-term legislators face election each period, whereas only one of the staggered-term legislators faces election each period.

A staggered-term legislator is denoted as EARLY when he is in the first period of his two-period term of office, and LATE when he is in the second (and final) period of his two-period term of office. In each period $t \geq 0$, therefore, one legislator is EARLY and the other LATE, and it is the period-t LATE legislator who comes up for reelection at the end of this period. If reelected, he becomes the period-$(t + 1)$ EARLY legislator, while the period-t EARLY legislator becomes the period-$(t + 1)$ LATE legislator. If, on the other hand, the period-t LATE legislator loses his election bid, then a new legislator is the period $(t + 1)$-EARLY legislator.[19]

It is assumed that in a simultaneous-term chamber, proposal power is conditioned only on the name of the district; thus the district i legislator is recognized each period to make a proposal with probability θ_i; in *every* period this is i's recognition probability. Alternatively, in the staggered-term legislature, proposal power is conditioned on the district name and the legislator's type: θ_{iE} and θ_{iL}, respectively, denote the probabilities with which the legislator from district i ($i = 1, 2$) makes the take-it-or-leave-it offer when he is EARLY and LATE, where $\theta_{iE} + \theta_{jL} = 1$ ($j \neq i$). Thus, i's recognition probability can possibly alternate from period to period according to his period-specific type. As noted earlier, recognition probabilities will typically depend on other factors such as legislative seniority, with more senior legislators possessing relatively greater agenda power and hence a larger recognition probability. We will discuss below how our results would change when account is taken of such factors.

This completes the description of the theoretical features of our basic framework. They define a stochastic game with a countably infinite number of agents, but only two agents (per chamber) are active in any one period, and the number of periods for which an agent is active is determined endogenously.[20]

6.4.7 Preliminary Results: Sequentially Rational Equilibria

The imperfect information assumption, assumption 6.3, implies that there are no proper subgames in our dynamic, stochastic game. As such we cannot use the subgame perfect equilibrium concept. But, as is now well established, it is desirable to work nonetheless with a solution concept that embodies the general notion of sequential rationality, which is the central element of the subgame perfect equilibrium concept. In the context of our stochastic game, the sequential rationality concept requires that in any period t and for any *observed* history, each legislator's actions are ex-post optimal (i.e., they maximize his expected payoff *from that period onward*). We define a sequentially rational, symmetric, pure-strategy equilibrium (henceforth equilibrium) to be a pure strategy, adopted by all legislators, which is sequentially rational.[21] We now state a main result concerning the structure of equilibria.

Proposition 6.1 *(Structure of Equilibria)*   *Fix the institutional choices made by the founding fathers in period* -1. *Any pure-strategy equilibrium of the subgame starting from period 0 is a Markov pure strategy.*

Proof.   See the Appendix. ▪

This remarkable and unexpected result implies that with imperfect information about the history of play, there cannot exist equilibria in which a legislator uses a non-Markov (history-dependent) pure strategy; that is, any pure strategy in which a legislator conditions his current actions on payoff-irrelevant past actions cannot be part of an equilibrium. This means, for example, that intertemporal cooperation is not sustainable in equilibrium.

We have formalized the notion of imperfect information about history in a particular manner, as defined in assumption 6.3. As noted earlier, this would be satisfied if, for example, legislators have finite memory. The method of proof of proposition 6.1 relies crucially on the implied feature that information about an action in period t is lost for sure after a finite number of periods; this allows us to deploy a backward-induction argument to establish that equilibrium actions in any period after $t + 1$ cannot be conditioned on period-t actions. While finite memory would seem to be a relatively reasonable assumption, it would be interesting to know whether or not the conclusion of proposition 6.1 is robust to alternative formalizations of imperfect information, such as when information is lost gradually and stochastically (for example, because each legislator knows the full history from the point at which he is first elected into the legislature).[22]

Given proposition 6.1, the set of pure-strategy equilibria is identical to the set of pure-strategy equilibria in Markov strategies. The following proposition characterizes the unique equilibrium.

Proposition 6.2 *(Unique Markov Equilibrium, ME)*   *Fix the institutional choices made by the founding fathers in period* -1. *In the unique pure-strategy ME of the subgame beginning in period 0, a legislator always agrees to any proposed demand, and when controlling the agenda always demands the whole cake.*

Proof.   See the Appendix.   ▪

Given these equilibrium consequences of any set of institutional choices made by the founding fathers in period -1, we now turn to characterize the payoff consequences to them of each possible set of choices, and then assess the relative merits of each such choice.

6.5   Unicameral Legislatures: Results

Without loss of generality in what follows, we normalize the utility of principal i, setting $u_i(1) = 1$ and $u_i(0) = 0$. Strict concavity implies that for any $x \in (0, 1)$, $u_i(x) > x$, a fact we use in the analysis below. We begin with unicameral legislatures where in each period the two legislators have the opportunity to partition a unit-sized cake.

First, we consider a unicameral, simultaneous-term chamber. Proposition 6.2 implies that a legislator will demand in any period the entire unit-sized cake when recognized to make a proposal, and will accept any proposal made to him when his counterpart is recognized. Thus, the representative citizen in district i (hereafter, principal i) will receive a sequence of 1s and 0s over time, sometimes securing the entire cake and other times getting none of it. Her Bellman equation is $U_i^S = \theta_i + \delta U_i^S$, and hence,

$$U_i^S = \frac{\theta_i}{1 - \delta}, \tag{6.1}$$

where U_i^S is the equilibrium discounted present value of principal i's payoffs under a unicameral, simultaneous-term institutional arrangement. (U is the mnemonic for "unicameral." The superscript identifies the chamber as simultaneous term.)

Computing the present value for principal i when her representative serves in a staggered-term legislature requires a bit more development as the legislator's recognition probability depends on his district and period-dependent type. Assume that as part of the constitutional determination at $t = -1$, one district is randomly denoted EARLY at $t = 0, 2, 4, ...$ and the other as EARLY at $t = 1, 3, 5, ...$ We may now compute two Bellman equations for each principal—one for U_{iE}^{St} and another for U_{iL}^{St}. These stand for the ex ante value to principal i at $t = 0$, depending on whether her district begins with the EARLY legislator or the LATE legislator respectively, under the unicameral staggered-term arrangement. From the assumption of random assignment of types, it follows that the present value for each district is simply the arithmetic average of the EARLY and LATE payoffs $U_i^{St} = [U_{iE}^{St} + U_{iL}^{St}]/2$.

Proposition 6.2 implies that the period-t EARLY principal, say principal i, will enjoy the entire cake with probability θ_{iE}, and thus the period-t LATE principal, principal j, will enjoy it with complementary probability, $\theta_{jL} = 1 - \theta_{iE}$. This implies the following Bellman equations for each principal:

$$U_{iE}^{St} = \theta_{iE} + \delta[\theta_{iL} + \delta U_{iE}^{St}] \rightarrow U_{iE}^{St} = [\theta_{iE} + \delta\theta_{iL}]/(1 - \delta^2)$$

$$U_{iL}^{St} = \theta_{iL} + \delta[\theta_{iE} + \delta U_{iL}^{St}] \rightarrow U_{iL}^{St} = [\theta_{iL} + \delta\theta_{iE}]/(1 - \delta^2).$$

Random assignment of EARLY and LATE to districts 1 and 2 implies

$$U_i^{St} = \frac{U_{iE}^{St} + U_{iL}^{St}}{2} = \frac{\theta_{iE} + \theta_{iL}}{2(1 - \delta)}. \tag{6.2}$$

Comparing (6.1) and (6.2), we note that in the absence of any frictions or constraints on parameter values, the payoff consequences of a unicameral, staggered-term legislature can be replicated by a unicameral, simultaneous-term legislature, and vice versa, by setting $\theta_i = (\theta_{iE} + \theta_{iL})/2$. Thus, in the (literal) context of the baseline model, the founding fathers should, in period -1, be indifferent between these two legislative term structures, given that choice is restricted to a unicameral legislature.[23]

But that would be a mistaken conclusion to arrive at in general, as this conclusion has been deduced from a baseline model that contains some restrictive features. This can be illustrated with a substantive extension to the baseline model. Suppose *legislative experience* is explicitly modelled (by, for example, the numbers of previous terms of office held by an incumbent legislator), and average experience positively affects the size of the cake available to the legislators—since it is plausible that a chamber with more experienced legislators is able to secure a larger-sized cake from the same set of resources ("more bang for the buck"). But how does that affect the conclusion that the principals, when restricted to selecting a unicameral legislature, are indifferent between adopting a simultaneous-term structure or a staggered-term structure?

The fundamental difference between these two term structures is that, in one structure, all legislators are up for reelection in the same period (simultaneous term), while in the other structure, not all legislators are up for reelection in the same period (staggered term). This key difference generates (potentially substantive) differences in expected legislative experience in the chamber. In our two-legislators-per-chamber setting, for example, consider the simultaneous-term chamber first. With positive probability both incumbent legislators will be defeated in any given period, and hence both legislators in the subsequent period will be newly minted ones. This implies a complete absence of legislative experience in the chamber. However, such a scenario is impossible in a staggered-term chamber. Consequently, when allowing for the size of the cake to be increasing in legislative experience, a staggered-term, unicameral legislature should have an advantage from the principals' perspective over a simultaneous-term, unicameral legislature. This, of course, was one of the virtues of a "partially renewed" chamber cited by Hamilton and Madison in *The Federalist*.

Another factor suggests that principals, at the constitutional moment, might prefer a staggered-term, unicameral legislature to a simultaneous-term, unicameral alternative: the former structure facilitates commitment to probabilistic alternation of agenda-setting powers between the two districts by making recognition likelihood type-dependent, a form of insurance preferred by risk-averse principals. We elaborate on this below.

We state one of the messages of this section informally since we have not elaborated our model in order to prove this as a result:

If restricted to select a unicameral legislature at the constitutional moment, there are circumstances under which founding fathers would choose one with a staggered-term structure rather than one with a simultaneous-term structure.

6.6   Bicameral Legislatures: Results

In the baseline model, the bicameral setting has two chambers each independently dividing half a cake. The payoff to a district is simply the sum of the chamber decisions. There are three cases to examine: (a) both chambers simultaneous term; (b) both chambers staggered term; (c) one simultaneous-term chamber and one staggered-term chamber.[24]

6.6.1 Two Simultaneous-Term Chambers

Define B_i^{SS} as the present value to district i of the flow of cake from two simultaneous-term chambers each allocating one half a cake. (B is the mnemonic for "bicameral." The superscript identifies both of the chambers as simultaneous term.) With probability θ_i^2, principal i's agent will be recognized in both chambers and receive the entire half-cake from each (following from proposition 6.2). With probability $(1 - \theta_i)^2$, she will receive no cake at all. And with probability $\theta_i(1 - \theta_i)$, she will receive half a cake from one chamber and none from the other (and this can occur in either of two ways). Thus,

$$B_i^{SS} = \theta_i^2 + 2\theta_i(1 - \theta_i)u_i(1/2) + \delta B_i^{SS} \rightarrow$$

$$B_i^{SS} = \frac{\theta_i^2 + 2\theta_i(1 - \theta_i)u_i(1/2)}{1 - \delta}. \tag{6.3}$$

A comparison of (6.1) and (6.3) verifies for each i that

$$B_i^{SS} > U_i^S, \tag{6.4}$$

since u_i is strictly concave.[25] Thus the bicameral legislature with both chambers operating under the simultaneous-term structure Pareto dominates (for the two principals) the unicameral legislature with the simultaneous-term structure. Since, as established above, principals are indifferent between simultaneous- and staggered-term structures when restricted to the choice of a unicameral legislature, we have the following result.

Proposition 6.3   *In the baseline model, at the constitutional moment the principals will select a bicameral legislature over a unicameral legislature.*

While the Pareto dominance of the bicameral, simultaneous-term legislature over the unicameral legislature of either term structure is established, we cannot yet say which term structures should operate in the bicameral setting until we determine the payoff consequences in the other two possible cases (all staggered and mixed). But before we turn to that, we provide some intuition for the result contained in proposition 6.3.

At the heart of the result lies the fact that principals are risk averse, and bicameralism, as modelled in our baseline model, reduces risk because it allows for the possibility that the agenda setters in the two chambers are different. If principal i's legislator in one chamber does not get proposal power in a particular legislative session, maybe her legislator in the other chamber will. This means that bicameralism—with two chambers each controlling the distribution of half a cake each period—provides better insurance for principals against getting nothing.[26]

6.6.2 Two Staggered-Term Chambers

Define B_{iEE}^{StSt} as the present value to district i of a two-staggered-term-chamber, bicameral arrangement where i's agent is EARLY in both. Define B_{iLL}^{StSt} and $B_{iEL}^{StSt} = B_{iLE}^{StSt}$ in a similar fashion. (The superscript identifies the arrangement as staggered term in each chamber, and the subscript identifies i's agent type in each chamber.) We obtain

$$B_{iEE}^{StSt} = \{\theta_{iE}^2 + 2\theta_{iE}(1 - \theta_{iE})u_i(1/2) +$$
$$\delta[\theta_{iL}^2 + 2\theta_{iL}(1 - \theta_{iL})u_i(1/2)]\}/(1 - \delta^2)$$

$$B_{iEL}^{StSt} = B_{iLE}^{StSt} = \left[(1 + \delta)\left(\theta_{iE}\theta_{iL} + [\theta_{iE}(1 - \theta_{iL}) +\right.\right.$$
$$\left.\left.(1 - \theta_{iE})\theta_{iL}]u_i(1/2)\right)\right]/(1 - \delta^2)$$

$$B_{iLL}^{StSt} = \{\theta_{iL}^2 + 2\theta_{iL}(1 - \theta_{iL})u_i(1/2) + \delta[\theta_{iE}^2 +$$
$$2\theta_{iE}(1 - \theta_{iE})u_i(1/2)]\}/(1 - \delta^2).$$

Summing these expressions (the second one twice), simplifying, and dividing by four, we obtain

$$B_i^{St\,St} = \frac{\hat{\theta}_i^2 + 2\hat{\theta}_i(2 - \hat{\theta}_i)u_i(1/2)}{4(1 - \delta)}, \tag{6.5}$$

where $\hat{\theta}_i = \theta_{iE} + \theta_{iL}$.[27] From (6.2) and (6.5), it is easy to verify for each i that (since $u_i(1/2) > 1/2$)

$$B_i^{St\,St} > U_i^{St}. \tag{6.6}$$

Consequently, we have established that principal i prefers the bicameral legislature with both chambers operating under the staggered-term structure over a unicameral, staggered-term legislature. By the same argument as the one establishing the Pareto dominance of the bicameral, simultaneous-term legislature over unicameral legislatures of either term structure (and hence proposition 6.3), it follows that the bicameral, staggered-term legislature Pareto dominates unicameral legislatures of either term structure.

Before proceeding further, we would like to note that the extent to which principal i prefers the bicameral, staggered-term legislature over the unicameral, staggered-term legislature strictly increases in her degree of risk aversion. More precisely, the difference $B_i^{St\,St} - U_i^{St}$ is directly proportional to the difference $u_i(1/2) - 1/2$. Indeed, the *risk-reduction* force is at work here as well.

6.6.3 A Simultaneous-Term Chamber and a Staggered-Term Chamber

Define B_{iE}^{SSt} as the present value to district i of a bicameral arrangement in which i's agent in the staggered-term chamber begins as the EARLY type; B_{iL}^{SSt} is the present value when i's agent begins as the LATE type. Given equal chances that i's agent will be of either type, $B_i^{SSt} = (B_{iE}^{SSt} + B_{iL}^{SSt})/2$.

From proposition 6.2, recognition in a chamber for a district's agent secures for her the entire half-cake from that chamber. Thus, assuming each chamber operates independently, the Bellman equations are

$$B_{iE}^{SSt} = \{\theta_i\theta_{iE} + [\theta_i(1 - \theta_{iE}) + (1 - \theta_i)\theta_{iE}]u_i(1/2)\}+$$

$$\delta\{\theta_i\theta_{iL} + [\theta_i(1 - \theta_{iL}) + (1 - \theta_i)\theta_{iL}]u_i(1/2)\} + \delta^2 B_{iE}^{SSt}$$

$$B_{iL}^{SSt} = \{\theta_i\theta_{iL} + [\theta_i(1 - \theta_{iL}) + (1 - \theta_i)\theta_{iL}]u_i(1/2)\}+$$

$$\delta\{\theta_i\theta_{iE} + [\theta_i(1 - \theta_{iE}) + (1 - \theta_i)\theta_{iE}]u_i(1/2)\} + \delta^2 B_{iL}^{SSt}.$$

Summing, simplifying, and dividing by two we obtain

$$B_i^{SSt} = \frac{B_{iE}^{SSt} + B_{iL}^{SSt}}{2} = \frac{\theta_i\hat{\theta}_i + [\theta_i(2 - \hat{\theta}_i) + (1 - \theta_i)\hat{\theta}_i]u_i(1/2)}{2(1 - \delta)}. \quad (6.7)$$

Proposition 6.3 established the payoff dominance of bicameralism over unicameralism (based on the risk-reduction argument). Having now completed the derivation of the payoffs to the principals from a bicameral legislature under the various alternative term structures, one can in principle assess the relative merits of the three possible kinds of bicameral legislatures. However, there are no general results to be obtained here, as matters in part depend on exact parameter values.

One interesting set of parameter values are those when $\theta_i = \hat{\theta}_i/2$ ($i = 1, 2$); that is, those that capture the notion that agenda power in a staggered-term chamber is on average the same as in a simultaneous-term chamber. For such parameter values, we obtain (via straightforward computations) for each i that

$$B_i^{StSt} = B_i^{SS} = B_i^{SSt} > U_i^{S} = U_i^{St},$$

and hence the following proposition.

Proposition 6.4   *If the parameters are such that agenda power to legislators from each district in a staggered-term chamber is to be the same on average as in a simultaneous-term chamber, then the principals are indifferent amongst the three possible bicameral legislatures.*

6.6.4 Summary and Discussion

Before we turn to study a few extensions of the baseline model, we provide a summary of the main insights established above. Perhaps the most important insight is the one contained in proposition 6.3, namely, that *bicameralism Pareto dominates unicameralism*. This result follows from the fact that on the one hand, bicameralism reduces risk and this benefits risk-averse principals, and on the other hand, there are no costs of having an additional chamber (in the baseline model). The greater the degree of risk aversion, the larger is the benefit from bicameralism. However, once costs of having an additional chamber are taken into account (see Section 6.7.2 below), a unicameral legislature can be preferred by the principals. In such circumstances, the principals may choose to operate the single chamber under a staggered-term structure rather than a simultaneous-term one, since, as noted above, that would provide for relatively greater legislative experience in the chamber in every period.

Given proposition 6.3, we then established a few results concerning the relative merits of the three possible kinds of bicameral legislature, relating to the term structures of its two chambers. One point to emphasize is that in general it is not possible to pin down which kind of bicameral legislature best serves the joint interests of the principals. It depends on parameter values. However, we showed in proposition 6.4 that for a class of parameter values, the principals are indifferent amongst the three possible kinds of bicameral legislatures.

6.7 Extensions

6.7.1 Risk Reduction: A Benefit from Dividing Power

In a unicameral legislature, all power is concentrated in the hands of the members of a single chamber. In contrast, in a bicameral legislature, power is divided between members of two chambers. What are the costs and benefits of dividing power between two chambers of a single legislature? To put it differently, what are the relative merits of unicameralism versus bicameralism? In the baseline model above, we identified and focused on one source of benefit of bicameralism over unicameralism to the principals, which is as follows. By dividing power between two chambers, there is the possibility of two distinctive agenda setters coexisting in each period. This, in turn, implies that each district has a relatively greater chance of securing some legislative agenda power, and this reduces the likelihood of receiving no (or little) cake in each period. Given that the principals are risk averse, the consequent reduction in risk afforded by this division of power is of strict benefit to each principal.

This logic of risk reduction extends beyond the comparative advantage of bicameralism over unicameralism, since dividing power further reduces risk further. To illustrate this point, consider a legislature composed of three chambers all of which operate under the simultaneous-term structure. We capture the division of power by assuming that each chamber controls, and independently divides, one third of the unit-sized cake. Since proposition 6.2 carries over to this context, the ex ante expected payoff to principal

i under simultaneous-term tricameralism is

$$T_i^{SSS} = \frac{3\theta_i(1-\theta_i)^2 u_i(1/3) + 3\theta_i^2(1-\theta_i)u_i(2/3) + \theta_i^3}{1 - \delta_i}. \tag{6.8}$$

Using (6.3), we obtain, after some simplification (and assuming that $0 < \theta_i < 1$), that

$$T_i^{SSS} \gtreqless B_i^{SS} \iff G(\theta_i) \equiv (1-\theta_i)u_i(1/3) + \theta_i u(2/3) - \frac{\theta_i}{3} - \frac{2}{3}u_i(1/2) \gtreqless 0.$$

Since u_i is strictly concave, it follows that $G(\theta_i) > 0$ (for all θ_i).[28] Hence, $T_i^{SSS} > B_i^{SS}$. So, in this version of the baseline model, where there are no costs of dividing power (see Section 6.7.2 below for that), tricameralism Pareto dominates bicameralism because of the risk-reduction factor. This point may generalize to some extent, as we now briefly show.

Suppose the legislature is composed of $n \geq 1$ chambers, all of which operate, for the sake of illustration, under the simultaneous-term structure. Furthermore, each chamber controls, and independently divides, $1/n$th of the unit-sized cake. Proposition 6.2 carries over, and it follows that the expected payoff to principal i at the constitutional moment from instituting a legislature with n such chambers is

$$V_i(n) = \frac{1}{1-\delta} \sum_{k=0}^{k=n} \left[\frac{n!}{k!(n-k)!} \right] (\theta_i)^k (1-\theta_i)^{n-k} u_i(k/n).$$

It is straightforward to show that for any finite n, $V_i(n) < u_i(\theta_i)/(1-\delta)$, and that as $n \to \infty$, $V_i(n) \to u_i(\theta_i)/(1-\delta)$.[29] These properties imply that there does not exist a finite n for which $V_i(n)$ is maximal. While we have not been able to establish whether in general $V_i(n)$ is monotonically increasing, these results imply that for any n there exists an $n' > n$ such that $V_1(n') > V_1(n)$ and $V_2(n') > V_2(n)$. In words, for any n there exists an $n' > n$ such that a legislature with n chambers is Pareto dominated by a legislature with $n' > n$ chambers. Of course, the risk-reduction benefit is at work here without the interference of any costs of increasing the number of chambers, an issue to which we now turn.

6.7.2 Excessive Taxation: A Cost from Dividing Power

There are several possible reasons why dividing power between two or more chambers can be costly from the principals' perspective, as evaluated at the constitutional moment. The calculus of the optimal number of chambers needs to trade off the benefits of dividing power, such as those derived from risk reduction, against the possible costs. To illustrate the possibility of such costs, we now extend the baseline model to enable us to see a few novel aspects of the relative merits of dividing power. To keep matters simple, we restrict attention to the choice between a bicameral legislature and a unicameral one; that is, we do not consider legislatures with three or more chambers. Furthermore, in this formal structure we will suppress the choice of term structure, and assume that legislators in any chamber operate under a simultaneous-term structure.[30]

The core feature of our extension is that the size of the cake is now endogenously determined through the tax rate chosen by the legislature. As in the baseline model, there are two districts, with possibly unequal population sizes, N_1 and N_2, where the income of each citizen in district i is $y_i > 0$.

If the legislature consists of a simultaneous-term, single chamber, then the legislator who is recognized to make the take-it-or-leave-it offer proposes a tax rate $\tau \in [0, 1]$ and a partition of the tax revenue (cake) between the two legislators (districts), where the size of the cake equals $\tau(y_1 N_1 + y_2 N_2)$. If the offer is rejected, then the status quo policy remains in force in the period in question, which is that no taxes are levied and no pork is thus available for distribution to the districts. As in the baseline model, the legislator from district i is recognized each period with probability θ_i.

If all that were involved was extracting revenue from citizens via taxes, repackaging it, and then returning it to the districts, then the process would be one of pure redistribution. However, it would then not be possible to improve upon the status quo for both districts; it is purely a money transfer. We are assuming something different. The legislature extracts revenues and then transforms these into a package of local public goods. If each district values its local public goods more than the tax revenue it loses, then a Pareto improvement is effected. That is, the legislature helps each district alleviate local-coordination/collective-action difficulties, enabling it to provide itself with public goods.

The probability that a legislator is reelected, Π, now depends on the amount x of per capita pork (local public goods) he brings to his district during his most recent, one-period term in office, and on the tax rate τ imposed in the period in question. It is natural to assume that Π is increasing in x but decreasing in τ. However, citizens, when deciding whether or not to reelect an incumbent legislator, tend to put relatively more weight on the amount of per capita pork that *he* secured for them (which we assume is observable) than on the tax rate set by the legislature (of which he is *one* member). We capture this by assuming that the marginal impact of x on Π is strictly greater than that due to τ. In summary, we make the following assumptions on this extended probability of reelection function.

Assumption 6.4 Π *is twice continuously differentiable, increasing in x and decreasing in τ. Furthermore, for any x, τ: $\|\Pi_1(x, \tau)\| > \|\Pi_2(x, \tau)\|$.*

Proposition 6.1 carries over and hence pure-strategy equilibria will necessarily be Markov. Given that, the following result may be established.

Proposition 6.5 *(Taxation and Pork Allocation under Unicameralism)*   In *the extension of the baseline model described above, in a unicameral, simultaneous-term legislature in which legislators finance pork spending via taxation, there is a unique equilibrium. In any period in which legislator i is recognized, his offer (x_i, τ_i), where x_i is the per capita pork for his district and τ_i is the proposed tax rate, is a solution to the maximization problem stated below, and this offer is accepted by the legislator from district j $(i \neq j)$:*

$$\max_{x_i, \tau_i} \Pi(x_i, \tau_i) \tag{6.9}$$

$$\text{s.t. } 0 \leq \tau_i \leq 1 \tag{6.10}$$

$$0 \leq x_i \leq \frac{\tau_i(y_1 N_1 + y_2 N_2)}{N_i} \quad \text{and} \tag{6.11}$$

$$\Pi\left(\frac{\tau_i(y_1 N_1 + y_2 N_2) - x_i N_i}{N_j}, \tau_i\right) \geq \Pi(0, 0). \tag{6.12}$$

Proof.   Given that equilibria are necessarily in Markov pure strategies, the formal argument parallels those in the proof of proposition 6.2. We thus omit that, but instead provide an informal argument. We first note that it follows from the *one-shot deviation* principle of dynamic programming that in a Markov equilibrium (ME, for short) each legislator's objective boils down to maximizing his current probability of reelection. Now, in any ME, the legislator from district i can always offer the status quo policy in which no taxes are raised and there is no pork available. Any different policy (x_i, τ_i) must thus offer the legislator from district j a probability of reelection that is at least as good as what it would be with the status quo policy. Hence, acceptable policies must satisfy legislator j's individual rationality constraint, inequality (6.12). Notice that total tax revenue raised is $\tau_i(y_1 N_1 + y_2 N_2)$ and the amount of per capita pork allocated to district j is as stated in the first argument in Π on the left-hand side of (6.12). Together with the feasibility constraints (6.10) and (6.11), the legislator from district i chooses an offer that maximizes his probability of reelection subject to satisfying these three conditions. ▪

Since our main objective is to compare and contrast the consequences in this extended setup of dividing power, we will shortly proceed to deriving the equilibrium solution for the bicameral setting. Once we have done that, we will then undertake a comparative analysis and during that process we will return to proposition 6.5 and provide a characterization of the solution of the optimization problem stated in this proposition. But there is one feature of the solution we would like to mention now.

In this extended setup, it is no longer the case that the agenda setter can allocate all the cake to his district (unlike in the baseline model in which the size of the cake was fixed and exogenously given; cf. proposition 6.2). Notice that if, for any $\tau_i > 0$, the legislator from district i sets x_i to its upper bound, then the individual rationality constraint of the legislator from district j, (6.12), would be violated (since, given assumption 6.4, Π is decreasing in the tax rate). Not surprisingly, raising some tax revenue across the two districts but without allocating any pork to a district is worse than the status quo policy from a legislator's perspective. So, in this extended setup, with multidimensional policy, extremal allocations of pork, which featured in the baseline model, cannot form part of the equilibrium solution. Having said that, at the solution to the maximization problem, the individual rationality constraint (6.12) binds (for otherwise the agenda setter could increase his reelection probability by allocating to his district a little more of the cake), and hence the agenda setter nonetheless extracts most of the surplus.

We now turn to the bicameral legislature, where power is divided between two chambers, which we assume are identical and both operating under the simultaneous-term structure. Here are the main features that are specific to the bicameral legislature. In each period, a legislator is randomly and independently recognized in each chamber. The probability that in each chamber the legislator from district i is recognized is θ_i. The two agenda setters simultaneously and independently make take-it-or-leave-it offers to their respective chamber partners, who simultaneously and independently decide whether or not to accept the proposals. There is no communication, cooperation, or collusion across the chambers. They operate separately.

We want to capture the notion that tax policy is determined "jointly" by the two chambers. We model this as follows. The offer of a legislator in each chamber contains a proposed tax rate. The actual tax rate announced by the legislature will be the average of the two proposed tax rates, which in turn determines the total tax revenue (the total size of the cake), which, as in the baseline model, is to be divided equally between the two chambers. It should be noted that the status quo policy—no taxation and no cake— is changed in any period if and only if in each of the two chambers, the respective offers made are accepted by the respective legislators. Thus, if the offer in either chamber is turned down, then the status quo policy remains in force in the period in question.

We assume that, in each period, after legislators from each chamber are recognized, this becomes known to all legislators in both chambers before any actions are taken. Hence, for example, the legislator who is recognized in a chamber can condition his offer on whether or not his counterpart has also been recognized in the other chamber. Indeed, since the actual tax rate will be the average of the proposed tax rates, the two agenda setters are in a game-theoretic situation, and we will, unlike in the baseline model, look for a Nash equilibrium in offers across the two chambers. Furthermore, it is assumed that when responding to an offer, a legislator knows the offer made in the other chamber, which thus allows him to calculate the actual tax rate if he and the responder in the other chamber accept their respective offers.

It is straightforward to verify that proposition 6.1 carries over here as well, and hence equilibria will necessarily be in Markov pure strategies. Given that, we can establish the following proposition.

Proposition 6.6 (*Taxation and Pork Allocation under Bicameralism*)   *In the extension of the baseline model described above under a bicameral legislature in which legislators finance pork spending via taxation and power is divided across the two chambers, there is a unique equilibrium in which, in any period, acceptable offers are made, which are as follows. Suppose that the legislators recognized in the two chambers are from districts i and j, where $i, j = 1, 2$. Then the equilibrium offers of legislators i and j, (x_i^j, τ_i^j) and $(\hat{x}_j^i, \hat{\tau}_j^i)$, re-*

spectively, are solutions to the following pair of (simultaneous) maximization problems:[31]

Problem 1:

$$\max_{x_i^j, \tau_i^j} \Pi\left(x_i^j, \frac{\tau_i^j + \hat{\tau}_j^i}{2}\right)$$

$$\text{s.t. } 0 \leq \tau_i^j \leq 1, \quad 0 \leq x_i^j \leq \frac{[(\tau_i^j + \hat{\tau}_j^i)/2](y_1N_1 + y_2N_2)}{2N_i}$$

$$\text{and } \Pi\left(\frac{[(\tau_i^j + \hat{\tau}_j^i)/2](y_1N_1 + y_2N_2) - 2x_i^j N_i}{2N_k}, \frac{\tau_i^j + \hat{\tau}_j^i}{2}\right)$$

$$\geq \Pi(0, 0), \text{ where } k \neq i.$$

Problem 2:

$$\max_{\hat{x}_j^i, \hat{\tau}_j^i} \Pi\left(\hat{x}_j^i, \frac{\tau_i^j + \hat{\tau}_j^i}{2}\right)$$

$$\text{s.t. } 0 \leq \hat{\tau}_j^i \leq 1, \quad 0 \leq \hat{x}_j^i \leq \frac{[(\tau_i^j + \hat{\tau}_j^i)/2](y_1N_1 + y_2N_2)}{2N_j}$$

$$\text{and } \Pi\left(\frac{[(\tau_i^j + \hat{\tau}_j^i)/2](y_1N_1 + y_2N_2) - 2\hat{x}_j^i N_i}{2N_l}, \frac{\tau_i^j + \hat{\tau}_j^i}{2}\right)$$

$$\geq \Pi(0, 0), \text{ where } l \neq j.$$

Proof. The argument is an extension of the proof of proposition 6.5 in which the offers made in each period by the two agenda setters in the two chambers are in a Nash equilibrium of the appropriate game. In an ME, it follows that each legislator's objective is to maximize his own current re-election probability. The solution to problem 1 defines i's reaction function to an arbitrary offer made by the agenda setter, j, in the other chamber. Symmetrically, problem 2 gives rise to j's reaction function. A fixed point of these reaction functions defines the equilibrium offers. ▪

As in the solution to the maximization problem that defines the equilibrium in the unicameral setting (cf. proposition 6.5), in each of two maximization problems stated in proposition 6.6 that together define an ME in the bicameral setting, the two individual rationality (IR) constraints bind, but the feasibility constraints don't. That is, while each agenda setter will extract as much of the surplus as possible, each needs to allocate some pork to the district of his chamber partner (for otherwise the status quo policy will be preferred).

Comparing the IR constraint of the maximization problem that defines the unicameral equilibrium with those that define the bicameral equilibrium, notice that, not surprisingly, for any pair of policies (x, τ), it is easier to satisfy the IR constraint in the unicameral setting than in the bicameral setting, because in the former setting there is twice as much pork from which a given x is deducted. This intuitive observation provides the key for the result that the set of acceptable and feasible offers under bicameralism is strictly contained in the corresponding set under unicameralism. This means it is possible that under bicameralism the status quo policy is the only feasible and acceptable policy while that is not the case under unicameralism. Consequently, there is relatively greater scope for gridlock under bicameralism. We summarize this in the following corollary.

Corollary 6.1 (*Gridlock under Bicameralism*)　*There is a relatively greater prospect of gridlock—no change from the status quo policy—under bicameralism than under unicameralism.*

We now consider scenarios in which the set of acceptable and feasible offers under bicameralism contains policy vectors other than the status quo policy. In such cases, the equilibrium tax rates under bicameralism will in general be higher than the equilibrium tax rates under unicameralism. The intuition for this result is straightforward and can be gleaned by comparing the maximization problems stated in these two propositions. It is this. Under bicameralism, each agenda setter gets to control and divide only one-half of the total tax revenues raised, and hence each has an incentive to set a higher tax rate than he would under unicameralism. It is "as if" the agenda setter in each chamber is being "held up" by the agenda setter in the other chamber, in having to relinquish one-half of the tax revenues raised.

Corollary 6.2 (*Higher Taxes under Bicameralism*)　*Tax rates under bicameralism will tend to be higher than under unicameralism.*

While the equilibrium policy (the tax rate and allocation of pork) will differ under these two alternative legislative structures, which one is preferred by the two principals at the constitutional moment, in period -1, depends on which policy is closer to the one they would jointly select (the first best). We assume that principals, as before, discount future payoffs with a common discount factor $\delta < 1$, and assume that their instantaneous utility is the sum of net income and utility from pork (as in the baseline model). That is, principal i's utility is $(1 - \tau)y_i + u_i(x)$. This implies that aggregate welfare per period is given by

$$(1 - \tau)(y_1 N_1 + y_2 N_2) + u_1(x_1)N_1 + u_2(x_2)N_2,$$
$$\text{where } x_1 N_1 + x_2 N_2 = \tau(y_1 N_1 + y_2 N_2).$$

It may be noted that since u_i is strictly increasing and strictly concave, the first-best tax rate will be strictly positive, and hence different from the status quo policy of a zero tax rate. The risk-reduction benefit from bicameralism will continue to arise in this extended baseline model. But now there is a potential cost from bicameralism, which is that the equilibrium policy vectors under a bicameral setting deviate further away from the first-best policy than the equilibrium policy vectors arrived at in a unicameral setting. Of course, this need not be the case, since this depends on the relative positions of the two sets of equilibrium policies and the first-best policy. And that, in turn, depends on the utility functions and the probability of reelection functions. But when the cost exists, then the optimal number of chambers (one or two) depends, in effect, on comparing the costs from excessive taxation against the benefits from risk reduction.

Conclusion   The concerns expressed by the authors of *The Federalist* in arguing for bicameral legislative arrangements centered on majority tyranny and delay. The results we have provided do so as well, but from a slightly different perspective. Bicameralism does, indeed, reduce the prospects of majority tyranny in the sense that two chambers provide greater insurance against domination by an agenda-setter agent of one (class of) principal to the exclusion of others. Bicameralism is associated with delay as well in the sense that there are circumstances in which a unicameral legislature will pass new legislation but a bicameral legislature is saddled with the status quo. Interestingly, Hamilton and Madison saw this, as they did the control of majority tyranny, as an *advantage* of bicameralism. We believe that, in their advocacy for the U.S. Constitution, they were not prepared to acknowledge the downside of delay, what modern scholars term *gridlock*. Nor were they prepared to speculate about taxation propensities in a bicameral legislature. So we have concluded that the risk-spreading virtues of multicameralism must be balanced against the prospects of inaction on the one hand, and the possibility of larger government on the other. Empirically, of course, most of the world's democracies have settled on a legislative branch with one or two chambers, though some have included some (partial) legislative powers in other branches of government (e.g., executive veto, judicial negativing of statutes).

We have had considerably less to say about the circumstances in which democracies choose a single chamber or multiple chambers, partial renewal or full renewal. As noted, such arrangements are ex ante optimal at any given constitutional moment depending upon "parameters," but we haven't offered much insight beyond this. We believe the next research step should be to build in heterogeneity among principals and thus diversity among agent objectives. Bicameralism, as we noted at the outset, is associated empirically with large states, with rich states, and with federal states—that is, with states that are nominally more complex economically and more layered politically. Unicameralism is found in states with a lower GDP per capita, with a more compact geography, and with more centralized governance. Under what circumstances would such factors induce constitution writers to make one set of institutional choices rather than another? We also believe it desirable to introduce more heterogeneity among agents. Re-elected incumbents are, in important ways, different from newly minted legislators—their human capital in the form of substantive expertise and legislative experience may well have performance effects that should be captured in an extension of the present model. Finally, it would be interesting to explore the possibility (and consequences thereof) of cooperation across space and time: cooperation, in any given session, amongst legislators within a single chamber and/or across chambers, and intertemporal cooperation. In order to sustain cooperative behavior in equilibrium, one needs to relax the informational assumption (assumption 6.3) that has underpinned the analysis in this chapter.[32]

Appendix

Proof of Proposition 6.1. Fix an arbitrary pure-strategy equilibrium, and fix an arbitrary period $t \geq 1$. We will show that the equilibrium actions in period t are conditioned on at most z_t (the amount of cake obtained by the period-t LATE legislator in period $t - 1$), but on no other bits of observed history, which then establishes the proposition. The argument involves induction. ∎

First, note that assumption 6.3 implies that there exists a $T \geq t + 2$ such that the equilibrium actions in any period from and including period T onward cannot be conditioned on the actions taken in any period before and including $t - 1$. Second, we establish the following inductive step:

Fix an arbitrary period s, where $s \geq t + 1$. If the equilibrium actions in any period from and including period $s + 1$ onward are not conditioned on the actions taken in any period before and including period $t - 1$, then the same is true of the equilibrium actions in period s.

Proof of inductive step. Since $s \geq t + 1$, none of the actions in any period before and including period $t - 1$ directly affects the payoffs of any legislator in period s. Given this and the hypothesis of the inductive step, it follows that the equilibrium expected payoff to a legislator from period s onward does not depend on the actions in any period before and including $t - 1$. Let h_{t-1} and h'_{t-1} denote two different histories till the end of period $t - 1$ that are observable to an arbitrary legislator in period s. Furthermore, let h denote a history of actions observed by the arbitrary legislator between and including periods t and $s - 1$. Hence, two different observed histories at the beginning of period s are (h_{t-1}, h) and (h'_{t-1}, h). The equilibrium expected payoffs to this arbitrary legislator from period s onward will be the same following either observed history (for any set of period s actions and given the equilibrium pure-strategy). Hence, given assumption 6.2, the legislator's equilibrium actions in period s following these two observed histories are the same. This completes the proof of the inductive step. ∎

Hence, it now follows from the principle of mathematical induction that the equilibrium actions in any period from and including period $t + 1$ are not conditioned on the actions taken in any period before and including period $t - 1$. The desired conclusion follows immediately.

Proof of Proposition 6.2. We first show that the strategy described in the proposition, when adopted by all legislators, is the unique stationary Markov equilibrium, and then we establish the nonexistence of nonstationary Markov equilibria. This then establishes the proposition. ▪

Since in the baseline model there is no payoff-relevant link between two chambers in a bicameral legislature, this means that a stationary Markov pure strategy of a legislator in a chamber is not conditioned on events or actions of legislators in the other chamber. Hence, it suffices to establish the result for a unicameral legislature. We do so below in the context of a unicameral, staggered-term chamber; the argument for a unicameral, simultaneous-term chamber is similar and hence omitted.

A stationary Markov pure strategy for a legislator from district i ($i = 1, 2$) in a unicameral, staggered-term chamber is made up of two numbers, k_{iE} and k_{iL}, and two functions, f_{iE} and f_{iL}. k_{in} denotes the legislator's demand when he is type n, and $f_{in} : [0, 1] \to \{\text{"Accept", "Reject"}\}$ such that $f_{in}(x)$ denotes whether the legislator accepts or rejects the demand x when he is type n, where $n = E, L$ (E stands for EARLY and L stands for LATE). Fix an arbitrary, stationary Markov equilibrium, and let W_i denote the expected payoff associated with this equilibrium to the legislator when he is EARLY at the beginning of any period (before the proposer is randomly selected). We first establish the following result:

Claim 6.1   If the probability of reelection Π satisfies assumption 6.1, then a legislator accepts any offer when EARLY and any offer when LATE.

Proof of Claim 6.1. To establish this claim, we need to show that the legislator, when EARLY and when LATE, respectively, accepts any demand $x \in [0, 1]$ made by the proposer. It follows from the *One-Shot Deviation Principle* that the legislator, when EARLY, accepts a demand $x \in [0, 1]$ if and only if $H_{iE}(x) \geq H_{iE}(1)$, where $H_{iE}(x) = b + [\theta_{jE}\Pi(1 - x, y_{iE}) + \theta_{iL}\Pi(1 - x, y_{iL})]W_i$, where

$$y_{iE} = \begin{cases} 1 - k_{jE} & \text{if } f_{iL}(k_{jE}) = \text{``Accept''} \\ 0 & \text{if } f_{iL}(k_{jE}) = \text{``Reject''} \end{cases} \quad \text{and}$$

$$y_{iL} = \begin{cases} k_{iL} & \text{if } f_{jE}(k_{iL}) = \text{``Accept''} \\ 0 & \text{if } f_{jE}(k_{iL}) = \text{``Reject''} \end{cases}.$$

Assumption 6.1 implies that for any $x \in [0, 1]$, $H_{iE}(x) \geq H_{iE}(1)$. Hence, this means that $f_{iE}(x) =$ "Accept" for all $x \in [0, 1]$. A legislator, when LATE, accepts an offer $x \in [0, 1]$ if and only if $H_{iL}(x) \geq H_{iL}(1)$, where $H_{iL}(x) = b + \Pi(z, 1 - x)W_i$, and z is the amount of cake received by the LATE legislator in the previous period. Assumption 6.1 implies that for any $x \in [0, 1]$, $H_{iL}(x) \geq H_{iL}(1)$. Hence, this means that $f_{iL}(x) =$ "Accept" for all $x \in [0, 1]$. This completes the proof of claim 1. ∎

Given claim 1, it follows from the One-Shot Deviation Principle that the pair (k_{iE}, k_{iL}) satisfy the following conditions:

$$k_{iE} \in \arg \max_{x \in [0, 1]} \left[b + [\theta_{jE}\Pi(x, 1 - k_{jE}) + \theta_{iL}\Pi(x, k_{iL})]W_i \right] \quad \text{and}$$

$$k_{iL} \in \arg \max_{x \in [0, 1]} \left[b + \Pi(z, x)W_i \right],$$

where z is the amount of cake earned by the LATE legislator a period earlier. That is,

$$k_{iE} \in \arg \max_{x \in [0, 1]} \left[\theta_{jE}\Pi(x, 1 - k_{jE}) + \theta_{iL}\Pi(x, k_{iL}) \right] \quad \text{and}$$

$$k_{iL} \in \arg \max_{x \in [0, 1]} \left[\Pi(z, x) \right].$$

Assumptions 6.1 and 6.2 thus imply that $(k_{iE}, k_{iL}) = (1, 1)$ is the unique solution.

ACKNOWLEDGMENTS

The authors are grateful to members of the Institutions, Organizations & Growth research group of the Canadian Institute for Advanced Research, an anonymous referee, and especially to Elhanan Helpman for very useful comments on an earlier draft. Shepsle acknowledges research support from the U.S. National Institute of Aging (RO1-AG021181).

NOTES

1. Empirically, each chamber of a bicameral legislature passes a legislative bill and there is an ex post reconciliation of these proposals. In the United States this resolution occurs in a *conference procedure*. In many distributive-politics situations, however, each chamber is effectively given a portion of the cake to divide, and their respective proposals are simply added together ex post. See Shepsle et al. (2007).

2. Tsebelis and Money (1997, 27) report the irony that all the North American colonial legislatures began as unicameral. By the time of the American Revolution, however, all but Georgia and Pennsylvania had become bicameral. The typical pattern was for the press of business to cause the creation of a subset of the unicameral legislative chamber as a separate "standing council." This was effectively a combined agenda-setting agent and executive committee, but was transformed over time into a second chamber.

3. This fails to account for why there were typically only two chambers. In fact, until reforms in the mid-nineteenth century, the Swedish Riksdag had *four* chambers. Tsebelis and Money (1997, 29–30) report that from the fifteenth century onward each chamber had a veto over decisions. In the eighteenth century this was relaxed with decisions requiring the assent of three of the four chambers. The 1865–66 creation of a two-chamber parliament is suggested by them to be the result of "the unwieldiness of decision making with four estates rather than by demands for electoral reform."

4. The author is believed to be either Alexander Hamilton or James Madison, but there is no definitive attribution.

5. Let x^0 be the status quo in a multidimensional policy space. Define $W(x^0)$ as the set of alternatives preferred to x^0 by any decisive coalition in a unitary legislature—the *winset of x^0*. Let $W_i(x^0)$, $i = H, S$ be the chamber-specific winsets of a House and Senate. The claim is $W_H(x^0) \cap W_S(x^0) \subset W(x^0)$.

6. Cutrone and McCarty (2006) demonstrate, as a positive claim (with no normative justification), that bicameralism produces a gridlock region that renders the status quo more robust to minor electoral perturbations than is the case in a unicameral arrangement.

7. One of the earliest treatments is Buchanan and Tullock (1962).

8. As a third institution, he suggests that the multipartism produced by proportional representation, even in a unicameral chamber, has similarities to both multicameralism and supermajority rule.

9. Riker makes a number of simplifying assumptions. He assumes, for example, that the distributions of legislative preferences are *identical* in both chambers. As Cutrone and McCarty (2006) show, even in a unidimensional world, when

this assumption is relaxed there is a gridlock region between the medians of the two chambers. So, the advantages attributed by Riker to bicameralism are not terribly robust.

10. In effect, the requirement is that there is clear "separation" between the preference distributions of the two chambers. That is, the majority winsets of the two chambers must have an empty intersection—an implausible condition.

11. Moral hazard is of interest because bargaining agents need not be "representative" of their parent chamber. Gailmard and Hammond (2006), for example, explore the ways in which intercameral bargaining has *intracameral* organizational consequences—in particular, that a chamber might wish to "tie its hands" by appointing a biased committee to bargain on its behalf. Impatience is of interest because it connects to the differing term structures of the two chambers of a bicameral legislature. In the United States, for example, the Senate might be thought the more patient body, since two-thirds of its members do not face their voters at the next election. In models of the Rubinstein variety, patience has its bargaining advantages.

12. Theirs is a vote-buying model in which politicians shake down interest groups for bribes and campaign contributions. Members of each chamber seek to arrange intracameral structures and procedures, taking other constitutional arrangements as fixed, to enable them to extract as much as possible. This involves creating intra-institutional hurdles optimally so as to encourage maximum contributions from special interests, making sure the hurdles are not so high as to discourage contributions.

13. There are many empirical papers in the American politics literature that explore legislative voting patterns, campaign practices, time allocations, and so on, conditional on where in the electoral cycle a senator is. Shepsle et al. (2007)—a study of divide-the-dollar pork-barreling activities among senators—cites some of these papers.

14. There are several restrictive features built into this baseline setup, which we initially adopt so as to allow us to focus attention on a few core points. In Section 6.7 on extensions we discuss several modifications. We raise the issue of the "optimal" number of chambers when more than two can be selected. It will be argued that frictions of various kinds arise as more chambers are added to the legislature, some of which can create costly gridlock. We explore the robustness of our results when in a bicameral legislature the two chambers are interlocked in the sense that to pass legislation the approval of both chambers (as is the case in many bicameral legislatures) is required. Finally we raise the prospect of allowing for a richer and more plausible composition of the legislature, which would involve chambers having different numbers of legislators and different bases of representation.

15. It would be useful to consider alternative procedures through which the unit-sized cake is partitioned, including procedures in which one chamber proposes an allocation while the other chamber decides on whether or not to approve it. Such procedures would mean that the two chambers are interlocked and connected and do not operate independently. Section 6.7 on extensions studies an extended setup in which some policy (tax rates) are determined "jointly" by the two chambers.

16. It may be noted that Π could alternatively be interpreted as the probability of reappointment by, say, a state legislature, as was the case in the nineteenth-century United States.

17. To be precise, there is a potential but minor loss of generality. By not entertaining discounting, we need to assume that the reelection probability never takes the value of 1. While such an assumption seems quite plausible, it does however rule out the cutoff voting rules used in the political agency literature (Barro 1973; Ferejohn 1986) in which a legislator is reelected with probability 1 if he performs sufficiently well (and fails to get reelected otherwise). The reelection probability function Π can of course approximate such a cutoff rule. We have chosen to proceed as we have in order to avoid carrying around an extra parameter (a discount factor for the legislators).

18. This formalization of imperfect information is adapted from Bhaskar (1998) who studies a version of Samuelson's OLG model with imperfect information.

19. The equilibria of this staggered-term legislature have been studied in Muthoo and Shepsle (2007).

20. Our stochastic game falls outside of the classes of stochastic games studied in the current literature (see, for example, Friedman 1986; Fudenberg and Tirole 1991; Dutta 1995). Thus, we cannot appeal to or apply results from that literature. However, some of our main results are derived using methods and ideas borrowed from that literature and from the theory of infinitely repeated games.

21. To simplify the formal analysis, we assume that the legislators in period t know the amount of cake the period-t LATE legislator obtained in period $t - 1$ (which comprises the payoff-relevant bits of the history at the beginning of period t in those cases when legislators have two-period terms of office); note this means that T in assumption 6.3 is strictly greater than $t + 1$. Given this, we do not need to invoke any beliefs regarding past actions in defining and implementing this equilibrium concept. For example, we do not need to employ the relatively more complex sequential equilibrium concept. Our adopted solution concept is essentially the same as that used in Bhaskar (1998).

22. It may be noted that any refinement of our equilibrium concept will *not*, by definition, sustain non-Markov equilibria involving intertemporal cooperation.

Proposition 6.1 only requires that players' strategies respect the standard notion of sequential rationality.

23. If the two legislators are treated equally, so that recognition probability depends only on a legislator's location in the electoral cycle, then $\theta_{1E} = \theta_{2E}$. Since $\theta_{iE} + \theta_{jL} = 1$, equation (6.2) becomes $U_i^{St} = 1/2(1 - \delta)$.

24. In case (ii) we will assume that the staggers are independently determined at $t = -1$. Thus, district i's agent begins EARLY in both chambers, LATE in both chambers, EARLY in the first chamber and LATE in the second, and LATE in the first chamber and EARLY in the second with equal probability.

25. The result also requires that $0 < \theta_i < 1$; that is, we rule out the possibility that either district has *all* the agenda power.

26. One might then wonder why we actually observe unicameral legislatures in many circumstances. That is, what weighs against the insurance advantages of bicameralism? We take up this extension in Section 6.7.

27. Note that while, by definition, $\hat{\theta}_1 + \hat{\theta}_2 = 2$, there is no reason why in general $\hat{\theta}_i = 1$. For example, it may be the case that LATE legislators receive higher agenda power than EARLY ones, but, at the same time, agenda power is increasing in population size. It is thus possible that if district i has a much smaller population, then while $\theta_{iL} > \theta_{iE}$, it nonetheless is the case that $\hat{\theta}_i < 1$.

28. This follows from the observations that G is linear, and that u_i strictly concave implies that $G(0) > 0$ and $G(1) > 0$.

29. The argument is as follows: $(1 - \delta)V_i(n) = E(u_i(k_n/n))$, where E is the expectation and k_n is a random variable with a binomial distribution with parameters n, θ_i. The expectation of k_n equals $n\theta_i$, and hence $E(k_n/n) = \theta_i$. It follows from Jensen's inequality (and since u_i is strictly concave) that for any finite n, $E(u_i(k_n/n)) < u_i(E(k_n/n))$. Hence, for any finite n, $(1 - \delta)V_i(n) < u_i(\theta_i)$. To show convergence, take any $\epsilon > 0$ and it is easy to show that as n tends to infinity, $Prob[k_n/n > \theta_i - \epsilon]$ converges to 1 (given continuity of u_i).

30. We conjecture that some of the main insights concerning the relative merits of bicameralism versus unicameralism established below, in the context of the extended setup, carry over to staggered-term structures. However, this needs to be formally established, and we leave that for future research.

31. (x_i^j, τ_i^j) is the offer of legislator i, who is the agenda setter in one of the chambers, say chamber 1, given that legislator j is the agenda setter in chamber 2. And $(\hat{x}_j^i, \hat{\tau}_j^i)$ is the offer of legislator j, who is the agenda setter in chamber 2, given that legislator i is the agenda setter in chamber 1.

32. In Muthoo and Shepsle (2007)—where we develop an analysis of intertemporal cooperative equilibria in staggered-term, unicameral legislatures—the role of information is assessed in some greater detail.

REFERENCES

Barro, Robert. 1973. "The Control of Politicians: An Economic Model." *Public Choice* 14:19–42.

Bhaskar, V. 1998. "Informational Constraints and the Overlapping Generations Model: Folk and Anti-Folk Theorems." *Review of Economic Studies* 65:135–49.

Buchanan, James, and Gordon Tullock. 1962. *The Calculus of Consent*. Ann Arbor, MI: University of Michigan Press.

Cutrone, Michael, and Nolan McCarty. 2006. "Does Bicameralism Matter?" *The Oxford Handbook of Political Economy*, eds. Barry Weingast and Donald Wittman, 180–95. New York: Oxford University Press.

Diermeier, Daniel, and Roger B. Myerson. 1999. "Bicameralism and Its Consequences for the Internal Organization of Legislatures." *American Economic Review* 89:1182–96.

Dutta, Prajit K. 1995. "A Folk Theorem for Stochastic Games." *Journal of Economic Theory* 66:1–32.

Ferejohn, John A. 1986. "Incumbent Performance and Electoral Control." *Public Choice* 50:5–25.

Fiorina, Morris P. 1981. *Retrospective Voting in American National Elections*. New Haven, CT: Yale University Press.

French Senat. 2000. "Bicameralism around the World: Position and Prospects." www.senat.fr/senatsdumonde.

Friedman. 1986. James, *Game Theory with Applications to Economics*. Oxford: Oxford University Press.

Fudenberg, Drew, and Jean Tirole. 1991. *Game Theory*. Cambridge, MA: MIT Press.

Gailmard, Sean, and Thomas Hammond. 2006. "Intercameral Bargaining and Intracameral Organization in Legislatures." Unpublished manuscript.

Gneist, Rudolf. 1886. *The English Parliament in Its Transformations through a Thousand Years*. Boston: Little, Brown.

Hamilton, Alexander, John Jay, and James Madison. [n.d.]. *The Federalist*. Modern Library Edition. New York: Random House.

Hammond, Thomas H., and Gary J. Miller. 1987. "The Core of the Constitution." *American Political Science Review* 81:1155–74.

Lascelles, F. W. 1952. "A Second Chamber." In *Parliament: A Survey*, Lord Campion et al., 202–19. London: George Allen & Unwin.

Levmore, Saul. 1992. "Bicameralism: When Are Two Decisions Better than One?" *International Review of Law and Economics* 12:145–62.

Muthoo, Abhinay, and Kenneth A. Shepsle. 2006. "Information, Institutions and Constitutional Arrangements." Unpublished manuscript.

Patterson, Samuel C., and Anthony Mughan, eds. 1999. *Senates: Bicameralism in the Contemporary World*. Columbus: Ohio State Press.

Persson, Torsten, and Guido Tabellini. 2000. *Political Economics*. Cambridge, MA: MIT Press.

———. 2005. *The Economic Effects of Constitutions*. Cambridge, MA: MIT Press.

Riker, William H. 1992. "The Justification of Bicameralism." *International Political Science Review* 13:101–16.

Shepsle, Kenneth A., Robert P. Van Houweling, Samuel J. Abrams, and Peter C. Hanson. 2007. "The Senate Electoral Cycle and Bicameral Appropriations Politics." Unpublished manuscript.

Tsebelis, George, and Jeannette Money. 1997. *Bicameralism*. New York: Cambridge University Press.

— 7 —

Economic Development, Insurgency, and Civil War

JAMES D. FEARON

7.1   Introduction

Civil war has been by far the most common and destructive form of violent military conflict in the last 60 years. About 40% of countries with a 1990 population of at least half a million have had at least one internal conflict that killed at least a thousand people. A large number of countries have had conflicts that killed tens or even hundreds of thousands. Civil war has been the major cause of forced migrations in this period, and those migrations have produced many millions of refugees. Overall, the damage to the health, economies, and lives of the survivors has been massive (Ghobarah, Huth, and Russett 2003).

A growing empirical literature has established a range of interesting facts and regularities about civil war since 1945, including the following. First, most civil wars in this period have been fought as guerrilla conflicts in which state counterinsurgent forces hunt for small, lightly armed rebel units operating in rural areas, often in rough terrain. Guerrillas tend to "control the night," while government forces operate by day and in urban strongholds in the war-affected region of the country. There are no clear front lines. Rebel units seek to ambush government units, assassinate or intimidate local government officials and other perceived collaborators, and to raise funds by collecting "revolutionary taxes" of various sorts (for example, from peasants or from businesses). Government forces may threaten or bribe locals for information about rebels, set up paramilitary "village guard" units, force peasants into "strategic hamlets," or massacre whole villages suspected of aiding or being sympathetic to the rebels. This pattern has been visible in Vietnam, Guatemala, El Salvador, Colombia, Algeria, Philippines (NPA and in Mindanao), southeast

292

Turkey, Peru, northeast India, Burma, Thailand, Kashmir, Nepal, Indonesia (Aceh and East Timor), Mozambique, Sierra Leone, Sudan, and many other places.

Conflicts akin to the U.S. Civil War in which conventional armies fight along well-defined fronts have been quite rare. The Biafran war is the clearest instance. Still, in accord with Mao's doctrine of "people's war," the later stages of some civil wars that began as guerrilla conflicts have tended in this direction (e.g., China 1945–49, Afghanistan, Ethiopia, and Uganda 1981–86). Another occasional pattern is conflict between militias organized on ethnic or regional lines (e.g., Lebanon, Turkey 1977–80, Bosnia, Tajikistan), although these have similarities and overlaps with both guerrilla and conventional civil wars.[1]

A second striking regularity is that poor countries have been much more likely to have civil wars than richer countries. Figure 7.1 shows how the frequency of civil war outbreaks has varied with per capita income for 161 countries observed between 1945 and 1999 (using data from Fearon and Laitin 2003). Of the richest fifth of the country years in the sample, only about 1.5% had a civil war erupt within the next five years. By contrast, among the poorest fifth of country years, 14.3% had a civil war start in the next five years.

Moreover, per capita income is the single best predictor of a country's odds of civil war outbreak, empirically dominating other factors that one might have expected to do better, such as level of democracy, degree of ethnic or religious diversity, nature of ethnic demography, or level of income inequality (Fearon and Laitin 2003).[2] Indeed, after controlling for income, none of these factors have any added purchase.

There are at least two important theoretical puzzles raised by these facts and regularities. First, how can we explain what is probably the modal civil war in this period—a persistent, small, stalemated guerrilla conflict? What prevents government and rebel groups from cutting deals that would allow them to avoid the enormous costs? Second, what explains the strong association between low per capita income and high civil war risk?

I address these questions with the help of a game model in which a government and a rebel leadership simultaneously choose how many soldiers and rebels to conscript or recruit. Counterinsurgency by government forces then yields the capture or death of a fraction of the rebel group. Uncaptured rebels proceed to tax peasants or businesses in their region of operation, and to exclude the government from collecting taxes.

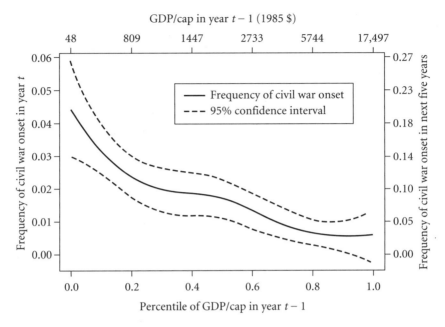

Figure 7.1 Income and civil war risk, 1945–1999.

The model is related to the "contest models" that Grossman (1991, 2002), Hirshleifer (1995), Skaperdas (1992), and other economists have used to analyze violent conflict, but it differs in two significant respects. First, in standard formulations, contest models of conflict do not actually have any violence in them. No one can get killed or captured. In some models, conflict is assumed to destroy resources, which can be interpreted as an effect of violence. But the implications of conflict for individual fighters are not modelled, making it impossible to analyze individual decisions to participate, or the trade-off between the risk and potential reward of becoming a rebel. This is a significant liability when the most common "explanations" for why low-income countries are civil war prone hold that poor young males find the option of rebellion more attractive, or that poor people are generally more aggrieved.

Second, in typical contest models, almost all the explanatory action is built into the *contest-success function*, which relates the players' fighting efforts to the final distribution of resources. By separating the extraction of resources from the violent interaction between government and rebel forces, the model here takes a step toward "unpacking" or opening up the standard contest-success function.

One benefit of this approach is that it forces us to consider what is distinctive about the mechanisms of violence in insurgency. I argue that in contrast to ordinary crime and conventional military confrontations, mafias and insurgencies face the problem that adding more fighters raises the risk of detection and thus capture for *all existing* fighters. In practice, the central problem of counterinsurgency is not to marshal adequate forces to defeat rebel units, but to gain good intelligence on who and where the active rebels are. If rebels are linked to each other, then adding more rebels increases risks of infiltration, betrayal, and detection for large parts of the organization. I argue that this information externality of adding more members provides a natural explanation for "diminishing returns" to guerrilla warfare, which is in turn necessary to explain how this kind of deadly conflict can remain small, stable, and stalemated.

On the question of why poor countries are civil war prone, I argue that common arguments in the empirical literature on civil war do not work. One of the main obstacles is that although richer people may have more to lose from civil strife, the fact that there is more wealth around to tax or appropriate also means that there is more to be gained by fighting. Conversely, if there is relatively little to fight for, as in an impoverished country, why fight? In contest models, the bigger the pie, the greater the equilibrium fighting efforts. This problem tends to undermine one of the most popular arguments proposed in the empirical literature on civil war, namely, that poverty makes for civil war because in poor countries there are more poor, underemployed people who find rebellion attractive as a "job" (e.g., Collier and Hoeffler 2004).

A possible reply holds that while there may be more to gain from rebellion in a wealthier economy, diminishing marginal utility, or risk aversion, means that greater per capita income makes citizens less willing to run risks of capture or death in a civil conflict. I show that, by itself, this assumption does not solve the puzzle either. One needs to make a stronger assumption about preferences, namely that richer people are *relatively more risk averse* than poorer people. Empirical support for this stronger assumption appears to be mixed and ambiguous; at any rate, it is certainly not a clear and powerful regularity.[3]

In the models presented below, the equilibrium level of insurgency and counterinsurgency is strongly influenced by the rebels' ability to collect taxes and by the government's ability to capture rebels. I argue that a plausible and internally coherent explanation for the empirical regularity is that in rich countries, much of the income being generated is not easily "taxed" using simple extortion, and in poor countries, rebels can more easily evade capture at given force levels, due to terrain, informational advantages of rural village as opposed to urban settings, and, possibly, government incompetence in running effective counterinsurgency campaigns.

In the next section, I introduce a simple contest model applied to civil war, and show why it produces no first-order result linking poverty and civil war risk. In Section 7.3, I discuss differences between the strategic logics of ordinary crime, mafias, insurgencies, and conventional military conflict. The main argument is that, as with mafias, adding new rebels to a small insurgency increases detection and denunciation risks for existing rebels, due to their network connections. Section 7.4 uses this argument in a model that explicitly represents the government's efforts to capture and kill rebels. Section 7.5 returns to the question of civil war risk and per capita income, modifying the model to allow for the recruitment of risk-averse rebels rather than conscription. Section 7.6 considers why more efficient peace deals are not obtainable in equilibrium in the model and considers obstacles to efficiency in the case where government and rebels interact over time and thus could in principle support cooperation by implicitly threatening to return to conflict.

7.2   Contest Models of Civil Conflict

In this section, I present a simple contest model applied to civil conflict and discuss its main implications and liabilities.

Consider a game with two strategic players, a government G and a rebel leadership R. They interact in a society with a continuum of individuals (normalized to size 1), each of whom has pretax income $y > 0$. Total potential tax revenues are thus ty, where $t \in [0, 1]$ is a fixed tax rate.[4] Suppose that R and G simultaneously choose to conscript $\alpha \in [0, 1]$ and $\beta \in [0, 1]$ rebels and soldiers, respectively, at marginal costs c_R and c_G.[5] Let the contest-success function be $p(\alpha, m\beta)$, which gives the share of tax revenue controlled by R when the force sizes are α and β; $m > 0$ is a parameter scaling the effectiveness of counterinsurgency. Rebel and government utility functions are then

$$u_R(\alpha, \beta) = p(\alpha, m\beta)ty(1 - \alpha - \beta) - c_R\alpha, \text{ and}$$
$$u_G(\alpha, \beta) = (1 - p(\alpha, m\beta))ty(1 - \alpha - \beta) - c_G\beta.$$

The standard assumption is that, holding the other side's force level constant, having more rebels or more soldiers gets one side more territory and tax revenue, though at a diminishing rate ($p_1 > 0$, $p_{11} < 0$, $p_2 < 0$, and $p_{22} > 0$).

Little more than inspection of the utility functions is necessary to understand how varying per capita income will affect equilibrium levels of conflict. Notice that increasing y (without changing anything else) increases the marginal returns to rebellion for R, and to counterinsurgency for G. That is, if $\alpha(\beta)$ was R's optimal force size given β before increasing y, then diminishing returns ($p_{11} < 0$) implies that after increasing y, $\alpha(\beta)$ will be larger.[6] The same logic holds for G, and the net effect in equilibrium is that higher y implies that a higher percentage of the population will be employed as rebels and as soldiers fighting them.

This is the exact opposite of the empirical regularity, but it is a general feature of contest models (including wars of attrition). On first glance, it does have a certain logical appeal. Isn't it natural to think that rational actors would fight harder and more for a bigger prize? Don't scholars in the civil war literature routinely explain the association between oil production (or other natural resources) and civil war by arguing that these increase the value of winning? Why wouldn't the same be true of the size of the economy?

On second glance, it should be noted that increasing per capita income y while holding constant c_R and c_G is equivalent to saying that the marginal cost of conscripting, feeding, and supplying combatants is lower in rich countries. Not surprisingly, if it is effectively cheaper to man armed forces, equilibrium levels of conflict will be higher. But surely these costs would be *higher* in richer countries. If we assume that they increase proportionally with income—say the marginal cost of conscription is $c_i y$ instead of c_i, $i \in \{G, R\}$—then varying income clearly has zero effect on equilibrium levels of conflict. In this case, we can divide y out of the utility functions above without changing R or G's incentives at all.

This result travels across a variety of alternative specifications. For example, suppose that G and R must hire labor rather than conscript it. Since the model as it stands does not involve any risk of death or jail for combatants, both G and R can offer a wage of $w = y$ (or infinitesimally more) to attract fighters, and this clearly leads to equilibrium levels of α and β being independent of y. Or suppose that incomes vary in the population, with y_i distributed by a cumulative distribution function F. If the shape of F does not change as per capita income $\bar{y}$ changes, we can again factor $\bar{y}$ out of the expressions for u_G and u_R, meaning that income level does not affect any marginal trade-offs and thus equilibrium force sizes.

To be more specific, let $w = (1-t)F^{-1}(\alpha + \beta)$ be the market-determined wage for rebels and soldiers when R hires α rebels and G hires β soldiers (for simplicity I am assuming that neither rebels nor soldiers pay taxes). At this wage, the $\alpha + \beta$ poorest fraction of the society prefers to sign up on one side or the other, while the $1 - \alpha - \beta$ richer (or more productive) fraction prefers to work in the regular economy.[7] Then $u_R(\alpha, \beta)$ becomes $p(\alpha, m\beta)t \int_{\alpha+\beta}^{1} F^{-1}(z)dz - w\alpha$. To examine the effect of changing per capita income without changing anything else (such as the shape of the income distribution), we define $F_0(y/\bar{y}) = F(y; \bar{y})$ as the "base" distribution. Then the market clearing condition becomes $\alpha + \beta = F(\frac{w}{1-t}; \bar{y}) = F_0(\frac{w}{\bar{y}(1-t)})$, and thus $w = \bar{y}(1-t)F_0^{-1}(\alpha + \beta)$. Using $F^{-1}(z) = \bar{y}F_0^{-1}(z)$, substitution into u_R yields

$$u_R(\alpha, \beta) = p(\alpha, m\beta)t \int_{\alpha+\beta}^{1} \bar{y}F_0^{-1}(z)dz - \bar{y}(1-t)F_0^{-1}(\alpha + \beta)\alpha.$$

Per capita income can be factored out of the rebel group's preferences without affecting any trade-offs and so does not affect equilibrium force levels. The same is true for the government.

Changing the *shape* of the income distribution does affect incentives for rebellion and counterinsurgency in the basic contest model. Holding per capita income constant while increasing inequality lowers marginal recruitment costs for both government and rebels, since there are more relatively poor people around and the total tax base is the same. Thus, greater inequality associates with higher equilibrium force levels.[8] In principle this could help explain the empirical regularity if richer countries are systematically more equal than poorer countries. The ambiguous empirical support for the Kuznet's curve suggests that there is some tendency in this direction, but it is not very strong. Also, as noted above, more-unequal countries have not been more prone to civil war in the last 60 years, at least using standard cross-national inequality measures.

On the other hand, this analysis suggests that the "bigger-prize" argument for why oil producers appear to have been more civil war prone does not work unless recast as an argument about oil creating big inequalities. If oil revenues are monopolized by a small group that controls the state, then $t\bar{y}$ is large relative to the marginal cost of recruiting rebels and soldiers, which favors larger rebellions, according to the model.[9]

To sum up, the contest-model approach points to two main effects of per capita income on the propensity for civil conflict. On the one hand, more income means more revenue for rebels to appropriate and government forces to defend. But on the other hand, the marginal costs of staffing a rebel or government force will be greater in a richer country. These effects work in opposite directions, tending to give the result of no net impact. This is a simple point, but I have not seen it stated or explored in the literature applying contest models to conflict.[10]

The basic contest model does suggest two second-order ways that low income might plausibly cause higher equilibrium levels of civil conflict. To see the first, note that the argument above implies that if you give the same amount of counterinsurgency funding to a poor and a rich state, the poor state should get a much bigger "bang for the buck" because it would be able to hire (or support) much more labor. Much anecdotal and case-based evidence suggests, by contrast, that richer countries are more efficient at using counterinsurgency funds, either because of higher levels of human capital, training, and organizational coherence, or because the strategic and tactical problems are more easily solved in an economically more developed setting, or both (see Section 7.5).

Second, it could be that individuals and businesses are less able to hide their income from insurgents in poor than in rich countries. The standard "appropriative technology" of insurgency consists of visits to households or businesses to collect revolutionary taxes, often in kind. This may yield a higher share of total product in a society of small-holding peasants than in a world of megacorporations and mobile, high-income-from-high-human-capital workers. If so, the effective tax rate that insurgents can impose would be higher in poor countries. It is easily shown in the contest model that higher tax rates lead to higher equilibrium levels of conflict.[11]

The standard contest model is a highly reduced-form approach to analyzing conflict. It hides the specifics of the interactions between combatants inside the black box of the contest-success function. With minor changes, the model could be redescribed as a model of interstate conflict, conflict between animals for territory, between firms for market share, between candidates for votes, or between lobbyists for policy. In all such cases, results follow from embedded assumptions about the shape of the contest-success function, and, in particular, the assumption of diminishing returns to effort and an assumption about the specifics of the cross-partial derivative of $p(\cdot, \cdot)$.[12]

The range of application of the contest model is a virtue in that it highlights the strategic similarities of a broad range of political and economic situations. But it can also be a vice if the contest-success function obscures important distinctions between types of conflict and violence. In the case at hand, we should not accept without argument that the returns to rebellion are diminishing, the assumption that makes possible a stable, interior equilibrium with a low level of insurgency in the contest model above. Many discussions of rebellion assume to the contrary that there are increasing returns, for example, a tipping point beyond which the government will fall. At a minimum we need a developed argument for why the returns to insurgency would be diminishing, and in the contest-model approach, this will at best be given "offstage."

I offer a model below that opens up the contest-success function, distinguishing between the violent interaction between government and rebel fighters and the interaction between surviving rebels and peasants over revenue. To justify some important assumptions that go into this model, I need first to discuss how the strategic logic of insurgency differs from several other kinds of conflict that have been modelled using contest-success functions.

7.3   Crime, Mafias, Insurgencies, and Conventional Warfare

In ordinary property crime, maintaining anonymity is the criminal's core strategy for avoiding arrest. Criminals seek to burgle unseen, to hold up banks wearing masks, or to mug quickly and then disappear into a large, anonymous urban population. They operate as individuals or in very small groups. The central motif of almost all crime drama is the finding and proving of "who done it."

The strategy of anonymity means that *repeat business* is not an option for ordinary criminals. They cannot repeatedly mug the same people, or return repeatedly to the same store or bank, without being identified and arrested. Mafias are an attempt to solve this problem. Mafia members must make themselves known to the individuals and business owners from whom they extort regular payments. Their strategy for avoiding arrest is then to threaten violent reprisal if their victims denounce them to the police and, in particular, if they testify in court. To make such threats credible, a mafia requires, in the first place, an organization. If one member is arrested due to testimony by a victim, there must be other members willing and able to punish the victim.

And given that there must be multiple members, there is a huge premium on loyalty within the organization. Since members know about and participate in the organization's violence and violent threats, *each member poses a denunciation risk to every other member*. Thus, there are the sacred oaths, long initiation periods, ethnic and family ties, and draconian punishments for suspected informers, as well as use of witness-protection programs as an antiracketeering strategy. Whereas increasing the total number of ordinary criminals may increase the expected returns to any given criminal (since police efforts are more diffused), adding mafiosi may decrease the expected returns to existing members because the network connections make for negative externalities regarding infiltration and betrayal.

Because mafiosi necessarily make themselves known to their targets, the problem for police is not primarily in identifying who the mafiosi are, but rather in acquiring solid evidence of criminal activity. They may face problems in locating a mafioso for arrest, but at least in urban environments, this is generally not so difficult. One implication is that if the state does not care that much about evidence or due process and its agents are relatively unbribable, mafias cannot survive. Such a state will just kill or throw suspected racketeers in jail. Mafias did not flourish in eastern Europe and much of the former Soviet Union until after the demise of Communist regimes. Mafias require either a political environment with the rule of law and due process or a state whose agents can be bribed to look the other way (or a combination of the two).

Insurgencies differ from mafias in espousing political goals. They seek either to become the formally recognized government in a region, to replace the current government in the country, or to force a change in its policies.[13] Their situation also differs from mafias in that even rule-of-law countries tend to have few scruples about attacking and detaining rebels without full due process. Combined with the fact that insurgencies start out and often remain small and militarily weak relative to government forces, this means that they have to be able to hide from government troops and intelligence. Rural settings with close access to mountains or jungles are thus strongly favored.

But rough terrain is rarely sufficient to allow the survival of a guerrilla band, since the guerrillas must interact with other people at least some of the time. They typically draw food and funds in the form of revolutionary taxes on households and businesses, engaging in "repeat business" with the same villages and people.[14] They require locals' information about government troop movements, and their own movements and activities are partly observed by local noncombatants. This means that a successful insurgency must address the same core problem that mafias face—the risk of denunciation to authorities. And like mafias, insurgents almost invariably threaten and carry out violent punishments against those who denounce (or are said to have denounced), in order to deter others (Kalyvas 1999; Kalyvas 2003). They may also provide more positive inducements to lessen the risk of denunciation, such as ideological training programs, control and discipline of individual rebels who injure civilians, and defense against marauding government troops. But the government's willingness to use force against civilians to acquire information about the rebels tends to quickly draw any rebel group into a competition of threats and violence with respect to noncombatant locals.[15]

As with mafias and in contrast to ordinary crime, adding new members to a small insurgent band raises denunciation and detection risks for the whole organization. More rebel units are more likely to be seen by locals or to try to "tax" individuals who are willing to run the risk of reporting to the government. Because rebels are linked to each other and because, in their early stages, guerrilla movements depend on being able to hide, the capture of one rebel can favor the capture of more.[16] In addition, monitoring and screening become more difficult as the size of the rebel organization expands. It is reasonable to suppose that the ideological commitment of additional rebels is diminishing (the more intensely committed types are already in the organization), which means that expansion increases the risks of informers, defections, and bad types who raise detection risks by overly abusing noncombatants.[17]

In sum, network connections and the need to hide imply that individual rebels may be made *less safe* rather than more safe when the rebel organization increases in size (other things being equal).[18] By contrast, ordinary criminals and soldiers in a conventional army are made more safe when more criminals or soldiers are added (holding police or the other military constant). In the case of criminals, police efforts are more diffused. In the case of a conventional military, a bigger army is more likely to win, and at a lower cost in lives.

The model of insurgency in the next section uses the assumption that adding rebels increases the share of the total rebel group that is captured or killed for a given government force size. As noted in the Introduction, in both Mao's theory and a number of internal conflicts in the last 50 years, small guerrilla movements have grown so large that they were able to reconfigure themselves as conventional military forces able to fight set-piece battles against state armies. A more sophisticated model might incorporate this possibility.

7.4 A Model of Insurgency

Again we consider a game with two strategic players, a government G and a rebel leadership R. They compete over control of tax revenues from a continuum of individuals (normalized to size 1), each of whom produces pretax income $y > 0$ if working in the private sector. Let $\alpha \in [0, 1]$ be the size of the rebel force, and $\beta \in [0, 1]$ be the size of government forces. When there are α rebels and β government soldiers, total tax revenues are $ty(1 - \alpha - \beta)$, where $t \in [0, 1]$ is a fixed tax rate.

The sequence of actions and events in the game is as follows:

1. R and G simultaneously choose to conscript α and β rebels and soldiers, at marginal costs $c_R y$ and $c_G y$, respectively.

2. A fraction of the rebels, $p(\alpha, m\beta)$, are captured or killed by government forces. As above, $m > 0$ is a parameter measuring the government's effectiveness at counterinsurgency.

3. The remaining rebel force, now of size $\alpha(1 - p(\alpha, m\beta))$, collects revolutionary taxes from a share of the population that did not join either the soldiers or the rebel group. Assume that one rebel collects from $\delta > 1$ peasants, so that R's total revenues are $ty\delta\alpha(1 - p(\alpha, m\beta))$, provided $\delta\alpha(1 - p(\alpha, m\beta))$ is less than the total number of producers, which is $1 - \alpha - b$. Otherwise the rebels collect from everyone.

Total revenues for the rebel group are thus $ty \min\{\delta\alpha(1 - p(\alpha, m\beta)), 1 - \alpha - \beta\}$.

4. The government collects tax revenues from peasants who are not "controlled" (here, taxed) by rebels. Thus G's total revenues are the larger of zero and $ty(1 - \alpha - \beta - \delta\alpha(1 - p(\alpha, m\beta)))$.

Two differences from the standard contest-model formulation should be stressed. First, notice that the model separates the interaction between insurgents and counterinsurgents from the interaction between insurgents and locals that produces revenues. Accordingly, $p(\alpha, m\beta)$ is no longer a contest-success function. It might instead be called a capture or capture-and-kill function, since it relates the size of rebel and government forces to the share of rebels captured or killed.

I assume that $p(\alpha, m\beta)$ is increasing in *both* its arguments. This is uncontroversial for β, since this just means that more government forces capture or kill a larger share of a given rebel force. The assumption that the share captured or killed increases with the size of the *rebel* force follows on the argument given above, that denunciation and detection are critical for rebel losses, and are harder to prevent as force size grows, other things being equal.

A second feature worth noting is the assumption that the rebels' tax collection technology has constant returns to scale up to the point at which the whole region is controlled by the rebels. One can imagine arguments for why there would be increasing returns (e.g., government is a natural monopoly), or decreasing returns (e.g., eventually there must be crowding, as occurs in this model), or perhaps increasing then decreasing returns. I don't see a decisive consideration one way or the other. Clearly, though, one way to "get" decreasing returns to rebellion would be to simply assume that the rebel's collection technology has quickly decreasing returns to scale, whereas the government's does not.

Let $k(\alpha, m\beta) = \alpha p(\alpha, m\beta)$ be the number (measure) of rebels captured or killed when the initial force sizes are α and β. Rebel and government utility functions are thus

$$u_R(\alpha, \beta) = ty \min\{1 - \alpha - \beta, \delta(\alpha - k(\alpha, m\beta))\} - c_R y\alpha \qquad (7.1)$$

$$u_G(\alpha, \beta) = ty \max\{0, 1 - \alpha - \beta - \delta(\alpha - k(\alpha, m\beta))\} - c_G y\beta. \qquad (7.2)$$

For the comparative statics results discussed below, I make three additional assumptions about the rate of change of the number killed or captured as force sizes vary; these assumptions parallel those made in typical contest-model formulations. They are as follows:

1. $k_{11} > 0$ when $\beta > 0$: The number captured increases at an increasing rate as R adds rebels, for a given (positive) government force size. By the arguments about network connections and the strategy of hiding given in Section 7.3, this is plausible, at least over the range where guerrilla tactics of hiding and hit-and-run attacks are necessary for the rebels. For instance, the assumption implies that adding more mafiosi increases the number prosecuted at an increasing rate.

2. $k_{22} < 0$ when $\alpha > 0$: The number captured increases at a decreasing rate as G increases the number of police or soldiers, for a given number of rebels. More soldiers or police are more likely to get good information about rebel-unit whereabouts, or are more likely to encounter them at random, but the "returns" are diminishing.

3. $k_{12} > 0$: The effect of increasing government forces on the number captured is higher when the number of rebels is larger. Or, likewise, the effect of increasing the number of active rebels on the number captured increases as there are more soldiers or police. (For instance, more FBI focused on the mafia means that adding more mafia becomes more dangerous for the mafia as a whole.)[19]

Analysis.   Figure 7.2 displays the rebel leadership's and government's best-reply functions for the type of case of interest here—that is, when the government has counterinsurgency capabilities sufficient to prevent its overrun by the rebel group. $\alpha(\beta)$ is the rebel leadership's optimal force size if there are β counterinsurgency personnel, and $\beta(\alpha)$ is the government's optimal force size if there are α rebels. Nash equilibrium levels are at the intersection (α^*, β^*). Note that for readability, the graph's x and y limits are "clipped" at 0.1 rather than 1. The rebel's best-reply $\alpha(\beta)$ continues on in the same way as β increases to 1, although at a β close to 1, $\alpha(\beta)$ changes course and heads to intersect the y axis at $\beta = 1$, due to an effect of the constraint in the utility function. By contrast, the government's best-reply $\beta(\alpha)$ discontinuously jumps down to and remains at 0 for rebel force sizes greater than a threshold value $\bar{\alpha}$, which in this example is outside the range of the graph and so is not shown.[20]

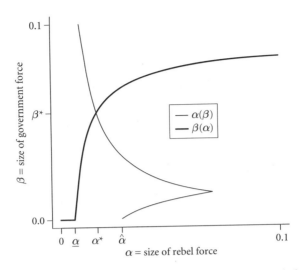

Figure 7.2 Best-reply functions for government and rebels.

A good way to grasp the logic of this model is to work through the logic of the best-reply functions. Beginning with the government, if the rebel movement is small enough (size less than $\underline{\alpha}$), then the group is so difficult for government forces to find and penetrate and the amount of tax revenue it appropriates is so small that counterinsurgency is not worth the cost— the government's best reply is zero effort. This cannot occur in equilibrium because the rebel group's best reply to zero government effort would be to mobilize a significantly larger force ($\hat{\alpha} = 1/(1 + \delta)$) that would allow it to tax and control the whole population.

As rebel forces surpass $\underline{\alpha}$, the returns to government counterinsurgency increase, making larger government forces increasingly worthwhile. A larger rebel force taxes more territory and faces greater penetration and capture risks, which makes a greater counterinsurgent response desirable for the government. Eventually, however, if the rebel force is large enough (above $\bar{\alpha}$), counterinsurgency is again not worth the cost for the government. The reason is that if the rebels have forces greater than $\hat{\alpha}$, they have more than enough to control the whole tax base. So for the government to take back any tax base, it has to fight enough to reduce the rebel forces below $\hat{\alpha}$ after captures and kills. When α is large enough, this can be so costly for the government that it is better off just giving up, as it were, and ceding control to the rebels. Once again, this situation cannot occur in equilibrium because the rebel leadership does not want to overhire forces if it faces no opposition (the rebels are in effect the government in this counterfactual in any event).

Now consider the rebel leadership's best replies to different levels of government effort. There are two cases, corresponding to whether the constraint in the utility function binds. The constraint binds if, after captures and kills, the rebel movement still has enough personnel to control the country's entire tax base. In this case, which corresponds to the part of $\alpha(\beta)$ that is increasing in β, the rebels want to set their force size so that they will have just enough to control the whole country after the fighting. This can obtain only when government forces are sufficiently small. By contrast, if government forces are large enough, the constraint in the rebels' utility function does not bind and the solution is interior, which means that the rebel group chooses the force size such that the marginal cost of another rebel equals the marginal gain in tax revenue. The larger the government presence, the smaller the marginal gain from adding another rebel due to capture and compromise risks, and thus the smaller the optimal rebel force size.

Proposition 7.1 asserts that if the game has a pure-strategy equilibrium, it is unique, and is either "interior" with positive government and rebel force levels, or a corner solution in which the "government" makes no effort and the rebels take over. (Proofs of propositions are in the appendix.)

Proposition 7.1   *If the game has a pure-strategy equilibrium, it is unique, and is either interior, satisfying the first-order conditions*

$$k_1(\alpha, m\beta) = 1 - c_R/\delta t \tag{7.3}$$

$$k_2(\alpha, m\beta) = \frac{t + c_G}{m\delta t}, \tag{7.4}$$

or the constraint in (7.1) and (7.2) binds and the equilibrium is $\alpha^* = 1/(1 + \delta)$, $\beta^* = 0$. In words, a pure-strategy Nash equilibrium involves either positive force levels on both sides or the rebels take over, controlling the whole country, which is ceded by the government. A necessary and sufficient condition for the latter is that $k_2(\hat{\alpha}, 0) \leq (t + c_G)/m\delta t$.

For certain parameter values, the game can have a unique, mixed-strategy equilibrium, which occurs "in between" the equilibria described in proposition 7.1. The equilibrium with $\beta^* = 0$ occurs when government counterinsurgency is highly inefficient (that is, has very low marginal return in terms of numbers captured or killed), whereas the pure-strategy equilibrium with positive force levels on both sides requires that the government be sufficiently capable. In between, it can happen that the government wants to raise forces $\beta(\hat{\alpha})$ if $\alpha = \hat{\alpha}$, but the rebel's best reply to $\beta(\hat{\alpha})$ is a force size such that the government's best reply would be to give up, setting $\beta = 0$, to which $\hat{\alpha}$ would again be a best reply by the rebels. The mixed-strategy Nash equilibrium involves R choosing $\bar{\alpha}$ while G mixes appropriately on $\{0, \beta(\bar{\alpha})\}$. In this case, either the rebels take over with no opposition, or there is a big conflict.[21]

The mixed-strategy equilibrium has little or no substantive relevance, however. It disappears, for example, in a Stackleberg version of the game that takes the government as the incumbent who can set police and counterinsurgent force levels prior to possible entry by a rebel group.[22] Moreover, both the mixed-strategy equilibrium and the equilibrium in which the government cedes control of the country to the rebels ($\beta^* = 0$) can occur only in a part of the parameter space where the core assumptions about the capture function $p(\alpha, m\beta)$ are not so reasonable. If the government is so weak or inept that rebel takeover is a strong possibility, then the assumption that adding rebel forces raises the probability of capture for each individual rebel is suspect. The assumption was offered as appropriate for conflicts that are at, or are stuck in, Mao's first two stages of guerrilla war. In these, the government remains dominant in terms of men and materiel; its difficulty is primarily in identifying and locating rebels, rather than in marshalling the forces to defeat them if found. In what follows, I focus on the comparative statics of the "interior" equilibrium that corresponds to the case of persistent, fairly low-level insurgency.[23]

Proposition 7.2   *An interior Nash equilibrium (α^*, β^*) has the following comparative statics:*

- *Government and rebel force levels, and thus the amount of conflict, do not vary at all with per capita income, y.*
- *Greater government efficiency or effectiveness in counterinsurgency, m, implies fewer rebels in equilibrium, and may associate with either a larger or smaller government army.*

- *Higher government costs for conscripting (or recruiting) and provisioning soldiers, c_G, imply fewer soldiers and more rebels in equilibrium.*

- *Higher costs of recruiting, training, and supplying rebels, c_R, imply fewer rebels and fewer soldiers in equilibrium.*

- *Higher tax yield t for rebels and government implies more soldiers in equilibrium, but may associate with a greater, smaller, or equal-sized rebel movement.*

- *Greater efficiency in the rebel organization's ability to collect revolutionary taxes, δ, implies more soldiers in equilibrium, but may associate with a larger, smaller, or equal-sized rebel movement.*[24]

These effects can mainly be anticipated from Figure 7.2, keeping in mind that an exogenous variable that makes insurgency more attractive for rebels tends to shift $\alpha(\beta)$ up (or right), and that a variable that makes counterinsurgency more attractive for the government tends to shift $\beta(\alpha)$ up (or left). So, for example, increasing the government's conscription costs reduces government effort for any level of rebel activity, leading to less counterinsurgency and more rebellion. The effects are different for an increase in the rebel group's costs of conscription or recruitment. For this change, the model predicts less rebellion and less counterinsurgency. Government reduces its effort when the rebellion shrinks because it becomes more difficult to find and attack a better-hidden opponent on which it is harder to get good intelligence.

Increasing the tax rate that both sides can extract, or increasing the rebel group's efficiency at collecting revolutionary taxes (δ), shifts the government's best-reply function upward and the rebels' best-reply function to the right. These changes make insurgency and counterinsurgency more productive at the margin for both sides. This unambiguously expands the equilibrium level of government forces, but because greater counterinsurgency lowers the marginal return of insurgency, the net effect on rebel force size may be positive, negative, or neutral.

The model as it stands assumes that the rebels and the government collect at the same tax rate from individuals in society. Rebel and government taxation technologies are often quite different, however. Rebels raise funds from house-to-house visits, contraband operations, or foreign patrons, whereas governments can use commodity taxation, sales taxes, or income taxes in more developed economies. If we modify the model so that the rebel group's tax extraction rate is $t_R > 0$ and the government's is $t_G > 0$, then it is easy to show that increasing t_R shifts the rebel group's best-reply function upward, making for an increase in equilibrium levels of both government and rebel forces. By contrast, increasing t_G while holding t_R fixed, shifts $\beta(\alpha)$ upward, increasing equilibrium counterinsurgency while reducing rebellion. If, as argued below, t_G tends to be smaller and t_R larger in poor than in rich countries, we would observe higher levels of civil conflict in poor countries even though their governments made less (or a similar amount of) police and counterinsurgent effort.

Per capita income makes no difference for civil conflict in the model for the same reason as before: a larger tax base is a positive incentive to fighting, but this is offset by the negative incentive that comes from greater costs for conscripting or otherwise staffing a force. In contrast, increasing the government's efficiency at counterinsurgency (m in the model) unambiguously reduces the amount of rebellion. If, as argued below, richer countries are more efficient at counterinsurgency due to features of the natural and social terrain in richer countries, this could help explain the association between income and civil peace.

7.5   Recruitment, Risk Attitudes, and Income

The model of the last section assumed that government and rebels conscript and provision their fighters at a fixed marginal cost. Conscription is typical for government forces involved in a civil conflict, and there are examples of rebel forces conscripting fighters as well. Child soldiers, who are frequently abducted or otherwise forced to join, are often used by rebel groups and sometimes in government forces.

Nonetheless, conscription is more problematic for rebels than for the government because, at least in the early stages, the rebel leadership does not control an administrative apparatus that can openly monitor a territory for deserters. Further, because hiding is so critical for the survival of guerrilla bands, the risks involved in conscripting fighters against their will can be unmanageable. Disgruntled conscripts would be inclined to defect to the government side, bringing information with them.[25]

So, especially in their small or early stages, guerrilla groups may depend on volunteers far more than conscripts. And volunteers need to be compensated, whether by the prospect of victory and subsequent reward, by the satisfaction of fighting for justice, or by the living that being a rebel provides. Regardless of the first two, joining an insurgency has to provide *some* material living to rebels since it is a long-term endeavor. Certainly potential rebels will take into account the comparison between the living provided by insurgency and the living provided by the regular economy, even if they also factor in considerations of justice and prospects for changing the government.

The game described above can be modified so that individuals choose whether to join the rebels in their fight. To keep with the spirit of a pure political economy model, I will consider potential rebels who care only about maximizing expected utility from income. They do not have idealistic motivations.[26]

Suppose that the rebel leadership R offers a wage w, which can be enjoyed only if the rebel is not captured or killed. Thus, individuals join the rebellion if their expected utility for the lottery on w and being killed or captured is at least as high as their utility for the disposable income $y(1 - t)$ they can earn in the regular economy. Let $u(x)$ be a concave, strictly increasing utility function for income, with $u(0) = 0$ set as the value for being killed or captured. For simplicity, and broadly consistent with the facts, I will continue to assume that government soldiers are conscripted and provisioned at marginal cost $c_G y$.

Expected utility for joining the rebels is thus $u(w)(1 - p(\alpha, m\beta))$, while the utility for not joining is $u(y(1 - t))$. Given government force size β, if R wants a force size of α, it needs to offer a wage of

$$w = u^{-1} \left(\frac{u(y(1 - t))}{1 - p(\alpha, m\beta)} \right).$$

The wage is increasing in α because the risk of capture increases with α for the reasons discussed above.

The rebel group leadership's utility function then becomes

$$u_R(\alpha, \beta) = u(t y \min\{1 - \alpha - \beta, \delta\alpha(1 - p(\alpha, m\beta))\} - w\alpha). \quad (7.5)$$

In terms of equilibrium logic, switching from conscription to recruitment does not change anything important. The only difference is that now the rebel group's marginal costs for adding rebels are increasing rather than constant. The effect will be similar to shifting $\alpha(\beta)$ left in Figure 7.2, implying fewer rebels and a smaller counterinsurgency in equilibrium.[27]

However, incorporating recruitment does allow us to analyze an initially plausible counter to the observation made above that while poor people have less to lose by rebelling, they also have less to gain (so why would there be any net effect?). Perhaps the marginal utility of additional income is smaller for wealthier people, making them less willing to risk the very bad outcomes of capture or death as a rebel. By contrast, for poorer people the possible gains from becoming a rebel are much more meaningful.

Another version of this argument is the claim that poverty itself makes for grievance and in consequence a greater willingness to take up arms. This is equivalent, I believe, to the proposition that poorer people are more risk acceptant. The idea is that they are willing to run higher risks of capture and death for the same proportional increase in income.

Consider the specific risk-averse utility function $u(x) = x^\rho$, $\rho \in (0, 1)$. This implies

$$w = \left(\frac{(y(1-t))^\rho}{1 - p(\alpha, m\beta)} \right)^{1/\rho} = \frac{y(1-t)}{(1 - p(\alpha, m\beta))^{1/\rho}}.$$

Yet again, R's marginal cost for adding rebels is linear in y, and thus R's net revenues are as well. R's marginal trade-offs concerning α are not affected by increasing y, and so the equilibrium force size for both rebels and government will again be independent of per capita income, despite our allowing for any degree of risk aversion. The only evident change from introducing risk aversion is that the rebel organization has to pay recruits more to compensate them for the risk of being captured. This will shift $\alpha(\beta)$ to the left in Figure 7.2, lowering both α^* and β^*.

The reason that the levels of rebellion and counterinsurgency are independent of income here is that the utility function $u(x) = x^\rho$ exhibits *constant relative risk aversion*. If a person's preferences satisfy this property, then her level of income y does not affect how she chooses between getting y for sure and a gamble that gives $\tau_1 y$ with some probability, and $\tau_2 y$ with the complementary probability, where $\tau_1 > 1 > \tau_2 \geq 0$.[28]

If we think that *increasing* relative risk aversion (IRRA) is empirically common and significant—that higher wealth makes one markedly less willing to take a gamble such as, say, a p chance of a 10% increase in wealth and a $1 - p$ chance of a 40% decline—then we have a possible explanation for why poor countries are much more civil war prone. When Arrow (1971) advanced the idea of relative risk aversion, he proposed that IRRA was empirically plausible, but subsequent investigations have produced mixed support at best.[29] Ogaki and Zhang (2001) point out that for households with incomes and wealth close to the subsistence level, relative risk aversion must be *decreasing* in income since falling below the subsistence level is so bad; they find empirical support for decreasing relative risk aversion in consumption data from India, and cite other studies with similar results. Behavioral economists argue on the basis of lab experiments and observation that "people do not display a consistent coefficient of relative risk aversion, so it is a waste of time to try to measure it" (Rabin and Thaler 2001, 225). The idea is that risk attitudes depend on contextual features of specific gambles, such as how they are framed.

So it seems unlikely that a general human propensity for IRRA could explain the empirical relationship between low levels of economic development and civil war, given that evidence for significant IRRA in other domains, such as financial assets and consumption, is weak. Alternatively, it could be that some general contextual feature of the specific decision to become a rebel makes for (effectively) greater risk acceptance about rebellion in poor countries. I cannot think of what this ad hoc feature would be, however.

Is there some more compelling way to account for the strong empirical association between low per capita income and the propensity for civil war? Income is plausibly linked to two other variables in the model besides y, in ways that might help explain the regularity.

First, as seen above, more efficient counterinsurgency (larger m) implies fewer rebels in equilibrium. In the context of the model, government forces are more efficient when they capture or kill more rebels for given force sizes. Efficiency in this sense will be determined by factors such as the physical and social terrain, by government and rebel organizational capabilities, and by doctrine.

Richer countries are more urbanized and more uniformly covered by road and communication networks. These factors favor counterinsurgency and government control by making it harder for a nascent guerrilla band to hide. Small, highly secretive terrorist cells can operate in cities, but the movements and operations of larger rebel bands will be visible to many urban dwellers, and the opportunities for anonymous denunciation plentiful. In rural villages, where everyone knows everything about everybody, it is much easier to credibly threaten reprisal for denunciation or to hold small groups collectively responsible. Road networks reduce the amount of land that is good for hidden rebel camps and allow government forces to concentrate more quickly in response to attacks.[30] In the last 60 years, richer countries have tended to have richer neighbors and better political relations with their neighbors, which may have reduced the options for foreign sanctuaries and support for guerrilla groups in wealthier countries.

Richer countries may also tend to have more efficient counterinsurgency due to better training, discipline, and, possibly, doctrine. Counterinsurgency is an extremely difficult political and military task. The main problems are acquiring the intelligence to distinguish reliably between active rebels and noncombatants, preventing military units from killing indiscriminately and so increasing support for the rebels, and preventing corruption in which military units loot and pillage from helpless populations. These problems may be more easily solved by a well-paid, well-trained, literate military with a strong chain of command and a strong sense of professionalism—all features that are plausibly correlated with per capita income.[31] This is not to say that the problems are easily solved even then, as the experience of the United States in Iraq and Vietnam, the former Soviet Union in Afghanistan, and the British in Northern Ireland testify. However, the comparison to counterinsurgency as practiced in Angola, Sudan, Liberia, Guatemala, El Salvador, or Peru—where government units regularly massacred, bombed, or strafed whole villages suspected of collaborating with rebels—is instructive.

A second variable in the model that might vary systematically with income is t, the share of income that rebels and government can extract from locals. Suppose we enrich the model by distinguishing between the rebel's effective tax rate t_R, and the rate the government can get, call it t_G. As noted above, these will often be different, since the government can tax cash-crop production of the region by having the state marketing board pay farmers less than the world price (Bates 1981), or by controlling extractive industries in the region such as oil or mining. In richer countries where income is directly taxed, the government has the advantage of an extensive, employer-based monitoring system. Also, income in a richer country may be less subject to extortion by rebels because it is hypothetical money kept in banks and cyberspace, and because a large corporation's decentralized structure makes it harder to threaten than a small business owner. In a richer economy with more income from human capital, individuals are more able to move in response to local extortion threats and the dangers of living in a conflict zone, making the effective tax rate for rebels lower. By contrast, farmers' income comes from immovable capital.

These examples suggest that economic modernization would tend to reduce t_R, the share of national income that a rebel group can extract through the standard taxation technologies of insurgency. In the model, this leads to fewer rebels and less police or counterinsurgent effort by the government.

7.6 What Prevents a Peaceful Settlement?

The insurgency equilibrium outcome in the model is inefficient; both rebels and governments could do better if they could contract with each other. In this simple and stylized model, inefficiency has only two sources: the diversion of labor from production to fighting, and the diversion of labor from production to tax collection by the rebel group, which is, in effect, assumed to be less efficient than the government's tax collection system.

Several minor modifications could introduce a larger and more realistic set of inefficiencies. First, I assumed that individuals are taxed either by the rebel group or by the government, but not both. Often this is not the case. For example, peasants in rebel-controlled areas may grow crops for market that are taxed by government marketing agencies. If so, then they will be overtaxed by a logic like that in Shleifer and Vishny (1993) and Olson (1993), and consequently will produce less than is optimal. Second, I assumed that the government is perfectly discriminate in its application of force (no one but rebels are captured or killed), and I neglected that, over time, rebel and government violence destroys physical and human capital, discourages investment and production, and encourages refugee flows. In a richer (though less tractable) model, it would be natural to have the violence between soldiers and rebels producing "collateral damage" to people and assets in the regular economy.

In the model at hand, an efficient outcome would be an agreement by R and G to conscript or recruit no rebels and no soldiers, and for G to distribute a portion of the total tax revenues ty to R that would leave both R and G at least as well off as they are in the insurgency equilibrium. This outcome cannot be achieved in the one-shot game analyzed here because neither side could credibly commit to the deal. The rebel leadership would want to take advantage of the government's weak military and police presence to grab control of territory, and the government would have no incentive to transfer funds to the rebel leaders if they had no force behind them.

In the real world, government–rebel interactions need not be "one shot." Could R and G use the fact of continuing interaction to construct a more efficient arrangement? If we make the model the stage game of a repeated game with discounting, then by the usual arguments, the repeated game will have efficient equilibria if the players are patient enough. For example, peace might be supported by having the government anticipate that failure to make transfers to the rebel leadership would lead to war, while the rebel leadership anticipates that arming and grabbing territory would be met by significant counterinsurgency.

But assuming a repeated-game structure assumes too much. If either side can hope to use force to eliminate or permanently disadvantage the other, then the mechanism that makes efficiency possible in a repeated game (conditional retaliation) can be undermined, essentially returning the situation to a "one shot" Prisoner's Dilemma–type problem.[32] Consider, for example, the following dynamic version of the model analyzed above. The game is repeated in successive periods, but suppose that if one side chooses zero forces and a public peace deal while the other chooses a positive level of forces, the side choosing zero is permanently eliminated while the other takes control of the whole country from that period forward. Then there is no way to support the efficient outcome described above using implicit threats of retaliation.

Thus, the rebel group fears accepting a peace deal because once its leadership becomes publicly visible (and findable) and once it disarms, it may be wiped out or permanently disadvantaged if the state reneges. This is arguably why rebel groups almost always demand political power rather than just policy changes or financial transfers to a region; they expect that only by gaining political power (or a perhaps a share of it) can they be assured of the policy changes or transfers they desire. Policy commitments are not credible unless the rebel group can somehow retain an adequate ability to return to war from peace.

Apart from attempting to crush the other side, the main way that combatants (and mediators) in civil wars attempt to resolve such commitment problems is by trying to construct political institutions that would share power between the former combatants. In wars over secession or regional autonomy, power-sharing proposals often envision regional political institutions that would be run in part or whole by the former rebels.[33] Providing a political institutional base for the former rebels increases their ability to "police" the deal. It may also, however, increase the former rebels' ability to demand even more from the government, making for another commitment problem that could prevent a deal in the first place.

In wars over control of a central government, power-sharing proposals seek to divide political offices and/or control of the military among the former combatants. Judging by the frequency with which such arrangements have been discussed but the rarity with which they are successfully implemented, it appears to be extremely difficult in practice to strike a balance that assures each side that it is not too exposed to the danger of reneging by the other (Fearon 2007, Walter 2002).

A spheres-of-influence agreement in which the rebels control less than what they could given the government's effort would seem to be the type of bargain most feasibly policed by an implicit understanding that violation would lead to more open and inefficient conflict. And in fact, "sitzkrieg" is a typical condition for rural guerrilla conflicts. Here, the rebels keep their arms and stay largely hidden, but restrain themselves from taking as much control as they could given the scale of government counterinsurgency in the short run. The government, on the other hand, does not conscript and employ the counterinsurgent force that would be short-run optimal given the size of the rebel force, understanding that if it did, the rebels would scale up and the conflict would escalate to the (α^*, β^*) equilibrium level. For example, the Burmese government cut a series of deals with hill-tribe rebel groups in the early 1990s in which the rebels kept their arms, and the two parties divided up revenues from the opium business.[34] Where feasible, such deals are still second best.

Another hypothetically plausible type of explanation for inefficient fighting in a dynamic version of the model examined here would argue that one or both sides possess private information about their capabilities or resolve to fight, leading to the use of fighting as a costly but credible signal of capabilities or resolve. For example, the government might be unsure about the replacement rate of rebel fighters, which might be affected by rebel organizational capabilities and regional popular support for the rebel aims, both of which could be hard to observe directly. Such "war of attrition" explanations are frequently given in the media and sometimes by combatants themselves. They become less persuasive over time, however, especially for a 5- or 10- or even 20-year fight that looks very much the same from year to year (Fearon 2004).

A final type of obstacle to a stable peace deal concerns the government's fear that if it cuts a deal with one rebel group, it may soon face other insurgent groups, or splinter groups, making similar demands and employing guerrilla tactics to control territory. R and G may not have the capability to prevent new "entrants" from using the same technology of rebellion, which could be just as profitable after their peace deal. The logic is that of the chain-store paradox. The government prefers inefficient conflict in case A in order to deter inefficient conflict in cases B, C, D, and so on.[35]

This mechanism would be expected to make for greater government intransigence in countries with a larger number of potentially secessionist minority groups. Walter (2005) empirically examines the relationship between the number of ethnic groups in a country and the government's propensity to grant a measure of regional autonomy, and finds that this is lower in more diverse countries. The logic also suggests that peace deals will be more difficult to reach in conflicts where there is no dominant rebel organization capable of suppressing or controlling challengers.[36]

Conclusion   The most common form of civil war in the post–World War II period has been a relatively small, stalemated guerrilla war confined to a rural periphery of a poor, postcolonial state. This is violence of a quite different sort from the French Revolution, the great model for theorizing about internal conflict. In the French Revolution paradigm, masses demonstrate in a capital city, which leads to violent encounters with the coercive arms of the old regime. Such conflicts still occur, as in Iran and perhaps Nicaragua in 1978, or China (Tiananmen) and Romania in 1989. But this pattern is far more the exception than the rule. Nor is the model of the U.S. Civil War—essentially an interstate war fought by conventional armies—at all common in this period.

I have argued that guerrilla warfare has distinct features and a distinct logic that, when incorporated in a model of the problem, help to explain its longevity and stability. In the French Revolution scenario, if the government is likely to collapse at a certain level of opposition, then there are "increasing returns" to adding more people to the opposition's protests. As a technology for attempting to change the government, revolution is an all-or-nothing affair, a matter of tipping points, focal points, and successful or unsuccessful mass coordination.

By contrast, in the guerrilla-war technology, a relatively small number of poorly armed rebels survive by hiding successfully from government forces, which, if they knew where the rebels were, could fairly easily destroy them. Rough terrain can help hide the rebel groups, but preventing informers and denunciation to authorities is also essential. The problem of denunciation and detection, I have argued, implies that adding more rebels can increase the risks for existing fighters and thus produce "decreasing returns" for the rebel movement (given a level of government resistance). This in turn leads to the possibility of a stable but violent equilibrium in which neither government nor rebels find it worthwhile to expand their efforts. Expansion would make the rebels too subject to detection and counterattack. A greater effort by the government would not yield enough new captures to make it worth the additional cost.

Higher per capita income means that there is, in principle, more stuff to appropriate if you are a member of a rebel band, and more stuff worth defending if you are on the government side. However, as argued above, the value of *not* fighting is also higher in a richer country, which raises the marginal costs of recruitment or conscription. These two considerations tend to offset each other, even when we consider risk aversion (and assuming that poorer people are not relatively more risk acceptant).

More plausible explanations for the empirical association between higher incomes and lower civil war risk pose an indirect link, via the association of high income with (a) natural and social terrains inimical to guerrilla hiding, (b) state military capability to conduct more efficient counterinsurgency, and (c) inability to appropriate as large a share of income through house-to-house visits by guerrillas, due in part to the mobility of human capital (as opposed to land).

At a theoretical level, the main innovation of this chapter is the opening up of the traditional contest-success function used to study an enormous variety of types of human and animal conflict. A natural next step would be to go further in this direction, developing a more explicit model of the information contest between rebels and government in this case of guerrilla war. In other words, can we "open up" the capture function used here, and so provide plausible microfoundations for the assumption that adding rebels increases the risks of capture for all?

Appendix

Proof of Proposition 7.1. Suppose that (α^*, β^*) is a Nash equilibrium and that the constraint binds in (7.1) and (7.2) so that $1 - \alpha^* - \beta^* \leq \delta(\alpha^* - k(\alpha^*, m\beta^*))$. Then G's payoff is $-c_G\beta^*$, which implies that $\beta^* = 0$ since otherwise G could do better by reducing β^*. $\beta^* = 0$ implies that R's problem is to choose α to maximize $t \min\{1 - \alpha, \delta\alpha\} - c_R\alpha$, which yields $\alpha^* =$

$1/(1 + \alpha)$. And given this α^*, G's utility function becomes $t \max\{0, -\beta + \delta k(\hat{\alpha}, \beta)\} - c_G \beta$. $\beta^* = 0$ is a best reply to $\hat{\alpha}$ if and only if this function slopes down in β at $\beta = 0$, which follows from $k_{22} < 0$ when the condition given in the proposition holds.

If (α^*, β^*) solves the first-order conditions and the constraint does not bind, then this is necessarily a Nash equilibrium, as the assumptions that $k_{11} > 0$ and $k_{22} < 0$ imply that the second-order conditions for maxima are satisfied. In addition, $k_{11} < 0$ implies that there is a unique $\alpha(\beta) > 0$ that solves (7.1) with equality when $k_1(0, \beta) \geq 1 - c_R/\delta t$, and $\alpha(\beta) = 0$ when this inequality does not hold. Likewise, $k_{22} > 0$ implies that there is a unique $\beta(\alpha)$ that satisfies (7.2) when the constraint does not bind. Thus if there is an interior Nash equilibrium, it is unique.

These arguments establish that there cannot be more than one interior pure-strategy Nash equilibrium, and that the only pure-strategy Nash equilibrium possible, such that the constraint binds, is $(\hat{\alpha}, 0)$. It remains to show that $(\hat{\alpha}, 0)$ and an interior equilibrium point (α^*, β^*) cannot both be equilibria for the same parameter values. Suppose the contrary. If $(\hat{\alpha}, 0)$ is an equilibrium, then $k_2(\hat{\alpha}, 0) \leq (t + c_G)/m\delta t$. $k_{12} > 0$ implies that this inequality also holds for any $\alpha < \hat{\alpha}$, so that it cannot be that $\alpha^* \leq \hat{\alpha}$.

Suppose now that $\alpha > \hat{\alpha}$. Then $k(\hat{\alpha}, 0) = 0$ and $k_{22} < 0$ imply that $k(\hat{\alpha}, m\beta^*) < m\beta^* k_2(\hat{\alpha}, 0)$. Subtracting $\beta^*(t + c_G)/\delta t$ from both sides leads to

$$k(\hat{\alpha}, mb^*) - \beta^* \frac{t + c_G}{\delta t} < \beta^* \left(mk_2(\hat{\alpha}, 0) - \frac{t + c_G}{\delta t} \right) \leq 0,$$

where the last inequality follows from $k_2(\hat{\alpha}, 0) \leq (t + c_G)/m\delta t$. Multiplying through by δt and adding the negative quantity $t(1 - \alpha^* - \delta\alpha^*)$ to both sides (negative because $\alpha^* > \hat{\alpha}$), we have

$$t(1 - \alpha^* - \delta\alpha^*) - \beta^* t + \delta t k(\hat{\alpha}, m\beta^*) - \beta^* c_G \leq t(1 - \alpha^* - \delta\alpha^*) < 0.$$

But this implies that the constraint in (7.2) binds for G, which means that $\beta^* > 0$ cannot be part of an equilibrium. ▪

Proof of Proposition 7.2. Let $(\alpha(c_G), \beta(c_G))$ solve (7.3) and (7.4), and then implicitly differentiate both equations in c_G. This yields

$$\frac{dk_1}{dc_G} = k_{11}\alpha' + k_{12}\beta' = 0$$

$$\frac{dk_2}{dc_G} = k_{21}\alpha' + k_{22}\beta' = 1/m\delta t.$$

From the first equation, $k_{11} > 0$ and $k_{12} > 0$ imply that α' and β' must have opposite signs or both be 0. From the second, $k_{21} > 0$, $k_{22} < 0$, and $1/m\delta t > 0$ rule out $\alpha' < 0$ and $\beta' > 0$, and also $\alpha' = \beta' = 0$. So it must be the case that $\alpha'(c_G) > 0$ and $\beta'(c_G) < 0$. Exactly the same type of argument yields the stated results for c_R, t, and δ.

Likewise, implicitly differentiating the first-order conditions at the equilibrium values in m yields

$$\frac{dk_1}{dm} = k_{11}\alpha' + k_{12}(\beta + m\beta') = 0$$

$$\frac{dk_2}{dm} = k_{21}\alpha' + k_{22}(\beta + m\beta') = -\frac{t + c_G}{m^2\delta t}.$$

From the first equation, $k_{11} > 0$ and $k_{12} > 0$ imply that if $\alpha' > 0$, it must be that $\beta + m\beta' < 0$. But then the second equation cannot hold, since $k_{21} > 0$ and $k_{22} < 0$. Nor can $\alpha' = 0$ since then the first equation would require $\beta + m\beta' = 0$, which is impossible by the second equation. So $\alpha' < 0$ and $\beta + m\beta' > 0$, which means that β' can have any sign depending on the functional forms. ▪

ACKNOWLEDGMENTS

I wish to thank Canadian Institute for Advanced Research and the Institutions, Organizations, and Growth group for comments, discussion, and material support for the research that went into this chapter, and also Avinash Dixit, David Laitin, and Michael Wallerstein for very helpful discussions. An earlier version of this chapter was presented at the annual meeting of the American Political Science Association, Washington, DC, September 1–4, 2005.

NOTES

1. See Kalyvas (2004) for a discussion of types of civil warfare that makes a similar set of distinctions.
2. The finding that level of economic development is a strong (typically the strongest along with total population) correlate of violent civil strife is one of

the most robust in the growing large-N literature on the subject. Some scholars used related variables such as life expectancy, education levels, or per capita
energy consumption, which are closely correlated with per capita income and
plausibly tap a common underlying dimension of level of economic development. See for examples Fearon and Laitin (2003), Collier and Hoeffler (2004),
and Hegre and Sambanis (2006).

3. One might get a certain amount of risk-seeking behavior by the poorest of the
   poor if one assumes that starvation is the likely alternative to joining a rebel
   band, but it seems implausible that this could explain much of the civil war we
   have seen in the last 60 years. Grossman and Mendoza (2003) develop essentially this argument to explain some anthropological observations of an association between resource scarcity and increased conflict in premodern societies
   where starvation was common.

4. We could assume that individuals can hide their income at marginal cost $h \in$
   $(0, 1)$, in which case government and rebels optimally set tax rates at $t = h$.

5. For completeness, assume that if R and G choose α and β such that $\alpha +$
   $\beta > 1$, then their realized force sizes are $\alpha' = \alpha/(\alpha + \beta)$ and $\beta' = \beta/(\alpha + \beta)$
   respectively. This is unimportant, however, since α and β such that $\alpha + \beta > 1$
   cannot be best replies given the utility functions below.

6. Diminishing returns also ensures that $\alpha(\beta)$ is unique.

7. An individual with pretax income (or ability) level $\hat{y}$ is indifferent between
   working in the regular economy and becoming a rebel or soldier at wage w
   when $w = (1 - t)\hat{y}$. At this wage everyone with $y < \hat{y}$ prefers to take w and
   fight, so that the fraction who are rebels or soldiers is $F(\hat{y}) = \alpha + \beta$, and thus
   $\hat{y} = F^{-1}(\alpha + \beta)$.

8. But it does not necessarily associate with greater inefficiency, which in this
   model comes from the fact that rebels and soldiers are not producing what they
   could. Greater inequality at a given per capita level means that there are more
   rebels and soldiers, but they would have been less productive in the regular
   economy anyway. Adding direct damage to the economy from conflict would
   change this, however, and in practice, these effects are probably far larger than
   that of labor displacement.

9. Fearon and Laitin (2003) and Fearon (2005) argue that oil exports favor civil
   war by increasing the "prize" value of capturing the state or region, and because, conditional on income level, oil producers tend to have less-developed
   state administrative apparatuses and capabilities. Humphreys (2005) considers
   a broader array of possible mechanisms. Olsson and Fors (2004) consider a contest model of civil conflict in which the ruler controls natural-resource rents;
   greater resource rents make for more conflict in their model, by the same logic
   as that described here.

10. Grossman and Mendoza (2003, 747–48) may be alluding to the issue when they write that "Surprisingly, the commonsensical hypothesis that resource scarcity causes a large allocation of time and effort to appropriative competition is not easy to formalize" and that "there is no reason to presume that in general the relative return to appropriative competition either increases or decreases with the size of the resource endowment."

11. Along similar lines, external funding from neighboring states and superpowers has been an important source for insurgencies since 1945, acting in a way similar to raising t or lowering c_R in the contest model. Another possible explanation for the concentration of civil wars in poorer countries since 1945 is that civil war has been a form of interstate war by proxy, and that the relative absence of civil war among richer countries is a by-product of the factors that have favored interstate peace among richer countries in this period.

12. The usual assumption is that $p_{12} > 0$ for $\alpha > m\beta$ and $p_{12} < 0$ for $\alpha < m\beta$. This gives rise to best-reply functions that increase and then decrease, and which intersect at an (α, β) such that $\alpha = m\beta$ when $p(\cdot, \cdot)$ is symmetric. (Here and below, f_i denotes the derivative of the function f with respect to argument i, and f_{ij} is the derivative of f taken first with respect to argument i and then with respect to argument j.)

13. There are cases, such as the RUF in Sierra Leone, where it is not clear whether the insurgent leaders are sincere about their political objections, but they nonetheless espouse them.

14. External funding from neighboring states, the United States and the former Soviet Union during the Cold War, or from ethnic diasporas are also quite significant for many insurgencies. See Weinstein (2005) and Hovil and Werker (2005) for studies of the implications of external funding for insurgent strategy and tactics, and Byman et al. (2001) for a study of external funding of insurgent groups after the cold war.

15. On this process, see for example Leites and Wolf (1970), Stoll (1993), and Kalyvas (2003). See Weinstein (2007) for a more general analysis of the determinants of different modes of rebel organization.

16. More evidence in favor of this characterization is provided by the cell structures that rebel organizations often use to lessen the network externalities of detection and infiltration.

17. Rebel organizations may devote considerable resources to ideological training of recruits (e.g., NPA in the Philippines, Museveni's NRA in Uganda) or use lower-tech methods such as requiring recruits to kill soldiers or even members of their own family (to make it very difficult for them to return to their former life).

18. Here is a very simple illustration of how network connections will tend to make the probability of capture increase with the size of the organization. Consider a country or region or village with n people, r of whom are active rebels. The government interrogates one person at random, and interrogation reveals if the person is an active rebel for sure. If there are no network connections between rebels at all, then ex ante a rebel's probability of capture is $1/n$. If, due to network connections, capture of any one rebel implies capture of the rest, then ex ante a rebel's probability of capture is r/n, which is increasing in r. A richer version of this setup has the government interrogating s people at random, and an expected share of other rebels captured if the government gets good information from interrogation. Again, individual risk of capture will be increasing in r.

19. All three properties are true of the capture model suggested in Note 17.

20. In this example, it is at $\bar{\alpha} \approx .56$. The example is generated using the capture function $p(\alpha, m\beta) = m\alpha\beta/(m\alpha\beta + 1)$ and parameters $t = .2$, $m = 1800$, $\delta = 35$, $c_R = 1$, $c_G = .3$.

21. The earlier, conference version of this chapter gives the details for the mixed-strategy equilibrium for the case of $p(\alpha, m\beta) = m\alpha\beta/(m\alpha\beta + 1)$. $\bar{\alpha}$ is defined as the α such that the constraint in (7.2) binds with equality at $(\bar{\alpha}, \beta(\bar{\alpha}))$, where $\beta(\cdot)$ solves G's first-order condition (7.4).

22. It can be shown that in the Stackleberg version, the government commits to a higher force level than in the simultaneous-move case, leading to a lower equilibrium level of rebellion. Comparative statics are the same as in the simultaneous-move case.

23. The model in the earlier version of this chapter considered the case of conflict over a region of a country beyond which the rebel group simply could not expand. In this case the $\beta^* = 0$ equilibrium has a natural interpretation as a situation where the government allows rebel control of the region because the tax base is too small, and counterinsurgency too difficult, to make governing it worthwhile. The British and French treated some peripheral zones in some of their colonies this way, as did some Latin American countries until fairly recently.

24. For the case of $p(\alpha, m\beta) = m\alpha\beta/(m\alpha\beta + 1)$, the equilibrium size of the rebel movement does not vary at all with changes in δ or t (in the interior equilibrium).

25. Thus, rebel groups that do try "conscription" tend to abduct children, who often do not know how to return home if they were to escape, and who are more easily scared or convinced to stay with the rebel group (Blattman 2007). In a few cases, such as the LTTE in Sri Lanka, the rebel group develops such

strong control of a region that conscription is made possible by the ability to threaten the conscript's family with retribution if he or she should defect.

26. These could easily be incorporated at the expense of more notation, and I doubt the implications would be surprising (that is, more idealism will imply more rebels and more counterinsurgency).

27. Analytic solutions are harder to obtain now; even with $u(x) = x$ and $p(\alpha, m\beta) = m\alpha\beta/(m\alpha\beta + 1)$, R's first-order condition requires solving a cubic equation. Note also that if we allow income to vary in the population, this creates another source of increasing costs for rebel recruitment, since they will draw first from the poor and have to offer increasing amounts to persuade additional recruits to join up.

28. More generally, constant relative risk aversion means that $-xu''(x)/u'(x)$ is constant.

29. See, for example, Meyer and Meyer (2005).

30. Fearon and Laitin (2003) find that the percentage of mountainous terrain in a country is positively related to civil war risk, although this is not one of the most robust predictors. Empirically, road density and urbanization are related to lower civil war risk, but these are so closely correlated with per capita income that the effects are hard to distinguish. Kocher (2004) argues that the income–civil war relationship is mainly due to urbanization disfavoring rebellion. A suggestive set of examples comes from South America in the 1970s, where intellectuals (especially in Argentina) tried to develop urban-based insurgencies. They were in all cases quickly penetrated and destroyed by state militaries and secret services. On Argentina, see Gillespie (1982). That said, there are a few cases of successful urban insurgency, such as in Northern Ireland and now, Iraq.

31. Felter (2005) uses extensive incident-level data from the Philippine military's wars in Mindanao and Luzon to show that local units with highly trained leadership cadres are the most effective at killing or capturing rebels while avoiding civilian deaths, especially when they are mixed with local forces with local knowledge and intelligence.

32. For models of inefficient civil and interstate conflict that rely on this mechanism, see Fearon (1994, 1995, 2004), and for a more general analysis, Powell (2004). The same mechanism is also at work in Acemoglu and Robinson's (2006) models of democracy and autocracy.

33. Some examples include the treatment of the Moro National Liberation Front in the Philippines, GAM in Aceh, Indonesia, the IRA in Northern Ireland, and arguably the PLO in the West Bank and Gaza.

34. See also Keen (1998) on Liberia and Sierra Leone.

35. In the classic chain-store–paradox models, the equilibrium outcome is efficient because no entrant challenges and thus fighting is off the equilibrium path. To

get inefficient fighting "on the path," we would need to allow for heterogeneous types of entrants, some of which are willing to fight if they have zero regional control even if they face resistance, and whose preferences are not publicly observable. The explanation then becomes a private-information story.

36. Peace negotiations for both Burundi and Somalia have been held up repeatedly by the appearance of new opposition groups demanding payoffs, just as an agreement is about to be signed.

REFERENCES

Acemoglu, Daron, and James Robinson. 2006. *Economic Origins of Dictatorship and Democracy*. New York: Cambridge University Press.

Arrow, Kenneth. 1971. *Essays in the Theory of Risk-Bearing*. Chicago: Markham.

Bates, Robert H. 1981. *Markets and States in Tropical Africa: The Political Basis of Agricultural Policies*. Berkeley: University of California Press.

Blattman, Christopher. 2007. "The Causes of Child Soldiering: Theory and Evidence from Northern Uganda." Unpublished manuscript, Yale University.

Byman, Daniel L., Peter Chalk, Bruce Hoffman, William Rosenau, and David Brannan. 2001. *Trends in Outside Support for Insurgent Movements*. Los Angeles: Rand Corporation.

Collier, Paul, and Anke Hoeffler. 2004. "Greed and Grievance in Civil War." *Oxford Economic Papers* 56:563–95.

Fearon, James D. 1994. "Ethnic War as a Commitment Problem." Presented at the 1994 Annual Meetings of the American Political Science Association, 2–5 September, New York.

———. 1995. "Rationalist Explanations for War." *International Organization* 49(3):379–414.

———. 2004. "Why Do Some Civil Wars Last So Much Longer Than Others?" *Journal of Peace Research* 41(3):275–301.

———. 2005. "Primary Commodity Exports and Civil War." *Journal of Conflict Resolution* 49(4).

———. 2007. "Iraq's Civil War." *Foreign Affairs* 86(2):2–16.

Fearon, James D., and David D. Laitin. 2003. "Ethnicity, Insurgency, and Civil War." *American Political Science Review* 97(1):75–90.

Felter, Joseph. 2005. "Taking Guns to a Knife Fight." PhD thesis, Department of Political Science, Stanford University.

Ghobarah, Hazem Adam, Paul Huth, and Bruce Russett. 2003. "Civil Wars Kill and Maim People—Long after the Shooting Stops." *American Political Science Review* 97(2):189–202.

Gillespie, Richard. 1982. *Soldiers of Perón: Argentina's Montoneros*. New York: Oxford University Press.

Grossman, Herschel I. 1991. "A General Equilibrium Model of Insurrections." *American Economic Review* 81(4):912–21.

———. 2002. "'Make Us a King': Anarchy, Predation, and the State." *European Journal of Political Economy* 18:31–46.

Grossman, Herschel I., and Juan Mendoza. 2003. "Scarcity and Appropriative Competition." *European Journal of Political Economy* 19:747–58.

Hegre, Håvard, and Nicholas Sambanis. 2006. "Sensitivity Analysis of the Empirical Literature on Civil War Onset." *Journal of Conflict Resolution* 50(4):508–35.

Hirshleifer, Jack. 1995. "Anarchy and Its Breakdown." *Journal of Political Economy* 103(1):26–52.

Hovil, Lucy, and Eric Werker. 2005. "Portrait of a Failed Rebellion: An Account of Rational, Sub-Optimal Violence in Western Uganda." *Rationality and Society* 17(1):5–34.

Humphreys, Macartan. 2005. "Natural Resources, Conflict, and Conflict Resolution: Uncovering the Mechanisms." *Journal of Conflict Resolution* 49(4):508–37.

Kalyvas, Stathis N. 1999. "Wanton and Senseless? The Logic of Massacres in Algeria." *Rationality and Society* 11(3):243–85.

———. 2003. "The Ontology of 'Political Violence': Action and Identity in Civil Wars." *Perspectives on Politics* 1(3):475–94.

———. 2004. "Memo for the October 2004 Sawyer Seminar on the Changing Nature of War." Unpublished manuscript, Yale University.

Keen, David. 1998. *The Economic Functions of Violence in Civil Wars*. London: Oxford University Press.

Kocher, Matthew Adam. 2004. "Human Ecology and Civil War." PhD thesis, Department of Political Science, University of Chicago.

Leites, Nathan, and Charles Wolf. 1970. *Rebellion and Authority*. Chicago: Markham.

Meyer, Donald J., and Jack Meyer. 2005. "Relative Risk Aversion: What Do We Know?" *Journal of Risk and Uncertainty* 31(3):243–62.

Ogaki, Masao, and Qiang Zhang. 2001. "Decreasing Relative Risk Aversion and Tests of Risk Sharing." *Econometrica* 69(2):515–26.

Olson, Mancur. 1993. "Dictatorship, Development, and Democracy." *American Political Science Review* 87(3):567–76.

Olsson, Ola, and Heather Congdon Fors. 2004. "Congo: The Prize of Predation." *Journal of Peace Research* 41(3):321–36.

Powell, Robert. 2004. "The Inefficient Use of Power: Costly Conflict with Complete Information." *American Political Science Review* 98(2):231–42.

Rabin, Matthew, and Richard H. Thaler. 2001. "Anomalies: Risk Aversion." *Journal of Economic Perspectives* 15(1):219–32.

Shleifer, Andrei, and Robert W. Vishny. 1993. "Corruption." *Quarterly Journal of Economics* 108(3):599–617.

Skaperdas, Stergios. 1992. "Conflict, Cooperation, and Power in the Absence of Property Rights." *American Economic Review* 82(4):720–39.

Stoll, David. 1993. *Between Two Armies in the Ixil Towns of Guatemala*. New York: Columbia University Press.

Walter, Barbara F. 2002. *Committing to Peace*. Princeton, NJ: Princeton University Press.

———. 2005. "Building Reputation: Why Governments Fight Some Separatists but Not Others." *American Journal of Political Science* 50(2):313–30.

Weinstein, Jeremy M. 2005. "Resources and the Information Problem in Rebel Recruitment." *Journal of Conflict Resolution* 49(4).

———. 2007. *Inside Rebellion: The Politics of Insurgent Violence*. New York: Cambridge University Press.

— 8 —

Party Discipline and
Pork-Barrel Politics

GENE M. GROSSMAN AND ELHANAN HELPMAN

8.1   Introduction

How do political institutions affect economic policy choices? This question frames much recent research in comparative political economics. Whereas political scientists working in comparative politics have long addressed the implications of different political institutions for *political* outcomes—such as the number of political parties, the stability of government, and the representation of minorities—political economists have more recently become interested in the institutional determinants of *policy* outcomes, such as income tax rates, national and local public spending, and industry rates of trade protection.

Much of the work on comparative political economy focuses on aspects of fiscal policy. For example, Persson, Roland, and Tabellini (2000) study the differences between presidential and parliamentary political systems for the provision of local public goods and the redistribution of income via transfer programs. Lizzeri and Persico (2001), Persson and Tabellini (2001, ch. 8), and Milesi-Ferretti et al. (2002) compare taxes, spending, and transfers in polities with majoritarian and proportionally representative (PR) electoral rules. Austen-Smith (2000) examines how tax and spending policies vary with the number of political parties represented in the law-making body.

We too are interested in the forces that shape fiscal policy, but we focus on a different political institutional feature. We note that polities differ in the extent to which political parties can pre-commit before elections to carry out certain policy actions if they take power. Commitment problems arise due to a divergence between ex ante and ex post incentives, which may reflect (among other things) a difference between the objectives of national parties, which seek to capture control of the legislature and thereby implement their ideological agendas, and the objectives of individual legislators, whose interests may be more parochial. At one extreme, as in the "Downsian" world, a party may be able to announce a policy platform to which its members will be fully committed if elected. At the opposite extreme, as with the "citizen-candidates" of Osborne and Slivinski (1996) and Besley and Coate (1997), the campaign promises of the political parties may be wholly nonbinding. In between these extremes, the extent to which the political parties can tie the hands of the politicians who are subsequently elected to office will depend on institutional characteristics of the political regime, such as the role of the national party in financing regional campaigns, in allocating the perquisites of election, and in choosing candidates for higher office.

For lack of a better term, we shall refer to the institutional variation that is of interest here as differences in "party discipline." We acknowledge that *party discipline* most often is used by political scientists and others to mean the extent to which parties (or the leaders of a legislative delegation) can induce members to toe the *current* party line.[1] With strict party discipline, party leaders can eliminate the scope for independent expression of opinions and interests by their fellow party members in the course of policymaking. Here we identify strict discipline with a party's ability to induce ex post adherence to a preannounced position. Parties have an ex ante incentive to make campaign announcements in order to further their electoral objectives, but the effectiveness of these announcements will reflect their ability to ensure compliance. Thus, the parties will want to use what tools they have at their disposal to induce the elected politicians to honor the party's promises.[2]

In this chapter and a companion paper (Grossman and Helpman 2005), we develop a new model of majoritarian elections and legislative policymaking that we hope will hold independent interest and prove useful for examining a variety of political-economic issues. In our model, winner-take-all elections occur in single-member legislative districts. The two political parties move first by announcing their policy platforms, with the aim of maximizing their chances of taking control of the legislature. Next, the heterogeneous voters in each district vote for the local candidate of one or the other party, with the goal of maximizing their personal expected welfare in the face of uncertainty about the relative popularity of the two parties in districts other than their own. Finally, the elected members of the legislature set policy to further the interests of their constituents, but in recognition of the political penalties that their national party will impose if they fail to deliver on the party's campaign promises. We introduce a parameter that measures the cost to the legislators of deviating from the party platform and so captures the degree of what we are calling party discipline. At one extreme value of this parameter, the legislators are fully committed; at the other, they behave like citizen candidates.

We use the model to examine pork-barrel spending, that is, projects that are financed by broad-based taxation but provide benefits that are geographically limited in scope.[3] We consider a polity with three districts that are symmetric ex ante. There are three public goods, each of which provides benefits to residents in one of the districts. Benefit functions are identical as are the costs of the public goods and the distributions of political preference among voters in the districts. Ex post, spending on the three public goods depends on the outcomes of the three regional elections. If, for example, the same political party wins the election in all three districts, then spending in every district will be the same. The spending levels typically will diverge from the efficient levels, however, because the parties will have made earlier promises that will affect the legislators' ex post choices. Depending on the degree of party discipline, the ex post spending in each district when the same party wins the election in all three can exceed or fall short of the efficient level.

When one party wins in two districts but loses in the third, the legislature will concentrate pork in the districts represented in the majority delegation, to the relative neglect of the district whose representative is a member of the minority party. Thus, there will be ex post inequality in spite of the ex ante symmetry—a kind of tyranny of the majority. For low levels of discipline, the majority delegation will not feel compelled to deliver any pork to the minority district, despite their party having made a campaign promise to spend there. When discipline reaches a certain level, however, the political cost to the elected representatives of completely ignoring their party's campaign promise becomes too great. Then spending in the minority district is positive, and is greater, the stricter the discipline. In the limit, as discipline becomes perfect, the campaign promise of spending in each district approaches the efficient level, and the elected politicians are compelled to deliver exactly what was promised. It follows that the spending in a minority district, when positive, is always less than the efficient level and approaches the efficient level (from below) only as discipline becomes strict.

An interesting implication of our analysis is that both the rhetoric and reality of pork-barrel spending bear a nonmonotonic relationship to the parameter that represents the ability of parties to commit to a campaign platform. The promised level of per-district spending is very high when party discipline is low but falls as discipline rises as long as anticipated spending in a minority district remains at zero. However, once the parameter representing discipline reaches the critical level at which the majority delegation will feel compelled to deliver positive pork, even to a district they do not represent, the relationship between discipline and promised spending is reversed. When the discipline parameter is high and grows even higher, the marginal electoral benefit that comes from being able to deliver more to a district that ultimately becomes part of a two-district majority exceeds the marginal electoral cost that comes when voters in a district realize that they do not need to be represented in the majority delegation to receive pork. In such circumstances, a rise in the discipline parameter leads the parties to promise more spending in each district.

Actual spending in a district that is represented in a two-member majority delegation also falls and then rises as a function of the parameter measuring the extent of pre-commitment possibilities. At low levels of discipline, the fall in the very high promise causes the delivered spending to decline, despite the fact that the majority delegation comes closer to delivering on its (more moderate) promises. At high levels of discipline, the positive relationship between the promise and discipline carries over to the actual policy response, as the majority delegation cannot bear to stray too far from its party's platform. Our analysis suggests, therefore, that the cross-sectional effects of political institutions cannot always be captured by simple correlations.

It is noteworthy too that the aggregate efficiency of fiscal policy bears a nonmonotonic relationship to the degree of party discipline. When discipline is lax, the parties make extravagant promises and actual spending in districts represented in a majority delegation is socially excessive. In fact, the lavish spending in these districts may leave a typical voter's expected welfare below what it would be were national spending on local public goods to be constitutionally prohibited. As discipline rises from these very low levels, the strong negative response of spending in districts represented in a two-member majority is sufficient to raise expected welfare. At the opposite extreme, when discipline is quite strict, spending in every district falls below the efficient level, which means that the extra spending that results from an increase in discipline again enhances expected welfare. But for intermediate levels of discipline, each party promises pork at the highest level consistent with ex post spending of zero in a district represented by a member of the minority party. Then spending in districts represented in the majority falls monotonically as a function of discipline from levels that are socially excessive to levels that are socially deficient. Expected welfare rises, then falls, as party discipline varies in this range.

The chapter is organized as follows. In Section 8.2 we describe the three stages—policy, campaign, and election—of our political game. We seek a subgame perfect equilibrium of the electoral game between political parties, so we describe the legislative deliberations first, the equilibrium voting behavior second, and the platform choices last. In Section 8.3, we derive the equilibrium platforms and policies as a function of the parameter representing the extent of party discipline. We refer to these respectively as the *rhetoric* and *reality* of pork-barrel policy. Then, in Section 8.4, we study how the announcements and policies vary with the political environment. We also examine the relationship between ex ante expected welfare and the degree of party discipline.

8.2 A Model of Pork-Barrel Spending

We study how party discipline affects pork-barrel spending in a majoritarian political system. Our model of public spending is a simple and familiar one—a central government can provide public goods that benefit citizens in specific geographic areas with funds raised by lump-sum levies on a national tax base.[4] In the political game, the national parties move first by announcing positions on the pork-barrel projects, with the goal of maximizing their chances of winning a majority in the national legislature. Then, the ideologically diverse voters elect representatives to the legislature. Finally, the members of the majority delegation in the legislature adopt a spending program to serve their constituents while taking into account the disciplines imposed by their national party. The legislators need not enact the projects endorsed by their party; thus, the political *rhetoric* may differ from the political *reality*.

Consider a polity with three geographic districts and two political parties. (We choose the number of districts to be three, because this eliminates the possibility of ties.) Citizens derive utility from consumption of private goods, consumption of a local public good, and from other policies enacted by the party in power. A resident i of district j has the quasi-linear preferences

$$u_{ij} = c_{ij} + H(g_j) + \beta_{ij}^K + v_j^K,$$

where c_{ij} denotes the individual's consumption of private goods, g_j is the size of a public project that yields benefits (only) to residents of district j, and $\beta_{ij}^K + v_j^K$ represents utility that the individual derives from other policies that will come into effect if party K captures a majority in the legislature. The function $H(\cdot)$ is increasing and concave.

Let the populations of the three districts be equal and each normalized to one. Funds raised by the tax system (in units of the private good) can be converted one for one into units of any of the three local public goods. Since the government levies lump-sum taxes, a program $\mathbf{g} = (g_1, g_2, g_3)$ requires a per capita levy of $\frac{1}{3} \sum_{j=1}^{3} g_j$. Thus, resident i of district j, who has (exogenous) income[5] I_{ij}, would consume $c_{ij}^K = I_{ij} - \frac{1}{3} \sum_{j=1}^{3} g_j^K$ units of private goods if party K were to gain power and enact the spending program $\mathbf{g}^K = (g_1^K, g_2^K, g_3^K)$.

We distinguish the (preelection) political objectives of the national parties from the (postelection) objectives of the individual politicians who are elected to office. The national party has an ideological agenda, which is reflected in the other policies it will enact (besides the pork-barrel spending) if elected. In order to pursue this agenda, the party must capture a majority of seats in the legislature. We assume, therefore, that a party's objective is to do just that, that is, to maximize the probability that it will win at least two of the district elections. The legislators, on the other hand, are beholden to their constituents. We do not model a sequence of elections and so cannot derive the politicians' objective functions endogenously. Instead, we assume that elected legislators pursue the interests of district residents but bear a political cost for any departures from party discipline. One way to reconcile this difference in objectives between the party and the elected legislators is by reference to the different times at which their decisions are taken. Suppose that all politicians care much more about the ideological issues of the day than about providing pork to their constituents. Then, before the election, the candidates from a given party will all agree to choose the vector of spending promises that maximizes their prospects to implement their ideological agenda. Once the election has passed, however, the victorious party will be in a position to enact these policies. At this stage, the majority delegation may turn its attention to providing pork to constituents, which, though of lesser importance to the legislators' overall concerns, still provides them with positive political welfare.

We seek a subgame perfect equilibrium of a three-stage game in which the parties A and B announce the spending programs $\mathbf{g}^A$ and $\mathbf{g}^B$, respectively, in the first stage; the voters in each district elect a single representative to the national legislature in the second stage; and the elected representatives supply the public goods $\mathbf{g}_L^K$ in the third stage, where K indicates the party that controls the legislature and L indicates the set of districts in which the candidates from party K garner a majority of votes.

8.2.1 The Policy Stage

Let us begin with the final, policy stage. At this stage, the majority delegation from party K comprises the representatives of two or three districts. Party K has previously announced a position $\mathbf{g}^K$ on the set of pork-barrel projects. The party sought competitive advantage by announcing its position, and it hopes to be able to use similar tactics in subsequent elections. Accordingly, it imposes such penalties as it can on elected party members when they deviate from the party's announced position. How much the party can penalize its members for pursuing their parochial objectives depends upon the institutional setting. If, for example, regional campaigns are financed by the national party, or if the party controls other resources such as committee assignments and patronage positions, then the party will have ample "sticks and carrots" with which to induce compliant behavior. We do not explicitly model the instruments of party discipline, but rather attempt to capture them in reduced form with a parameter δ. If the legislators from majority party K enact a pork-barrel program $\mathbf{g}$ after their party has announced a position $\mathbf{g}^K$, then, collectively, they bear a political cost $\frac{\delta}{2} \sum_{j=1}^{3} \left(g_i - g_i^K \right)^2$. If, for example, $\delta = 0$, then discipline is lacking, and the legislators are free to serve their local constituents with complete impunity. As $\delta \to \infty$, a party has the wherewithal to keep its individual politicians fully in line. Then the party can commit to actions that its candidates surely will take if they are elected.

We assume that each legislator has as his objective to maximize the aggregate welfare of the residents of his district less the costs he will bear for failing to deliver on his party's promises. We also assume that members of a given political party have the ability to transfer (political) utility among themselves, for example, by sharing patronage benefits. In contrast, members of different political parties lack the means to effect such transfers.[6] Then a majority delegation of party K comprising representatives from the set of districts L will choose a spending program to maximize their joint political welfare given by

$$\sum_{j \in L} \left[I_j + H(g_j) - \frac{g_1 + g_2 + g_3}{3} \right] - \frac{\delta}{2} \sum_{m=1}^{3} \left(g_m - g_m^K \right)^2,$$

where I_j is aggregate income in district j. The interests of those residing in districts represented by legislators in the minority party are neglected in the process of distributing pork.

We can now link the policy outcomes to the composition of the legislature and the announced positions of the majority party. If party K captures all three seats in the legislature, then

$$g_{\{1,2,3\},j}^K = \arg \max_{g_j \geq 0} H(g_j) - g_j - \frac{\delta}{2} \left(g_j - g_j^K \right)^2, \qquad (8.1)$$

where $g_{L,j}^K$ denotes spending on the public project in district j when party K holds a majority comprising the set of districts L. If party K captures the seats in districts j and k, but not in ℓ, then

$$g_{\{j,k\},j}^K = \arg \max_{g_j \geq 0} H(g_j) - \frac{2}{3} g_j - \frac{\delta}{2} \left(g_j - g_j^K \right)^2 \qquad (8.2)$$

and

$$g_{\{j,k\},\ell}^K = \arg \max_{g_\ell \geq 0} -\frac{2}{3} g_\ell - \frac{\delta}{2} \left(g_\ell - g_\ell^K \right)^2. \qquad (8.3)$$

8.2.2 The Election Stage

Citizens enter the voting booth knowing the announced positions of each party. They anticipate the links between possible election outcomes and policy choices, as described in (8.1), (8.2), and (8.3). However, they are imperfectly informed about the preferences of the average voter in each district. This uncertainty is what makes the voter's problem meaningful.

Each individual votes for the candidate who, if elected in her district, would offer her the highest level of expected utility.[7]

Voters differ in their tastes for the parties' ideological positions, as noted above. The taste disparities have idiosyncratic and regional components. We define $\beta_{ij} = \beta_{ij}^B - \beta_{ij}^A$ as the idiosyncratic component of the relative preference of voter i in district j for the ideological positions and other characteristics of party B compared to party A. Similarly, $v_j = v_j^B - v_j^A$ represents the relative preference for the positions of party B (positive or negative) shared by all residents of district j. We assume that β_{ij} has mean zero in every district j and that it is distributed uniformly on values ranging from $-1/2h$ to $1/2h$. The parameter h measures (inversely) the extent of preference diversity among citizens in any district. The residents of a district know their own preferences, of course, by the time they enter the voting booth, but they are not sure of the mean preferences of those residing in other districts. Each voter in district j views v_k and v_ℓ as independent, random variables drawn from a common, cumulative distribution function $F(\cdot)$. To preserve the symmetry of the two parties in the eyes of the (average) voter, we take the density function associated with $F(\cdot)$ to be single-peaked and symmetric about $v = 0$.

Consider the problem facing voter i in district 1. If the candidate for party A wins in district 1, her utility will depend on the election results in districts 2 and 3 and on the positions previously announced by the two parties (since these will affect the subsequent legislative deliberations). Let $V_j(\mathbf{g}^K) = H(g_j^K) - \left(g_1^K + g_2^K + g_3^K\right)/3$ be the common component of utility for any individual in district j that arises from the spending program $\mathbf{g}^K$. Using this notation, the expected utility for voter i, conditional on a victory by party A in district 1, can be written as

$$U_{i1}^A = I_{i1} + \rho_2\rho_3 \left[V_1\left(\mathbf{g}_{\{1,2,3\}}^A\right) + \beta_{i1}^A + v_1^A \right]$$

$$+ \rho_2\left(1 - \rho_3\right)\left[V_1\left(\mathbf{g}_{\{1,2\}}^A\right) + \beta_{i1}^A + v_1^A \right]$$

$$+ \left(1 - \rho_2\right)\rho_3\left[V_1\left(\mathbf{g}_{\{1,3\}}^A\right) + \beta_{i1}^A + v_1^A \right]$$

$$+ \left(1 - \rho_2\right)\left(1 - \rho_3\right)\left[V_1\left(\mathbf{g}_{\{2,3\}}^B\right) + \beta_{i1}^B + v_1^B \right],$$

where ρ_j is the probability that party A will win in district j as perceived by a voter outside that district. Here, the term in the first set of square brackets is the utility that voter i in district 1 would derive from all of the policy actions (pork barrel and other) that would be enacted by party A were it to win in all three districts. This is multiplied by the probability that party A will win in both districts 2 and 3, since we are conditioning on the event of a victory by party A in district 1. The other terms in the expression for U_{i1}^A can be understood similarly. Note especially the last term, which represents the probability of a victory by party B in districts 2 and 3 multiplied by the voter's evaluation of the policies that would be enacted by party B (*not* party A) in this eventuality.

Similarly, we can evaluate the expected utility for voter i in district 1, conditional on an electoral victory by the candidate from party B in this district, which is

$$
\begin{aligned}
U_{i1}^B = I_{i1} &+ \rho_2\rho_3 \left[V_1\left(\mathbf{g}_{\{2,3\}}^A\right) + \beta_{i1}^A + v_1^A \right] \\
&+ \rho_2\left(1 - \rho_3\right) \left[V_1\left(\mathbf{g}_{\{1,3\}}^B\right) + \beta_{i1}^B + v_1^B \right] \\
&+ \left(1 - \rho_2\right)\rho_3 \left[V_1\left(\mathbf{g}_{\{1,2\}}^B\right) + \beta_{i1}^B + v_1^B \right] \\
&+ \left(1 - \rho_2\right)\left(1 - \rho_3\right) \left[V_1\left(\mathbf{g}_{\{1,2,3\}}^B\right) + \beta_{i1}^B + v_1^B \right].
\end{aligned}
$$

Voter i casts her ballot for the candidate from party A if and only if $U_{i1}^A \geq U_{i1}^B$, that is, if and only if

$$
\beta_{i1} \leq \frac{\Delta_1}{\theta_1} - v_1, \tag{8.4}
$$

where

$$
\begin{aligned}
\Delta_1 = \rho_2\rho_3 &\left[V_1\left(\mathbf{g}_{\{1,2,3\}}^A\right) - V_1\left(\mathbf{g}_{\{2,3\}}^A\right) \right] \\
&+ \rho_2\left(1 - \rho_3\right) \left[V_1\left(\mathbf{g}_{\{1,2\}}^A\right) - V_1\left(\mathbf{g}_{\{1,3\}}^B\right) \right] \\
&+ \left(1 - \rho_2\right)\rho_3 \left[V_1\left(\mathbf{g}_{\{1,3\}}^A\right) - V_1\left(\mathbf{g}_{\{1,2\}}^B\right) \right] \\
&+ \left(1 - \rho_2\right)\left(1 - \rho_3\right) \left[V_1\left(\mathbf{g}_{\{2,3\}}^B\right) - V_1\left(\mathbf{g}_{\{1,2,3\}}^B\right) \right]
\end{aligned}
$$

and

$$
\theta_1 = \rho_2(1 - \rho_3) + \rho_3(1 - \rho_2).
$$

Inequality (8.4) gives the upper bound on a voter's idiosyncratic relative preference for the ideological positions of party B such that she nonetheless votes for the candidate from party A. This bound depends on the relative preference of voters in district 1 for the announced spending program of party A, the district-wide average preference among voters in district 1 for the ideological positions of party B, and the probability θ_1 that district 1 will prove to be pivotal in determining which party controls a majority in the legislature.

Considering that β_{i1} is distributed uniformly on $[-1/2h, 1/2h]$, the fraction of votes that party A will capture in district 1 (as a function of v_1 and the announced platforms) is given by $s_1 = 1/2 + h\Delta_1/\theta_1 - hv_1$. The probability that party A will capture the seat in district 1 (as viewed from outside the district) is the probability that $s_1 \geq 1/2$, or the probability that $v_1 \leq \Delta_1/\theta_1$. Thus, $\rho_1 = F\left(\Delta_1/\theta_1\right)$. More generally, we can write

$$\rho_j = F(\Delta_j/\theta_j), \tag{8.5}$$

where Δ_j and θ_j are defined analogously to Δ_1 and θ_1, respectively, with j in place of 1, k in place of 2, and ℓ in place of 3, $j \neq k$, $j \neq \ell$, and $k \neq \ell$.

8.2.3 The Campaign Stage

We turn to the initial stage of the political game, when the parties announce their positions on the pork-barrel projects. At this stage, the party leaders are uncertain about the relative popularity of the two parties among voters in the three districts. The leaders regard each v_j as randomly and independently distributed with distribution $F(\cdot)$. Thus, each party sees a link between the pair of announcements $\mathbf{g}^A$ and $\mathbf{g}^B$ and the probability of a victory by party A in district j such as is given in equation (8.5). Party A chooses its positions on the pork-barrel projects to maximize the probability that it will win in at least two districts, which is

$$\rho = \rho_1\rho_2\rho_3 + \rho_1\rho_2(1 - \rho_3) + \rho_1(1 - \rho_2)\rho_3 + (1 - \rho_1)\rho_2\rho_3.$$

Party B seeks to minimize ρ.

Consider the choice of g_1^A, which is the proposal by party A for spending on projects in district 1. The party's first-order condition for maximizing ρ is[8]

$$\frac{\partial \rho}{\partial g_1^A} = \sum_{j=1}^{3} \theta_j \frac{\partial \rho_j}{\partial g_1^A} = 0. \tag{8.6}$$

Party B has an analogous first-order condition for minimizing ρ.

Since the parties have the same average popularity among voters and similar incentives in regard to pork-barrel spending, it is natural to focus on a symmetric equilibrium. In a symmetric equilibrium, the parties announce identical positions, that is, $\mathbf{g}^A = \mathbf{g}^B = \mathbf{g}$. Then the economic platforms of the two parties have equal appeal to voters, and thus $\Delta_j = 0$ for all j. In the event, each party has a 50 percent chance of winning in each district; that is, $\rho_j = F(0) = 1/2$ for all j. But then the first-order condition (8.6) can be written more simply as

$$\sum_{j=1}^{3} \frac{\partial \Delta_j}{\partial g_1^A} = 0. \tag{8.7}$$

We shall also describe an equilibrium in which the parties treat the three districts similarly. It may seem natural that they should do so, inasmuch as the three districts have equal populations of voters, similar distributions of ideological preferences, and similar tastes for the local public goods. However, Myerson (1993) has shown in a different but related context that candidates might prefer to target "goodies" to a subset of otherwise similar voters. In his model, there exists no pure-strategy equilibrium in which voters are treated symmetrically. Our setting differs from his, because voters have preferences for one party or the other apart from their evaluation of the goodies they are promised in the course of the electoral competition. We find that the parties have strong incentives to concentrate their promises of public spending in only two districts when $F'(0)$ is large (the density of the regional popularity shock is high at zero), but that they prefer to treat the districts similarly when $F'(0)$ is small.[9] In what follows, we focus on the latter case.

Let g denote the level of pork-barrel spending promised by both parties to every district in a symmetric equilibrium. Note that g is just rhetoric, while the reality of public spending varies with the composition of the elected legislature. The spending on a particular project will depend on whether the elected representative from the district is a member of the majority party or not, and if so, whether the majority delegation comprises two or three legislators. In the symmetric environment we describe, the spending is the same in each of the two districts included in a two-member majority no matter which two districts happen to be in the majority, and the spending in a district represented by a minority legislator is the same no matter which district that is. We denote by $\bar{g}_3$ the actual spending in each district when the majority delegation comprises three legislators, by $\bar{g}_2$ the actual spending in a district included in a two-member majority delegation, and by $\bar{g}_0$ the spending in a district excluded from the majority delegation.

We can now use the definitions of Δ_j and V_j to rewrite the first-order condition (8.7) for party A's choice of promised spending in district 1 as

$$\frac{1}{4}\left[H'(\bar{g}_3) - 1\right]\frac{\partial g_{\{1,2,3\},1}^A}{\partial g_1^A} + \frac{1}{2}\left[H'(\bar{g}_2) - \frac{1}{3}\right]\frac{\partial g_{\{1,2\},1}^A}{\partial g_1^A}$$

$$-\frac{1}{4}\left[H'(\bar{g}_0) + \frac{1}{3}\right]\frac{\partial g_{\{2,3\},1}^A}{\partial g_1^A} = 0. \tag{8.8}$$

The three terms in the expression on the left-hand side give the marginal effect of a change in g_1^A on the electoral prospects of party A via the induced changes in spending in district 1 in the event that this district is included in a three-member majority, included in a two-member majority, and excluded from the majority, respectively. The impact on the party's prospects comes not only from the marginal effect on voters in district 1 who are affected by these changes, but also from the marginal effect on voters in districts 2 and 3, who must share in the cost of providing public goods to district 1. Finally, note that the solution to (8.8) gives not only the optimal choice of g_1^A, but also the Nash equilibrium value of g, since the parties behave similarly in the symmetric equilibrium and they treat all districts the same.

8.3 Equilibrium Platforms and Policies

To simplify the exposition, we adopt a quadratic form for the (per capita and aggregate) benefits from the local public goods. We assume that $H(g) = \alpha g - \beta g^2/2$ for $g \leq \alpha/\beta$ and $H(g) = \alpha^2/2\beta$ for $g \geq \alpha/\beta$. Concavity requires $\beta > 0$. We also take $\alpha > 1$, so that a social planner would provide a positive amount $(\alpha - 1)/\beta$ of each public good.

Suppose that some party has announced the platform $\mathbf{g} = (g, g, g)$ and now it wins the election in all three districts. Then, by (8.1), the legislature will spend an amount $\bar{g}_3(g)$ in each district, where

$$\bar{g}_3(g) = \begin{cases} \frac{1}{\beta+\delta}(\alpha + \delta g - 1) & \text{for } g \leq \frac{1}{\delta} + \frac{\alpha}{\beta} \\ g - \frac{1}{\delta} & \text{for } g \geq \frac{1}{\delta} + \frac{\alpha}{\beta} \end{cases}. \tag{8.9}$$

The chosen spending level equates the marginal benefit from spending, $\alpha - \beta \bar{g}_3$ (if $\bar{g}_3 < \alpha/\beta$), to the marginal cost, $1 + \delta(\bar{g}_3 - g)$, where the latter includes not only the unit cost of the goods, but also the (marginal) political cost to the legislators of deviating from the promised spending level, g.

If the party wins, instead, in only two districts, it will spend

$$\bar{g}_2(g) = \begin{cases} \frac{1}{\beta+\delta}\left(\alpha + \delta g - \frac{2}{3}\right) & \text{for } g \leq \frac{2}{3\delta} + \frac{\alpha}{\beta} \\ g - \frac{2}{3\delta} & \text{for } g \geq \frac{2}{3\delta} + \frac{\alpha}{\beta} \end{cases} \tag{8.10}$$

in each of the two districts represented by a member of the majority delegation and

$$\bar{g}_0(g) = \begin{cases} 0 & \text{for } g \leq \frac{2}{3\delta} \\ g - \frac{2}{3\delta} & \text{for } g \geq \frac{2}{3\delta} \end{cases} \tag{8.11}$$

in the remaining district. Notice that $\bar{g}_2 > \bar{g}_3$ for all finite δ and all g. The perceived benefits from spending in a district are the same no matter how many districts are represented in the majority delegation, but the perceived costs of the spending are smaller when the taxes borne by residents of one district are neglected in the policymaking calculus; the unit cost of 1 that appears in the formula for $\bar{g}_3$ is replaced by 2/3 in the formula for $\bar{g}_2$. Also, $\bar{g}_0 = 0$ unless g is sufficiently large, that is, unless $g > 2/3\delta$. The majority delegation perceives no political benefit from delivering pork to a district represented by a member of the minority party. It will undertake spending in such a district only if the party had promised some reasonably high level of public goods and if the political cost of neglecting that promise is sufficiently great. Finally, note that all spending levels are strictly increasing in the announcement, g, except when g is small so that $\bar{g}_0 = 0$.

Equations (8.9), (8.10), and (8.11) relate the various possible policy outcomes to the policy announcement. We can now use these equations to find the announcement that satisfies the first-order condition, (8.8). In so doing, we recognize that symmetry implies $g^A_{\{1,2,3\},1} = \bar{g}_3(g)$, $g^A_{\{1,2\},1} = \bar{g}_2$, $g^A_{\{2,3\},1} = \bar{g}_0$, and $g^A_1 = g$. We note that $H'(\bar{g}) = \alpha - \beta\bar{g}$ if $\bar{g} < \alpha/\beta$ and that $H'(\bar{g}) = 0$ otherwise. Also, $\partial\bar{g}_3/\partial g = \delta/(\beta + \delta)$ for $g < 1/\delta + \alpha/\beta$ and $\partial\bar{g}_2/\partial g = \delta/(\beta + \delta)$ for $g < 2/3\delta + \alpha/\beta$. For $g > 2/3\delta + \alpha/\beta$, $\partial\bar{g}_2/\partial g = 1$ and for $g > 1/\delta + \alpha/\beta$, $\partial\bar{g}_3/\partial g = 1$. The change in responsiveness of local spending in a district to changes in the campaign promise is due to the assumed satiation of voters when the quantity of their local public good reaches α/β. Finally, note that $\partial \bar{g}_0/\partial g = 0$ for $g < 2/3\delta$, while $\partial \bar{g}_0/\partial g = 1$ for $g > 2/3\delta$. This fact, which will prove to be important for understanding our findings below, reflects that a district not represented in the majority delegation receives no pork whatsoever for low levels of the announcement, but spending there rises one for one with the announcement once g is so high that the legislators provide pork even to this district to mitigate the costs of reneging on their party's promise.

Let $\Gamma(g)$ denote the left-hand side of (8.8), that is, (a positive multiple of) the marginal electoral benefit to a party from increasing the size of its campaign promise to a typical district. There are four segments of $\Gamma(g)$ according to whether the supply of public goods to a minority district responds to a change in the campaign promise or not, and whether the response of the supply to represented districts reflects a positive marginal value of the good in the district or just the positive marginal cost of deviating from the party's promise. For $g < 2/3\delta$, $\bar{g}_0$ does not respond to g. For $2/3\delta < g < 2/3\delta + \alpha/\beta$, $\bar{g}_0$ responds, but only as a reflection of party discipline. For $2/3\delta + \alpha/\beta < g < 1/\delta + \alpha/\beta$, $\bar{g}_0$ and $\bar{g}_2$ respond only for disciplinary reasons, and for $g > 1/\delta + \alpha/\beta$, $\bar{g}_0, \bar{g}_2$, and $\bar{g}_3$ all respond only because the legislators wish to mitigate the rising discipline costs. Substituting the relevant expressions into (8.8), we find

$$
\Gamma(g) = \begin{cases}
\frac{\delta}{3(\beta+\delta)^2} [2\beta + 9\delta(\alpha - \beta g) - 5\delta] & \text{for } g < \frac{2}{3\delta}, \\[2ex]
\frac{\delta}{3(\beta+\delta)^2} [2\beta + 9\delta(\alpha - \beta g) - 5\delta] & \\[1ex]
\quad - \left(\frac{2\beta}{3\delta} + \alpha - \beta g + \frac{1}{3}\right) & \text{for } \frac{2}{3\delta} < g < \frac{2}{3\delta} + \frac{\alpha}{\beta}, \\[2ex]
\frac{\delta^2}{(\beta+\delta)^2}(\alpha - \beta g - 1) - 1 & \text{for } \frac{2}{3\delta} + \frac{\alpha}{\beta} < g < \frac{1}{\delta} + \frac{\alpha}{\beta}, \\[2ex]
-2 & \text{for } g > \frac{1}{\delta} + \frac{\alpha}{\beta}.
\end{cases}
$$

Figure 8.1 depicts $\Gamma(g)$ for a polity with little party discipline, that is, $\delta < 4\beta/(9\alpha - 5)$. Note that $\Gamma(0) > 0$ and that $\Gamma(g)$ declines linearly with g for $g < 2/3\delta$ and for $2/3\delta + \alpha/\beta < g < 1/\delta + \alpha/\beta$. For $\delta < 4\beta/(9\alpha - 5)$, $\Gamma(g)$ rises linearly with g for $2/3\delta < g < 2/3\delta + \alpha/\beta$. Finally, for $g > 1/\delta + \alpha/\beta$, $\Gamma(g)$ is flat and equal to -2. It is easy to show that the curve jumps downward at $g = 2/3\delta$, again at $2/3\delta + \alpha/\beta$, and again at $g = 1/\delta + \alpha/\beta$. For this case of low discipline, $\Gamma(g) < 0$ for g slightly below $2/3\delta$

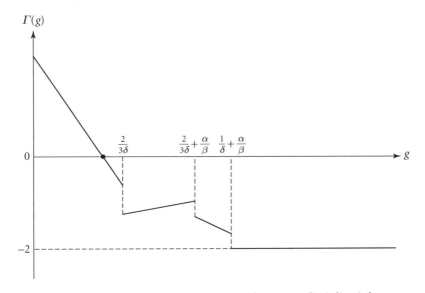

Figure 8.1 Equilibrium announcement when party discipline is low.

and $\Gamma(g) < 0$ for all $g > 2/3\delta$. Therefore, there is a unique equilibrium announcement, which is

$$g = \frac{2}{9\delta} + \frac{9\alpha - 5}{9\beta} \quad \text{for} \quad \delta \le \frac{4\beta}{9\alpha - 5}. \tag{8.12}$$

Next suppose that party discipline is moderate, that is, that $4\beta/(9\alpha - 5) < \delta \le \beta(3 + 3\alpha + \sqrt{3 + 6\alpha + 27\alpha^2})/(6\alpha - 6)$. In this case, $\Gamma(g)$ takes the form shown in Figure 8.2. This figure is qualitatively similar to Figure 8.1, except that $\Gamma(g)$ is positive for values of g slightly to the left of $2/3\delta$ while g is negative for values slightly to the right of $2/3\delta$, for δ in this range. It follows that each party has an electoral incentive to increase its promises of local public spending for all $g < 2/3\delta$, but an incentive to decrease its promises of local public spending for all $g > 2/3\delta$. Evidently, the equilibrium announcement is

$$g = \frac{2}{3\delta} \quad \text{for} \quad \frac{4\beta}{9\alpha - 5} < \delta \le \frac{\beta\left(3 + 3\alpha + \sqrt{3 + 6\alpha + 27\alpha^2}\right)}{6(\alpha - 1)}. \tag{8.13}$$

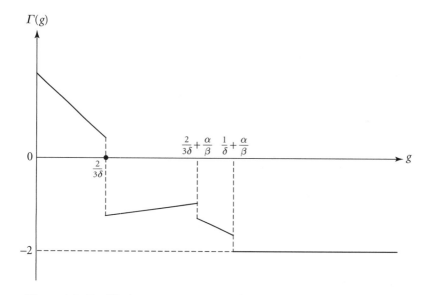

Figure 8.2 Equilibrium announcement when party discipline is moderate.

Finally, suppose that party discipline is strict, that is, $\delta > \beta(3 + 3\alpha + \sqrt{3 + 6\alpha + 27\alpha^2})/(6\alpha - 6)$. In this case, $\Gamma(g)$ appears as in Figure 8.3. For such high values of δ, $\Gamma(g)$ is downward sloping in every region except when $g > 1/\delta + \alpha/\beta$, where it is flat. We find that $\Gamma(g) > 0$ for all $g < 2/3\delta$ and $\Gamma(g) < 0$ for all $g > 2/3\delta + \alpha/\beta$. The unique equilibrium falls between these values, where

$$g = \frac{6\delta^3(\alpha - 1) - 2\delta^2\beta(1 + 3\alpha) - \delta\beta^2(5 + 3\alpha) - 2\beta^3}{3\delta\beta(2\delta^2 - 2\beta\delta - \beta^2)}$$

$$\text{for } \delta > \frac{\beta\left(3 + 3\alpha + \sqrt{3 + 6\alpha + 27\alpha^2}\right)}{6(\alpha - 1)}. \tag{8.14}$$

We can substitute the equilibrium values of g into (8.9), (8.10), and (8.11) to solve for the equilibrium spending in a district whose elected representative is a member of a three-member majority delegation, a two-member majority, and a minority delegation, respectively. We study the relationship between party discipline and pork-barrel spending in the section that follows.

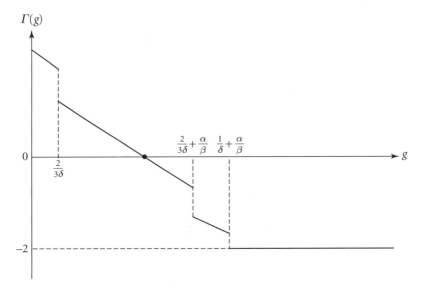

Figure 8.3 Equilibrium announcement when party discipline is high.

8.4   Party Discipline and Pork-Barrel Spending

8.4.1 Policy Rhetoric

We use (8.12), (8.13), and (8.14) to plot the relationship between the level of spending on local public goods that each party announces in a Nash equilibrium and the parameter that measures the strength of party discipline. We do so in Figure 8.4 for the case of $\alpha = 2$ and $\beta = 1$. As we shall now explain, the qualitative features of the figure—including the apparent nonmonotonicity in the relationship between the size of the announcement and δ—hold for all values of $\alpha > 1$ and $\beta > 0$.

When party discipline is lax, the political rhetoric is shrill. Each party promises extravagant spending on local public goods, with $g \to \infty$ as $\delta \to 0$. But voters recognize that the promises will not be fully honored. Indeed, the modest penalties for deviating from the platform will allow elected legislators to turn their backs entirely on a district that is not included in the majority ($\bar{g}_0 = 0$). Nonetheless, anticipated pork-barrel spending in a district that does end up represented in a majority—be it a two-district majority or a three-district majority—is quite lavish. We shall find in Sec-

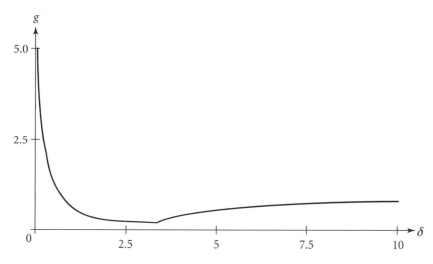

Figure 8.4 Equilibrium platform as a function of party discipline for $\alpha = 2$ and $\beta = 1$.

tion 8.4.2 that, for δ small, $\bar{g}_3$ exceeds the efficient level of spending and $\bar{g}_2$ exceeds the level of spending that maximizes the well-being of residents of the two districts that comprise a two-member majority. In other words, the promises induce the legislators to opt for greater pork-barrel spending than even their own constituents would like. Why would the parties make such extravagant promises? The answer is that each party chooses g_j not only to make the anticipated spending attractive to residents of district j, but also to make it unattractive for voters in other districts to elect the candidate of the opposing party. An increase in party A's promised spending in district 1, for example, raises the expected tax bill and thus lowers welfare for voters in district 2 in the event that the candidates from party A win in districts 1 and 3 but not in their own.

In the region of lax discipline, (8.12) implies that promised spending in each district is a decreasing function of δ. In such circumstances, the parties and voters recognize that a district whose representative is not included in a majority delegation will be allocated no pork-barrel spending. Thus, a change in δ has no effect on $\bar{g}_0$ in this range. Since $\partial\bar{g}_3/\partial g = \partial\bar{g}_2/\partial g = \delta/(\beta + \delta) > 0$ for $g < 2/3\delta$, the first-order condition (8.8) is satisfied if and only if $H'(\bar{g}_3) - 1 + 2\left[H'(\bar{g}_2) - 1/3\right] = 0$. But an increase in δ causes both

$\bar{g}_3$ and $\bar{g}_2$ to rise at constant g. This reduces both $H'(\bar{g}_3)$ and $H'(\bar{g}_2)$, and so it shifts the first segment of $\Gamma(g)$ downward in Figure 8.1. The result is a lower equilibrium value of g.

To understand why the parties temper their promises as discipline increases (for low δ), we note that $g > \bar{g}_2 > \bar{g}_3$ when δ is small. Then, if a party were to hold its promise constant, a tightening of discipline would raise anticipated spending in any majority district for all possible election outcomes. But public goods have diminishing marginal value to voters and constant marginal cost. So the increase in anticipated spending would reduce the attractiveness of the party's platform in all districts. The party avoids this by moderating its promise.

As δ rises and g falls, the maximum announcement consistent with zero spending in a district not represented in the majority delegation (call it $\hat{g}$) falls even faster than g. Eventually, a δ is reached such that, if a party were to promise a spending level $g = 2/9\delta + (9\alpha - 5)/9$ as it does for low values of δ, $\bar{g}_0$ would turn positive. But once $\bar{g}_0$ is positive and responds to g, an additional term enters into the marginal electoral effect of a change in the announcement. Thus, we reach the region of moderate δ, where a cut in a party's campaign promise induces an anticipated change in spending only in districts included in a majority, but an increase in the promise induces an anticipated change in spending in all three districts. This is the region in which Figure 8.2 applies.

In the region of moderate discipline, the marginal electoral benefit of an increase in g is strictly positive for $g < \hat{g}$ and strictly negative for $g > \hat{g}$ (see Figure 8.2). Accordingly, each party chooses the largest policy announcement that yields zero spending in a district represented by a member of the minority party. As discipline strengthens in this range, the pressure on an elected legislature to provide positive public goods to a district that is not represented in the majority intensifies as well. The parties must promise ever less to ensure that spending will be zero in an excluded district. In other words, $g = \hat{g} = 2/3\delta$ falls with δ in this region. Thus, the equilibrium promises continue to moderate as party discipline strengthens.

So too do the anticipated levels of spending in majority districts, as we shall see in Section 8.4.2. Indeed, $\bar{g}_3$ and $\bar{g}_2$ fall to levels that are below the efficient levels of spending. Why would a party announce a platform that leads to so little anticipated spending when it knows that voters in every district would prefer more? Again, the answer has to do with a party's desire not only to reward districts that elect its candidates but also to punish those that fail to give their support. An increase in, say, party A's promise of spending in district 1 would increase the welfare of voters in that district for those election outcomes in which party A wins both in district 1 and in at least one other district. But the higher promise would also benefit voters in district 1 if party A were to capture a majority in the legislature while losing in district 1. This latter effect reduces the cost to residents of district 1 of voting against party A, and the party takes this into account when formulating its platform.

Finally, we reach a δ large enough such that $\Gamma > 0$ for g slightly above $\hat{g}$. This is the region of high discipline—illustrated in Figure 8.3—in which the parties find it optimal to announce a platform that yields positive spending even in a district represented by a legislator in the minority party. In this region, there are conflicting forces at work on the parties' choices of campaign promises in response to changes in δ. Recall that $\Gamma(\delta)$ has three terms:

$$\Gamma(g) = \frac{1}{4}\left[H'(\bar{g}_3) - 1\right]\frac{\partial\bar{g}_3}{\partial g} + \frac{1}{2}\left[H'(\bar{g}_2) - \frac{1}{3}\right]\frac{\partial\bar{g}_2}{\partial g}$$
$$- \frac{1}{4}\left[H'(\bar{g}_0) + \frac{1}{3}\right]\frac{\partial\bar{g}_0}{\partial g}.$$

When δ is large, $\partial\bar{g}_3/\partial g = \partial\bar{g}_2/\partial g = \delta/(\beta + \delta)$, and $\partial\bar{g}_0/\partial g = 1$. Thus, an increase in δ raises the responsiveness of spending in a majority district— be it one that is part of a three-district majority or one that is part of a two-district majority—to changes in the campaign announcement. Since, as we shall see, $H'(\bar{g}_3) > H'(\bar{g}_2) > 1$ in this range, this tends to raise $\Gamma(g)$, the marginal electoral value of the announcement. The actual spending levels ($\bar{g}_3$, $\bar{g}_2$, and $\bar{g}_0$) all move in the direction of the announcement, g, as δ rises for given g. But since $\bar{g}_3$ and $\bar{g}_2$ may exceed or fall short of the campaign promise for high δ, these changes in spending may contribute to an increase or a decrease in Γ. The increase in δ unambiguously pulls $\bar{g}_0$ toward the higher promised level of spending, thereby reducing the marginal valuation $H'(\bar{g}_0)$, and thus contributing to a higher value of Γ via an increase in the last term. Despite the conflicting forces on the marginal electoral value of the announcement level, we are able to prove that an increase in δ shifts $\Gamma(g)$ upward at constant g throughout the region of high party discipline.[10] Thus, promised pork rises with a strengthening of party discipline once party discipline is already sufficiently strict. It is likely that the unambiguously positive relationship between g and δ in this range reflects our choice of a quadratic form for the benefit function, H.

To summarize, we find that the campaign promise of pork-barrel spending in each district bears a nonmonotonic relationship to the severity of party discipline. When discipline is lax, the parties anticipate that the elected legislature will provide public goods only to districts represented in the majority. Then, the level of promised spending declines with a strengthening of party discipline. But, at some critical level of δ, the party recognizes that the promise far exceeds the zero spending that will actually occur in a minority district. With yet further increases in party discipline, a majority delegation comprising two legislators will find it too politically costly to withhold all pork-barrel spending from the minority district. Anticipating this, the parties respond to further increases in party discipline by elevating their promises. As $\delta \to \infty$, the parties are able virtually to pre-commit their candidates to a level of pork-barrel spending in each district, regardless of the composition of the elected legislature. Then $g \to (\alpha - 1)/\beta$, the spending level that would be chosen by a social planner. This is in keeping with the findings of Lindbeck and Weibull (1987), who show that parties commit to efficient policies when their campaign promises are fully credible.

8.4.2 Policy Reality

Now we can examine the relationship between party discipline and the pork-barrel spending that results for the different possible election outcomes. For this, we use equations (8.9), (8.10), and (8.11), together with the expressions for the equilibrium value of g.

Consider first the spending in any district when all three seats in the legislature are captured by the same party. Since the equilibrium announcement g never exceeds $2/3\delta + \alpha/\beta$, (8.9) implies that per-district spending $\bar{g}_3$ never reaches the satiation level. Substituting the equilibrium value of g into (8.9), we find

$$\bar{g}_3 = \begin{cases} \frac{9\alpha-5}{9\beta} - \frac{2}{9(\beta+\delta)} & \text{for } \delta \le \frac{4\beta}{9\alpha-5}, \\[2ex] \frac{3\alpha-1}{3(\beta+\delta)} & \text{for } \frac{4\beta}{9\alpha-5} < \delta \le \frac{\beta\left(3+3\alpha+\sqrt{3+6\alpha+27\alpha^2}\right)}{6(\alpha-1)}, \\[2ex] \frac{6(\alpha-1)\delta^3-8\beta\delta^2-(9\alpha-1)\beta^2\delta-\beta^3(3\alpha-1)}{3\beta(2\delta^2-\beta^2-2\beta\delta)(\beta+\delta)} & \text{for } \delta > \frac{\beta\left(3+3\alpha+\sqrt{3+6\alpha+27\alpha^2}\right)}{6(\alpha-1)}. \end{cases}$$

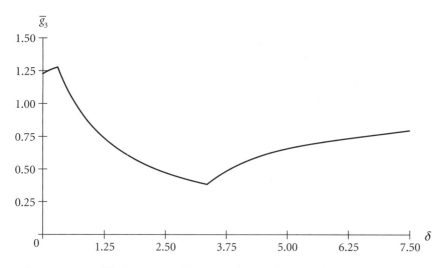

Figure 8.5 Equilibrium $\bar{g}_3$ as a function of party discipline for $\alpha = 2$ and $\beta = 1$.

Figure 8.5 shows the relationship between per-district spending and party discipline for the case $\alpha = 2$ and $\beta = 1$.

As the figure illustrates, spending in a district that is part of a three-district majority exceeds the efficient level of $(\alpha - 1)/\beta$ when $\delta \to 0$, and it grows with δ when party discipline is low. In this range of low δ, a strengthening of discipline causes the parties to moderate their promises (g falls), but the legislators have greater incentive to deliver on what has been promised. When all three legislators are members of the same party, the latter effect must dominate. To see this, recall that the first-order condition for the optimal platform requires $H'(\bar{g}_3) - 1 + 2\left[H'(\bar{g}_2) - 1/3\right] = 0$, because the parties set their platforms in anticipation that the legislature will allocate no pork to a district that ends up outside the ruling coalition. For this condition to be satisfied following an increase in δ, exactly one of $\bar{g}_3$ and $\bar{g}_2$ must rise and the other must fall. But it is easy to see that $d\bar{g}_3/d\delta > d\bar{g}_2/d\delta$ when δ is small, which means that $d\bar{g}_3/d\delta > 0$.[11]

When party discipline is in an intermediate range in which the promised level of spending per district is the largest amount consistent with zero ex post spending in a minority district, $\bar{g}_3$ falls with increases in δ. Again, the tightening of discipline causes each party to moderate its promises, but now the decline in g must result in decreased delivery to majority districts as well. However, when discipline is sufficiently strong that spending in a minority district would be positive, the per-district spending in case of a three-district majority rises with further increases in δ. In this case, the campaign promise rises with δ as we have seen, and even if the legislators are delivering more than what is promised, the net effect of an increase in δ will be for $\bar{g}_3$ to rise.[12]

Using (8.10), we can similarly derive the relationship between party discipline and public spending in either of the two districts that happen to be included in a two-district majority. When a party wins the local elections in exactly two districts, the legislator allocates pork of $\bar{g}_2$ to each of those districts, where

$$
\bar{g}_2 = \begin{cases} \dfrac{9\alpha-5}{9\beta} + \dfrac{1}{9(\beta+\delta)} & \text{for } \delta \le \dfrac{4\beta}{9\alpha-5}, \\[3ex] \dfrac{\alpha}{\beta+\delta} & \text{for } \dfrac{4\beta}{9\alpha-5} < \delta \le \dfrac{\beta\left(3+3\alpha+\sqrt{3+6\alpha+27\alpha^2}\right)}{6(\alpha-1)}, \\[3ex] \dfrac{6(\alpha-1)\delta^3-6\beta\delta^2-\beta^2(1+9\alpha)\delta-3\alpha\beta^3}{3\beta\left(2\delta^2-2\beta\delta-\beta^2\right)(\beta+\delta)} & \text{for } \delta > \dfrac{\beta\left(3+3\alpha+\sqrt{3+6\alpha+27\alpha^2}\right)}{6(\alpha-1)}. \end{cases}
$$

Figure 8.6 depicts the relationship between $\bar{g}_2$ and δ for $\alpha = 2$ and $\beta = 1$; the qualitative features of the figure apply more generally. Specifically, we see that spending in a majority district falls with δ when party discipline is low or moderate, but rises with δ once discipline is strong enough that spending in a minority district turns positive.[13] For δ near zero, $\bar{g}_2$ exceeds $(\alpha - 2/3)/\beta$, the level of spending that maximizes welfare for the residents of the two districts represented in the majority delegation. Yet when δ is in the upper end of the moderate range, $\bar{g}_2$ falls short of even the socially efficient level of spending, $(\alpha - 1)/\beta$.

Finally, we can use (8.11) to examine pork-barrel spending in a district whose representative is not a member of the majority party. Using (8.14), we find

$$
\bar{g}_0 = \begin{cases} 0 & \text{for } \delta \le \dfrac{\beta\left(3+3\alpha+\sqrt{3+6\alpha+27\alpha^2}\right)}{6(\alpha-1)}, \\[3ex] \dfrac{6(\alpha-1)\delta^2-6\beta(1+\alpha)\delta-\beta^2(1+3\alpha)}{3\beta\left(2\delta^2-\beta^2-2\beta\delta\right)} & \text{for } \delta > \dfrac{\beta\left(3+3\alpha+\sqrt{3+6\alpha+27\alpha^2}\right)}{6(\alpha-1)}. \end{cases}
$$

As we have seen, the legislature does not provide any public goods to a minority district when party discipline is low or moderate. But when δ grows sufficiently large, the legislators will provide pork even to the district that they do not represent in order to moderate the discipline costs. In this

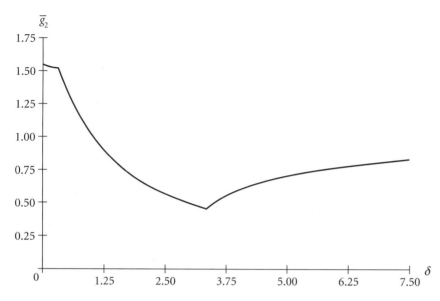

Figure 8.6 Equilibrium $\bar{g}_2$ as a function of party discipline for $\alpha = 2$ and $\beta = 1$.

range, the allocation of pork to the minority district grows monotonically with the degree of party discipline.[14]

What happens to spending as discipline becomes nearly perfect? We have seen that as $\delta \to \infty$, $g \to (\alpha - 1)/\beta$, the per-district spending level that would be chosen by a social planner. Moreover, it becomes prohibitively costly for the elected legislature to deviate from what their party has announced. Accordingly, spending in every district approaches the efficient level of $(\alpha - 1)/\beta$, irrespective of the election outcome and whether a district's representative is included in the majority or not. The reader can verify that our expressions for $\bar{g}_3$, $\bar{g}_2$, and $\bar{g}_0$ all converge to $(\alpha - 1)/\beta$ as δ approaches infinity.

8.4.3 Expected Welfare

We can use our analysis of the equilibrium policy choices for the different possible election outcomes to examine the relationship between party discipline and the efficiency of government spending on local public goods. From an ex ante perspective, each voter has a one-quarter probability that his district will be represented in the legislative delegation of a three-member majority, a one-half probability that his district will be represented in a two-member majority, and a one-quarter probability that his district's elected representative will not be a member of the majority delegation. Thus, the expected welfare from public spending for the typical voter is given by

$$EV = \frac{1}{4} \left[H \left(g_3 \right) - g_3 \right] + \frac{1}{2} \left[H \left(g_2 \right) - \frac{1}{3} \left(2g_2 + g_0 \right) \right]$$

$$+ \frac{1}{4} \left[H \left(g_0 \right) - \frac{1}{3} \left(2g_2 + g_0 \right) \right]$$

$$= \frac{1}{4} \left[H \left(g_3 \right) - g_3 \right] + \frac{1}{2} \left[H \left(g_2 \right) - g_2 \right] + \frac{1}{4} \left[H \left(g_0 \right) - g_0 \right] .$$

Figure 8.7 plots expected welfare as a function of δ for $\alpha = 2$ and $\beta = 1$. As the figure shows, welfare is quite low when the parties have little ability to constrain the spending behavior of the legislators. More generally, as $\delta \to 0$, $EV \to \left(9\alpha^2 - 18\alpha + 7 \right) / 24\beta$, which is positive if and only if $\alpha > 1 + \sqrt{2}/3$. In other words, if α is small, a polity with little party discipline delivers lower expected welfare than one that is unable to provide any local public goods whatsoever. The low level of expected welfare results from overspending in districts that are represented in majority delegations and underspending in districts that are not represented in the majority.

In the region of low discipline, expected welfare rises monotonically with an increase in party discipline. In this region, $\bar{g}_3$ and $\bar{g}_2$ both exceed the efficient level, and the former rises with δ while the latter falls. But the net effect is always positive.[15] As δ rises into the region of moderate discipline, where the parties' announcements are such as to keep the level of spending in a minority district just equal to zero, expected welfare continues to rise.[16] Here, both $\bar{g}_3$ and $\bar{g}_2$ remain above the efficient level of spending, and both fall when discipline strengthens. But $\bar{g}_3$ will eventually fall below the efficient level of spending when δ passes $2\beta/[3 \left(\alpha - 1 \right)]$, and even the spending in a district represented in a two-member majority delegation will fall below the efficient level when δ exceeds $2\beta/[3 \left(\alpha - 1 \right)]$. Both of these values of δ fall within the region of moderate discipline, and both $\bar{g}_3$ and $\bar{g}_2$ are declining throughout the region. Thus, there must come a critical level of δ between $2\beta/[3 \left(\alpha - 1 \right)]$ and $\beta/[\left(\alpha - 1 \right)]$ at which expected welfare reaches a local maximum. Thereafter, further increases in discipline that do not cause spending in a minority district to turn positive must reduce ex-

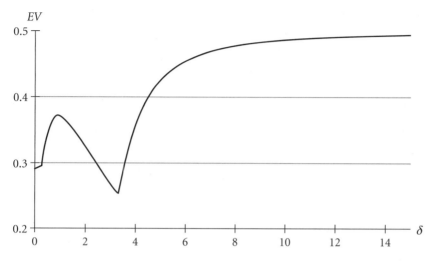

Figure 8.7 Expected welfare as a function of party discipline for $\alpha = 2$ and $\beta = 1$.

pected welfare. In the figure, expected welfare reaches a local maximum at $\delta = 46/51$.[17]

Finally, we reach the region of high δ, where discipline is sufficiently strong that the parties' promises induce positive spending even in a district that is not represented in the majority delegation. Throughout this region, $\bar{g}_3$, $\bar{g}_2$, and $\bar{g}_0$ all rise monotonically with δ from levels that are inefficiently small. Thus, expected welfare must be rising with δ in the region of high discipline. As we have noted before, spending levels converge to the efficient levels as $\delta \to \infty$. Thus, expected welfare asymptotes to the first-best level.

In short, we find that when political parties have limited ability to pre-commit the actions of elected representatives, the legislature delivers quite inefficient levels of local public goods and the outcome can be worse even than if national spending on district projects were impossible. At the opposite extreme, when the political parties have full ability to pre-commit public spending, then the spending level in each district is efficient. But the relationship between party discipline and expected welfare is not monotonic.

Conclusion   In this chapter, we have developed a three-stage model of political campaigns, voting, and legislative deliberations to study the determinants of national spending on local public goods. The key variable of interest in our analysis is the degree to which political parties can pre-commit the policy actions of their members during the course of the political campaign. We assume that political parties are differentiated by ideology and that the leaders of the two parties seek to gain majority control of the contested legislature in order to pursue their ideological agendas. Electoral competition motivates their promises of pork-barrel spending. After the election, the victorious candidates pursue more parochial concerns, namely to provide goodies to their local constituents. Thus, members of the majority delegation will want to steer pork-barrel spending to the districts they represent, regardless of what their party may have promised. A party's ability to pre-commit to policy reflects its ability to discipline its members when the party succeeds in gaining control of the legislature.

We conceive of this ability as reflecting political institutions, although we do not model the institutions explicitly. Rather, we represent party discipline by a parameter that measures the size of a penalty that the party imposes on its members if they deviate from the party's campaign platform. We imagine that the party imposes this penalty to preserve its ability to use campaign promises for electoral benefit in future elections. Presumably, the size of the penalty reflects the degree to which the national party controls resources that are valuable to the individual politicians. In future work, it would be desirable to model explicitly the instruments available to the party and the incentives to use them. By doing so, we could endogenize the degree of pre-commitment ability as a function of more primitive features of the political system.

Our reduced-form approach yields a very tractable model and some interesting conclusions. We find that a party's platform, as well as actual spending in districts represented in a majority delegation, bear a nonmonotonic relationship to the parameter representing the degree of party discipline. At low levels of discipline, the parties promise lavish pork-barrel spending in every district. If a given party wins in all three districts, the legislature spends more than is optimal in every district. If the majority party controls only two seats, the legislators allocate even more pork to the two districts they represent but do not spend at all in the third district. As the parameter reflecting party discipline rises from these low levels, initially the qualitative features of the equilibrium remain the same, although the promises moderate and so does spending in a district represented by a legislator in a two-member majority delegation.

As discipline rises, eventually the penalties for deviating from the party platform become sufficiently great that the legislators in a two-member majority delegation would not choose to eschew spending in the remaining district (that they do not represent). For this and higher levels of discipline, public spending is positive in every district, although greater in those represented in a majority delegation than in those that are not. Further increases in discipline cause the parties to raise their campaign promises (from levels that are quite low) and to deliver greater pork to every district for all possible election results. As the penalties for failure to deliver on campaign promises become prohibitive, the promised level of spending per district approaches the socially efficient level, as does the actual spending in every district after any possible election outcome.

We also examined the relationship between parties' ability to pre-commit their fiscal policies and the expected welfare of voters. At low levels of discipline, the excessive spending in districts represented in a majority, and the absence of spending in a district that is excluded from the majority, result in a highly inefficient fiscal regime. Indeed, expected welfare can be lower due to tyranny of the majority than what would result from a constitutional prohibition on all public spending on local public goods. As discipline strengthens, promises moderate and so does the inefficiency that results from excessive spending. But further increases in discipline cause the spending levels to fall to and below the efficient levels, and expected welfare then falls. However, once discipline is so strict that the legislature allocates pork even to a minority district, subsequent increases in discipline cause spending levels to rise again, and expected welfare converges to the first-best level.

Our chapter fills a gap in the literature between the pre-commitment models in the Downsian tradition and the no-commitment models of Osborne and Slivinski (1996), Besley and Coate (1997), and others. Our findings urge a cautionary note about the use of correlations in comparative political analysis. The relationship between political institutions and policy outcomes can be subtle and complex even in a relatively simple political environment.

ACKNOWLEDGMENTS

We are grateful to Itay Fainmesser and Ran Melamed for outstanding research assistance and to Ken Shepsle, Dennis Epple, and other participants at the meeting of the Political Institutions and Economic Policy (PIEP) Research Group for helpful comments and suggestions. We acknowledge with thanks the support of the National Science Foundation (SES 0211748 and SES 0451712) and the U.S.-Israel Binational

Science Foundation (2002132). Helpman also thanks the Canadian Institute for Advanced Research (CIFAR) for support. Helpman's work for this chapter was done when he was Sackler Visiting Professor at Tel Aviv University.

NOTES

1. See, for example, McGillivray (1997), Snyder and Groseclose (2000), and Mc-Carty, Poole, and Rosenthal (2001).
2. We might have referred to our institutional variable as "the extent of commitment to party platforms," but we felt that this alternative terminology would be too cumbersome.
3. In Grossman and Helpman (2005) we use a similar model to study the determination of trade protection when industries are geographically concentrated.
4. This is the same model of local public goods that was used extensively in Persson and Tabellini (2000) to address a variety of political-economic questions.
5. For simplicity, we consider public (consumption) goods that provide utility directly, rather than public (investment) goods that raise the productivity of firms and thereby enhance income. However, the distinction between public consumer goods and public investment goods is not important for our analysis.
6. Of course, this is just an extreme case of a less controversial claim, that members of a political party have better means to transfer utility among themselves than do members of opposing parties.
7. An individual's vote often will make no difference to the electoral outcome, but when it does, it will determine the victor in the voter's own district. Therefore, when an individual's vote matters, it decides between the expected utility from having the candidate from party A represent the voter's own district versus the expected utility from having the candidate from party B do so. A rational voter will cast her ballot for her preferred choice among these two alternatives. Technically speaking, the assumed voting behavior is a *weakly dominant strategy* in our electoral environment.
8. More formally, a maximum requires $\partial \rho / \partial g_1^A \geq 0$ for a small downward deviation in g_1^A from the equilibrium value, and $\partial \rho / \partial g_1^A \leq 0$ for a small upward deviation in g_1^A from the equilibrium value. This detail will become important for certain parameter values, as $\partial \rho / \partial g_1^A$ is not everywhere continuous.
9. More specifically, we have used numerical methods to evaluate the best response by party A when party B chooses a spending program that satisfies the first-order condition in (8.7). We find in numerous such examples that the second-order conditions for maximizing ρ are violated when $F'(0)$ is large, but that they are satisfied when $F'(0)$ is sufficiently small. In these latter cases, the platform that satisfies (8.7) is a (global) best response for party A.

10. We have proved directly that $dg/d\delta > 0$ for high party discipline, using the formula for g in equation (8.14). The derivative of the expression on the right-hand side of (8.14) with respect to δ equals zero at exactly four points, only one of which is positive, namely, $\delta = \beta/2$. Moreover, this expression attains a local minimum at $\delta = \beta/2$, because its second derivative, evaluated at this point, is positive. Note also that

$$\frac{\beta}{6\,(\alpha - 1)}\left(3 + 3\alpha + \sqrt{3 + 6\alpha + 27\alpha^2}\right) > \frac{\beta}{2}$$

for $\alpha > 1$. Therefore g is an increasing function of δ when party discipline is high.

11. From (8.9) and (8.10), $\left(d\bar{g}_3/d\delta\right) - \left(d\bar{g}_2/d\delta\right) = 1/3(\beta + \delta)^2 > 0$.

12. When $\delta > \beta\left(3 + 3\alpha + \sqrt{3 + 6\alpha + 27\alpha^2}\right)/(6\alpha - 6)$,

$$\frac{d\bar{g}_3}{d\delta} = \frac{2\left(\beta^3 + 4\delta^3 + 6\beta\delta^2 + 6\beta^2\delta\right)(\beta + 2\delta)}{3\left(2\delta^2 - \beta^2 - 2\beta\delta\right)^2 (\beta + \delta)^2} > 0.$$

13. When $\delta > \beta\left(3 + 3\alpha + \sqrt{3 + 6\alpha + 27\alpha^2}\right)/(6\alpha - 6)$,

$$\frac{d\bar{g}_2}{d\delta} = \frac{\beta^4 + 12\delta^4 + 40\beta\delta^3 + 12\beta^3\delta + 36\beta^2\delta^2}{3\left(2\delta^2 - \beta^2 - 2\beta\delta\right)^2 (\beta + \delta)^2} > 0.$$

14. When $\delta > \beta\left(3 + 3\alpha + \sqrt{3 + 6\alpha + 27\alpha^2}\right)/(6\alpha - 6)$,

$$\frac{d\bar{g}_0}{d\delta} = \frac{4\left(4\beta\delta + \beta^2 + 6\delta^2\right)}{3\left(2\delta^2 - \beta^2 - 2\beta\delta\right)^2} > 0.$$

15. It is straightforward to show that

$$\frac{dEV}{d\delta} = \frac{\beta}{54(\beta + \delta)^3} > 0 \qquad \text{for } \delta < \frac{4\beta}{9\alpha - 5}.$$

16. At $\delta = 4\beta/(9\alpha - 5)$,

$$\frac{dEV}{d\delta+} = \frac{\left(54\alpha^2 - 9\alpha - 1\right)\beta}{18\left(9\alpha - 5\right)(\beta + \delta)^3} > 0.$$

17. More generally, the turning point comes at

$$\delta = \frac{2\beta(12\alpha - 1)}{27\alpha^2 - 30\alpha + 3} \in \left(\frac{4\beta}{9\alpha - 5}, \frac{\beta\left(3 + 3\alpha + \sqrt{3 + 6\alpha + 27\alpha^2}\right)}{6\,(\alpha - 1)}\right).$$

REFERENCES

Austen-Smith, David. 2000. "Redistributing Income under Proportional Representation." *Journal of Political Economy* 108:1235–69.

Besley, Timothy, and Stephen Coate. 1997. "An Economic Model of Representative Democracy." *Quarterly Journal of Economics* 112:85–114.

Grossman, Gene M., and Elhanan Helpman. 2005. "A Protectionist Bias in Majoritarian Politics." *Quarterly Journal of Economics* 120:1239–82.

Lindbeck, Assar, and Jörgen Weibull. 1987. "Balanced Budget Redistribution and the Outcome of Political Competition." *Public Choice* 52:273–97.

Lizzeri, Alessandro, and Nicola Persico. 2001. "The Provision of Public Goods under Alternative Electoral Incentives." *American Economic Review* 91:225–45.

McCarty, Nolan, Keith T. Poole, and Howard Rosenthal. 2001. "The Hunt for Party Discipline in Congress." *American Political Science Review* 95:673–87.

McGillivray, Fiona. 1997. "Party Discipline as a Determinant of the Endogenous Formation of Tariffs." *American Journal of Political Science* 41:584–607.

Milesi-Ferretti, Gian Maria, Roberto Perotti, and Massimo Rostagno. 2002. "Electoral Systems and Public Spending." *The Quarterly Journal of Economics* 117:609–57.

Myerson, Roger. 1993. "Incentives to Cultivate Favored Minorities under Alternative Electoral Systems." *American Political Science Review* 87:856–69.

Osborne, Martin J., and Al Slivinski. 1996. "A Model of Political Competition with Citizen-Candidates." *Quarterly Journal of Economics* 111:65–96.

Persson, Torsten, Gerard Roland, and Guido Tabellini. 2000. "Comparative Politics and Public Finance." *Journal of Political Economy* 108:1121–61.

Persson, Torsten, and Guido Tabellini. 2000. *Political Economics: Explaining Economic Policy.* Cambridge MA: MIT Press.

Snyder, James M., and Tim Groseclose. 2000. "Estimating Party Influence in Congressional Role-Call Voting." *American Journal of Political Science* 44:193–211.

— 9 —

Policy Persistence in Multiparty Parliamentary Democracies

DANIEL DIERMEIER AND POHAN FONG

9.1 Introduction

Recent theoretical and empirical studies on comparative constitutions have deepened our understanding of how political institutions shape economic policies. Models by Persson and Tabellini (1999), Lizzeri and Persico (2001), and Milesi-Ferretti et al. (2002), for example, compared how different electoral rules lead to different fiscal policies, such as the size of general public goods, targeted transfers, local public goods, and corruption. Pagano and Volpin (2006) investigated how electoral rules shape government regulations on corporate governance. A few studies have also investigated the economic effects of legislative institutions. Persson, Roland, and Tabellini (2000) compared the consequences of presidential versus parliamentary constitutions on fiscal policy. More recently, Battaglini and Coate (2007, 2008) analyzed inefficient public investment and the dynamics of public debt resulting from legislative bargaining. Finally, Fong (2006) and Baron, Diermeier, and Fong (2007) showed how coalition formation and voting under proportional representation can lead to policy inefficiency. This last approach combined both legislative and electoral institutions in a single, integrated model.

These theoretical advances have been accompanied by related empirical investigations. In some cases, the purpose was to test some of the theoretical predictions of the models, in others, to establish new relationships. Persson and Tabellini (2001, 2003, 2004), for example, created a comprehensive dataset on political institutions and then used the data to empirically investigate how constitutional arrangements shape fiscal policies.

Most of the existing studies, however, were based on static models or focused on static policy issues like the sizes of total government spending or welfare expenditures, or the levels of waste and corruption.[1] This is in marked contrast to the earlier generations of political economy models with their emphasis on dynamic phenomena such as political business cycles (Rogoff 1990; Alesina, Roubini, and Cohen 1997), accumulation of public debt (Persson and Svensson 1989; Aghion and Bolton 1990; Alesina and Tabellini 1990; Alesina and Drazen 1991), dynamics of welfare programs (Hassler et al. 2003, 2005), and economic growth (Alesina and Rodrik 1994; Persson and Tabellini 1994; Krusell and Rios-Rull 1996). However, these earlier models relied on very simplified models of political decision making, such as the median-voter theorem and two-party electoral competition, that were unable to capture constitutional differences across countries. To model constitutional differences, an institutionalist approach is necessary.

This state of affairs leaves an important gap in our understanding of the relationship between political institutions and economic policy. It seems that we can either focus on institutional accounts of static economic policy-making or on dynamic policy models without institutional details, but not both.[2] This state of affairs is particularly lamentable as recent work by, for example, Persson and Tabellini (2001, 2003, 2004) provided some empirical evidence of the constitutional effects on political business cycles, fiscal deficits, and the responsiveness of government to income shocks. The main difficulty is the absence of suitable political economy frameworks, that is, institutionally rich models with changing economic state variables. Existing legislative decision-making approaches run into technical difficulties once we enrich the choice space to include dynamic economic policy. Continuing policies in multiperiod models usually generate discontinuity or lack of concavity of equilibrium value functions and policy rules that make the characterization of equilibria a challenging task (Baron and Herron 2003; Kalandrakis 2004; Fong 2006; Baron, Diermeier, and Fong 2007; Duggan and Kalandrakis 2007).

In this chapter, we introduce a new model of legislative decision making (Diermeier and Fong 2007) to investigate the institutional determinants of economic policy choice. The focus of this chapter is the so-called *ratchet effect* of government spending, that is, the observation that in some countries, government spending, measured as a fraction of GDP, increases during recessions but does not decrease during cyclical upturns, leading to a stepwise increase in overall public spending. The ratchet effect was first established by Persson and Tabellini (2001, 2003, 2004).

Specifically, Persson and Tabellini divide democratic countries into four constitutional groups defined by their respective electoral rules (majoritarian or proportional representation) and their legislative systems (presidential or parliamentary). The United States, for example, would fall in the majoritarian-presidential category, the United Kingdom in the majoritarian-parliamentary, Argentina in the proportional-presidential category, and Germany in the proportional-parlimentary. Persson and Tabellini then show that the ratchet effect only occurs in one of the groups: parliamentary countries with proportional-representation electoral rules. More precisely, they find the following differences: First, government expenditure, fiscal deficit, and welfare spending are more persistent in this group than in the others. Second, downturns lead to a lasting expansion of outlays and welfare spending in proportion to GDP that are not reversed during upturns. Third, the difference in the size of government between this group and the others grew particularly large in the per iod up to the early 1980s (or the early 1990s in the case of welfare spending).

What could account for the special status of proportional-parliamentary democracies? In this chapter, we develop a formal model of policy choice in parliamentary democracies with proportional representation and then show that this model can explain the ratchet effect. Our model is based on two distinct observations. The first observation is related to the political institutions that characterize proportional-parliamentary democracies. This group is distinct in two respects, one related to the electoral, the second to the legislative process. The first feature is a consequence of the electoral rule: proportional representation. It is well known that proportional representation leads to minority parliaments, that is, multiple represented parties with no party controlling a majority of seats in parliament (Duverger 1952). This is true even if voters can vote strategically (Austen-Smith and Banks 1988; Baron and Diermeier 2001), and if governments can strategically manipulate future status quos (Fong 2006; Baron, Diermeier, and Fong 2007). Therefore government policy needs to be conceptualized as bargaining among multiple parties, either among *all* parties represented in the parliament (Diermeier and Merlo 2000) or among the parties represented in the governing coalition (Baron and Diermeier 2001; Fong 2006; Baron, Diermeier, and Fong 2007). In contrast, majoritarian systems, for example, the plurality rule used in the United Kingdom or United States, usually lead to two major political parties (Duverger 1952). Except for the rare case of a hung parliament, the party who controls a majority of seats usually has full control over policy.

The second feature focuses on the particular structure of agenda setting that is typical of the legislative process in parliamentary democracies. Comparative scholars have long observed that compared to presidential systems, the constitutional features of parliamentary systems lead to high levels of agenda control for the executive, that is, the cabinet (Doering 1995). In many cases, that power is concentrated within the prime minister. We capture this feature formally by considering a single, persistent agenda setter during a given legislative period. On the other hand, presidential democracies (whether multiparty or two-party) lack the constitutional feature of effective agenda control by the executive. So, our model combines the features typical of parliamentary democracies (the government's agenda control) with multiparty bargaining typical of proportional representation.

The second observation is related to the composition of government budgets. In modern democratic countries, a majority proportion of total government spending is conducted in the form of entitlement programs. For example, in 2007 the U.S. government spent $586 million on social security, $394.5 million on Medicare, $276.4 million on Medicaid, $367 million on unemployment insurance and other welfare programs, and $72.6 million on veteran subsidies. Taken together these entitlement programs comprise more than 60 percent of the total budget of $2.8 trillion. In entitlement programs, benefits are distributed and once the programs are enacted, they are in effect until they are reformed in subsequent legislative periods. In many cases, for example, the U.S. Social Security Act of 1935, beneficiaries can sue the government if benefits are withheld.

Our model of the political process is based on the legislative bargaining framework of Diermeier and Fong (2007). The model has three important features. First, the default policy of legislative bargaining is endogenous and evolves over time. Second, any policy may be revisited and changed after it is passed in the first place. Third, any legislator with agenda-setting power is allowed to make a new policy proposal at any time and as frequently as possible; there is no well-defined last round of policymaking. The first two features are reminiscent of Bernheim, Rangel, and Rayo's (2006) concept of an evolving default policy. The passage of a bill does not stop the legislature from revisiting the same policy issue. The passed bill simply serves as a new default policy as the legislators negotiate in the next round. The third feature distinguishes our model from Bernheim, Rangel, and Rayo's.

Here we investigate equilibrium behavior in a public-goods environment with a distortionary income tax. One of the key findings of our analysis is how in a dynamic legislative bargaining equilibrium, the initial status quo policy may lead to policy persistence and inefficiencies. The intuition is a resistance of the government to reducing government spending due to corner solutions. That is, if the initial status quo government size is large due to some exogenous reason, for example, a war or economic crisis, in equilibrium, the agenda setter may not be able to further reduce expenditures because the other groups are already at their constraint. To further reduce expenditures, the agenda setter has to cut down spending on his own group, whereas reduced deadweight loss is shared by all. In this case the agenda setter does not internalize all the economic benefits from reducing an inefficiently large budget. The reverse, however, is not true. If the status quo government size is too small, the agenda setter is always able to increase expenditures, although he may also raise spending on some other groups in order to compensate the additional tax burden they bear.

We then expand the model to a dynamic policy environment that captures the government's response to random shocks that may affect the marginal cost of taxation. As discussed above, a sizable fraction of total government expenditure is related to continuing entitlement programs. When an economy is hit by a temporary negative income shock, the party that controls agenda setting faces a strong resistance on expenditure cuts. This is because a more stringent entitlement program on any socioeconomic group implies a worse status quo in the future and therefore a permanently lower bargaining power of that group or party. Fiscal adjustment in response to a temporary shock has a permanent effect. This makes it even more difficult for a persistent agenda setter to cut spending on the other groups. On the other hand, with a temporary positive income shock, the leading party can easily satisfy its coalition partners' reservation values and pass a more generous entitlement program to benefit the socioeconomic group it represents. An asymmetric, upward movement of public spending thus results.

9.1.1 Comparison to Existing Approaches: Models of Political Bargaining

Our point of departure is the Baron and Ferejohn (1989) model. They analyzed how legislators under majority rule bargain over division of a pie and find stationary equilibria where only a bare majority of legislators receive positive shares of the pie, while the agenda setter captures a disproportionate share. The seminal paper was recently tested by Knight (2005) using

U.S. data on the distribution of the portion of the budget earmarked for transportation projects. The evidence supports the key qualitative prediction that proposal power is valuable but more constrained than predicted by the model. In our model, we show that the possibility of reconsidering a policy issue substantially weakens the proposal power of an agenda setter, even if he has the sole authority to make policy proposals throughout the whole legislative session. In existing legislative bargaining models, a single proposer would always be able to capture the entire pie. However, this is not the case in our model, as legislators, out of fear that the agenda setter will use his agenda-setting power to exploit legislators with low reservation values in the future, do not approve any policy that substantially lowers the reservation values of others.

This chapter belongs to the literature of dynamic legislative bargaining with a moving status quo where intertemporal trade-offs between current legislation and future policymaking may lead to complex patterns of policy dynamics. With a one-dimensional policy space and single-peaked preferences, Baron (1996) showed that, in the long run, the policy will converge to the alternative preferred by the median voter. Baron and Herron (2003) and Fong (2004) studied the game in a multidimensional policy space. Recently, Duggan and Kalandrakis (2007) established general existence results for models with a moving status quo and provided a technical characterization of equilibrium strategies and value functions in these models. Kalandrakis (2004) analyzed an infinitely repeated Baron-Ferejohn legislative bargaining game where three players with linear utility divide a dollar in each period. The Markov perfect equilibrium in his model has the characteristic that irrespective of the discount factor or the initial division of the dollar, eventually in all periods, the proposer extracts the whole dollar. In contrast, in the dynamic version of our model, full expropriation by the agenda setter rarely occurs. The distribution is more egalitarian.

In models of a parliamentary democracy with proportional representation, Fong (2006) showed that an incumbent coalition government strategically manipulates to lower the bargaining position of the outside parties in order to create cheap coalition partners in the future. The incentive leads to more noncentral policy outcomes and inefficiency. Baron, Diermeier, and Fong (2007) showed that with strategic voters the problem of inefficiency is worsened, since a more extreme status quo favors the incumbent parties in future elections.

Bernheim, Rangel, and Rayo (2006) examined legislative policymaking in institutions with real-time agenda setting and evolving default. Assuming finite rounds of proposal making and voting within a pork-barrel model of redistributive politics, the last proposer is able to pass his favorite policy under relatively weak conditions. As a consequence, the final policy outcome is highly unequal, and the last proposer is able to obtain his ideal policy. As the authors point out in their concluding section, it is natural to wonder whether particular procedures effectively promote a more egalitarian distribution of political power. Our model maintains the idea of an evolving default policy but assumes an agenda setter with persistent power throughout the legislative session and no ex ante known last round of negotiation. Surprisingly, this framework does not necessarily lead to extreme proposal power, but constrains the agenda setter. Specifically, we show that legislators have indirect preferences over the distribution of benefits to third parties. That is, each legislator cares not only about his own allocation of benefits but also about the allocation to other legislators. This holds, not because of altruistic preferences, but because current distributions affect each legislator's bargaining power in the future. As a consequence, in equilibrium, the legislators not included in the winning coalition are not fully expropriated, and the value of agenda setting can be significantly smaller than what is predicted in other legislative bargaining models such as Baron and Ferejohn (1989) or Bernheim, Rangel, and Rayo (2006). This result of constrained proposal power is consistent with some recent empirical findings (e.g., Knight 2005).

9.1.2 Comparison to Existing Approaches: Policy Inertia

This chapter belongs to the literature of policy inertia. There have been other political economy theories that account for the failure to adopt socially beneficial economic reforms or the long delay before an adoption.[3]

Fernandez and Rodrik (1991) argued that the status quo bias of economic policies may result from uncertainty caused by potential reforms. If voters or interest groups are uncertain about the ex post distribution of costs and benefits, they may vote against the reform even if they believe it to be a socially beneficial reform ex ante. Their argument does not necessarily depend on the assumption of risk aversion. Note however, that this approach does not explain why such uncertainty would be higher in proportional-parliamentary democracies.

Inspired by Olson's (1982) *The Rise and Decline of Nations,* a common view is that policy inertia results when vested interest groups oppose a policy reform. Krusell and Rios-Rull (1996) presented a dynamic model in which vested interest groups who have invested in old technologies support policies that block the entry of newer superior technologies and thus cause stagnation.

Policy persistence may result when there are conflicts over the burden of reform as well as asymmetric information. Alesina and Drazen (1991) as well as Drazen and Grilli (1993) presented a model in which the government is running a deficit due to the failure of interest groups to agree on a deficit-reduction program. There is disagreement on how the burden of higher taxes should be distributed across groups or which government programs should be cut. As different groups are unsure about the others' preferences, they wait for the others to concede and accept a reform with unfavorable distributional implications. While Alesina and Drazen (1991) assumed that consensus (unanimity) is required to pass a reform, we assume a simple majority rule. Nevertheless, in the impulse-response analysis, we show that the proposer of a fiscal reduction may face strong resistance from the other groups so that he may have to reduce the size of government programs for his own group. This equilibrium implication of our model may provide a microfoundation for Alesina and Drazen's ad hoc assumption that any proposer of stabilization has to bear an unequally large burden resulting from the reform.

Riboni and Ruge-Murcia (2007) applied a two-player bargaining model with unanimity rule and random shocks to show that preference heterogeneity and dynamic consideration generate inertial monetary policy and explain why the nominal interest rate under the central bank's control is infrequently adjusted. Their argument relies on the fact that, in a stochastic environment, a policy superior for the current moment may not be as efficient in the future. If the central bank committee members foresee that in the future it will be difficult to reverse a policy change made today, they will behave inactively even now. We model how fiscal policies can persist even under majority rule.

9.1.3 Comparison to Existing Approaches: Political Economy of Government Size

This chapter also speaks to the political economy literature on government size. A central question in this literature is, what are the fundamental factors, either political or economic, that determine the size of total government expenditure? This literature begins with the seminal paper by

Meltzer and Richard (1981), who applied the median-voter theorem to a simple macroeconomic setup. They assume that the policy issue is a one-dimensional variable, the size of government, so that the policy choice is dictated by the voters with median income level. As voting rights are extended from the elite groups to a broader electorate, or as income distribution becomes more unequal so that the median voters are relatively poorer, there is more redistribution of income through government programs, which leads to a larger government size. Krusell and Rios-Rull (1996) extended this model to a dynamic setup in which voters also have to trade off consumption and savings.

Hassler et al. (2003) studied the dynamics of redistributive policy and explained the survival of a big welfare program, again, in the analytical framework of the median-voter theorem. Their model demonstrates how beliefs about future political outcomes and policymaking may affect current private investment decisions, which affect the sizes of different groups (for example, the rich and the poor) and therefore fulfill the beliefs in the first place. They use multiple equilibria to explain different possible patterns of policy dynamics. Hassler et al. (2005) addressed the same issues with a probabilistic model in the spirit of Lindbeck and Weibull (1987). All these studies deepen our understanding of policy dynamics, but institutional details are lacking in the respective models. The median-voter setup not only relies on a very restrictive policy space, but also leaves no room for us to understand the different policy patterns resulting from different political institutions.

Another branch of this literature does provide theories about how different constitutions shape fiscal policies and government sizes. Persson and Tabellini (1999) and Persson, Roland, and Tabellini (2000) theoretically investigated how different electoral rules (majoritarian vs. proportional representation) and political regimes (presidential system vs. parliamentary system) affect the sizes of total government expenditure, general public-goods provision, and targeted transfers. They concluded that parliamentary systems and/or proportional electoral rules lead to a larger government. These empirical implications were then tested and confirmed by Persson and Tabellini (2001, 2003, 2004). The theoretical approach of Persson and Tabellini was also applied by Pagano and Volpin (2006) to study the composition of public expenditure and regulation over protection of employees and investors. All these models explicitly stress institutional details and compare different political institutions. However, most theories along this line are based on static models or focus on static policy issues like the sizes of total government spending, welfare expenditures, or the level of waste and corruption. Our model investigates how political institutions affect policy dynamics, for example, the *change* of government expenditure over time.

Battaglini and Coate (2007, 2008) provided a dynamic model of public investment and public debt with a legislative bargaining institution. They illustrated how inefficiency results from the institutions and presented rich dynamics of fiscal policies. However, their models do not apply to the ratchet effect investigated here.

In the next section we define both the policy environment and the legislative decision-making model. We then characterize the model's equilibrium and briefly discuss its implications. This is followed by a brief conclusion.

9.2   The Model

9.2.1   The Policy Environment

Consider a policy environment with three distinct socioeconomic groups, indexed by $\ell = a, b, c$. Each group, formed by a continuum of identical individuals with a measure one-third, sends a representative to the legislature. Time is discrete, with two periods. In every period, the representatives collectively decide on the size as well as the distribution of the government budget among the groups.

The government can implement three distinct public programs, each of which targets a different socioeconomic group. As an example, imagine that the society is divided into retirees, the working poor, and the working rich. The government may enforce a social security policy that redistributes resources to the retired elderly, provides public education and a medicare system that especially benefit the low income families, and engages in some other public programs that benefit the wealthy group. Let $x_{\ell,t} \geq 0$ be the size of the public program for group ℓ in period t. Note that the total government budget is endogenous but not fixed. Therefore, any feasible policy in period t is a triplet $\mathbf{x}_t = (x_{a,t}, x_{b,t}, x_{c,t})$. We assume a discrete policy space for technical convenience. The minimal spending units can be as small as necessary, for example, one cent. We normalize an indivisible unit to 1, and the policy space is $X = \mathbb{Z}_+^3$.

All government expenditure is financed by a distortionary income tax. For any amount $\Pi_t > 0$ of tax revenue collected, the taxation system results in a deadweight loss of $C_S(\Pi_t) > 0$, where the cost function is continuous, differentiable, strictly increasing, and strictly convex. A balanced budget implies that the tax revenue exactly covers the total public expenditure: $\Pi_t = \sum_{\ell=a}^c x_{\ell,t}$. With symmetry, each group bears one-third of the deadweight loss, $\frac{1}{3} C_S(\Pi(\mathbf{x}_t))$.

The subscript S of the cost function refers to the state of the economy, which affects the marginal deadweight loss of taxation. This parameter could reflect the technological productivity of the economy, severity of fiscal deficits, efficiency of government bureaucrats, and other economic or policy variables. We discuss various specifications of the economic state variable S in Section 9.2.3.

In addition to distributional concerns, we are also interested in efficiency properties. The size of the government budget may be too large or too small, compared to its socially optimal level. If the public policy was chosen by a benevolent dictator, the total government budget would be G_S^* such that $C_S'(G_S^*) = 1$. At this efficient expenditure level, the social deadweight loss incurred by the last dollar spent is equal to the additional utility contributed by that dollar through government programs. In contrast, if the public policy was solely determined by a single socioeconomic group without any checks and balances by the others, the total government budget would be $\overline{G}_S$ such that $\frac{1}{3} C_S'(\overline{G}_S) = 1$. A single group internalizes only its part (one-third) of the deadweight loss and therefore overspends ($\overline{G}_S > G_S^*$), leading to an inefficient allocation. Regardless of the legislative institution, $\overline{G}_S$ is the upper bound of any politically feasible government size.

We do not assume electoral competition and assume that the representatives are perfect delegates. Given the constraints imposed by the balanced-budget requirement and the political process, they maximize the expected utilities of their respective groups. In any period t with economic state S_t, the preferences of group ℓ are assumed to be quasi-linear and given by

$$u_\ell(\mathbf{x}_t; S_t) = x_{\ell,t} - \frac{1}{3} C_{S_t}\left(\sum_{\ell=a}^c x_{\ell,t}\right).$$

The total two-period utility is given by

$$(1 - \beta) u_\ell(\mathbf{x}_1; S_1) + \beta u_\ell(\mathbf{x}_2; S_2),$$

where $\beta \in [0, 1)$ represents a common discount factor.

9.2.2 The Political Process

The political process is modeled as legislative bargaining between the three representatives. We focus on a particular proposal protocol that is typical of parliamentary democracies where agenda setting is concentrated in the executive. Formally, we assume a single, persistent agenda setter during a legislative session. A legislative session refers to the lifetime of a government, that is, the time period between two parliamentary elections. In our model, a session consists of two periods. We assume that the government will last the entire session. In other words, we do not consider issues of cabinet stability. Therefore, the agenda setter is unchanged throughout the two periods. Without loss of generality, let the representative of group a be the sole agenda setter.

Legislative bargaining proceeds in potentially multiple rounds of proposal making and voting. The number of rounds depends on both exogenous factors that may randomly terminate the session and the decision by the agenda setter. Note that in a multiperiod model, each *period* may potentially have multiple *rounds* of proposing and voting.

At the beginning of period t, there is an initial default policy $\mathbf{d}_t^0$. A *default* is the policy that will be implemented if no new policy proposal is passed subsequently in the same period. Consider an arbitrary round r of negotiation and denote the prevailing default by $\mathbf{d}_t^{r-1}$. The agenda setter can choose to make a new policy proposal $\widetilde{\mathbf{x}}_t^r \in X$ or to pass. To simplify the mathematical formulation, a *pass* is modeled as a proposal identical to the prevailing default; that is, $\widetilde{\mathbf{x}}_t^r = \mathbf{d}_t^{r-1}$. Once a proposal (different from the default) is made, it is voted on against the default. Voting is by simple majority rule. If a new proposal passes, it becomes the default in the next round; that is, $\mathbf{d}_t^r = \widetilde{\mathbf{x}}_t^r$. Otherwise the original default remains; that is, $\mathbf{d}_t^r = \mathbf{d}_t^{r-1}$. Collective decision making then continues in the same fashion conditional on the continuation of the period. The default evolves as legislation in a period progresses. The default policy that survives until the end of the period is the final policy outcome for that period. We denote the policy outcome in period t by $\mathbf{x}_t$.

The assumption of an evolving default is similar to the approach proposed by Bernheim, Rangel, and Rayo (2006). Intuitively, the passage of a bill does not prevent the legislature from revisiting the issue at a later date; rather, it changes the default for subsequent deliberations. Bernheim, Rangel, and Rayo assumed an exogenously fixed, commonly known num-

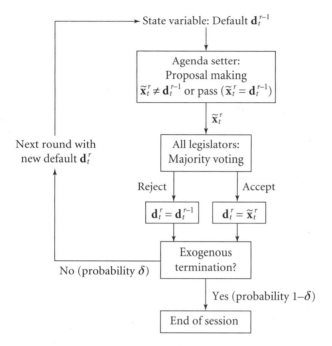

Figure 9.1 The flow chart: Sequence of events in round r of period t.

ber of bargaining rounds. In our model, however, there is no well-defined last round. Rather, the number of actual bargaining rounds is determined as follows.

There are two ways to terminate a legislative session. First, the period ends *endogenously* if the ongoing default is such that the agenda setter no longer wants to propose any new policy to defeat it. Second, at the end of each round of negotiation, the period may end *exogenously* with probability $(1-\delta)$, where $\delta \in [0, 1)$. In other words, conditional on any round of negotiation, with probability δ, a period continues and the agenda setter gets a chance to revisit the same policy and make a new proposal to replace the current policy. Following Diermeier and Fong (2007), we assume that the probability of reconsideration is sufficiently close to 1. Figure 9.1 summarizes the sequence of events in this game.

In any period t, we refer to a policy that has been enacted as a *status quo* and denote it by $\mathbf{q}_t$. Following this definition, the status quo in period two is the policy outcome in period two; that is, $\mathbf{q}_2 = \mathbf{x}_1$. We assume that, once enacted, a policy is in effect until it is reformed. Such an assumption captures the feature of a broad set of welfare programs and entitlement policies that comprise a majority proportion of the government expenditures in well-developed democracies, and especially in multiparty, parliamentary countries. Given this, it is natural to assume that, in any period t, the initial default policy is simply the status quo alternative at that point; that is, $\mathbf{d}_t^0 = \mathbf{q}_t$. In the beginning of the first period, we assume an exogenous initial status quo $\mathbf{q}_1$.

Note that in the existing dynamic bargaining literature, "status quo" and "default" are the same thing (e.g., Baron 1996; Kalandrakis 2004; Fong 2006; Baron, Diermeier, and Fong 2007; Duggan and Kalandrakis 2007). However, this is not the case in our model. For example, suppose that in year 2007 the legislature passes a social security reform that will become effective in year 2009. The status quo is the ongoing policy that has been working, and the default is the new bill, which may be reconsidered or even replaced before it is enacted. A separation of the concepts of status quo and default allows us to distinguish policy dynamics *within* and *across* periods.

9.2.3 An Impulse Analysis Setup

The goal of this chapter is to provide mechanisms, resulting from bargaining frictions, that could possibly account for the persistence of government size and inaction of government policy in response to a change of economic environment in multiparty, parliamentary countries. Therefore, instead of a full, dynamic characterization of a model with changing economic state variables, we consider only an impulse-response analysis.

We assume that the economy could be in one of three states: H, N, and L. We assume that for any spending level Π, $C_H'(\Pi) < C_N'(\Pi) < C_L'(\Pi)$. Therefore, $G_H^* > G_N^* > G_L^*$ and $\overline{G}_H > \overline{G}_N > \overline{G}_L$. We refer to $S = H$ as a *good state* where it is cheaper to provide government programs ceteris paribus and therefore the efficient government expenditure is at a higher level. We refer to $S = L$ as a *bad state* in which it is more costly to tax in order to finance the same amount of government expenditure and therefore the efficient government expenditure is at a lower level.

To conduct an impulse-response experiment, we assume that before the first period, the economy had been in a normal state $S_0 = N$, and the government size had been stabilized at G_N^*. In this way, the initial status quo $\mathbf{q}_1$ is a policy associated with a government size $\sum_{\ell=a}^c q_{\ell,1} = G_N^*$. In the first period, a temporary shock strikes that affects the marginal social cost of public expenditure. The shock is temporary in the sense that it lasts for only one period. In the second period, the economy reverts to its normal state. This means that we assume $S_2 = N$. We want to know how the government would respond to the change of economic environment by making a new policy in the first period. Given very few theories available in the literature, we believe this is a reasonable starting point from which to approach the key questions.

We characterize the equilibrium for three different possible states of the economy in the first period. The exact interpretation of this shock is not critical. What really matters is that the economy temporarily deviates from its long-run trend. We now want to investigate how this fluctuation results in a fluctuation of government spending.

As a normative benchmark, in the first-best solution, in every period with economic state S_t, the total size of government expenditure should be equal to $G^*_{S_t}$ regardless of the specific allocation. Public spending should be fully responsive to the state of the economy. In our model, the policy is chosen by the political process of legislative bargaining. We want to show how the equilibrium policy deviates from the first-best solution and identify possible sources of inefficiency and policy persistence resulting from the political institutions that characterize the legislative bargaining environment.

9.3 Equilibrium Concept

9.3.1 Equilibrium Definition

Consider any period t and an arbitrary round r of proposal making and voting with a prevailing default $\mathbf{d}_t^{r-1}$ and economic state S_t. If no new bill is passed in the rest of this period, $\mathbf{d}_t^{r-1}$ will be implemented and the utility of group ℓ is given by $d_{\ell,t}^{r-1} - \frac{1}{3}C_{S_t}\left(\sum_{\ell=a}^{c}d_{\ell,t}^{r-1}\right)$. Since the probability that this period may exogenously end is constant across time, the legislature faces an identical dynamic choice problem in legislative bargaining rounds r and $r' \neq r$ if the default policies in the two rounds are the same, that is, $\mathbf{d}_t^{r-1} = \mathbf{d}_t^{r'-1}$. Therefore, we restrict analysis to cases in which the legislators condition their strategies only on the prevailing default as well as the economic state S_t. In other words, we assume stationarity *within* a legislative period. From now on, we drop the superscript for bargaining rounds.

The equilibrium we are going to define involves not only stationarity within periods but also subgame perfection across periods. *Subgame perfection* implies that in any period, the representatives maximize their discounted sums of expected utilities and take into consideration the effect of their current policy choice on legislation in the subsequent period.

Moreover, following Diermeier and Fong (2007), we focus on the limiting legislative equilibrium as the probability of reconsideration, δ, goes to 1. The reason for this assumption is mainly technical as the limiting equilibrium has various appealing properties. However, for very significant legislation (such as entitlement programs), a δ close to 1 provides a reasonable approximation.

For tractability, when formulating the equilibrium definition, we assume that in any period the representatives and socioeconomic groups they represent foresee a limiting equilibrium to follow in a subsequent period but precisely perceive a sufficiently high probability of reconsideration in the current period. This assumption makes the model very tractable, although it is not binding in a more general model.

Let $\mathbf{g}_t(\mathbf{d}_t; S_t)$ be the new bill passed in any round of negotiation in period t with a prevailing default $\mathbf{d}_t$. It will also be the new default in the subsequent rounds if the current legislative period continues. For any S_t, we refer to $\mathbf{g}_t : X \to X$ as the policy rule in period t. Let

$$\mathbf{g}_t^*(\mathbf{d}_t; S_t) \equiv \lim_{\delta \to 1} \mathbf{g}_t(\mathbf{d}_t; S_t) \tag{9.1}$$

be the limiting policy rule in period t.

Let $U_{i,t}(\mathbf{x}_t; S_t)$ be the expected utility of group i if a policy $\mathbf{x}_t$ is passed in any round of negotiation in period t, and

$$U_{i,t}^*(\mathbf{x}_t; S_t) \equiv \lim_{\delta \to 1} U_{i,t}(\mathbf{x}_t; S_t) \tag{9.2}$$

be the limiting counterpart. In a two-period model, set $U_{i,3}^*(\mathbf{x}_3; S_3) \equiv 0$ for any $\mathbf{x}_3$, any S_3, and any i. With probability $(1 - \delta)$, the legislative session in period t exogenously ends, and this group receives a utility of $x_{i,t} - \frac{1}{3}C_{S_t}\left(\sum_{\ell=a}^{c}x_{\ell,t}\right)$ in the current period and an expected utility of $U_{i,t+1}^*\left(\mathbf{g}_{t+1}^*(\mathbf{x}_t; S_{t+1}); S_{t+1}\right)$ in the subsequent period. With probability δ, the agenda setter has a chance to revisit the policy issue and $\mathbf{g}_t(\mathbf{x}_t; S_t)$ will be passed in the next round of negotiation. In this case, group i will receive an expected utility of $U_{i,t}\left(\mathbf{g}_t\left(\mathbf{x}_t; S_t\right); S_t\right)$. Thus, for any $i = a, b, c$,

$$U_{i,t}\left(\mathbf{x}_t; S_t\right) = (1 - \delta)(1 - \beta)\left(x_{i,t} - \frac{1}{3}C_{S_t}\left(\sum_{\ell=a}^c x_{\ell,t}\right)\right) \tag{9.3}$$

$$+ (1 - \delta)\beta U_{i,t+1}^*\left(\mathbf{g}_{t+1}^*\left(\mathbf{x}_t; S_{t+1}\right); S_{t+1}\right) + \delta U_{i,t}\left(\mathbf{g}_t\left(\mathbf{x}_t; S_t\right); S_t\right).$$

Note that, for any prevailing default $\mathbf{d}_t$, $U_i\left(\mathbf{d}_t; S_t\right)$ is the reservation value of group i in period t since this is the group's expected utility if the default remains.

We make two behavioral assumptions regarding proposal making and voting. First, a legislator votes against a policy proposal if and only if passage of the bill makes him strictly worse off. This is equivalent to a case in which a legislator has to overcome an infinitesimal cost in order to vote against the agenda setter. Second, an agenda setter never makes a proposal that is destined to be vetoed in the majority voting. The agenda setter could always propose the prevailing default and achieve the same result.

Given any prevailing default $\mathbf{d}_t$, the agenda setter makes a policy proposal to maximize his expected utility $U_{a,t}\left(\mathbf{d}_t; S_t\right)$. Given the second assumption above, the maximization problem is subject to a constraint that the proposal be approved by majority voting. Given the assumption on voting behaviors, this is equivalent to a constraint that at least one other legislator is weakly better off with the proposed policy than with the default. In other words, majority voting can be modeled by an incentive compatibility constraint. To sum up, the policy rule $\mathbf{g}_t\left(\mathbf{d}_t; S_t\right)$ solves

$$\max_{\mathbf{x}_t' \in X} U_{a,t}\left(\mathbf{x}_t'; S_t\right)$$

$$\text{s.t. } U_{i,t}\left(\mathbf{x}_t'; S_t\right) \geq U_{i,t}\left(\mathbf{d}_t; S_t\right) \text{ for some } i \in \{b, c\}. \tag{9.4}$$

Note that the prevailing default $\mathbf{d}_t$ always satisfies the incentive compatibility constraint. If the default policy is such that an agenda setter cannot pass any proposal that leaves him a (weakly) higher expected utility than his reservation value, he "proposes," and trivially, "passes" the default policy. In this case, the default policy solves the constrained maximization problem and $\mathbf{g}_t\left(\mathbf{d}_t; S_t\right) = \mathbf{d}_t$.

We are now ready to summarize the equilibrium definition.

Definition   *A limiting legislative equilibrium is a pair of policy rules* $\{\mathbf{g}_t^*\}_{t=1}^2$, *and a set of expected utility functions* $\left\{U_{a,t}^*, U_{b,t}^*, U_{c,t}^*\right\}_{t=1}^2$ *such that these functions are the limit given by equations (9.1) and (9.2), where* $\{\mathbf{g}_t\}_{t=1}^2$ *and* $\left\{U_{a,t}, U_{b,t}, U_{c,t}\right\}_{t=1}^2$ *satisfy the following conditions:*

1. *Given any* $t \in \{1, 2\}$, $\mathbf{g}_t$ *and* $\left\{U_{\ell,t+1}^*\right\}_{\ell=a}^c$, *for any* S_t *and any* $\mathbf{x}_t \in X$, $U_{i,t}\left(\mathbf{x}_t; S_t\right)$ *satisfies equation (9.3) for any* $i = a, b, c$.
2. *Given any* $t \in \{1, 2\}$ *and* $\{U_{\ell,t}\}_{\ell=a}^c$, *for any* $\mathbf{d}_t \in X$, $\mathbf{g}_t\left(\mathbf{d}_t\right)$ *solves maximization problem (9.4).*

9.3.2 An Equivalent Problem

A limiting legislative equilibrium exists. The proof is an extension of Diermeier and Fong (2007) and here omitted. In the rest of the chapter, we only characterize necessary conditions for the limiting equilibrium. These necessary conditions demonstrate the mechanisms that lead to the persistence of public expenditures.

In analogy with the analysis in Diermeier and Fong (2007), the following holds.

First, even though the agenda setter has the ability to have current policies reconsidered, in equilibrium, there exists at most one round of proposal making and voting in every period. In other words, if the agenda setter ever desires to change the status quo, he makes one proposal immediately without reconsidering it in any further round.

Second, in any period, the equilibrium spending levels for both of the two groups with no proposal power are identical. This is an important difference compared to the results in all models in the Baron–Ferejohn tradition, in which all legislators whose votes are not needed to pass a proposal are fully expropriated. The nature of legislative bargaining is different in our model, however. It is still true that the agenda setter has an incentive to expropriate as much as possible from any socioeconomic group, say k, whose vote he does not need in order to pass a new policy. However, the group, say j, from which the agenda setter seeks a voting support, may not permit him to expropriate group k too much. This is explained in the following example based on Diermeier and Fong (2007).

Let's suppose that the three socioeconomic groups are dividing a fixed budget with size normalized to 6 units. Assume a single period with a status quo (the initial default) $\mathbf{d} = (3, 2, 1)$. In a static Baron–Ferejohn model with closed rule, the policy outcome would be (5, 0, 1). Legislator c is most disadvantaged by the default policy and therefore becomes the cheapest coalition partner for the agenda setter. Excluded from the coalition, legislator b is fully expropriated since her vote is not needed to pass the proposal. The agenda setter leaves legislator c just enough benefit to be indifferent between accepting and rejecting the proposal. In subgame perfect equilibrium, c accepts with probability 1 and the proposer takes the rest of the budget.

In our limiting legislative equilibrium, however, the agenda setter could never pass the policy (5, 0, 1). To see why, consider counterfactually what would happen if legislator c approved the proposal. With probability $1 - \delta$, the proposer would not have been able to revisit the policy issue and therefore (5, 0, 1) would be the final policy outcome. With probability δ, however, the agenda setter would be able to propose a new policy (6, 0, 0), which would be accepted by the fully expropriated legislator b. This implies that by accepting the policy (5, 0, 1), legislator c becomes vulnerable to further expropriation in the future. Foreseeing such an adverse consequence, legislator c will always vote against the proposal of (5, 0, 1) even though according to this proposal he does not lose any benefit right away. By similar arguments, we can conclude that legislator c will not accept any new policy where legislator b receives strictly less benefit than legislator c, assuming that the probability for reconsideration is sufficiently high. Therefore, the agenda setter can guarantee himself at most 4 units and only pass the policy (4, 1, 1). Surprisingly, the possibility of reconsideration, in fact, constrains the agenda setter and leads to an equal distribution of public resources between the two groups that have no proposal power.

Combining these observations, we can simplify the formulation of our model. It is as if the equilibrium policy outcome results from an equivalent problem in which in every period the agenda setter makes a policy proposal once and for all with a "limited expropriation" constraint. This additional constraint should specify that the agenda setter's policy proposal has to offer both of the other groups an equal expected utility, that is, targeted government programs of an equal size. Given that Diermeier and Fong (2007) suggest multiple equilibria in this class of games, we focus on the pure-strategy equilibrium in which proposal power has the greatest value. An analysis based on any other pure-strategy equilibrium will not qualitatively change the results.

In the second period and for status quo $\mathbf{q}_2 \in X$, the equilibrium policy rule $\mathbf{g}_2^* (\mathbf{q}_2; N)$ solves

$$\max_{\mathbf{x}_2' \in X} x_{a,2}' - \frac{1}{3} C_N \left(\sum_{\ell=a}^c x_{\ell,2}' \right)$$

$$s.t. \ x_{b,2}' = x_{c,2}',$$

$$x_{i,2}' - \frac{1}{3} C_N \left(\sum_{\ell=a}^c x_{\ell,2}' \right) \geq$$

$$q_{i,2} - \frac{1}{3} C_N \left(\sum_{\ell=a}^c q_{\ell,2}' \right) \ \text{for some} \ i \in \{b, c\}.$$

(9.5)

In a similar way, in the first period and for any status quo $\mathbf{q}_1 \in X$ and any economic state S_1, the equilibrium policy rule $\mathbf{g}_1^* (\mathbf{q}_1; S_1)$ solves

$$\max_{\mathbf{x}_1' \in X} (1 - \beta) \left(x_{a,1}' - \frac{1}{3} C_{S_1} \left(\sum_{\ell=a}^c x_{\ell,1}' \right) \right)$$

$$+ \beta \left(g_{a,2}^* (\mathbf{x}_1'; N) - \frac{1}{3} C_N \left(\sum_{\ell=a}^c g_{\ell,2}^* (\mathbf{x}_1'; N) \right) \right)$$

(9.6)

$$s.t. \ x_{b,1}' = x_{c,1}',$$

$$W_i (\mathbf{x}_1'; S_1) \geq W_i (\mathbf{q}_1; S_1) \ \text{for some} \ i \in \{b, c\},$$

where

$$W_i (\mathbf{q}_1; S_1) = (1 - \beta) \left(q_{i,1}' - \frac{1}{3} C_{S_1} \left(\sum_{\ell=a}^c q_{\ell,1}' \right) \right)$$

$$+ \beta \left(g_{i,2}^* (\mathbf{q}_1; N) - \frac{1}{3} C_N \left(\sum_{\ell=a}^c g_{\ell,2}^* (\mathbf{q}_1; N) \right) \right)$$

is the equivalent reservation value of group $i \in \{b, c\}$, and

$$W_i (\mathbf{x}_1'; S_1) = (1 - \beta) \left(x_{i,1}' - \frac{1}{3} C_{S_1} \left(\sum_{\ell=a}^c x_{\ell,1}' \right) \right)$$

$$+ \beta \left(g_{i,2}^* (\mathbf{x}_1'; N) - \frac{1}{3} C_N \left(\sum_{\ell=a}^c g_{\ell,2}^* (\mathbf{x}_1'; N) \right) \right)$$

is the expected utility of the same group if policy $\mathbf{x}_1'$ is chosen, and $\mathbf{g}_2^* (\mathbf{x}_1'; N)$ is the solution to (9.5), the agenda setter's equivalent maximization problem in the second period.

9.4 The Second Period

We characterize the equilibrium by backward induction and start the analysis from the second period. This case also provides us with a complete analysis of a legislative session with only one period.

9.4.1 General Intuition

In the period-two equilibrium, either the nonnegativity constraint or the incentive compatibility constraint is binding. With a period-two status quo $\mathbf{q}_2$, the agenda setter chooses a policy $\mathbf{x}_2' \in X$ such that either $x_{b,2}' = x_{c,2}' = 0$, or

$$x_{b,2}' - \frac{1}{3}C_N \left(\sum_{\ell=a}^{c} x_{\ell,2}' \right) = x_{c,2}' - \frac{1}{3}C_N \left(\sum_{\ell=a}^{c} x_{\ell,2}' \right)$$

$$= \min \{q_{b,2}, q_{c,2}\} - \frac{1}{3}C_N \left(\sum_{\ell=a}^{c} q_{\ell,2} \right).$$

If this was not true, the agenda setter could always reduce the provision of government programs to the other groups by a small amount and still obtain a voting support from the more disadvantaged group.

For any status quo $\mathbf{q}_2$ and any government size Π_2', let

$$\bar{x} (\mathbf{q}_2, \Pi_2'; S_2) \equiv \min \{q_{b,2}, q_{c,2}\} + \frac{1}{3}C_{S_2} (\Pi_2') - \frac{1}{3}C_{S_2} \left(\sum_{\ell=a}^{c} q_{\ell,2} \right).$$

Then in equilibrium, the agenda setter must choose $\mathbf{x}_2'$ such that

$$x_{b,2}' = x_{c,2}' = \max \left\{ 0, \bar{x} \left(\mathbf{q}_2, \sum_{\ell=a}^{c} x_{\ell,2}'; N \right) \right\}, \tag{9.7}$$

and

$$x_{a,2}' = \sum_{\ell=a}^{c} x_{\ell,2}' - 2 \max \left\{ 0, \bar{x} \left(\mathbf{q}_2, \sum_{\ell=a}^{c} x_{\ell,2}'; N \right) \right\}. \tag{9.8}$$

We can now apply this approach and transform the original problem into a maximization problem in which the agenda setter directly chooses the size of the total government budget $\Pi_2' = \sum_{\ell=a}^{c} x_{\ell,2}'$. Once Π_2' is chosen, the relative magnitudes of government programs for all socioeconomic groups are pinned down by (9.7) and (9.8).

For any government size Π_2' to be feasible, it must be that

$$\Pi_2' \in \mathcal{F}_2 \left(\mathbf{q}_2; N \right) \equiv \left\{ \Pi \in \mathbb{N} : 2\overline{x} \left(\mathbf{q}_2, \Pi; N \right) \leq \Pi \right\},$$

so that the spending level on the agenda setter's group is nonnegative. The transformed problem then can be stated as follows:

$$\max_{\Pi_2' \leq \mathbb{N}} \Pi_2' - 2 \max \left\{ 0, \overline{x} \left(\mathbf{q}_2, \Pi_2'; N \right) \right\} - \frac{1}{3} C_N \left(\Pi_2' \right)$$

$$s.t. \ \Pi_2' \in \mathcal{F}_2 \left(\mathbf{q}_2; N \right).$$

In the subsections that follow, we characterize the period-two equilibrium policy and relate it to the status quo government size. We divide the discussion into three parts according to the status quo government size in relation to its socially optimal level.

9.4.2 An Efficient Status Quo Government Size

Consider any status quo $\mathbf{q}_2 \in X$ for the second period such that $\sum_{\ell=a}^{c} q_{\ell,2} = G_N^*$. Here, the status quo government size is socially optimal since $C_N' \left(G_N^* \right) = 1$, that is, the social cost of the last dollar spent is equal to its social benefit. Would an efficient government budget persist through the political process? We answer this question in two steps.

In the first step, suppose the agenda setter was restricted by the existing government size but that he could change the allocations of the budget among the socioeconomic groups. Note that $G_N^* \in \mathcal{F}_2 \left(\mathbf{q}_2; N \right)$, so keeping the same size of government expenditure is always feasible, though not necessarily optimal, for the agenda setter. With a fixed budget of G_N^*, the agenda setter's problem is identical to the one analyzed by Diermeier and Fong (2007). Their result shows that the agenda setter would spend

$$\widehat{x}_{i,2} = \overline{x} \left(\mathbf{q}_2, G_N^*; N \right) = \min \left\{ q_{b,2}, q_{c,2} \right\}$$

for each of the other groups $i = b, c$, and leave his own group with

$$\widehat{x}_{a,2} = G_N^* - 2\overline{x} \left(\mathbf{q}_2, G_N^*; N \right)$$

$$= q_{a,2} + \max \left\{ q_{b,2}, q_{c,2} \right\} - \min \left\{ q_{b,2}, q_{c,2} \right\}.$$

With policy $\widehat{x}_2$, the group more disadvantaged by the status quo would be indifferent, and the third group would be expropriated up to the status quo allocation of the more disadvantaged group. This is the maximal amount of expropriation still acceptable to the more disadvantaged group. The fact that $\widehat{x}_{b,2} = \widehat{x}_{c,2}$ ensures that the agenda setter will not be able to pass any new policy in the remainder of the legislative session to expropriate any of the other groups (including the current coalition partner) further. The agenda setter can then allocate an amount equal to $\max\{q_{b,1}, q_{c,1}\} - \min\{q_{b,1}, q_{c,1}\}$ more on his own group compared to the status quo allocation. The larger is the difference between spending levels for the other two groups, the larger is the room for expropriation and therefore the value of proposal power.

In the second step, we ask if the agenda setter ever has an incentive to shift his proposal from $\widehat{x}_2$ to some other policy that leads to a different government size from G_N^*. If the answer is yes, there must be some policy with which the agenda setter could derive a utility greater than

$$G_N^* - 2\min\{q_{b,2}, q_{c,2}\} - \frac{1}{3}C_N\left(G_N^*\right).$$

We can show that this is not possible. To see that, suppose that instead of choosing and dividing a government budget, the agenda setter chooses and divides a total social surplus through policymaking. Observe that policy $\widehat{x}_2$ already maximizes the social surplus defined as the summation of the three groups' period-two utilities, that is, $\sum_{\ell=a}^{c} x_{\ell,2} - \frac{1}{3}C_N\left(\sum_{\ell=a}^{c} x_{\ell,2}\right)$, and also that in order to pass any new policy, the agenda setter has to offer each of the other groups at least a constant utility of $\min\{q_{b,2}, q_{c,2}\} - \frac{1}{3}C_N\left(G_N^*\right)$. By strict concavity of the social surplus, increasing or decreasing the size of government expenditure from its efficient level reduces the total surplus and therefore that must leave the agenda setter's group with a strictly smaller utility if this policy is passed. Therefore, $\widehat{x}_2$ is the best policy alternative the agenda setter can make for himself.

The following proposition summarizes the findings.

Proposition 9.1   *For any status quo q_2 in the second period such that $\sum_{\ell=a}^{c} q_{\ell,2} = G_N^*$:*

1. *The equilibrium government size is the same as its default, which is socially optimal; efficiency is sustainable.*

2. *Among the two groups with no proposal power, the one more disadvantaged by the status quo, say group j, is left in the same condition as that given by the status quo, and expenditure on the other group is cut to match that on group j. In particular,*

$$g_{b,2}^* \left(\mathbf{q}_2; N \right) = g_{c,2}^* \left(\mathbf{q}_2; N \right) = \min \left\{ q_{b,2}, q_{c,2} \right\}.$$

3. *The agenda setter's group gets* $\max \left\{ q_{b,1}, q_{c,1} \right\} - \min \left\{ q_{b,1}, q_{c,1} \right\}$ *more than the amount given by the status quo. In particular,*

$$g_{a,2}^* \left(\mathbf{q}_2; N \right) = G_N^* - 2 \min \left\{ q_{b,2}, q_{c,2} \right\}.$$

9.4.3 An Inefficiently Small Status Quo Government Size

Now consider any status quo $\mathbf{q}_2$ in the second period such that $\sum_{\ell=a}^c q_{\ell,2} < G_N^*$. The status quo government size is inefficient since $C_N' \left(\sum_{\ell=a}^c q_{\ell,1} \right) < 1 = C_N' \left(G_N^* \right)$, that is, the social cost of the last dollar spent is smaller than its social benefit. If the status quo remains, there is underprovision of government programs. Would bargaining in the legislature improve efficiency and lead to a larger size of government expenditure? We answer this question by analysis in parallel with that of the previous subsection.

First, if the agenda setter was restricted to maintaining the same government size as given by the status quo whenever he makes any proposal, the policy outcome would be

$$\widehat{x}_{i,2}^- = \overline{x} \left(\mathbf{q}_2, \sum_{\ell=a}^c q_{\ell,2}; N \right) = \min \left\{ q_{b,2}, q_{c,2} \right\},$$

for each of the other groups $i = b, c$, and

$$\widehat{x}_{a,2}^- = \sum_{\ell=a}^c q_{\ell,2} - 2\overline{x} \left(\mathbf{q}_2, \sum_{\ell=a}^c q_{\ell,2}; N \right)$$

$$= q_{a,2} + \max \left\{ q_{b,2}, q_{c,2} \right\} - \min \left\{ q_{b,2}, q_{c,2} \right\}.$$

This policy, $\widehat{x}_2^-$, serves as a reference point. If the agenda setter ever wants to choose a different government size from $\sum_{\ell=a}^c q_{\ell,2}$, his group must be able to derive at least a utility of

$$\sum_{\ell=a}^c q_{\ell,2} - 2 \min \left\{ q_{b,2}, q_{c,2} \right\} - \frac{1}{3} C_N \left(\sum_{\ell=a}^c q_{\ell,2} \right)$$

from such a deviation.

We claim that the agenda setter is both willing and able to *increase* the size of government expenditure from its status quo value. As long as the government size is strictly smaller than the socially optimal level G_N^*, a small increase in total government expenditure enlarges the total social surplus to be divided by the three groups. At the same time, the agenda setter can adjust the size of government programs for groups b and c so as to retain a constant utility of

$$\min \{q_{b,2}, q_{c,2}\} - \frac{1}{3}C_N \left(\sum_{\ell=a}^{c} q_{\ell,2}\right),$$

which is just enough for the disadvantaged group to break even. Therefore, it is to the agenda setter's interest to maximize social surplus by increasing the government expenditure to G_N^*.

As total government expenditure rises, the more disadvantaged group has to bear more deadweight loss resulting from distortionary taxation. As a consequence, in order to obtain agreement from this group, the agenda setter has to offer

$$\bar{x}\left(\mathbf{q}_2, G_N^*; N\right) = \min \{q_{b,2}, q_{c,2}\} + \frac{1}{3}C_N\left(G_N^*\right) - \frac{1}{3}C_N\left(\sum_{\ell=a}^{c} q_{\ell,2}\right)$$

to both groups b and c. Since $\sum_{\ell=a}^{c} q_{\ell,2} < G_N^*$ by supposition and the fact that the cost function is strictly increasing, the government program targeted at the more disadvantaged group is more generous than its status quo.

The agenda setter's group, a, then takes the residual of

$$G_N^* - 2\bar{x}\left(\mathbf{q}_2, \sum_{\ell=a}^{c} q_{\ell,2}; N\right).$$

Notice that group a also has to share the burden of a rising total expenditure. Given that it is better off with expansion, it must be that the government program for group a is more generous than its status quo as well. These findings are summarized in the following proposition.

Proposition 9.2   *For any status quo $\mathbf{q}_2$ in the second period such that $\sum_{\ell=a}^{c} q_{\ell,2} < G_N^*$:*

1. The period-two government size rises to its socially optimal level G_N^*.

2. *The spending level on each of the groups with no proposal power, $i = b, c$, is given by*

$$g_{i,2}^*(\mathbf{q}_2; N) = \bar{x}_2(\mathbf{q}_1, G_N^*; N)$$

$$\equiv \min\{q_{b,2}, q_{c,2}\} + \frac{1}{3}C_N(G_N^*) - \frac{1}{3}C_N\left(\sum_{\ell=a}^{c}q_{\ell,2}\right).$$

The government program for the group disadvantaged by the status quo, say j, always becomes more generous than its status quo. On the other hand, the government program for the other group, k, may shrink. This happens under two conditions: (a) The status quo government size is not far below its socially optimal level so that there is not much room to expand total public spending; and (b) the disadvantaged group j is initially allocated very little by the status quo so that the agenda setter has sufficient ability to expropriate group k. In particular, group k is harmed if

$$C_N\left(\sum_{\ell=a}^{c}q_{\ell,2}\right) + 3\left(\max\{q_{b,2}, q_{c,2}\} - \min\{q_{b,2}, q_{c,2}\}\right)$$

$$> \frac{1}{3}C_N(G_N^*).$$

3. *The agenda setter's group is allocated strictly more, compared to the status quo. In particular,*

$$g_{a,2}^*(\mathbf{q}_2; N) = G_N^* - 2\min\{q_{b,2}, q_{c,2}\}$$

$$- \frac{2}{3}C_N(G_N^*) + \frac{2}{3}C_N\left(\sum_{\ell=a}^{c}q_{\ell,2}\right).$$

Proposition 9.2 implies that if the status quo is associated with underprovision of public goods and government programs, through the legislative institution, it is easy for the government to expand. Whenever taxing more enhances social welfare, the agenda setter raises distortionary taxes, spends part of the extra tax revenues on the other groups just enough to obtain a majority support, and leaves the rest of the additional resources to his own group. Of course, such an adjustment while expanding the size of the government will be efficient. The key question is whether optimal contraction of the government size can also be a political economy equilibrium. If not, we have an explanation for the ratchet effect. We answer this question in the next subsection.

9.4.4 An Inefficiently Large Status Quo Government Size

Consider any status quo $\mathbf{q}_2$ in the second period such that $\sum_{\ell=a}^{c} q_{\ell,2} > G_N^*$. The status quo government size is inefficient since $C_N' \left(\sum_{\ell=a}^{c} q_{\ell,1} \right) > 1 = C_N' \left(G_N^* \right)$, that is, the social cost of the last dollar spent is greater than its social benefit. If the status quo remains, there is overprovision of government programs.

Again, the reference point is a policy $\widehat{\mathbf{x}}_2^+$ such that

$$\widehat{x}_{i,2}^+ = \overline{x} \left(\mathbf{q}_2, \sum_{\ell=a}^{c} q_{\ell,2}; N \right) = \min \left\{ q_{b,2}, q_{c,2} \right\},$$

for each of the other groups $i = b, c$, and

$$\widehat{x}_{a,2}^+ = G_N^* - 2\overline{x} \left(\mathbf{q}_2, \sum_{\ell=a}^{c} q_{\ell,2}; N \right)$$
$$= q_{a,2} + \max \left\{ q_{b,2}, q_{c,2} \right\} - \min \left\{ q_{b,2}, q_{c,2} \right\}.$$

Intuitions developed in the previous subsections may suggest that the agenda setter would cut total public spending to its socially optimal level in order to "maximize the aggregate surplus," offer each of the other groups just enough utility to obtain a majority support, and then leave the rest of the public resources to his own group. However, this intuition is incomplete as the agenda setter may be constrained from doing this. Notice that the argument above presupposes that the agenda setter is able to make the disadvantaged group, j, indifferent. When the total government expenditure is decreased, group j (as well as the other groups) is released from a heavy tax burden. To make this group indifferent between the status quo policy and the new proposal, the agenda setter has to cut the size of the government program for j. But if the initial spending level on group j is sufficiently small, the agenda setter may not have room to substantially reduce it. In other words spending on j will be constrained at 0. At this corner solution, group j may be strictly better off with a smaller government size than with the status quo. Whenever such a corner solution occurs, the agenda setter must instead rely on cutting his own group's expenditure to reduce the budget, but this may be too costly for him. Ironically, although the agenda setter *does increase* the total social surplus by adjusting total government expenditure downward, the additional surplus created by a smaller government may in fact be enjoyed by all the groups that have no proposal power. Such an outcome will not be the case in the legislative equilibrium.

The results are summarized in the following proposition.

Proposition 9.3 *For any period-two status quo $\mathbf{q}_2$ such that $\sum_{\ell=a}^{c} q_{\ell,2} > G_N^*$, the following holds:*

1. *If $\sum_{\ell=a}^{c} q_{\ell,2} > \overline{G}_N$ and $\overline{x}\left(\mathbf{q}_2, \overline{G}_N; N\right) \leq 0$, then*

$$g_{b,2}^*\left(\mathbf{q}_2^*; N\right) = g_{c,2}^*\left(\mathbf{q}_2; N\right) = 0,$$

$$g_{a,2}^*\left(\mathbf{q}_2; N\right) = \overline{G}_N, \text{ and}$$

$$\sum_{\ell=a}^{c} g_{\ell,2}^*\left(\mathbf{q}_2; N\right) = \overline{G}_N.$$

2. *If $\overline{x}\left(\mathbf{q}_2, \overline{G}_N; N\right) > 0$ and either $\overline{x}\left(\mathbf{q}_2, G_N^*; N\right) \leq 0$ or $G_N^* - 2\overline{x}\left(\mathbf{q}_2, G_N^*; N\right) \leq 0$, then*

$$\sum_{\ell=a}^{c} g_{\ell,2}^*\left(\mathbf{q}_2; N\right) = \max\left\{\widehat{G}\left(\mathbf{q}_2\right), \widetilde{G}\left(\mathbf{q}_2\right)\right\},$$

where

$$\overline{x}\left(\mathbf{q}_2, \widehat{G}\left(\mathbf{q}_2\right); N\right) = \min\left\{q_{b,2}, q_{c,2}\right\}$$
$$- \left(\frac{1}{3}C_N\left(\sum_{\ell=a}^{c} q_{\ell,2}\right) - \frac{1}{3}C_N\left(\widehat{G}\left(\mathbf{q}_2\right)\right)\right) = 0,$$

and $\widetilde{G}\left(\mathbf{q}_2\right)$ is defined as the minimal total spending level such that

$$\frac{1}{2}\widetilde{G}\left(\mathbf{q}_2\right) - \frac{1}{3}C_N\left(\widetilde{G}\left(\mathbf{q}_2\right)\right) = \min\left\{q_{b,2}, q_{c,2}\right\} - \frac{1}{3}C_N\left(\sum_{\ell=a}^{c} q_{\ell,2}\right).$$

In this case, if $\widetilde{G}\left(\mathbf{q}_2\right) > \widehat{G}\left(\mathbf{q}_2\right)$, then

$$g_{b,2}^*\left(\mathbf{q}_2; N\right) = g_{c,2}^*\left(\mathbf{q}_2; N\right) = \frac{1}{2}\widetilde{G}\left(\mathbf{q}_2\right),$$

$$g_{a,2}^*\left(\mathbf{q}_2; N\right) = 0.$$

Instead, if $\widetilde{G}\left(\mathbf{q}_2\right) < \widehat{G}\left(\mathbf{q}_2\right)$, then

$$g_{b,2}^*\left(\mathbf{q}_2; N\right) = g_{c,2}^*\left(\mathbf{q}_2; N\right) = 0,$$

$$g_{a,2}^*\left(\mathbf{q}_2; N\right) = \widehat{G}\left(\mathbf{q}_2\right).$$

3. If $\bar{x}\left(\mathbf{q}_2, G_N^*\right) > 0$ and $G_N^* - 2\bar{x}\left(\mathbf{q}_2, G_N^*; N\right) > 0$, then

$$g_{b,2}^*\left(\mathbf{q}_2; N\right) = g_{c,2}^*\left(\mathbf{q}_2; N\right) = \min\left\{q_{b,2}, q_{c,2}\right\}$$

$$+ \frac{1}{3}C_N\left(G_N^*\right) - \frac{1}{3}C_N\left(\sum_{\ell=a}^c q_{\ell,2}\right),$$

$$g_{a,2}^*\left(\mathbf{q}_2; N\right) = G_N^* - 2\min\left\{q_{b,2}, q_{c,2}\right\} - \frac{2}{3}C_N\left(G_N^*\right)$$

$$+ \frac{2}{3}C_N\left(\sum_{\ell=a}^c q_{\ell,2}\right), \text{ and}$$

$$\sum_{\ell=a}^c g_{\ell,2}^*\left(\mathbf{q}_2; N\right) = G_N^*.$$

4. *Starting with an efficiently large status quo government size, the equilibrium total spending level may end up being greater than its socially optimal level. Everything else being equal, this will happen if the status quo government size is sufficiently large, if the more disadvantaged group is given a sufficiently small government program by the status quo, and if the marginal social cost of government spending is sufficiently large.*

5. *If the equilibrium government size is strictly greater than its socially optimal level, then nothing is spent on either of the two groups that have no proposal power or on the agenda setter's group. If the equilibrium government size is socially optimal, then the sizes of the government program for both of the two groups that have no proposal power are cut but are still positive, to make the more disadvantaged group break even. The government program for the agenda setter's group may increase or decrease.*

The intuition for the result can easily be grasped in the special case where $\sum_{\ell=a}^c q_{\ell,2} > \overline{G}_N$. Then, even if the agenda setter was restricted to reducing expenditure on his own group, he would have an incentive to do so. This follows because $\frac{1}{3}C_N'\left(\sum_{\ell=a}^c q_{\ell,2}\right) > 1$, that is, even if the last dollar is spent solely on the agenda setter's group, the cost of the dollar incurred on the agenda setter is greater than the utility derived from the dollar. Therefore, the upper bound of equilibrium government size in the second period is always $\overline{G}_N$. The agenda setter always wants to reduce expenditures at least to this level.

We follow with a marginal analysis and characterize the conditions under which the agenda setter is both willing and able to reduce government expenditure and, if so, to what extent.

Consider two cases regarding the allocation of government budget with a fixed budget of $\overline{G}_N$.

Case A   If $\overline{x}\left(\mathbf{q}_2, \overline{G}_N; N\right) \leq 0$, *the agenda setter would spend nothing on any of the other groups but spend all of $\overline{G}_N$ on his own group.*

Case B   If $\overline{x}\left(\mathbf{q}_2, \overline{G}_N; N\right) > 0$, *the agenda setter has to offer each of the other groups $\overline{x}\left(\mathbf{q}_2, \overline{G}_N; N\right)$ to make the disadvantaged group indifferent, which leaves $\overline{G}_N - 2\overline{x}\left(\mathbf{q}_2, \overline{G}_N; N\right)$ to his own group, assuming that $\overline{G}_N - 2\overline{x}\left(\mathbf{q}_2, \overline{G}_N; N\right) \geq 0$.*

We now need to investigate if the agenda setter ever wants to cut total expenditure further. In case A, he is not willing to do so since the expenditure on the other groups is already zero. If the agenda setter continues cutting spending to reach some government size $\Pi < \overline{G}_N$, then he would be able to reduce the government program only for his own group, a, in order to achieve that goal. Group a would lose a utility of 1 from the last dollar cut but only save a cost of $\frac{1}{3}C'_N(\Pi)$, which is strictly smaller than $\frac{1}{3}C'_N\left(\overline{G}_N\right) = 1$. This is not optimal for group a.

In case B, the agenda setter is both willing and able to continue reducing government expenditure as long as the final total spending level $\Pi < \overline{G}_N$ is such that $\overline{x}\left(\mathbf{q}_2, \Pi; N\right) > 0$ and $\Pi - 2\overline{x}\left(\mathbf{q}_2, \Pi; N\right) \geq 0$. It is in the agenda setter's interest to do that because by reducing the government size by a small amount, the total social surplus increases, and at the same time the other groups have an incentive to agree to a tighter budget. Consider two subcases below.

Case B1   If $\max\left\{\widehat{G}\left(\mathbf{q}_2\right), \widetilde{G}\left(\mathbf{q}_2\right)\right\} \leq G^*_N$, *then $\overline{x}\left(\mathbf{q}_2, G^*_N; N\right) \geq 0$ and $G^*_N - 2\overline{x}\left(\mathbf{q}_2, G^*_N; N\right) \geq 0$. Therefore the agenda setter can successfully propose a policy that leads to an efficient government size by spending $\overline{x}\left(\mathbf{q}_2, G^*_N; N\right)$ on each of the other groups and $G^*_N - 2\overline{x}\left(\mathbf{q}_2, G^*_N\right)$ on his own group.*

Case B2   If $\max\left\{\widehat{G}\left(\mathbf{q}_2\right), \widetilde{G}\left(\mathbf{q}_2\right)\right\} > G^*_N$, *then either $\overline{x}\left(\mathbf{q}_2, G^*_N\right) < 0$ or $G^*_N - 2\overline{x}\left(\mathbf{q}_2, G^*_N; N\right) < 0$. Before the agenda setter reduces total government expenditure to its efficient level, he hits the corner. There are two possibilities. In one case, the agenda setter has no incentive to propose a policy that leads to a* *government smaller than* $\widehat{G}\left(\mathbf{q}_2\right)$, *since otherwise the lost utility due to the last dollar cut is 1, but the cost savings are strictly smaller than* $\frac{1}{3}C'_N\left(\overline{G}_N\right) = 1$. *In the other case, the agenda setter wants to cut total expenditure, but the expenditure on his group is already down to zero and the other two legislators do not allow him to cut expenditures on their groups. In the latter case, the equilibrium government size is* $\widetilde{G}\left(\mathbf{q}_2\right)$.

This establishes the result for a status quo government size of $\sum_{\ell=a}^{c} q_{\ell,2} > \overline{G}_N$. An analogous argument holds for the case of $G_N^* < \sum_{\ell=a}^{c} q_{\ell,2} \leq \overline{G}_N$.

9.5   The First Period

Throughout this section, consider an initial status quo $\mathbf{q}_1 \in X$ such that $\sum_{\ell=a}^{c} q_{\ell,1} = G_N^*$. That is, assume that the economy has been in a normal state, and the government size has reached its socially optimal level. We now conduct an impulse-response analysis by assuming that the economy is hit by some temporary random shock S_1 in the first period, but reverts to its normal state at $S_2 = N$ in the second period.

9.5.1   General Intuition

As in the previous section, it is useful to transform the agenda setter's maximization problem.

First, note that if the initial status quo $\mathbf{q}_1$ remains in the first period, according to Section 9.4.2, the second-period equilibrium policy will be $g_{i,2}^*\left(\mathbf{q}_1; N\right) = \min\left\{q_{b,1}, q_{c,1}\right\}$ for each of the other groups $i = b, c$, and $g_{a,2}^*\left(\mathbf{q}_1; N\right) = G_N^* - 2 \min\left\{q_{b,1}, q_{c,1}\right\}$. Therefore, the discounted sum of utility of group $i \in \{b, c\}$ will be

$$W_i\left(\mathbf{q}_1; S_1\right) = (1 - \beta)\left(q_{i,1} - \frac{1}{3}C_{S_1}\left(G_N^*\right)\right)$$

$$+ \beta\left(\min\left\{q_{b,1}, q_{c,1}\right\} - \frac{1}{3}C_N\left(G_N^*\right)\right).$$

In the period-one equilibrium, either the nonnegativity constraint or the incentive compatibility constraint is binding. In other words, the agenda setter must choose a policy $\mathbf{x}'_1 \in X$ with $\Pi'_1 = \sum_{\ell=a}^c x'_{\ell,1}$ such that for any $i \in \{b, c\}$, either $x'_{i,1} = 0$, or

$$W_i \left(\mathbf{x}'_1; S_1\right) = (1 - \beta) \left(x'_{i,1} - \frac{1}{3} C_{S_1} \left(\Pi'_1\right)\right)$$

$$+ \beta \left(g^*_{i,2} \left(\mathbf{x}'_1; N\right) - \frac{1}{3} C_N \left(\sum_{\ell=a}^c g^*_{\ell,2} \left(\mathbf{x}'_1; N\right)\right)\right)$$

$$= \min \left\{W_{b,1} \left(\mathbf{q}_1; S_1\right), W_{b,1} \left(\mathbf{q}_1; S_1\right)\right\}.$$

To see that this claim holds, suppose otherwise. In that case, the agenda setter could always reduce the provision of government programs to the other groups by a small amount and still obtain support from the more disadvantaged group, which would be a contradiction. For the moment, ignore the nonnegativity constraint and let $\tilde{x} \left(\mathbf{q}_1, \Pi'_1; S_1\right)$ be such that, for any initial status quo $\mathbf{q}_1$, any period-one economic state S_1, and any chosen government size Π'_1,

$$(1 - \beta) \left(\tilde{x} \left(\mathbf{q}_1, \Pi'_1; S_1\right) - \frac{1}{3} C_{S_1} \left(\Pi'_1\right)\right)$$

$$+ \beta \left(g^*_{i,2} \left(\tilde{\mathbf{x}}'_1; N\right) - \frac{1}{3} C_N \left(\sum_{\ell=a}^c g^*_{\ell,2} \left(\tilde{\mathbf{x}}'_1; N\right)\right)\right)$$

$$= \min \left\{W_{b,1} \left(\mathbf{q}_1; S_1\right), W_{c,1} \left(\mathbf{q}_1; S_1\right)\right\},$$

where

$$\tilde{x}'_{b,1} = \tilde{x}'_{c,1} = \tilde{x} \left(\mathbf{q}_1, \Pi'_1; S_1\right),$$

and

$$\tilde{x}'_{a,1} = \sum_{\ell=a}^c \tilde{x}'_{\ell,1} - 2\tilde{x} \left(\mathbf{q}_1, \Pi'_1; S_1\right).$$

Then, in equilibrium

$$x'_{b,1} = x'_{c,1} = \max \left\{0, \tilde{x} \left(\mathbf{q}_1, \sum_{\ell=a}^c \tilde{x}'_{\ell,1}; S_1\right)\right\}, \tag{9.9}$$

and

$$\tilde{x}'_{a,1} = \sum_{\ell=a}^c \tilde{x}'_{\ell,1} - 2 \max \left\{0, \tilde{x} \left(\mathbf{q}_1, \sum_{\ell=a}^c \tilde{x}'_{\ell,1}; S_1\right)\right\}. \tag{9.10}$$

We can now apply this argument and transform the original problem into a maximization problem in which the agenda setter directly chooses the size of the total government budget $\Pi'_1 = \sum_{\ell=a}^c x'_{\ell,1}$. Once Π'_1 is chosen, the respective sizes of government programs for all socioeconomic groups are now determined by (9.9) and (9.10).

For any government size Π_1' to be feasible, it must be that $2\widetilde{x}\left(\mathbf{q}_1, \Pi_1'; S_1\right)$ $\leq \Pi_1'$, so that the spending level on the agenda setter's group is nonnegative. Let

$$\mathcal{F}_1\left(\mathbf{q}_1; S_1\right) = \left\{\Pi \in \mathbb{N} : 2\widetilde{x}\left(\mathbf{q}_1, \Pi; S_1\right) \leq \Pi\right\}.$$

The transformed problem is then as simple as

$$\max_{\Pi_1' \leq \mathbb{N}} (1 - \beta)\left(x_{a,1}' - \frac{1}{3}C_N\left(\Pi_1'\right)\right)$$

$$+ \beta\left(g_{a,1}^*\left(\mathbf{x}_1'; N\right) - \frac{1}{3}C_N\left(\sum_{\ell=a}^c g_{\ell,1}^*\left(\mathbf{x}_1'; N\right)\right)\right)$$

s.t. $\Pi_1' \in \mathcal{F}_1\left(\mathbf{q}_1; S_1\right)$.

$$x_{a,1}' = \Pi_1' - 2\max\left\{0, \widetilde{x}\left(\mathbf{q}_1, \Pi_1'; S_1\right)\right\},$$

$$x_{b,1}' = x_{c,1}' = \max\left\{0, \widetilde{x}\left(\mathbf{q}_1, \Pi_1'; S_1\right)\right\}.$$

In the subsections that follow, we characterize the period-two equilibrium policy and relate it to the status quo government size. Again we divide the discussion into three parts according to whether the status quo government budget is efficient, too small, or too large.

9.5.2 Stable Economy Benchmark

Suppose $S_1 = N$, that is, there is no shock and the economy is stable in the normal state. By an argument analogous to that above (Section 9.4.2), we can show that, in equilibrium, the efficient status quo government size is retained in both periods.

Proposition 9.4   *Suppose $S_1 = N$. For any $\mathbf{q}_1 \in X$ such that $\sum_{\ell=a}^c q_{\ell,1} = G_N^*$:*

1. *In equilibrium, the status quo government size remains and the socially optimal government size is attained in both periods. That is,*

$$\sum_{\ell=a}^c x_{\ell,1} = \sum_{\ell=a}^c x_{\ell,2} = G_N^*.$$

2. *The period-one equilibrium policy is*

$$g_{b,1}^*\left(\mathbf{q}_1; N\right) = g_{c,1}^*\left(\mathbf{q}_1; N\right) = \min\left\{q_{b,1}, q_{c,1}\right\}, \text{ and}$$

$$g_{a,1}^*\left(\mathbf{q}_1; N\right) = q_{a,1} + \max\left\{q_{b,1}, q_{c,1}\right\} - \min\left\{q_{b,1}, q_{c,1}\right\}.$$

If the agenda setter ever deviated from the efficient status quo government size, he would actually make the total social surplus smaller. Note that the agenda setter has to satisfy each of the other groups by $\min \{W_{b,1} (\mathbf{q}_1; N), W_{c,1} (\mathbf{q}_1; N)\}$, which is a constant, in order to pass any new policy. If the total social surplus were smaller, the agenda setter's group would have to take a smaller residual. This shows why the agenda setter would like to maintain the status quo government size. Given this, the remaining open issue pertains only to the distribution of the budget among the socioeconomic groups. The agenda setter simply satisfies the more disadvantaged group and expropriates the other group as much as possible.

Proposition 9.4 implies that, with a persistent agenda setter, if the state of the economy does not change, the policy remains the same over time. If the agenda setter ever adopts a new policy, this is done at the very beginning of the legislative session.

9.5.3 A Temporary Positive Shock

Suppose $S_1 = H$, that is, a temporary positive shock occurs in the first period. This means that the status quo government size $\sum_{\ell=a}^{c} q_{\ell,1} = G_N^* < G_H^*$ is too small compared to the efficient solution. We now need to derive the equilibrium response to this temporary shock. Will the total government budget rise in the first period and then drop in the second? The next proposition answers this question.

Proposition 9.5   *Suppose $S_1 = H$. For any $\mathbf{q}_1 \in X$ such that $\sum_{\ell=a}^{c} q_{\ell,1} = G_N^*$ and $\min \{q_{b,1}, q_{c,1}\}$ sufficiently large:*

1. *In equilibrium, the government size rises to $\sum_{\ell=a}^{c} x_{\ell,1} = G_H^*$ in the first period and drops to $\sum_{\ell=a}^{c} x_{\ell,2} = G_N^*$ in the second period. In both periods, the government size is socially optimal and fully responsive to the change of economic environment.*

2. *The period-one equilibrium policy is*

$$g_{b,1}^* (\mathbf{q}_1; N) = g_{c,1}^* (\mathbf{q}_1; N)$$

$$= \min \{q_{b,1}, q_{c,1}\} + \frac{1}{3} ((1-\beta) (C_H (G_H^*) - C_H (G_N^*))$$

$$+ \beta (C_N (G_H^*) - C_N (G_N^*)))$$

$$> \min \{q_{b,1}, q_{c,1}\},$$

and

$$g^*_{a,1}(\mathbf{q_1}; N) = G^*_H - g^*_{b,1}(\mathbf{q_1}; N) - g^*_{c,1}(\mathbf{q_1}; N) > q_{a,1}.$$

Both the agenda setter's group and the more disadvantaged group receive more than their status quo allocations.

3. *The period-two equilibrium policy is*

$$g^*_{b,2}(\mathbf{q^*_2}; H) = g^*_{c,2}(\mathbf{q_1}; H)$$

$$= \min\{q_{b,1}, q_{c,1}\} - \frac{1}{3}(1-\beta)\left((C_N(G^*_H) - C_N(G^*_N))\right.$$

$$\left. - (C_H(G^*_H) - C_H(G^*_N))\right)$$

$$< \min\{q_{b,1}, q_{c,1}\},$$

and

$$g^*_{a,2}(\mathbf{q_1}; H) = G^*_H - g^*_{b,2}(\mathbf{q_1}; H) - g^*_{c,2}(\mathbf{q_1}; H) > q_{a,1}.$$

In the second period, the agenda setter's group receives more than its status quo allocations, while both of the other groups receive strictly less.

With a temporary positive shock, total expenditure expands accordingly. With a larger total spending level, all groups have to bear a larger cost than with the status quo. Therefore, the agenda setter has to increase spending on the other groups just enough to obtain majority support. He can then spend the remaining additional tax revenues on his own group. After the shock ceases to have an effect, total spending is back to its normal level. However, the spending levels on the other groups *do not* return to their original status quo level. Instead, they drop to some level below the initial status quo. In other words, from an efficiency point of view, government spending is fully elastic, but from a distributional point of view, the agenda setter's group benefits.

9.5.4 A Temporary Negative Shock

Suppose $S_1 = L$, that is, a temporary negative shock occurs in the first period. This means that the status quo government size $\sum^c_{\ell=a} q_{\ell,1} = G^*_N > G^*_L$ is too large compared to the efficient case. We want to know how the government responds to this temporary shock. Will it also be fully elastic, that is, will the total government budget drop in the first period to the efficient level and then rebound in the second?

Suppose that the agenda setter chooses a policy $x_1' \in X$ such that $\sum_{\ell=a}^{c} x_{\ell,1}' = \Pi_1'$. First, it is straightforward to show that $\Pi_1' \leq G_N^*$. Suppose otherwise. Then the agenda setter reduces the total social surplus while he still has to offer the other groups a constant value of min $\{W_{b,1}(\mathbf{q}_1; L)$, $W_{c,1}(\mathbf{q}_1; L)\}$ in order to pass any new policy. This is not beneficial to the agenda setter. Since $\Pi_1' \leq G_N^*$, by propositions 9.1 and 9.2, we know that in the second period the agenda setter is able to implement a policy with a total government budget G_N^*. Therefore, the government size will drop in the first period and then rebound when the negative shock goes away. The remaining question is: to what extent?

The analysis in Section 9.5.1 showed that the agenda setter will expropriate as much as possible by giving

$$x_{b,1}' = x_{c,1}' = \tilde{x}\left(\mathbf{q}_1, \Pi_1'; L\right)$$

$$\equiv \min\{q_{b,1}, q_{c,1}\} - \frac{1}{3}(1-\beta)\left(C_L\left(G_N^*\right) - C_L\left(\Pi_1'\right)\right)$$

$$- \frac{1}{3}\beta\left(C_N\left(G_N^*\right) - C_N\left(\Pi_1'\right)\right)$$

to each of the other groups. Note that for x_1' to be feasible, it must be that $\tilde{x}\left(\mathbf{q}_1, \Pi_1'; L\right) \geq 0$ and $x_{a,1}' = \Pi_1' - 2\tilde{x}\left(\mathbf{q}_1, \Pi_1'; L\right) \geq 0$, so that all nonnegativity constraints are satisfied. This imposes constraints on the feasible set of government sizes. Let $\underline{G}^+(\mathbf{q}_1; L)$ be such that $\tilde{x}\left(\mathbf{q}_1, \underline{G}^+(\mathbf{q}_1; L); L\right) = 0$. Then $\tilde{x}\left(\mathbf{q}_1, \Pi_1'; L\right) \geq 0$ if and only if $\Pi_1' \geq \underline{G}^+(\mathbf{q}_1; L)$. Also let $\underline{G}^-(\mathbf{q}_1; L)$ be such that $\tilde{x}\left(\mathbf{q}_1, \underline{G}^-(\mathbf{q}_1; L); L\right) = \frac{1}{2}\underline{G}^-(\mathbf{q}_1; L)$. Then $\Pi_1' - 2\tilde{x}\left(\mathbf{q}_1, \Pi_1'; L\right) \geq 0$ if and only if $\Pi_1' \geq \underline{G}^-(\mathbf{q}_1; L)$. The equilibrium government size then solves the following problem:

$$\max_{\Pi_1' \in \mathbb{N}} (1-\beta)\left(\Pi_1' - x_{b,1}' - x_{c,1}' - \frac{1}{3}C_L\left(\sum_{\ell=a}^{c} x_{\ell,1}'\right)\right)$$

$$+ \beta\left(G_N^* - \sum_{\ell=b}^{c} g_{\ell,2}^*\left(x_2'; N\right) - \frac{1}{3}C_N\left(G_N^*\right)\right)$$

s.t. $\max\{\underline{G}^-(\mathbf{q}_1; L), \underline{G}^+(\mathbf{q}_1; L)\} \leq \Pi_1' \leq G_N^*$,

$$x_{b,1}' = x_{c,1}' = \tilde{x}\left(\mathbf{q}_1, \Pi_1'; L\right).$$

As long as the period-one government expenditure is above its socially optimal level, the agenda setter can gain additional utility by reducing the government size. With a smaller government budget, all groups are released from a heavy tax burden. In order to fully take advantage of this, the agenda setter would like to reduce government programs for the other groups at the same time. However, the agenda setter would face strong resistance from the other groups. The reason lies in the dynamic nature of bargaining, that is, the fact that equilibrium distributions in future periods depend on the status quo allocation, which is determined in the current period. In other words a "temporary" cut in government expenditures has a "permanent" effect in political equilibrium. If the government program on group b is reduced, in the subsequent period group b would be faced with a lower reservation value. This would reduce the bargaining power of group b, which implies that the spending level of group b would be permanently low. Foreseeing this, group b will not allow the agenda setter to substantially cut its allocation and neither will group c. Given this, when decreasing the total government budget, the agenda setter can only slightly reduce allocations to the other groups, which means he has to substantially reduce his own allocation. Eventually, a corner solution is reached, that is, the spending level on the agenda setter's group is 0, and the agenda setter will have no room to cut expenditures any further. This happens when β is sufficiently large and the agenda setter's initial government program is sufficiently small.

It is also possible that the spending levels on the other groups have reached 0, so that to reduce the total government budget, the agenda setter has to rely solely on cutting allocations to his own group. As long as the government size is smaller than $\overline{G}_L$, it is not beneficial for him to do that. This is another possible corner solution. This case happens when β and the initial program for one of the other groups are sufficiently small.

These results are summarized in proposition 9.6.

Proposition 9.6   *Suppose $S_1 = L$. For any $\mathbf{q}_1 \in X$ such that $\sum_{\ell=a}^{c} q_{\ell,1} = G_N^*$:*

1. *In equilibrium, the government size is $\max\left\{\max\left\{\underline{G}^-\left(\mathbf{q}_1; L\right),\right.\right.$*
   *$\left.\underline{G}^+\left(\mathbf{q}_1; L\right)\right\}, G_L^*\right\}$ *in the first period, and G_N^* in the second period. The government size in the second period is always socially optimal. In the first period, the government size is insufficiently adjusted downward if $\underline{G}^-\left(\mathbf{q}_1; L\right) > G_L^*$ or $\underline{G}^+\left(\mathbf{q}_1; L\right) > G_L^*$. That is, policy persistence is more likely to happen if the initial status quo leads to an unequal distribution of public resources in the sense that the spending level on the most disadvantaged socioeconomic group is sufficiently small.*

2. The period-one equilibrium policy is

$$g_{b,1}^* \left(\mathbf{q}_1; L \right) = g_{c,1}^* \left(\mathbf{q}_1; L \right)$$

$$= \min \left\{ q_{b,1}, q_{c,1} \right\} - \frac{1}{3} \left(1 - \beta \right) \left(C_L \left(G_N^* \right) - C_L \left(\Pi_1^* \right) \right)$$

$$- \frac{1}{3} \beta \left(C_N \left(G_N^* \right) - C_N \left(\Pi_1^* \right) \right),$$

$$g_{a,1}^* \left(\mathbf{q}_1; L \right) = \Pi_1^* - g_{b,1}^* \left(\mathbf{q}_1; L \right) - g_{c,1}^* \left(\mathbf{q}_1; L \right) > q_{a,1},$$

where Π_1^* refers to the equilibrium government size in the first period. Both of the groups without proposal power get less in the first period than their status quo allocation.

9.6   Discussion

Our theory has two separate components. First, notice that the period-two equilibrium can be interpreted as the equilibrium in a one-period model. Even in that case, we are able to provide an explanation for the ratchet effect. The key insight is that the equilibrium government size depends on the status quo allocation, but in an asymmetric manner: it is easy for government spending to rise but difficult for it to fall. If the status quo spending level is too low, that is, smaller than the efficient level, then through legislative bargaining, the government programs will expand in equilibrium. The agenda setter can always seek support by spending part of the additional tax revenues on the other socioeconomic groups. However, the situation is different when the status quo spending level is too high. In order for the agenda setter to enjoy the benefits of budget contraction, he has to be able to cut down the government programs targeted at some other socioeconomic group. If the status quo policy already gives the other groups very few public resources, the agenda setter will not have sufficient leeway to do this. In an extreme case, the agenda setter can reduce total government expenditure to the point that nothing is spent on the other groups and the agenda setter has to bear any additional cuts solely by himself. However, because the agenda setter is only able to partially capture the net benefits from such a contraction, he does not reduce the government size to the efficient level.

The key mechanism in this single-period model may be further developed and integrated into a fully specified macroeconomics or public finance model. Suppose that for certain periods there is an extraordinary need for a certain public good x_i so that the spending level on this good rises substantially and the spending levels of the other goods are cut down. Consider, for example, national security crises or wars, which will lead to a dramatic increase in defense spending including significant long-term health care and pension benefits for veterans. Unless the increase in spending has a predefined termination clause (a so-called sunset provision), this policy will be in effect until a new law is passed. However, now the increased budget has become the status quo, with a high total spending level, and there is an unequal allocation of the total budget on different spending items. Our model shows not only how this status quo spending level will get locked in, but how it may lead to further increases. This provides an explanation for the ratchet effect.

The one-period model is a good approximation for the case where a policy takes effect after the legislative session ends. For example, a parliament that is in session for two years may make a change (say, to the social security system) that will take place three years from now. However, in many cases a sitting parliament will have to revisit a policy within its current session. This includes, of course, the annual budget. In this case, a one-period model may not capture all the relevant dynamics. The key point is that by adopting a policy for the current period, parliament is endogenously determining the status quo for the next period when it is still in session. This may lead to additional strategic effects as a change in the status quo affects each representative's future bargaining position. This leads to a second explanation for the ratchet effect and provides insights for the persistence of high levels of government spending in multiparty, parliamentary democracies.

In the multiperiod case, nonproposing parties need to take into account that any reduction made now, even if it is efficient for the whole society in the current period, will permanently lock them into a lower level of allocated spending. This follows because the current sizes of continuing public programs will be the status quo in future periods. As the economy rebounds from a recession, making it easier to raise taxes, the agenda setter will exploit the lower reservation values of the other socioeconomic groups so that public programs for those groups will never rebound accordingly. But with every group foreseeing this effect, downward adjustment of public expenditures has to be achieved by disproportionately cutting the public program for the agenda setter's group. At most, the agenda setter can reduce total government expenditure down to the point where nothing is spent on his own group. Beyond this point, any fiscal adjustment faces a strong resistance from the groups without agenda control. Policy persistence thus results.

In our model, policy persistence occurs in a corner solution where some of the nonnegativity constraints are binding. Either nothing is spent on the groups that have no proposal power or nothing is spent on the agenda setter's group. Of course this finding should not be interpreted literally. The agenda setter may have to provide some minimum allocation to the other groups or to his own group for other (unmodeled) reasons. For example, with a large senior population with little personal savings, it may be difficult or constitutionally prohibited to literally reduce social security benefits to zero. In other words, our model only captures that part of the budget that realistically and legally can be cut. Another important point is that our model does not capture positive externalities of government programs across different socioeconomic groups. If the agenda setter's group partially benefits from spending on other groups, for example, by providing education subsidies, he may not want to fully eliminate those programs. Finally, the quasi-linear assumption may be too much of a simplification. If the utilities derived from public programs have diminishing marginal returns, when the expenditure on some group ℓ is sufficiently small, the marginal utility of group ℓ on its public program may be sufficiently high. In this case, a corner solution will never be reached, yet we will still observe the ratchet effect as an interior solution.

Even our simple model yields various testable empirical implications. First and importantly, it generates a version of the ratchet effect of total spending. As the economy is hit by an unexpected temporary positive shock, the total spending expands and the extra spending disproportionately benefits the agenda setter's group. As the economy is hit by an unexpected temporary negative shock, the total spending may not be fully adjusted downward.

Second, in empirical studies, Persson and Tabellini (2001, 2003, 2004) identify the ratchet effect in parliamentary democracies that have proportional representation. Our intuition suggests that what matters, strictly speaking, is the form of government that makes fiscal policy decisions. In other words, what is important is not proportional representation per se but multiparty legislative bargaining. Proportional representation is only important as it usually leads to multiparty parliaments without a majority party. In other words, the ratchet effect *should* also be observed in the case of a hung parliament in the majoritarian-parliamentary case and *should not* be observed in the rare cases where elections under proportional representation yield a majority party. To test this intuition, we could possibly look at fiscal policy dynamics in countries during different regimes: regimes with a majority party, and regimes with a minority parliament and coalition governments. We conjecture that the ratchet effect is more prevalent when fiscal policy is determined by a coalition government.

Third, ratchet effects are particularly pronounced for large negative shocks. If we relate the larger marginal cost of public expenditure to a negative income shock, the model predicts that government expenditure is inertial if the income level of the economy substantially deviates from and gets below its long-run trend. The intuition is that the agenda setter may have difficulty cutting spending on the other legislators; he can mainly cut his own benefit. If the negative shock is small, the agenda setter is able to do so and adjust total spending to its new socially optimal value. However, if the negative shock is sufficiently large, the agenda setter leaves zero benefit to himself and, at this corner solution, he is not able to further reduce public spending. As a consequence, there is overspending compared to the first-best solution.

Fourth, our model also implies that, whenever the government size is not fully downward elastic, the allocation of public resources on various socioeconomic groups will be highly unequal. Therefore, there is a positive relationship between policy persistence and inequality of public budget allocation.

It should be noted that as long as the status quo government size is not too big compared to its efficient level, the equilibrium policy attains socially optimal public fiscal policies. This is due to the possibility of reconsideration by the agenda setter. In order to obtain voting support from group j, the agenda setter is forced not to expropriate group k. As a consequence, the agenda setter faces equilibrium spending constraints on both of the other groups. These constraints make the agenda setter fully internalize all costs and benefits of public expenditure, whenever the expenditure on any group is strictly positive. It is easy to verify that, without possibility of reconsideration, the equilibrium government size is always larger than its socially optimal level regardless of the status quo, leading to inefficiency in all cases. Paradoxically, granting some political actors more power may be social-welfare enhancing.

Note also that the agenda setter would be better off if he were able to commit to a certain allocation (this is what happens in models without reconsideration). However, this is ruled out by the ongoing possibility of reconsideration. While it is commonly accepted that lack of commitment by the policymaker is a source of inefficiency,[4] our model shows that lack of commitment by the agenda setter with persistent proposal power in fact may lead to more egalitarian divisions and more efficient government size.

Finally, our analysis also demonstrates the general point that in order to understand the size of government expenditures in a political economy framework, it is important to look at its composition as well. The issues of efficiency and distribution cannot be separated.

Conclusion   In this chapter we provide an institutional explanation for the so-called ratchet effect: the observation that in proportional-parliamentary democracies, economic downturns lead to a lasting expansion of outlays and welfare spending in proportion to GDP that is not reversed during upturns. We model proportional-parliamentary democracies as a multiparty legislative bargaining game with reconsideration and a single agenda setter. The political economy model is then applied to the case of public-goods provision with distortionary taxes. We show that in contrast to other bargaining models, in equilibrium proposers are less able to expropriate other members of the legislature. This makes it more difficult for proposers to secure approval for a contraction of government spending in cyclical downturns. On the other hand, spending increases in upturns can always be supported in equilibrium. We then extend our analysis to a multiperiod model where the government needs to respond to random temporary income shocks. We show that these dynamic considerations create additional incentives for strategic behavior consistent with the ratchet effect.

An immediate next step of this research agenda is to investigate how the bargaining frictions identified in this chapter can *quantitatively* account for policy persistence in multiparty parliamentary countries. Such a numerical project requires a more specific macroeconomic or public finance setup than the reduced forms assumed in this chapter. It would also require an infinite-horizon model so that we could look at an equilibrium that is stationary not only within periods (as in the current model) but also across periods.

Second, our current model implicitly assumes balanced budgets in every period. How the ability to use public debt as an additional fiscal instrument would change the analysis is an open question.

Third, since economic policy is made through the political process, a complete understanding of policy dynamics in democracies also requires an understanding of how political power transits from one group to another.

Whatever policy is chosen in one period may affect not only the status quo in the next period but also which group captures agenda control in the future. In other words, the identity of the agenda setter would be endogenous. If the incumbent can manipulate fiscal policies so that he is more likely to obtain or retain power in the future, we may expect more inertia in fiscal policies. To answer this question, two approaches can be followed. First, we can explicitly model parliamentary elections with sophisticated voters, as in the model of Baron, Diermeier, and Fong (2007). Second, different socio-economic groups may directly spend resources or exert efforts to compete for political power (Yildirim 2007).

ACKNOWLEDGMENTS

We wish to thank the Canadian Institute for Advanced Research (CIFAR) for generous funding, and members of CIFAR's Institutions, Organizations, and Growth Program group for their insightful comments.

NOTES

1. Among the cited papers, Fong (2006), Battaglini and Coate (2007, 2008), and Baron, Diermeier, and Fong (2007) presented dynamic models.
2. See, however, the recent work by Fong (2006), Battaglini and Coate (2007, 2008), and Baron, Diermeier, and Fong (2007).
3. For an extensive survey of related studies see Drazen (2000).
4. See Alesina and Tabellini (1990) and Persson and Svensson (1989) on public debt manipulation, Besley and Coate (1998) for commitment problems in a citizen-candidate modeling framework, Acemoglu and Robinson (2001) for an example about the emergence of inefficient redistribution, and Fong (2006) and Baron, Diermeier, and Fong (2007) for the commitment problem in legislative bargaining institutions. For a comprehensive literature survey see Acemoglu (2003).

REFERENCES

Acemoglu, Daron. 2003. "Why Not a Political Coase Theorem? Social Conflict, Commitment and Politics." *Journal of Comparative Economics* 31:620–762.

Acemoglu, Daron, and James A. Robinson. 2001. "Inefficient Redistribution." *American Political Science Review* 95:649–61.

Aghion, Philippe, and Patrick Bolton. 1990. "Government Domestic Debt and the Risk of Default: A Political-Economic Model of the Strategic Role of Debt."

In *Capital Markets and Debt Management*, eds. R. Dornbusch and M. Draghi. Cambridge, MA: MIT Press.

Alesina, A., and A. Drazen (1991). "Why Are Stabilizations Delayed?" *The American Economic Review* 81:1170–88.

Alesina, Alberto, and D. Rodrik. 1994. "Distributive Politics and Economic Growth." *Quarterly Journal of Economics* 109:465–90.

Alesina, A., N. Roubini, and G. Cohen. 1997. *Political Cycles and the Macroeconomy.* Cambridge, MA: MIT Press.

Alesina, A., and G. Tabellini. 1990. "A Positive Theory of Fiscal Deficits and Government Debt." *Review of Economic Studies* 57:403–14.

Austen-Smith, David, and Jeff Banks. 1988. "Elections, Coalitions, and Legislative Outcomes." *American Political Science Review* 82:405–22.

Baron, David P. 1996. "A Dynamic Theory of Collective Goods Programs."*American Political Science Review* 90:316–30.

Baron, David P., and Daniel Diermeier. 2001. "Elections, Governments, and Parliaments in Proportional Representation Systems." *Quarterly Journal of Economics* 116(3):933–67.

Baron, David P., Daniel Diermeier, and Pohan Fong. 2007. "Policy Dynamics and Inefficiency in a Parliamentary Democracy with Proportional Representation." Working paper, Stanford University.

Baron, David P., and John Ferejohn. 1989. "Bargaining in Legislatures." *American Political Science Review* 83:1181–1206.

Baron, David P., and Michael Herron. 2003. "A Dynamic Model of Multidimensional Collective Choice." In *Computational Models of Political Economy*, eds. Ken Kollman, John H. Miller, and Scott E. Page. Cambridge, MA: MIT Press, 13–47.

Battaglini, Marco, and Stephen Coate. 2007. "Inefficiency in Legislative Policy-Making: A Dynamic Analysis." *American Economic Review* 97(1):118–49.

———. 2008. "A Dynamic Theory of Public Spending, Taxation and Debt." *American Economic Review* 98(1):201–36.

Bernheim, Douglas, Antonio Rangel, and Luis Rayo. 2006. "The Power of the Last Word in Legislative Policy Making." *Econometrica* 74:1161–90.

Besley, Timothy, and Stephen Coate. 1998. "Sources of Inefficiency in a Representative Democracy." *American Economic Review* 88:139–56.

Diermeier, Daniel, and Pohan Fong. 2007. "Legislative Bargaining with Reconsideration." Mimeo, Concordia University.

Diermeier, Daniel, and Antonio Merlo. 2000. "Government Turnover in Parliamentary Democracies." *Journal of Economic Theory* 94:46–79.

———. 2004. "An Empirical Investigation of Coalitional Bargaining Procedures." *Journal of Public Economics* 88:783–97.

Doering, Herbert. 1995. "Time as a Scarce Resource: Government Control of the Agenda." In *Parliaments and Majority Rule in Western Europe*, ed. Herbert Doering. New York: St. Martin's Press.

Drazen, A. 2000. *Political Economy in Macroeconomics*. Princeton, NJ: Princeton University Press.

Drazen, A., and V. Grilli. 1993. "The Benefits of Crises for Economic Reform." *American Economic Review* 83:3.

Duggan, John, and Tasos Kalandrakis. 2007. "A Dynamic Model of Legislative Bargaining." Working paper, University of Rochester.

Duverger, Maurice. 1952. "Public Opinion and Political Parties in France." *American Political Science Review* 46:1069–78.

Fernandez, R., and D. Rodrik. 1991. "Resistance to Reform: Status Quo Bias in the Presence of Individual-Specific Uncertainty." *American Economic Review* 81(5): 1146–55.

Fong, Pohan. 2004. "Dynamic Legislation through Bargaining." Mimeo, Concordia University.

———. 2006. "Dynamics of Government and Policy Choice." Mimeo, Concordia University.

Hassler, J., P. Krusell, K. Storesletten, and F. Zilibotti. 2005. "The Dynamics of Government." *Journal of Monetary Economics* 52(7):1331–58.

Hassler, J., J. Mora, K. Storesletten, and F. Zilibotti. 2003. "The Survival of the Welfare State." *American Economic Review* 93(1):87–112.

Kalandrakis, Anastassios. 2004. "A Three-Player Dynamic Majoritarian Bargaining Game." *Journal of Economic Theory* 16:294–322.

Knight, Brian. 2005. "Estimating the Value of Proposal Power." *The American Economic Review* 95(5):1639–52.

Krusell, P., and V.-J. Rios-Rull. 1996. "Vested interests in a positive theory of stagnation and growth." *Review of Economic Studies* 63(2):301–29.

Lindbeck, Arthur, and Jorgen W. Weibull. 1987. "Balanced-budget Redistribution as the Outcome of Political Competition." *Public Choice* 52(3):273–97.

Lizzeri, Alessandro, and Nicola Persico. 2001. "The Provision of Public Goods under Alternative Electoral Incentives." *American Economic Review* 91(March): 225–39.

Meltzer, A. H., and S. F. Richard. 1981. "A Rational Theory of the Size of Government." *Journal of Political Economy* 89(5):914–27.

Milesi-Ferretti, Gian Maria, Roberto Perotti, and Massimo Rostagno. 2002. "Electoral Systems and Public Spending." *Quarterly Journal of Economics* 117(2):609–57.

Olson, M. 1982. *The Rise and Decline of Nations*. New Haven, CT: Yale University Press.

Pagano, M., and P. F. Volpin. 2006. "The Political Economy of Corporate Governance." *American Economic Review* 95(4):1005–30.

Persson, Torsten, Gerard Roland, and Guido Tabellini. 2000. "Comparative Politics and Public Finance." *Journal of Political Economy* 108:1121–61.

Persson, Torsten, and L. Svensson. 1989. "Why a Stubborn Conservative Would Run a Deficit: Policy with Time-Inconsistent Preferences." *Quarterly Journal of Economics* 104(2):325–45.

Persson, Torsten, and Guido Tabellini. 1994. "Is Inequality Harmful for Growth?" *American Economic Review* 84(3):600–21.

———. 1999. "The Size and Scope of Government: Comparative Politics with Rational Politicians." *European Economic Review* 43:699–735.

———. 2001. "Political Institutions and Policy Outcomes: What Are the Stylized Facts?" Banca D'Italia working paper no. 412.

———. 2003. *The Economic Effects of Constitutions. The Munich Lectures in Economics*. Cambridge, MA: MIT Press.

———. 2004. "Constitutional Rules and Fiscal Policy Outcomes." *American Economic Review* 94(1):25–45.

Rogoff, Kenneth. 1990. "Equilibrium Political Budget Cycles." *American Economic Review* 80:21–36.

Riboni, Allesandro, and F. Ruge-Murcia. 2007. "The Dynamic (In)efficiency of Monetary Policy by Committee." Working paper, University of Montreal.

Yildirim, Huseyin. 2007. "Proposal Power and Majority Rule in Multilateral Bargaining with Costly Recognition." *Journal of Economic Theory* 136(1): 167–96.

— III —

Contemporary Evidence

— 10 —

Formalizing Informal Institutions

Theory and Evidence from a Kenyan Slum

SIWAN ANDERSON AND PATRICK FRANCOIS

10.1 Introduction

Since Weber, the rise of the West has been associated with a rise in formalism in everything from the arts and music to the governing of personal relations, political relations, and economic ties. Yet why formalization matters for long-term growth and how the process of formalization unfolds are only beginning to be understood. The works of Acemoglu and Robinson, Greif, Besley, Persson and Tabellini, and other contributors to this volume have been key in defining the perspective from which institutions are studied by economists today, and have framed the questions on which progress will be defined in future. We bring these questions back to the details of development in one of the world's poorest locations, Kibera, a slum of over one million inhabitants, which sits on the outskirts of Nairobi.

We study the degree of formalism that self-sustaining groups invoke to help govern their relations in Kibera. We are interested in knowing what features of self-sustaining groups make some choose informal structures of governance, while others choose formal ones. By formalism, we mean implementing rules, procedures, and codified adjudication methods that clearly specify actions to be taken in contingencies, rather than relying on the discretion of decision makers when such contingencies arise. Generally such formalism is hard to measure, but here we bring concrete data to the investigation of the phenomenon. The data provide a snapshot of steps of increased formalization being taken by otherwise informal groups.[1] A place like Kibera is one of the best to study the behavior of informal groups, because groups formed here can be set up beyond the direct reach of the usual instruments of coercion, both political and legal. They are thus a relatively pure example of self-enforcing institutions, which can autonomously decide on the structure of their decision-making protocols and collective rules.

The information we have on them contains numerous variables that are good proxies for this formalization process. We have information about groups' attempts to codify their rules on expected behavior, their attempts to spell out clear punishments in case of transgression, and perhaps most importantly, their attempts to provide external oversight regarding decision making by inviting outside scrutiny over group behavior and decisions.

Our study relates broadly to the study of institutional development, which is increasingly seen as a key to economic development. At the countrywide level, the usual institutions of interest are the macropolitical and legal ones, whose development has long been known to be correlated with income levels and which are increasingly evidenced as having an important causative role.[2] Micro-level institutions, where our study is focused, though necessarily of more localized impact, have the advantage of allowing a deeper characterization of institutional details.[3] But what is unique here is our focus on a set of institutions where the first steps of formalization seem to be emerging. This may help us better understand the conditions under which these formal components are useful and why they might arise. Avner Greif's work over the long historical spread of western European institutional formation is explicitly concerned with the dynamics of institution formation too; see Greif (1994, 2006) and his contribution to the present volume (chapter 1). By analyzing the historical underpinnings of western European market institutions in medieval trade, his work illuminates the process by which institutions may have morphed into the complex structures that we observe today. Though only a static picture is provided by the work here, this may still have implications for this dynamic process if we are glimpsing the first steps from fully discretionary decision making to something more restricted.

Relatedly, others have noted that, in successful community development programs, linkages by informal groups to outside authorities are forged incrementally (Rao and Woolcock 2001). Here we unearth reasons why these and other actions of formalization may arise. One key determinant seems to be a group's ethnic structure. A reasonable conjecture emanating from the literature on social capital is that groups of homogeneous ethnic structure, presumably rich in social ties, should find relying on formalization less necessary.[4] Formalization instead should arise to strengthen group cohesion in places where individuals do not bring strong, externally based interconnections to their informal groups. This is consistent with anecdotal observations comparing formalization (which is strong in the developed West, where traditional or ethnic ties are weak) with lower formalization in less developed countries (LDCs) (where traditional or ethnic ties are strong). The first striking and robust empirical finding here is that, contrary to the conjecture above, the groups constituted along ethnic lines are the ones most likely to choose these formal procedures. Groups formed among unrelated individuals, with presumably weaker interindividual connections, seem more content to persist with informal decision making and procedures.[5]

We conjecture that this is because the ties that are usually seen as beneficial in overcoming agency, moral hazard, and enforcement problems in informal groups can also have a downside. Specifically, these ties, which consist of social links between kin members that extend beyond the workings of the group, impose social and psychological costs on individuals when it comes to punishing recalcitrant group members. Lacking formal sanctions, punishment in self-enforcing groups amounts to exclusion from future interaction with the group. We posit that when an individual from a group organized along kin lines is excluded from the group, both the individual being punished and the remaining members of the group suffer these costs.

The effects of these nonpecuniary costs on the punished are well known and have been thoroughly analyzed previously. They raise the cost of cheating, and thus help in sustaining informal group functioning. However, the effects of these costs on the punishers have, to our knowledge, not received any attention in the economics literature.[6] Costs that are similar to the ones we posit have, however, come to increasing prominence in recent work in organizational science. Schulze et al. (2001), for example, identify the cost imposed on agency relationships when members are linked by altruistic tendencies toward each other in the context of family firms. One of these costs is difficulty in disciplining family members, which they argue can make agency problems in family firms worse than those in standard firms. According to them, connections between family members can get in the way: "Altruism, on the other hand, can make parent owner-managers unable or unwilling to properly administer incentive programs. The altruist's ability to enforce agreements is often compromised by the ramifications that such actions might have on familial relationships, both within and among extended family. Both phenomenons, if carried into the family firm, make it difficult for owner managers to discipline family agents and enforce agreements" (p. 111).[7]

In the formal model that we develop, the main impact of these connections is to raise the costs of dismissing, and hence weaken the credibility of punishing, recalcitrant group members. Since the credibility of punishment is key to the effective functioning of such groups, the informal groups seek to respond by altering their governance protocols. We analyze two ways in which they do this. The first is by formalizing decision making, in the ways outlined above, and the second is by strengthening decision makers' incentives to follow through on promised punishments by asking members to post membership fees as bonds.

The chapter is also related to work on the interaction between formal and informal institutions. For example, Arnott and Stiglitz (1991) argued that, in the context of insurance, well-functioning informal insurance mechanisms that provide protection against small shocks could undermine the diffusion of formal insurance by compromising the ability of formal insurers to impose deductibles on clients.[8] In contrast, we are not directly concerned with the interaction between the formal and informal institutions here, but instead with the means by which the formal may emerge from the informal.

Our emphasis on ethnicity also relates this to previous work on the role of ethnic ties in sustaining cooperation between individuals in informal groups (for example, La Ferrara 2003; Fafchamps 1992; Udry 1994; Bates 1990). The literature on informal group formation and social capital has pointed to the role of kinship ties. The theoretical underpinnings of sustaining cooperative outcomes in informal settings relates back to the folk theorem and the benefits of information flows both within and outside the group (for example, Kandori 1992). A standard result theoretically, which has been confirmed in empirical settings, is that improvements in the quality of information flows between group members should help in creating functional institutions. Such information flows are often thought to be linked to the quality of social and extrasituational ties between the individuals (for example, Besley and Coate 1995). Similar insights underlie attempts to improve lending to the poor by exploiting their information sharing in setting up joint-liability lending (for example, Ghatak 1999; Morduch 1999). Our focus is instead on the effects that such ties have on the credibility of punishing recalcitrant group members rather than on their effects in aiding information flows.

Alternative means of supporting cooperative behavior have been the invoking of bonding technologies (Kranton 1996). A type of bond also plays an important role in the groups we study—however, once again, for different reasons than have been emphasized in the previous literature. Bonds are usually seen to help in ensuring that individuals liable to moral hazard have an incentive to take the actions they promise (or forfeit their bond).[9] Here the bonds we analyze aid the credibility of following through on threatened punishments once moral hazard has occurred.

This chapter is also related to the downside of the social capital created by ties of ethnicity, though for different reasons than have previously been suggested. Previously the extent of ties between individuals, and the lack of these ties across other individuals, have been seen to stifle the extent to which production can move beyond the kin group. Woolcock and Narayan (2000) survey this literature, and Francois and Zabojnik (2005) develop a theory emphasizing the role these ties play in the implementation of modern technologies. Here, however, the cost we identify is more direct, in that the flip side of the benefit they generate in imposing costs on morally hazardous behavior is the imposition of similar costs on those who must punish the deviators.

We first develop a simple model to analyze our claims that kinship ties may create problems with punishment, and to tease out empirical implications. A natural issue that arises is how these posited problems of kinship interact with the well-known benefits that such ties create in raising the costs of morally hazardous behavior. The model we develop makes clear that the beneficial side of kinship is that it is useful in helping sustain interactions that are of relatively low intrinsic value to members. Groups of higher intrinsic value will be sustainable both with and without ethnic homogeneity. However, it is at these high values where kin groups encounter the additional difficulty that arises from the credibility of enforcement—although this is also a difficulty that all informal groups will have, it is worse for them. Consequently, formalization is a means to overcome this and, though used by all groups, will be more intensively used by the kin groups. The alternative to formalization is providing internal (to the group) incentives for individuals to punish transgressors. As will be seen, this is costly in the present context—with the costs being proxied by membership fees—but there is a trade-off between providing this internally costly incentive to punish versus relying on costly formalization procedures to take over the role from the outside.

The model makes clear predictions about what sort of groups will choose formalism, how these should relate to membership fees, the value of groups, and the capacity that groups have to punish. We explore these conjectures in the data. The chapter proceeds as follows. The next two sections outline the data and the key variables and relationships that will form the basic building blocks of our model. The model is then built to explore the ways in which these key features interact. Specifically, what are the reduced-form relationships between the key variables we observe: ethnicity, formalization, membership fees, and the value of groups. We then test these implications on the data in section 10.5 and subsequently discuss these implications and certain other observed correlations. We then conclude.

10.2   The Context

We exploit unique data that comes from a survey of households conducted in 1997 in the slum of Kibera, which is located on the outskirts of Nairobi, Kenya.[10] The slum is one of the largest in Africa, extends over 250 hectares of land, and is purported to house a population of more than one million people. The inhabitants are very poor. They live with enormous risks to their health and income, with no access to formal insurance or credit institutions. There is little activity by the state to improve the well-being of the slum population. Individuals are left to their own devices to meet their most basic needs. These circumstances have given rise to the formation of numerous informal groups that come together for the purposes of savings, insurance, and investment.

Individuals from approximately 520 households were interviewed, all living in the same area of Kibera, namely the village of Kianda.[11] In addition to the standard household survey information, the survey asked individuals details of informal group membership and details about the characteristics of the groups in which they participate. Over 80% of households in the slum had at least one member in at least one informal group, and from this process, information on approximately 600 groups was collected. Characteristics of these groups include information on function of the group, ethnic composition, membership fees, group duration, disputes, punishments, and formalization attempts.

The groups provided three distinct functions and are thus divided into three categories. About 60% of the groups have a savings role. These function as rotating savings and credit associations (ROSCAs). The groups meet regularly, and each member attends the meeting with an equivalent prespecified monetary amount. The total contribution of all individuals is then taken home by one individual. The identity of the individual changes each time there is a meeting until a cycle of all members is completed. This method of saving is one of the most common in the developing world and is the subject of a considerable literature in economics.[12]

Approximately 30% of groups serve an insurance function. These generally provide two types of insurance. The first is medical insurance for individuals who fall sick. These groups may cover the costs of medical treatment for household members, as well as support for dependents in case of lost earnings due to incapacity. The second type of insurance is covering funeral and body transport costs in case of death. Most members of the slum still have some ties to their home village in their tribal area. It is a strongly held belief that the deceased should be interned in their home villages, and the costs of paying for the transport and funeral proceedings are met out of the fund.

The final function, comprising about 25% of groups, is an investment one.[13] Members of investment groups collect their savings into a larger pool, which is then used to generate income for the members. The two main income-generating sources are a bank account and lending to other residents of the slum. The table below lists some summary statistics on the different groups.

We see from Table 10.1 that insurance groups are the largest and have existed the longest in the slum. Membership fees and monthly contributions are in (year 1996) Kenyan shillings, when there were approximately 55 Kenyan shillings to the U.S. dollar. Monthly contributions to these groups are significant as average individual monthly income for a typical household member in the slum is 3526 Kenyan shillings so that group contributions reflect around 15%–20% of earnings. Membership fees are roughly 10% of earnings.

A key variable that will be exploited here is the measure of formalism in groups. A direct measure of this is the binary variable "registered." Groups

Table 10.1 Summary statistics on characteristics of groups

	Savings group	Insurance group	Investment group
Membership	16.1 (11.6)	67.0 (53.7)	34.3 (32.6)
Years existed	2.3 (2.6)	7.6 (7.7)	4.1 (4.6)
Membership fee	219.3 (361.6)	241.2 (503.0)	346.4 (595.7)
Monthly contributions	595.3 (733.4)	655.2 (901.9)	498.4 (588.1)
Number of observations	365	196	143

Note: Standard deviations are in parentheses. Monthly contributions for insurance groups come in two forms. The first is the regular contribution; the second is the average monthly contribution in the form of a spot fund, where members voluntarily contribute funds when an emergency occurs. The membership fees average is computed for the subset that pay such fees.

that are registered are subject to some degree of external oversight. The oversight is usually performed by a social worker, of which there are many active in the slum. If the group is registered, individuals aggrieved with behavior of leaders or administrators in the group, or upset with the treatment they have received, are able to appeal directly to a social worker for interventions. A registered group pays a fixed amount to the government and is, nominally at least, required to do a number of other things. Registered groups are required both to keep minutes of their meetings and to have a set of written rules that determine the way in which the group members should act in certain contingencies. These actions can be undertaken by nonregistered groups as well, and it turns out that not all registered groups follow these guidelines. Both having written rules and keeping minutes are measured in the data as well; these are the variables "Written rules" and "Minutes" respectively. Additionally, there is information on whether groups have formal penalties for individuals that do not directly comply with the rules of the group; this is the variable "Penalties." A final variable that aids in enforcement is whether groups have a bank account. An account helps in monitoring the fees and contributions collected by the group and is denoted as the variable "Bank account."

Some groups in our data are almost entirely informal (11%), in the sense of having implemented none of these procedures, whereas others (28%) have implemented them all. We see from Table 10.2 that the majority of

Table 10.2 Summary statistics on measures of formalism

	Mean	Standard deviation
Registered	0.39	0.49
Written rules	0.68	0.47
Minutes	0.64	0.48
Penalties	0.76	0.43
Bank account	0.40	0.49

Table 10.3 Correlations between measures of formalism

	Registered	Written rules	Minutes	Penalties	Bank account
Registered	1				
Written rules	0.546	1			
Minutes	0.807	0.586	1		
Penalties	0.219	0.104	0.182	1	
Bank account	0.542	0.810	0.561	0.070	1

groups have written rules, keep minutes of their meetings, and impose penalties on their members, whereas only 40% of groups are registered and have a bank account. As expected, these variables are positively correlated, as seen from Table 10.3.

Since the formalization processes that we study each entail some costs to the groups—either in terms of flexibility, time, or resources—we hypothesize that these will only be borne if they help in achieving the groups' goals. Since these groups are largely self-sustaining and self-enforcing, the successful ones (i.e., the ones we observe) are somehow able to sustain collectively beneficial outcomes by ensuring that members forego individually beneficial deviations that would hurt other members. Successful repeated interaction corresponds to a set of individual behaviors, along the equilibrium path, that are mutually beneficial and become individually rational within the confines of the group. How is this sustained? It is sustained by ensuring that individuals who deviate from the required path are (1) detected and (2) punished by the other members of the group. With (1) and (2) in place, individuals have incentives to act as promised, and groups can succeed in realizing objectives.

Table 10.4 Summary statistics on measures of social connectedness

	Mean	Standard deviation
Same ethnicity	0.47	0.50
Majority local	0.56	0.50
Started with relatives	0.23	0.42
Started with friends	0.43	0.50

When such groups choose formalization, we conjecture that it is because it helps in achieving one, or both, of these actions. But when one looks at the nature of the formalization process that we measure, it seems unlikely that these could help with detection. The capacity to detect deviations from prescribed behavior seems more like an immutable feature of the information environment these groups face than a variable affected by formalization procedures. It is conceivable that formalization could bring with it improved means of detection, for instance if it allowed members to access a technology that enhanced observation or allowed the monitoring of members' actions, but in the present context this seems unlikely. Instead we think a much more likely benefit to formalization is in helping groups punish individuals straying from prescribed behavior.

There is reason to believe that this may be particularly relevant in the African context. Relatedly, another important detail that we observe in the present context is information regarding the measure of social connectedness in groups. We have a number of measures of this, two that relate to the current composition of the group and two that relate to the group's formation as shown in Table 10.4. The variable "Same ethnicity" measures whether the group is ethnically homogeneous or heterogeneous. There are five main ethnic groups in the slum: Kikuyu (local to Nairobi and surrounds), Luhya, Luo, Kamba, and Kisii. Additionally there are a number of smaller ethnicities. A second measure, "Majority local," pertains to whether a majority of members of the group live in the part of the slum, Kianda, where the data was collected. Two remaining binary variables, "Started with relatives" or "Started with friends," pertain to the formation of the group.

In general, groups seem to be comprised in one of two ways. Either they are formed by individuals who are ethnically related, or they are formed by individuals who are friends and/or live close to each other. Approximately 20% of groups are organized around both same ethnicity and local area,

Table 10.5 Correlations between measures of social connectedness

	Same ethnicity	Majority local	Started with relatives	Started with friends
Same ethnicity	1			
Majority local	−0.236	1		
Started with relatives	0.510	−0.3067	1	
Started with friends	−0.149	0.1700	−0.481	1

whereas 17% of groups are not organized around either of these two measures of social connectedness. These latter groups are more likely to have been started with friends. The correlations between measures of social connectedness are shown in Table 10.5. The table shows that there is a positive correlation between starting with relatives and being a group of homogeneous ethnicity, and that both of these factors are negatively correlated with the group starting with friends and being composed of members who are from the same part of the slum.

10.3   Relationship between Formalism and Social Connectedness

We see from Table 10.4 that links of ethnicity and kinship are important determinants of group formation. In the African context, kin groups are powerful levels of authority. These groups are able to provide enforcement, both by threat of social ostracism and by exclusion from other beneficial group activities—see Garg and Collier (2005). We use kin information to allow inference regarding the extent of noneconomic ties between members. A reasonable conjecture emanating from the literature on social capital is that groups rich in such ties should find it less necessary to rely on formalization. Formalization, it is conjectured, instead should arise to strengthen group cohesion in places where individuals do not bring strong externally based interconnections to their informal groups. This is consistent with anecdotal observations comparing formalization (which is strong in the developed West, where traditional or ethnic ties are weak) with lower formalization in LDCs (where traditional or ethnic ties are strong).

The first striking and robust empirical finding is that, contrary to the conjecture above, the groups constituted along ethnic lines are the ones most likely to choose these formalization procedures. The tables below demonstrate the significant positive correlation between formalism and ethnic homogeneity. We first present correlation results for each measure of formalism independently and then for estimations on an index of formalism.

Table 10.6 presents results from a probit estimation on the binary variables that measure formalism as a function of ethnic homogeneity and other controls that include the membership and existence of the group, the primary function of the group, and the other main measure of social connectedness, that is, the majority of members being from the local area.

The results demonstrate the significant positive correlation between ethnic homogeneity and our five separate measures of formalism. We see that the other measure for social connectedness, where groups instead organize around local proximity, is negatively but insignificantly related to measures of formalism. These results are robust to including other measures of social connectedness, such as whether the group started with friends or with relatives. Other controls such as membership size are positively related to formalism for some of the measures. Relative to savings groups (the category left out of these Table 10.6 regressions), insurance and investment groups are significantly more likely to use formalism. Nevertheless, it is important to point out that the positive correlation between ethnic homogeneity and measures of formalism is robust if we break the data up into subsamples defined by the function of the group. That is, even for just savings groups, for example, the positive correlation holds.

The regressions in Table 10.7 instead use an index of formalism as the key dependent variable. We constructed this index using principal-component analysis on our five binary measures of formalism. We see that the positive correlation between ethnic homogeneity and formalism holds for this index. There is also a negative and significant relationship between starting the group with friends and formalism. The longer the group has existed is also positively related to the index of formalism. Similar relationships to those in Table 10.6 between the function of the group and this index of formalism still hold.

Starting from the somewhat puzzling empirical observation that the groups constituted along ethnic lines are the ones most likely to choose these formalization procedures, we conjecture that kinship ties, while beneficial for group formation, can be detrimental to enforcement. In our context of self-sustaining groups, kinship ties may manifest as an inability,

Table 10.6 Probit estimations on measures of formalism

	Registered	Written rules	Minutes	Penalties	Bank account
Same ethnicity	0.39 (0.14)***	0.58 (0.14)***	0.44 (0.13)***	0.24 (0.13)*	0.31 (0.14)**
Majority local	−0.12 (0.14)	−0.014 (0.15)	−0.087 (0.14)	−0.13 (0.13)	−0.26 (0.14)*
Membership	0.002 (0.001)**	0.012 (0.005)***	0.0016 (0.0018)	−0.0003 (0.0002)	0.003 (0.001)**
Years existed	0.014 (0.012)	−0.018 (0.021)	0.044 (0.023)*	−0.013 (0.010)	0.013 (0.015)
Insurance	1.61 (0.16)***	1.51 (0.25)***	1.61 (0.22)***	0.055 (0.15)	1.99 (0.18)***
Investment	1.10 (0.15)***	1.38 (0.18)***	1.37 (0.17)***	0.93 (0.17)***	1.045 (0.15)***
Constant	−1.48 (0.16)***	−0.62 (0.16)***	−0.63 (0.15)***	0.55 (0.13)***	−1.46 (0.17)***
Observations	582	582	582	582	582
$\overline{R}^2$	0.37	0.36	0.35	0.07	0.47

Note: Standard errors are in parentheses. A triple asterisk (***) denotes significance at the 1% level, double (**) for the 5% level, and single (*) for the 10% level.

Table 10.7 OLS estimations on formalism index

	Formalism	Formalism
Same ethnicity	0.45 (0.10)***	0.39 (0.11)***
Majority local	−0.19 (0.10)*	−0.16 (0.10)
Started with friends		−0.20 (0.11)*
Started with relatives		0.20 (0.16)
Membership	0.0001 (0.0001)	0.0001 (0.0001)
Years existed	0.017 (0.008)**	0.015 (0.008)*
Insurance	2.10 (0.12)***	1.97 (0.13)***
Investment	1.46 (0.11)***	1.48 (0.11)***
Constant	−1.27 (0.11)***	−1.16 (0.13)***
Observations	582	582
$\overline{R}^2$	0.55	0.55

or unwillingness, to punish group members who have been wayward and/or irresponsible in their actions vis-à-vis the group. If that is the case, then we conjecture that perhaps, by instituting formal modes of punishment, procedures, and decision-making rules that are beyond discretion, formalism can overcome this lack of credibility in punishing transgressors.

To analyze this conjecture, we first develop a simple model to explore this consequence of formalization. A natural issue that arises at first is why, given the excessive (and hence damaging) commitment individuals may feel toward their kin groups, do kin-based organizations arise at all? The answer is easily obtained by looking at the more standard literature on enforcement in repeated interaction.[14] An advantage of kin-based groups is that, in addition to the direct benefits from forming the groups that we see here—insurance, savings, and investment—individuals who are connected by kinship also have more social and personal connections that can help in sustaining the interaction. That is, kin connections bring additional surplus to the engagement, surplus that can be used as a type of collateral allowing other useful, but difficult to sustain, interactions between group members to occur. However, this of course depends on the credibility of the group members spending that collateral in the event of a transgression, that is, on the problem of the credibility of punishment within groups, referred to above. The theoretical model develops a simple mechanism of enforcement that groups can use to overcome this problem, a mechanism whose measurement we can proxy by observing membership fees. The model explores how groups with high collateral (like the ethnically homogeneous) will choose strategies that contrast with those that are heterogeneous in this context.

A basic implication of the model is that kin groups will be useful in sustaining interactions that are of less, but still positive, intrinsic value to members. Interactions of higher intrinsic value will be sustainable both with and without ethnic homogeneity. However, kin groups create the additional difficulty of credible enforcement—although this is also a difficulty that all informal groups will have, it is worse for kin groups. Consequently, formalization is a means to overcome this, and though used by all groups, will be more intensively used by the kin groups. The alternative to formalization is to provide internal (to the group) incentives for individuals to punish transgressors. As will be seen, this is costly in the present context—with the costs being proxied by membership fees—but there is a trade-off between providing this internally costly incentive to punish versus relying on costly formalization procedures to take over the role from the outside.

The model makes clear predictions about what sort of groups will choose formalism, how these should relate to membership fees, the value of groups (measured by monthly contributions), and the capacity that groups have to punish. We explore these conjectures in the data in Section 10.5.

10.4 The Model

Apart from controls on group size and age, the key variables that we have at our disposal relate to the value of groups, their ethnic composition, the formalization procedures they use, and the size of membership fees (what we think of as bonds), which they demand. We want the model we develop here to suggest the ways in which these observables might be related. Our conjecture, as already stated, is that ethnicity increases ties between individuals, which creates higher nonpecuniary costs when things go badly between group members. These costs fall on those committing morally hazardous acts (deviations from prescribed behavior), and also on those whose task it is to punish the deviations. A natural context in which to explore these issues is the repeated prisoner's dilemma setting.

The usual repeated prisoner's dilemma game (with a cooperative outcome that is not a Nash equilibrium, due to a collectively costly but individually beneficial deviation) sustains the cooperative outcome by trigger strategies. If any player deviates from the cooperative strategy in a stage game, all others play the noncooperative strategy from then on. Since the noncooperative outcome is an equilibrium of the stage game, this is also an equilibrium of the repeated game, and moreover, since sustained reversion to the noncooperative outcome minimizes payoffs, this represents the harshest punishment for single-period deviations. This punishment thus sustains the cooperative outcome for the widest range of parameter values. But for the context we are studying, this will not do. Since our hypothesis is that a key issue for informal groups is the credibility of punishment, focusing on the usual optimal punishment schemes with permanent reversion to the noncooperative stage game is of little use.

To look at the issues we are concerned with, we will allow for limited commitment on the part of the other members of the group when facing a deviation. Specifically, though groups may threaten deviators with permanent dismissal from the group, since such actions are costly to the dismissors as well as the dismissed—in both pecuniary and nonpecuniary ways—the other group members will have trouble committing. This will be a problem if, following a deviation, the deviator will be able to credibly commit to reverting back to the cooperative outcome. Our focus will thus be on the means that groups use to sustain the credibility of such threats.

Though we are, of course, focusing on subgame perfect equilibria, by allowing the possibility of reversion back to cooperative play once a deviation has occurred, we are not studying equilibria that are on the possibilities frontier of the simple framework that we have set up. In the present context we think this is defensible for two reasons. Firstly, there is the reason of simplicity. Since our aim is primarily to explore data where such problems of credibility seem to arise, it is plainly not possible to do this in the usual, simple, repeated prisoner's dilemma framework where the issue of credibility of commitment to punishments does not arise. The frontier is characterized by reversion to the noncooperative outcome, where credibility of commitments does not come up since the noncooperative outcome is an equilibrium of the stage game. Secondly, it would certainly be possible in a more complex form of the repeated prisoner's dilemma to allow for punishments along the equilibrium path. In that case, reversion to the harshest punishment—permanent exclusion from the group—is unlikely to be optimal. There, the credibility of punishment comes into play more directly. We have not followed that modelling strategy here primarily for reasons of simplicity. Though we do think that it would be potentially interesting to build the more complex model with equilibrium punishments, for our present goal, which is to build a simple theory to guide us through a first pass at the data, the standard repeated prisoner's dilemma game is sufficient.

10.4.1 Primitives

Individuals who are identical and infinitely lived are randomly allocated into potential groups of size N, which we treat as exogenous. Each potential group has the possibility of forming in order to undertake a mutually beneficial activity. At time 0, when formation of the group is decided upon, each individual j in the group has wealth W. The wealth can be used to buy numeraire consumption goods, or can be invested in setting up the group, which we shall see can involve incurring fixed costs. There is no other storage technology. If the group is formed, the group can ask for a membership fee M_i, to be paid by each member. The level of this fee is determined endogenously. This is our representation of a bonding technology. We proxy the bonds through membership fees as this is what we observe in the data.[15] More generally, the bond corresponds to anything the individual has invested in the group and which is forfeited and redistributed to other members on dismissal.

Individuals value consumption, and they also derive nonpecuniary value from social interactions. Such interactions are organized around ethnicity. We model the valuations of nonpecuniary social interactions in a simple binary form. The value of these interactions for i at t is denoted by $\phi_i(t)$. Individual i either has good relations with members of her ethnic group, and hence derives some value, $\phi_i(t) = v > 0$, or not, $\phi_i(t) = 0$. Finer gradations of quality in these relationships could be introduced without altering this chapter's main results. Preferences are represented by a quasilinear utility function, where i's period t utility, denoted $\Upsilon_i(t)$, rises with consumption, $c_i(t)$, and the quality of social relations with own group members, $\phi_i(t)$:

$$\Upsilon_i(t) = U\left(c_i(t)\right) + \phi_i(t).$$

Per-period consumption enters utility in an increasing and concave manner: $U' > 0$, $U'' \leq 0$, and the future is discounted by factor β per period.

If individuals choose not to form a group, they receive income w each period. If forming a group, the structure of the game played between members of the group is a prisoner's dilemma.[16] The per-period value of group activity to each member of group i, if all individuals act in good faith (i.e., cooperate), is denoted V_i. The variable V_i is a random variable drawn before the group forms from some well-defined distribution with supports $(w, \widehat{V})$. Once drawn, this value remains constant for each period that the group continues to function.

The group activity is susceptible to individually beneficial deviations. Specifically, if a single individual cheats, that is, deviates from prescribed actions, the cheater has stage-game income $\widehat{V}$, and their partners all obtain $\underline{V}$, in the period. If more than one individual deviates, the payoffs are $(0, 0)$. Assuming that no one else has cheated, player j chooses between the following two actions and income levels:

$$
\begin{bmatrix}
\text{Player j\textbackslash Players } \_j & \text{Cooperate} \\
\text{Cooperate} & V_i, V_i \\
\text{Cheat} & \widehat{V}, \underline{V}
\end{bmatrix}
$$

This stage game is repeated each period that the group stays together, and stops as soon as the group is disbanded. Individuals can also be dismissed from the group by means that we outline below. Dismissal is costly since $V_i > w$. We also assume that it is costly to the dismissors, that is, the remaining $N - 1$ members of the group who continue on. These members then have a lower per-period payoff, $V_{i-1} < V_i$, from the cooperative outcome in every period that the group continues. This reduction in group size due to dismissal is roughly equal in its effect on group value irrespective of the V_i. Formally, we shall assume throughout that the ordering over the V_i is also imposed over the V_{i-1}.

Without a storage technology, consumption simply equals income each period. Consequently, $c_i = w$ for individuals not in groups, and equals output derived from the group if an individual is in one.

10.4.2 Ethnicity

The existence of ties to individuals that extend beyond the group has only one effect in the present context. Individuals forming groups along ethnic

lines suffer a decline in the quality of their social relations if they are themselves dismissed from, or they dismiss, a group member. If an individual is
dismissed from an ethnically homogeneous group at time t, then $\phi_i(\tau) = 0$
for all $\tau \geq t$ and for all i members of the group. This captures the cost borne
both by the dismissed individual and by the dismissors.[17]

10.4.3 Feasibility of Group Formation

Assuming that a group i can be made incentive-compatible (the conditions
of which are to be explored below) its feasibility when asking for a one-off
membership fee of M_i requires

$$U\left(V_i + W - M_i\right) + \phi_i + \frac{\beta}{1-\beta}\left(U\left(V_i\right) + \phi_i\right)$$

$$\geq U\left(w + W\right) + \phi_i + \frac{\beta}{1-\beta}\left(U\left(w\right) + \phi_i\right), \qquad (10.1)$$

$$\text{s.t. } W \geq M_i.$$

This simply depends upon the benefits of formation V_i being high enough
relative to the outside option, w, and, due to concavity, on the individual
having enough wealth at period 0 to be able to bear the cost of any required
membership fee M_i.

10.4.4 Incentive Compatibility of Cooperative Behavior

Given that cheaters will be punished by removal from the group, behaving
cooperatively depends on the cost of that punishment relative to the benefits from cheating. We derive the incentive compatibility of cooperative
behavior assuming, for now, that punishments are credible, and we shall
explore the credibility of punishments below. The usual factors determine
the credibility of cooperative behavior: that is, if future discounting is low
enough, the value of sustained interaction high enough, and the gains from
deviating and the cost of being in autarky both low enough. That is, for
each member j of group i we require

$$\frac{U(V_i) + \phi_j}{1-\beta} \geq U(\widehat{V}) + \phi_j + \frac{\beta}{1-\beta}\left(U(w) + \phi_j\right). \qquad (10.2)$$

Groups formed along the same ethnic lines differ from groups that are heterogeneous in terms of incentive compatibility. Assuming that all j incoming members of any group start with social relations intact, then $\phi_j = v$; however, once dismissed from an ethnically homogeneous group then $\phi_j = 0$. Consequently, incentive compatibility for an ethnically homogeneous group requires

$$\frac{U(V_i) + v}{1 - \beta} \geq U(\widehat{V}) + v + \frac{\beta}{1 - \beta} (U(w)). \qquad (10.3)$$

The comparable condition for groups not formed along ethnic lines is the harder to satisfy:

$$\frac{U(V_i) + v}{1 - \beta} \geq U(\widehat{V}) + v + \frac{\beta}{1 - \beta} (U(w) + v). \qquad (10.4)$$

Consequently, as is standard, social relations make it easier (i.e., feasible for lower V_i) to make a group incentive-compatible. This, however, is contingent on punishments being credible, which we now explore.

10.4.5 Credibility of Punishment If Group Is Cheated

Since $V_i > V_{i-1}$, punishing is costly to both homogeneous and ethnically mixed groups. Enacting punishments in ethnically homogeneous groups imposes additional costs; both the punished and the punishers suffer a deterioration in social relations from $\phi_i = v$ to $\phi_i = 0$. Credibility of punishments is therefore an issue with which groups are concerned. Specifically, we are implicitly allowing for a deviating member, who is threatened with punishment by perpetual exclusion from the group, to approach the other members of his group and offer to never commit the deviation again. Moreover, we implicitly allow that the members of the group believe this offer to be true. Since repeated cooperation is an equilibrium outcome, these beliefs are rational. Credibility of punishments will thus only be possible if the group of $N - 1$ members find it in their interests to punish a cheating member even though they believe that the member will never again deviate to cheating.

Here, we explore two means by which groups maintain credibility in light of these problems. The first method is to ask joining members for a membership fee that is held as a bond and forfeited in the event of punishment with dismissal. The second is to implement formalization procedures that effectively reduce group discretion in evoking punishments.

10.4.5.1 Method 1: Membership Fees (Bonds)

At time 0, each member of group i is required to pay an amount of membership fee M_i. Each member's payment is then kept in abeyance as a fund. If $N - 1$ members of the group agree, they can dismiss one member of the group and share that member's fee among themselves. In that case, each receives $\frac{1}{N-1}M_i$. Once the member has been removed, the group can choose to continue at the lower per-period value V_{i-1} or disband and receive w from then on. For the bond to both make punishment credible and at the same time not lead to incentives for abuse by a coalition of $N - 1$ members, it is necessary that (1) an individual who cheats is punished by having his or her membership fee expropriated by the others, and then by being dismissed from the group from then on, and (2) an individual who has not cheated does not have his or her membership fee expropriated.

10.4.5.2 Method 2: Formalization

We interpret formalization as the group taking actions in setting up governance provisions that help in providing some degree of external oversight to the administration of the group's rules and procedures. The data includes information on (1) whether the group has written rules, (2) whether it is registered as a group with the government, (3) whether it keeps written minutes of meetings, (4) whether it has formal penalties, and (5) whether it has a bank account. Registration of informal groups is, strictly speaking, a legal requirement. However, less than half of the groups in our sample choose to do so. Registration allows for some oversight of group activities and requires that the group be open to visits from a social worker in the slum. Third-party oversight helps negate individual group members' discretionary power. Having well-defined rules and penalties helps to make clear both what a transgression is and the expected group behavior in case of transgression; keeping minutes of meetings helps to establish an account of previous decisions and actions that is observable by outsiders; having a bank account helps to ensure the location and size of the group's funds. In the data, we explore various ways of treating these binary variables, each of which we think of as capturing formalization. In the theoretical part of the model, we treat formalization as a binary choice.

Having such formal procedures involves a cost, which we call the formalization cost, denoted by an amount F, per member. In return for such a payment, we assume that the group obtains full credibility in enforcing of the rules. Thus, when formalized, punishments will be credible and, in the event that no transgression has occurred, there will not be any false punishments.

Since both formalization and holding membership fees as bonds can be used to achieve the same end—that is, making punishments credible—they are substitutes. Groups will choose either to use the bonding technology or to formalize. We return to the optimal choice in section 10.4.7, but first we consider the level of membership fees necessary for the bonding technology to work.

10.4.6 Optimal Membership Fees

The first function of the membership fee is to ensure that when a single member cheats, the remaining $N - 1$ members have incentive to punish. Suppose individual k cheats. The remaining $N - 1$ individuals will exclude the cheating member from future group activities and expropriate his membership fee if and only if, for each one of these, j,

$$U\left(\underline{V} + \frac{1}{N-1}M_i\right) + \phi_j + \frac{\beta}{1-\beta}\left(U\left(V_{i-1}\right) + \phi_j\right)$$

$$\geq U\left(\underline{V}\right) + \phi_j + \frac{\beta}{1-\beta}\left(U\left(V_i\right) + \phi_j\right). \tag{10.5}$$

For any M_i satisfying this, when cheating occurs, the $N - 1$ cheated individuals will dismiss the cheater and allocate his membership fees among the remaining members.

At the same time, it should not be the case that the membership fee makes it attractive for individuals to form $N - 1$ member coalitions in order to expropriate membership fees from noncheaters. To see whether this occurs, the condition is

$$U\left(V_i + \frac{1}{N-1}M_i\right) + \phi_j + \frac{\beta}{1-\beta}\left(U\left(V_{i-1}\right) + \phi_j\right)$$

$$\geq U\left(V_i\right) + \phi_j + \frac{\beta}{1-\beta}\left(U\left(V_i\right) + \phi_j\right). \tag{10.6}$$

The difference between these expressions is that, in the latter, the first term on both sides of the expression has $V_i > \underline{V}$. This makes the condition harder to satisfy for (10.6) than for (10.5). Intuitively, when no cheating has occurred, consumption of the $N - 1$ members is higher. Consequently, due to concavity, their valuation of marginal consumption in condition

(10.6) is lower than in (10.5). Thus, if the membership fee is set at a level that is just sufficient to ensure punishment when cheating has occurred, that is, when (10.5) binds, punishment will not occur when cheating has not happened, that is, when (10.6) fails. We summarize with the following proposition.

Proposition 10.1   *At a membership fee M such that (10.5) just binds, it is credible for an individual to be dismissed from the group when he cheats. However, the group would have no incentive to punish and exclude a member who has not cheated.*

Proof.   Follows directly from concavity of U.   ▪

Since membership fees held as bonds are costly, and do not benefit group members other than through ensuring punishment, the group will find it optimal to set them such that condition (10.5) binds. By doing so, they also ensure that a supermajority of $N - 1$ members will also not have an incentive to expropriate a fee from a member when cheating has not occurred. It is then immediate that if individuals are wealthy enough to afford the membership fee, it will be possible to find values of V_i for which group formation is feasible. We summarize with the following proposition.

Proposition 10.2   *There exists a critical level of initial wealth W, denoted W^*, such that, for $W > W^*$, for some values of group membership valuation $V_i \subset (w, \widehat{V})$: (a) condition (10.1) holds, so that it is worthwhile for individuals to start a group; (b) there exists a membership fee M_i such that condition (10.5) holds, so that individuals who cheat will be dismissed by the $N - 1$ others, even if the others believe that without dismissal the cheater will revert to the cooperative outcome from then on; and (c) no one will be dismissed if cheating did not occur.*

For these values of V_i, groups will be able to function without cheating by imposing membership fees that solve

$$U\left(\underline{V} + \frac{1}{N-1}M_i\right) + \phi_j + \frac{\beta}{1-\beta}\left(U\left(V_{i-1}\right) + \phi_j\right)$$

$$= U\left(\underline{V}\right) + \phi_j + \frac{\beta}{1-\beta}\left(U\left(V_i\right) + \phi_j\right). \tag{10.7}$$

10.4.7 Comparing Bonds and Formalization

By paying the amount F per member and formalizing, the group avoids having to raise M_i from members to ensure credibility of punishments through bonds. Groups thus face a simple choice: if $F < M_i$ from equation (10.7), then formalize. If not, keep a fund of amount M_i as a bond for each member. In case of cheating, the individual is dismissed from the group, and if the M_i is held as a bond, it is shared among the remaining $N - 1$ group members. A direct implication of this is that it should be the relatively high-value groups, ceteris paribus, who choose formalization. This is addressed specifically in proposition 10.3.

Proposition 10.3   *Ceteris paribus, groups with high valuations V_i should be most likely to choose formalization, and groups that are formalized have the highest membership fees.*

This follows because the membership fee required to ensure the credibility is higher for groups of high value. These will thus be the ones most likely to prefer to pay F and instead to use the alternative means of ensuring credibility; that is, formalism will be chosen when $F < M_i$.

10.4.8 Implications of Ethnicity

The first implication of "same ethnicity" is that the membership fee required to ensure credibility of punishments, M_i, must be higher for an equivalent V_i, if groups are ethnically homogeneous. To see this, note that in the ethnically homogeneous case, M_i solves

$$U\left(\underline{V} + \frac{1}{N-1}M_i\right) + v + \frac{\beta}{1-\beta}\left(U\left(V_{i-1}\right)\right)$$

$$= U\left(\underline{V}\right) + v + \frac{\beta}{1-\beta}\left(U\left(V_i\right) + v\right), \tag{10.8}$$

which is greater than that required in the ethnically heterogeneous case, where dismissal does not impose a cost on social relations. That is, in the heterogeneous case, the last term on the left-hand side above is replaced with

$$\frac{\beta}{1-\beta}\left(U\left(V_{i-1}\right) + v\right).$$

This is the cost of homogeneous ethnicity.

Proposition 10.4 *Conditional upon a group not being formalized, membership fees among the ethnically homogeneous are, on average, higher than among the ethnically diverse.*

Proof. Consider the lowest value of V_i at which a group of homogeneous ethnicity is viable. From equation (10.3) this is given by V_i solving

$$\frac{U(V_i) + v}{1 - \beta} = U(\widehat{V}) + v + \frac{\beta}{1 - \beta} (U(w)).$$

For this value of V_i, compute the value of M_i that is just required for this group to have credible punishments. This is given from equation (10.8) by

$$U\left(\underline{V} + \frac{1}{N-1} M_i\right) + v + \frac{\beta}{1-\beta} \left(U\left(V_{i-1}\right)\right)$$

$$= U\left(\underline{V}\right) + v + \frac{\beta}{1-\beta} \left(U\left(V_i\right) + v\right).$$

Substituting out for V_i from the previous equation yields

$$U\left(\underline{V} + \frac{1}{N-1} M_i\right) + \frac{\beta}{1-\beta} U\left(V_{i-1}\right)$$

$$= U\left(\underline{V}\right) + \beta \left(U(\widehat{V}) + v + \frac{\beta}{1-\beta} (U(w))\right). \tag{10.9}$$

This value of M_i is that required for the lowest feasible ethnically homogeneous group. Denote it by M_i^S *(low)*. Now compute the corresponding value of M_i for the heterogeneous groups. For these groups, the lowest V_i at which they are viable is

$$\frac{U(V_i) + v}{1 - \beta} = U(\widehat{V}) + v + \frac{\beta}{1 - \beta} (U(w) + v),$$

and the corresponding membership fee solves

$$U\left(\underline{V} + \frac{1}{N-1} M_i\right) + v + \frac{\beta}{1-\beta} \left(U\left(V_{i-1}\right) + v\right)$$

$$= U\left(\underline{V}\right) + v + \frac{\beta}{1-\beta} \left(U\left(V_i\right) + v\right).$$

Substituting for V_i as we did above yields

$$U\left(\underline{V}+\frac{1}{N-1}M_i\right)+\frac{\beta}{1-\beta}U\left((V_{i-1})+v\right)$$

$$=U\left(\underline{V}\right)+\beta\left(U(\widehat{V})+v+\frac{\beta}{1-\beta}\left(U(w)+v\right)\right)$$

$$\Rightarrow U\left(\underline{V}+\frac{1}{N-1}M_i\right)+\frac{\beta}{1-\beta}U(V_{i-1})+\beta v$$

$$=U\left(\underline{V}\right)+\beta\left(U(\widehat{V})+v+\frac{\beta}{1-\beta}\left(U(w)\right)\right).\qquad(10.10)$$

Denote this value M_i^M (*low*). It is immediately clear from (10.9) and (10.10) that M_i^M (*low*) $< M_i^S$ (*low*). Since both the heterogeneous and homogeneous V_i are drawn from the same distribution, and since any high draws yielding a V_i for which $M_i > F$ will be formalized, it then follows that the set of homogeneous ethnicity groups who are not formalized will, on average, have higher membership fees than the heterogeneous ones that are not formalized.   ▪

Though, for a given V_i, membership fees are clearly higher among the homogeneous groups, since these groups will be viable at lower values of V_i, it is not immediately clear that, when averaging across all groups that are not formalized, the ethnically homogeneous will have higher membership fees. The higher fees required for a given V_i are offset by the fact that the homogeneous groups also form for lower V_i. Proposition 10.4 shows that this offsetting effect will not be sufficiently great. This depends critically on the difference in nonpecuniary costs of the dismissors being not too much less than such costs for the dismissed.[18]

Corollary 10.1   *Membership fees are, on average, higher among the ethnically homogeneous groups, independent of formalization. But, conditional upon being formalized, membership fees between ethnically homogeneous and mixed groups are identical.*

This follows because, for the V_i where formalization is chosen, both groups simply pay the fixed amount F. However, over the lower ranges where groups find it better to remain unformalized, the homogeneous will have higher membership fees for all V_i.

A further implication can be obtained by comparing the levels of V_i that make ethnically heterogeneous and homogeneous groups just indifferent to formalizing. Since from proposition 10.4, groups of the same ethnicity require higher bonds for a given V_i for credibility of punishments, they will choose formalism for lower values of V_i than the heterogeneous groups.

Proposition 10.5   *The unconditional probability of a group formalizing is higher if it is of homogeneous ethnicity.*

The benefit of ethnic ties is that they make it possible for groups that might otherwise not be viable to form. Specifically, consider the value of V_i just required to make a homogeneous ethnicity group viable, which we denote by V_i^S, and compare it with the equivalent, marginally viable, mixed-ethnicity group, denoted V_i^M. The marginal group for the homogeneous ethnicity is given from (10.3):

$$\frac{U(V_i^S) + v}{1 - \beta} = U(\widehat{V}) + v + \frac{\beta}{1 - \beta}(U(w)). \qquad (10.11)$$

The comparable V_i for the heterogeneous ethnicity group is from (10.4):

$$\frac{U(V_i^M) + v}{1 - \beta} = U(\widehat{V}) + v + \frac{\beta}{1 - \beta}(U(w) + v). \qquad (10.12)$$

It follows immediately from these two conditions that $V_i^S < V_i^M$.

Intuitively, the lowest-value groups are those for which it is barely feasible to sustain the cooperative outcome. In the homogeneous groups, the extra cost of cheating (i.e., the loss of v in all subsequent periods) increases the feasible range of V_i for which the group will work. We thus have the following.

Proposition 10.6   *The lowest-value groups will be of the same ethnicity, so that the value of sustainable groups will, on average, be higher if they are of mixed ethnicity.*

We summarize the implications of the model in Figure 10.1.

For low values of V_i, no groups are sustainable. For V_i between the first and second vertical line in Figure 10.1, only same-ethnicity groups will be viable, and they will be informal. At some higher value of V_i, beyond the second vertical line in Figure 10.1, the mixed-ethnicity groups also become

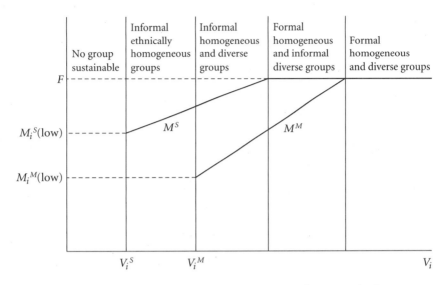

Figure 10.1 Bonds versus formalism by group ethnicity and value.

viable, and they form too. These will be viable without the need for formalism. At some higher level of V_i, beyond the third vertical line in Figure 10.1, the same-ethnicity groups will find it cheaper to use formal procedures rather than informal ones to maintain the credibility of punishments. At an even higher level of V_i, beyond the final vertical line in Figure 10.1, mixed-ethnicity groups will also choose formalism.

10.5   Econometric Results

The model makes clear predictions about what sort of groups will choose formalism, how these should relate to membership fees, the value of groups, and the capacity that groups have to punish. We explore these conjectures in this section. Since many of the variables we analyze are endogenous and could easily be affected by idiosyncratic group components that we do not observe, most of our results involve simple comparisons of means that test the consistency between the conditional conjectures of the model and the data. The econometric regressions demonstrate that these correlation results are robust to the inclusion of our available controls, but the data do not allow us to properly address sample selection and endogeneity issues, so the conclusions here are tempered and suggestive of future directions.

10.5.1 Membership Fees

In this section, we explore some of the implications derived from the theoretical framework regarding membership fees. To this end, we have four main predictions generated from the model and we briefly restate the intuition for each in turn.

The following is from corollary 10.1:

Conjecture 10.1   *Groups of homogeneous ethnicity have higher membership fees than heterogeneous groups, ceteris paribus.*

Ethnic ties make it more costly to dismiss members who have cheated; consequently, to offset this, groups of same ethnicity have to provide greater incentives for the cheated members to dismiss cheaters by allowing the cheated to claim a higher forfeited membership fee.

The following is from proposition 10.3:

Conjecture 10.2   *Groups that are formalized have higher membership fees.*

According to the theory, it is the groups that have greatest difficulty committing to punishments that will need the highest membership fees to make punishment credible. Consequently, it is these groups that will make use of the fees to evoke formal procedures. The groups able to sustain the commitment to punishment with low fees will use these instead and will not formalize.

The following is from proposition 10.4:

Conjecture 10.3   *Among the nonformalized groups, those with the same ethnicity have higher membership fees.*

Conditional upon not being formalized, for a given V_i, groups with the same ethnicity have higher membership fees on average.

Table 10.8 Equivalence of means tests on membership fees

	Membership fees	Equivalence of means
Same ethnicity	166.88	86.75 (23.11)***
Mixed ethnicity	80.13	
High formalism	262.81	195.80 (24.77)***
Low formalism	67.01	
Same ethnicity/high formalism	296.05	88.63 (62.94)
Mixed ethnicity/high formalism	207.42	
Same ethnicity/low formalism	92.64	44.07 (19.98)**
Mixed ethnicity/low formalism	48.57	

Note: The variable high formalism takes on the value of 1 if the group adopts all five of the measures of formalism. This is the case for approximately 30% of the groups.

From corollary 10.1 we also have the following:

Conjecture 10.4   *Among the groups that are formalized, ethnicity has no impact on membership fees.*

This is because being of the same ethnicity does not affect the cost of formalization, F. Ethnicity affects the choice of formalization but not costs once formalized. Consequently, if of high enough V_i to find it worthwhile to formalize, the group simply pays F and ethnicity plays no role.

Table 10.8 provides some evidence in support of conjectures 10.1 through 10.4. The first two rows compare average membership fees by ethnicity of the group, and the second two rows, by the degree of formalism. We see that, as stipulated by conjectures 10.1 and 10.2, membership fees are higher for groups of the same ethnicity and for those which are more formal. The last two pairs of rows compare membership fees across groups by ethnicity, first for those with high formalism and then for those with low formalism. Consistent with conjectures 10.3 and 10.4, average membership fees are not significantly different for ethnically homogeneous groups compared to heterogeneous ones if the groups are highly formalized, whereas same-ethnicity groups have larger membership fees if they have less formalization.

The results from tobit estimations on membership fees as a function of same ethnicity and additional controls are listed in Table 10.9. The first column lists the results for the sample of all groups, and thus tests conjec-

Table 10.9 Tobit estimations on membership fees

	Entire sample	High formalism	Low formalism
Same ethnicity	97.6 (37.0)***	90.4 (70.6)	69.3 (40.8)*
Majority local	−156.7 (36.5)***	−208.2 (67.2)***	−92.7 (41.2)**
Membership	0.03 (0.03)	0.20 (0.27)	0.03 (0.03)
Years existed	−3.4 (2.7)	−6.9 (4.2)	−1.6 (3.5)
Insurance	336.4 (41.4)***	−30.5 (85.6)	346.4 (53.5)***
Investment	383.9 (39.1)***	170.4 (77.6)**	332.9 (46.4)***
Constant	−202.1 (43.3)***	257.1 (108.7)**	−241.1 (46.8)***
Observations	576	160	416
$\overline{R}^2$	0.04	0.01	0.04

ture 10.1. The second column considers only groups with high formalism, and the third is for groups with low formalism. The insignificant relationship between same ethnicity and membership fees for high-formalism groups and the positive significant relationship for low-formalism groups is consistent with conjectures 10.3 and 10.4.

10.5.2 Monthly Contributions

Assuming that the net value of the group is correlated with the amount of regular monthly contributions by individual group members, we have the following prediction from proposition 10.6:

Conjecture 10.5 *Groups of the same ethnicity have lower net value on average.*

This is because ethnicity makes groups viable that would not be viable without the connections that ethnicity provides. It extends the range of groups at the lower end of the distribution, as high-value groups are able to formalize anyway. Since the left tail of the feasible distribution for homogeneous ethnicity groups is longer, their values are, on average, lower.

Table 10.10 provides mixed support for this conjecture. The first two rows compare average monthly contributions by ethnicity of the group. We see that, unconditionally, ethnically homogeneous groups have significantly lower average monthly contributions. The last two pairs of rows

Table 10.10 Equivalence of means tests on monthly contributions

	Monthly contributions	Equivalence of means
Same ethnicity	328.33	−182.76 (51.40)***
Mixed ethnicity	511.33	
Same ethnicity/low formalism	392.52	−80.29 (66.66)***
Mixed ethnicity/low formalism	572.80	
Same ethnicity/high formalism	218.42	−46.0 (65.8)
Mixed ethnicity/high formalism	264.42	

make the same comparison for groups with low formalization and high formalization, respectively. The significance of the difference in means persists for the low-formalization groups only. However, the model predicts that we should see it for the high ones as well.

Table 10.11 further tests this conjecture by presenting estimation results of regular contributions as a function of same ethnicity as well as additional controls. The first column presents results for the entire sample of groups, the second column is for the subsample of groups with low formalism, and the third for high formalism. We see that the relationship between average contributions and ethnic homogeneity (reflected in the sample means) survives with the additional controls. The fourth column describes results from a regression that includes the additional controls, which represent the function of the group. When these variables are included, the result is no longer robust, the negative relationship between same ethnicity and contributions is only significant at the 11% level, and when we further divide the sample by formalism, the results are even less significant.

10.5.3 Discussion

The model lines up with the data reasonably well in terms of the predicted relationships between group value, membership fees, ethnicity, and formalization. Note that, for all of these results, we have controlled for the function of the group, its age, and its membership size. As mentioned earlier, however, we have no means of controlling for selection into groups nor for the possibility that omitted variables may be leading to the correlations we observe. So, though somewhat encouraging of the formal theory, we view the results presented here as preliminary.

Table 10.11 Ordinary Least Squares estimations on monthly contributions

	Entire sample	Low formalism	High formalism	Entire sample
Same ethnicity	−153.85 (53.13)***	−139.16 (68.37)**	−96.23 (69.72)	−83.23 (52.48)
Majority local	−128.45 (53.81)**	−154.04 (70.09)**	−187.95 (69.33)***	−205.70 (53.05)***
Membership	−0.02 (0.05)	−0.01 (0.06)	−0.19 (0.28)	−0.02 (0.05)
Years existed	−18.82 (4.19)***	−21.66 (6.28)***	−9.59 (4.41)**	−8.79 (4.30)**
Insurance				−409.22 (60.95)***
Investment				−118.58 (57.26)**
Constant	653.93 (53.69)***	731.10 (68.59)***	446.64 (72.99)***	784.99 (56.49)***
Observations	576	160	416	576
$\overline{R}^2$	0.05	0.04	0.06	0.12

The data also includes information about what happens in the event that groups have problems. This also seems consistent with the basic premise followed here, that credibility of punishments is a greater problem in homogeneous ethnicity groups and it is mitigated by formalism. However, it is not possible to derive formal propositions regarding this from the theoretical model. This is because, along the equilibrium path of our model, there are no deviations, no reported problems, therefore no punishments, and no difficulty punishing. However, in the data, we observe all of these things. Thus, here we simply report the information on these variables and note how they correlate with formalism and ethnicity.

10.5.4 Additional Variables of Interest

10.5.4.1 Attendance and Payments

The variable "Attendance" denotes irregular meeting attendance, and the variable "Payments" denotes irregular payments of dues. The summary statistics for these two variables are listed in Table 10.12. We also include a binary variable for if the group has expelled members in the past.

Although a large proportion of groups have faced problems of irregular attendance and failure to meet monthly contributions, only a small number of them have actually expelled members due to poor behavior. The proportion of groups who expelled members increases to 22% if we condition on the fact that the group has faced problems of attendance or payments in the past.

The first observation is that having homogeneous ethnicity seems to create problems in enforcement relative to being heterogeneous. This is assumed to be perfectly mitigated, in the model, by using formalism or raising membership fees. However, if this is less than perfect (for instance, if it only works proportionally some of the time), then groups of the same

Table 10.12 Summary statistics on problems faced by the groups

	Mean	Standard deviation
Attendance	0.32	0.47
Payments	0.41	0.49
Expelled members	0.13	0.34

Table 10.13 Equivalence of means tests on group problems

	Attendance	Equivalence of means	Payments	Equivalence of means
Same ethnicity	0.39	0.14 (0.04)***	0.48	0.14 (0.04)***
Mixed ethnicity	0.25		0.34	
Same ethnicity/ high formalism	0.45	0.07 (0.08)	0.53	0.10 (0.08)
Mixed ethnicity/ high formalism	0.38		0.43	
Same ethnicity/ low formalism	0.36	0.14 (0.04)***	0.45	0.14 (0.05)***
Mixed ethnicity/ low formalism	0.22		0.32	

ethnicity should have more problems. Also, groups that use formalism should be able to mitigate these problems of ethnicity.

Table 10.13 compares the prevalence of the two main problems the group faces, irregular attendance and missed payment of contributions, by ethnicity of the group. As consistent with the basic premise of our chapter, groups of homogenous ethnicity are significantly more likely to face problems, but this is only the case for those groups with low formalism. Tables 10.14 and 10.15 demonstrate that this result is robust to controlling for other determinants of problems. In Table 10.14, the dependent variable is the probability that the group faced attendance problems. We see that there is a positive relationship between this probability and ethnic homogeneity, which is significant only at the 15% level for the overall sample, but statistically significant at the 10% level for those groups with low formalism. There is no significant relationship for those groups with high formalism, as would be consistent if formalism helps in overcoming problems.

In Table 10.15, the dependent variable is the probability that the group faced problems of irregular payment of contributions by group members. We see that there is a significant and positive relationship between this probability and ethnic homogeneity for the overall sample, and for the subsample of groups with low formalism. However, this relationship is statistically insignificant for the subsample of groups with high formalism, which is again consistent with the basic premise of our investigation here. Groups of same ethnicity should face greater difficulties because of the

Table 10.14 Probit estimations on attendance problems

	Entire sample	High formalism	Low formalism
Same ethnicity	0.18 (0.12)	−0.15 (0.25)	0.27 (0.14)*
Majority local	−0.22 (0.12)*	−0.46 (0.23)**	−0.16 (0.14)
Membership	−0.00005 (0.0002)	0.0004 (0.0009)	−0.0001 (0.0002)
Years existed	−0.002 (0.009)	−0.023 (0.014)	0.03 (0.01)**
Insurance	0.49 (0.13)***	0.63 (0.30)	0.16 (0.20)
Investment	−0.30 (0.14)**	−0.46 (0.26)*	−0.31 (0.18)*
Constant	−0.56 (0.13)***	−0.11 (0.38)	−0.68 (0.14)***
Observations	582	163	419
$\overline{R}^2$	0.06	0.10	0.05

Table 10.15 Probit estimations on payment problems

	Entire sample	High formalism	Low formalism
Same ethnicity	0.31 (0.11)***	0.08 (0.24)	0.35 (0.13)***
Majority local	−0.27 (0.11)**	−0.63 (0.23)***	−0.14 (0.14)
Membership	−0.0001 (0.0002)	0.0007 (0.0009)	−0.0002 (0.0003)
Years existed	0.002 (0.009)	−0.03 (0.01)**	0.03 (0.01)**
Insurance	−0.04 (0.13)	−0.08 (0.28)	−0.41 (0.20)**
Investment	0.05 (0.12)	−0.20 (0.26)	0.03 (0.16)
Constant	−0.24 (0.12)*	0.45 (0.37)	−0.41 (0.14)***
Observations	582	163	419
$\overline{R}^2$	0.02	0.06	0.03

problems they have with punishment, but they should be able to be mitigate these difficulties with sufficient use of formalism.

10.5.4.2 Expulsion

Expulsion is again something that is not analyzable in our model. This is because deviations from cooperative behavior that would induce expulsion should never occur on the equilibrium path. Nonetheless, a basic premise of our analysis is that formalism is evoked in order to make such actions more credible. It is thus interesting to see if there is a relationship between expulsion and formalism. We see in Table 10.16 that this relationship is

Table 10.16 Probit estimations on the rate of expulsion

	Expulsion	Expulsion
Formalism index	0.09 (0.05)*	0.14 (0.07)**
Same ethnicity		−0.23 (0.18)
Majority local		0.02 (0.18)
Membership		−0.0003 (0.001)
Years existed		−0.03 (0.02)*
Insurance		−0.03 (0.25)
Investment		0.18 (0.21)
Constant	−0.80 (0.08)***	−0.59 (0.21)***
Observations	298	298
$\overline{R}^2$	0.01	0.04

significant and positive. The result is robust to including other control variables, and the regressions only include the sample of groups who have faced problems in the past.

Considering these additional elements of the data that go beyond the simple model provides some indications that are consistent with the basic premise of our analysis, that is, that formalism is a means that groups utilize to help carry out punishments of recalcitrant members. Formalizing seems to make punishment by exclusion more likely, and to make it less likely that groups would have faced problems in the past.

Conclusion Informal groups in Kibera, one of the largest slums in the developing world, seem to use steps of formalization in ways that help them credibly enforce punishments for transgressors of group rules. The problem of credibly committing to punishments seems to be greatest for groups of homogeneous ethnicity. A simple theoretical model consistent with this basic observation generates a number of other implications that we were able to explore in the data. It seems that the pattern of group behavior, both across formalized and unformalized groups, and across groups of homogeneous and mixed ethnicity, is consistent with many of the implications of the theoretical model.

Future work would ideally address the shortcomings of our current study. There are econometric problems arising from selection and endogeneity. The empirical treatment we have taken has necessarily had to treat group formation as exogenous. Conceptually, we assume that groups of identical, otherwise connected individuals simply have an opportunity for mutual gain presented to them exogenously, which they either exploit or not. In reality, individuals may actively seek out groups, have heterogeneous characteristics, bring their histories of past behavior with them, and develop reputations across multiple groups. These possibilities are beyond the data and are not considered here, but they would clearly be of importance to analyze in future. At a theoretical level, we have taken shortcuts that should be rectified in future work. We have analyzed problems of punishment credibility in a standard, repeated prisoner's dilemma game in which optimal punishments should never allow such problems to arise. According to optimal punishments, individuals who deviate from prescribed behavior should be dismissed from groups in perpetuity. The principle advantage of this is simplicity, but a more complete treatment would allow for credibility to be analyzed when punishments are realized along the equilibrium path. In that case, optimal punishments need not imply perpetual expulsion.

Despite these shortcomings, we have learned considerably from this undertaking. At least for the informal groups in this environment, these small steps of formalization seem to serve the function of taking some of the authority in decision making out of the hands of group members. This may be helpful in stopping abuse, but the pattern of its occurrence also seems to be consistent with ensuring that promised punishments actually occur. Similar considerations may be behind the movement from informal kin-based organizations to formal ones in other historical contexts, or in other contemporary environments. Given the strength of tribal and kin loyalties in the African context, it may be that this difficulty in punishing kin members, which is also consistent with other kin-based difficulties, is peculiar to the African context. But the strength of familial ties actually being a hindrance to collective undertakings is suggested in Western family firms as well, so it is at least possible that such motives for formalization may have arisen elsewhere.

More broadly, the investigation here is consistent with a theme that pervades all forms of organizations. All need to design mechanisms that mediate conflicts of interest between group members, whether these organizations are states (as in Acemoglu and Robinson 2005) or informal groups as we see here. At a normative level, if the conjectures here are correct, outsiders may be able to play a helpful role in improving the function of informal groups. The process of registration, and the oversight of group decision making by social workers, seem to be services that groups actively sought out because they helped the groups to function. Since improving the performance of such groups may significantly improve the welfare of the very poor, governments should be encouraged to experiment with alternative means of providing such services, especially if, as is the case in Kibera, groups are effectively free to choose or reject the use of such services as they see fit.

ACKNOWLEDGMENTS

We thank Tim Besley, Avner Greif, and an anonymous referee for extensive comments on an earlier draft. This paper has also benefited from discussions with the participants of the Institutions, Organizations, and Growth Program of the Canadian Institute for Advanced Research (CIFAR).

NOTES

1. This is related to sociological explanations of institutional development, which have focused on the need for intense ties at institutional inception but then note that such intensity hampers further institutional expansion. Authors such as Granovetter (1998), Woolcock and Narayan (2000), and Rao and Woolcock (2001) have emphasized the need for groups to move from the reliance on the personal links to more anonymous and codified means of decision making.

2. Acemoglu, Johnson, and Robinson (2001) demonstrated this causation in a sample of ex-colonies, and their emphasis on identifying causation has characterized the best subsequent work in the field. In this volume, the works of Nunn (chapter 4), Persson and Tabellini (chapter 13), and Besley and Kudamatsu (chapter 11), further demonstrate the insights that can be extracted by country-level perspectives.

3. An early seminal work is Greif (1994), and Besley (1995) surveys microstudies of risk-sharing institutions. The chapters by Acemoglu, Bautista, Querubín, and Robinson (chapter 5) and Drelichman and Voth (chapter 3) in this volume exemplify the advantages afforded by the detail that such micro-level approaches allow.

4. A similar theme is advanced by Mokyr's chapter in the present volume (chapter 2). There he argues that high degrees of trust in Industrial Revolution Britain augmented formal institutional developments in providing the foundation for Britain's sustained economic development.

5. See also the related work on problems of tribal links in Africa. That literature emphasizes the power of familial obligation in restraining, not just opportunistic behavior, but behavior that might be beneficial. Specifically, it emphasizes how familial ties and claims to wealth provide disincentives to personal wealth accumulation. Such ties make it hard for individuals to refuse the demands of family members, no matter how unreasonable those demands may be. For a recent economic analysis of this aspect, see Hoff and Sen (2005). Platteau (2000, ch. 15) has emphasized the role of migration in creating physical distance between kin members and in freeing them of these onerous obligations. In our context of self-sustaining groups, such "unreasonable" or detrimental demands may manifest as an inability, or unwillingness, to punish group members who have been wayward and/or irresponsible in their actions vis-à-vis the group. If that is the case, then we conjecture that perhaps, by instituting formal modes of punishment, procedures, and decision-making rules that are beyond discretion, formalism can overcome this lack of credibility in punishing transgressors.

6. An exception is a recent survey by Cox and Fafchamps (2006), which touches upon this issue, but it is not their focus.

7. Other indications are provided by Gomez-Mejia, Nunez-Nickel, and Gutierrez (2001), who show, using the entire population of Spanish newspapers during a 27-year period (1966–1993), that firm performance and business risk are much stronger predictors of executive tenure in nonfamily versus family firms. Schulze et al. (2001) show that the majority of U.S. family firms offer employed family members short- and long-term, performance-based incentive pay. They draw on household economics and altruism literature to explain why family firms might feel compelled to do so. They provide a theory to explain how altruism influences agency relations within the family.

8. See also Stiglitz (1999) for a thorough discussion of this interaction between formal and informal institutions.

9. See, for example, Carmichael (1989).

10. This data was collected by Jean-Marie Baland from the University of Namur in Belgium.

11. The slum is divided into 12 main villages.

12. See, for example, Besley, Coate, and Loury (1993). Anderson and Baland (2002) analyze ROSCAs in this slum.

13. The total adds up to over 100% because some groups have multiple functions.

14. An important contribution to this literature in a similar context to the present is provided by Greif (1994). Treating institutions as self-enforcing constructs has led to many valuable insights into their functioning; see for example Greif (2006) and North (1990) for extensive discussion and illustration.

15. These are relatively small in the data but are likely to be correlated with the total amount of bond that an individual has invested in the group.

16. Even though the groups in our sample have widely varying functions (insurance, investment, savings), all report problems with opportunistic behavior and have structured their groups to help overcome this moral hazard. The prisoner's dilemma stage game is a simple and well understood means of representing such problems.

17. It is not essential for the results presented here that the nonpecuniary costs of dismissal are equivalent to both the dismissed and the dismissors. It is possible for these costs to be greater for the dismissed, as we detail after the main results are established.

18. Stated somewhat loosely, the required condition is that ϕ(dismissed heterogeneous) $-$ ϕ(dismissed homogeneous) $<$ $\frac{1}{\beta}$(ϕ(dismissor heterogeneous)$-$ ϕ (dismissor homogeneous)). But since ϕ(dismissed heterogeneous) $-$ ϕ(dismissed homogeneous) $=$ (ϕ(dismissor heterogeneous) $-$ ϕ(dismissor homogeneous)) $= -v$, the condition clearly holds here.

REFERENCES

Acemoglu, D., S. Johnson, and J. Robinson. 2001. "Colonial Origins of Comparative Development: An Empirical Analysis." *American Economic Review* 91:1369–1401.

Acemoglu, D., and J. Robinson. 2005. *Economic Origins of Dictatorship and Democracy*. Cambridge: Cambridge University Press.

Anderson, S., and J.-M. Baland. 2002. "The Economics of Roscas and Intra-household Resource Allocations." *Quarterly Journal of Economics* 117(3):963–95.

Arnott, Richard, and Joseph Stiglitz. 1991. "Moral Hazard and Non-market Institutions: Dysfunctional Crowding Out of Peer Monitoring." *American Economic Review* 81(1):179–90.

Bates, R.H. 1990. "Capital, Kinship, and Conflict: The Structuring Influence of Capital in Kinship Societies." *Canadian Journal of African Studies* 24(2):151–64.

Besley, T. 1995. "Nonmarket Institutions for Credit and Risk Sharing in Low Income Countries." *Journal of Economic Perspectives* 9(3):115–27.

Besley, T., and S. Coate. 1995. "Group Lending, Repayment Incentives and Social Collateral." *Journal of Development Economics* 46(1):1–18.

Besley, T., S. Coate, and G. Loury. 1993. "The Economics of Rotating Savings and Credit Associations." *American Economic Review* 83(4, Sep.):792–810.

Carmichael, L. 1989. "Self-Enforcing Contracts, Shirking, and Life-Cycle Incentives." *Journal of Economic Perspectives* 3(4):65–83.

Cox, D., and M. Fafchamps. 2006. "Extended Family and Kinship Networks: Economic Insights and Evolutionary Directions." Mimeo, Oxford University.

Fafchamps, M. 1992. "Solidarity Networks in Preindustrial Societies: Rational Peasants with a Moral Economy" *Economic Development and Cultural Change* 41(1):147–74.

Francois, P., and J. Zabojnik. 2005. "Trust, Social Capital and Economic Development." *Journal of the European Economics Association* 3(1, Mar.):51–94.

Garg, A., and P. Collier. 2005. "On Kin Groups and Employment in Africa, Centre for the Study of African Economies." Working paper 95–16, Oxford, UK.

Ghatak, M. 1999. "Group Lending, Local Information, and Peer Selection." *Journal of Development Economics* 60.

Gomez-Mejia, L.R., M. Nunez-Nickel, and I. Gutierrez. 2001. "The Role of Family Ties in Agency Contracts." *Academy of Management Journal* 44(1):81–95.

Granovetter, M. 1998. "The Economic Sociology of Firms and Entrepreneurs." In *The Economic Sociology of Immigration: Essays on Networks, Ethnicity, and Entrepreneurship*, ed. Alejandro Portes. New York: Russell Sage Foundation.

Greif, A. 1994. "Cultural Beliefs and the Organization of Society: A Historical and Theoretical Reflection on Individualist and Collectivist Societies." *Journal of Political Economy* 102(5):912–50.

———. 2006. *Institutions and the Path to the Modern Economy: Lessons from Medieval Trade*. Cambridge: Cambridge University Press.

Hoff, K., and A. Sen. 2005. "The Kin System as a Poverty Trap." World Bank Policy Research working paper, 3575.

Kandori, Michihiro. 1992. "Social Norms and Community Enforcement." *Review of Economic Studies* 59(1):63–80.

Kranton, Rachel. 1996. "The Formation of Cooperative Relationships." *Journal of Law, Economics, and Organization* 12(1):214–33.

La Ferrara, Eliana. 2003. "Kin Groups and Reciprocity: A Model of Credit Transactions in Ghana." *American Economic Review* 93(5):1730–51.

Morduch, J. 1999. "The Microfinance Promise." *Journal of Economic Literature* 37:1569–1614.

North, D. 1990. *Institutions, Institutional Change and Economic Performance*. Cambridge: Cambridge University Press.

Platteau, Jean-Phillipe. 2000. *Institutions, Social Norms, and Economic Development*. Amsterdam: Harwood.

Rao, Vijayendra, and Michael Woolcock. 2001. "Social Networks and Risk Management Strategies in Poor Urban Communities: What Do We Know?" Working paper, the World Bank.

Schulze, W.S., M.H. Lubatkin, R.N. Dino, and A.K. Buchholz. 2001. "Agency Relationships in Family Firms: Theory and Evidence." *Organizational Science* 12(2):99–116.

Stiglitz, J. 1999. "Formal and Informal Institutions." In *Social Capital: A Multifaceted Perspective*, eds. P. Dasgupta and I. Serageldin, 59–68. Washington, D.C.: World Bank Publications.

Udry, Christopher. 1994. "Risk and Insurance in a Rural Credit Market: An Empirical Investigation in Northern Nigeria." *Review of Economic Studies* 61(3):495–526.

Woolcock, Michael. 1998. "Social Capital and Economic Development: Towards a Theoretical Synthesis and Policy Framework." *Theory and Society* 27:151–208.

Woolcock, Michael, and Deepa Narayan. 2000. "Social Capital: Implications for Development Theory, Research, and Policy." *World Bank Research Observer* 15(2):225–49.

— 11 —

Making Autocracy Work

TIMOTHY BESLEY AND MASAYUKI KUDAMATSU

11.1   Introduction

One of the goals of political economy is to understand how institutional arrangements shape policy outcomes and human well-being. A large literature has now emerged that studies aspects of this. For the most part, this literature has concentrated on studying democratic institutions where elections are the main institution that shapes policy choices. However, throughout most of human history, elections have served a fairly modest role. Far more common are systems based on coercive power—such as monarchies, military dictatorships, or one-party rule—where elections are either a veil or nonexistent.

Recent history has seen a significant move toward open and free elections as a means of determining who should hold power. The case for such institutional arrangements is partly based on liberal values that emphasize the political freedoms that such institutions embody. Indeed, this intrinsic case for democracy, emphasized by Sen (1999), would stand regardless of whether it delivered concrete policy benefits to its citizens. But the case for democracy would be cemented further if there were demonstrable benefits in terms of outcomes.

A key observation that motivates this chapter is that autocratic government is not always a disaster in economic terms. Indeed, there are examples of growth and development in autocratic systems of government throughout history. For example, the British Industrial Revolution predates the introduction of free and fair elections with mass participation. Modern China is also a case in point with a spectacular growth performance in a nondemocratic setting. Whether these observations damage the instrumental case for democracy is moot. After all, it is the counterfactual that matters—growth and development might have proceeded at a greater pace had democracy been present. But it is equally clear that whether one looks at democracy or

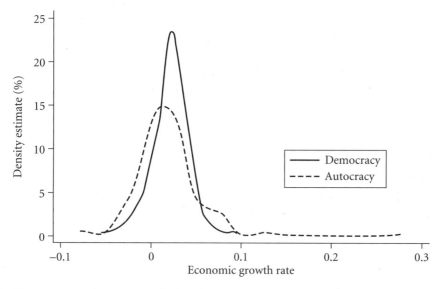

Figure 11.1 Economic growth distributions among democracies and autocracies. *Source*: Penn World Table 6.2 (Heston, Summers, and Aten 2006) and Polity IV (version 2004; see Marshall and Jaggers 2005). *Note*: Plotted are the density functions estimated by using the Gaussian kernel and the bandwidth that minimizes the mean integrated squared error (the *kdensity* command in Stata with the *gaussian* option).

autocracy, there is a great deal of heterogeneity in their performance that cries out for explanation.

This fact is illustrated in Figure 11.1, which shows estimated density functions for real GDP per capita growth rates among autocratic and democratic regimes that lasted five full calendar years or longer.[1] A *regime* is defined as a period in which the authority characteristics of a country stay the same, according to the Polity IV dataset.[2] Regimes are democratic if their Polity score is positive and autocratic if it is nonpositive.[3] The striking fact that we will explore in more detail is that the distribution has fatter tails for autocracies than for democracies—autocracies are more likely than democracies to be either very good or very bad.[4]

A key challenge for students of political economy is to extract lessons from historical and contemporary experience about what makes government work in the general interest of its citizens. There is little doubt that building infrastructure, managing macroeconomic policy, facilitating

private trade and investment, and protecting the vulnerable are all facilitated by effective government. In this chapter, we will focus somewhat
narrowly on the issue of why autocracy can sometimes be successful. This
project is not intended as a defense of autocracy, but as a means of gaining further insights into the institutional basis of good government. It also
contributes to broader discussions about the differences in policy and performance between democracies and autocracies.

The main focus of the chapter is on the institutions that make government accountable—specifically, on finding a means of removing poorly
performing leaders from office. Democracies organize this through regularized contests for power in elections. However, the means of achieving
accountability are more murky in autocratic settings. The analysis emphasizes accountability from a "selectorate" comprised of insiders who have the
ability to depose a leader.[5] We show that autocratic government works well
when the power of the selectorate does not depend on the existing leader remaining in office. This framework can be used to contrast the performance
of autocracy and democracy in terms of the accountability of leaders.

We then turn to identifying successful autocracies empirically. We look
at a variety of methods and use these to pick out regimes that are robustly
high performers. This sample of regimes provides a structured basis for
some case study analysis. We are also able to look statistically at the patterns
of successful autocracies across countries. We then examine the idea that
successful autocracies are able to generate accountability mechanisms in the
absence of open contests for power.

The background to this chapter is a large body of studies on the way in
which government and the economy interact.[6] There are two standard ways
of looking at how political institutions work—in terms of representation
and of accountability. In the context of an autocracy/democracy comparison, Acemoglu and Robinson (2005) focus on representation, modeling
autocracy as a dictatorship of the rich and democracy as a dictatorship of
the poor or middle classes. An accountability perspective is taken in Bueno
de Mesquita et al. (2002, 2003), characterizing political institutions by the
numbers of citizens with the right to choose the government (the selectorate) and of those whose support is necessary for the government to stay
in power. Our theory below emphasizes the interplay of accountability and
representation in making government work. In common with the large
literature on autocracy by political scientists and sociologists, our model
emphasizes heterogeneity among autocracies.[7]

The remainder of this chapter is organized as follows. In Section 11.2, we develop the model. In Section 11.3, we look empirically at successful autocracies and how far their incidence can be explained. Section 11.4 explores links between the theory and the characteristics of successful autocracies. We then offer some concluding remarks.

11.2 The Model

We lay out a simple agency model of autocracy, which studies the incentives for an incumbent policymaker to implement a costly action that yields benefits to all citizens. It differs from a standard model of democracy as in Besley (2006, ch. 3) in that there is no regularized contest for public office. We begin by assuming that such contests only arise when the ruling group replaces its leader. We will show that this institutional feature can lead to autocracy working in the interests of all citizens (Section 11.2.1). After discussing the robustness of our results (Section 11.2.2), we compare the outcome of this model with a stylized representation of democracy where power is contested regularly (Section 11.2.3).

The world comprises N citizens each of whom belongs to either group A or B. Group A comprises a fraction β of the population. There are two time periods denoted by $t \in \{1, 2\}$. In each period, there is a policymaker in office who is a member of one of the two groups of citizens. Without loss of generality, we assume that the period-one policymaker is from group A.[8]

The policymaker in office in period t makes two policy decisions. The first is a discrete "general interest" policy denoted by $e_t \in \{0, 1\}$. This could be thought of as a wealth-creation decision for the citizens, which requires the policymaker to forego private benefits such as bribery by a special interest. The payoff to citizens and the policymaker from this policy depends on a state of the world, $s_t \in \{0, 1\}$, which is observed only by the policymaker. Each state occurs with equal probability. Citizens and the policymaker receive a payoff Δ if $e_t = s_t$ and 0 otherwise.

The second policy decision is purely distributive. This divides an exogenous revenue of size T between the groups. Let $\sigma_{Jt} \in [\underline{\sigma}, \bar{\sigma}]$ denote the fraction of this revenue allocated to group $J \in \{A, B\}$ in period t. In the most extreme case, $\bar{\sigma} = 1$ and $\underline{\sigma} = 0$. However, institutionalized checks and balances may limit this possibility.

As well as having a group identity, each policymaker is either good or bad. This is not observed by the citizens. Let π be the probability that a randomly picked individual from either group is good.[9] Both types of policymakers receive Δ as a citizen if they choose $e_t = s_t$. However, a good policymaker gets the payoff of 0 by choosing $e_t \neq s_t$. We think of this as having a moral stance so that they get no utility from earning rents. Hence, a good politician will always act in the interests of all citizens on the general-interest issue. A bad politician gets a private benefit of r from picking $e_t \neq s_t$, where r is drawn independently each period from a distribution whose cumulative distribution function is $G(r)$ with $E(r) = \mu$, $G(\Delta) = 0$, and $G(r) > 0$ for $r > \Delta$.[10] Denote the realized value of the rent available in period t by r_t.

A fraction of the citizens in each group is enfranchised, that is, endowed with the power to influence the choice of policymaker when there is a contest for power. Let $n \leq N$ be the total number of enfranchised citizens, of which a fraction ϕ belongs to group A. Enfranchised citizens from the ruling group (A) decide whether to retain the incumbent as the policymaker for period two. If they so choose, then the incumbent remains in power. However, if group A's enfranchised citizens decide to replace the incumbent, there is an "open" contest between two candidates, one from group A and the other from group B. Again, following Bueno de Mesquita et al. (2003), we refer to group A's enfranchised citizens as the selectorate.[11]

Suppose that in the event of an open contest, group A's candidate has the support of a fraction κ of the enfranchised citizens. We allow for a uniformly distributed shock to the popularity of group B's candidate to affect the outcome, which we denote by $\eta \in \left[-\frac{1}{2}, \frac{1}{2}\right]$. The group A candidate then wins if

$$\kappa > (1 - \kappa) + \eta.$$

Then the probability that a candidate from group A wins the contest, denoted by $\gamma(\kappa)$, is

$$\gamma(\kappa) = \begin{cases} 1 & \text{if } \kappa > \frac{3}{4} \\ 2\kappa - \frac{1}{2} & \text{otherwise} \\ 0 & \text{if } \kappa < \frac{1}{4}. \end{cases}$$

This model conveniently nests the standard probabilistic voting model of democracy in which all citizens are enfranchised and each citizen has one vote. Then if all citizens vote along group-identity lines, the probability that group A wins is $\gamma\,(\beta)$.[12]

In an autocratic world, not all citizens are enfranchised (e.g., as in South Africa during apartheid), in which case $\kappa = \phi$ if all enfranchised citizens support their own group's candidate. We also allow for group B's enfranchised citizens being repressed by being denied access to polling stations or because group A monopolizes coercive forces. We represent this simply by a repression parameter $(\upsilon \geq 1)$ with $\kappa = \upsilon\phi/(\upsilon\phi + (1 - \phi)) \geq \phi$. If most enfranchised citizens are from group A (a large ϕ) or if there is strong repression (large enough υ), then $\gamma\,(\kappa) = 1$; that is, group A is certain to hold on to power in the second period. This represents the case of an effectively institutionalized autocracy along the lines of, say, modern-day China.

Finally, if the period-one policymaker is removed from office, he receives a period-two payoff as a citizen from group A.

The timing of the game is as follows:

1. Nature determines (s_1, r_1) and whether the period-one policymaker is good or bad. This is private information, known to the policymaker.

2. The policymaker picks $(\sigma_{A1}, \sigma_{B1}, e_1)$, and period-one payoffs are realized.

3. Members of the selectorate decide whether to retain the policymaker.

4. If the policymaker is removed from office, then nature determines whether two candidates in an open contest are good or bad. An open contest then ensues in which enfranchised citizens of groups A and B decide which candidate to support. The group A candidate wins with probability $\gamma\,(\kappa)$.

5. Nature determines (s_2, r_2).

6. The period-two policymaker chooses $(\sigma_{A2}, \sigma_{B2}, e_2)$, and period-two payoffs are realized.

A key feature of the model is that there is a contest for power only if the selectorate of group A chooses to replace the current leader. It is the absence of a guaranteed contest at the end of period one that characterizes autocracy in the model. Below, we contrast this with a situation where there is an election at the end of period one, as in the standard agency model of democracy.

11.2.1 Equilibrium

We solve for the perfect Bayesian equilibrium of our model. This requires that, in every period, each type of policymaker behaves optimally given the contest rule in place. Members of the selectorate use Bayes' rule to update their beliefs on the type of the period-one policymaker, accordingly, and decide optimally whether to replace the policymaker at the end of period one.

It is very easy to work out the equilibrium behavior of policymakers in period two. In terms of the general-interest policy, each kind of policymaker takes his short-term optimal action. Thus, $e_2 = s_2$ for a good politician, and $e_2 = 1 - s_2$ for a bad politician. In terms of the distributive policy, the policymaker of group J chooses $\sigma_{J2} = \bar{\sigma}$ and $\sigma_{K2} = \underline{\sigma}$ for $K \neq J$, that is, giving the biggest reward that he can to his own group.

Given these period-two policy choices, consider the decision of enfranchised citizens in an open contest between two randomly chosen candidates from groups A and B. As the type of the candidates is unknown to them, both candidates will produce Δ with probability π if elected. Group J citizens prefer their own group's candidate (who will choose $\sigma_{J2} = \bar{\sigma}$) to the other group's candidate (who will choose $\sigma_{J2} = \underline{\sigma}$). Therefore, all group A enfranchised citizens support the group A candidate while all group B enfranchised citizens support the group B candidate, implying that the share of support that a group A candidate receives is $\upsilon\phi/(\upsilon\phi + (1 - \phi))$. The probability that group A retains power in an open contest is therefore

$$\gamma\left(\frac{\upsilon\phi}{(\upsilon\phi + (1 - \phi))}\right) \equiv \Gamma(\phi, \upsilon).$$

This probability is key to understanding whether autocracy is successful.

Turning now to period one, the distributive policy is again straightforward. As the period-one policymaker is a member of group A, he will set $\sigma_{A1} = \bar{\sigma}$ and $\sigma_{B1} = \underline{\sigma}$. Good policymakers always make the right decision on the general-interest policy so that $e_1 = s_1$. The only issue concerns how bad policymakers behave. To work out the bad policymaker's incentive to produce Δ, we must compare his payoffs from the good and bad actions. If he stays in power, his expected period-two payoff is $\mu + \bar{\sigma}T$. If he is removed from office, then he will get the payoff of a group A citizen: $\pi\Delta + \bar{\sigma}T$ with probability $\Gamma(\phi, \upsilon)$, and $\pi\Delta + \underline{\sigma}T$ with probability $1 - \Gamma(\phi, \upsilon)$.

Let $\rho(\delta)$ be the probability that the period-one policymaker will stay in office if he produces a payoff of $\delta \in \{0, \Delta\}$ from the general-interest policy. The bad policymaker's period-two payoff from producing a payoff of δ to the citizens in period one is[13]

$$\rho(\delta)(\mu + \bar{\sigma}T) + (1 - \rho(\delta))\left[\pi\Delta + \Gamma(\phi, \upsilon)\bar{\sigma}T + (1 - \Gamma(\phi, \upsilon))\underline{\sigma}T\right].$$

Using this, it is easy to see that the bad policymaker will produce the good action in period one if

$$[\rho(\Delta) - \rho(0)][\mu - \pi\Delta + (1 - \Gamma(\phi, \upsilon))(\bar{\sigma} - \underline{\sigma})T] + \Delta > r_1.$$

Consequently, the probability that a bad policymaker chooses the right general-interest action in period one, denoted by λ, is

$$\lambda = G([\rho(\Delta) - \rho(0)][\mu - \pi\Delta + (1 - \Gamma(\phi, \upsilon))(\bar{\sigma} - \underline{\sigma})T] + \Delta).$$

The bad politician is motivated to choose the right general-interest policy by two sources of future rents. The first is the personal rent μ that he earns. The second is the group-specific rent $(\bar{\sigma} - \underline{\sigma})T$. The latter is relevant only if his group may lose office in an open contest, that is, if $\Gamma(\phi, \upsilon) < 1$.

To understand $\rho(\Delta) - \rho(0)$, we need to examine the behavior of the group A selectorate. Observe that if the policymaker generates Δ, then it is always optimal to retain him. He creates higher group-specific rents from the redistributive policy (strictly so if $\Gamma(\phi, \upsilon) < 1$), and there is a higher probability of good behavior than would arise in an open contest. To see the second point, the posterior probability that the incumbent policymaker is good after having produced the good outcome in period one (by Bayes' rule) is

$$\frac{\pi}{\pi + (1 - \pi)\lambda},$$

which is at least as large as π. Therefore, we have $\rho(\Delta) = 1$. If the policymaker does not generate Δ, then the selectorate will fire him if

$$(1 - \Gamma(\phi, \upsilon))(\bar{\sigma} - \underline{\sigma})T < \pi\Delta.$$

Thus, $\rho(0) = 0$. Poor-quality policymakers will be fired as long as the selectorate has a sufficient grip on power so that they will keep their group-specific rents if they decide to replace the policymaker. Otherwise, $\rho(0) = 1$.[14]

For notational simplicity, define $\tau \equiv (\bar{\sigma} - \underline{\sigma}) T$, which captures the degree of salience of the distributional policy. The above discussion then leads us to the following result.

Proposition 11.1   *In the unique perfect Bayesian equilibrium, the probability that a bad policymaker picks the right general-interest action in period one is given as follows:*

1. If $(1 - \Gamma(\phi, \upsilon)) \tau < \pi \Delta$, then

$$\lambda = G (\mu - \pi \Delta + (1 - \Gamma(\phi, \upsilon)) \tau + \Delta) . \tag{11.1}$$

2. If $(1 - \Gamma(\phi, \upsilon)) \tau \geq \pi \Delta$, then

$$\lambda = 0. \tag{11.2}$$

This result says that the selectorate will be able to discipline policymakers in autocracy, leading to a good general-interest policy choice, if their grip on power is sufficiently strong. If not, they will fear that removing the policymaker will trigger a contest in which the other group can seize power.[15] This suggests that successful autocracies will tend to be those with strong selectorates who can commit to removing bad leaders.

The case where $\Gamma(\phi, \upsilon) = 0$ is interesting here and could be thought of as a case of personal rule where the selectorate's grip on power is dependent on the specific policymaker remaining in power. If $\tau \geq \pi \Delta$, then personal rule in this sense will always result in $\lambda = 0$. This is because the accountability mechanism via the selectorate has no bite. This accords with intuition and the often-made empirical claim that personal rule is not conducive to good government. We develop a case study to illustrate this in Section 11.4.3 below.

The role of checks and balances $(\bar{\sigma} - \underline{\sigma})$ in disciplining autocrats turns out to be subtle. First, if group A retains power for sure ($\Gamma(\phi, \upsilon) = 1$), there is no role for constraints on distributional policymaking in improving the quality of government. The complete lack of checks and balances could still lead to good policy outcomes if the selectorate is securely in power. Otherwise, improvements in checks and balances have a nonmonotonic impact on the incentive of autocrats to make a good policy. On the one hand, improvements in checks and balances make autocracies more likely to be successful. On the other hand, once checks and balances start disciplining bad politicians, further improvements in checks and balances actually undermine bad politicians' incentive to take the good action. This is because a high level of checks and balances makes an autocrat less concerned about the seizure of power by group B as a result of his bad performance. Finally, if we compare two autocracies with the same level of checks and balances, we could see a stark difference in performance between the two, depending on how salient the distributional issue is due to the size of T.

As we observed above, a key feature of our model is the assumption that a contest for power is triggered only if there is a decision to replace the leader in period one. The role of this assumption can now be assessed. Suppose instead that there is a probability ξ that a contest ensues even if the selectorate chooses to retain the incumbent. The incumbent then competes with a challenger from group B for office in period two. This does not change the optimal strategy of enfranchised citizens in the contest if $(1 - \pi) \Delta < \tau$.[16] However, it weakens the incentive of the leader in case 1 of proposition 11.1 since we would now have

$$\lambda = G\left([\xi\Gamma(\phi, \upsilon) + (1 - \xi)][\mu - \pi\Delta + (1 - \Gamma(\phi, \upsilon))\tau] + \Delta\right),$$

which is decreasing in ξ. Thus the model predicts that, conditional on having an effective selectorate disciplining the leader, political stability (low ξ) is an asset. This offers a perspective on autocracy that is reminiscent of Olson (1993) who put weight on the power of longer time horizons in improving the quality of government within autocracy.[17] However, the exact mechanism in which political stability induces a better quality of autocratic government is different. In Olson's theory (1993), political stability allows an autocrat to internalize the benefit from good economic policies through an increased amount of tax revenue. In our model, political stability allows the selectorate to discipline an autocrat who otherwise chooses bad policies for private gain.

11.2.2 Repression and Bribery of the Selectorate

The basic model assumes that the selectorate is powerful enough to replace the leader if they want to. But autocratic leaders frequently take actions to entrench their power. If such actions were costless, then the leader would always stay in office while setting $\lambda = 0$. However, in reality, such tactics—whether repression by force or bribery—are costly. We now explore the implications of this to illustrate how the good performance of autocracy in proposition 11.1 depends on limiting actions by incumbents to entrench their power.

Assume that the period-one policymaker can pay a cost $b > 0$ to repress the selectorate when the latter wishes to remove him from power. If $(1 - \Gamma(\phi, \upsilon)) \tau < \pi \Delta$, then the bad policymaker prefers repression to choosing the bad policy and being ousted, as long as the cost of repression is not too high, specifically

$$b < \mu - \pi \Delta + (1 - \Gamma(\phi, \upsilon))\tau.$$

Under this condition, the bad policymaker will choose repression if

$$r_1 - b > \Delta.$$

As a result, the probability that the bad leader chooses the good policy is

$$\lambda = G \left(\Delta + \min \{b, \mu - \pi \Delta + (1 - \Gamma(\phi, \upsilon)) \tau \} \right).$$

It is clear from this that the possibility of repression (weakly) reduces the incidence of good period-one behavior under autocracy. Thus if $b = 0$ (costless repression), then $\lambda = 0$ and we are back to the case of bad autocracy (case 2 in proposition 11.1).

Bribery to stay in office is also a possibility. Suppose that the policymaker can make a transfer to each member of the selectorate in exchange for supporting him to stay in office after he has taken the bad action. Then he may prefer this strategy to taking the good action if the bribe that he would have to pay is small enough. Since each member of the selectorate must be compensated for keeping a bad leader in office, the total cost of bribing the selectorate is

$$n\phi \left[\pi \Delta - (1 - \Gamma(\phi, \upsilon)) \tau \right].$$

This makes bribery preferable if

$$\left[\pi \Delta - (1 - \Gamma(\phi, \upsilon)) \tau \right] (1 + n\phi) < \mu.$$

This is more likely to be satisfied when the selectorate is small—the result in proposition 11.1 still holds for large enough $n\phi$. This case, in particular, emphasizes that it need not be the benevolence of the selectorate that drives good autocracy but having a large enough selectorate so as to make bribery unattractive.

This extension further emphasizes the need for an effective group to manage leadership transitions. To the extent that prevention of repression and bribery can be institutionalized, we expect autocracy to work better. This analysis also makes clear that μ (the future value of staying in office) is important in shaping incentives. Severe punishments for poorly performing leaders after they leave office are double-edged. On the one hand, they improve incentives conditional on tactics like bribery and corruption not being used. On the other, they increase the incentive to use such tactics in the first place. Thus the model shows why negotiating attractive exit arrangements for bad leaders could sometimes improve policy outcomes.

11.2.3 Comparison with Democracy

We now contrast the model above with a stylized representation of democracy. This is a nontrivial comparison since it is well known from the literature on political agency models (see, for example, Besley 2006) that elections are an imperfect way of providing incentives for good policies.

Now assume that all citizens are enfranchised with each having one vote: $n = N$, $\phi = \beta$, and $\upsilon = 1$.[18] The key feature of democracy that we model here is a guaranteed contest for power at the end of period one even when group A citizens prefer retaining the incumbent policymaker. The timing of the game is the same except for steps 3 and 4, which are now as follows:

3. Citizens from group A decide whether to support the incumbent policymaker or a randomly picked citizen from group A whose type (good or bad) is unobservable to citizens (i.e., a primary election).

4. All citizens decide which candidate to support, the group A candidate chosen in step 3 or a randomly picked citizen from group B whose type (good or bad) is unobservable to citizens. The group A candidate wins with probability $\gamma\,(\kappa)$.

The remaining structure of the game is otherwise the same as before.

If group A citizens decide not to support the incumbent in a primary election, the electoral outcome that follows is exactly the same as that of an open contest in the model of autocracy, with group A's winning probability being $\Gamma(\beta, 1) = \gamma(\beta)$. The difference comes from a case in which group A

citizens decide to support the incumbent in a primary election. This case emerges if the incumbent takes a good action in period one, because otherwise group A citizens are strictly better off by replacing the incumbent with a randomly picked candidate.[19] A key issue in a democracy is whether citizens from group B reward the group A incumbent for taking the general-interest action. This depends on how salient is the general-interest policy relative to the distributional policy.

We first look at the case in which the distributional policy is more salient:

$$(1 - \pi)\,\Delta < \tau.$$

This condition says that group B voters will always support a candidate from their own group even if the group A candidate is known to be good. In this case, the share of votes the incumbent undertaking a good action in period one obtains will be $\kappa = \beta$. Consequently, if a bad incumbent chooses a good policy so that group A citizens support him in a primary election, his expected period-two payoff is

$$\gamma(\beta)(\mu + \bar{\sigma}T) + (1 - \gamma(\beta))(\pi\Delta + \underline{\sigma}T).$$

If he chooses a bad policy, he will be removed in a primary election and his expected period-two payoff is therefore

$$\gamma(\beta)(\pi\Delta + \bar{\sigma}T) + (1 - \gamma(\beta))(\pi\Delta + \underline{\sigma}T).$$

Comparing these two payoffs, it is straightforward to see that the probability that a bad incumbent chooses a good action is

$$\lambda = G\left(\gamma(\beta)(\mu - \pi\Delta) + \Delta\right). \tag{11.3}$$

Since group B citizens are not responsive to the policymaker's reputation, only private rents motivate good behavior. This is because the distribution of group-specific rents does not depend on which general-interest policy is adopted in period one. In addition, private rents are discounted by the probability of reelection, $\gamma(\beta)$, which can be less than one. The regularized contest for power coupled with the lack of responsiveness by group B citizens even undermines the motivation of policymakers stemming from private gains.

We next turn to a situation where the general-interest policy is more salient:

$$(1 - \pi)\,\Delta \geq \tau.$$

Table 11.1 Comparison of autocracy and democracy

	Good democracy $\tau \leq (1-\pi)\Delta$	Bad democracy $\tau > (1-\pi)\Delta$
Good autocracy $(1-\Gamma(\phi, \upsilon))\tau < \pi\Delta$	Democracy if $\Gamma(\phi, \upsilon) > \gamma(\beta)$	Autocracy
Bad autocracy $(1-\Gamma(\phi, \upsilon))\tau \geq \pi\Delta$	Democracy	Democracy if $\gamma(\beta) > 0$

We will look at the best performance of democracy that can be sustained in this case. Suppose that all group B citizens will support a candidate from group A who takes the good action in period one. Then, the outcome is equivalent to the good autocracy case in Section 11.2.1. It is straightforward to see that

$$\lambda = G\left(\mu - \pi\Delta + (1-\gamma(\beta))\tau + \Delta\right). \tag{11.4}$$

Good behavior by the period-one policymaker is now rewarded with personal rents in period two for sure and by an increase in the probability of retaining group-specific rents. This will be an equilibrium consistent with Bayes' rule provided that at this value of λ,

$$\pi\left[\frac{(1-\pi)(1-\lambda)}{\pi + (1-\pi)\lambda}\right]\Delta > \tau,$$

which will always hold for a sufficiently low value of τ.[20]

We now compare the performance of autocracy and democracy in terms of the probability of disciplining the bad incumbent. Table 11.1 shows which political system is better in each of four main parameter regions. When the distributional issue is of little importance (a very small τ as in the top-left cell), democracy performs better as long as $\gamma(\beta) < \Gamma(\phi, \upsilon)$ (compare equations (11.1) and (11.4)); that is, power is more contestable in a democracy. Thus democracy is better insofar as it strengthens the power of the opposition and increases the group-specific rent that motivates a bad politician to stay in office.

When the distributional issue is very important (a very large τ as in the bottom-right cell in Table 11.1), we see, by comparing equations (11.2) and (11.3), that democracy performs better as long as democratic competition does not entirely prevent group A from holding power ($\gamma(\beta) > 0$). When the distributional issue is very salient, the selectorate in autocracy is unable to discipline the policymaker. However, in democracy, the fact that group A citizens regularly face competition from group B allows them to discipline a bad politician.

Determining which of the off-diagonal cells in Table 11.1 is the relevant parameter region depends on the size of $\Gamma(\phi, \upsilon)$. If $(1 - \pi)(1 - \Gamma(\phi, \upsilon)) \geq \pi$, then the bottom-left cell is relevant. In this case, democracy always performs better (compare (11.2) and (11.4)). In this case, $\Gamma(\phi, \upsilon)$ is not large enough for the selectorate to credibly threaten to remove a bad politician if he behaves badly. On the other hand, in democracy, group B citizens are responsive to the policymaker's good behavior, giving the incumbent an incentive to behave well. Broader political participation in a democracy is beneficial in this case.

If $\Gamma(\phi, \upsilon)$ is large enough so that $(1 - \pi)(1 - \Gamma(\phi, \upsilon)) < \pi$, we are in the top-right cell in which autocracy performs better than democracy (compare (11.1) and (11.3)). In this case, the distributional issue is relatively important, making group B citizens unresponsive to the good action by the incumbent. In democracy, this unresponsiveness undermines a bad politician's incentive for good action. In autocracy, however, group B has very little influence on leadership selection due to a high $\Gamma(\phi, \upsilon)$. This exclusion of group B from political participation creates an incentive for a bad politician to undertake good policy because group A does not fear losing power after replacing the leader.

The above analysis suggests that, as long as the selectorate has a strong hold over power, autocracy is a better form of government if the distributional issue is neither too salient nor too irrelevant. In all other cases, however, democracy is a better form of government under the plausible condition that $0 < \gamma(\beta) < \Gamma(\phi, \upsilon)$. Thus, while the approach that we have taken shows why successful autocracy is a possibility, it is suggestive of why democracy is broadly superior in promoting general-interest policies.

While the analysis is very simple indeed, it gives a novel take on the difference between autocracy and democracy in delivering policies. There is no easy ranking between democracy and autocracy—it depends on the institutional setting and the environment in which each system of government is implemented. For a given level of the salience of the distributional issue (a fixed τ), the model suggests a natural ordering among a cross section of democracies and autocracies in terms of implementation of general-interest policies. Best of all is responsive democracy where general-interest policies are salient (a large Δ). Second best is successful autocracy, requiring an effective selectorate. Next is polarized democracy where elections do not reward good, general-interest policies. Worst of all is bad autocracy where leaders are able to hold on to power regardless of their performance while in office. This could explain the longer lower tail of the performance distribution among autocracies, as seen in Figure 11.1.

However, Figure 11.1 also shows that autocracy has a longer upper tail in the performance distribution. Our model can explain this by assuming that the extent of the constraints on distributional issues (as proxied by $(\bar{\sigma} - \underline{\sigma})$) is lower in a political system without regularized contests for power. Comparing equations (11.1) and (11.4) reveals that even if $\gamma(\beta) < \Gamma(\phi, \upsilon)$, autocracy can perform better because the policymaker is motivated more by group-specific rents. The lack of constraints on autocratic leaders in making distributional policies may explain why some autocracies perform better than the best of all democracies. Thus there are likely to be important interaction effects between the different dimensions of government institutions as measured in datasets like Polity IV.

11.2.4 Discussion

Padro-i-Miquel (2006) is closely related to this chapter. Although it is not discussed explicitly, his model also predicts that a secure selectorate (high $\Gamma(\phi, \upsilon)$) improves the policymaker's performance. In his model, institutionalized participation by the opposition prevents an autocrat from expropriating his opponents at will, which in turn reduces the ruling group's fear of losing power and allows them to discipline the autocrat. However, allowing the opposition to participate in leadership selection in our model may not improve the policy choice if the distributional policy is more salient. The difference stems from our assumption that distributional policymaking depends on checks and balances and the group identity of the policymaker. Moreover, the contest for power does not discipline the incumbent in this policy dimension.

Our model has deliberately focused on the incidence of common-interest policy decisions in democracy and autocracy. This makes sense since the performance metric that it invokes is uncontroversial. However, it is clear that the distributional outcomes under all the cases that we have studied may be quite different. Thus, there could be a preference for one regime or another on distributional grounds. For example, in the case of successful autocracy, power is monopolized by group A and this may not be good from a social point of view. A more complete treatment of the issues would clearly have to widen the perspective that we have taken here by taking a stance on a welfare criterion that pays attention to distributional issues.

We also assumed that the fraction of good politicians π is fixed when we compare political regimes. However, the model makes clear that π can affect the quality of government, both directly in determining whether good actions are taken and indirectly by changing the political equilibrium. Besley (2005) emphasizes the importance of selection mechanisms in political regimes both in history and in a comparison of contemporary political regimes. More open access to political life could be an important difference between autocracy and democracy, which would affect the comparison in a way that is not modeled in our baseline case.[21]

Perhaps the most interesting possibility for future work is to appraise the way in which this framework predicts the evolution of institutional choices over time. We should expect autocracy and democracy to prevail when these choices are successful. Thus there should be a bias (among long-lived regimes) toward cases where (in terms of the model) the equilibrium policy outcomes are (11.1) and (11.4). But for that, democracy requires good checks and balances with general-interest policies being more salient. Equally, successful autocracy requires a strong, hard-to-repress or hard-to-bribe selectorate. However, weak checks and balances (and polarization) should be less of an issue for producing general-interest actions in autocracy.

11.3   Successful Autocracies?

In this section, we look at autocracies empirically. This analysis serves two purposes. The first is to show that there are indeed cases of successful autocracy according to objective criteria. Although we have some sense of which autocracies are more successful than others (e.g., the Chinese communist regime versus African dictatorships), to the best of our knowledge, there has been no systematic analysis to identify good autocracies empirically. The second aim of this section is to identify the cases of successful autocracy that we will use to investigate the validity of our theory in Section 11.4. By relying on objective criteria to identify successful autocracies, we avoid arbitrarily selecting only cases that are consistent with our theory.

To identify successful autocracies, we first need to decide how to define an autocracy empirically. Ideally, the definition should closely follow the characterization of autocracy in our theory: the absence of regularized contests for leadership. In addition, to capture heterogeneous institutional features among autocracies, we should classify periods of autocratic rule by the degree of constraint on the executive in making distributional policy $(\bar{\sigma} - \underline{\sigma})$, the proportion of the selectorate among enfranchised citizens (ϕ), and the way enfranchised citizens exercise their power (υ).

Due to lack of such data covering a long period of time, however, we rely on the Polity IV database (version 2004; see Marshall and Jaggers 2005) because its coverage of the sample period is the longest among appropriate datasets. We adopt the following procedure to divide country-years into autocratic and democratic regimes. First, for each country, we divide the years from 1800 or independence until 2004 between democratic and autocratic periods according to the Polity score. The Polity score, ranging from -10 to 10, measures the degree of democracy.[22] If the Polity score is positive, we treat such a year as democratic. Years with a nonpositive Polity score are autocratic.[23] To capture heterogeneity among autocracies and democracies, we further divide consecutive democratic and autocratic years into different regimes if there is a change in authority characteristics according to the Polity dataset: the method of chief-executive recruitment (EXREC), the constraint on the chief executive (EXCONST), and political participation (POLCOMP). These three dimensions of authority characteristics measured in the Polity database loosely correspond to institutional features of autocracy in our model: EXREC for the presence of regularized contests for executive power, EXCONST for checks and balances on the distributional policy, and POLCOMP for the probability that the selectorate stays in power when the incumbent is replaced $(\Gamma(\phi, \upsilon))$.

In sum, we define a *regime* as consecutive years with the same authority characteristics. A regime is autocratic if its Polity score is nonpositive. Below, we restrict our attention to regimes that lasted at least five full calendar years. Autocratic regimes of shorter length may perform very well simply because of luck or just by "inheriting" a good performance from the previous regime.

In the following subsections, we first identify autocracies successful in achieving economic growth. We then turn to autocracies successful in human development: health and education. These two investigations identify the core set of successful autocracies, successful in at least two dimensions of performance among the three (growth, health, and education). We check the robustness of the selection of these autocracies to alternative definitions of autocracy. Finally, we show that "standard" exogenous characteristics of countries identified by the literature as reflecting the quality of government and institutions do not fully predict whether a country has a successful autocracy.

11.3.1 Economically Successful Autocracies

We measure each regime's economic performance as follows. Suppose that a regime starts in year s and ends in year t. We calculate the regime's annual economic growth rate as

$$\frac{\ln Y_{t-1} - \ln Y_s}{t - 1 - s}, \tag{11.5}$$

where Y_t is real GDP per capita in year t, taken from the Penn World Table version 6.2 (the variable RGDPCH; see Heston, Summers, and Aten 2006).[24]

We then obtain the 80th percentile of the distribution of annual growth rates among all regimes, including democratic ones (313 in total). We regard an autocratic regime as successful if its annual growth rate exceeds this 80th percentile of the distribution.[25]

Table 11.2 shows the list of economically successful autocracies obtained by the above procedure. There are 35 autocratic regimes whose annual growth rate is above the 80th percentile of the distribution. The list includes east Asian autocracies well known for high economic growth, such as China, Indonesia, Singapore, South Korea, Taiwan, and Thailand. Dictatorships in southern Europe are also in the list. On the other hand, there are lesser-known autocracies as well: a couple of African countries in the 1960s (Gabon and Togo), those in the Middle East (Iraq in the 1970s, Syria in the 1960s), communist regimes in eastern Europe (Poland, Romania), and a few Latin American countries (Ecuador in the 1970s, Peru and Venezuela in the 1950s). Overall, the table shows that there are indeed successful autocracies in terms of economic growth.

Measuring success based on annual growth rates may not be an accurate way of assessing the economic performance of regimes, however. One concern is that a regime's growth rate may pick up the effect of country characteristics. Whatever regime may exist, it can be that a country's economy grows anyway. Another concern is that an economy under a certain regime may grow rapidly solely due to the convergence effect if the regime starts with very low per capita GDP. Finally, a regime may perform well simply because it succeeds the previous regime that devastated the economy.

Table 11.2 Economically successful autocracies

Regime	Years of observations	Annual growth (%)	Robustness 1	2	3
Equatorial Guinea (1996–2004)	1996–2003	28.04	Y	Y	Y
Rwanda (1994–2000)	1994–1999	12.56	Y	Y	N
Gabon (1960–1968)	1960–1967	8.59	Y	Y	—
Belarus (1996–2004)	1996–2003	8.15	N	Y	—
Liberia (1997–2003)	1997–2002	7.94	Y	Y	Y
China (1976–2004)	1976–2004	7.87	Y	Y	—
Greece (1967–1974)	1967–1973	7.85	Y	Y	Y
Ecuador (1972–1979)	1972–1978	7.73	Y	Y	Y
Romania (1948–1977)	1960–1976	7.63	Y	Y	—
South Korea (1981–1987)	1981–1986	7.23	Y	Y	Y
Azerbaijan (1998–2004)	1998–2003	7.15	Y	Y	Y
Taiwan (1975–1987)	1975–1986	6.81	N	Y	—
Niger (1974–1981)	1974–1981	6.27	Y	Y	N
Iraq (1968–1979)	1970–1978	6.17	Y	Y	—
Taiwan (1949–1975)	1951–1974	5.98	N	Y	—
Brazil (1965–1974)	1965–1973	5.89	Y	Y	Y
Spain (1939–1975)	1950–1974	5.77	Y	Y	—
Poland (1947–1980)	1970–1979	5.76	Y	Y	—
Portugal (1930–1974)	1950–1973	5.75	Y	Y	—
Togo (1960–1967)	1960–1966	5.68	Y	Y	—
South Korea (1973–1981)	1973–1980	5.50	N	Y	Y
Thailand (1958–1968)	1958–1967	5.34	Y	Y	Y
Venezuela (1941–1958)	1950–1957	4.93	Y	Y	—
Singapore (1965–2004)	1965–2004	4.80	N	Y	—
Indonesia (1967–1998)	1967–1997	4.56	Y	Y	—
Vietnam (1976–2004)	1989–2003	4.47	N	Y	—
Bhutan (1953–2004)	1970–2003	4.28	N	Y	—
China (1969–1976)	1969–1975	4.04	N	Y	N
Iran (1955–1979)	1955–1978	4.01	Y	Y	—
Tunisia (1971–1981)	1971–1980	3.86	N	N	Y
Syria (1963–1970)	1963–1969	3.82	Y	Y	Y
North Korea (1966–2004)	1970–2003	3.75	N	Y	—
Peru (1950–1956)	1950–1955	3.73	Y	N	—
Pakistan (1977–1985)	1977–1984	3.70	Y	Y	Y
UAE (1971–2004)	1971–2003	3.70	N	N	—

Note: Years of observations indicates the period for which the annual economic growth rate is calculated. Robustness 1 is "Y" if the regime's growth rate minus the country average is above the 80th percentile of the distribution; it is "N" otherwise. Robustness 2 is "Y" if the regime's growth rate minus the average among regimes in the same initial income quintile is above the 80th percentile; it is "N" otherwise. Robustness 3 is "Y" if the growth rate during the three-year period preceding the regime is positive; it is "N" if negative; and "–" if either the regime lasted 10 years or longer, or there is no data on GDP for the preceding period.

To deal with these concerns, we conduct three alternative assessments of success. First, we subtract the *country*'s annual economic growth rate from each regime's growth rate, obtain the 80th percentile of the demeaned growth rates among all regimes, and check whether autocratic regimes in Table 11.2 are above the 80th percentile. This procedure removes "country fixed effects" from the measure of performance of each regime. Second, we group regimes into five quintiles according to their initial GDP per capita (Y_s in equation (11.5)), obtain each quintile's average growth rate, subtract it from each regime's growth rate, calculate the 80th percentile of the demeaned growth rates among all regimes, and check whether autocratic regimes in Table 11.2 are above the 80th percentile. As a result, the convergence effect is removed from each regime's performance measure.[26] Finally, we discount a regime's success if it does not survive ten years or longer *and* if it follows a three-year period of negative growth (i.e., $Y_s - Y_{s-3} < 0$), because such a regime can perform well simply due to a "reconstruction" effect.[27]

The three rightmost columns in Table 11.2 show the results from these three robustness checks. Among the 35 successful autocracies, 21 survive all the robustness checks that are applicable. The first robustness check turns out to be tough for east Asian autocracies since these countries grew consistently over time. Notwithstanding, China since 1976, South Korea in the 1980s, Thailand in the 1960s, and Indonesia since 1967 survive this test, proving to be very successful autocracies.

11.3.2 Autocracies Successful in Human Development

We now turn to human development. To measure success in this sphere, we first remove the effect of real GDP per capita by obtaining the residuals from the following equation estimated for each cross section of countries in year t:

$$H_t = \alpha + \beta Y_t + \gamma (Y_t)^2 + \varepsilon_t, \qquad (11.6)$$

where H_t is either life expectancy at birth in year t, obtained from the World Bank's *World Development Indicators* (September 2006 edition), or the gross primary school enrollment ratio in year t, obtained from UNESCO Institute for Statistics (through the EdStats website maintained by the World Bank).[28] We include the squared term of per capita income as a regressor because health and education exhibit a strong nonlinear relationship with income in a cross section of countries.[29] We can interpret the residuals as partly reflecting government efforts to promote human development through public health interventions and through developing schooling systems.

We average the residuals for each regime and calculate the 80th percentile of its distribution among all regimes (307 for health and 275 for education).[30] We also perform the first of the three robustness checks that we conducted for economic performance (i.e., removing "country fixed effects"). Tables 11.3 and 11.4 list successful autocracies in terms of health and education, respectively. Communist regimes in China, Cuba, Poland, Romania, and Vietnam appear in these tables. For health, regimes in the Middle East and north Africa enter the list (Algeria, Iraq, Jordan, Morocco, Syria, Tunisia), while the list for education includes a number of African regimes.

11.3.3 Robustness

In order to identify autocracies that are successful in at least two dimensions of performance among the three (economic growth, health, and education), we assign a success score to each regime that is equal to the number of league tables (i.e., Tables 11.2, 11.3, and 11.4) in which that regime appears. If a regime passes all the applicable robustness checks in each table, one more point is added to its score in each case. The highest score is, therefore, 6. We choose 4 as the cutoff because this ensures success in at least two dimensions and at least one robust success. Table 11.5 shows the list of autocracies whose score is 4 or higher. The list includes dictatorships in southern Europe (Greece, Portugal, and Spain), communist regimes (China, Cuba, Poland, and Romania), and military dictatorships in Latin America (Brazil, Chile, and Panama) and in east Asia (South Korea and Thailand).

Below, we check the robustness of this list to alternative definitions of autocratic regimes.

11.3.3.1 Definition of Regimes

Our definition of a regime entirely depends on the coding in the Polity database. As the original aim of the Polity dataset is to analyze the duration of regimes (see Marshall and Jaggers 2005, 3), we have much confidence in the

Table 11.3 Autocracies successful in health production

Regime	Years of observations	Conditional life expectancy	Robust	Economic success
Cuba (1961–1976)	1970–1972	17.48	Y	N
Romania (1948–1977)	1960–1972	17.48	Y	Y
Taiwan (1949–1975)	1960–1972	16.34	Y	Y
China (1969–1976)	1970–1972	13.89	N	Y
Poland (1947–1980)	1970–1977	12.68	Y	Y
China (1976–2004)	1977–2004	12.43	N	Y
Paraguay (1954–1967)	1960–1962	12.28	Y	N
Syria (1970–2000)	1972–1997	11.89	N	N
Azerbaijan (1998–2004)	2000–2003	11.83	N	Y
Vietnam (1976–2004)	1990–2003	11.49	N	Y
North Korea (1966–2004)	1970–2003	11.35	N	Y
Cuba (1977–2004)	1980–2003	11.22	N	N
Panama (1969–1978)	1970–1977	11.03	Y	N
Thailand (1958–1968)	1960–1967	10.69	Y	Y
Taiwan (1975–1987)	1977–1985	10.08	Y	Y
Jordan (1992–2004)	1995–2003	9.67	Y	N
Morocco (1998–2004)	2000–2003	8.73	Y	N
Paraguay (1967–1989)	1970–1987	8.49	N	N
Kyrgyzstan (1991–2004)	1995–2002	8.09	N	N
Greece (1967–1974)	1970–1972	7.88	Y	Y
South Korea (1973–1981)	1977–1980	7.80	Y	Y
Chile (1973–1981)	1977–1980	7.67	Y	N
Uzbekistan (1991–2004)	1997–2003	7.58	N	N
Spain (1939–1975)	1960–1972	6.80	Y	Y
Morocco (1992–1998)	1995–1997	6.79	Y	N
Syria (1963–1970)	1967	6.39	N	Y
Portugal (1930–1974)	1960–1972	6.15	Y	Y
Tunisia (1987–1993)	1990–1992	6.08	N	N
Algeria (1995–2004)	1997–2003	6.00	Y	N
Iraq (1979–2003)	1980–1997	5.85	N	N
Tunisia (1993–2002)	1995–2000	5.82	N	N

Note: Years of observations indicates the first and last years of observations on life expectancy at birth for each regime. Conditional life expectancy is the number of years in life expectancy at birth unexplained by the Preston curve (the quadratic function of per capita real GDP). Robust is "Y" if the regime is above the 80th percentile of the distribution of conditional life expectancy minus the country average; it is "N" otherwise. Economic success is "Y" if the regime appears in Table 11.2; it is "N" otherwise.

Table 11.4 Autocracies successful in education

Regime	Years of observations	Conditional enrollment ratio	Robust	Economic success
Equatorial Guinea (1969–1993)	1990	81.55	Y	N
Congo-Brazzaville (1963–1979)	1970–1975	57.44	Y	N
Congo-Brazzaville (1979–1991)	1980–1990	50.68	Y	N
Cuba (1961–1976)	1970–1975	48.13	Y	N
Brazil (1965–1974)	1970	42.25	Y	Y
Uganda (1996–2004)	1999–2003	40.87	Y	N
China (1969–1976)	1970–1975	38.01	N	Y
Romania (1948–1977)	1970–1975	34.27	Y	Y
Madagascar (1975–1991)	1980–1990	32.39	Y	N
Mongolia (1952–1990)	1970–1985	31.72	Y	N
China (1976–2004)	1980–2004	30.98	N	Y
Panama (1969–1978)	1970–1975	29.78	Y	N
Spain (1939–1975)	1970	29.58	Y	Y
Lesotho (1973–1986)	1975–1985	29.40	N	N
Peru (1968–1976)	1970–1975	28.87	N	N
Philippines (1972–1981)	1975–1980	28.59	N	N
Togo (1979–1991)	1980–1990	28.12	N	N
Laos (1975–2004)	1980–2003	27.62	N	N
Equatorial Guinea (1996–2004)	1999–2002	26.74	N	Y
Mexico (1930–1977)	1970–1975	25.41	Y	N
South Korea (1973–1981)	1975–1980	24.98	Y	Y
Ecuador (1972–1979)	1975	24.60	N	Y
Gabon (1991–2004)	1999–2004	24.52	N	N
Dominican Republic (1966–1978)	1970–1975	24.41	Y	N
Mexico (1977–1988)	1980–1985	23.96	Y	N
Zimbabwe (1987–2000)	1990–1999	23.77	N	N
Tunisia (1981–1987)	1985	23.77	Y	N
Indonesia (1967–1998)	1970–1996	23.64	N	Y
Chile (1973–1981)	1975–1980	23.15	Y	N
Togo (1993–2004)	1994–2004	22.77	N	N
Paraguay (1967–1989)	1970–1985	22.29	N	N
Vietnam (1976–2004)	1990–2003	22.13	N	Y
Cameroon (1966–1972)	1970	21.82	Y	N
Syria (1970–2000)	1975–1999	21.03	N	N

Note: Years of observations indicates the first and last years of observations on gross primary school enrollment ratio for each regime. Conditional enrollment ratio is the percentage points in gross primary school enrollment ratio unexplained by the quadratic function of per capita real GDP. Robust is "Y" if the regime is above the 80th percentile of the distribution of conditional enrollment ratio minus the country average; it is "N" otherwise. Economic success is "Y" if the regime appears in Table 11.2; it is "N" otherwise.

Table 11.5 Core set of successful autocracies

Regime	Score	Economic growth		Health		Education	
		Success	Robust	Success	Robust	Success	Robust
Romania (1948–1977)	6	Y	Y	Y	Y	Y	Y
Spain (1939–1975)	6	Y	Y	Y	Y	Y	Y
South Korea (1973–1981)	5	Y	N	Y	Y	Y	Y
Brazil (1965–1974)	4	Y	Y	N	—	Y	Y
Chile (1973–1981)	4	N	—	Y	Y	Y	Y
China (1976–2004)	4	Y	Y	Y	N	Y	N
Cuba (1961–1976)	4	N	—	Y	Y	Y	Y
Greece (1967–1974)	4	Y	Y	Y	Y	N	—
Panama (1969–1978)	4	N	—	Y	Y	Y	Y
Poland (1947–1980)	4	Y	Y	Y	Y	N	—
Portugal (1930–1974)	4	Y	Y	Y	Y	N	—
Thailand (1958–1968)	4	Y	Y	Y	Y	—	—

Note: For each performance measure (Economic growth, Health, Education), Success is "Y" if the regime's performance is above the 80th percentile, "N" if not, and "—" if data is unavailable. For Economic growth, Robust is "Y" if the regime does not fail to pass the three robustness checks shown in Table 11.2, "N" if it does, and "—" if Success is "N." For Health and for Education, Robust is "Y" if the regime passes the robustness check of subtracting the country average (see tables 11.3 and 11.4), "N" if it does not, and "—" if Success is "N." Score is calculated as the number of "Y" in each row.

coding of regime-change timing in the dataset. However, defining the beginning and end of regimes in a different way may yield a different list of successful autocracies. To check this possibility, we use an alternative definition of regimes. We first divide years for each country between democratic and autocratic periods according to the Polity variable as we did above. For autocratic periods, we then divide them into different regimes if chief executives of government are different according to the Archigos dataset (version 2.5).[31] Consequently, each autocratic regime now represents one dictator. For a democratic period, we treat it as one regime, because leadership changes are so frequent in democracies that many democratic regimes would not survive five full calendar years or longer if we divided them by leadership changes.

With this definition of a regime, we conduct exactly the same analysis as in the previous subsections. Table 11.6 lists dictators under whose rule annual economic growth exceeds the 80th percentile of the growth distribution among all regimes. The table also reports whether human development performances are above the 80th percentile of the distribution and whether each autocrat passes the robustness checks. The majority of successful autocratic regimes identified in Table 11.5 also appear in this table and perform well in health and/or education, too. Brazil (1965–1974) and Thailand (1958–1968) do not appear here because both regimes have relatively frequent leadership changes and are therefore split into multiple regimes of less than five full calendar years. Chile (1973–1981) and Cuba (1961–1976) are dropped because these regimes are part of a dictator's long-lived rule (Pinochet and Castro) and these dictators perform less successfully during the rest of their rule.

Since our theory in Section 11.2 emphasizes the role of leadership changes under the fixed parameters of regime characteristics, we prefer the definition of regimes according to the authority characteristics coded by the Polity dataset, which allows leadership changes to happen within each autocratic regime. However, Table 11.6 shows that the definition of regimes does not affect the list of successful autocratic regimes substantially.

11.3.3.2 Definition of Democracy

We define democracies as regimes whose Polity score is positive. However, this definition allows some dubious cases to be classified as democracies and it also does not strictly coincide with the presence of regularized contests for executive power as our model characterizes democracy. Table 11.7 shows the list of regimes whose Polity score is between 1 and 5 inclusive and whose growth rate is above the 80th percentile of the distribution of all regimes. Ten more regimes now enter the league table for economic growth. Among them, South Korea (1963–1972) and Greece (1949–1967) join the core set of successful autocracies in Table 11.5.

We further check the robustness of our definition of democracy to the use of a completely different democracy dataset, the one by Przeworski et al. (2000).[32] We define a regime as a period in which three aspects of political institutions remain the same: (1) how the chief executive is elected (directly, indirectly, or not elected by popular elections); (2) how the legislature is elected (elected by popular elections, not elected, nonexistent); and (3) the number of legal political parties (more than one, one, none).[33] A regime is democratic if all of the following five conditions are met: (1) the chief executive is elected directly or indirectly; (2) the legislature is elected by popular elections; (3) there is more than one legal political party; (4) the

Table 11.6 Successful autocrats

Country	Years	Name of autocrat	Annual growth (%)	Robust for growth	Health Success	Health Robust	Education Success	Education Robust
Rwanda	1994–2004	Paul Kagame	10.19	N	N	—	N	—
China	1980–1997	Deng Xiaoping	8.51	Y	Y	Y	Y	N
Equatorial Guinea	1969–1979	Macias Nguema	8.07	Y	N	—	—	—
Liberia	1997–2003	Charles Taylor	7.94	Y	N	—	N	—
Greece	1967–1973	Papadopoulos	7.90	Y	Y	Y	N	—
South Korea	1972–1979	Park Chung Hee	7.74	Y	Y	Y	Y	Y
Belarus	1995–2004	Lukashenko	7.23	N	N	—	N	—
China	1997–2003	Jiang Zemin	7.20	Y	Y	N	Y	N
Portugal	1968–1974	Caetano	7.03	Y	Y	Y	N	—
Equatorial Guinea	1979–2004	Nguema Mbasogo	7.02	N	N	—	Y	N
South Korea	1980–1987	Chun Doo Hwan	6.61	Y	N	N	N	—
Taiwan	1978–1988	Chiang Ching-Kuo	6.25	N	Y	N	N	—
Iraq	1968–1979	Hassan Al-Bakr	6.17	Y	N	—	N	—
Swaziland	1968–1982	Subhuza II	6.14	Y	N	—	N	—
Taiwan	1950–1975	Chiang Kai-shek	5.98	N	Y	Y	—	—
Nicaragua	1947–1956	Anastasio Somoza Garcia	5.91	Y	—	—	—	—
North Korea	1948–1994	Kim Il-Sung	5.83	Y	Y	N	—	—
Spain	1939–1975	Franco	5.77	Y	Y	Y	Y	Y
Singapore	1965–1990	Lee Kuan Yew	5.77	N	N	—	N	—
Poland	1970–1980	Gierek	5.76	Y	Y	Y	N	—

Country	Years	Name of autocrat	Annual growth (%)	Robust for growth	Health		Education	
					Success	Robust	Success	Robust
Romania	1965–1989	Ceaușescu	5.68	Y	Y	N	Y	Y
Vietnam	1991–1997	Do Muoi	5.55	N	Y	N	Y	Y
Portugal	1932–1968	Salazar	5.01	N	Y	Y	—	—
Venezuela	1950–1958	Perez Jimenez	4.93	Y	—	—	—	—
Qatar	1995–2004	Amad Al Thani	4.87	Y	N	—	N	—
Bhutan	1972–1998	Jigme Singye Wangchuck	4.83	N	N	—	—	—
Mexico	1976–1982	Lopez Portillo	4.63	Y	N	—	Y	Y
Indonesia	1966–1998	Suharto	4.30	N	N	—	Y	N
Iran	1989–1997	Rafsanjani	4.17	Y	N	—	N	—
Congo-Brazzaville	1969–1977	Ngouabi	4.16	Y	N	—	Y	Y
Iran	1955–1979	Mohammad Reza	4.01	N	N	—	N	—
Pakistan	1977–1988	Zia	3.78	Y	N	—	N	—
Nigeria	1966–1975	Gowon	3.73	Y	N	—	N	—
Peru	1950–1956	Odria	3.73	N	—	—	—	—
UAE	1971–2004	An-Nahayan	3.70	N	N	—	N	—
Panama	1968–1981	Torrijos Herrera	3.68	N	Y	Y	Y	Y
Mexico	1952–1958	Ruiz Cortines	3.65	N	—	—	—	—

Note: Included in the list are autocrats under whose rule annual growth rate exceeds the 80th percentile of the distribution. Years indicates the period in which an autocrat rules the country nondemocratically. Robust for growth is "Y" if an autocrat's rule does not fail to pass the three robustness checks described in the note for Table 11.2. For columns titled Health and Education, see the note for Table 11.5.

Table 11.7 Successful regimes with their polity score between 1 and 5

Regime	Annual growth (%)	Robust for growth	Health Success	Health Robust	Education Success	Education Robust
South Korea (1963–1972)	6.57	Y	Y	Y	Y	Y
Greece (1949–1967)	5.33	Y	Y	Y	—	—
Pakistan (1962–1969)	4.66	Y	N	—	—	—
Malaysia (1971–1995)	4.63	N	N	—	N	—
Turkey (1954–1960)	4.55	Y	—	—	—	—
France (1958–1969)	4.27	Y	N	—	—	—
Cambodia (1998–2004)	4.14	Y	N	—	Y	N
Brazil (1947–1958)	3.77	N	—	—	—	—
Sri Lanka (1982–2001)	3.62	N	Y	N	Y	N
Thailand (1978–1988)	3.59	N	Y	N	N	—

Note: Listed in the table are regimes whose Polity score is between 1 and 5 inclusive, and whose annual economic growth exceeds the 80th percentile of the distribution. See also notes for Table 11.5 for the last five columns in the table.

current chief executive will not establish nonparty or one-party rule or unconstitutionally close the legislature in subsequent years; and (5) there was, or will be, partisan power alternation via elections.[34] Otherwise a regime is autocratic.

Table 11.8 provides the list of successful autocracies when we define democratic and autocratic regimes in this way. Since the data from Przeworski et al. (2000) ends in 1990, none of the autocracies since then appear in this table.[35] Autocracies in Romania, Spain, South Korea, China, Panama, Portugal, and Thailand appear in this table as well. Except for South Korea, however, the robustness of their good performances is more tenuous than in Table 11.5. Brazil and Greece drop off the list because these two regimes are split into multiple autocracies according to the coding in Przeworski et al. (2000). Chile and Poland drop off the list because the less successful period of autocracy (the 1980s) is now integrated into the same regime. Cuba drops off due to the lack of coding in Przeworski et al. (2000).

11.3.4 Correlates of Successful Autocracies

In what kind of countries do successful autocracies tend to emerge? In this section, we seek exogenous characteristics of countries that are correlated

Table 11.8 Successful autocracies defined by Przeworski et al. (2000)

Regime	Annual growth (%)	Robust for growth	Health		Education	
			Success	Robust	Success	Robust
Botswana (1966–1990)	7.90	N	Y	N	N	—
Ecuador (1972–1979)	7.73	Y	N	—	N	—
South Korea (1981–1988)	7.67	Y	N	—	N	—
South Korea (1973–1980)	7.41	Y	Y	Y	Y	Y
Jordan (1955–1966)	7.21	Y	N	—	N	—
Singapore (1965–1981)	7.05	N	N	—	N	—
Iraq (1963–1980)	.6.77	Y	Y	N	N	—
South Korea (1963–1972)	6.57	N	Y	Y	Y	Y
Taiwan (1952–1990)	6.20	N	Y	N	N	—
Portugal (1951–1974)	5.60	Y	N	—	N	—
Romania (1961–1990)	5.31	N	Y	N	N	—
China (1961–1990)	5.18	N	Y	N	Y	N
Spain (1951–1977)	5.01	N	N	—	N	—
Niger (1974–1983)	4.96	N	N	—	N	—
Morocco (1956–1963)	4.85	Y	N	—	N	—
Thailand (1957–1969)	4.71	N	Y	Y	N	—
Togo (1961–1967)	4.70	Y	N	—	N	—
Panama (1978–1984)	4.67	Y	Y	N	N	—
Pakistan (1962–1969)	4.66	Y	N	—	N	—
Singapore (1981–1990)	4.35	N	N	—	N	—
Malaysia (1971–1990)	4.31	N	Y	N	N	—
Iran (1963–1979)	4.28	N	N	—	N	—
Uruguay (1976–1982)	4.11	Y	N	—	N	—
Indonesia (1971–1990)	4.02	N	N	—	Y	N
Lesotho (1970–1984)	3.95	N	N	—	Y	N
Philippines (1972–1978)	3.93	N	N	—	Y	Y
Syria (1963–1970)	3.82	Y	Y	N	N	—
Egypt (1979–1990)	3.34	N	N	—	N	—

Successful in human development only

Panama (1969–1978)	2.59	—	Y	Y	Y	Y
Togo (1979–1990)	−3.76	—	Y	Y	Y	Y

Note: Listed in the table are autocracies, as defined by Przeworski et al. (2000), whose annual economic growth exceeds the 80th percentile of the distribution. Also included are autocracies successful in human development only (the last two rows). Also see notes for Table 11.5.

with the incidence of successful autocracies. It turns out that exogenous country characteristics often used in the literature to explain socioeconomic performances, on the whole, do not seem to explain (in a statistical sense) the emergence of successful autocracies.

We estimate the following probit regression for the sample of autocratic regimes (defined by the Polity dataset), to see if any country characteristics predict successful autocracies:

$$\Pr(SUCCESS_{ic}^k = 1) = \Phi(\alpha + \mathbf{X}_c\beta + \mathbf{Z}_{ic}\gamma), \qquad (11.7)$$

where $SUCCESS_{ic}^k$ is 1 if an autocratic regime i in country c appears in the list in Table 11.k, where $k \in \{2, 3, 4, 5\}$, and 0 otherwise, $\Phi(\cdot)$ is the cumulative distribution function of the standard normal distribution, α is a constant, and $\mathbf{Z}_{ic}$ is a vector of controls including region dummies[36] and dummies for the decades (1960s, 1970s, 1980s, 1990s) in which regime i emerges. $\mathbf{X}_c$ is a vector of the exogenous characteristics of country c that are known as determinants of the quality of government and institutions in the literature (ethnic fractionalization, legal origins, European settlers' mortality).

Table 11.9 shows the results from this analysis. Columns 1 to 3 look at success in economic growth ($k = 2$). Column 1 shows that ethnic fractionalization, which Alesina et al. (2003) identify as a significant determinant of economic growth, does not predict the emergence of successful autocracies. Column 2 shows that European settlers' mortality, which Acemoglu, Johnson, and Robinson (2001) argue affects the degree of secure property rights and thus the level of economic development today, does not predict the economic success of autocracies, either.

In column 3, we deal with a concern that economically successful autocracies simply reflect oil booms. Autocratic regimes in oil-producing countries like Ecuador, Equatorial Guinea, Gabon, Indonesia, Iran, Iraq, UAE, and Venezuela appear in Table 11.2. It may be the case that these successful autocracies simply coincide with periods of high oil prices. To deal with this concern, we replace $\mathbf{X}_c$ in equation (11.7) with the interaction term between a dummy for oil-exporting countries and the deviation of the average world oil price during the period in which regime i exists from the 1960–2004 average.[37] If the coefficient on this interaction term is positive, then successful autocracies simply reflect the oil-price boom that these regimes enjoy. Column 3 shows that the coefficient is significantly *negative*, suggesting that oil-price booms actually make autocracies less likely to be

Table 11.9 Exogenous country characteristics and successful autocracy

Dependent variable	(1) Growth	(2) Growth	(3) Growth	(4) Health	(5) Health	(6) Education	(7) Education	(8) Core	(9) Core
Ethnic fractionalization	−0.12 [0.16]			−0.54** [0.25]		−0.01 [0.19]		−0.35 [0.47]	
Log European settlers' mortality		−0.0270 [0.0336]							0.0377 [0.1599]
French legal origin					−0.10 [0.25]		0.12 [0.09]	0.89*** [0.11]	
Socialist legal origin					0.52* [0.28]		0.40 [0.30]	0.98*** [0.02]	
German legal origin					0.59*** [0.15]		−0.16 [0.11]	0.78*** [0.08]	
Oil price boom			−0.02** [0.01]						
Constant	Yes	Yes	Yes	Yes	Yes	Yes	Yes	Yes	Yes
Decade dummies	Yes	Yes	Yes	Yes	Yes	Yes	Yes	Yes	Yes
Region dummies	Yes	Yes	Yes	Yes	Yes	Yes	Yes	Yes	Yes
Observations	176	74	170	89	90	148	149	38	19
Pseudo R^2	0.25	0.15	0.3	0.19	0.22	0.16	0.20	0.32	0.12

Note: Reported are the marginal effect for continuous regressors and the discrete change in the probability of success for dummy regressors (legal origins), both evaluated at the mean of all regressors. Robust standard errors are reported in brackets. The unit of observation is an autocratic regime. The dependent variables are a dummy for success in economic growth (included in Table 11.2) in columns 1–3, a dummy for success in health production (included in Table 11.3) in columns 4–5, a dummy for success in education (included in Table 11.4) in columns 6–7, and a dummy for being included in the core set of successful autocracies (Table 11.5). Decade dummies refers to dummies indicating the decade in which the regime begins (1960s, 1970s, 1980s, 1990s, with decades before 1960 omitted). Region dummies include east Asia and Pacific, eastern Europe and central Asia, south Asia, Middle East and north Africa, sub-Saharan Africa, and Latin America and the Caribbean (with western Europe omitted). Depending on the specification, some dummies perfectly predict the dependent variable, which causes reductions in the number of observations. Asterisks indicate significance: * at the 10% level; ** at 5%; *** at 1%.

successful.[38] If we interpret oil export revenues as the source of distributional conflict (a large T in our model), this finding is consistent with our theory though we cannot exclude alternative explanations such as Caselli (2006).

In columns 4 and 5, we look at success in health production ($k = 3$). La Porta et al. (1999) find that ethnic fractionalization and French legal origin are positively correlated with infant mortality. Column 4 shows that autocratic regimes successful in health production tend to be in countries with lower ethnic fractionalization. Thus, the performance of autocracies in terms of health partly reflects the effect of ethnic homogeneity. However, as a low value of the Pseudo R^2 indicates, it is not the whole story. Column 5 shows that French legal origin does not explain the success of autocracies in health production. Countries with a socialist legal origin tend to have autocracies successful in terms of health. This result may be in line with our theory to the extent that Communist regimes tend to have a strong selectorate. The positive correlation of German legal origin and success in health is difficult to interpret because only regimes in South Korea and Taiwan have German legal origin in the sample.

The dependent variable in columns 6 and 7 is success in education ($SUCCESS_{ic}^4$). La Porta et al. (1999) also find that ethnic fractionalization and French legal origin are negatively correlated with school enrollment. We do not find that these two exogenous country characteristics are correlated with success in education among autocracies, either.[39]

Finally, columns 8 and 9 investigate whether the core set of successful autocracies identified in Table 11.5 have any particular characteristics ($k = 5$). Since the number of successful autocracies is very limited in these regressions, a large number of observations are dropped because some decade dummies and region dummies perfectly predict success. Neither ethnic fractionalization nor European settlers' mortality is significantly correlated with success. Compared to British legal origin, countries with French legal origin are *more* likely to see successful autocracies, contrary to the negative correlation between French legal origin and the quality of government, found by La Porta et al. (1999). Countries with socialist or German legal origins are also more likely to have successful autocracies than those with British legal origin. Indeed, only Thailand has British legal origin among the countries listed in Table 11.5.

A positive correlation between socialist legal origin and the likelihood of successful autocracy might seem counterfactual. Our theory implies that Communist regimes are successful to the extent that the ideology of Communism ensures the secure hold of power by the selectorate (typically top Communist-party officials). Perhaps Communism encourages groups of citizens outside the regime to accept autocratic rule, while opposition groups in dictatorships without any ideology find it hard to accept such rule and thus pose a significant threat to the selectorate. Alternatively, the presence of an ideology such as Communism may enhance coordination among members of the ruling group to establish an effective mechanism to repress the opposition. Either way, our model does not predict that Communism per se breeds success. The later years of Ceaușescu's rule in Romania (see Section 11.4.1.3 below) is an example of a Communist regime being transformed into a regime based on personal rule.

These results suggest that the previous literature on the quality of government and institutions cannot fully explain why some autocracies are successful in achieving high economic growth, better health, and better education. A theory to explain successful autocracies is necessary to make further progress. We now investigate how well institutional features identified in our model relate to cases of successful autocracy as identified by this empirical exercise.

11.4   Link to the Theory

The previous section identified the core set of successful autocracies. In this section, we link these autocracies to our theory in Section 11.2. We first provide several case studies of successful autocracies to motivate the institutional context suggested by our theory. Next, we provide evidence that autocracies are more likely to be successful if the rate of leadership change is high, which is consistent with our theory. Finally, we exploit the natural death of leaders as a natural experiment to see if the selectorate's grip on power is indeed secure in successful autocracies, as predicted by our theory.

11.4.1   The Selectorate in Successful Autocracies: Some Case Studies

A core idea in our model is the role of the selectorate in organizing leadership contests *within* regimes in successful autocracies. We begin by looking at five case studies suggested by Table 11.5. Of these, we will argue that Brazil (1965–1974), China (1976–2004), and Romania (1948–1977) appear to be consistent with our theory. On the other hand, Spain (1939–1975) does not seem to match very well with our theoretical predictions. Finally, we consider South Korea (1973–1981). Although this does not seem to fit with our theory either, the advent of this autocratic regime can be explained by our theoretical framework.

11.4.1.1 Brazil (October 1965–January 1974)

According to the Polity dataset, the Brazilian military dictatorship from 1964 to 1985 went through three regime changes, in 1965, 1974, and 1982. Tables 11.2 and 11.4 reveal that the second phase was successful in economic development and primary school enrollment. During this period, Humberto Castelo Branco, Artur da Costa e Silva, and Emilio Garrastazu Medici were the chief executives (presidents) according to the Archigos dataset.

The de facto selectorate of this regime was the armed forces. The national legislature (Congress) had the formal right to elect a president.[40] However, it was only allowed to rubber-stamp the sole presidential candidate presented by the military both when the presidential term for Castelo Branco came to an end in 1967 and when Costa e Silva was incapacitated due to a stroke in 1969. In both cases, top military officers chose a candidate behind whom the armed forces could be united (Skidmore 1988, 18–21, 51–53; Stepan 1971, 248–52).

The replacement of Castelo Branco in 1967 appears to be consistent with our theoretical prediction that the selectorate can oust a poorly performing incumbent in a successful autocracy. Kaufman (1979, 172–73) argues that Castelo Branco's economic policy resulted in only a moderate reduction in inflation and that the recession in the industrial southeast showed few signs of abating. Castelo Branco was determined to step down in 1967 (Stepan 1971, 248), but he tried to nominate his successor and prevent Costa e Silva from assuming office (Skidmore 1988, 51–52). It appears that he failed to do so in part due to the unpopularity of his economic policies among military officers. Upon assuming the presidency, Costa e Silva appointed Delfim Neto as finance minister, under whose economic management the Brazilian economy grew rapidly.

The presidential succession after the incapacitation of Costa e Silva also shows that the Brazilian armed forces' grip on power was secure. Although the Constitution stipulated that the vice president would succeed the incapacitated president, the military did not allow Vice President Pedro Aleixo, a veteran congressman, to take office. Those outside the regime, including congressmen, had no say in leadership selection.

This episode is consistent with our theory in that successful autocracies are those with a selectorate whose power is secure in the case of a leadership replacement.

11.4.1.2 China (since September 1976)

Since the death of Mao Zedong, who had been Communist Party chairman since the proclamation of the People's Republic of China in 1949, China has been a stable autocratic regime according to the Polity dataset. As tables 11.2 to 11.4 show, the Communist regime of China during this period was successful in economic and human development (though success in human development was less spectacular than in Mao's era). According to the Archigos dataset, Hua Guofeng, Deng Xiaoping, Jiang Zemin, and Hu Jintao were the chief executives under this regime.

Members of the Politburo of the Chinese Communist Party appear to correspond to the selectorate in our theory. Formally, the party's leader (party chairman until 1982 and general secretary afterward) is elected by the Central Committee of the party whose several hundreds of members are in turn elected by the Party Congress. However, members of the Central Committee are de facto appointed by around 20 members of the Politburo.[41]

After the death of Mao Zedong, Hua Guofeng assumed party chairmanship by the Politburo's appointment.[42] During the subsequent years until his resignation as party chairman in June of 1981, Hua's power was gradually transferred to Deng Xioaping, apparently because the Politburo members were dissatisfied with Hua's attempt to continue Mao's policies (Lieberthal 2004, 125–27). This gradual power transfer paralleled the replacement of Hua's supporters with Deng's in the Politburo membership.[43]

As Deng never assumed leadership formally, it is hard to tell whether members of the Politburo disciplined him during his rule. However, the selection of general secretary of the party does appear to have been in the hands of the Politburo. Hu Yaobang, Deng's designated successor and general secretary since 1982, resigned in January of 1988, when several members of the Politburo were dissatisfied with his economic policies and tolerance on pro-democracy student protests.[44] Zhao Ziang, who succeeded

Hu as general secretary, was in turn dismissed by the Politburo for similar reasons in May of 1989.[45]

The handover of power from Deng to Jiang Zemin, who was appointed as general secretary in June of 1989, took place gradually.[46] Jiang was formally reelected as general secretary by the Central Committee in October of 1992 and September of 1997. Given that Central Committee members are effectively appointed by the Politburo, the reelection of Jiang implies that the Politburo supported him. In November of 2002, Hu Jintao became general secretary. Lieberthal (2004, 156) notes that "Jiang reportedly tried to convince his colleagues to allow him to stay on as general secretary." But he failed, indicating that members of the Politburo supported Hu's succession.

In every case of leadership succession over this period, the opposition to the Communist Party rule did not manage to participate in leadership selection. In our model's term, $\Gamma(\phi, \upsilon)$ was close to 1 because the opposition group is effectively disenfranchised ($\phi \approx 1$) and/or their voice counts little ($\upsilon \approx 0$). When Zhao Ziang was dismissed in May of 1989, for example, there had been student-led antigovernment demonstrations in Beijing since April. The Communist government, however, managed to stay in power by mobilizing the army to suppress the demonstrations (the Tiananmen Square massacre).[47]

Overall, China since 1976 fits well with our model of autocracy and with case 1 of proposition 11.1.

11.4.1.3 Romania (January 1948–January 1977)

From the proclamation of the People's Republic of Romania until Nicolae Ceauşescu consolidated his personal rule, Romania's Communist rule is coded as one regime by the Polity dataset. According to the Archigos dataset, Gheorghe Gheorghiu-Dej and Nicolae Ceauşescu were the rulers during this period. As tables 11.2 to 11.4 show, the regime's performance is impressive in all three dimensions of development.

Top officials in the Communist Party were clearly the selectorate under this regime. At a meeting in October of 1945, the party's Central Committee secretaries agreed that Gheorghiu-Dej would become general secretary, the top position to lead the party (Tismaneanu 2003, 121). At the Central Committee plenum in March of 1956, two members of the Politburo (Iosif Chisinevschi and Miron Constantinescu) openly challenged Gheorghiu-Dej's authority. When Gheorghiu-Dej died of lung cancer in

March of 1965, members of the Politburo chose Ceaușescu as his successor (ibid., 185–86).

It appears that Gheorghui-Dej decided to promote industrialization after his Stalinist background became the source of criticism due to Khrushchev's Secret Speech, denouncing Stalinism, in 1956. In this context, the leadership challenge by Chisinevschi and Constantinescu, mentioned above, took place. Determined to promote industrialization, Gheorghui-Dej even resisted Khrushchev's plan to transform Romania into the agricultural base in the Soviet bloc.[48]

Ceaușescu continued this effort of industrialization. By the time this centrally planned industrialization had caused economic problems in the late 1970s, however, Ceaușescu had managed to consolidate his power and had established his personal cult, appointing his wife as the number two in the Communist Party hierarchy and promoting his son as heir apparent.[49] The selectorate's grip on power appears to have become dependent on Ceaușescu, unable to discipline his devastating economic policies in the 1980s.

11.4.1.4 Spain (April 1939–November 1975)

Franco ruled Spain during this period (from the end of the Civil War until his death). Although the regime began in 1939, the data that we used to identify Franco as a successful autocrat comes from the 1950s at the earliest.

We are unable to find any characteristics of Franco's regime consistent with our theory. The formal rule of leadership succession (Law of Succession), adopted in a popular referendum on July 6, 1947, stipulated that Spain was a monarchy that Franco would govern until his death and that Franco had the right to appoint his successor.[50] Therefore, there was no selectorate, at least formally.

Franco's supporters consisted of Falangists (Spanish fascists), the military, the Catholic church, and monarchists. These groups might be seen as the selectorate, but there is little evidence that any of them seriously challenged Franco's leadership (Grugel and Rees 1997, 30–43, 51–58). Franco's balancing act looks like the divide-and-rule tactic, which Acemoglu, Robinson, and Verdier (2004) identify as the source of long-lasting kleptocracy.

Given the personal-rule characteristics of the regime, Franco's flexibility on economic policies is remarkable. When the policy of autarky and import-substitution industrialization ended up with government deficits, inflation, and current-account imbalances by the mid-1950s, culminating in strikes and student protests, Franco shuffled the cabinet, appointing two technocrats, Alberto Ullastres and Mariano Navarro Rubio, as economic ministers in 1957. When the two ministers proposed the abandonment of the autarky policy and the plan for macroeconomic stabilization, Franco accepted the proposal even though this was against his ideology (Payne 1987, 470). We cannot relate this policy change to the selectorate's pressure on Franco. If any, there appears to have been pressure from the opposition outside the regime—protesting workers and students in the 1950s. Weirdly enough, the logic of successful democracy in our model seems to apply here, although it is not through regularized elections but through strikes and protests. Alternatively, Franco might have been a good policymaker in the terms of our model.

11.4.1.5 South Korea (February 1973–March 1981)

According to the Polity dataset, the South Korean military dictatorship, initiated by a coup in 1961, went through four changes of authority characteristics (1963, 1972, 1973, 1981).[51] We have identified the fourth regime as the most successful.[52] During this period, Archigos identifies four leaders ruling the country: Park Chung Hee until his assassination in 1979, Choi Kyu Hah from 1979 to 1980, Park Chung Hun briefly in 1980, and Chun Doo Hwan from 1980 (who continued to rule the country until 1988).

Formally, the selectorate was an electoral college, the National Conference for Unification (NCU), whose members were elected by popular vote on a nonpartisan basis. The Constitution (proposed by Park Chung Hee and approved in a referendum in November 1972) stipulated that the NCU would elect the president for six years with no term limits. Elections for the NCU took place in December 1972 (5,876 candidates contested the 2,359 seats with 225 unopposed in their constituencies) and in May 1978 (boycotted by opposition parties); both were followed by the reelection of Park as president.[53] (Park had been president since 1961.) After Park's assassination, the NCU elected Choi Kyu Hah, who had been prime minister since 1975, as the new president in December 1979. After the resignation of Choi in August 1980, the NCU elected Chun Doo Hwan as the new president in the same month.[54] It is not entirely clear whether members of the NCU had any influence on leadership selection, however.[55]

Informally, the Korean CIA (KCIA), the regime's secret police organization, could have been the selectorate. It was the KCIA chief who assassinated

Park in 1979. However, the assassin's predecessors as KCIA chief had been repeatedly purged by Park (Clifford 1998, 80–90). There is little evidence that anyone within the regime credibly threatened to oust Park.

A threat does appear to have come from those outside the regime, especially the opposition party leader Kim Dae Jung.[56] He ran for the presidency in the 1971 election, only narrowly defeated by Park, even though Park's export-led industrialization policy since the mid-1960s had been successful. This electoral result appears to have prompted Park to abolish multiparty direct presidential elections in 1972.[57] We can interpret this series of events in terms of our model. South Korea in the early 1970s could have been a case of high polarization where $(1 - \pi) \Delta < \tau$. Although the economy grew rapidly and therefore the size of the pie to share among the population, T, became larger, workers did not benefit much from it due to wage suppression by the regime.[58] The opposition group, therefore, would never reward the incumbent's good behavior. Park's supporters, including the business community (and Park himself if he was a good policymaker in the terms of our model), therefore preferred the autocratic regime in which the selectorate could discipline the incumbent (or Park as a good policymaker could keep choosing a good policy without being ousted).

11.4.2 Turnover

Our theory predicts that autocracies are successful if the selectorate can credibly remove poorly performing leaders. This implies that an autocratic regime with a high rate of leadership change is more likely to be successful on average than those with less turnover.[59]

To test this empirical implication, we obtain the number of leadership changes for each autocratic regime from the Archigos dataset.[60] We then calculate the number of leadership changes per year for each regime. The raw data support the idea that there are turnover differences in successful and unsuccessful autocracies (as identified in the base case of Section 11.3.1 above). The probability of turnover in a successful autocracy is 13% compared to 7% in an unsuccessful autocracy (the difference being statistically significant at 5%). This implies that leaders in successful autocratic regimes spend, on average, seven-and-a-half years in office compared to nine years for unsuccessful autocratic regimes. Interestingly, this contrasts with a much higher rate of annual turnover of leaders (26%) in regimes classified as democracies, implying an average leadership tenure of just over four years.

To examine this further, we estimate equation (11.7) where $\mathbf{X}_c$ is replaced with the number of leadership changes per year for regime i. Table 11.10 shows the estimated marginal effect of the rate of leadership change. The dependent variable in column 1 is a dummy indicating economic success (whether an autocratic regime is listed in Table 11.2). The higher rate of leadership change is significantly associated with a higher likelihood of economic success, consistent with our theoretical prediction. One standard deviation in the number of leadership changes per year (0.11) changes the probability of economic success by around 11 percentage points.

If we restrict economic success to robust cases, the significant positive correlation between leadership turnover and success remains (column 2). For success in health and education, however, columns 3 to 6 show no significant correlation between the rate of leadership change and regime performance. In column 7, the dependent variable is a dummy indicating whether an autocratic regime is in the core set of successful ones identified in Table 11.5. There is no correlation for this group either.[61]

In sum, this evidence suggestively supports a key idea from our theory when economic success is used as the outcome. The results on health and education suggest that the selectorate in autocracy is less responsive to leadership performance in human development, perhaps because members of the selectorate can afford private alternatives to state health and education.

11.4.3 Death of the Leader as a Natural Experiment

Our theory predicts that an autocracy is successful if the selectorate's grip on power is secure ($\Gamma(\phi, \upsilon)$ is high). More specifically, an autocrat is disciplined by the selectorate if overthrowing him does not lead to the seizure of power by citizens outside the selectorate.

Observing $\Gamma(\phi, \upsilon)$ for each autocratic regime is not an easy task. We may observe a leadership change in a poorly performing autocracy with the selectorate remaining in power afterward. This may be interpreted as an unsuccessful autocracy with a high $\Gamma(\phi, \upsilon)$, which is apparently inconsistent with our theory. However, it can also be interpreted as an equilibrium outcome of our model where the policymaker chooses the bad policy and thus gets removed from office by the selectorate with a high $\Gamma(\phi, \upsilon)$. The problem here is that leadership changes are endogenous to the regime performance.

Table 11.10 Leadership turnover and successful autocracies

Dependent variable	(1) Success in growth	(2) Robust success in growth	(3) Success in health	(4) Robust success in health	(5) Success in education	(6) Robust success in education	(7) Core success
Number of leadership changes per year	0.99*** [0.28]	0.61*** [0.20]	−0.22 [0.57]	−0.34 [0.58]	−0.29 [0.38]	0.08 [0.28]	0.09 [0.96]
Constant	Yes	Yes	Yes	Yes	Yes	Yes	Yes
Decade dummies	Yes	Yes	Yes	Yes	Yes	Yes	Yes
Region dummies	Yes	Yes	Yes	Yes	Yes	Yes	Yes
Observations	177	177	90	84	149	149	38
Pseudo R^2	0.31	0.26	0.15	0.20	0.17	0.12	0.23

Note: Reported are the marginal effects evaluated at the mean of all regressors. Robust standard errors are reported in brackets. The unit of observation is an autocratic regime. The dependent variables are: in column 1, a dummy for being included in Table 11.2; in column 2, a dummy for being included in Table 11.2 and not failing to pass any robustness checks; in column 3, a dummy for being included in Table 11.3; in column 4, a dummy for being included in Table 11.3 and passing the robustness check; in column 5, a dummy for being included in Table 11.4; in column 6, a dummy for being included in Table 11.4 and passing the robustness check; in column 7, a dummy for being included in Table 11.5. See Table 11.9 for details on decade and region dummies. Asterisks indicate significance: * at the 10% level; ** at 5%; *** at 1%.

However, if a leader dies or becomes incapacitated due to natural causes, whether the selectorate remains in power afterward does indicate $\Gamma(\phi, \upsilon)$. Our theory, therefore, predicts that an autocratic regime performs well if a random death or incapacitation of the leader does not lead to the loss of power by the selectorate. It also should be the case that after a poorly performing dictator dies due to natural causes, the selectorate is likely to change.[62]

Table 11.11 shows the list of autocratic regimes (with data on either growth, health, or education) under which the chief executive died in office due to natural causes, according to the Archigos dataset. Among the core set of successful autocracies identified in Table 11.5, regimes in China, Poland, Portugal, Romania, Spain, and Thailand went through a natural death of the leader. We already saw above that the deaths of Deng Xiaoping in China and Gheorghe Gheorghiu-Dej in Romania did not lead to the loss of power by the selectorate, indicating that these two regimes had a high value of $\Gamma(\phi, \upsilon)$, and this might have allowed the selectorate to discipline their leader. We find that Portugal and Thailand are also consistent with our theory.[63] To see whether unsuccessful autocracies confronted with a random death reveal a poorly entrenched selectorate, we also look at Guinea.

We proceed as follows. For each autocratic regime, we (1) describe the performance of an autocrat who died in office; (2) identify the selectorate under the dead leader's rule; and (3) investigate whether the selectorate remained in power after the death.

11.4.3.1 Portugal (July 1930–April 1974)

Prime Minister Oliveira Salazar suffered a cerebral thrombosis and hemorrhage, lapsing into a coma on September 16, 1968.[64] Salazar had been premier since 1932. His rule was successful in economic growth and health production as seen in Table 11.6 (though in growth, success was not robust).

The selectorate under Salazar's rule appears to have been the armed forces,[65] which controlled the government since its seizure of power in 1926. The Constitution of 1933 stipulated that the ceremonial president had the power to appoint and remove premiers, and the post of presidency was consistently given to military men (Wiarda 1977, 100, 122–23).

The armed forces retained control of the country after Salazar's incapacitation (Wiarda 1977, 253–54). President Americo Thomaz, a retired admiral, summoned the Council of State, a constitutional advisory body consisting of the nation's prominent figures, and also met with other powerful figures of the regime. On September 26, Thomaz announced publicly that he had released Salazar from his post and had appointed Marcello Caetano as prime minister. Caetano remained in power until 1974.[66]

This sequence of events after the incapacitation of Salazar indicates that the selectorate's grip on power was rather secure. Salazar, whose rule could be seen as personal rule, may actually have been disciplined by the military and thus had an incentive to promote economic development and improve people's health.

11.4.3.2 Thailand (October 1958–February 1968)

Prime Minister Sarit Thanarat died from heart and lung ailments on December 8, 1963 (Lentz 1994, 749). Sarit, a military officer, seized power in a bloodless coup in October 1958. His dictatorial rule performed well in economic growth and health production.[67]

The selectorate under Sarit's regime appears to have been King Bhumibol Adulyadej and the military. In February 1959, Sarit was formally elected prime minister by the Constituent Assembly, whose members were appointed by royal decree.[68] According to Chaloemtiarana (2007, 187), 152 out of the 220 members of the assembly were military officers. Chaloemtiarana (2007, ch. 6) argues that Sarit needed the support of the military and the king. The support of the king appears to have been the most crucial for Sarit, as he "accorded the throne much more power and prestige than [his] predecessors had" to seek the military regime's legitimacy (ibid., 205).

After the death of Sarit, the selectorate remained the same. The king's influence got even stronger. Thanom Kittikachorn, a military officer who had been deputy minister and defence minister since 1959, succeeded Sarit by King Bhumibol's appointment.[69] Thanom "turned increasingly to the king for support and advice" (ibid., 217). The military had the last say in keeping Thanom in power. When Thanom's government faced student demonstrations in 1973, the military refused to suppress them, forcing Thanom to flee the country (Nelson 2001, 262).[70]

The above episode suggests that the selectorate—the king and the military—had a tight grip on power. Our theory implies that this allowed them to credibly threaten to oust Sarit or Thanom in the case of a poor

Table 11.11 Autocratic regimes with leader's natural death

Regime	Year of leader's death	Score	Annual growth (%)	Economic growth Success	Economic growth Robust	Conditional life expectancy	Health Success	Health Robust	Conditional enrollment ratio	Education Success	Education Robust
Romania (1948–1977)	1965	6	7.63	Y	Y	17.48	Y	Y	34.27	Y	Y
Spain (1939–1975)	1975	6	5.77	Y	Y	6.80	Y	Y	29.58	Y	Y
China (1976–2004)	1997	4	7.87	Y	Y	12.43	Y	N	30.98	Y	N
Poland (1947–1980)	1956	4	5.76	Y	Y	12.68	Y	Y	19.82	N	—
Portugal (1930–1974)	1968	4	5.75	Y	Y	6.15	Y	Y	8.46	N	—
Thailand (1958–1968)	1963	4	5.34	Y	Y	10.69	Y	Y		—	—
China (1969–1976)	1976	3	4.04	Y	N	13.89	Y	N	38.01	Y	N
Taiwan (1949–1975)	1975	3	5.98	Y	N	16.34	Y	Y		—	—
Taiwan (1975–1987)	1978	3	6.81	Y	N	10.08	Y	Y	5.56	N	—
Vietnam (1976–2004)	1986	3	4.47	Y	N	11.49	Y	N	22.13	Y	N
Gabon (1960–1968)	1967	2	8.59	Y	Y	−26.81	N	—		—	—
Jordan (1992–2004)	1999	2	0.89	N	—	9.67	Y	Y	−6.92	N	—
Morocco (1998–2004)	1999	2	1.19	N	—	8.73	Y	Y	2.24	N	—
North Korea (1966–2004)	1994	2	3.75	Y	N	11.35	Y	N		—	—
Syria (1970–2000)	2000	2	2.18	N	—	11.89	Y	N	21.03	Y	N
Bhutan (1953–2004)	1972	1	4.28	Y	N	0.92	N	—		—	—
Lao PDR (1975–2004)	1992	1	1.35	N	—	−3.72	N	—	27.62	Y	N

Regime	Year of leader's death	Score	Annual growth (%)	Economic growth Success	Robust	Conditional life expectancy	Health Success	Robust	Conditional enrollment ratio	Education Success	Robust
Algeria (1965–1989)	1978	0	1.35	N	—	-0.75	N	—	4.01	N	—
Egypt (1952–1976)	1970	0	1.29	N	—	-0.20	N	—	-3.77	N	—
Guinea (1958–1984)	1984	0	-0.67	N	—	-14.59	N	—	-44.54	N	—
Haiti (1961–1971)	1971	0		—	—	-3.24	N	—	-15.74	N	—
Iran (1982–1997)	1989	0	0.86	N	—	1.78	N	—	11.13	N	—
Kenya (1969–1979)	1978	0	-0.47	N	—	3.66	N	—	12.64	N	—
Kuwait (1965–1971)	1965	0		—	—	2.25	N	—	8.57	N	—
Liberia (1909–1980)	1971	0	-1.13	N	—	-9.03	N	—	-35.24	N	—
Mauritania (1962–1991)	1979	0	-0.19	N	—	-5.44	N	—	-42.17	N	—
Nepal (1962–1981)	1972	0	0.49	N	—	-4.75	N	—	-18.18	N	—
Nicaragua (1936–1979)	1966	0	2.45	N	—	-7.86	N	—	-6.87	N	—
Saudi Arabia (1926–2004)	1953, 1982	0	0.20	N	—	-12.30	N	—	-40.52	N	—
Swaziland (1973–1993)	1982	0	3.31	N	—	-9.63	N	—	10.28	N	—

Note: Listed are autocratic regimes under which the chief executive died in office due to natural causes. Year of leader's death is self-explanatory. For the rest of the columns, see notes for tables 11.3 to 11.5.

performance. The impressive performance of the Thai military regime by Sarit and Thanom on economic growth and health may have been due to the discipline imposed by the king and the military.

11.4.3.3 Guinea (October 1958–April 1984)

On March 26, 1984, President Ahmed Sekou Toure died in a U.S. hospital to which he had been taken by air from Guinea after suffering a heart attack the day before.[71] Sekou Toure had ruled Guinea since its independence. As Table 11.11 shows, the performance of his rule was miserable: a negative economic growth rate (-0.67%), lower life expectancy, and lower primary school enrollment compared to countries with the same level of real GDP per capita.[72]

The ruling selectorate appears to have been members of the Political Bureau of the sole legal party, the Parti Democratique de Guinea (PDG).[73] By Constitution, the Political Bureau of the PDG would meet to choose a new leader within 45 days after the incapacitation of the president.[74]

After the death of Sekou Toure, Prime Minister Lansana Beavogui became interim president and was supposed to succeed formally by the appointment of the PDG Political Bureau.[75] On April 3, however, young military officers staged a bloodless coup with Colonel Lansana Conte becoming the new president. The PDG was then dissolved.

This episode indicates that the selectorate, the PDG Political Bureau, stayed in power solely due to Sekou Toure's presence. They plausibly expected that they would lose power if they removed Sekou Toure ($\Gamma(\phi, \upsilon) \approx 0$). This lack of secure power on the part of the selectorate may explain why Sekou Toure performed so badly while remaining in office.[76]

Conclusion This chapter is a contribution to ongoing debates about the institutional basis of successful government. It tries to clarify and explain differences between good and bad autocracies in terms of the forces that shape accountability in the absence of regularized elections. It does so in three steps. The first is to develop a simple model of incentives to generate good policy when the decision to retain the leader is vested in a selectorate comprising citizens from some ruling "group." Second, it identifies "successful autocracies" using objective empirical criteria. Third, it uses the group of autocracies identified from this exercise as a basis for case studies in successful autocracy with a view to matching the theory to real-world experience.

Our modeling approach makes clear that democracies can be better or worse than autocracies in terms of accountability although it suggests a presumption in favour of democracy on this basis. This is consistent with the raw data. In our model, successful autocracies are those where poor-quality leadership leads to removal of leaders from office. While it is asking too much of a simple theory to do justice to the richness of the real-world experience, we find some suggestive evidence that the forces shaping leadership replacement in the way that the model suggests may be at work in successful autocracies. Leadership turnover is greater in successful compared to unsuccessful autocracies. Moreover, studying the sample of successful autocracies that handled leadership deaths from natural causes reinforces the view that successful autocracies are those where the ruling group has a hold on power.

The analysis in this chapter is a first step in a wider project. It seems essential in collecting data that characterizes differences in political regimes to be guided by what theory suggests could be important. Among the large array of impressive data-collection exercises, there is very little that provides a persuasive mapping between things that shape political incentives and outcomes. For a broad category like autocracy, it is essential to further bridge this gap in future work to understand the lessons for the genesis of good government.

This chapter provides a complement to other ongoing work in this area. The approach emphasizes the value of rooting our understanding in simple theoretical models, not least as a lens to focus empirical exercises. It also suggests a way of applying agency models to the democracy–autocracy comparison, which may have other fruitful applications. While it is evident that much remains to be done to bring theory and data together in understanding the forces that shape the quality of government, the theoretical tools that are being developed in political economy and the rich data now available provide a secure starting point for this endeavour.

ACKNOWLEDGMENTS

Timothy Besley is grateful for support from the Canadian Institute for Advanced Research (CIFAR). The authors received much helpful feedback from members of CIFAR's Institutions, Organizations, and Growth Program to which a preliminary version of this chapter was presented. Useful comments from Madhav Aney, Fernando Aragon, Peter Evans, Valentino Larcinese, Gabriel Leon, Adam Przeworski, Konstantin Sonin, and Guido Tabellini are gratefully acknowledged.

NOTES

1. The density functions are estimated by using the Gaussian kernel and the bandwidth that minimizes the mean integrated squared error. Including regimes that lasted less than five years does not change the distributions substantially except for the inclusion of democratic regimes that existed less than three years, which tend to perform very badly (growth rates less than -1%).

2. Section 11.3 provides details.

3. The shapes of the two estimated density functions are similar if we define a democratic regime as one whose Polity score is higher than 5, as Fearon (2006) does.

4. Rodrik (1997, 2000), Almeida and Ferreira (2002), and Glaeser et al. (2004, table 8) make similar observations, although the unit of observation in their analysis is a country rather than a regime. If we look at the distributions of performances in health and education conditional on per capita income, autocracies have fatter tails as well (see figures 2 and 3 of Besley and Kudamatsu [2007]).

5. The term "selectorate" is borrowed from Bueno de Mesquita et al. (2003).

6. See Besley and Kudamatsu (2007) for a more complete review of the literature.

7. See Wintrobe (1990, 1998), Egorov and Sonin (2005), and Dixit (2006) for other political economy approaches that emphasize the different forms that autocracy can take.

8. Whether group A is in the majority does not affect our analysis.

9. We require that $\pi > 0$. However, π could be very small, and many people plainly believe that it is in many practical settings. The key issue, however, is that the *possibility* of a good policymaker existing creates a role for signalling.

10. We could think of r as embezzling public funds that are supposed to be spent on public goods provision. Making Δ the lower bound on rents guarantees that it is never possible to motivate a bad policymaker to act in the general interest on the basis of his personal payoff in the current period only.

11. As we assume the same preference among citizens of each group, we do not allow a faction from the selectorate to join with the opposition to topple the regime. This possibility is interesting because a power struggle within the ruling elite in an autocracy is often cited as a force leading to democratization (see O'Donnell and Schmitter 1986).

12. The purpose of making the contest outcome probabilistic is to allow the probability of group A's candidate winning to be between 0 and 1 even if the size of support for candidate A exceeds that for B. With a finite number of citizens in our model, group A's winning probability can be a step function of κ. This

does not affect our analysis because κ only changes discretely in response to the period-one policies in our model.

13. Note that $\Gamma(\phi, \upsilon)$ does not depend on δ. This is because in an open contest, both candidates are equally likely to be good. Group B enfranchised citizens, therefore, only care about the distributional policy and always support their own candidate regardless of δ. This is no longer the case if an open contest ensues even when the selectorate of group A prefers keeping the incumbent in office. See Section 11.2.3.

14. We assume that if

$$(1 - \Gamma(\phi, \upsilon)) \left(\bar{\sigma} - \underline{\sigma}\right) T = \pi \Delta,$$

then the selectorate chooses to retain the incumbent.

15. Padro-i-Miquel (2006) uses the same logic to analyze why African dictators have implemented inefficient policies.

16. This condition implies that the policymaker's group membership is the salient issue if there is a contest for power. Were this not the case, then the group B enfranchised citizens would be content to support a group A incumbent who had taken the good general-interest action in period one if there were a contest for power at the end of period one. Thus, a guaranteed contest would strengthen incentives for good behavior in autocracy as it does in the analysis of democracy with low polarization presented in Section 11.2.3.

17. This idea is later formalized in McGuire and Olson (1996).

18. If $\upsilon > 1$, the model of democracy in this subsection can be what Levitsky and Way (2002) call *competitive authoritarianism*, a regime in which elections with universal suffrage are regularly held, with opposition groups systematically harassed so that the number of effective votes per person is less than one for opposition groups.

19. To see this, let $\gamma(\kappa')$ be the probability that the incumbent who did not produce Δ wins in an election, and $\gamma(\kappa'')$ be the probability that a randomly picked group A candidate wins. Group A citizens' expected period-two payoff is

$$\gamma(\kappa')\bar{\sigma}T + (1 - \gamma(\kappa'))(\pi \Delta + \underline{\sigma}T)$$

if they let the incumbent run for reelection, and

$$\pi \Delta + \gamma(\kappa'')\bar{\sigma}T + (1 - \gamma(\kappa''))\underline{\sigma}T$$

if they support a randomly picked candidate. Therefore, they prefer kicking out the incumbent in a primary election if

$$\gamma(\kappa')\pi \Delta + [\gamma(\kappa'') - \gamma(\kappa')](\bar{\sigma} - \underline{\sigma})T > 0.$$

We always have $\gamma(\kappa'') = \gamma(\beta)$. And we have $\gamma(\kappa') = \gamma(\beta)$ if group A never supports a group B candidate (i.e., $\pi\Delta < (\bar{\sigma} - \underline{\sigma})T$). If group A prefers a group B candidate to a bad group A politician (i.e., $\pi\Delta \geq (\bar{\sigma} - \underline{\sigma})T$), then we have $\gamma(\kappa') = 0$. Therefore, the inequality above always holds.

20. If this condition does not hold, then there will be a mixed-strategy equilibrium with a lower level of λ. This is a little tricky as it is not entirely obvious how to put mixed strategies together with probabilistic voting. However, define

$$\pi \left[\frac{(1 - \pi)(1 - \hat{\lambda})}{\pi + (1 - \pi)\hat{\lambda}} \right] \Delta = \tau.$$

Then we require that $\hat{\lambda}$ is a fixed point of the mapping

$$\hat{\lambda} = G(\psi(\hat{\lambda})(\mu - \pi\Delta) + (\psi(\hat{\lambda}) - \gamma(\beta))\tau + \Delta),$$

where $\psi\lambda) < 1$ is the probability of reelection given that the incumbent has produced Δ. Since all group B voters are, by construction, indifferent between group A and group B candidates at $\hat{\lambda}$, we suppose that a proportion ζ of the group B voters support the group A candidate ex ante (i.e., before the aggregate shock takes place) so that

$$\psi(\hat{\lambda}) = \gamma\ (\beta + \zeta(1 - \beta) - (1 - \zeta)(1 - \beta)).$$

The key observation is that any equilibrium where $\lambda = \hat{\lambda}$ must have less good behavior by the leader so that the equilibrium behavior in equation (11.4) is an upper bound on the performance of democracy consistent with the level of checks and balances in place.

21. Rauch (2001) can be seen as an attempt to endogenize π in our model in the context of autocratic regimes.

22. If the Polity score is either -66 (foreign occupation), -77 (anarchy), or -88 (regime transition periods), we see it as a year without a regime.

23. See Section 11.3.3.2 for the robustness to choosing a different cutoff value.

24. We choose $t - 1$ rather than t as the end year for calculating annual growth rate because Y_t may reflect economic turmoil caused by the regime change and/or the succeeding regime. In a few cases where the succeeding regime starts on January 1 of the next year, we use Y_t instead of Y_{t-1}. If GDP observations are not available for the entire period of a regime, we use the first and/or the last observation to calculate the growth rate. In doing so, we drop regimes with less than five years of GDP observations.

25. Note that this procedure would yield very few successful autocracies if most regimes in the top quintile of the growth distribution were democratic.

26. Grouping regimes into ten or twenty categories by initial income does not yield substantially different results.

27. Note that this procedure is not applicable to regimes for which Y_{s-3} is not available in the data.

28. For life expectancy, years 1960, 1962, 1967, 1970, 1972, 1977, 1980, 1982, 1985, 1987, 1990, 1992, 1995, 1997, 2000, 2002, 2003, and 2004 are chosen because data for a sizable number of countries is available for these years. For primary school enrollment ratio, years 1970, 1975, 1980, 1985, 1990–1996, and 1999–2004 are chosen for the same reason. For Taiwan, we use data taken from issues of the *Statistical Yearbook of the Republic of China*: for health (1987), for education (1994), and for both (2005). (See Republic of China, relevant years.)

29. Preston (1975) finds this nonlinear relationship for health. It turns out that a similar nonlinear relationship can be found for primary school enrollment.

30. In calculating the average residual for each regime, we exclude the residuals in the first year of each regime because they may reflect political instability caused by regime change or the achievement by the previous regime.

31. Jones and Olken (2007) use this dataset, which is downloadable at Hein Goemans's website: http://mail.rochester.edu/~hgoemans/data.htm. See also Goemans, Gleditsch, Chiozza (forthcoming).

32. The dataset was obtained from Jose Cheibub's website in December of 2005. www.ssc.upenn.edu/~cheibub/data/Default.htm.

33. These three aspects correspond to variables EXSELEC, LEGSELEC, and PARTY in their dataset, respectively.

34. See Przeworski et al. (2000, ch. 1) for details.

35. The updated versions of the Przeworski et al. (2000) data by Boix and Rosato (2001) and by Cheibub and Gandhi (2004) do not provide information on disaggregated aspects of political institutions. Therefore, we cannot exploit heterogeneity across autocracies in terms of institutional characteristics.

36. The regions are east Asia and the Pacific, eastern Europe and central Asia, south Asia, the Middle East and north Africa, sub-Saharan Africa, and Latin America and the Caribbean (with western Europe—Greece, Portugal, and Spain—omitted). We follow the World Bank's classification of regions.

37. See our discussion paper—Besley and Kudamatsu (2007)—for details on how this variable was constructed.

38. The standard deviation of the oil price is 12.4 U.S. dollars per barrel. Therefore, a one standard deviation increase in the oil price decreases the probability of economic success by 24.8 percentage points for autocracies in oil-exporting countries.

39. If we redefine $SUCCESS_{ic}^{k}$ for $k = 2, 3, 4$ by making it 0 if regime i's success is not robust, results for economic and educational success do not substantially change. For health success, the coefficient on ethnic fractionalization is no longer significant. If we run OLS regressions with economic growth rates, conditional life expectancy, or school enrollment ratio as the dependent variable, results for educational success do not change. Ethnic fractionalization and French legal origin are now negatively correlated with economic growth and health performance, respectively. These results imply that aside from top performers, the negative effect of ethnic fractionalization on economic growth and that of French legal origin on health outcomes persists among autocratic regimes. The correlation between the oil-price boom and economic success, and between ethnic fractionalization and health success, on the other hand, is no longer significant.

40. *Keesing's Contemporary Archives*, 21063, 21939, 23706.

41. See Lieberthal (2004, 173–75) for the formal organizational structure of the party.

42. See *Keesing's Contemporary Archives*, 28205–28207 and 28719.

43. Deng's supporters (Chen Yun, Deng Yingchao, Hu Yaobang, and Wang Zhen) joined the Politburo in December of 1978 (*Keesing's Contemporary Archives*, 30488). Lieberthal (2004, 126) regards Wang Dongxing, Wu De, Ji Dengkui, and Chen Xilian as Politburo members supporting Hua. All of them resigned from the Politburo in February of 1980 (*Keesing's Contemporary Archives*, 30498).

44. See the account by Ruan (1994, 165–69, 175–76), who was Hu's friend.

45. *Keesing's Record of World Events*, 36640. An immediate reason for Zhao's dismissal was his support for pro-democracy student protests in Tiananmen Square. However, Zhao's support had already waned since late 1988 due to his too-radical economic reform, which caused inflation. Also, Zhao's sons were alleged to be corrupt businessmen in Guangdon Province. See Gilley (1998, 129–31) and Lieberthal (2004, 144–45).

46. By the end of 1995, Deng was effectively incapacitated and no longer commented on policies (Gilley 1998, 288).

47. *Keesing's Record of World Events*, 36587, 36640, 36720.

48. See Tismaneanu (2003, 142–80) for a series of events from the Secret Speech to the adoption of industrialization plans.

49. See Fischer (1989) for a series of events leading to the consolidation of Ceaușescu's power. It is perhaps not just a coincidence that Ion Gheorghe Mauer and Emil Bondras, two members of the Politburo instrumental to the appointment of Ceaușescu as Gheorghiu-Dej's successor in 1965 (Tismaneanu 2003, 185–86), voluntarily resigned from the Politburo and died in office, respectively,

in the mid-1970s (ibid., 193), after which Ceauşescu's rule became outside the control of any member of the Communist Party.

50. See Payne (1987, 372–75), Grugel and Rees (1997, 42–43), and Fusi (1987, 66–67) for the background of the adoption of the Law of Succession.

51. Park Chung Hee staged a military coup and became president in 1961; held multiparty presidential elections and won in 1963; disbanded the national legislature, banned political parties temporarily, and introduced the indirect presidential election by nonpartisan electoral college in 1972; and held multiparty legislative elections for two-thirds of the seats in 1973 (the remaining one-third are appointed by the president). In 1981, members of the electoral college were allowed to be affiliated with political parties.

52. Table 11.6 shows that, if we define democracy as a regime whose Polity score is larger than 5, the second phase (1963–1972) is also a successful autocracy.

53. See *Keesing's Contemporary Archives*, 25747, 29795.

54. Chun Doo Hwan seized control of the military in December 1979 and imposed martial law in May 1980, shortly after which he became the head of an advisory body (consisting of military officers) to President Choi. See Clifford (1998, 143–63).

55. We are unable to find any scholarly research on the NCU, which Korea specialists appear to dismiss as a rubber-stamping organization.

56. Clifford (1998, 86) notes that, according to a former KCIA director, Park feared two things: Kim Dae Jung and the U.S. Congress.

57. Sohn (1989, 31–32) quotes Park's remark on the 1971 electoral result: ". . . I have done my best to get rid of poverty. . . . [D]o I deserve only this margin against Kim Dae Jung?"

58. See the account of worker protests in the early 1970s by Sohn (1989, 34–36).

59. Note that if we look at the *same* successful autocratic regime over time, our theory predicts the opposite: leadership change follows a bad performance. This prediction is *not* what we try to provide empirical support for here. Also note that leadership turnover and regime performance are jointly determined in our theoretical model. The aim of empirical analysis in this subsection is, therefore, not to establish causality but to show correlations that are consistent with our theory.

60. We match Polity IV and Archigos on a daily basis to avoid assigning leadership changes to regimes that emerge later in the same year. If a leadership change and the emergence of a new regime take place on the same date, we assign the leadership change to the preceding regime. Finally, if the Archigos dataset indicates that there is no national leader, we regard only the beginning of such a period as a leadership change, rather than counting two leadership changes at

the beginning and the end, because we are interested in whether the selectorate can replace the incumbent.

61. These results are robust to excluding leadership changes due to natural causes (natural deaths, resignation for health reasons, and suicides) from the calculation of the rate of leadership turnover.

62. Jones and Olken (2005) first exploit the random death of leaders as a natural experiment.

63. A random death in Poland occurred before we observe performance measures. The death of Franco in Spain does not fit with our theory as it led to democratization.

64. Salazar was alive until 1970. Wiarda (1977, ch. 9, n. 3) notes, however, that "he no longer made decisions and . . . had no impact on the policies of the new government."

65. Maxwell (1986, 112) provides an alternative view, however, by noting that "[t]he Portuguese dictatorship was preeminently civilian and legalistic."

66. Maxwell (1986, 112) notes that the appointment of Caetano as premier was conditional on his acceptance of the military's position on what to do with Portugal's territories in Africa. This further suggests that the selectorate was the military.

67. Thailand's economic growth rate from 1958 to 1962 was 5.5%. Life expectancy at birth conditional on real GDP per capita was 11.4 years (the average of 1960 and 1962), comparable to the whole regime performance (see Table 11.3). Sarit does not enter Table 11.6 because his rule did not last more than five full calendar years.

68. *Keesing's Contemporary Archives*, 16691.

69. *Keesing's Contemporary Archives*, 19814.

70. Although the Polity dataset codes 1968 as the end of the Thai military regime, Thanom remained in power by holding multiparty parliamentary elections in which his party won. He then dissolved the Parliament and banned political parties in 1971, restoring the military dictatorship.

71. *Africa Research Bulletin*, March 1–31, 1984, 7178.

72. Kaba (1977, 40) lists Sekou Toure's failures in health production: the shortage of hospital beds in the capital city, the appointment of inexperienced individuals to hospital administration, medicine shortage, and Sekou Toure's denial of a cholera epidemic in 1973.

73. Sekou Toure was a founding member of the PDG and became secretary general of the party in 1952 (Johnson 1970, 350). In 1957, the PDG won multiparty elections for the Territorial Assembly under French rule. In November of 1958,

one month after independence, the PDG became the sole legal party by Constitution (see Brune 1999).

74. *Keesing's Record of World Events*, 32955.

75. According to Momoh (1984, 757), "the powerful Toure family including the ambitious Minister of Mines and Geology, Ismael Toure, had persuaded . . . Beavogui to accept the post of acting president. . . . Beavogui, as it was understood, would have held the post for two or three years. . . . "

76. According to Jackson and Rosberg (1982, 210), Guinea under Sekou Toure's rule saw "persistent attempts by the government to hold to the ruler's ideological approach while ignoring the lessons to be learned from economic and planning failures."

REFERENCES

Acemoglu, Daron, Simon Johnson, and James A. Robinson. 2001. "The Colonial Origins of Comparative Development: An Empirical Investigation." *American Economic Review* 91(5):1369–1401.

Acemoglu, Daron, and James Robinson. 2005. *Economic Origins of Dictatorship and Democracy*. Cambridge: Cambridge University Press.

Acemoglu, Daron, James Robinson, and Thierry Verdier. 2004. "Kleptocracy and Divide-and-Rule: A Model of Personal Rule." *Journal of the European Economic Association* 2(2–3):162–92.

Alesina, Alberto, Arnaud Devleeschauwer, William Easterly, Sergio Kurlat, and Romain Wacziarg. 2003. "Fractionalization." *Journal of Economic Growth* 8:155–94.

Almeida, Heitor, and Daniel Ferreira. 2002. "Democracy and the Variance of Economic Performance." *Economics and Politics* 14(3):225–57.

Besley, Timothy. 2005. "Political Selection." *Journal of Economic Perspectives* 19(3):43–60.

———. 2006. *Principled Agents? The Political Economy of Good Government*. Oxford: Oxford University Press.

Besley, Timothy, and Masayuki Kudamatsu. 2007. "Making Autocracy Work." STICERD Development Economics discussion paper, no. 48.

Boix, Carles, and Sebastián Rosato. 2001. "A Complete Data Set of Political Regimes, 1800–1999." Unpublished dataset.

Brune, Stefan. 1999. "Guinea." In *Elections in Africa: A Data Handbook*, eds. Dieter Nohlen, Michael Krennerich, and Bernhard Thibaut. Oxford: Oxford University Press.

Bueno de Mesquita, Bruce, James D. Morrow, Randolph M. Siverson, and Alastair Smith. 2002. "Political Institutions, Policy Choice and the Survival of Leaders." *British Journal of Political Science* 32:559–90.

Bueno de Mesquita, Bruce, Alastair Smith, Randolph M. Siverson, and James D. Morrow. 2003. *The Logic of Political Survival*. Cambridge, MA: MIT Press.

Caselli, Francesco. 2006. "Power Struggles and the Natural Resource Curse." Unpublished paper.

Chaloemtiarana, Thak. 2007. *Thailand: The Politics of Despotic Paternalism*. Ithaca, NY: Southeast Asia Program Publications.

Cheibub, Jose Antonio, and Jennifer Gandhi. 2004. "Classifying Political Regimes: A Six-Fold Measure of Democracies and Dictatorships." Unpublished dataset.

Clifford, Mark L. 1998. *Troubled Tiger: Businessmen, Bureaucrats, and Generals in South Korea*, rev. ed. Armonk, NY: M.E. Sharpe.

Dixit, Avinash. 2006. "Predatory States and Failing States: An Agency Perspective." Unpublished paper.

Egorov, Georgy, and Konstantin Sonin. 2005. "The Killing Game: Reputation and Knowledge in Non-Democratic Succession." Unpublished paper.

Fearon, James. 2006. "Self-Enforcing Democracy." Unpublished paper.

Fischer, Mary Ellen. 1989. *Nicolae Ceaușescu*. Boulder, CO: Lynne Rienner Publishers.

Fusi, J. P. 1987. *Franco: A Biography*. London: Unwin Hyman.

Geddes, Barbara. 1999. "Authoritarian Breakdown: Empirical Test of a Game Theoretic Argument." Unpublished paper.

Gilley, Bruce. 1998. *Tiger on the Brink: Jiang Zemin and China's New Elite*. Berkeley: University of California Press.

Glaeser, Edward L., Rafael La Porta, Florencio Lopez-de-Silanes, and Andrei Shleifer. 2004. "Do Institutions Cause Growth?" *Journal of Economic Growth* 9(3):271–303.

Goeman, H. E., Kristian Skrede Gleditsch, and Giacomo Chiozza. Forthcoming. "Introducing Archigos: A Data Set of Political Leaders." *Journal of Peace Research*.

Grugel, Jean, and Tim Rees. 1997. *Franco's Spain*. London: Arnold.

Heston, Alan, Robert Summers, and Bettina Aten. 2006. *Penn World Table*, version 6.2. University of Pennsylvania, Center for International Comparisons of Production, Income and Prices. http://pwt.econ.upenn.edu.

Jackson, Robert H., and Carl G. Rosberg. 1982. *Personal Rule in Black Africa*. Berkeley: University of California Press.

Johnson, R. W. 1970. "Sekou Toure and the Guinean Revolution." *African Affairs* 69:350–65.

Jones, Benjamin F., and Benjamin A. Olken. 2005. "Do Leaders Matter? National Leadership and Growth Since World War II." *Quarterly Journal of Economics* 120(3):835–64.

———. 2007. "Hit or Miss? The Effect of Assassinations on Institutions and War." BREAD working paper, no. 150.

Kaba, Lansine. 1977. "Guinean Politics: A Critical Historical Overview." *Journal of Modern African Studies* 15(1):25–45.

Kaufman, Robert R. 1979. "Industrial Change and Authoritarian Rule in Latin America: A Concrete Review of the Bureaucratic Authoritarian Model." In *The New Authoritarianism in Latin America*, ed. David Collier. Princeton, NJ: Princeton University Press.

Keesing's Contemporary Archives and *Keesing's Record of World Events*. Available at //www.keesings.com.

La Porta, Rafael, Florencio Lopez-de-Silanes, Andrei Shleifer, and Robert W. Vishny. 1999. "The Quality of Government." *Journal of Law, Economics & Organization* 15(1):222–79.

Lentz, Harris M. 1994. *Heads of States and Governments: A Worldwide Encyclopedia of Over 2,300 Leaders, 1945 through 1992*. Jefferson, NC: McFarland.

Levitsky, Steven, and Lucan A. Way. 2002. "The Rise of Competitive Authoritarianism." *Journal of Democracy* 13(2):51–65.

Lieberthal, Kenneth. 2004. *Governing China: from Revolution through Reform*, 2nd ed. New York: W.W. Norton.

Marshall, Monty G., and Keith Jaggers. 2005. "Polity IV Project: Political Regime Characteristics and Transitions, 1800–2004." www.cidcm.umd.edu/polity.

Maxwell, Kenneth. 1986. "Regime Overthrow and the Prospects for Democratic Transition in Portugal." In *Transitions from Authoritarian Rule: Southern Europe*, eds. Guillermo O'Donnell, Philippe C. Schmitter, and Laurence Whitehead. Baltimore, MD: Johns Hopkins University Press.

McGuire, Martin C., and Mancur Olson, Jr. 1996. "The Economics of Autocracy and Majority Rule: The Invisible Hand and the Use of Force." *Journal of Economic Literature* 34:72–96.

Momoh, Eddie. 1984. "A Dawn Descends, A Myth Broken." *West Africa* 9 (April):756–57.

Nelson, Michael H. 2001. "Thailand." In *Elections in Asia and the Pacific: A Data Handbook*, vol. 2, eds. Dieter Nohlen, Florian Grotz, and Christof Hartmann. Oxford: Oxford University Press.

O'Donnell, Guillermo A., and Philippe C. Schmitter. 1986. *Transitions from Authoritarian Rule: Tentative Conclusions about Uncertain Democracies*. Baltimore, MD: Johns Hopkins University Press.

Olson, Mancur. 1993. "Dictatorship, Democracy, and Development." *American Political Science Review* 87(3):567–76.

Padro-i-Miquel, Gerard. 2006. "The Control of Politicians in Divided Societies: The Politics of Fear." NBER working paper, no. 12573.

Payne, Stanley G. 1987. *The Franco Regime: 1936–1975*. Madison: University of Wisconsin Press.

Preston, Samuel H. 1975. "The Changing Relationship between Mortality and Level of Economic Development." *Population Studies* 29(2):231–48.

Przeworski, Adam, Michael E. Alvarez, Jose Antonio Cheibub, and Fernando Limongi. 2000. *Democracy and Development: Political Institutions and Well-Being in the World, 1950–1990*. New York: Cambridge University Press.

Rauch, James E. 2001. "Leadership Selection, Internal Promotion, and Bureaucratic Corruption in Less Developed Countries." *Canadian Journal of Economics* 34(1):240–58.

Republic of China. *Statistical Yearbook of the Republic of China*. Taipei: Directorate General of Budget, Accounting and Statistics, Executive Yuan.

Rodrik, Dani. 1997. "Democracy and Economic Performance." Unpublished paper.

———. 2000. "Participatory Politics, Social Cooperation, and Economic Stability." *American Economic Review* 90(2):140–44.

Ruan, Ming. 1994. *Deng Xiaoping: Chronicle of an Empire*. Boulder, CO: Westview Press.

Sen, Amartya K. 1999. *Development as Freedom*. Oxford: Oxford University Press.

Skidmore, Thomas E. 1988. *The Politics of Military Rule in Brazil, 1964–85*. Oxford: Oxford University Press.

Sohn, Hak-Kyu. 1989. *Authoritarianism and Opposition in South Korea*. London: Routledge.

Stepan, Alfred. 1971. *The Military in Politics: Changing Patterns in Brazil*. Princeton, NJ: Princeton University Press.

Tismaneanu, Vladimir. 2003. *Stalinism for All Seasons: A Political History of Romanian Communism*. Berkeley: University of California Press.

Wiarda, Howard J. 1977. *Corporatism and Development*. Amherst: University of Massachusetts Press.

Wintrobe, Ronald. 1990. "The Tinpot and the Totalitarian: An Economic Theory of Dictatorship." *American Political Science Review* 84(3):849–72.

———. 1998. *The Political Economy of Dictatorship*, New York: Cambridge University Press.

World Bank. *Ed Stats*. Available at www.worldbank.org/education/edstats.

———. 2006. *World Development Indicators Online*. http://go.worldbank.org/IW6ZUUHUZ0.

— 12 —

Democracy, Technology, and Growth

PHILIPPE AGHION, ALBERTO ALESINA,
AND FRANCESCO TREBBI

12.1   Introduction

There are two main open questions in the debate on the relationship between economic development and democratic institutions. One is whether or not countries become democratic only at high levels of per capita income, and the second is whether or not (or when) democracy enhances economic development, captured by per capita GDP growth.

On both questions there are disagreements among scholars. Most observers would agree that richer countries are democracies and therefore economic development favors transitions toward political freedom, as argued by Lipset (1959) and Barro (1999). However, Acemoglu et al. (2005) suggest that this cross-sectional evidence is not robust to controlling for factors affecting, simultaneously, income and political institutions. When they add country fixed effects in repeated cross-country regressions, they find no effect of the level of income on democracy. Admittedly this procedure loses all the information arising from cross-country comparisons, which seems crucial in this context. Huntington (1991) argues that the progress toward democratization is not linear and there are back and forth waves of democratization.

On the second question the evidence is mixed at best.[1] Perhaps democratic institutions increase redistributive pressures[2] that may be harmful to growth, especially for middle-income countries, and this is one of the reasons why Barro (1996) argues that countries cannot become democracies too "soon" in terms of their level of income per capita. However, Mulligan, Sala-i-Martin, and Gil (2004) do not find much of a difference in public policies between democracies and nondemocracies, questioning therefore any link between form of government and economic performance.[3] Glaeser

511

et al. (2004) also question the causal effects of political institutions on economic growth.

Very few studies address both questions jointly. Two exceptions are Przeworski et al. (2000) and Bueno de Mesquita et al. (2003). Persson and Tabellini (2006) use the transition from democracy to dictatorship and the concept of the accumulated stock of democratic capital, concluding that the latter is conducive to growth and consolidation of democratic institutions at the same time.[4] Giavazzi and Tabellini (2005) analyze the timing of economic and political liberalizations.

In this chapter, we will focus mostly on the second question of whether or when democracy enhances economic growth. Most of the existing papers on the subject employ aggregate data on income levels and economic growth. A first point of departure of this chapter is its use of disaggregated data to shed new light on the debate. A second point of departure is the idea that political institutions, and democracy in particular, may have different effects on different sectors of the economy, possibly depending on the specific characteristics of the technology and the industry's market. Our results can be summarized in three points. First, we find that democratic institutions and political rights enhance growth of more advanced sectors, namely sectors close to the technological frontier in the sense of Acemoglu, Aghion, and Zilibotti (2006). Second, we uncover that an important channel of this effect is freedom of entry in markets. Political rights are associated with freedom of entry, and the latter is especially important for sectors close to the technological frontier. In fact, entry of new firms and competition are especially beneficial in spurring innovation at high levels of technological development, whereas it may discourage innovation in more backward sectors as argued by Aghion et al. (2006). Third, and this is an implication of the first two results, more advanced economies benefit more from democratic institutions and therefore the demand for democracy should increase with the level of per capita income in a country, calling into question, indirectly at least, the result by Acemoglu et al. (2005) suggesting that development does not bring about democratic institutions.

That democracy may entail both positive and negative effects on growth has already been stressed, for example by Acemoglu (2007). There, higher democracy tends to be good for growth because it reduces the extent to which existing oligarchies can prevent entry by potential competitors. On the other hand, democracy leads to higher tax rates in equilibrium, which in turn tends to discourage innovation, everything else remaining equal. However, unlike in our analysis below, in Acemoglu (2007), the comparison between the costs and benefits of democracy does not interact with the economy's proximity to the world technological frontier.

The chapter is organized as follows. Section 12.2 presents a model of democracy and entry that blends the entry model of Aghion et al. (2006), henceforth ABRZ, with the model of vested interests in Acemoglu, Aghion, and Zilibotti (2006), henceforth AAZ. Section 12.3 discusses the empirical evidence. We then conclude.

12.2   The Model

The point of the model is to show that freedom of entry is especially growth enhancing in sectors closer to the technological frontier. Freedom of entry is correlated with political rights, as we assume in the model and we show below in the empirical part. Therefore the model derives the relationship between sectorial growth and democratic institutions, which we then test.

12.2.1 Production and Profits

Time is discrete, and all agents live for one period. One final good is produced competitively using a continuum of intermediate inputs, indexed from 0 to 1, according to the following technology:

$$y_t = \frac{1}{\alpha} \int_0^1 A_{it}^{1-\alpha} x_{it}^{\alpha} \, di,$$

where x_{it} is the quantity of intermediate input produced in sector i at date t, A_{it} is a productivity parameter that measures the quality of the intermediate input i in producing the final good, and the parameter $\alpha \in (0, 1)$. The final good can be used either for consumption or as an input in the process of production of intermediate goods or for investments in innovation. We normalize the price of the final good to one.

In each intermediate sector i, only one firm (a monopolist) is active in each period, and produces intermediate input i using final output as input, one for one. Since the final-good sector is competitive, the intermediate monopolist i sells its intermediate good to the final-good sector at a price equal to its marginal cost. The first-order condition for the final-sector producers reads as follows:

$$p_{it} = (A_{it}/x_{it})^{1-\alpha}. \tag{12.1}$$

Then profit maximization for intermediate-good producers yields the choice:

$$x_{it} = A_{it} \left(\frac{1}{\alpha} \right)^{-\frac{1}{1-\alpha}},$$

and the equilibrium profit:

$$\pi_{it} = \delta A_{it}, \tag{12.2}$$

where $\delta \equiv \left(\frac{1}{\alpha} - 1 \right) \left(\frac{1}{\alpha} \right)^{-\frac{1}{1-\alpha}}$.

Substituting for x_{it} in the production function for final output, we also get

$$y_t = \zeta A_t, \tag{12.3}$$

where

$$A_t = \int_0^1 A_{it} di$$

is the average productivity at date t and $\zeta = \left(\frac{1}{\alpha} \right)^{1-\frac{\alpha}{1-\alpha}}$ is a constant.

12.2.2 Entry and Incumbent Innovation

Let p denote the probability of a potential entrant appearing in any intermediate sector. In the model, the government directly chooses this parameter in a way described below. This is of course a shortcut that captures different policies that may favor or hinder competition and entry. There are only two types of intermediate firms: advanced firms, with productivity $A_{it} = \overline{A}_t$, and backward firms, with productivity $A_{it} = \frac{1}{\gamma} \overline{A}_t$, and we focus on technologically advanced entry; accordingly, each potential entrant arrives with the leading-edge technology parameter $\overline{A}_t$, which grows by the factor γ with certainty each period. An advanced firm can use a first-mover advantage to block entry and retain its monopoly. But if the firm is backward, then entry will occur, Bertrand competition will ensue, and the technologically dominated incumbent will be eliminated and replaced by the entrant.

A new innovation costs $c_{it} A_{it-1}$ and allows the innovating incumbent firm to improve productivity by factor γ. We assume c_{it} to be random and independently and identically distributed across intermediate sectors with support $\{0, \overline{c}\}$, with

$$\Pr(c_{it} = 0) = \Pr(c_{it} = \overline{c}) = \frac{1}{2}.$$

The effect of entry threat p on incumbent innovation will depend on the marginal benefit v_{it}, which the incumbent expects to receive from an innovation. Note that firms know their cost of innovation when they decide whether to innovate (i.e., there's no uncertainty).

Consider first an incumbent that was an advanced firm last period. If it innovates, then it will remain on the frontier, and hence will be immune to entry. Its profit will then be $\delta \overline{A}_t = \delta \gamma \overline{A}_{t-1}$. If it fails to innovate then with probability p, it will be eliminated by entry and earn zero profit, while with probability $1 - p$, it will survive as the incumbent earning a profit of $\delta \overline{A}_{t-1}$. Dividing through by $\overline{A}_{t-1}$, an advanced firm with innovation cost c_{it} will innovate whenever

$$\delta(\gamma - (1 - p)) = \delta(\gamma - 1 + p) > c_{it}. \qquad (12.4)$$

In particular, an increase in entry threat encourages this incumbent to innovate. Intuitively, a firm close to the frontier responds to increased entry threat by innovating more in order to escape the threat.

Next, consider an incumbent that was a backward firm last period and that will therefore remain behind the frontier even if it manages to innovate, since the frontier will also advance by the factor γ. For this firm, profits will be zero if entry occurs, whether it innovates or not, because it cannot catch up with the frontier. Thus, it will innovate whenever

$$\delta (1 - p) (\gamma - 1) > c_{it}, \qquad (12.5)$$

where the left-hand side is the profit gain from innovation that will be realized with probability $(1 - p)$, the probability that no potential entrant shows up. Thus, in this case, innovation incentives depend negatively on the entry threat p. Intuitively, the firm that starts far behind the frontier is discouraged from innovating as much by an increased entry threat because it is unable to prevent the entrant from destroying the value of its innovation.

Assumption 12.1 *We assume that initially, the entry rate p is equal to zero, and that*

$$\delta(\gamma - 1) < \bar{c},$$

so that, absent any entry threat, no firm with innovation cost equal to $\bar{c}$ ever innovates.

Using these assumptions, one can determine the steady-state fraction of advanced firms conditional upon $p = 0$. Following ABRZ, suppose that an advanced firm that successfully innovates at date t starts out in period $t + 1$ as an advanced firm. All other firms start out as backward firms. Moreover, with exogenous probability h, a backward firm at the end of period t is replaced by a new, advanced firm at date $t + 1$. If a_t denotes the fraction of advanced firms at t, then it satisfies the dynamic equation (see ABRZ):

$$a_{t+1} = z_A a_t + h \left(1 - z_A a_t\right),$$

where

$$z_A = \Pr(c = 0) = \frac{1}{2}$$

is the probability that an advanced firm innovates if $p = 0$. Thus, the steady-state fraction of advanced firms is

$$a^* = \frac{h}{1 - \frac{1}{2}(1 - h)} = \frac{2h}{1 + h}.$$

12.2.3 Politics and the Equilibrium Probability of Entry

Suppose that entry policy, p, is determined each period by a politician who cares about the current consumption but may also respond to bribes. Following AAZ, we assume that the politician's payoff is equal to $H\overline{A}_{t-1}$, where $H > 0$, if she chooses the policy that maximizes current output y_t, and to B_t otherwise, where B_t denotes the bribe that the politician may receive from private firms to limit entry. The parameter H reflects the aggregate welfare concerns of politicians, or the effectiveness of checks and balances that the political system imposes on politicians. It is our proxy for democracy in this model, and we discuss this below. To compute the equilibrium bribe incumbent firms are willing to pay to prevent moving from initial entry probability $p_0 = 0$ to $p > 0$, we need to compute the equilibrium payoffs for each type of firm (advanced or backward) and for each cost realization $c_{it} = 0$ or $\bar{c}$, as a function of p.

Consider first an advanced firm. If this firm's innovation cost is zero, then the firm will always innovate and its postinnovation profit $\delta\gamma\bar{A}_t$ is independent of the entry probability. However, if the innovation cost is $\bar{c}$, this firm will lose from higher entry only if the threat p becomes sufficiently high that condition (12.4) holds. Then, indeed, the firm will lose the amount

$$\bar{A}_{t-1}[\bar{c} - \delta(\gamma - 1)],$$

which is positive by assumption 12.1. Thus, the maximum bribe advanced firms would be ready to pay as a whole to prevent an increase in entry threat from zero to p is given by

$$B_a(p) = \bar{A}_{t-1}a^*\frac{1}{2}[\bar{c} - \delta(\gamma - 1)] \cdot 1_{(\delta(\gamma-1+p)>\bar{c})},$$

where $\frac{1}{2}$ is the probability that $c_{it} = \bar{c}$ and $1_{(\delta(\gamma-1+p)>\bar{c})}$ is equal to one whenever equation (12.4) holds and to zero otherwise.[5]

Now, consider a backward firm. Such a firm will innovate if and only if $c = 0$ by assumption 12.1 no matter the entry probability. And it will lose from a higher threat of entry, whether it innovates or not, just because this reduces its probability of survival. The maximum bribe backward firms will be willing to pay to prevent an increase in entry threat from zero to p is equal to

$$B_b(p) = \bar{A}_{t-1}(1 - a^*)\left[\frac{1}{2}\delta p + \frac{1}{2}\frac{\delta p}{\gamma}\right],$$

where the first (respectively, second) term in the bracket is the expected loss incurred by backward firms with low (respectively, high) innovation cost.[6]

Altogether, incumbent firms will successfully prevent the increase in entry threat from zero to p whenever p is greater than p^* such that

$$B(p^*) = B_a(p^*) + B_b(p^*) = \bar{A}_{t-1}H. \tag{12.6}$$

Given that $B(p)$ is strictly increasing in p, equation (12.6) defines the equilibrium entry probability p^* as an increasing function of H.

12.2.4 Democracy, Distance to Frontier, and Growth

The above analysis tells us that more democracy, as measured by a higher H, increases the probability of entry. But this in turn encourages innovation by advanced firms, whereas it discourages innovation by backward firms (from (12.4) and (12.5) above). The overall effect on aggregate innovation and growth will then depend upon the fraction of advanced firms a^* in the economy, which also measures the economy's proximity to the world technology frontier: for a^* sufficiently close to one, the overall effect of entry and therefore democracy on innovation will be positive, whereas it will be negative if a^* (i.e., h) is close to zero.

12.2.5 Main Prediction and Discussion

Combining (12.6) with (12.4) and (12.5) yields the prediction that an increase in "democracy" as measured by H will stimulate innovation by advanced firms but not by backward ones. One should thus expect a higher impact of democracy on productivity growth in sectors that are closer to the world technological frontier.

We identify with democratic institutions the parameter H in our model. This parameter captures the benefits of investing in a new technology relative to those of bribing a policymaker to make him raise the barrier to entry. Bribes are certainly not unknown in democracies, but since democracies are more open, are associated with more freedom of the press, and involve alternation in power of different groups, democratic leaders are generally less likely to be permanently captured by incumbents. A different way of interpreting the evidence that we present below is to say that democracy enhances growth in technologically advanced sectors when democracy is associated with policies that allow more competition and more freedom of entry. In the empirical section that follows, we do indeed review evidence that implies a strong correlation between freedom of entry and democratic institutions as measured by indicators of political rights.

12.3   Empirical Analysis

12.3.1 Data

We use industry employment and value-added data from the Industrial Statistics database collected by the UNIDO (revision 2).[7] The data include

28 ISIC (level 3) manufacturing sectors at the three-digit level for 180 countries for the period 1963 to 2003. UNIDO is arguably the most comprehensive source of sectorial data available in a cross-country-sector panel format.[8] The UNIDO database provides the most extensive coverage of developing countries sectorial output data available, a very important subsample for our study as most of the countries are partially free or not free from a political standpoint. However, a drawback of this source is the extensive use of national statistics, which tend to be especially noisy for industry-level data of developing countries.

For our empirical analysis, there are two key independent variables: democracy and the distance to the technological frontier. In measuring the former, we use standard, well-established measures of democracy in political economics, such as the aggregate indicators from the Polity IV database and the Freedom House measures of civil liberties and political rights. The Polity IV project records various regime characteristics for every independent state above a half-million total population. In particular we make use of the combined polity index[9] ranging from -10 to 10 ($-10 =$ high autocracy; $10 =$ high democracy). Such an index incorporates more specific subindexes concerned with constraints on the executive, open political competition, effectiveness of legislature, and so on. The Freedom in the World data by Freedom House reports annual analysts' assessments of both political dimensions[10] and civil dimensions[11] since 1972 for more than 192 countries. For the political rights and civil liberties indexes, 1 represents the most-free and 7 the least-free rating. For consistency we rescale both indexes in order to have 7 as the most-free rating.

As for distance to the technological frontier, we consider the logarithm of the value added per worker (VA/EMP) of a sector divided by the maximum of the log of the same variable in the same sector across all countries in each year and take one minus this ratio as a proxy for distance to frontier. Specifically we define

$$DISTANCE_{ict} = 1 - \frac{\left(VA_{ict}/EMP_{ict}\right)}{\max_{c'}\left(VA_{ic't}/EMP_{ic't}\right)},$$

where i indicates the industry; c, the country; and t, the year. We also substitute log value added per worker with the logarithm of output per worker in order to construct an alternative measure of distance to frontier. We do not report results employing this variable, however, as they tend to be similar.

Finally, we make use of measures of entry barriers and costs-of-entry estimates as constructed by Djankov et al. (2002) and of real gross domestic product per capita in international dollars as reported in the Penn World Tables, mark 6.2. Summary statistics for the sample are reported, classified by year, in the Appendix (see Table 12.A1).

12.3.2 Specification

On the left-hand side of our regression, we have the growth rate of either output (Y), value added (VA), or employment (EMP) in the industrial sector. On the right-hand side, we have a measure of democracy (and other measures of political or civil rights), a measure of distance to the technological frontier, and the interaction term between the two. This term allows the marginal effect of democracy to vary with the proximity to the world's most productive technology. We also include time and country-industry fixed effects in order to account for contemporaneous shifts in world growth rates and unobserved heterogeneity across countries and industries. Thus, the empirical specification is as follows, where with y_{ict} we mean either output, value added, or employment, in industry i of country c at time t:

$$\Delta_s \log y_{ict} = \beta_0 + \beta_1 DISTANCE_{ict} + \beta_2 POL_{ct} \qquad (12.7)$$
$$+ \beta_3 DISTANCE_{ict} * POL_{ct} + \alpha X_{ict} + u_{ict}$$
$$\Delta_s \log y_{ict} = \log y_{i,c,t+s} - \log y_{ict}$$
$$u_{ict} = \delta_t + \gamma_{i,c} + \varepsilon_{i,c,t+s}$$
$$s = \{5, 10\}.$$

In the analysis we study 5-year and 10-year output, value-added, and employment sectorial growth rates. We compute growth rates over nonoverlapping periods, and in particular, 5-year growth rates are computed over the periods 1970–75, 1975–80, 1980–85, 1985–90, 1990–95, and 1995–2000. For the 10-year growth rates, we use alternatively the 1975–85, 1985–95 (odd) years and the 1980–90 and 1990–2000 (even) years. Given the somewhat measurement-error–prone nature of the data, we perceive this sample segmentation as a conservative approach. By employing this segmentation approach, we are able to exclude issues of mechanical serial correlation present in a moving average setting. As we show below, indeed the results are sometimes influenced by the specific assumptions on sample periods. In a series of results that we do not report, we also reestimate our main specification with yearly growth rates ($s = 1$). By and large, the main implications of our discussion hold for this sampling choice as well. However, the degree of measurement error is substantial in UNIDO data at the yearly level, mostly because idiosyncrasies at the national statistical level are present, and results sometimes (and expectably) tend to be sensitive in this respect. By employing growth rates over longer periods of time, signal-to-noise ratios tend to improve and ameliorate measurement-error issues.

All the standard errors are robust and clustered at the country or country-industry level whenever possible in order to account for general variance-covariance structures at the country-industry level within the panel setup. This approach is useful in order to address arbitrary forms of serial correlation in the error terms by allowing general variance-covariance structures within any industry-country error term.

The set of controls that we systematically include in any industry-country regression, X_{ict}, include the level of real GDP per capita and its interaction with distance to frontier. The empirical model (12.7) is essentially a reduced-form specification, and we do not intend to overemphasize any channel of causation. A two-way causation mechanism is surely at work within a growth-democracy (or income-democracy) aggregate specification. The aim of this chapter is to emphasize a significant differential role in the correlation between growth and democracy; this does not require the reader assigning a causal interpretation to our finding.

12.3.3 Basic Results

Table 12.1 shows, in accordance with Acemoglu et al. (2005), that there is no effect of democracy on growth rates for manufacturing in a fixed-effects regression at the country level (obtained aggregating the UNIDO sectorial data at country-year level). If any, the effect of democracy on growth appears to be negative, since a few of the coefficients in the various regressions are significantly negative (even though most coefficients on democracy are insignificant different from zero). Specifically, the upper panel (5-year growth rates) presents a split picture between value-added and employment growth rates regressions. In the notation for this table (and the following ones), we employ the $L\ j$ operator notation for j−years lagged values. The middle panel (10-year growth rate for odd years) appears mostly positive, and the lower panel (10-year growth rate for even years)

Table 12.1 Aggregate manufacturing growth and democracy

1975-80-85-90-95-00	Fixed effects, country-year								
	5-year output growth rate			5-year value-added growth rate			5-year employment growth rate		
L5. Democracy	0.001 [0.006]			−0.003 [0.005]			−0.009 [0.005]*		
L5. Political rights		0.023 [0.024]			−0.014 [0.023]			0.003 [0.016]	
L5. Civil liberty			0.029 [0.031]			−0.036 [0.033]			−0.008 [0.022]
Observations	627	591	591	405	362	362	438	411	411
Number of countries	133	148	148	106	111	111	116	130	130
R^2	0.08	0.08	0.08	0.34	0.26	0.27	0.12	0.06	0.06

1975-1985-1995	10-year output growth rate			10-year value-added growth rate			10-year employment growth rate		
L10. Democracy	−0.003 [0.007]			0.007 [0.013]			0.001 [0.012]		
L10. Political rights		0.05 [0.038]			0.002 [0.081]			0.102 [0.055]*	
L10. Civil liberty			0.05 [0.051]			0.057 [0.065]			−0.046 [0.077]
Observations	277	226	226	181	142	142	190	157	157
Number of countries	111	121	121	82	82	82	87	92	92
R^2	0.13	0.14	0.14	0.37	0.29	0.3	0.09	0.03	0.02

Fixed effects, country-year

1980-1990-2000	10-year output growth rate			10-year value-added growth rate			10-year employment growth rate		
L10. Democracy	0.02 [0.010]*			-0.009 [0.008]			-0.022 [0.008]***		
L10. Political rights		0.087 [0.051]*			-0.028 [0.053]			-0.07 [0.046]	
L10. Civil liberty			0.098 [0.089]			-0.04 [0.053]			-0.084 [0.042]**
Observations	290	217	217	184	121	121	194	133	133
Number of countries	111	119	119	82	77	77	89	85	85
R^2	0.04	0.05	0.04	0.45	0.01	0.01	0.27	0.15	0.15

Note: Clustered standard errors in brackets; * significant at 10%; ** significant at 5%; *** significant at 1%.

presents mostly negative coefficients. These results are therefore consistent with what is found in the literature—no robust effects of democracy on aggregate growth.

Table 12.2 reports results on the effect of democracy on growth at the country-industry disaggregated level. The unit of observation becomes now a particular industry in a country at a specific moment in time. Still no effect of democracy is statistically or quantitatively significant in the data. Once again, some of the coefficients of democracy (or political/civil rights) are negative and statistically different from zero. This table then shows that adding an extra dimension (industry-level data) does not produce a departure from standard fixed-effects country-level results per se. Notice that Table 12.2 introduces a control for the level of real gross domestic product per capita. We include a control for income levels (and its interactions when necessary) in order to partial out the effects of political institutions and of the level of economic development.

Table 12.3 introduces, in specification at the country-industry level (equation (12.7)), an interaction term between democracy and distance from the technological frontier. We report results concerning output, value added, and employment for all sample periods (5-year and the odd and even 10-year). This interaction matters statistically and quantitatively in most specifications and enters with a negative and significant coefficient. The table shows that introducing a differential effect of distance to the technological frontier and democracy explains the data better in terms of fit. The sign of the interaction between distance to frontier and democracy is usually negative, while the level of democracy is positive. The result indicates that when close to the technological frontier, the effect of democracy on growth is positive. However, far away from the technological frontier, the effect of democracy may be growth diminishing. This can be interpreted as the basic reduced-form implication of the theoretical model we built. Finally, we interpret the positive sign of the coefficient associated with the regressor *DISTANCE* as evidence of convergence, a robust and recurrent finding in the empirical economic-growth literature. Notice also that a component of convergence is also captured (predictably) by the level of GDP per capita, which presents a negative sign (growth rates are lower in countries with higher levels of GDP per capita). The interaction term between GDP per capita and distance to frontier is usually negative, although mostly insignificant.

Concerning quantitative implications of Table 12.3, let us begin from the first panel (5-year growth rates), recalling that the Polity index ranges from

−10 to +10, increasing in the level of democratic freedom. The statistically and quantitatively significant results concern the value added and the employment growth regressions (columns 4–9) and the political rights and civil liberty indexes. In general, output growth regressions tend to appear more noisy and so do regressions employing the Polity IV index as a proxy for democracy in the right-hand side.

Column 5 implies that the effect of an increase of a unit point on the Polity IV scale of democracy for a sector that operates with the most advanced technology (i.e., distance from the frontier is 0) has the effect of increasing the growth rate of value added by 1.2%. However, at the mean distance to frontier in the sample (0.16), the effect of a similar increase in democracy on the growth rate of value added decreases to −1%. Notice that this figure is roughly consistent with the results of Table 12.2. Considering a technology at half the productivity of the world frontier, we would find a really substantial effect of an increase of a Polity IV unit of democracy: a drop of −5.7%. The unit measure for political rights and civil liberties is different from the Polity IV index, ranging from 1 to 7 (rescaled so that 7 indicates full democracy and 1 full autocracy). Once the coefficients are scaled for the unit of measurement, the results employing Freedom House data (columns 2 and 3) confirm the column 1 estimates.

Results systematically present more beneficial effects of democracy when we use as the left-hand-side variable the sector's employment growth. In column 8, the effect of an increase of a unit point on the Polity IV scale of democracy for a sector that operates with the most advanced technology (i.e., distance from the frontier is 0) has the effect of increasing the growth rate of value added by 3.9%. At the mean distance to the frontier, the effect of a similar increase in democracy on the growth rate of employment is −0.7%.

Considering the 10-year growth rates for both the even-year and the odd-year samples, we maintain the finding of a negative interaction term and a positive coefficient on the level of democracy in the majority of the specifications, albeit with some exceptions that we tend to attribute to the demanding nature of our three-way, fixed-effects specification. The results confirm a positive role of democracy, especially when close to the technological frontier. Consider column 1 of the odd-years panel. The estimated effects are consistent with the 5-year growth rates but not statistically significant. Again the results on employment growth rates are stronger.

Table 12.2 Growth by sector and democracy

	Fixed effects SIC, country-year								
1975-80-85-90-95-00	5-year output growth rate			5-year value-added growth rate			5-year employment growth rate		
L5. Democracy	0.002 [0.002]			0.001 [0.002]			-0.008 [0.001]***		
L5. Political rights		-0.004 [0.009]			-0.006 [0.009]			-0.012 [0.006]*	
L5. Civil liberty			-0.015 [0.010]			-0.015 [0.011]			-0.012 [0.007]*
L5. Real GDP per capita	-0.321 [0.048]***	-0.518 [0.057]***	-0.505 [0.058]***	-0.155 [0.049]***	-0.397 [0.059]***	-0.384 [0.060]***	-0.141 [0.031]***	-0.178 [0.038]***	-0.17 [0.038]***
Observations	9250	8234	8234	9412	8078	8078	10097	8932	8932
Number of countries	2579	2650	2650	2408	2447	2447	2619	2779	2779
R^2	0.3	0.26	0.26	0.26	0.22	0.22	0.08	0.05	0.05
1975-1985-1995	10-year output growth rate			10-year value-added growth rate			10-year employment growth rate		
L10. Democracy	0.003 [0.006]			-0.002 [0.006]			0.007 [0.004]*		
L10. Political rights		-0.001 [0.031]			-0.043 [0.031]			0.017 [0.019]	
L10. Civil liberty			0.104 [0.031]***			0.135 [0.030]***			0.008 [0.022]
L10. Real GDP per capita	-0.239 [0.119]**	-0.142 [0.182]	-0.163 [0.184]	-0.04 [0.113]	0.064 [0.171]	0.04 [0.173]	-0.428 [0.085]***	-0.356 [0.129]***	-0.35 [0.129]***
Observations	4103	3217	3217	4164	3183	3183	4386	3486	3486
Number of countries	1963	1950	1950	1941	1867	1867	2038	2032	2032
R^2	0.19	0.07	0.07	0.17	0.07	0.08	0.1	0.01	0.01

Fixed effects SIC, country-year

1980-1990-2000	10-year output growth rate			10-year value-added growth rate			10-year employment growth rate		
L10. Democracy	−0.001 [0.003]			−0.006 [0.003]*			−0.013 [0.003]***		
L10. Political rights		−0.006 [0.020]			−0.012 [0.021]			−0.044 [0.016]***	
L10. Civil liberty			0.01 [0.024]			−0.028 [0.026]			−0.049 [0.018]***
L10. Real GDP per capita	−0.715 [0.096]***	−1.044 [0.159]***	−1.059 [0.160]***	−0.592 [0.101]***	−0.984 [0.166]***	−0.958 [0.166]***	−0.379 [0.072]***	−0.203 [0.103]**	−0.165 [0.106]
Observations	4060	2661	2661	4294	2682	2682	4485	2874	2874
Number of countries	1873	1685	1685	1962	1693	1693	2087	1811	1811
R^2	0.45	0.1	0.1	0.37	0.09	0.09	0.17	0.03	0.03

Note: Clustered standard errors in brackets; * significant at 10%; ** significant at 5%; *** significant at 1%.

Table 12.3 Differential effect of democracy depending on distance to frontier

1975-80-85-90-95-00	(1)	(2)	(3)	(4)	(5)	(6)	(7)	(8)	(9)
				Fixed effects SIC, country-year					
	5-year output growth rate			5-year value-added growth rate			5-year employment growth rate		
L5. Distance to frontier in value added/employment	4.283 [1.259]***	5.939 [1.588]***	6.044 [1.588]***	5.06 [1.308]***	6.307 [1.707]***	6.262 [1.700]***	0.873 [0.952]	1.845 [1.142]	1.626 [1.159]
L5. Distance to frontier x democracy				−0.022 [0.023]			−0.056 [0.018]***		
L5. Democracy				0.005 [0.004]			0.004 [0.003]		
L5. Distance to fronter x political rights		−0.076 [0.076]			−0.138 [0.080]*			−0.29 [0.052]***	
L5. Political rights		0.006 [0.014]			0.01 [0.014]			0.039 [0.010]***	
L5. Distance to frontier x civil liberty			−0.128 [0.087]			−0.21 [0.093]**			−0.249 [0.063]***
L5. Civil liberty			0.003 [0.015]			0.019 [0.016]			0.04 [0.011]***
L5. Distance to frontier x real GDP per capita	−0.192 [0.147]	−0.269 [0.179]	−0.256 [0.175]	−0.063 [0.153]	−0.047 [0.192]	−0.007 [0.190]	−0.155 [0.110]	−0.1 [0.130]	−0.104 [0.128]
L5. Real GDP per capita	−0.148 [0.061]**	−0.298 [0.070]***	−0.29 [0.070]***	0.087 [0.059]	−0.11 [0.069]	−0.117 [0.069]*	−0.218 [0.044]***	−0.223 [0.051]***	−0.237 [0.050]***
Observations	8110	7449	7449	8427	7649	7649	8607	7893	7893
Number of industry-countries	2205	2295	2295	2250	2318	2318	2257	2368	2368
R^2	0.34	0.31	0.31	0.33	0.3	0.3	0.09	0.07	0.06

Fixed effects SIC, country-year

1975-1985-1995	10-year output growth rate			10-year value-added growth rate			10-year employment growth rate		
L10. Distance to frontier in value added/employment	13.985 [2.278]***	15.496 [3.945]***	16.527 [4.212]***	10.689 [2.503]***	11.224 [5.250]**	12.987 [5.384]**	1.274 [1.713]	−3.171 [2.997]	−1.676 [3.181]
L10. Distance to frontier x democracy	−0.04 [0.057]			−0.066 [0.053]			−0.035 [0.044]		
L10. Democracy	0.01 [0.010]			0.012 [0.009]			0.017 [0.007]**		
L10. Distance to frontier x political rights		−0.58 [0.216]***			−0.447 [0.223]**			−0.469 [0.157]***	
L10. Political rights		0.105 [0.040]***			0.046 [0.042]			0.095 [0.027]***	
L10. Distance to frontier x civil liberty			−0.387 [0.266]			−0.334 [0.266]			−0.576 [0.198]***
L10. Civil liberty			0.157 [0.040]***			0.172 [0.041]***			0.123 [0.029]***
L10. Distance to frontier x real GDP per capita	−1.319 [0.277]***	−1.073 [0.450]**	−1.318 [0.441]***	−0.655 [0.296]**	−0.362 [0.600]	−0.654 [0.580]	−0.309 [0.209]	0.529 [0.339]	0.395 [0.335]
L10. Real GDP per capita	0.183 [0.147]	0.218 [0.214]	0.219 [0.216]	0.305 [0.139]**	0.399 [0.226]*	0.413 [0.225]*	−0.422 [0.104]***	−0.523 [0.151]***	−0.5 [0.151]***
Observations	3803	3045	3045	3900	3114	3114	3999	3238	3238
Number of industry-countries	1835	1812	1812	1864	1831	1831	1896	1868	1868
R^2	0.22	0.13	0.13	0.22	0.15	0.16	0.09	0.03	0.03

Table 12.3 (*continued*) Differential effect of democracy depending on distance to frontier

1980-1990-2000	(1)	(2)	(3)	(4)	(5)	(6)	(7)	(8)	(9)
					Fixed effects SIC, country-year				
	10-year output growth rate			10-year value-added growth rate			10-year employment growth rate		
L10. Distance to frontier in value added/employment	6.672	11.612	11.296	4.619	13.327	13.666	8.025	15.233	15.414
	[2.682]**	[4.183]***	[4.117]***	[2.955]	[4.260]***	[4.234]***	[2.196]***	[3.648]***	[3.612]***
L10. Distance to frontier x democracy	0.158			0.147			0.062		
	[0.047]***			[0.046]***			[0.039]		
L10. Democracy	−0.027			−0.033			−0.021		
	[0.006]***			[0.007]***			[0.005]***		
L10. Distance to frontier x political rights		−0.676			−0.763			−0.683	
		[0.201]***			[0.194]***			[0.161]***	
L10. Political rights		0.064			0.067			0.004	
		[0.023]***			[0.024]***			[0.022]	
L10. Distance to frontier x civil liberty			−0.697			−0.852			−0.841
			[0.214]***			[0.214]***			[0.166]***
L10. Civil liberty			0.115			0.1			0.023
			[0.033]***			[0.037]***			[0.026]
L10. Distance to frontier x real GDP per capita	−0.483	−0.444	−0.411	−0.121	−0.427	−0.414	−1.083	−1.263	−1.197
	[0.306]	[0.428]	[0.414]	[0.334]	[0.451]	[0.432]	[0.246]***	[0.395]***	[0.378]***
L10. Real GDP per capita	−0.542	−0.89	−1.071	−0.511	−0.83	−0.959	−0.254	0.151	0.099
	[0.127]***	[0.179]***	[0.173]***	[0.140]***	[0.180]***	[0.172]***	[0.111]**	[0.142]	[0.141]
Observations	3546	2499	2499	3662	2546	2546	3729	2638	2638
Number of industry-countries	1737	1599	1599	1784	1634	1634	1782	1619	1619
R^2	0.47	0.22	0.22	0.4	0.25	0.25	0.18	0.08	0.09

Note: Clustered standard errors in brackets; * significant at 10%; ** significant at 5%; *** significant at 1%.

Overall, these results, including many other specification tests that we performed and which are available upon request,[12] suggest that our intuition of a differential effect of democracy in different sectors as a function of distance from the frontier is plausible. However, as the last part of Table 12.3 shows, some degree of sensitivity of the results to certain specification or measurement issues remains evident.

12.3.4 Entry and Democracy

The previous section presents evidence of differential effects of political institutions on sectorial performance, depending on the specific characteristics of each industry. In this section, we make some progress in the investigation of a channel, especially focusing on entry barriers.

In the model of Section 12.2, we discussed the role of freedom of entry and we assumed a correlation between freedom of entry and political freedom. In the Appendix (Table 12.A2), we report evidence that democracies do indeed have lower barriers and cost of entry by employing the Djankov et al. (2002) cross-country data on regulation of entry. Indeed, a table similar to 12.A2 is also present in the original Djankov et al. (2002) paper, and here it is reported only for completeness of the argument. The left-hand-side variable is a measure of the cost of entry given by the number of bureaucratic procedures needed for a firm to enter the market (number of procedures necessary to start up a business), available from the Doing Business project by the World Bank. All measures of democratic development (constraints on the executives, political and civil rights, and similar) present a negative correlation with entry costs, even controlling for income levels. Notice that in addition to the Polity IV autocracy index and Freedom House political and civil rights indexes, we also report results employing all the additional measures of democracy and political liberties that Djankov et al. (2002) employ, such as the Polity IV subindexes of executive de facto independence, constraints on executive power, effectiveness of legislature, government effectiveness, and competition in the legislative nominating process.

Perotti and Volpin (2006) study in detail the cross-national determinants of investor protection and entry. They present convincing evidence that "countries with more accountable political institutions have better investor protection and lower entry costs." Note that, as they point out, poor investor protection is indirectly a barrier for entry since new investors face higher risks in entering a new market. Perotti and Volpin (2006) also use Polity IV as a measure of political accountability, but they also experiment with several other measures, finding a strong correlation between democracy and freedom of entry.

A direct way of relating our approach to past literature would be to consider the differential effect of democracy and entry using, as a proxy for the probability of entry of a competitor, the number of procedures needed to start up a business in the country as reported by Djankov et al. (2002). We could check whether, controlling for a differential effect of entry, the role of democracy and the significance of the interaction term changed. Given the cross-sectional nature of the cost-of-entry variables, only the interaction term between entry cost and distance can be added to the specification of Table 12.3.

Although promising in principle, this approach did not yield any statistically relevant result in our attempts. In tables available from the authors, we considered this approach, with and without controls for GDP levels. The estimates of the coefficients on democracy and its interaction with distance seemed to be unaffected by introducing this particular measure of entry costs interacted with distance. Considering the 5-year growth-rate sample and the 10-year rates for both even and odd dates presents a noisy picture at best: the marginal effects of democracy at different distances become somewhat smaller, but the proxy for entry is always insignificant and often with the wrong sign. This is also true if we add further interactions on property-rights protection, which we explored as well. The results on democracy and the interaction with distance remain generally significant and with a positive and a negative sign, respectively. These results taken together suggest either that the Polity IV and Freedom House variables capture something more general than the number of procedures regarding the possibility of entry and competition or that a purely cross-sectional measure of cost of entry, as the one proposed by Djankov et al. (2002), does not present sufficient variation to allow our three-way panel setup (industry-country-time, which is indeed fairly demanding in this respect) to pick up any significant relationship with growth.

In order to provide a reasonable amount of variation in the data in Table 12.4, we replace the number of procedures with the effective level of entry in the sector, measured by the 5-year or 10-year growth rates in the number of establishments. Notice that the growth rate in the number of establishments is a realized (ex post) measure of entry, and one could argue whether or not it is the relevant covariate to influence the pattern of innovation discussed in the model, as opposed to ex ante proxies. Clearly a point in favor of our approach is the scarcity of alternatives in terms of time-varying proxies of entry.

The time-varying entry variable allows to control for both the level of entry and its interaction with distance to frontier. However, the UNIDO data do not include information on the number of establishments before the 1980s, therefore limiting the sample period for the analysis. In addition, casual inspection of the original data indicates a somewhat more noisy nature of the establishment figures relative to employment and value-added figures, with somewhat large (abnormal) jumps (which we decide not to censor in the analysis).

The effect of democracy is now reduced substantially. If we interpret effective entry as a precise proxy for entry costs, this finding tends to support our interpretation of the data. However, only for the 10-year sample did the marginal effects of entry depend on the distance to frontier in a direction in line with the model's prediction. Entry in levels has a positive and significant effect in all regressions, and the interaction with distance is instead negative. Statistically significant coefficients on the interaction between entry and distance are present for both sectorial output and value added. The effect of democracy is generally negative at the mean distance to frontier (0.16), but the coefficients on democracy and its interaction with distance are significant only in the case of political rights. This suggests that indeed an entry channel may explain why democracy is conducive to growth in sectors closer to the technological frontier rather than other less-advanced sectors, at least over relatively long periods of time (10 years).

Conclusion   This chapter investigates a different approach to and some novel empirical evidence on the relationship between democracy, level of development, and economic growth by employing disaggregated data on industrial sectors' growth rates. We have argued (and shown empirically with some degree of success) that democratic institutions favor growth in sectors of the economy that are particularly advanced in terms of value added per worker, or in our terminology, close to the world technological frontier. Our interpretation is that it is in sectors close to the technological frontier that democracy is more beneficial, possibly through fostering entry, competition, and innovation, which are relatively more important

Table 12.4 Growth, democracy, and actual entry

1985-90, 1990-95, 1995-2000	5-year output growth rate			5-year value-added growth rate			5-year employment growth rate		
	Fixed effects SIC, country-year								
L5. Distance to frontier in value added/employment	-16.168	-10.385	-0.197	-15.656	-11.037	0.732	-0.187	2.102	3.607
	[9.651]*	[7.660]	[8.171]	[10.027]	[9.887]	[9.496]	[7.299]	[5.304]	[5.394]
L5. Distance to frontier x 5-yr growth in no. estab.	-0.296	-0.372	-0.448	0.236	0.13	0.163	-0.192	-0.381	-0.33
	[0.549]	[0.514]	[0.526]	[0.450]	[0.462]	[0.451]	[0.465]	[0.453]	[0.480]
L5. 5-year growth in no. of establishments	-0.058	-0.066	-0.055	-0.143	-0.165	-0.176	-0.055	-0.047	-0.046
	[0.081]	[0.078]	[0.080]	[0.045]***	[0.045]***	[0.046]***	[0.053]	[0.051]	[0.054]
L5. Distance to frontier x democracy	-0.368			-0.36			-0.208		
	[0.205]*			[0.200]*			[0.150]		
L5. Democracy	0.105			0.137			0		
	[0.033]***			[0.030]***			[0.028]		
L5. Distance to frontier x political rights		0.497			0.611			0.062	
		[0.283]*			[0.274]**			[0.149]	
L5. Political rights		-0.111			-0.119			0.05	
		[0.070]			[0.066]*			[0.047]	
L5. Distance to frontier x civil liberty			-0.453			-0.394			-0.206
			[0.340]			[0.368]			[0.254]
L5. Civil liberty			-0.074			-0.1			0.022
			[0.048]			[0.049]**			[0.032]
L5. Distance to frontier x real GDP per capita	2.577	1.749	1.086	2.83	2.102	1.288	0.103	-0.24	-0.266
	[1.115]**	[0.867]**	[0.913]	[1.164]**	[1.088]*	[1.044]	[0.883]	[0.620]	[0.624]
L5. Real GDP per capita	-1.673	-1.478	-1.731	-1.791	-1.777	-2.01	-0.864	-0.575	-0.624
	[0.347]***	[0.224]***	[0.217]***	[0.309]***	[0.225]***	[0.219]***	[0.201]***	[0.158]***	[0.164]***
Observations	1694	1789	1789	1742	1835	1835	1819	1910	1910
Number of industry-countries	1117	1161	1161	1145	1187	1187	1184	1228	1228
R^2	0.31	0.33	0.34	0.37	0.4	0.41	0.12	0.1	0.1

Fixed effects SIC, country-year

1985-95, 1990-2000	10-year output growth rate			10-year value-added growth rate			10-year employment growth rate		
L10. Distance to frontier in value added/employment	-8.102 [9.748]	-7.676 [9.374]	-7.387 [10.137]	-10.077 [9.889]	-8.546 [8.825]	-13.865 [9.523]	1.111 [5.762]	0.285 [4.884]	-6.124 [5.726]
L10. Distance to frontier x 10-yr growth in no. estab.	-1.916 [0.646]***	-1.985 [0.639]***	-2.332 [0.652]***	-1.939 [0.689]***	-1.857 [0.638]***	-1.983 [0.664]***	-0.217 [0.616]	-0.56 [0.631]	-0.612 [0.649]
L10. 10-yr growth in no. of establishments	0.691 [0.104]***	0.637 [0.112]***	0.695 [0.113]***	0.565 [0.119]***	0.521 [0.117]***	0.555 [0.119]***	0.486 [0.119]***	0.486 [0.128]***	0.505 [0.127]***
L10. Distance to frontier x democracy	-0.277 [0.140]**			-0.071 [0.124]			-0.022 [0.082]		
L10. Democracy	0.029 [0.021]			0.014 [0.019]			-0.009 [0.015]		
L10. Distance to frontier x political rights		-1.335 [0.466]***			-1.611 [0.328]***			-0.283 [0.198]	
L10. Political rights		0.288 [0.096]***			0.31 [0.056]***			0.152 [0.036]***	
L10. Distance to frontier x civil liberty			-0.639 [0.393]			-1.148 [0.362]***			-0.53 [0.248]**
L10. Civil liberty			0.136 [0.062]**			0.172 [0.054]***			0.153 [0.034]***
L10. Distance to frontier x real GDP per capita	1.524 [1.131]	2.025 [1.269]	1.525 [1.276]	2.079 [1.135]*	2.733 [1.068]**	2.994 [1.158]***	-0.334 [0.653]	-0.005 [0.538]	0.748 [0.686]
L10. Real GDP per capita	-1.478 [0.307]***	-1.965 [0.254]***	-1.994 [0.298]***	-1.671 [0.267]***	-1.763 [0.245]***	-1.963 [0.272]***	-0.562 [0.184]***	-0.757 [0.155]***	-0.944 [0.185]***
Observations	1718	1852	1852	1732	1838	1838	1837	1980	1980
Number of industry-countries	1186	1267	1267	1170	1225	1225	1220	1314	1314
R^2	0.55	0.49	0.47	0.57	0.52	0.5	0.5	0.45	0.44

Note: Clustered standard errors in brackets; * significant at 10%; ** significant at 5%; *** significant at 1%.

for growth in those sectors. Thus our analysis introduces a technological motive for the survival of political freedom, a dimension that has not received much attention in the wide empirical literature on democratization. It also suggests that the demand for democracy should be higher in richer countries, that is, those countries in which more sectors are closer to the technological frontier.

In a general sense, this chapter contributes to the strand of the politico-economic literature focusing on the differential effects of political institutions on economic outcomes. The same institutional features may have quite different effects on different components of the economy.

Natural next steps in this research program would be, first, to dig further into the various channels whereby democracy fosters growth in more advanced sectors and, second, to analyze the process by which the economic demand for democracy may or may not translate into a real transition to democracy.

ACKNOWLEDGMENTS

The authors are particularly grateful to Daron Acemoglu for his comments. We also benefitted from discussions with Matilde Bombardini, Allan Drazen, Elhanan Helpman, Guido Tabellini, and seminar participants at a meeting of the Canadian Institute for Advanced Research (CIFAR) in Toronto, and we thank Daron Acemoglu, Simon Johnson, Jim Robinson, and Pierre Yared for sharing their data. Andrea Asoni provided excellent research assistance. Trebbi gratefully acknowledges financial support from the Initiative on Global Financial Markets.

NOTES

1. See for instance Helliwell (1994), Barro (1996), and Papaioannou and Siourounis (2004) and the references cited therein.
2. For some results consistent with this observation, see Aghion, Alesina, and Trebbi (2004) and Boix (2003).
3. They consider education spending, spending on pensions and welfare, and trade openness, among other variables.
4. On a related topic, see also Rodrik and Wacziarg (2005).
5. Indeed, the firm's expected profit if the entry probability is p, is equal to

$$(\delta\gamma - \overline{c}) \, \overline{A}_{t-1}$$

whereas it is just

$$\delta \overline{A}_{t-1}$$

if the firm does not innovate. The difference between the latter and the former is just equal to

$$(\overline{c} - \delta(\gamma - 1)) \, \overline{A}_{t-1}.$$

6. A backward firm's ex ante expected profit is

$$\left(\frac{1}{2}\delta(1 - p) + \frac{1}{2}\delta\gamma(1 - p) \right) \overline{A}_{t-1}$$

whenever the entry probability is p.

7. Rajan and Zingales (1998) is one of the early seminal papers employing sectorial growth rate analysis.

8. Other well-recognized sources of country-sector panels include OECD and ILO. However UNIDO employs OECD data for the relevant subsample, while ILO produces employment data aggregated to the ISIC, level 2, which is therefore more coarse than the data we employ here.

9. We exclude special polity conditions such as transitions, interruptions, and interregnums as coded in the Polity IV database $-66; -77; -88$.

10. Participate freely in the political process; vote freely in legitimate elections; have representatives who are accountable to them.

11. Exercise freedoms of expression and belief; be able to freely assemble and associate; have access to an established and equitable system of rule of law; have social and economic freedoms, including equal access to economic opportunities and the right to hold private property.

12. Among the additional tests we performed are change of sampling frequency (yearly panel results; modified dates for the computation of the sample changes); specification changes (including quadratic terms of the democracy index); and exclusion of country or sector fixed effects.

APPENDIX

We now introduce the supplementary tables for the Appendix.

Table 12A.1 Summary statistics by year

Year	1975					1980				
Variable	Obs	Mean	St. dev.	Min	Max	Obs	Mean	St. dev.	Min	Max
logY	2249	19.16	2.75	8.15	26.73	2348	19.60	2.73	9.04	26.76
logVA	2272	18.09	2.63	10.26	25.66	2269	18.52	2.63	10.50	25.97
logEmp	2494	8.45	2.43	0.00	15.79	2576	8.63	2.41	0.00	15.79
logEsta	0					0				
dlogY	2176	0.04	0.32	-3.54	4.25	2184	0.06	0.34	-3.58	7.79
dlogVA	2238	0.03	0.33	-3.18	4.13	2133	0.04	0.35	-3.19	7.96
dlogEmp	2428	0.04	0.26	-2.85	3.76	2469	0.02	0.26	-2.84	6.58
dlogEsta	0					0				
d5logY	1869	0.61	0.58	-2.35	5.39	2054	0.41	0.57	-3.48	4.44
d5logVA	2074	0.57	0.60	-2.70	4.48	2101	0.39	0.60	-3.21	4.15
d5logEmp	2191	0.26	0.47	-1.61	3.24	2342	0.16	0.50	-3.67	6.92
d5logEsta	0					0				
d10logY	1429	0.93	0.78	-2.42	5.59	1812	0.98	0.81	-3.49	6.99
d10logVA	1475	0.90	0.77	-1.67	5.71	1971	0.91	0.84	-3.64	6.51
d10logEmp	1584	0.44	0.63	-2.45	4.38	2143	0.41	0.70	-3.64	6.45
d10logEsta	0					0				
distfront	2171	0.15	0.08	0.00	0.45	2159	0.15	0.08	0.00	0.49
db_proc_99	1911	10.19	4.51	2.00	21.00	1969	10.22	4.45	2.00	21.00
polityIV	2837	-0.91	7.83	-10.00	10.00	2836	-0.33	7.98	-10.00	10.00
pr	3168	3.64	2.24	1.00	7.00	3262	3.96	2.20	1.00	7.00
cl	3168	3.98	1.94	1.00	7.00	3262	3.95	1.96	1.00	7.00

Year	1985					1990				
Variable	Obs	Mean	St. dev.	Min	Max	Obs	Mean	St. dev.	Min	Max
logY	2249	19.51	2.69	9.31	26.85	2286	19.73	2.79	10.20	26.88
logVA	2067	18.51	2.54	10.34	25.94	2124	18.89	2.62	9.29	25.96
logEmp	2387	8.73	2.44	0.00	15.80	2441	8.88	2.31	0.00	16.11
logEsta	2069	4.37	2.24	0.00	11.02	2202	4.38	2.25	0.00	10.97
dlogY	2179	−0.02	0.32	−2.50	4.78	2048	0.00	0.43	−5.83	3.49
dlogVA	1992	−0.04	0.36	−2.40	4.86	1941	0.03	0.43	−6.08	4.46
dlogEmp	2309	0.01	0.21	−3.89	3.82	2159	0.02	0.26	−3.21	2.99
dlogEsta	1892	0.03	0.21	−1.61	1.72	1912	0.09	0.42	−4.62	3.76
d5logY	2008	−0.26	0.58	−4.94	4.30	1787	0.32	0.63	−7.91	4.47
d5logVA	1868	−0.31	0.63	−5.15	4.52	1701	0.34	0.66	−7.12	3.35
d5logEmp	2181	−0.01	0.43	−3.60	4.91	1881	0.09	0.45	−6.38	3.93
d5logEsta	0					1576	0.23	0.67	−4.31	4.27
d10logY	1875	0.15	0.77	−4.11	4.68	1736	0.07	0.76	−4.62	7.27
d10logVA	1835	0.11	0.79	−2.78	3.85	1717	0.05	0.82	−6.09	7.39
d10logEmp	2086	0.15	0.65	−4.22	5.15	1871	0.07	0.61	−4.97	7.76
d10logEsta	0					0				
distfront	2100	0.15	0.08	0.00	0.47	1953	0.16	0.09	0.00	0.53
db_proc_99	1989	10.20	4.43	2.00	21.00	2133	10.19	4.33	2.00	21.00
polityIV	2861	0.37	7.93	−10.00	10.00	2806	2.45	7.41	−10.00	10.00
pr	3287	4.12	2.23	1.00	7.00	3151	4.46	2.19	1.00	7.00
cl	3287	3.90	2.05	1.00	7.00	3151	4.53	1.86	1.00	7.00

Table 12A.1 (continued) Summary statistics by year

Year	1995					2000				
Variable	Obs	Mean	St. dev.	Min	Max	Obs	Mean	St. dev.	Min	Max
logY	2289	19.31	2.99	8.35	27.00	1649	19.71	3.05	6.68	27.12
logVA	1982	18.69	2.85	8.00	26.04	1405	19.16	2.71	8.70	26.20
logEmp	2408	8.68	2.39	0.00	15.77	1780	8.90	2.38	0.00	15.41
logEsta	2225	4.40	2.50	0.00	11.38	1695	5.05	2.44	0.00	11.47
dlogY	2171	0.08	0.49	−7.69	6.70	1579	0.03	0.31	−2.31	2.31
dlogVA	1877	0.07	0.51	−6.60	5.68	1312	−0.01	0.27	−1.92	1.73
dlogEmp	2280	0.00	0.34	−4.12	4.20	1674	0.00	0.20	−2.39	1.78
dlogEsta	2109	0.10	0.48	−2.69	3.84	1621	0.05	0.36	−3.76	2.68
d5logY	1709	0.06	0.91	−5.92	5.09	1495	−0.07	0.75	−7.10	6.02
d5logVA	1654	0.04	0.80	−6.47	4.08	1246	−0.07	0.63	−4.64	3.94
d5logEmp	1944	−0.11	0.68	−5.89	4.30	1613	−0.07	0.50	−4.69	2.78
d5logEsta	1673	0.33	0.97	−4.23	4.87	1396	0.15	0.70	−4.22	5.46
d10logY	1546	0.43	1.03	−10.86	5.31	1233	0.02	1.11	−5.82	5.68
d10logVA	1486	0.47	0.97	−6.89	4.67	1126	0.05	0.83	−4.87	5.29
d10logEmp	1677	0.12	0.73	−6.20	4.33	1417	−0.14	0.78	−5.37	3.43
d10logEsta	1328	0.50	1.13	−3.57	5.01	1289	0.53	1.11	−4.25	5.23
distfront	1969	0.18	0.10	0.00	0.82	1410	0.16	0.10	0.00	0.85
db_proc_99	2194	10.30	4.34	2.00	21.00	1954	10.17	4.39	2.00	21.00
polityIV	3241	3.79	6.54	−10.00	10.00	2542	4.96	6.07	−10.00	10.00
pr	3576	4.74	2.06	1.00	7.00	2729	5.11	2.06	1.00	7.00
cl	3576	4.48	1.79	1.00	7.00	2729	4.87	1.64	1.00	7.00

Table 12A.2 Explaining the differential: Entry and democracy

	Procedures number							
GDP per capita, log	-0.544 [0.337]	-0.687 [0.367]*	-0.111 [0.382]	-0.367 [0.511]	-0.757 [0.320]**	-0.853 [0.338]**	-1.094 [0.440]**	-0.783 [0.383]**
Executive de facto independence	-0.853 [0.270]***							
Constraints on executive power		-0.658 [0.290]**						
Effectiveness of legislature			-2.553 [0.661]***					
Government effectiveness				-1.88 [0.933]**				
Competition in the legislative nominating process					-2.051 [0.963]**			
Autocracy						0.322 [0.185]*		
Political rights average 1972–99							-0.655 [2.263]	
Civil rights average 1972–99								-4.171 [2.362]*
Observations	84	84	73	85	73	84	84	84
R^2	0.26	0.24	0.3	0.25	0.22	0.22	0.2	0.23

Note: Robust standard errors in brackets; * significant at 10%; ** significant at 5%; *** significant at 1%.

REFERENCES

Acemoglu, Daron. 2008. "Oligarchic Versus Democratic Societies." *Journal of the European Economic Association* 6(1):1–44.

Acemoglu, Daron, Philippe Aghion, and Fabrizio Zilibotti. 2006. "Distance to Frontier, Selection and Economic Growth." *Journal of the European Economic Association* 4(1):37–74.

Acemoglu, Daron, Simon Johnson, James Robinson, and Pierre Yared. 2005. "Income and Democracy." Mimeo, MIT.

Aghion, Philippe, Alberto Alesina, and Francesco Trebbi. 2004. "Endogenous Political Institutions." *Quarterly Journal of Economics* 119(2):565–611.

Aghion, Philippe, Robin Burgess, Stephen Redding, and Fabrizio Zilibotti. 2006. "The Unequal Effects of Liberalization: Evidence from Dismantling the License Raj in India." NBER working paper, no. 12031.

Barro, Robert. 1996. "Democracy and Growth." *Journal of Economic Growth* 1:1–27.

———. 1999. "The Determinants of Democracy." *Journal of Political Economy* 107:S158–S183.

Boix, Carlos. 2003. *Democracy and Redistribution.* Cambridge: Cambridge University Press.

Bueno de Mesquita, Bruce, Alastair Smith, Randolph Siverson, and James Morrow. 2003. *The Logic of Political Survival.* Cambridge: MIT Press.

Djankov, Simon, Raphael LaPorta, Florencio Lopez-de-Silanes, and Andrei Shleifer. 2002. "The Regulation of Entry." *Quarterly Journal of Economics* 113:1–37.

Giavazzi, Francesco, and Guido Tabellini. 2005. "Economic and Political Liberalizations." *Journal of Monetary Economics* 52:1297–1330.

Glaeser, Edward, Rafael La Porta, Florencio Lopez-de-Silanes, and Andrei Shleifer. 2004. "Do Institutions Cause Growth?" *Journal of Economic Growth* 9:271–304.

Helliwell, John. 1994. "Empirical Linkages Between Democracy and Economic Growth." *British Journal of Political Science* 24:225–48.

Huntington, Samuel. 1991. *The Third Wave: Democratization in the Late Twentieth Century.* Norman: University of Oklahoma Press.

Lipset, Seymour Martin. 1959. "Some Social Requisites of Democracy: Economic Development and Political Legitimacy." *American Political Science Review* 53:69–105.

Mulligan, Casey B., Xavier Sala-i-Martin, and Richard Gil. 2004. "Do Democracies Have Different Public Policies than Nondemocracies?" *Journal of Economic Perspectives* 18:51–74.

Papaioannou, Elias, and Gregorios Siourounis. Forthcoming. "Democratization and Growth." *Economic Journal*.

Perotti, Enrico, and Paolo Volpin. 2006. "Investor Protection and Entry." Tinbergen Institute Discussion Paper TI 2007–006/2.

Persson, Torsten, and Guido Tabellini. 2006. "Democratic Capital: The Nexus of Political and Economic Change." NBER working paper, no. 12175.

Przeworski, Adam, Michael Alvarez, Jose Cheibub, and Fernando Limongi. 2000. *Democracy and Development: Political Institutions and Well-Being in the World, 1950–1900*. Cambridge: Cambridge University Press.

Rajan, Raghuram, and Luigi Zingales. 1998. "Financial Dependence and Growth." *American Economic Review* 88:559–86.

Rodrik, Dani, and Romain Wacziarg. 2005. "Do Democratic Transitions Produce Bad Economic Outcomes?" *American Economic Review Papers and Proceedings* 95:50–56.

— 13 —

The Growth Effect of Democracy

Is It Heterogenous and
How Can It Be Estimated?

TORSTEN PERSSON AND GUIDO TABELLINI

13.1 Introduction

Political regimes can change suddenly because of coups, popular revolts, or the death of leaders. Such changes provide an opportunity to assess whether economic policies or performance are influenced by political institutions. A number of recent papers have exploited this opportunity. Using more or less the same difference-in-difference methodology, they have all estimated the average effects of democratic transitions on economic growth, or some other measures of economic performance, using a postwar panel dataset (see, e.g., Giavazzi and Tabellini 2005, Papaioannou and Siourounis forthcoming, Persson 2005, Persson and Tabellini 2006a, Rodrik and Wacziarg 2005). While the difference-in-difference strategy yields interesting results, which are considerably more credible than those from a standard cross-sectional regression, it still rests on strong identifying assumptions.[1]

The goal of this chapter is to reassess the relation between democracy and growth, while relaxing some of these strong identifying assumptions. To reach this goal, we reestimate the average effect of political transitions on economic growth by means of semiparametric methods. Broadly speaking, we combine aspects of difference-in-difference methods with aspects of propensity-score methods, by giving more weight to the comparisons of reforming and nonreforming countries that have similar probabilities of experiencing democratic reform. Specifically, we first estimate the probability of regime change conditional on a number of observable variables. We then use this estimated probability, the propensity score, to evaluate the difference in growth performance between the countries with and without a regime change. Under the standard assumptions in the propensity-score literature (the selection-on-observables and common-support assumptions), this empirical strategy yields consistent estimates of the average effect of political regime changes, in cases when a standard difference-in-difference strategy would not. A theoretical paper by Abadie (2005) further discusses this approach to estimation.[2] Heckman et al. (1997) evaluate similar nonexperimental estimators, using data from a large-scale U.S. social experiment with job training. Blundell et al. (2004) apply a combination of matching and difference in differences when estimating the effect of UK job-training programs. To our knowledge, the present chapter is the first to apply matching *cum* difference-in-difference methods in a macroeconomic context.[3] The macro setting raises specific issues that are not present is standard microeconomic applications, such as a relatively small sample and different treatment (reform) dates for different observations.

Our empirical findings suggest that empirically relevant heterogeneities are indeed present across countries, meaning that the flexibility allowed by semiparamatric methods is important. We show that transitions from autocracy to democracy are associated with an average growth acceleration of about 1 percentage point, producing a gain in per capita income of about 13% by the end of the sample period. This 1% growth effect is imprecisely estimated, but larger than most of the estimates in the literature using straight difference-in-difference methods (see the references mentioned above). The effect of transitions in the opposite direction is even larger: a relapse from democracy to autocracy slows down growth by almost 2 percentage points on average, which implies an income fall of about 45% at the end of the sample. These effects are much larger than those commonly found in the literature.

The chapter proceeds to discuss the main econometric issues (Section 13.2), describe the data (Section 13.3), and provide a benchmark with the straight difference-in-difference approach (Section 13.4). We then discuss some preliminaries in the matching procedure (Section 13.5), present the chapter's main results on how democracy affects growth (Section 13.6), and conclude.

13.2   Econometric Methods

This section introduces a number of econometric issues and methods to deal with them. Most of it can probably be skimmed by econometrically proficient readers who are familiar with the methods used in the treatment literature.

Our goal is to estimate the average causal effect on economic growth of becoming a democracy. To simplify the argument, we assume throughout the section that we have access to a sample consisting of data from only two types of countries: "treated" countries that experience a single transition from autocracy into democracy and "control" countries that remain autocracies throughout the sample period.[4] For each country in this sample, we observe economic growth in country i and year t, $y_{i,t}$, a dummy variable equal to one under democracy, $D_{i,t}$, and a vector of covariates, $\mathbf{x}_{i,t}$.

13.2.1 Difference-in-Difference Estimates

Several recent papers (see Section 13.1) have estimated the average effect of democracy on growth from a panel regression like

$$y_{i,t} = \phi D_{i,t} + \rho \mathbf{x}_{i,t} + \alpha_i + \theta_t + \varepsilon_{i,t}, \tag{13.1}$$

where α_i and θ_t are country and year fixed effects. This specification seeks to estimate the parameter ϕ by difference in differences: economic growth after the democratic transition minus growth before the transition in the treated countries is compared to the change in economic growth in the control countries over the same period.

This estimation method allows for any correlation between the democracy dummy $D_{i,t}$ and time-invariant country features—for example, that fast-growing countries are more likely to become democratic than slow-growing ones—since the growth effects of these country features are all captured by the country fixed effect, α_i. Nevertheless, identification rests on an important assumption: the selection of countries into democracy has to be uncorrelated with the *country-specific and time-varying* shock to growth, $\varepsilon_{i,t}$.

This in turn corresponds to two restrictive assumptions. First, absent any regime change, average growth in treated countries should (counterfactually) have been the same as in control countries (conditional on $\mathbf{x}_{i,t}$). This would fail if democratic transitions are enacted by far-sighted leaders, who have a lasting impact on growth irrespective of the regime change, or if political transitions coincide with other events—such as the economic transitions toward free markets in former socialist countries—that may have a lasting impact on economic growth.

To make this assumption more credible, the existing literature typically attempts to increase the similarity between treated and controls by including, in the vector $\mathbf{x}_{i,t}$, several covariates, such as initial per capita income, indicators for war years or socialist transitions, indicator variables for continental location (Africa, Asia, and Latin America) interacted with year dummy variables, and so on.

The second restrictive assumption is that heterogeneity in the effects of democracy should not be systematically related to the occurrence of democracy itself. Circumstances of regime change differ widely across time and space as do the types of political institutions adopted or abandoned. Thus, the effects of a crude democracy indicator are likely to differ across observations. If we neglect this heterogeneity and estimate the average effect of democracy as in (13.1), the unexplained component of growth, $\varepsilon_{i,t}$, also includes the term $(\phi_{i,t} - \phi)D_{i,t}$, where $\phi_{i,t}$ is the country-specific effect of democracy in country i and year t. Identification of ϕ now requires heterogeneity in the effect of reforms to be uncorrelated with their occurrence. This assumption fails, for example, if countries self-select into democracy based on the growth effect of regime changes (i.e., $D_{i,t} = 1$ is more likely when $\phi_{i,t} > \phi$).

To cope with this assumption, the dummy variable for democratic transitions is sometimes interacted with other observable features of democratic transitions (such as the nature of the democratic institutions that are acquired, or the sequence of economic and political reforms). But this strategy quickly runs into the curse of a dimensionality problem. The possible interactions and covariates are simply too many, relative to the limited number of democratic transitions.

13.2.2 Matching Estimates Based on the Propensity Score

To circumvent the curse of dimensionality, the recent microeconometric literature has often come to rely on semiparametric methods based on the propensity score. Typically these applications concern a cross section of individuals. But a few recent papers have combined difference-in-difference estimates with matching based on the propensity score, exploiting repeated observations for the same individuals. Abadie (2005) discusses an estimation strategy that uses the propensity score to carry out estimates in the spirit of difference in differences, while Heckman et al. (1997) and Blundell et al. (2004) provide theory as well as microeconometric applications.

The general idea is very intuitive. Performance—growth, in our case—before and after the treatment date is observed for the treated group and the control group. Conventional difference in differences compare the average change in performance for all the treated with the average change in performance for all the controls, on the two sides of a common treatment date. The matching approach instead compares each treated individual with a set of "similar" controls, and a difference-in-difference estimate is computed with reference only to the matched controls. This way, controls similar to the treated are given large weight, and controls very dissimilar to any treated observation may even be deemed entirely noncomparable; that is, they are left unmatched and given zero weight. Similarity is measured by the one-dimensional metric of the propensity score, that is, the probability of receiving treatment conditional on a set of covariates. Basically, the effect of treatment is estimated by comparing groups of individuals with similar distributions of those covariates that enter the estimation of the propensity score.

The microeconometric papers mentioned above discuss the econometric theory behind this methodology, and we refer the reader to these papers for more details. In this section, we confine ourselves to stating and explaining the main identifying assumptions. For this purpose, we need some notation adapted from Persson and Tabellini (2003) and Abadie (2005).

13.2.2.1 The Parameter of Interest

As above, let D be an indicator for democracy ($D = 1$) or autocracy ($D = 0$). Time is indexed by k, which corresponds to (an average over) years before ($k = 0$) and after ($k = 1$) the year of democratic transition. Let $Y_{i,k}^D$ denote *potential* growth of country i in period k and democratic state D (we use the symbol Y, in distinction from y in the previous subsection, since growth in period k is now an average of yearly growth rates during k). The individual treatment effect of democracy in country i and period k is then $Y_{i,k}^1 - Y_{i,k}^0$, the effect on growth in period 1 if this country switched from autocracy to democracy.

Consider a subset of the treated countries (i.e., countries with $D_{i,1} = 1$) with similar (time-invariant) characteristics, $\mathbf{X}_i$. The expected effect of democracy on growth in each of these countries is

$$\alpha(\mathbf{X}_i) = E(Y_{i,1}^1 - Y_{i,1}^0 | \mathbf{X}_i, \, D_{i,1} = 1),$$

where the expectations operator E refers to unobserved determinants of growth in democracy. Our parameter of interest is the *average effect of treatment on the treated*, namely,

$$\alpha = E\alpha(\mathbf{X}_i) = E\left\{E(Y_{i,1}^1 - Y_{i,1}^0 | \mathbf{X}_i, D_{i,1} = 1)\right\}, \qquad (13.2)$$

where the outer expectations operator E is taken over $\mathbf{X}$ in the part of the sample treated with democracy. This parameter measures the effect of democracy on growth in the countries that actually experienced the transition, relative to what would have happened had they remained autocracies. In other words, the relevant counterfactual is remaining under autocracy. Without additional assumptions, the parameter α does not say anything about what growth would have been if the countries that remained autocracies had instead become democracies (this would be a statement about the effect of treatment on the nontreated).

The fundamental problem of causal inference is that potential growth in the counterfactual regime is not observed. We only observe *actual* growth in one of the two possible political regimes. In particular, in period 1 we only observe $Y_{i,1}^1$ in the countries that actually became democratic (the treated) and $Y_{i,1}^0$ in the countries that actually had no transition (the controls). But the term $Y_{i,1}^0$ (counterfactual growth in a democracy if it had remained an autocracy) on the right-hand side of (13.2) is not observed.

13.2.2.2 Selection on Observables

To come up with an observable counterpart to $Y_{i,1}^0$, we can make the key identifying assumption (cf. Abadie 2005):

$$E(Y_{i,1}^0 - Y_{i,0}^0 | \mathbf{X}_i, D_{i,1} = 1) = E(Y_{i,1}^0 - Y_{i,0}^0 | \mathbf{X}_i, D_{i,1} = 0). \quad (13.3)$$

The right-hand side of (13.3) is the (observed) average change in growth between periods 1 and 0 in countries that remained autocracies throughout (the control group). The left-hand side is the (unobserved) average change in growth that the countries that actually became democracies (the treated group) COUNTERFACTUALLY would have experienced had they remained autocratic. Thus, the critical assumption is that, *conditional on* $\mathbf{X}$, without their democratic transition, the treated countries would have followed a growth path parallel to that of the control countries. This is the analog of the *selection-on-observables* assumption in a simple cross-sectional context.[5]

Decomposing the expectations operators on both sides of (13.3), all the terms are observable except for one: $E(Y_{i,1}^0|X_{i,}, D_{i,1} = 1)$. Thus, assumption (13.3) enables us to obtain an observable counterpart of this unobserved counterfactual, which can be used to estimate the parameter of interest in (13.2). Intuitively, by conditioning on a large enough set of covariates X, we can replace unobserved period 1 growth under autocracy in the treated countries (the term $E(Y_{i,1}^0|X_{i,}, D_{i,1} = 1)$) with observed growth under autocracy over the same period (the term $E(Y_{i,1}^0|X_i, D_{i,1} = 0)$) in those control countries that have similar covariates X_i.

Importantly, this argument does not impose any functional-form assumption on how democracy impacts growth. Because the relevant conditional expectations in (13.3) can all be computed nonparametrically, we can estimate our parameter of interest, α, nonparametrically just by comparing (weighted) mean outcomes. This is the central difference between matching and linear regression. Matching allows us to draw inferences from *local* comparisons only: as we compare countries with similar values of X, we do not rely on counterfactuals very different from the observed factuals. However, this desirable property requires that any *unobserved* heterogeneity in the response of growth to democracy be nonsystematic across the two groups of countries.

13.2.2.3 Propensity Score and Common Support

In practice, however, the dimension of X is too large for direct matching to be viable. This is where the propensity-score methodology is helpful. An important result due to Rosenbaum and Rubin (1983) implies that comparing countries with the same *probability of democratic transition* (*treatment*), given the controls X, is equivalent to comparing countries with similar values of X.

Specifically, let

$$p_i = p(X_i) = \text{Prob}[D_{i,1} = 1|X_i]$$

be the conditional probability that country i has a democratic transition during our sample period, given the vector of controls, X_i. This conditional probability is also called the *propensity score*. Assume that the propensity score is bounded away from 0 and 1 for all countries, an assumption known as the so-called *common-support* condition:

$$0 < p(X_i) < 1, \quad \text{for all } X_i. \tag{13.4}$$

Rosenbaum and Rubin (1983) show that, in a cross-sectional setting, conditioning on the vector $\mathbf{X}$ is equivalent to conditioning on the scalar p. If (13.4) is satisfied in our two-period context, (13.3) implies

$$E(Y^0_{i,1} - Y^0_{i,0}|p(\mathbf{X}_i),\ D_{i,1} = 1) = E(Y^0_{i,1} - Y^0_{i,0}|p(\mathbf{X}_i),\ D_{i,1} = 0). \quad (13.5)$$

For countries with similar propensity scores, realized transitions to democracy are random and uncorrelated with growth. We can thus replace the unobserved counterfactual on the left-hand side of (13.5) with the observed factual on the right-hand side of (13.5).

13.2.2.4 What Do We Gain?

The main advantage of this semiparametric (semiparametric because we have to estimate the propensity score) approach over the parametric difference-in-difference approach is that it relaxes linearity. We can thus allow for any heterogeneity in the effect of democracy, as long as it is related to the observable covariates $\mathbf{X}$. Suppose, for example, that richer countries are more likely to become democracies, and that democracy also works better in richer countries. Then the linear estimates corresponding to equation (13.1) would be biased unless we also included an interaction term between income and the democracy dummy. This bias is removed if income is included among the covariates $\mathbf{X}$ used to estimate the propensity score. Of course, unobserved heterogeneity remains a problem. Any omitted variable *uncorrelated with* $\mathbf{X}$ that influences both the adoption and the effects of democracy would violate selection on observables. But since—as a practical matter—economic, social, and cultural characteristics tend to cluster a great deal across countries, unobserved differences among countries may well correlate with observed differences.

A second advantage of this approach is that it allows a simple diagnostic to check that the distribution of observed covariates is balanced between the countries in the treated group and the control group. If the distribution of a specific covariate is very unbalanced in the two samples of countries, it is important to check if the results are robust to including this variable when estimating the propensity score. Intuitively, if the treated and controls have similar covariates, the linearity assumption entailed in conventional difference in difference is just a convenient local approximation. If they do not, the dissimilarity may bias the results.

Of course, there is no free lunch. The main cost of a semiparametric approach is that the estimates are less efficient than parametric estimates (under the null of the assumed functional form). Given the small samples in macroeconomics relative to standard micro applications, the loss in precision is nonnegligible.

13.2.2.5 Implementation in Practice

Our actual sample—unlike the stylized example and typical microeconomic applications like training programs—has different transition dates T_i for different observations $i = 1, \ldots, I$. Of course, our estimation procedure will have to cope with this additional complication. Also different from the example in this section, the actual sample includes transitions from democracy to autocracy. This presents no conceptual problems (see further detail in Section 13.3), however, so we can continue to think about treatment as a transition into democracy. In practice, we implement the estimation in five steps:

1. We begin by defining a group of treated and a group of control countries and estimate the probability of treatment. This is done in a cross section by means of a logit regression, where the dependent variable equals one for all countries making a transition at some time within the sample and zero for those that don't, and where all the covariates are time invariant. The estimated probability of a transition to democracy is our measure of the propensity score.

2. Next, for each country treated with democracy, we compute average growth before and after the date of transition, T_i. The difference between these two averaged growth rates is denoted by g_i. Thus, we measure

$$g_i = \frac{1}{N_i^a} \sum_{t > T_i} y_{i,t} - \frac{1}{N_i^b} \sum_{t < T_i} y_{i,t}, \tag{13.6}$$

where $y_{i,t}$ is the yearly growth in period t and N_i^b and N_i^a are the number of years before and after the transition date in country i. (The next section describes how we deal with multiple transitions, so for now, think about the procedure as applying to a setup where each country has at most one transition in the sample period.)

3. Subsequently, we match each treated country with some of the controls. For each of these controls, we compute the difference in average growth over the periods before and after the transition date in the

treated country they are matched with: the expression is thus identical to (13.6), except that $y_{i,t}$ is replaced with $y_{j,t}$. We denote the resulting variable as g_i^j where the j superscript refers to a certain country j among the controls and i refers to the treated country. In doing this, we make sure that the years over which g_i and g_i^j are computed exactly coincide.

4. For each treated country, we then compute the weighted average of the nonparametric difference-in-difference estimator $\hat{\alpha}_i$:

$$\hat{\alpha}_i = g_i - \sum_j w_{i,j} g_i^j, \tag{13.7}$$

where $w_{i,j} \geq 0$, and $\sum_j w_{i,j} = 1$, are weights based on the propensity score. These weights differ depending on the detailed properties of the matching estimators, and some controls may receive zero weight if they are very different from the treated country with which they are matched. The parameter $\hat{\alpha}_i$ is our estimate of the effect of democratic transition on growth in country i. Intuitively, it measures how growth in country i changed after the transition, relative to a weighted average of the (similar) controls it is matched with.

5. Finally, we compute the average estimated effect of transitions to democracy in the group of treated countries, $\hat{\alpha}$, as a simple average of the individual $\hat{\alpha}_i$ estimates, namely

$$\hat{\alpha} = \frac{1}{I} \sum_i \hat{\alpha}_i, \tag{13.8}$$

where I denotes the number of treated countries in our sample. This is our estimator of the average effect of democracy on growth (the average effect of treatment on the treated).

Clearly, this procedure may use each control country several times, as the same controls may be matched with several treated countries and possibly at different dates. This matters for the computation of the standard error of our estimators, since it may introduce correlation between g_i^j and g_k^j—that is, between growth in control country j when it is used as a control for treated countries i and k. Of course, the correlation will be positive and higher the closer are the transition dates of i and k, while the correlation between g_i^j and g_k^j might even be negative if the transition dates are far apart. The Appendix provides analytic expressions for the standard error of α under two alternative assumptions: (a) the variables g_i^j and g_k^j are independent and (b) the variables g_i^j and g_k^j are perfectly correlated. While (b) certainly yields an upper bound, the true standard errors might be lower than under (a) if negative correlation between g_i^j and g_k^j is prevalent. When computing the standard errors, we assume that all treated countries have the same variance, as do all control countries. We also neglect that the weights are estimated in a first step (i.e., we treat the propensity score as known). Both assumptions are standard in the applied literature (see, e.g., Lechner 2001).[6]

13.3   Data and Sample Definitions

Our panel dataset includes annual data on economic growth and political regimes for as many countries as possible over the years 1960–2000. Economic growth is measured as the yearly growth rate of per capita income, and the source is the Penn World Tables. We classify a country as democratic if the *polity2* variable in the Polity IV dataset is strictly positive. The threshold of 0 for *polity2* corresponds to a generous definition of democracy, but has the advantage that many large changes in the *polity2* are clustered around 0. This is important, since we want to identify the causal effect of regime transitions on growth, exploiting the time variation in the data. A definition of democracy based on a higher threshold for *polity2* would also classify as democratic transitions very gradual changes in the underlying indicators of *polity2* that are unlikely to be associated with significant changes in political regimes.[7]

We also include some other covariates, which will be introduced and defined in context. The resulting panel is unbalanced, partly because of data availability and partly because countries do not enter the dataset until their year of independence.

From this panel dataset we construct two partly overlapping samples, which are used to study transitions to democracy and autocracy, respectively. When studying transitions into democracy, we include as control countries those that remain autocracies throughout the sample period, while the treated countries are those that experience at least one transition from autocracy to democracy. We call this sample the *democratic transitions* sample. When studying transitions into autocracy, the control countries remain democracies throughout, while the treated countries have at least one transition from democracy to autocracy. This is called the *autocratic transitions* sample.

In selecting these two samples, we had to deal with a number of complications. A few countries experience transitions close to the beginning or the end of the period for which growth data are available. Since we expect it to take some time for transitions to influence growth, we discard the transitions that take place in the last three years of the available sample. We also discard reforms in the first three years of the panel to avoid a poor estimate of growth before the transition. Specifically, we treat the observations of growth after (or before) a transition as missing if the transition is not followed (or preceded) by at least three years of growth data. The country is then considered a control, as if the transition did not occur.

In a few countries, especially in Africa and Latin America, we observe transitions that last only for a few years. We discard those lasting (strictly) less than four years, to avoid hinging the estimation on very short growth episodes. As in the beginning or end of sample transitions, we treat growth during the years of these short transitions as missing, and classify the country as if the transition did not occur.

In another few countries, we observe more than one long spell of democracy or autocracy. Chile, for instance, starts out as a democracy in 1960, it becomes an autocracy in 1973 (the Pinochet regime), and it returns to democracy in 1989. This means that Chile is a treated country both when treatment is defined as transition to democracy and when treatment is defined as transition to autocracy. Therefore, Chile is included as treated in the democratic transitions sample for the years from 1973 (when it first becomes an autocracy) until the end of the sample. It is also included in the autocratic transitions sample from 1960 until 1988 (the last year of autocracy). We apply similar sample-selection rules to other countries that experience more than one spell in the same regime lasting more than three years.

When transitions are defined in this way, most countries have no more than a single transition in one or both directions. Guatemala, Uganda, and Nigeria, however, have two transitions in the same direction. We deal with the transitions in these three countries in two different ways: they are either excluded because the propensity score is outside of the common-support range (see Section 13.5), or included with the transitions but treated as independent cases (as if each transition applied to a different, treated country).

13.4   Difference-in-Difference Estimates

To provide a benchmark, Table 13.1 presents results from traditional difference-in-difference estimation with yearly data. These results correspond to estimates of equation (13.1) in various samples. Besides country and year fixed effects, the covariates $x_{i,t}$ include per capita income lagged once, year fixed effects interacted with indicators for Latin America and Africa, indicators for war years and lagged war years, and an indicator for formerly socialist countries in central and eastern Europe and the Asian provinces of the former Soviet Union after 1989. This specification is similar to those in the existing literature (e.g., Giavazzi and Tabellini 2005; Persson and Tabellini 2006a).

Column 1 imposes the assumption that the effect on growth of a transition into democracy is the same as the negative of the effect on growth of a transition into autocracy. The effect of democracy is thus estimated in the full sample. As in the earlier papers cited above, we find that the effect of democratic transitions is positive, inducing a growth acceleration of about 0.5 percentage points. Although not statistically significant, the point estimate is not a trivial effect from an economic point of view. The long-run effect is dampened by the relatively high estimated convergence rate, however. With a convergence rate of 5.5% per year, a growth acceleration of about 0.5 percentage points implies a long-run positive effect of democracy on the level of per capita income of almost 10%.[8]

The remainder of Table 13.1 does not impose the symmetry constraint, but estimates the effect of democracy separately from transitions to democracy (columns 2 and 3) and transitions to autocracy (columns 4 and 5), allowing these two effects to differ. Note that when estimating the effect of autocratic transitions in columns 4 and 5, we still display the effect of being a democracy, computed as the negative growth effect of transitions away from democracy. In column 2, we let the sample include only the countries that became democracies plus the countries that remained autocracies throughout.[9] In column 3, we add to the sample those countries that remained democratic throughout. Analogously, the sample behind column 4 includes the countries that became autocracies and the more restricted set of countries that remained democratic throughout, while the sample behind column 5 includes both permanent democracies and autocracies. All the estimates in Table 13.1 convey a similar message: democracy induces

Table 13.1 Democracy and growth: Difference-in-difference estimates on yearly data

	(1)	(2)	(3)	(4)	(5)
			Growth		
Democracy	0.48	0.58	0.73	0.26	0.35
	(0.34)	(0.54)	(0.42)*	(0.65)	(0.63)
Lagged income	−5.45	−6.20	−5.38	−5.04	−6.06
	(0.62)***	(0.81)***	(0.65)***	(0.97)***	(0.93)***
Treatment	Transition to democracy and autocracy	Transition to democracy	Transition to democracy	Transition to autocracy	Transition to autocracy
Control group	Permanent autocracy or democracy	Permanent autocracy	Permanent autocracy or democracy	Permanent democracy	Permanent autocracy or democracy
Observations	4,323	2,554	4,000	1,985	2,924
Number of countries	138	76	123	70	97
Adjusted R^2	0.08	0.08	0.08	0.13	0.08

Note: Robust standard errors in parentheses: * significant at 10%; ** significant at 5%; *** significant at 1%. Other covariates: country and year fixed effects; year fixed effects interacted with indicators for Latin America and for Africa, indicators for war years and lagged war years, and an indicator for formerly socialist countries in central and eastern Europe and the Asian provinces of the former Soviet Union after 1989.

a positive, but small and generally insignificant, growth acceleration. The positive effect of transitions to democracy appears larger in absolute value (and in one case statistically significant) than the negative effect of transitions to autocracy.

13.5   Matching Preliminaries

We now turn to the main contribution of this chapter, namely, the matching approach to estimating the growth effects of democracy. Before getting to the actual estimates, however, we need to go through a number of preliminary steps, including some diagnostics. This section is devoted to these preliminaries.

13.5.1 Estimating the Propensity Score

As explained in Section 13.2.2.5, the first step in implementing a matching *cum* difference-in-difference estimator is to estimate the propensity score, the probability of treatment, in a cross section of countries (i.e., ignoring the time dimension). We do this separately for the events of becoming a democracy and becoming an autocracy, because we want to allow the effect of the covariates on the probability of transition to be different for the two events. In the democratic transitions sample, the dependent variable is thus zero for the countries that remained autocracies, and one for the countries that experienced at least one transition toward democracy. In the autocratic transitions sample, the dependent variable is zero for the countries that remained democracies throughout, and one for the countries that experienced at least one transition toward autocracy. Thus, the samples are partly overlapping (because some countries, like Chile, appear in both samples).

We estimate the propensity score with a logit regression. The selection of the covariates to enter this regression is a crucial decision that trades off two opposite concerns. On the one hand, the selection-on-observables assumption would suggest the inclusion of many covariates to ensure that the propensity score is indeed a balancing function. On the other hand, we don't want to predict treatment too well, so as not to violate the common-support assumption. Here is an instance where the macroeconomic setting makes a difference. Most microeconomic applications concentrate on the first concern, because the sample is large enough that even rare events—like an actual transition for an observation with a low propensity score—would still occur in large enough numbers to allow meaningful comparisons (and small standard errors). But in our context we also have to worry about not excluding too many countries for which a state is predicted too well. Thus, we include a limited number of variables that are likely to influence both the occurrence of regime transitions and their economic effects, and we check the robustness of the results to two alternative specifications. The set of covariates is the same in the democratic and autocratic transitions samples.

To capture differences in economic development, we include real per capita income at the beginning of the sample. As explained above, different countries enter our samples at different dates, depending on political history or data availability. To increase comparability, we measure each country's per capita income in the first year it enters a given sample, relative to U.S. per capita income in the same year. We call the resulting variable *income relative to the United States*.

The countries in these samples have very different political histories. Some of them have a long history with entry into democracy in the distant past; some have a prolonged autocratic spell. Others became independent some time during the sample period or a few years before. To mitigate this important source of heterogeneity, we condition on what Persson and Tabellini (2006b) call *domestic democratic capital*, which measures the incidence of democracy in each country since 1800 (or since the year of independence, if later). This variable is assumed to accumulate in years of democracy, but to depreciate under autocracy. The depreciation rate is estimated by Persson and Tabellini (2006b) to fit the hazard rates in a time series regression where the dependent variable is exit from democracy and from autocracy. This variable is rescaled to lie between 0 and 1, where a 1 corresponds to the steady-state value of a country never exiting from democracy. In this chapter, we measure *domestic democratic capital* in the first year that a country enters the sample.

Transitions to democracy or autocracy often occur in waves that include several neighboring countries. To capture this phenomenon, we include a variable measuring the geography of democracy around 1993 (the first year in our sample, when we have data for all formerly socialist countries in central and eastern Europe). This variable, called *foreign democratic capital*, is a slight variation on a similar measure used in Persson and Tabellini (2006b). For each country, it is defined as the incidence of democracy in 1993 among all other countries within a 1,750 km radius (the radius refers to the distance between the capitals). By the definition of a share, this variable too lies between 0 and 1, where a 1 captures the case where all countries in the neighborhood are democratic.

Since the sample period varies in length across countries, and since the probability of a regime transition is higher the longer is the duration of the relevant time period, we also control for the length of the period during which we have available data for each country, a variable called *length of sample*. This variable is introduced to eliminate the possibility that sample length covaries systematically with growth performance.

Wars are often destabilizing for political regimes and, of course, they also hurt economic activity. Thus, we include as a covariate the fraction of war years (including both interstate and civil wars) over the total-period length for which growth data are available, a variable called *war years*.

Finally, regime transitions are more likely for countries that start out with a value of our democracy index, *polity2*, closer to the threshold of zero. At the same time, a high value of *polity2* at the outset might have an independent effect on the economic consequences of regime changes (for instance because a regime change might correspond to a more gradual transition). For this reason, we also consider including the value of *polity2* in the first year a country enters the sample. As we shall see, however, the inclusion of this variable increases a great deal the predictive power of the logit regressions in the sample of autocratic transitions. This, in turn, leads to a much smaller set of treated countries that safely meet the common-support condition. Hence, we discuss results with and without the *initial value of polity2*.

The results of the logit regressions are displayed in Table 13.2. Columns 1 and 2 refer to the democratic transitions sample, with and without the inclusion of the *initial value of polity2*. *Domestic democratic capital* considerably raises the probability of a transition toward democracy, as expected. *Foreign democratic capital* has a similar positive effect, but this effect is not statistically significant. The frequency of wars discourages democratic transitions, an effect that is statistically significant. *Income relative to the United States* has no effect. Finally, the inclusion of the *initial value of polity2* makes no difference. Overall, the pseudo R^2 (the improvement in the likelihood associated with the inclusion of the covariates in addition to a constant) is 0.17, suggesting that these covariates leave a lot of residual variation unexplained.

Columns 3 and 4 refer to the autocratic transitions sample, with and without the *initial value of polity2*. Here *income relative to the United States* has strong predictive power, with richer countries less likely to relapse into autocracy, as expected.[10] *Foreign democratic capital* also helps to predict transitions to autocracy, although here the sign is opposite of what one would expect. As anticipated, the inclusion of the *initial value of polity2* makes a big difference: the variable is highly significant and with the expected sign, and when it is included, the pseudo R^2 jumps from 0.43 to 0.61. Overall, these covariates help to predict transitions from democracy to autocracy much better than transitions in the opposite direction. As already discussed, this is a mixed blessing, since it makes the selection-on-

Table 13.2 Estimates of the propensity score

	(1)	(2)	(3)	(4)
	Democratic transition		Autocratic transition	
Length of sample	2.40	2.52	2.63	4.08
	(1.97)	(1.95)	(1.50)*	(2.20)*
Income relative to the	−0.002	−0.003	−0.03	−0.02
United States	(0.005)	(0.005)	(0.01)***	(0.01)**
War years	−8.35	−8.14	−3.69	−10.33
	(4.71)*	(4.84)*	(5.58)	(7.13)
Domestic democratic capital	8.73	8.82	0.65	−0.35
	(4.25)**	(4.20)**	(2.29)	(2.05)
Foreign democratic capital	1.73	1.90	3.26	2.42
	(1.21)	(1.24)	(1.26)***	(1.31)*
Initial value of polity2		0.04		−0.89
		(0.06)		(0.22)***
Observations	77	77	70	70
Pseudo R^2	0.17	0.17	0.43	0.61

Note: Robust standard errors in parentheses: * significant at 10%; ** significant at 5%; *** significant at 1%. *Income relative to the United States, domestic democratic capital,* and *initial value of polity2* are measured in first year of sample. *Foreign democratic capital* is measured in 1993.

observables assumption more credible, but at the same time strains the credibility of the common-support assumption.

Figure 13.1 depicts the density of the estimated-propensity score from columns 1 and 3, respectively, of Table 13.2 (i.e., the specification that does not include the *initial value of polity2*), for both treated and control countries. Observations outside of the common support we impose are dropped and not displayed in Figure 13.1 (see the discussion in Section 13.5.2). As one would expect from the estimation results, the distribution of the propensity scores for the treated and the controls are more similar in the sample of democratic transitions, where treatment is predicted less well, than in the sample of autocratic transitions. Both samples display considerable overlap between treated and control countries, however. Overall, the figure suggests that matching should work well, at least if the local comparisons are made within relatively broad regions of the propensity score (a coarse balancing function), so as to guarantee overlap.

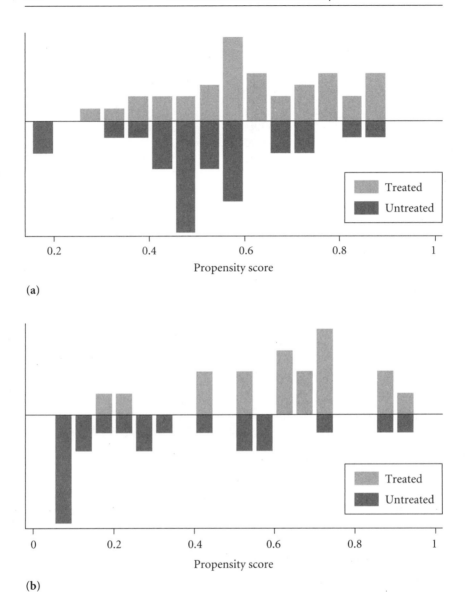

(a)

(b)

Figure 13.1 Estimated-propensity scores: (a) treated with democracy; (b) treated with autocracy. *Note*: The estimates correspond to columns 1 and 3, respectively, of Table 13.2.

13.5.2 Countries Inside the Common Support

The first column of Tables 13.3a and 13.3b report the full list of countries in each of the two samples. These are sorted in ascending order of the
estimated-propensity scores, which are displayed in the third column. To
facilitate reading the table, the names of treated countries are indicated by
boldface font, whereas the names of control countries are not. The same
information is given in column 2: the variable "Treated" in the second column equals 0 for the countries in the control group and 1 for the countries
in the treated group. The last two columns of each table report the change
in *polity2* in the year of the regime transition, and the year of that (those)
transition(s).

It is important to verify that the common-support assumption is not obviously violated, and possibly to drop observations for which the estimated-
propensity score is too close to its bounds of 0 and 1. Consider the democratic transitions sample in Table 13.3a. At the lower bound (the top of the
table), we are comfortably away from 0. The first observation, Yemen, is a
control with an estimated propensity score of 0.17. The third observation,
Iran, is the first treated country (according to our generous definition, Iran
became a democracy in 1997), with an estimated propensity score of 0.28.
At the upper end (the bottom of the table), instead, several treated countries
are strongly predicted to switch into democracy. There is no firm rule for
how to deal with this situation. We choose to drop all treated observations
with a propensity score above 0.9; that is, they become the observations
outside the common support in Table 13.3a. This has the advantage of not
drawing inferences from Guatemala (the unique country to experience two
long spells of democracy), and gives a fair margin away from unity. Adopting a higher upper bound and including more countries would not affect
the estimates. But the results are sensitive to a more conservative, lower upper bound, essentially because Haiti (with an estimated-propensity score
of 0.887) is a large outlying observation, which makes some difference. We
comment more on this in Section 13.5.7.

Next, consider the autocratic transitions sample in Table 13.3b, where
we face the opposite problem. The controls (that remained democracies
throughout) are predicted very well around 0, and there is little overlap
with treated countries, while at the upper end, the lack of overlap is less serious. Here, we choose to drop all observations with an estimated-propensity
score below 0.075 and above 0.93. At the upper end, the choice is made

Table 13.3a Transitions from autocracy to democracy

Country	Treated	Propensity score	Change in polity2	Date of reform
Yemen	0	0.1712141	.	
Angola	0	0.1947455	.	
Iran	1	0.2785125	9	1997
Chad	0	0.3203447	.	
Mozambique	1	0.3398073	12	1994
Comoros	1	0.354881	11	1990
Vietnam	0	0.3581062	.	
Uganda	1	0.3897252	10	1980
El Salvador	1	0.4127302	2	1982
Sierra Leone	0	0.4226772	.	
Equatorial Guinea	0	0.424049	.	
Guinea-Bissau	1	0.4358898	11	1994
Zaire	0	0.4407421	.	
Tanzania	0	0.4520402	.	2000
Morocco	0	0.4527073	.	
Central African Republic	1	0.4552693	12	1993
Rwanda	0	0.470873ö	.	
Mauritania	0	0.4757592	.	
Algeria	0	0.4805619	.	
Guinea	0	0.4810042	.	
Nicaragua	1	0.4910639	7	1990
Burundi	0	0.4922749	.	
Thailand	1	0.5017168	4	1978
Syria	0	0.5023594	.	
Niger	1	0.5082768	8	1991
Bangladesh	1	0.5125053	11	1991
Senegal	0	0.5249349	.	2000
Gabon	0	0.537788	.	
Ivory Coast	0	0.5521293	.	2000
Togo	0	0.5554183	.	
Benin	1	0.555422	6	1991
Congo	1	0.5571044	6	1992
Mali	1	0.5590481	7	1992
Cameroon	0	0.5675696	.	
Ghana	1	0.5689386	3	1996
Jordan	0	0.5769697	.	
Nigeria	1	0.5864162	7	1979
Madagascar	1	0.594099	8	1991
Burkina Faso	0	0.5977144	.	1977
Poland	1	0.5982632	11	1989

Table 13.3a *(continued)* Transitions from autocracy to democracy

Country	Treated	Propensity score	Change in polity2	Date of reform
Hungary	1	0.6095265	6	1989
Taiwan	1	0.611932	8	1992
Malawi	1	0.6158609	15	1994
Cyprus	1	0.638754	7	1968
Zambia	1	0.653224	15	1991
Singapore	0	0.6654041	.	
Indonesia	0	0.6893978	.	1999
Portugal	1	0.69704	6	1975
Lesotho	1	0.7038091	15	1993
Nepal	1	0.7060294	7	1990
Dominican Republic	1	0.7089661	9	1978
China	0	0.7145793	.	
Tunisia	0	0.7278883	.	
Romania	1	0.7553898	7	1990
Mexico	1	0.7785828	4	1994
Philippines	1	0.7795237	7	1986
South Korea	1	0.799453	6	1987
Pakistan	1	0.8041176	12	1988
Paraguay	1	0.8284625	10	1989
Egypt	0	0.8383721	.	
Cuba	0	0.8655669	.	
Ethiopia	1	0.8730649	1	1993
Haiti	1	0.8866652	14	1994
Panama	1	0.8921999	16	1989
Guyana	1	0.8947882	13	1992
Outside common support				
Guatemala	1	0.9190304	8	1966
Guatemala	1	0.9190304	4	1986
Ecuador	1	0.9237149	14	1979
Honduras	1	0.9413305	2	1980
Brazil	1	0.9437772	10	1985
Spain	1	0.9685184	4	1976
Argentina	1	0.979982	16	1983
Uruguay	1	0.9839289	16	1985
Bolivia	1	0.9866512	15	1982
Peru	1	0.9885088	5	1979
Greece	1	0.9948298	8	1974
Chile	1	0.9977797	9	1989

Note: The Propensity score is estimated as in column 1 of Table 13.2.

Table 13.3b Transitions from democracy to autocracy

Country	Treated	Propensity score	Change in polity2	Date of reform
Outside common support				
New Zealand	0	0.0014931	.	
Australia	0	0.0016789	.	
Iceland	0	0.0040472	. .	
South Africa	0	0.0105352	.	
Switzerland	0	0.0115997	.	
Czech Republic	0	0.0148975	.	
Slovenia	0	0.0238694	.	
United States	0	0.0261698	.	
Luxembourg	0	0.0281385	.	
Israel	0	0.0299115	.	
Denmark	0	0.0345439	.	
Germany	0	0.0352485	.	
Sweden	0	0.0398666	.	
Papua New Guinea	0	0.0476861	.	
France	0	0.04837	.	
United Kingdom	0	0.0497661	.	
Netherlands	0	0.0540976	.	
Fiji	0	0.0557607	.	1987
Canada	0	0.0612058	.	
Venezuela	0	0.0615961	.	
Slovak Republic	0	0.063058	.	
Latvia	0	0.063171	.	
Ukraine	0	0.0654528	.	
Italy	0	0.0667572	.	
Belarus	1	0.0720809	−7	1995
Russia	0	0.0729471	.	
Inside common support				
Austria	0	0.0757894	.	
Finland	0	0.0819311	.	
Norway	0	0.0822244	.	
Belgium	0	0.0840312	.	
Japan	0	0.0974352	.	
Bulgaria	0	0.0998625	.	
Estonia	0	0.1184082	.	
Namibia	0	0.1368068	.	
Trinidad and Tobago	0	0.180688	.	

Table 13.3b *(continued)* Transitions from democracy to autocracy

Country	Treated	Propensity score	Change in polity2	Date of reform
Greece	1	0.1918558	−11	1967
Macedonia	0	0.2195661	.	
Uruguay	1	0.2241872	−6	1972
Ireland	0	0.2807057	.	
Sri Lanka	0	0.2912095	.	
Malaysia	0	0.3415968	.	
Zimbabwe	1	0.4292819	−7	1987
Turkey	0	0.4345146	.	1980
Armenia	1	0.4382235	−9	1996
Peru	1	0.5047568	−12	1968
Chile	1	0.5215374	−13	1973
Costa Rica	0	0.52407	.	
Mauritius	0	0.541923	.	
Jamaica	0	0.553453	.	
Colombia	0	0.5750838	.	
Guatemala	1	0.6118631	−4	1974
Sierra Leone	1	0.6188506	−7	1971
Panama	1	0.6420545	−11	1968
Zambia	1	0.6628014	−2	1968
Philippines	1	0.6917624	−11	1972
Congo	1	0.7105513	−11	1997
South Korea	1	0.717416	−12	1972
Albania	0	0.7235891	.	1996
Gambia	1	0.729219	−15	1994
Brazil	1	0.7480876	−6	1964
India	0	0.8504922	.	
Kenya	1	0.8767781	−2	1966
Guyana	1	0.878488	−1	1978
Botswana	0	0.9226773	.	
Pakistan	1	0.9228303	−15	1977
Outside common support				
Nigeria	1	0.9312006	−14	1966
Nigeria	1	0.9312006	−14	1984
Lesotho	1	0.9540992	−18	1970
Uganda	1	0.9912787	−7	1966
Uganda	1	0.9912787	−3	1985

Note: The Propensity score is estimated as in column 3 of Table 13.2.

so that Nigeria and Uganda (the only two treated countries with multiple spells of autocracy) are dropped from the sample. But adopting a higher or lower threshold would not change the results. At the lower end, one outlying observation matters quite a bit for the results: Belarus, which starts out as a (weak) democracy and drops into dictatorship after a few years. Since the time period where we have data for Belarus is very short, and since the next treated country is Greece with a much higher propensity score (0.19 versus 0.07 for Belarus), we choose to be conservative and exclude Belarus from the common support. At the low end, we thus start the sample with Austria, a control with a propensity score slightly above 0.075. Adopting an even more conservative higher bound for the common support does not affect the final results.

13.5.3 The Balancing Property

To what extent is the propensity score a balancing function? That is, how well does our matching on the propensity score balance the distribution of relevant covariates across treated and control countries? The answer to this question is important, because this is where the value added of this methodology lies. Tables 13.4a and 13.4b provide the answer for our two samples of democratic and autocratic transitions.

Each double row in the table refers to a specific covariate. We consider all covariates included in the logit regressions of Table 13.2 (including the *initial value of polity2*), plus three dummy variables for continental location (in Latin America or Asia or Africa). The upper, single row (labeled "Unmatched") for each variable displays the simple average of that variable in the treated and control groups, respectively, plus the *t* statistic and the *p*-value for the null hypothesis that these averages are the same in the treated and control groups. This first set of statistics is calculated over the full set of countries listed in Tables 13.3a and 13.3b, respectively, before imposing the common-support assumption. Clearly, the null of equal means is rejected for many variables in either or both of the tables. Thus, treated and control countries differ systematically with regard to economic development (*relative income*), political history (*domestic democratic capital*), and political geography (*foreign democratic capital*). Initial democracy as measured by *polity2* is also very different in the treated and control groups in the autocratic transitions sample. Finally, the treated and control groups also seem

Table 13.4a Treated versus controls: Countries that became democracies

Variable	Sample	Mean		t-test	
		Treated	Control	t	p > |t|
Relative income	Unmatched	−201.16	−228.1	1.59	0.116
	Matched	−222.22	−220.4	−0.12	0.91
Domestic democratic	Unmatched	0.12	0.02	3.01***	0.00
captial	Matched	0.05	0.03	0.64	0.53
Foreign democratic	Unmatched	0.60	0.43	2.55***	0.01
capital	Matched	0.51	0.48	0.44	0.66
Length of sample	Unmatched	0.92	0.87	1.25	0.22
	Matched	0.90	0.90	0.01	0.99
War years	Unmatched	0.04	0.05	−0.50	0.62
	Matched	0.04	0.04	−0.08	0.94
Initial value of	Unmatched	−4.78	−5.07	0.29	0.77
polity2	Matched	−5.03	−5.43	0.39	0.70
Latin America	Unmatched	0.37	0.04	3.45***	0.00
	Matched	0.22	0.06	1.99*	0.05
Asia	Unmatched	0.14	0.14	0.00	1.00
	Matched	0.19	0.20	−0.08	0.93
Africa	Unmatched	0.33	0.71	−3.49***	0.00
	Matched	0.43	0.67	−2.05**	0.04

Note: Initial value of polity2, relative income, and domestic democratic capital are measured in first year of sample. Foreign democratic capital is measured in 1993. Matching is based on the estimates reported in column 1 of Table 13.2. When computing the unmatched means, we do not impose the common-support restriction, while we do when computing the matched means.

to be drawn from different continents (in particular with regard to Latin America and Africa).

The lower single row for each variable (labeled "Matched") presents a similar set of statistics calculated in a different way. First, we impose the common-support assumption for both the treated and the control countries, as discussed above. We then calculate the means for the treated countries. Clearly, this changes the means for the treated group. Second, we display the matched means for the control countries, namely, a weighted average where each control country receives a weight based on its propensity

Table 13.4b Treated versus controls: Countries that became autocracies

Variable	Sample	Mean		t-test	
		Treated	Control	t	p > |t|
Relative income	Unmatched	−217.89	−95.43	−6.50***	0.00
	Matched	−194.20	−185.44	−0.41	0.69
Domestic democratic	Unmatched	0.10	0.25	−2.49**	0.01
capital	Matched	0.137	0.16	−0.33	0.74
Foreign democratic	Unmatched	0.57	0.69	−1.44	0.15
capital	Matched	0.61	0.71	−0.97	0.34
Length of sample	Unmatched	0.84	0.75	1.13	0.26
	Matched	0.88	0.80	0.99	0.33
War years	Unmatched	0.05	0.03	1.46	0.15
	Matched	0.04	0.05	−0.09	0.93
Initial value of	Unmatched	4.12	8.68	−6.67***	0.00
polity2	Matched	3.39	8.13	−4.41***	0.00
Latin America	Unmatched	0.28	0.11	1.90*	0.06
	Matched	0.39	0.33	0.37	0.71
Asia	Unmatched	0.16	0.09	0.96	0.34
	Matched	0.17	0.19	−0.17	0.87
Africa	Unmatched	0.44	0.09	3.83**	0.00
	Matched	0.33	0.20	0.88	0.39

Note: Initial value of polity2, relative income, and *domestic democratic capital* are measured in first year of sample. *Foreign democratic capital* is measured in 1993. When computing the unmatched means, we do not impose the common support; when computing the matched means, we do.

score, corresponding to the matching procedure described in Section 13.6.1 (see also equations (13.7) and (13.8) above).

Clearly, matching equalizes the means of all covariates used in the logit regression. Interestingly, it also reduces the difference in means of some of the other covariates: Latin America in Table 13.4a, Africa and Latin America in Table 13.4b. This gives some credence to our earlier expectation that observed (included among the covariates) and unobserved (not included among the covariates) country characteristics may be correlated. In the autocratic transitions sample, however, the variable *initial value of polity2* retains a very different distribution in the treated and control groups, which suggests the importance of also conditioning on the *initial value of polity2* in this sample.

Overall, and with the caveat just mentioned on *initial value of polity2*, matching seems indispensable to achieve a balanced distribution of covariates between treated and control countries—the so-called balancing property. Without matching based on the propensity scores, the two samples are quite different. This means that the assumption of linearity cannot be treated as an innocuous linear approximation. Various interaction effects may thus bias the inference drawn from traditional difference-in-difference regressions.

13.6   Matching Estimates

With the preliminaries of the previous section in hand, we are ready to estimate the effect of political transitions on the treated countries. This section is devoted to the estimation results.

13.6.1 Democratic Transitions

We start with transitions toward democracy. To get a benchmark, we start by reporting linear regression estimates obtained with a two-step procedure suggested in a recent paper by Bertrand, Duflo, and Mullainathan (2004). The purpose of that procedure is not to address bias in the coefficients due to heterogeneity, but to address serial correlation yielding (upward) bias in the standard errors. The procedure treats the data in a similar way, however, in its averaging of the outcome of interest before and after the treatment. Because they impose the parametric assumptions of a linear regression, these estimates provide a useful perspective on the final results from the nonparametric matching procedure.

Specifically, the Bertrand, Duflo, and Mullainathan (2004) estimates are obtained as follows. In a first step, growth is regressed against country and year fixed effects in a sample with yearly data from *all* countries, treated and controls. Then, the estimated residuals of the treated countries only are retained and averaged before and after each country's transition date. This yields a panel of two periods with only treated countries. Finally, the averaged residuals in this panel are regressed against a constant and a dummy variable, which is equal to 1 in the second period (after the transition) and 0 in the first (before the transition). The estimated coefficient and standard errors thus correspond to the difference-in-difference estimator of the average effect of transition in the treated countries. As explained by Bertrand,

Duflo, and Mullainathan (2004), this procedure removes the serial correlation in the yearly residuals—a potential problem in the yearly regressions of Table 13.1.

Column 1 of Table 13.5 implements this procedure for all countries in the democratic transitions sample, where the control countries are those that remained autocracies throughout and the treated are those that made a transition to democracy. The estimated coefficient, although not statistically significant, implies an average growth acceleration of 0.6 percentage points after transition to democracy. Despite the different procedure and specification, this estimate is remarkably similar to that reported in Table 13.1, column 2 (contrary to Table 13.1, the first step does not include initial income, indicators for wars, socialist transitions, and continents interacted with years). In the democratic transitions sample, the average date of reform is in the late 1980s, with about 12 years of posttransition growth. This implies an average effect on per capita income at the end of the sample of about 7%–8%. This estimate is consistent with the long-run effects on income implied by Table 13.1. In column 2 of Table 13.5, we drop the control and treated countries that are outside of the common support defined in Section 13.5 (cf. Table 13.3a). The point estimate increases a bit, but remains statistically insignificant.

Columns 3 to 6 of Table 13.5 present the matching estimates. In columns 3 and 4, the underlying specification of the propensity score does not condition on the *initial value of polity2*, while in columns 5 and 6 it does. All estimators are based on Kernel matching, that is, the weights on specific controls are declining in their distance in propensity score to the treated country they are matched with. Columns 3 and 5 weigh control countries with the Epanechnikov measure, which gives zero weight to all controls whose estimated propensity score differs by more than 0.25 to that of the treated country. Columns 4 and 6 use a Gaussian kernel, which gives all control countries weights that approach zero for the more distant controls—see Leuven and Sianesi (2003) for more detailed information. Note that each country in the control group is used several times in the matching, particularly when we use the Gaussian kernel. As explained in Section 13.2, we compute two sets of standard errors: the lowermost parenthesis below each point estimate corresponds to an upper bound.

All our estimates form a consistent picture despite the different covariates and matching procedures. The point estimate of the effect of democratic transitions ranges between 0.83 and 1.08, an economically relevant

Table 13.5 Democracy and growth: Ordinary Least Squares (OLS) and matching estimates of the growth effect of becoming a democracy

	(1)	(2)	(3)	(4)	(5)	(6)
			Growth			
Growth effect of democracy in the group of treated countries	0.60 (0.54)	0.74 (0.68)	1.08 (0.78) (1.24)	1.19 (0.77) (1.25)	0.83 (0.79) (1.25)	1.01 (0.77) (1.26)
Estimation	Two-step diff-in-diff	Two-step diff-in-diff	Matching	Matching	Matching	Matching
Kernel			Epanechnikov	Normal	Epanechnikov	Normal
Propensity score conditional on *initial value of polity2*	No		No	No	Yes	Yes
Inside common support		Yes	Yes	Yes	Yes	Yes
Number of treated countries	49	37	37	37	36	36
Number of control countries			28	28	28	28
Number of controls including repetitions			651	937	639	910

Note: Columns 1–2: Standard errors in parenthesis.

Columns 3–6: First parenthesis: standard errors estimated assuming independent observations; second parenthesis: standard errors estimated assuming perfect correlations of repeated observations in control countries.

Columns 1–2: Outcome variable: averaged residual of a regression of growth on country and year fixed effects, in a sample that also includes the control countries; first step of Two-step diff-in-diff: OLS of yearly growth on country and year fixed effects, in the treated countries only (averaged before and after treatment, respectively), on dummy variable equal to 1 after treatment; second step: OLS of averaged residuals in the treated countries only (averaged before and after treatment, respectively), on dummy variable equal to 1 after treatment.

Columns 3–6: Outcome variable: change in average growth (after − before reform year).

Common support imposed (according to Table 13.3a) as indicated in all columns.

effect that is considerably higher than the linear estimates. Recalling that the effect refers to average growth during an average posttransition period, which lasts about twelve years, a growth acceleration of 1% implies that per capita income is 13% higher at the end of the sample. Despite the magnitude of the point estimate, the standard errors are large enough that the effect remains statistically insignificant. This is not unexpected, given that matching estimators are not likely to be very precise in such a small sample. To say it differently: we are trading off unbiasedness against efficiency.

An important property of the matching estimation procedure is that it directs our attention to heterogenous effects of democratic transitions in different countries, pointing to influential observations and to other relevant features of the data. Figures 13.2 and 13.3 explore these issues.

Figure 13.2a,b displays histograms of the distribution of the variables g_i and g_i^j, defined in Section 13.2. Intuitively, Figure 13.2 shows the change in average growth after democratic transitions in the groups of (a) treated countries, and (b) control countries at comparable dates. The treated countries have observations symmetrically distributed around zero, except for a large positive outlier, namely Haiti, where democracy was associated with a growth acceleration of about 19%. There are some outliers in the group of control countries as well, but these are less influential because the control group is much larger than the treated group. More important, the distribution of the change in growth in the control countries is clearly tilted to the left and has its mass below zero. Thus, the positive point estimate in Table 13.5 is not due to an improvement in growth in the countries that became democratic (with the exception of Haiti), but rather due to a deterioration of growth in the control countries that remained autocracies. In other words, under a causal interpretation, by becoming democracies, the treated countries avoided the growth slump that hit the permanent autocracies in the control group.

Figure 13.3 displays the contribution to the average growth effect of treated countries by their propensity scores. Specifically, the vertical axis plots the estimator $\hat{\alpha}_i$ defined above, namely, the estimated effect in treated country i expressed as the average change in growth rate (in percentage points per year), while the horizontal axis reports the estimated propensity score in country i.[11] This figure reveals that there is no systematic relationship between the individual treatment effect and the estimated probability of treatment. This is reassuring, because selection into treatment is not systematically correlated with performance, in accordance

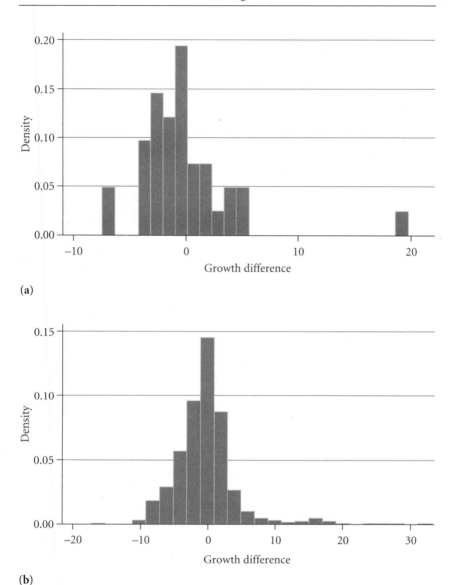

(a)

(b)

Figure 13.2 Change in growth after transition to democracy: (a) in the treated countries; (b) in the control countries. *Note*: The horizontal axis in each histogram plots the difference between growth after and before reform dates (expressed in percentage points per year).

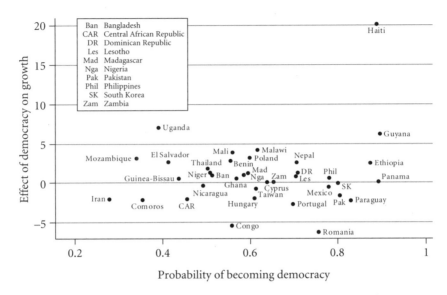

Figure 13.3 Effect of democratic transitions on growth in each treated country. *Note*: The vertical axis measures the yearly growth effect of democracy in percentage points. Estimates refer to column 3 in Table 13.5.

with the identifying assumption. The figure also shows that the growth effects of democratic transition are very heterogenous across countries, with impact effects ranging from −5 to +5 percentage points. Together with the unbalanced distribution of covariates across treated and control countries (cf. Tables 13.4a and 13.4b), this suggests that the linear estimates are quite fragile. As already noted, Haiti remains an influential outlier even after matching (dropping Haiti from the sample would reduce the estimated growth effect almost by half). Finally, note that much of the heterogeneity in the effect of treatment derives from less developed countries with rather fragile democratic institutions, such as Uganda, Guyana, Congo, and Romania. This is not unexpected, because growth is likely to be more volatile in such countries, and autocracies are likely to be associated with highly corrupt dictatorships. It is reassuring, however, that we find no systematic relationship between these heterogenous effects and some of the observed covariates, such as per capita income or the intensity of the treatment (as measured by the change in the *polity2* score associated with democratic transitions). This can be guessed already by a cursory look at the symmetric distribution of countries in Figure 13.3, and is confirmed by a more careful analysis where we regress the individual treatment effect against the observed covariates.

13.6.2 Autocratic Transitions

Finally, we turn to the autocratic transitions sample with countries treated with a transition to autocracy and a control group of democracies that are politically stable during the sample period. The estimates are displayed in Table 13.6, with columns exactly analogous to those of Table 13.5. Here, the estimates capture the effect of transition to autocracy, and thus we expect them to have a negative sign.

Consider the two-step linear estimates in columns 1 and 2. In this case, it makes a big difference whether or not we impose the common support. When all observations are included (column 1), the effect of a relapse into autocracy is essentially zero (a point estimate of 0.17, with a large standard error). Dropping all observations outside of the common support (column 2), however, turns the estimate negative and almost statistically significant: according to the point estimate, a transition to autocracy cuts average yearly growth by 0.84%. As shown in Table 13.3b, the observations outside the common support are made up of a large group of very solid democracies: Belarus (which was very unlikely to receive treatment), and a few African countries at the opposite extreme of the propensity score. Belarus in particular is a very influential observation, because its growth rate accelerates dramatically toward the end of the sample when it also turns to autocracy. These countries are indeed very different from most of the other countries in the sample. Thus the estimates in column 2, which restrict attention to countries on the common support, may be the most reliable.

The remaining columns of Table 13.6 report the matching estimates, which all deliver a similar and robust message. A transition into autocracy cuts average yearly growth by a statistically significant and large amount, which ranges from −1.6 to −2.4 percentage points. The average year of autocratic transition is about 1975. This makes the level effects at the end of the sample very large: a reduction in the posttransition growth rate of, say, −1.8 percentage points sustained for 25 years corresponds to a 45% loss of per capita income.

The estimated treatment effect is not particularly sensitive to including the *initial value of polity2* among the covariates in the underlying propensity

Table 13.6 Democracy and growth: Ordinary Least Squares (OLS) and matching estimates of the growth effect of becoming an autocracy

	(1)	(2)	(3)	(4)	(5)	(6)
			Growth			
Growth effect of autocracy in the group of treated countries	0.17	−0.84	−1.97	−1.85	−2.38	−1.55
	(0.72)	(0.42)*	(0.58)***	(0.53)***	(1.31)**	(0.75)**
			(1.00)**	(0.92)**	(3.59)	(1.57)
Estimation	Two-step diff-in-diff	Two-step diff-in-diff	Matching	Matching	Matching	Matching
Kernel			Epanechnikov	Normal	Epanechnikov	Normal
Propensity score conditional on *initial value of polity2*			No	No	Yes	Yes
Inside common support	No	Yes	Yes	Yes	Yes	Yes
Number of treated countries	20	18	18	18	14	14
Number of control countries			18	18	15	15
Number of controls including repetitions			107	289	34	176

Note: Columns 1–2: Standard errors in parenthesis.

Columns 3–6: First parenthesis: standard errors estimated assuming independent observations; second parenthesis: standard errors estimated assuming perfect correlations of repeated observations in control countries.

Columns 1–2: Outcome variable: averaged residual of a regression of growth on country and year fixed effects; first step of Two-step diff-in-diff: OLS of yearly growth on country and year fixed effects, in a sample that also includes the control countries; second step: OLS of averaged residuals in the treated columns only (averaged before and after treatment, respectively), on dummy variable equal to 1 after treatment.

Columns 3–6: Outcome variable: change in average growth (after − before reform year).

Common support imposed (according to Table 13.3a) as indicated in all columns, except in columns 5–6, where it is [0.11, 0.98].

score. This is reassuring, in light of the unbalanced distribution of this variable across the treated and control groups (cf. Table 13.4b). However, when the *initial value of polity2* enters the estimated propensity score, the number of countries on the common support shrinks further, because treatment is predicted quite well.[12] As a result, the estimates become more sensitive to the weighting procedure (cf. columns 5 and 6).

Figures 13.4 and 13.5 illustrate the contribution of individual countries to these estimates, in the same way as figures 13.2 and 13.3. Figure 13.4 contrasts with the democratic transition case in Figure 13.2, in that the treated group has a distribution with mass mostly below a zero change in growth, while the distribution for the group of control counties seems centered at, or slightly above, zero. Thus, the estimated negative growth effect of autocracy is mainly due to a growth deceleration in countries that relapsed into autocracy. Once we impose the common support, there appear to be no influential outliers in the group of treated countries.

Figure 13.5 plots the estimates of the individual treatment effects against the estimated propensity scores.[13] As in Figure 13.3, there is considerable heterogeneity. But we detect no systematic relation to the estimated-propensity score (nor against other covariates). Moreover, no single treated country appears particularly influential. Instead, most countries have a large and negative effect of treatment, suggesting that the large negative estimate of the average effect in Table 13.6 is quite robust.

Conclusion   We have estimated the effect of political regime transitions on growth in a new way, paying close attention to heterogenous effects. Our nonparametric matching estimates suggest that previous parametric estimates may have seriously underestimated the growth effects of democracy. In particular, we find an average negative effect on per capita income of leaving democracy as large as 45% percent over the sample. We also find clear indications that the discrepancies relative to the parametric results are driven by large differences in the composition of the treatment and control groups, making linearity a doubtful assumption. While our matching estimates do allow for heterogeneity in a very general way, it is important to recall that they rest on the specific assumption of selection on observables.

As far as we know, our chapter is the first to combine matching and difference in differences in a macroeconomic context. This seems a promising avenue for further work on the effects of reform. In the context of political reforms and growth, it would be natural to investigate the effects of

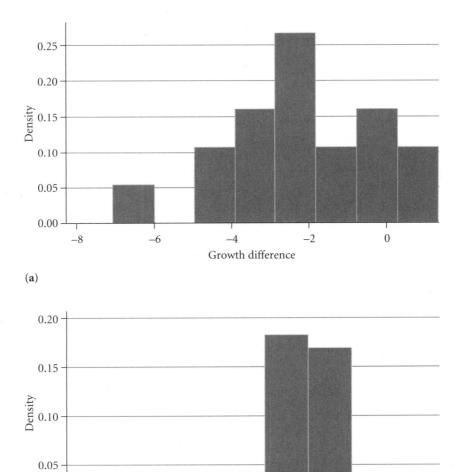

(a)

(b)

Figure 13.4 Change in growth after becoming autocracy: (a) in the treated countries; (b) in the control countries. *Note*: The horizontal axis in each histogram plots the difference between growth after and before reform dates (expressed in percentage points per year).

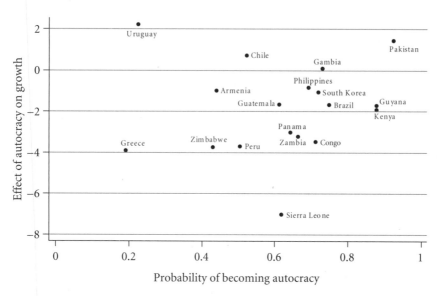

Figure 13.5 Effect of autocratic transitions on growth in each treated country. *Note*: The vertical axis measures the yearly growth effect of autocracy in percentage points. Estimates refer to column 3 in Table 13.6.

different types of democracy (or different types of autocracy, as do Besley and Kudamatsu 2008). But similar estimation techniques also could be used to empirically analyze other types of reform, where we might suspect the effects to be quite heterogenous. Reforms introducing central bank independence and/or inflation targeting may be a particular case in point.

ACKNOWLEDGMENTS

We thank participants in a seminar at the Canadian Institute for Advanced Research (CIFAR), and especially Dan Trefler, for helpful comments. Financial support from the Swedish Research Council, the Tore Browaldh Foundation, Bocconi University, and CIFAR is gratefully acknowledged.

NOTES

1. It is hard to find good instruments for regime changes. Jones and Olken (2005, 2006) imaginatively use unexpected deaths of leaders, and the contrast between successful and unsuccessful assassination attempts on leaders, respectively. The

latter approach allows them to estimate the likelihood of a democratic transition, but it is likely to generate too weak an instrument (too few successful assassinations and too imprecise timing) for democracy.

2. Athey and Imbens (2006) generalize the difference-in-difference methodology along related but different lines. Their nonparametric approach also allows for hetereogeneous treatment effects, but relies on estimating the entire distribution of counterfactual outcomes for the treatment group in the absence of treatment.

3. Persson and Tabellini (2003) apply propensity-score methods to evaluate the effect of alternative constitutional features, but they compare a cross section of countries and do not exploit temporal variation in the data.

4. For the time being, we thus neglect transitions from democracy to autocracy, and exclude from the sample countries that always remained democracies. We also neglect multiple transitions and consider only countries that had a single transition from autocracy to democracy. These complications are all dealt with in later sections.

5. As Abadie (2005) notes, equation (13.3) coincides with the so-called *selection-on-observables* assumption used in cross-sectional studies if in addition we also have $E(Y_{i,0}^0 \mid \mathbf{X}_i, D_{i,1} = 1) = E(Y_{i,1}^0 \mid \mathbf{X}_i, D_{i,1} = 0)$.

6. An alternative—to be pursued in future work—would be to compute the standard errors by bootstrapping. Doing so would take into account that the weights $w_{i,j}$ are uncertain, since they are based on (logit) estimates of the propensity score.

7. An alternative would be to use a classification of political regimes, based on a finer subdivision of the 21-step scale for the *polity2* score. This would turn the analysis into the domain of multiple treatments (see, e.g., Lechner 2001).

8. The coefficient ϕ on the democracy indicator D measures the impact effect on growth $y_t - y_{t-1}$. Because lagged (log) income y_{t-1} enters on the right-hand side of the estimated equation with coefficient β, the long-run effect on income can be computed as

$$\frac{dy}{dD} = -\frac{\phi}{\beta}.$$

With estimates $\widehat{\phi} = 0.5$ and $\widehat{\beta} = -0.055$, we obtain a long-run income gain of 0.09, that is, about 9%. Since the convergence rate β is likely overestimated in yearly data (due to cyclical fluctuations in income), this is almost surely an underestimate of the long-run income gain.

9. This is, of course, the democratic transition sample defined in Section 13.3. In this section, we avoid the term "control countries," however, since in a difference-in-difference estimation with different treatment dates, all countries

that do not have a reform in period t effectively serve as controls for those countries that do have a reform in t.

10. The results on income are consistent with the results in the annual hazard rates estimated by Persson and Tabellini (2006b), who find that income does not explain transitions out of autocracy but does slow down transitions out of democracy.

11. The growth estimates refer to column 3 in Table 13.5.

12. When we condition also on the *initial value of polity2*, we change the range corresponding to the common support to those treated and control countries with an estimated common support in the range (0.11–0.98). In Table 13.5, the definition of the common support remains, instead, the same irrespective of whether we condition or not on the *initial value of polity2*.

13. The estimates refer to column 3 in Table 13.6.

APPENDIX

Here we compute the standard error of the estimator $\hat{\alpha}$ given in (13.8)—see also Lechner (2001) for a similar derivation. Combining (13.8) and (13.7), we have

$$\hat{\alpha} = \frac{1}{I} \sum_i g_i - \frac{1}{I} \sum_i \sum_j w_{i,j} g_i^j. \tag{13.9}$$

Suppose that all treated countries have the same variance $\sigma_T^2 = Var(g_i | i$ is treated), and that all control countries also have the same variance, $\sigma_C^2 = Var(g_i^j | i$ is treated, j is a control). Assume further that $w_{i,j}$ are known scalars, and that all g_i observations are mutually uncorrelated. If g_i^j and g_k^j are also mutually uncorrelated for $i \neq k$ and all j, then

$$Var(\hat{\alpha}) = \frac{\sigma_T^2}{I} + \sigma_C^2 \frac{\sum_i \sum_j (w_{i,j})^2}{I^2}. \tag{13.10}$$

This is our lower bound for the estimated variance of α.

Suppose instead that g_i^j and g_k^j are perfectly correlated for $i \neq k$, but that g_i^j and g_i^l are mutually uncorrelated for $j \neq l$ (i.e., observations corresponding to different control countries are mutually uncorrelated, while observations drawn from the same control are perfectly correlated when that control is used several times for different treated countries). Then

$$Var(\hat{\alpha}) = \frac{\sigma_T^2}{I} + \sigma_C^2 \frac{\sum_j \left(\sum_i w_{i,j}\right)^2}{I^2}. \tag{13.11}$$

This is our upper bound for the estimated variance of $\hat{\alpha}$.

REFERENCES

Abadie, A. 2005. "Semiparametric Difference-in-Difference Estimators." *Review of Economic Studies* 72:1–19.

Athey, S., and G. Imbens. 2006. "Identification and Inference in Nonlinear Difference-in-Difference Models." *Econometrica* 74: 431–97.

Bertrand, M., E. Duflo, and S. Mullainathan. 2004. "How Much Should We Trust Difference-in-Differences Estimates?" *Quarterly Journal of Economics* 119:249–75.

Besley, T., and M. Kudamatsu. 2008. "Making Autocracy Work." (See Chapter 11 in this volume.)

Blundell, R., M. Costa Dias, C. Meghir, and J. Van Reenen. 2004. "Evaluating the Employment Impact of a Mandatory Job Search Assistance Program." *Journal of the European Economic Association* 2:596–606.

Giavazzi, F., and G. Tabellini. 2005. "Economic and Political Liberalizations." *Journal of Monetary Economics* 52:1297–1330.

Heckman, J., H. Ichimura, J. Smith, and P. Todd. 1997. "Matching as an Econometric Evaluation Estimator: Evidence from a Job Training Program." *Review of Economic Studies* 64:605–54.

Jones, B., and B. Olken. 2005. "Do Leaders Matter? National Leadership and Growth since World War II." *Quarterly Journal of Economics* 120:835–64.

———. 2006. "Hit or Miss? The Effects of Assassinations on Institutions and Wars." Mimeo, Harvard University.

Lechner, M. 2001. "Identification and Estimation of Causal Effects of Multiple Treatments under the Conditional Independence Assumption" In *Econometric Evaluation of Labor Market Policies*, eds. M. Lechner and F. Pfeiffer. Heidelberg: Springer.

Leuven, E., and B. Sianesi. 2003. "PSMATCH: Stata Module to Perform Full Mahalanobis and Propensity Score Matching, Common Support Graphing and Covariate Imbalance Testing." http://ideas.repec.org/c/boc/bocode/s432001.html.

Papaioannou, E., and G. Siourounis. Forthcoming. "Democratization and Growth." *Economic Journal*.

Persson, T. 2005. "Forms of Democracy, Policy and Economic Development." NBER working paper, no. 11171.

Persson, T., and G. Tabellini. 2003. *Economic Effects of Constitutions*. Cambridge: MIT Press.

———. 2006a. "Democracy and Development: The Devil in the Details." *American Economic Review Papers and Proceedings* 96:319–24.

———. 2006b. "Democratic Capital: The Nexus of Political and Economic Change." NBER working paper, no. 12175.

Rodrik, D., and R. Wacziarg. 2005. "Do Democratic Transitions Produce Bad Economic Outcomes?" *American Economic Review Papers and Proceedings* 95:50–56.

Rosenbaum, P., and D. Rubin. 1983. "The Central Role of the Propensity Score in Observational Studies for Causal Effects." *Biometrika* 70:41–55.

List of Contributors

DARON ACEMOGLU, Charles P. Kindleberger Professor of Applied Economics, Department of Economics, Massachusetts Institute of Technology; and CIFAR

PHILIPPE AGHION, Robert C. Waggoner Professor of Economics, Department of Economics, Harvard University; and CIFAR

ALBERTO ALESINA, Nathaniel Ropes Professor of Political Economy, Department of Economics, Harvard University

SIWAN ANDERSON, Assistant Professor of Economics, Department of Economics, University of British Columbia; and CIFAR

MARÍA ANGÉLICA BAUTISTA, PhD Candidate, Department of Political Science, Brown University

TIMOTHY BESLEY, Kuwait Professor of Economics and Political Science, Department of Economics, London School of Economics; and CIFAR

DANIEL DIERMEIER, IBM Distinguished Professor of Regulation and Competitive Practice, Department of Managerial Economics and Decision Sciences, Kellogg School of Management, Northwestern University; and CIFAR

MAURICIO DRELICHMAN, Assistant Professor of Economics, Department of Economics, University of British Columbia; and CIFAR

JAMES D. FEARON, Theodore and Frances Geballe Professor in the School of Humanities and Sciences, Stanford University, and Professor, Department of Political Science, Stanford University; and CIFAR

POHAN FONG, Assistant Professor of Economics, Department of Economics, Concordia University

PATRICK FRANCOIS, Associate Professor, Department of Economics, University of British Columbia; and CIFAR

587

AVNER GREIF, Bowman Family Endowed Professor in Humanities and Sciences, and Professor of Economics, Department of Economics, Stanford University; and CIFAR

GENE M. GROSSMAN, Jacob Viner Professor of International Economics, Department of Economics and Woodrow Wilson School of Public and International Affairs, Princeton University

ELHANAN HELPMAN, Galen L. Stone Professor of International Trade, Department of Economics, Harvard University; and CIFAR

MASAYUKI KUDAMATSU, Assistant Professor of Economics, Institute for International Economic Studies, Stockholm University

JOEL MOKYR, Robert H. Strotz Professor of Arts and Sciences, and Professor of Economics and History, Northwestern University; and CIFAR

ABHINAY MUTHOO, Professor of Economics, Department of Economics, University of Essex

NATHAN NUNN, Assistant Professor of Economics, Department of Economics, Harvard University

TORSTEN PERSSON, Director, Institute for International Economics Studies, Stockholm University; Centennial Professor of Economics, London School of Economics; and CIFAR

PABLO QUERUBÍN, PhD Candidate, Department of Economics, Massachusetts Institute of Technology

JAMES A. ROBINSON, Professor of Government, Department of Government, Harvard University; and CIFAR

KENNETH A. SHEPSLE, George D. Markham Professor of Government, Department of Government, Harvard University; and CIFAR

GUIDO TABELLINI, Professor of Economics, Department of Economics, Bocconi University; and CIFAR

FRANCESCO TREBBI, Assistant Professor of Economics, University of Chicago Graduate School of Business

HANS-JOACHIM VOTH, ICREA Research Professor of Economics and Economic History, Department of Economics, Universitat Pompeu Fabra

Author Index

Page numbers with an "n" indicate citations in notes; page numbers with an "r" indicate citations in references.

Subject Index